GREAT HEAVENS IT'S YOU!
YAS'M. RECKON AS HOW IT IS. HOW DOES YO' DO?

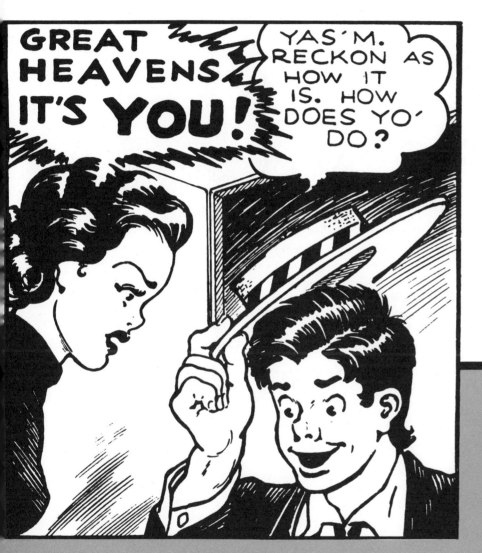

LI'L ABNER

Dailies

Volume One: 1934-1936

Al Capp

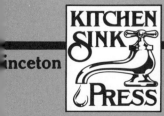

KITCHEN SINK PRESS
inceton Wisconsin

ISBN 0-87816-036-1 (hardcover)
ISBN 0-87816-037-x (softcover)

The complete reprinting of Al Capp's Li'l Abner commences with this volume of the first dailies, covering the inception of the strip in August, 1934 through the first week of January, 1936. The series is being issued by Kitchen Sink Press, **Denis Kitchen**, publisher. The series editor is **Dave Schreiner**. The cover for the first volume was designed and colored by **Peter Poplaski**. The strips were shot by **Jan Manweiler** and **Ray Fehrenbach**, with Fehrenbach assembling and retouching the material for publication. We wish to thank the Capp estate for their cooperation in publishing this series. They have provided rare proof sheets for the best possible reproduction in this volume. In addition, **Catherine Capp** graciously provided the Introduction, and **Julie Capp Cairol** loaned us photos from the Capp family album. Finally, we wish to thank **Bill Blackbeard** of the San Francisco Academy of Comic Art for supplying us with the few missing strips we needed to complete the volume; the Li'l Abner promotional art; and the examples of Capp's work on Joe Palooka.

The black and white daily *Li'l Abner* strips are being collected chronologically in their entirety. At some point we will begin a separate series of volumes of chronological Sunday strips, hopefully in full color. Readers should note that the Sunday strips involved a separate continuity from the Monday through Saturday adventures. Any readers possessing original *Li'l Abner* artwork, related merchandise, Al Capp correspondence or other related historical material are encouraged to contact the publisher.

Yearly subscriptions covering four volumes of *Al Capp's Li'l Abner* are available from Kitchen Sink Press, Inc., No. 2 Swamp Rd., Princeton WI 54968. If you are interested, please send us a card and we will forward the information. We also have available a free 16-page catalog of all our books and comics, including the work of Milton Caniff, Will Eisner and Harvey Kurtzman.

Library of Congress Cataloging-in-Publication Data

Capp, Al, 1909-
    Li'l Abner : dailies.

    Includes index.
    Contents: v. 1. 1934-1936
    I. Title.
PN6728.L5C29   1988   741.5'973   88-12831
ISBN 0-87816-036-1 (v. 1)
ISBN 0-87816-037-X (pbk. : v. 1)

Hardcover: second printing January, 1989

Softcover: third printing January, 1989

Introduction

by Catherine Capp Halberstadt

I met Alfred Gerald Caplin—Al Capp—when we were both students at the Designers Art School in Boston. This was in 1930, when we were 20 years old. Drawing had been very important to me ever since I was a small girl. I was studying fine arts at the school, working at figure drawing and portraits. I wasn't interested in the cartoon field at all. Of course, Al was going to the Designers School specifically to draw the human figure for use in cartoons. From the time I knew him, and considerably before that, he wanted to be a cartoonist. Not only that, he wanted to be the best. He had already spent years working at it, and by the time I met him he had been to three other art schools in Philadelphia and Boston for training in anatomy and perspective.

Although he had never graduated from high school, Al was extremely well-read and was well informed both about the classics of literature and current events. He had strong opinions about nearly everything, and was a good judge of character, very perceptive. He had spent much of his youth drawing, reading, and observing people.

We were both in the fine arts class at the school, and we became better acquainted at lunchtime. I was living in a girl's boarding house, and I didn't get out much at night, so lunchtime was very nearly the only social time we had at first. I had come from my home in Amesbury, Massachusetts, and was living on a small allowance from my family. Al would bring some wonderful chopped liver sandwiches his mother made, and other good food. So I used my allowance and his mother's sandwiches to get by. We *both* got by. One day, a fire broke out somewhere in the building that housed the school. Everybody had to leave the classroom, down a fire escape. Since Al had a wooden leg, he was a bit slower than the others, so I stayed with him while we escaped. He managed it by himself, though. I remember also one time he ripped a hole in the seat of his pants at school and I loaned him my artist's smock so he could cover it up. These are all little things, not very important, but out of them grew a relationship. We were together as much as we could be, and it all happened because we were in that fine arts class.

After graduating, he went to New York and got a job ghosting for a very short time with Bud Fisher on *Mutt and Jeff*. Eventually, in 1932, he caught on at the Associated Press, where he began drawing a panel cartoon called *Mr. Gilfeather*. He didn't like it, but he earned enough for us to get married that same year. When he left the AP and came back to Boston, he studied some more at another art school, and he did some freelance work at the Boston *Post*. He went back to New York in 1933, and got a job assisting Ham Fisher on *Joe Palooka*. Our daughter, Julie, was born around this time, and Al found a two-room basement apartment on the west side, where we set up housekeeping. Al would come home from work, and sometimes he talked to me a bit about Ham Fisher. He was constantly amazed at Fisher's lifestyle—sometimes amused and often angry, but there's not much in that area that I want to write about.

Catherine and Al at Seabrook Beach, New Hampshire, 1931.

3

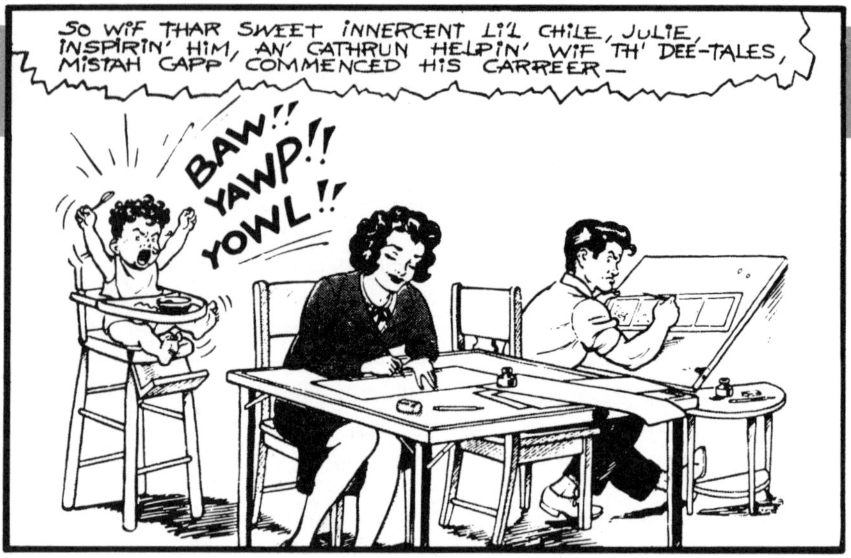
SO WIF THAR SWEET INNERCENT LI'L CHILE, JULIE, INSPIRIN' HIM, AN' CATHRUN HELPIN' WIF TH' DEE-TALES, MISTAH CAPP COMMENCED HIS CARREER—
BAW!! YAWP!! YOWL!!

Above is a panel from "Al Capp by Li'l Abner," done in the 1940s by Capp for servicemen-amputees. At right, Catherine and Al in the mid-1930s.

One night while Al was working for Fisher, we went to a vaudeville theater in Columbus Circle. One of the performances was a hillbilly act. A group of four or five singers/musicians/comedians were playing fiddles and Jews harps and doing a little soft shoe up on stage. They stood in a very wooden way with expressionless deadpan faces, and talked in monotones, with Southern accents. We thought they were just hilarious. We walked back to the apartment that evening, becoming more and more excited with the idea of a hillbilly comic strip. Something like it must have always been in the back of Al's mind, ever since he had thumbed his way through the Southern hills as a teenager, but that vaudeville act seemed to crystallize it for him. Eventually, he produced some samples about a hillbilly family, and called it *Li'l Abner.* "Abner" was what we had nicknamed the baby when I was pregnant; it's what we called Julie before she was born. I don't recall any great difficulty when he went to sell the strip, but I do remember giving a sigh of relief when the contract was signed. I thought "Now we're going to be all right for many years."

Al and I conferred about the characters while he was drawing his samples. I'll take credit for naming Daisy Mae and Pansy Yokum, although contrary to popular belief, I was *not* the model for Daisy. The closest I came to being a model in the strip happened later, when Al used my hair for Moonbeam McSwine. For the first six months, and possibly for the first year, I assisted Al with the art on the strip. I drew the backgrounds; all of the outdoor country scenes were mine—the trees and log cabins and such. Neither of us were very good with cars or more technical things. In addition, Al was always terribly fussy about the lettering. I did it in the beginning, but I don't think it satisfied him, because he took it over. We struggled along for a number of months that way. I think we were both happy when he acquired another assistant, Moe Leff.

I'm happy Al's work is being presented again in this extensive collection. *Li'l Abner* was a big part of our lives for many years. It *did* make things all right for a long time.

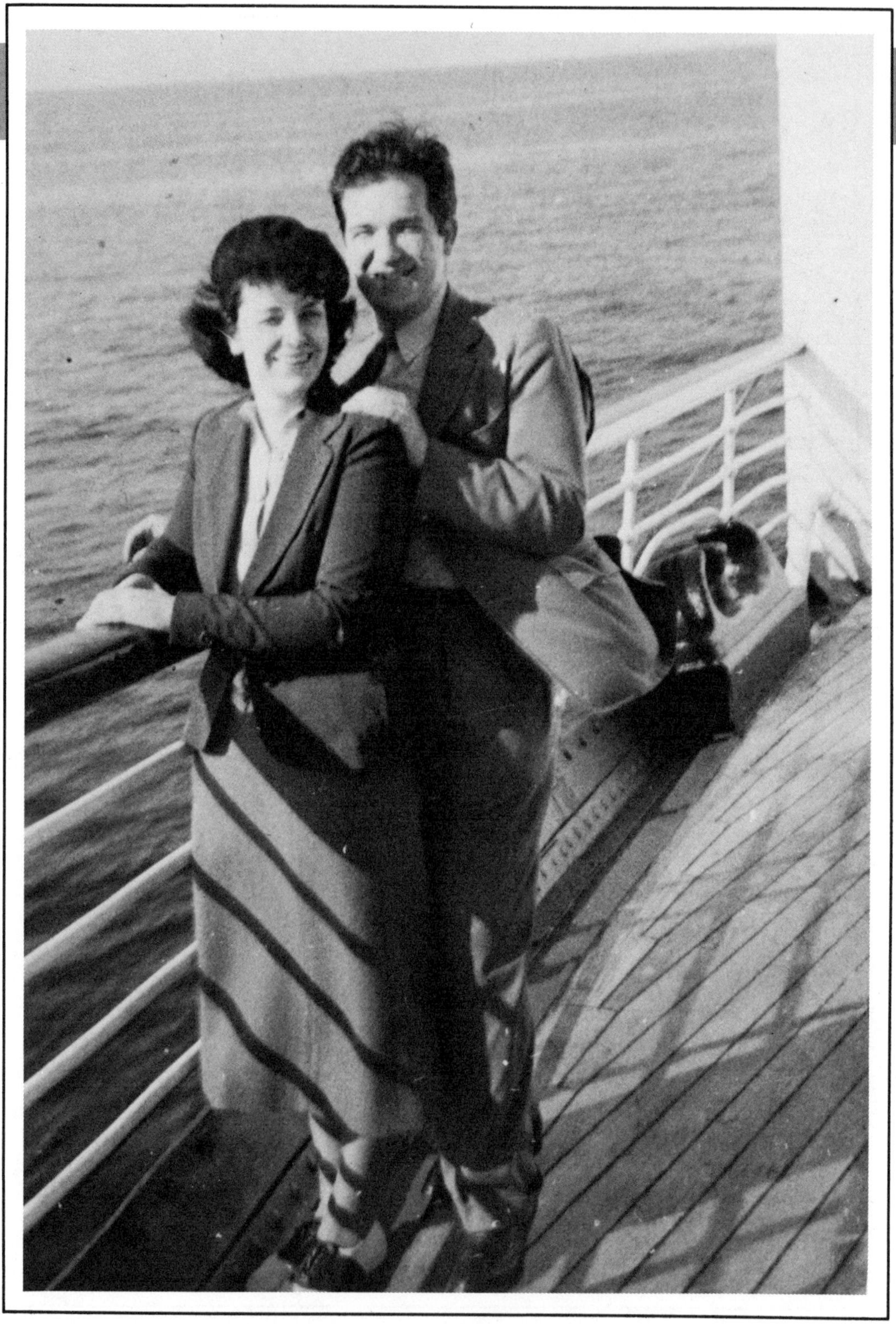

Innocents in Peril

by Al Capp

(In 1952, an edited collection of strips called The World of Li'l Abner *was published with an introduction by John Steinbeck and a foreword by Charles Chaplin. Al Capp's reflections about comic strips and the "formula" for* Li'l Abner *appeared there under the above title.)*

Over fifteen years ago, before *Li'l Abner* was born, comics adopted a New Order of the Day as they discovered SUSPENSE! Maybe they caught it from *The Perils of Pauline*, but anyhow it was as much of a change as from silent movies to "talkies."

Newspaper publishers discovered that the populace bought more papers more regularly if they were worried by a comic strip than if they were just amused. A citizen who laughed in delight at one of Rube Goldberg's great inventions was able to put his paper down with a chuckle, eat dinner with a placid mind, and sleep the sleep of the peaceful.

The same citizen, however, who read Chester Gould's magnificent *Dick Tracy*, didn't laugh when he reached the last panel of that strip—he moaned or gasped. Who wouldn't worry at the sight of a bullet whizzing out through his favorite detective's forehead, accompanied by a fine spray of Tracy's brains and bits of his skull (Tracy had been shot from behind, of course). You may be sure *that* reader didn't eat *his* dinner in peace. He did *not* spend a restful night. *That* harassed soul couldn't wait until dawn came and, with it, the next edition. Only then was his agony relieved. And then, while the next strip revealed that it was an unimportant section of Tracy's skull that had been shattered and that he could get along just as well without those particular bits of brain, the reader's relief was short-lived. In the last panel of the new strip, the walls of the room into which Tracy had been lured began slowly and relentlessly to *close in on him*, with no escape possible, while the maniacal laughter of the criminal fiends operating the death-dealing levers outside was ringing in Tracy's helpless ears.

Again no peace for the reader—until he could rush out in a fresh dawn to buy the next day's paper—and the next and the next.

When you multiply one harassed soul by several million and when you realize that newspaper publishers *love* to have millions of people rushing out to buy their papers at dawn, you can understand why—having discovered that worrying the hell out of people paid off a lot more in circulation than simply amusing them did—publishers declared a New Order for the comic page. Out went the simple fun, the pratfalls, the gentle satire, and in came the "suspense continuity."

This was the situation that faced young, starry-eyed, starving Al Capp, when at twenty-three, fifteen years ago, he decided to become a professional, or three-meals-a-day, cartoonist. Our hero was confused. He'd been brought up on Rube Goldberg, Fred Opper, Milt Gross, Rudy Dirks, Cliff Sterrett—the great funny guys. He wanted to be like them. But with the coming of the New Order, the comedians had been banished from the comic page—and in came the detectives, the ape-men, the big, lovable prize-fighters who sobbed as they slaughtered their opponents because they didn't really want to hurt anybody and were doing it only because their mothers needed expensive treatments for leprosy, and the little orphan girls with no daddy but the N.A.M. [National Association of Manufacturers] to guide them.

Out went the laugh, the guffaw and the chuckle that were the purpose of the old-time comic strips—and in came the gasp, the shudder, the cold sweat on the brow, the sick feeling in the pit of the stomach that were the *new* purposes of the "suspense continuity" comic strips.

How could a kid who wanted to draw *comic* comic strips sell one to a comic strip world that wanted only terrifying, heartbreaking, blood-curdling comic strips? There was only one kind of comic strip for him to do and that was to do both kinds—in the same strip.

Therefore, while the *Li'l Abner* characters themselves are broad burlesques in the tradition of my ideals, the immortal Goldberg, Opper, Milt Gross, Maurice Ketten—the situations in which I plunge 'em are macabre, horrible, thrilling and chilling in the new "suspense continuity" fashion. The problems that face the Yokums are monstrous enough to worry readers delightedly enough to get 'em to rush out and buy the paper to find out what happens next, and that makes publishers happy; while the characters' naive solutions and reactions to these problems provide the comedy that makes *me* happy.

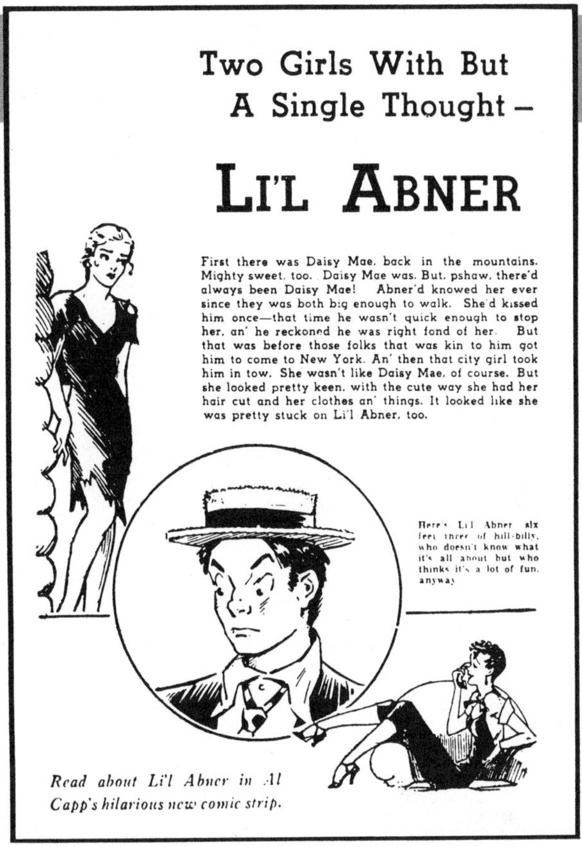

Two Girls With But
A Single Thought –
LI'L ABNER
First there was Daisy Mae, back in the mountains. Mighty sweet, too. Daisy Mae was. But, pshaw, there'd always been Daisy Mae! Abner'd knowed her ever since they was both big enough to walk. She'd kissed him once—that time he wasn't quick enough to stop her, an' he reckoned he was right fond of her. But that was before those folks that was kin to him got him to come to New York. An' then that city girl took him in tow. She wasn't like Daisy Mae, of course. But she looked pretty keen, with the cute way she had her hair cut and her clothes an' things. It looked like she was pretty stuck on Li'l Abner, too.
Here's Li'l Abner six feet three of hill-billy, who doesn't know what it's all about but who thinks it's a lot of fun, anyway
Read about Li'l Abner in Al Capp's hilarious new comic strip.

Promotional ad for newspapers about to carry the new strip from United Features Syndicate, "Li'l Abner," 1934.

My family of innocents is surrounded by a world of super-average people. This innocence of theirs is indestructible, so that while they possess all the homely virtues in which we profess to believe, they seem ingenuous because the world around them is irritated by them, cheats them, kicks them around. They are trusting, kind, loyal, generous and patriotic. It's truly a bewildering world in which they find themselves. Of course, what they don't know is that it takes more than innocence to be truly virtuous—but that's another story.

If a point of view can be called anything as neat as a formula, mine for writing *Li'l Abner* is to throw comedy characters into melodramatic situations and to show them solving their monstrous tribulations in a simple-minded way. I imagine most of us feel just like the Yokums now and then, don't we?

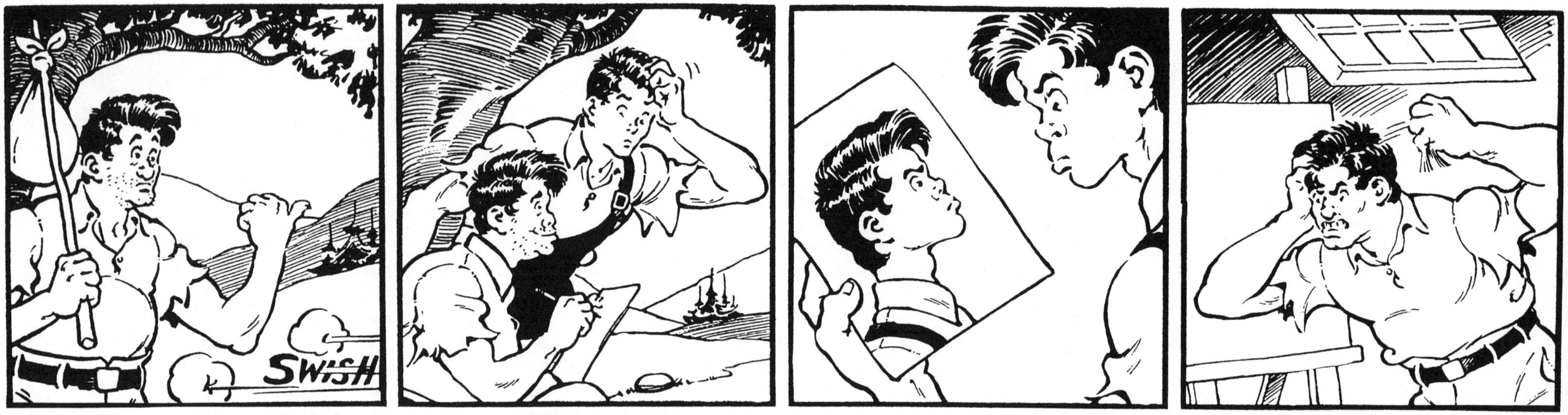
SWISH

"About the time my first crop of whiskers began to come up, I took a walking trip through the Kentucky mountains. Take it from me, it was thumb experience!"

"I sketched the hillbilly people there, the prototypes of Li'l Abner and the folks of his world. My skill amazed them—till they saw the drawings."

"One youngster—I guess he was the real Abner—said, when I showed him his picture, 'The picture ain't as good-lookin' as me. Looks more like you.'"

"In Greenwich Village later, between wondering where the next meal was coming from, I tore my hair searching for a comic strip idea."

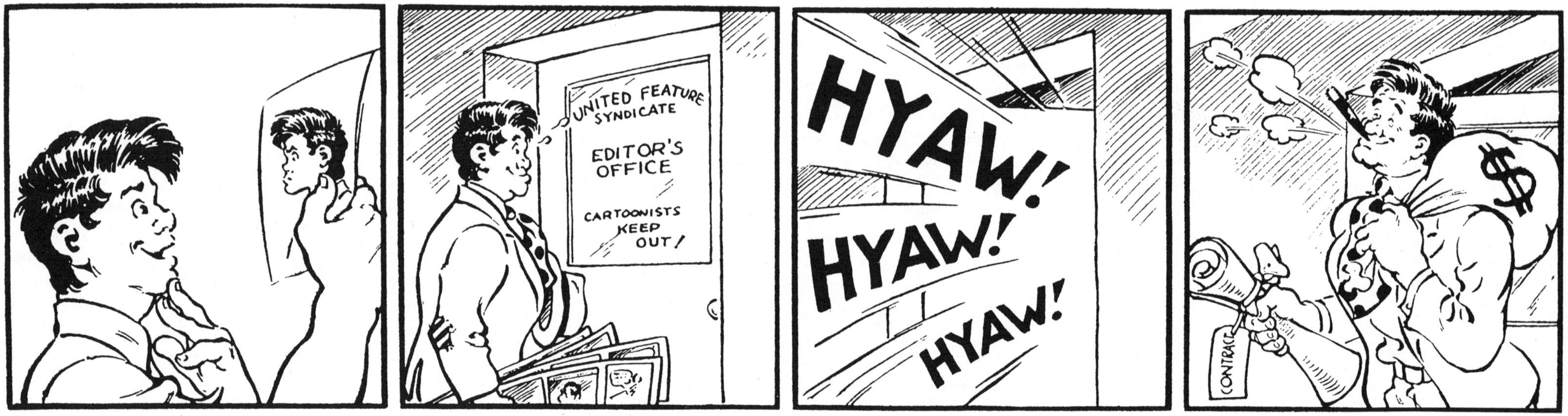
UNITED FEATURE SYNDICATE
EDITOR'S OFFICE
CARTOONISTS KEEP OUT!
HYAW!
HYAW!
HYAW!
$
CONTRACT

"I remembered my hillbilly. And I knew nobody had ever built a comic around one. So I did. Once started, the strip seemed just to write and draw itself."

"But would it sell itself? With all my strips and my hat in hand, I set siege to United Features. They put up a game fight, mom, but I got in."

"Loud laughter ensued—so loud as to have me worried Li'l Abner couldn't be as funny as all that. I suddenly concluded the cause must be me."

"But I guess it wasn't. I came out lugging a contract and more money than I ever believed existed. I'd have pinched myself, only I had both hands full."

One of Capp's first versions of the creation and sale of "Li'l Abner," done for a 1937 United Features Syndicate promotional book. As he did many times, the artist mixed fact and hyperbole to tell a good story of how things "really" happened.

The Storyteller

by Dave Schreiner

Al Capp may have been his own greatest creation. He built around himself and his personal history a pyramid of truth, near-truth and myth which helped transform the already colorful and interesting Alfred Gerald Caplin into the controversial and legendary Al Capp, world's best-known newspaper cartoonist. In 1947, *New Yorker* writer E.J. Kahn Jr. quoted a close friend of Capp's as saying, "I have it on the very best of information that Al was born in three different places." This is not necessarily bad, although it tends to drive chronologists crazy. Capp was one of the very best storytellers, and he did not confine his enormous talent to the funny pages. He mixed plausibility with outrageousness in his work, and when he related anecdotes and incidents from his life, the same rules applied. He had the master tale-spinner's ability to make what he said believable.

On August 21, 1919, just short of his tenth birthday, he lost his left leg in an accident. Capp's official version, written for *Life* magazine in 1960, went this way: "That day my father, a vague and unworldly man, gave me 50 cents to get a haircut: 35 cents for the haircut, 5 cents for a tip, 10 cents for trolley fare. At least that was the way he figured it. I, a calculating and worldly kid, figured it a little different. I had seen a tantalizing offer on a sign in a downtown New Haven window: 'Prof. Amoroso, Barber Academy—Haircuts 15 cents—No Tipping.' By hitching a ride on the back of an ice wagon, I could step into Professor Amoroso's with 50 cents and, with luck, step out again with most of the money (and possibly some of my scalp) intact. Clutching that 50-cent piece, blinded with dreams of riches and power, I hopped off the ice cart in front of the barber academy—and directly in the path of a huge old-fashioned trolley car. I was caught under the wheels and before the car could be stopped my left leg was severed at the thigh.

"During the ride to the hospital and later while I was under anesthetic, I never once unclutched that half dollar. My mother finally took it from me. For years afterward she kept that coin, the kind of melancholy memento that only mothers understand, in the drawer of her sewing machine. I used to find her now and then, staring into the open drawer and quietly weeping. A dozen years later, during the Depression and a particularly severe family financial crisis, she opened the drawer again, stared at the coin for the last time, and marched to the grocery store with it."

The artist with the hated "Mr. Gilfeather" pinned under his pen. Photo taken at the AP office in New York, 1932.

If that is not a true story, it should be. The important parts are true: the terrible accident and loss suffered by a child; the trauma in the family. It is possible that the story of the coin is not true; the usual explanation is that he jumped the wagon to snatch a shard of ice on a hot day, then fell off. If so, the fable is artful. It has romance and drama; it is poignant and sentimental, and then it takes a patented Capp-veer into worldly reality. It reveals much about the family's fortunes, and it also seems to say something about a young man's conception of the value of a buck and the birth of his motivation to leave poverty permanently behind him.

Everyone now agrees that he was born September 28, 1909, in New Haven, Connecticut, the eldest of four children born to Tillie and Otto Caplin. From some accounts, Otto was a good amateur artist who delighted and entertained his children with hand drawn comic strips. For a living, he sold industrial oil, a job that took him on the road a great deal, and also forced family moves to Bridgeport, Brooklyn and eventually Boston, all during the time Al was growing up.

Brooklyn is the setting for the legend about Miss Mendelsohn, the teacher. His younger brother, Elliot Caplin, says he was put in a class of retarded children there "because he wasn't normal—he had only one leg." Capp said he was the victim of a school administrator's experiment in which 25 brilliant students were put in a class with 25 "degenerates. I think I was supposed to be one of the smart kids, and the morons were supposed to benefit by association with us. It worked the other way around." Both accounts agree that it was a brutal class, not designed for learning. Because Al could draw, he was coaxed or bullied or paid to draw nude pictures of the teacher, Miss Mendelsohn, and thus escaped beatings or earned good money or learned a lesson about art that sells.

Bridgeport is the stepping off place for his fabled trip to the South when he was 15. Elliot says he went out one day for a pack of cigarettes "and we didn't hear from him for two weeks." He called them from Virginia, telling his mother that he and a friend were thumbing a ride down to the corner when a man going to Memphis picked them up. He and his friend, Donald Munson ("Gus" in the Elliot version), decided to go along. Eventually, they wound up in Memphis with Al's Uncle George, a rabbi, who is also credited with giving Al his first drawing utensils years before. Curiously, Capp himself always omitted the colorful start of the journey, concentrating instead on the people he met and the sights he saw. The trip was essential to his origin tale of *Li'l Abner*, one version of which is reprinted in this volume from a United Features Syndicate promotional book of the 1930s. Some have questioned the ability of a young man with a wooden leg to travel the South, even if he was hitchhiking. He was not an expert at moving with it, and was quite self-conscious about it. However, he was always adventurous and took his share of chances before and after this period. While he may not have met Abner on the trip, it seems he did indeed take it.

In Boston, he grew to maturity, taking art classes at various schools and devouring every book he could get his hands on. Ever since the accident, he had been reading and drawing. His taste in literature was wide-ranging, from the classics to the comics. From early on, he wanted to be a cartoonist. He explained this by saying "I heard Bud Fisher of *Mutt and Jeff* made $3,000 a week and was constantly marrying French countesses [or chorines in the Ziegfield Follies]. I decided that was for me." He seems to have had, even before the accident, a burning desire to succeed. The accident perhaps served to focus his attention even more.

In Boston, he met Catherine Wingate Cameron of Amesbury at the Designers Art School, and would later marry her. Before that happened, he would try his luck in getting a job in his chosen profession. The place to go was New York, where the syndicates which serviced the newspapers were headquartered. The fact that it was the worst possible time to be looking for any sort of work anywhere did not stop him. It was 1932 and the United States—the world—was in the grip of the Great Depression.

In fact, he had little trouble finding work that first trip. Another uncle provided him with an introduction to the Associated Press, and Capp's own talent and a bit of luck got him a job writing and drawing a justly-forgotten panel called *Mr. Gilfeather*. Begun as *Col. Gilfeather* a few years before, it was the AP's knockoff of another syndicate's successful *Major Hoople*. Capp created a younger brother for the colonel, dropped the military man, and changed the name of the feature.

Then he suffered for six months, missing deadlines, agonizing over the art and words, having a miserable time. He was faced not only with his own inexperience, but was working on a cartoon he hated. The editors who bought it hated it, too. In the mid-1930s, when *Abner* was already a success and jokes about the bad old days could be made, Capp claimed he lost a subscribing paper a week during the *Gilfeather* era, a record. He said newspaper editors universally condemned it as the worst feature ever offered by any syndicate. If they said that, they were mistaken; there were many worse strips and panels floating around—including the original *Col. Gilfeather*. But it wasn't very good and Capp's epitaph acknowledged that "it was simply a case of a young fellow with some raw talent shoved into the spotlight before he knew enough to carry on." *Gilfeather* had made Capp the youngest syndicated cartoonist in the nation, but it was small consolation.

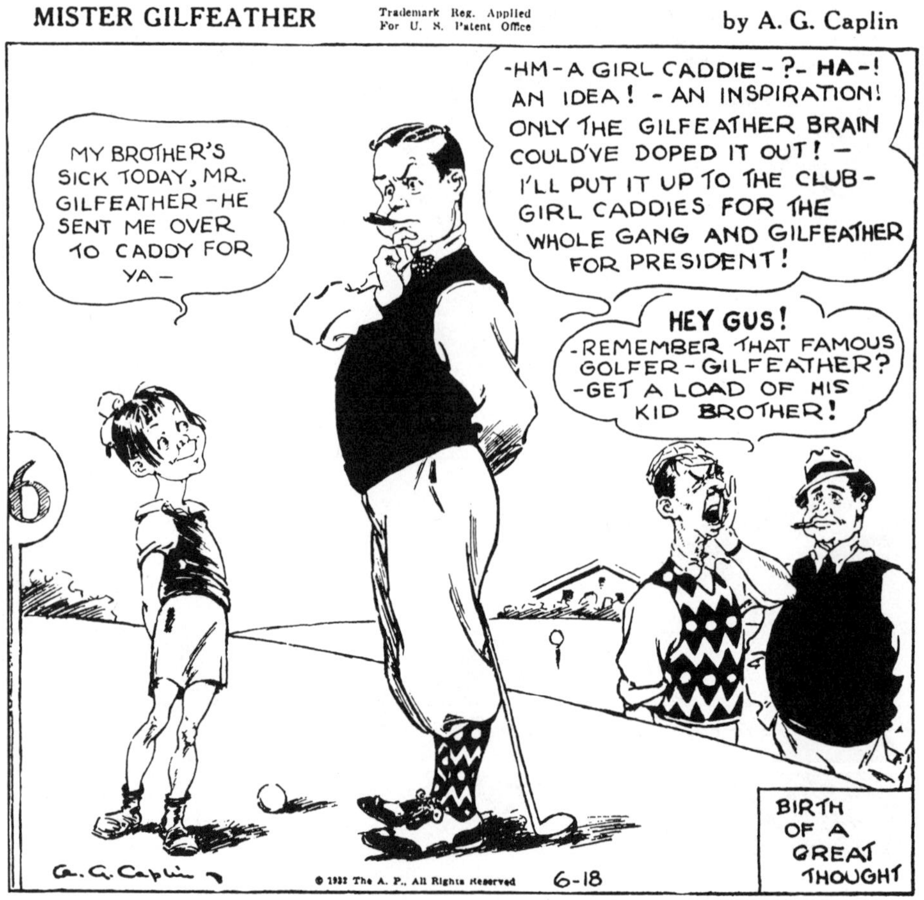
MISTER GILFEATHER
Trademark Reg. Applied For U. S. Patent Office
by A. G. Caplin
MY BROTHER'S SICK TODAY, MR. GILFEATHER — HE SENT ME OVER TO CADDY FOR YA —
-HM - A GIRL CADDIE - ?- HA-! AN IDEA! - AN INSPIRATION! ONLY THE GILFEATHER BRAIN COULD'VE DOPED IT OUT! — I'LL PUT IT UP TO THE CLUB - GIRL CADDIES FOR THE WHOLE GANG AND GILFEATHER FOR PRESIDENT!
HEY GUS! - REMEMBER THAT FAMOUS GOLFER - GILFEATHER? - GET A LOAD OF HIS KID BROTHER!
6
BIRTH OF A GREAT THOUGHT
A. G. Caplin
© 1932 The A. P., All Rights Reserved
6-18

An example of "Mr. Gilfeather," by Al Capp. June, 1932.

He quit abruptly and went back to Boston to study art at the Museum School. In the context of the times, that was a riskier move than any trip he took through the South. There were benefits from his term at the AP, though. For one thing, he met Milton Caniff, and they began their lifelong friendship. (Caniff, in fact, took over *Gilfeather*, and after a decent interval, changed it himself to *The Gay 30's*. But that's another story.) In addition, Capp said later that after he left the AP, he knew "more about anatomy, plots, perspective. I had *enough*, anyway, that I thought I could hit the syndicates again." He married Catherine on his return to Boston, and picked up freelance jobs for local newspapers. Soon enough, he was travelling back to New York, leaving Catherine for the time being with her parents in Amesbury.

He arrived in New York virtually penniless, but was extremely fortunate in finding a place to stay. A former landlady in Greenwich Village, who had "sublime confidence in my abilities, agreed to put the rent for my garret on the cuff and staked me besides to a dollar a day for carfare, cakes and coffee." He would later describe the garret as "an airless rat hole," but he doubtless needed the woman's largesse. More than one account says he was desperate for work during this time. Milton Caniff says he haunted Village cafeterias looking for cheap food, and one day an elderly woman, a newspaper seller, approached him and gave him a few coins for his evening meal. It was gratefully accepted. Capp would treat this time with humor and irony later, but living it must have been downright frightening. In that year, 29 people starved to death in New York City, and another 110 died more slowly of malnutrition. Most of them were children. There were one million jobless in the city, served by 82 breadlines. There was little else in the way of relief for the poor. Nationwide, there were 14 million unemployed and *Fortune* magazine said that 34 million men, women and children had no income at all. At the time Capp returned to New York, there was at least a glimmer of hope on the horizon because a new, confident administration was about to take over in Washington. In 1932, when he quit in frustration at the AP, there was not even that.

It was during this period of desperate personal and national poverty that Capp encountered Ham Fisher, the artist responsible for the strip *Joe Palooka*. Fisher had built the daily and Sunday strip about a heavyweight boxer into one of the most popular features in the country. It was a humorous adventure continuity, built around what can only be called the hero's good-natured stupidity and his hard fists. *Joe Palooka* was a good enough feature to be made into an early "all talking" movie starring Jimmy Durante as the hero's fast-talking, slightly bent manager, Knobby Walsh. Ham Fisher was one rich cartoonist when he gazed out from the back seat of his chauffered limo at the seedy-looking young man walking with a sheaf of drawings wrapped in paper under his arm.

The Fisher-Capp relationship was one that started in discord and slowly soured into bitterness over decades. It would climax in wild charges, devastating magazine articles and bitter in-fighting in the 1940s and 1950s. In 1933, it began with disagreement about how they met. There are even varying stories as to who was present at this historic occurrence. Fisher would claim later that he bet his chauffeur that the man walking down the street was a cartoonist, identified by the blue paper used by his own syndicate to wrap rejected art. The earliest story, from the mid-1930s, said Fisher was with a "smartly-dressed woman" and he bet *Capp* he was a cartoonist. In this version, Capp coldly turned him down because he thought the man was making fun of him. Besides, he didn't have the money for a wager — and he would have lost anyway. Fisher would say later that if it hadn't been for his stopping, Capp would have jumped off a bridge. This doesn't seem even remotely plausible, knowing even a little bit about Capp and his history, but it might reflect the desperate straits of a man with a wife to support and a baby on the way. Whatever happened, after Fisher told Capp not to "get sore" and identified himself, Capp was offered $10 to finish a *Joe Palooka* Sunday page.

With Catherine at Seabrook Beach, New Hampshire, 1932.

When Capp passed that test, he was hired as Fisher's assistant. He was put on either a $22.50 or $25 a week salary to work on the Sunday page, after which Fisher left promptly on an extended vacation. At least, so the legend goes. Fisher would have had to break the new man in, working at Fisher's luxurious apartment. Capp would also need some time for what Catherine Capp calls his "amazement, amusement and anger" at Fisher's lifestyle to grow. But grow it did; it seems a basic personality clash is mixed up in all that was to happen later.

It's unclear if Capp and Catherine saw the vaudeville show she chronicles in her introduction to this volume before or after Fisher went on vacation. Whatever the chronology, when Fisher left for six weeks, Capp filled the gap with a story involving a hillbilly named Big Leviticus, his family and friends. Capp did all the writing and art — even the lettering — on these pages. The roots of *Li'l Abner* are in that sequence; the characters and setting are echoes of what would follow in 1934. Big Leviticus lives in Minesburg, Kentucky, and is big and strong and stupid, like Abner. However, all resemblances end there. Unlike Abner and the rest of the Yokums, the characters created for *Joe Palooka* carry shootin' irons constantly, and are not averse to shootin' them. Ever alert for revenooers, they are sly and cunning and they likes their likker. They resemble the Scragg clan more than the innocent and amiable Yokums, who fight with their fists and don't intentionally drink. The Leviticus characters are ignorant predators, figures of ridicule. A reader is not supposed to like them, just be amused and at the same time repelled by them. The Abner clan is crucially different, victims who muddle through because they're "good," as Capp well knew. Yet Leviticus and his feral kin are the first incarnations of Abner and his family, and are the basis of the New York-style feud between Fisher and Capp. The *Joe Palooka* pages appeared in November of 1933, so Al and Catherine could well have been discussing and even working on *Li'l Abner* samples before or at the same time these pages appeared. According to the mid-1930s piece, Capp had 12 weeks of samples when he went shopping around with *Li'l Abner*, and the strip appeared in August of 1934. That reflects an intense period of work —

9

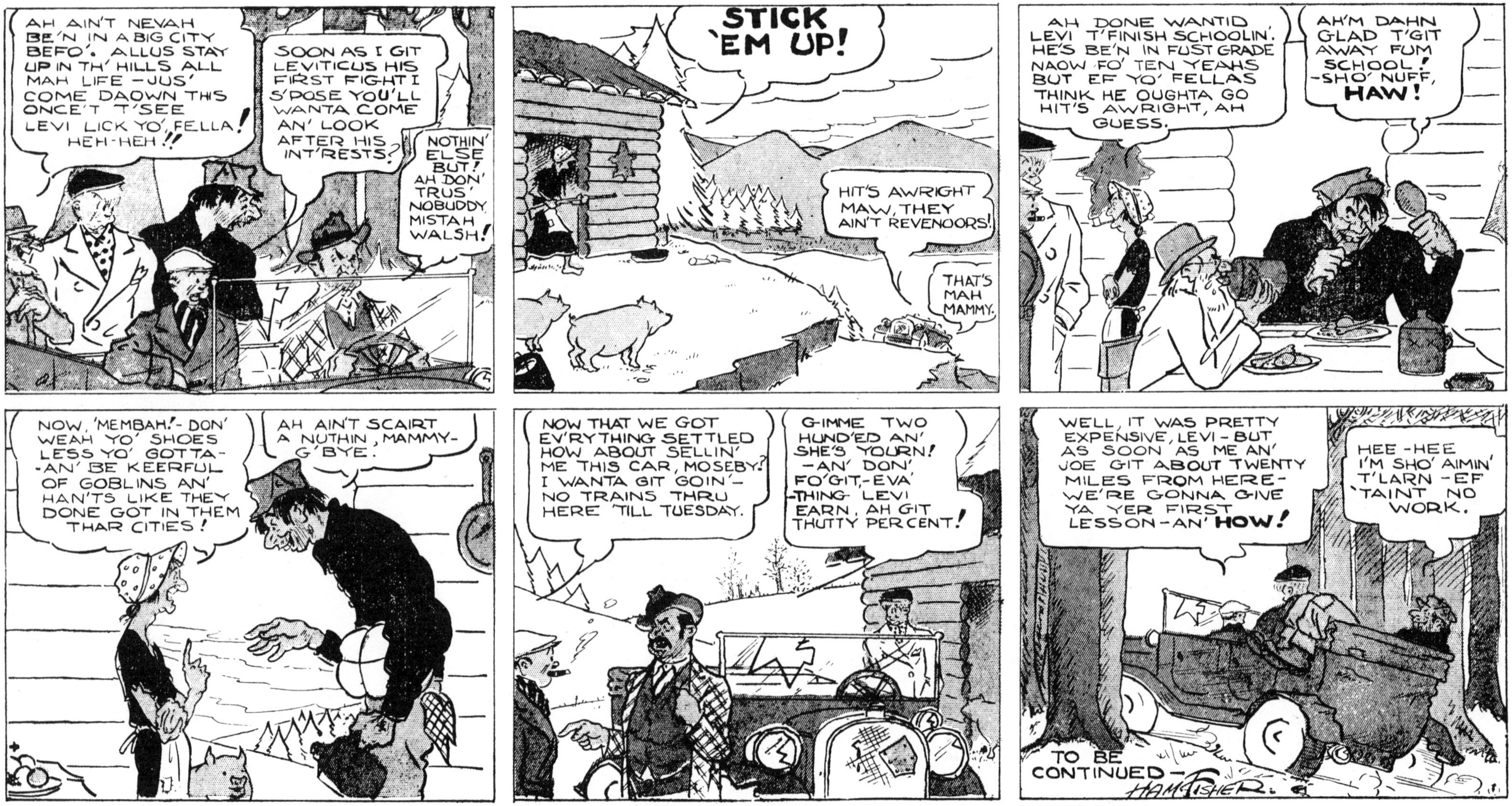
AH AIN'T NEVAH BE'N IN A BIG CITY BEFO'. ALLUS STAY UP IN TH' HILLS ALL MAH LIFE —JUS' COME DAOWN THIS ONCE'T T'SEE LEVI LICK YO' FELLA! HEH-HEH!!
SOON AS I GIT LEVITICUS HIS FIRST FIGHT I S'POSE YOU'LL WANTA COME AN' LOOK AFTER HIS INT'RESTS?
NOTHIN' ELSE BUT! AH DON' TRUS' NOBUDDY, MISTAH WALSH!
STICK 'EM UP!
HIT'S AWRIGHT MAW, THEY AIN'T REVENOORS!
THAT'S MAH MAMMY.
AH DONE WANTID LEVI T'FINISH SCHOOLIN'. HE'S BE'N IN FUST GRADE NAOW FO' TEN YEAHS BUT EF YO' FELLAS THINK HE OUGHTA GO HIT'S AWRIGHT, AH GUESS.
AH'M DAHN GLAD T'GIT AWAY FUM SCHOOL! -SHO' NUFF, HAW!
NOW, 'MEMBAH!- DON' WEAH YO' SHOES LESS YO' GOTTA- -AN' BE KEERFUL OF GOBLINS AN' HAN'TS LIKE THEY DONE GOT IN THEM THAR CITIES!
AH AIN'T SCAIRT A NUTHIN, MAMMY- G'BYE.
NOW THAT WE GOT EV'RYTHING SETTLED HOW ABOUT SELLIN' ME THIS CAR, MOSEBY? I WANTA GIT GOIN'— NO TRAINS THRU HERE 'TILL TUESDAY.
GIMME TWO HUND'ED AN' SHE'S YOURN! -AN' DON' FO'GIT,-EVA' THING LEVI EARN, AH GIT THUTTY PER CENT!
WELL, IT WAS PRETTY EXPENSIVE, LEVI - BUT AS SOON AS ME AN' JOE GIT ABOUT TWENTY MILES FROM HERE- WE'RE GONNA GIVE YA YER FIRST LESSON-AN' HOW!
HEE-HEE I'M SHO' AIMIN' T'LARN -EF 'TAINT NO WORK.
TO BE CONTINUED—
HAM FISHER

Section of the "Joe Palooka" page from November 12, 1933. Written and drawn by Al Capp, it features Big Leviticus, his Mammy and Pappy, and assorted pigs. Capp created the characters and drew a six-page Sunday adventure with them while "Palooka" artist Ham Fisher was on an extended vacation. After Capp left Fisher to create "Li'l Abner," Fisher would claim the young artist had stolen the characters. Capp felt that since he had created the hillbillies, he could use them. Actually, the Leviticus characters are very different from the Abner clan in personality, but the disagreement between the two artists eventually soured into a bitter feud.

producing, selling the strip to the syndicate and marketing the strip to newspapers—between November of 1933 and the official beginning of *Li'l Abner* nine months later.

Shortly after Fisher returned, Capp quit and began devoting his full time to generating the samples. It was not an amicable parting. When *Li'l Abner* appeared, Fisher felt that Capp had stolen characters which rightfully belonged to him; after all, the hillbillies "first" appeared in *Joe Palooka*. In 1933, however, Fisher was angered at the mere fact that Capp left him. He wasn't used to such ingratitude from his assistants, underpaid or not. The time would come when Fisher would resurrect the Leviticus troupe each year and claim they were the "first" hillbilly comic strip characters, ignoring the fact that Capp created them and that there had been other hillbillies in other strips well before Leviticus tromped across the page. The Capp-Fisher feud would get much worse from there, and will be detailed in future volumes. But in 1934, it was not in full bloom, and as late as 1937, Capp would allow himself to be quoted as saying: "He [Fisher] was a great artist. His work was then and is now right up with the best in the world. To him I owe all my success."

Although it was the first comic strip to utilize hillbillies as central characters, the creation of *Li'l Abner* did not happen in a vacuum. The vaudeville show jogged a young cartoonist's memories of a trip to the South. It has also been written that Capp heard a radio playing "Good Old Mountain Music" while at his apartment one day. In fact, the South was a presence in many places on the national scene in the early 1930s.

Erskine Caldwell's novel *Tobacco Road* was published in 1932. His *God's Little Acre* followed in 1933. Perhaps significantly, both garnered much publicity after being banned from sale in Boston, where Capp was living at least part of the time. Both were controversial (that is, they were bawdy and "naturalistic") best sellers. Another Southern novel, William Faulkner's *Light in August* was also published in 1932. It decidedly was not a best seller; but his scandalous 1931 Southern novel *Sanctuary* was, featuring as it did a torturing and tortured villain named "Popeye." Eugene O'Neill's play, *Ah, Wilderness*, had dual premieres in New York and San Francisco in 1933. Songs like "When the Moon Comes Over the Mountain," "Good Old Mountain Music," and "Stars Fell on Alabama" were popular.

In 1933, the Tennessee Valley Authority was created, and it would eventually bring electrification to *Li'l Abner* country. To help justify the TVA in 1933, the living conditions in the country's real Dogpatches were publicized, and Americans were shown hamlets and backward settlements which were very much like Abner's hometown, only not as cheerful.

The most prominent Southern man of the era, a man watched nervously by everyone who opposed him and loved as a god by everyone who followed him, was Senator Huey Long of Louisiana. Long had a cornpone facade that was backed by more than low cunning. An extremely intelligent man born into redneck poverty, he became one of the foremost demagogues of the 20th century. He called himself "Kingfish," after the scheming character on radio's *Amos 'n Andy* and his slogan was "every man a king, but no man wears a crown." His Share Our Wealth program promised much to the dispossessed by limiting everyone's money and spreading the surplus around. Privately, he wanted to be dictator of America; publicly, he helped steer the Democratic nomination to Franklin Roosevelt in 1932, and then was instrumental in forming the Social Security program and agitating for higher tax rates in the wealthy brackets. He ran Louisiana like a police state; his opponents were not safe at home or on the street. And he provided roads, schools, and relief for the poor. He got his percentage of every public works deal; and the people loved him. It was projected that he would get over six million votes in his presumed third party run in 1936, but an assassin killed him in 1935. There is no question that of all the political opponents FDR had after 1932, Long was by far the strongest and most dangerous. He had the followers and the brains to use them. Then and now, Long's right wing and lunatic fringe mates blamed the new president for the bullet, but the killer was the son of a man Long ruined in a local Louisiana election. The killer was instantly shot by the legion of Long's bodyguards.

Al Capp always followed what was happening on the national scene and in the culture, and it would be naive to think he wasn't aware of any of this. He probably read about and had an opinion on all of it. More important, while a song and a show may have jogged his memory, he was shrewd enough to know that a syndicate might jump at a strip set in the South. Such a strip might also prove complementary to Capp's own sense of humor and artistic ability.

Capp first took the strip to King Features, and according to legend, told syndicate head Joseph Connolly that "Ham Fisher says I am the most promising young cartoonist he has seen in 25 years." The tale goes on that Connolly liked the strip and offered Capp $200 or $250 a week for it, but only if he made a few changes. He wanted Abner in a suit, Daisy Mae in a dress, Mammy in a new personality, and the whole strip set in the suburbs. Capp, faced with a moral dilemma, left with his integrity unsullied and went to United Features Syndicate. After sitting around their office for two days, he barged into syndicate head Monte Bourjai-

Al Capp and his first daughter, Julie, in 1934.

ly's office and demanded he look at the strip. Bourjaily and his salesmen liked *Li'l Abner* just as it was, and offered Capp $50 a week. Capp thus took less money for more control of his own vision.

Catherine Capp says she doesn't remember this particular difficulty in selling the strip. It seems the story about King Features was gilded by Capp. According to writer Rick Marschall, who conducted Al Capp's last interview, Capp submitted the strip to King and then heard nothing while they were deciding whether to buy it or not, a normal if sadistic procedure in publishing. He then tried United Features. The story of his storming the fortress of Bourjaily's office is true, and taking that into account along with King's delay, it points to one overpowering motive on Capp's part: economic desperation. Julie Capp was on the scene by this time, and the Capp family had little income. The hair tearing episode Capp humorously depicted in a 1937 UFS press book, printed in this volume, is probably quite close, in its way, to the truth.

The syndicate salesmen approached their clients with *Li'l Abner* and could only generate eight sales. If that had happened today, *Li'l Abner* would have been stillborn. But someone at UFS must have had faith in the strip, and on Monday, August 13, 1934, *Li'l Abner* began its run.

Al Capp was 25 years old.

In the first week of *Li'l Abner*, all the main characters are in place, and though their physical appearances would change over the next 43 years, their personalities never did. Mammy's the boss, Pappy's the stooge, Abner's the lovable boob and Daisy Mae is a clinging vine. The only relationship that would change between the main characters would happen in 1952, when Abner finally married Daisy Mae (Capp's first attempt to marry them took place on Valentine's Day, 1935). The first volume also sees the introduction of Marryin' Sam, the terrible Scragg family, Hairless Joe and Abijah Gooch. Their personalities don't change much over the years, either. Capp's sense of his own characters—how they relate to each other and to the stories he would write for them—was already well-developed.

As soon as possible, Capp propelled Abner to New York and kept him there until December. The adventures of a bumpkin in a big city, an innocent abroad, reaches back to the earliest days of the European novel, if not before, and Capp would return Abner to New York in April of 1935 and yet again later in the year. Besides contrasting his innocent against the ways of sophisticates, Capp was also taking advantage of the vogue in "screwball" comedies Hollywood was cranking out. *It Happened One Night* was popular that year, and *My Man Godfrey* was around the corner. The Marx Brothers cavorted in the playgrounds of the rich in *Animal Crackers* and *Duck Soup*, and there were many more. These movies poked fun at the rich for being fools and congratulated the poor for their common sense. Phony nobility was part of that scene, and so Capp provided Baron Slinkovitch and his valet, Scarloff. The rich were venal, concerned with proprieties and procedures no longer relevant, and they were plain silly, so Capp trotted out Aunt Bessie and Mrs. Eppingham, who becomes a "love pirate" to Lem Scragg, of all people. The storyteller was already poking at facades.

The first volume is dotted with references to the times. There are women aviators (Amelia Earhart had flown the Atlantic solo in 1932), kidnappings (the Lindbergh case was reaching its climax at this time), and a character named Baby Face Floydinger (the Dillinger gang, with prominent members Baby Face Nelson, Pretty Boy Floyd and John Dillinger had been broken up in 1933, and Dillinger died in Chicago in the summer of 1934). There is only one specific event referred to in the strip. That is the sequence beginning in May of 1935, which addresses itself to the Gloria Vanderbilt custody case. In time, Capp would treat real events satirically; not here. His heart is worn prominently on his sleeve for the little girl, defenseless before her relatives, warring over her millions of dollars in trust. Abner is used for comic relief, and to provide a voice of sanity and love for the orphan. This sequence is soap opera, rather than broad satire. In fact, the first years of *Li'l Abner* are, as Capp points out in "Innocents in Peril," adventure stories with comic overtones. Certainly the strongest stories here are the Astorbux/Vanderbilt tale and the adventure with Babs, the aviator (who bears more than a passing resemblance to Catherine Capp). Capp would later complain that he "used to kill the most charming gags for the sake of suspense. It was a policy I invariably and grimly followed, and it was heartbreaking, but it paid off." He was learning what he called "dirty tricks" at this time, the most prominent one being where Abner is shot on a Saturday, and readers have to wait till Monday to find out if he survived.

Technically, *Li'l Abner* shows improvement in art and presentation from day one. Stiff at first, the art loosens up considerably as the months flow by. Capp always acknowledged the work of his assistants, and he had them from the very beginning. Yet, his own art—principally in the faces and in the human figures—shows ever growing confidence. As Catherine Capp notes, he was fussy about his lettering, and here he would be staking out new territory. As the stories progress, the dialogue becomes bolder and bolder within the balloons. Words are emphasized and leap out at the reader. Marschall pointed out in Capp's last interview that the artist was concerned about "infant mortality" in comic strips, and wanted his own to draw attention away from all the competing strips around it on the comics page. One way to do that was in the balloons. It gave the reader the notion that something exciting was going on all the time. Usually, that was true. Capp was a real student of the form, taking it very seriously, and as he became more comfortable with his work, he was able to implant little nuggets of interest into nearly every strip he wrote.

His first art assistant was Catherine Capp. His second was Moe Leff, a UFS artist who was also drawing the sports strip *Joe Jinks*. As nearly as can be determined, Leff began to work with Capp in early 1935, around March. Catherine notes that both she and Capp had trouble with cars, and in March, cars are shown in full, as are trains and other mechanical objects. More important, the art in general becomes more rounded and the strip in general more smooth at this time. The shadings and the animation in the figures all point to Leff coming aboard at this time. Capp was still vitally involved with the art, of course, and improving all the time. His work shows up most frequently in the faces and the figure of Abner himself. But Leff's strong, bold inking and his backgrounds began to make *Li'l Abner* a slick-looking strip.

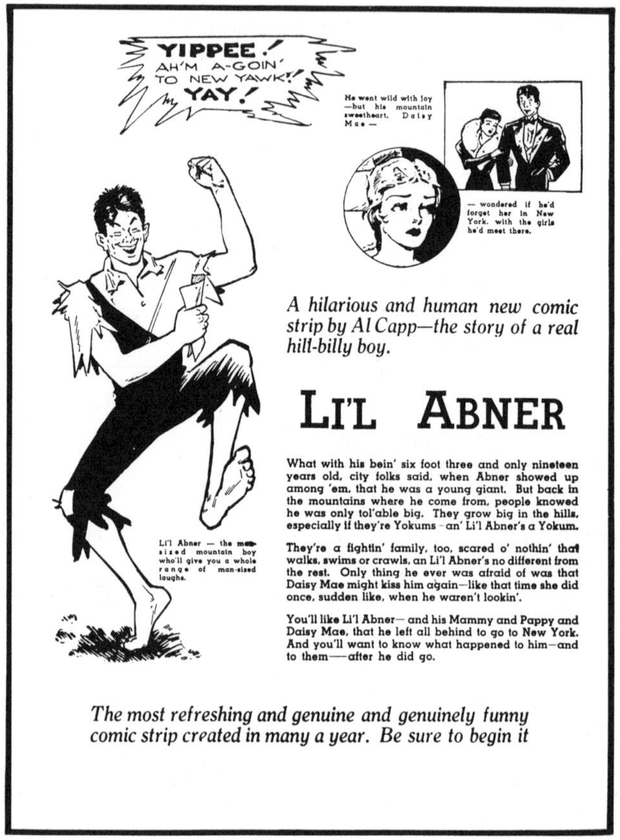

YIPPEE! AH'M A-GOIN' TO NEW YAWK!! YAY!
He went wild with joy —but his mountain sweetheart, Daisy Mae—
— wondered if he'd forget her in New York, with the girls he'd meet there.
A hilarious and human new comic strip by Al Capp—the story of a real hill-billy boy.
LI'L ABNER
What with his bein' six foot three and only nineteen years old, city folks said, when Abner showed up among 'em, that he was a young giant. But back in the mountains where he come from, people knowed he was only tol'able big. They grow big in the hills, especially if they're Yokums—an' Li'l Abner's a Yokum.
They're a fightin' family, too, scared o' nothin' that walks, swims or crawls, an Li'l Abner's no different from the rest. Only thing he ever was afraid of was that Daisy Mae might kiss him again—like that time she did once, sudden like, when he waren't lookin'.
You'll like Li'l Abner— and his Mammy and Pappy and Daisy Mae, that he left all behind to go to New York. And you'll want to know what happened to him—and to them—after he did go.
Li'l Abner — the man-sized mountain boy who'll give you a whole range of man-sized laughs.
The most refreshing and genuine and genuinely funny comic strip created in many a year. Be sure to begin it

Promotional ad for the new strip, "Li'l Abner," 1934.

As 1936 began, *Li'l Abner* was gaining in popularity. Soon, newspaper articles about Capp, generated by the syndicate, would appear. The client list was growing steadily and the artist was becoming confident with his strip. The salad days were ahead.

Bibliography

Caplin, Elliot, "We Called Him Alfred," Cartoonist ProFiles, 1979.
Capp, Al. "Al Capp by Li'l Abner," excerpted in *Life* magazine, June 24, 1946.
———"My Well-Balanced Life on a Wooden Leg," *Life*, May 23, 1960.
Grun, Bernard. *The Timetables of History*, Touchstone/Simon & Schuster, 1982.
Kahn, E.J. "Ooff!!! (Sob!!) Eep!!! (Gulp!!) Zowie!!!!—II," *New Yorker*, Dec. 6, 1947.
Maloney, Russell. "Li'l Abner's Capp," *Life*, June 24, 1946.
Marschall, Richard, "Saying Something About the Status Quo," *Nemo*, April, 1986
"Die Monstersinger," *Time* magazine, November 6, 1950.
United Features Syndicate press book. "How Al Capp Came to Create Li'l Abner," 1937.

LI'L ABNER

By Al Capp

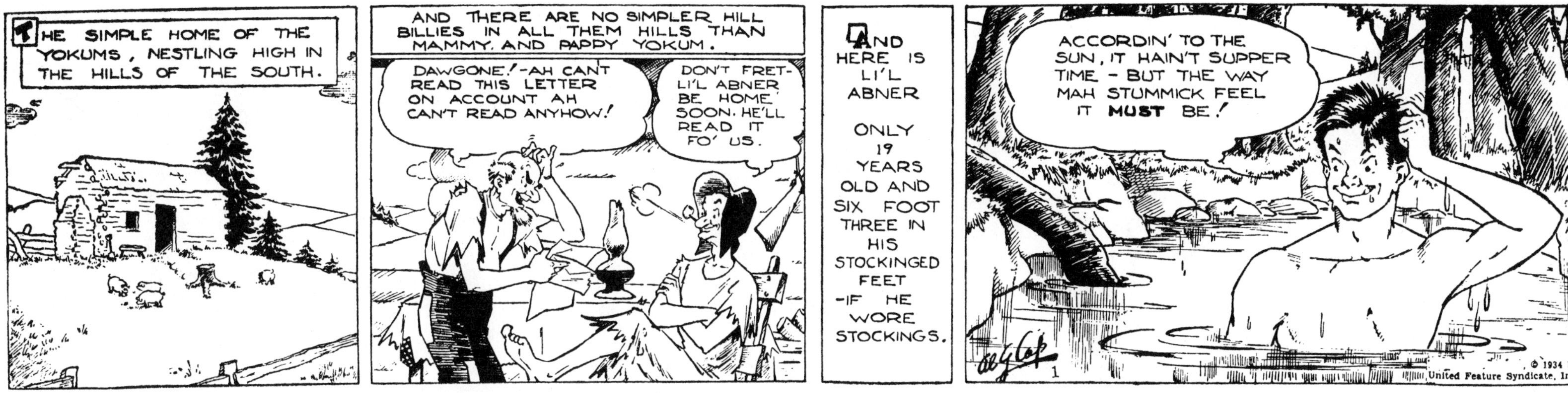
THE SIMPLE HOME OF THE YOKUMS, NESTLING HIGH IN THE HILLS OF THE SOUTH.
AND THERE ARE NO SIMPLER HILL BILLIES IN ALL THEM HILLS THAN MAMMY AND PAPPY YOKUM.
DAWGONE!-AH CAN'T READ THIS LETTER ON ACCOUNT AH CAN'T READ ANYHOW!
DON'T FRET- LI'L ABNER BE HOME SOON. HE'LL READ IT FO' US.
AND HERE IS LI'L ABNER ONLY 19 YEARS OLD AND SIX FOOT THREE IN HIS STOCKINGED FEET -IF HE WORE STOCKINGS.
ACCORDIN' TO THE SUN, IT HAIN'T SUPPER TIME - BUT THE WAY MAH STUMMICK FEEL IT MUST BE!
© 1934 by United Feature Syndicate, Inc.

LI'L ABNER

By Al Capp

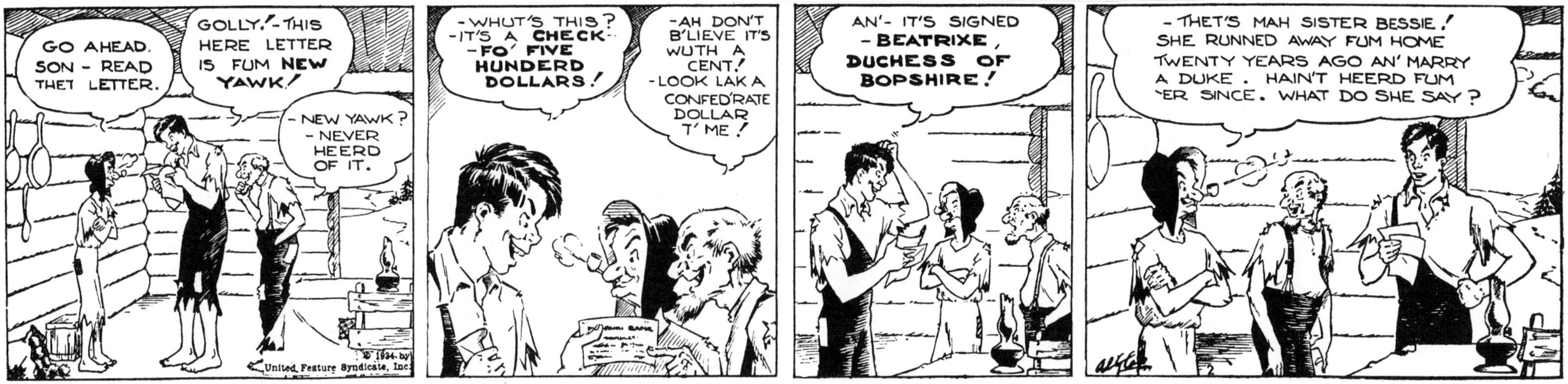
GO AHEAD, SON - READ THET LETTER.
GOLLY!-THIS HERE LETTER IS FUM NEW YAWK!
-NEW YAWK? -NEVER HEERD OF IT.
© 1934 by United Feature Syndicate, Inc.
-WHUT'S THIS? -IT'S A CHECK -FO' FIVE HUNDERD DOLLARS!
-AH DON'T B'LIEVE IT'S WUTH A CENT! -LOOK LAK A CONFED'RATE DOLLAR T'ME!
AN'- IT'S SIGNED -BEATRIXE, DUCHESS OF BOPSHIRE!
-THET'S MAH SISTER BESSIE! SHE RUNNED AWAY FUM HOME TWENTY YEARS AGO AN' MARRY A DUKE. HAIN'T HEERD FUM 'ER SINCE. WHAT DO SHE SAY?

LI'L ABNER *Daisy Mae Disappears* By Al Capp

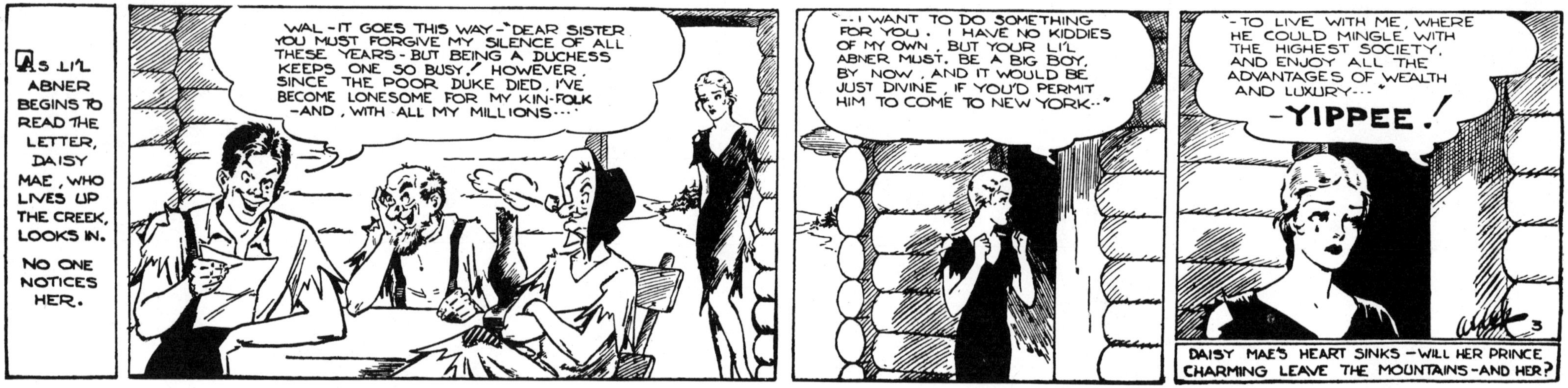
AS LI'L ABNER BEGINS TO READ THE LETTER, DAISY MAE, WHO LIVES UP THE CREEK, LOOKS IN.
NO ONE NOTICES HER.
WAL - IT GOES THIS WAY - "DEAR SISTER YOU MUST FORGIVE MY SILENCE OF ALL THESE YEARS - BUT BEING A DUCHESS KEEPS ONE SO BUSY! HOWEVER, SINCE THE POOR DUKE DIED, I'VE BECOME LONESOME FOR MY KIN-FOLK -AND, WITH ALL MY MILLIONS---
"--I WANT TO DO SOMETHING FOR YOU. I HAVE NO KIDDIES OF MY OWN, BUT YOUR LI'L ABNER MUST BE A BIG BOY, BY NOW, AND IT WOULD BE JUST DIVINE, IF YOU'D PERMIT HIM TO COME TO NEW YORK--"
"-TO LIVE WITH ME, WHERE HE COULD MINGLE WITH THE HIGHEST SOCIETY, AND ENJOY ALL THE ADVANTAGES OF WEALTH AND LUXURY---"
-YIPPEE!
DAISY MAE'S HEART SINKS - WILL HER PRINCE CHARMING LEAVE THE MOUNTAINS - AND HER?

LI'L ABNER **Just Like a Gal!** By Al Capp

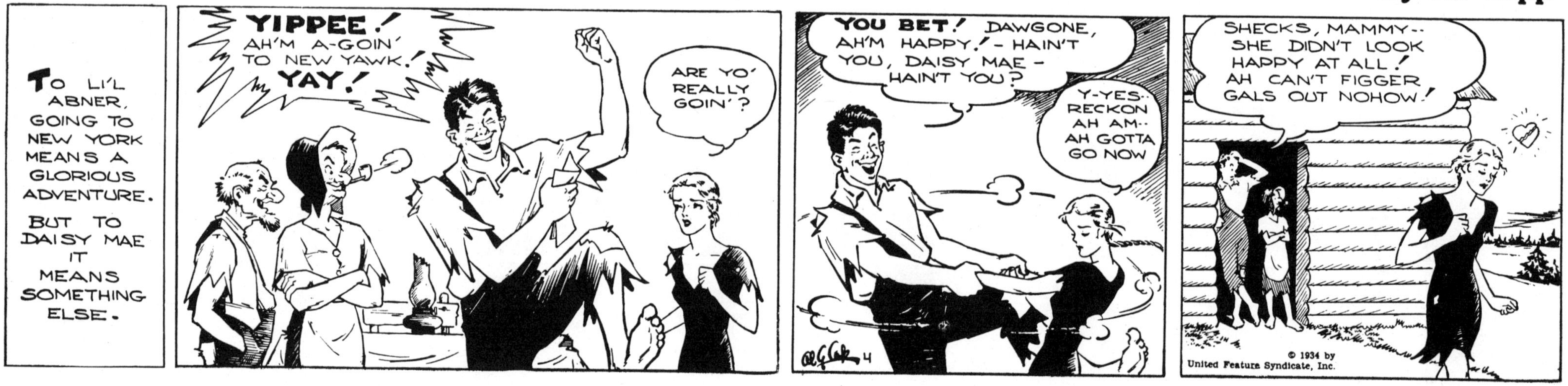
TO LI'L ABNER, GOING TO NEW YORK MEANS A GLORIOUS ADVENTURE.
BUT TO DAISY MAE IT MEANS SOMETHING ELSE.
YIPPEE! AH'M A-GOIN' TO NEW YAWK! YAY!
ARE YO' REALLY GOIN'?
YOU BET! DAWGONE, AH'M HAPPY! - HAIN'T YOU, DAISY MAE - HAIN'T YOU?
Y-YES- RECKON AH AM-- AH GOTTA GO NOW
SHECKS, MAMMY-- SHE DIDN'T LOOK HAPPY AT ALL! AH CAN'T FIGGER GALS OUT NOHOW!
© 1934 by United Feature Syndicate, Inc.

LI'L ABNER Pore Daisy! By Al Capp

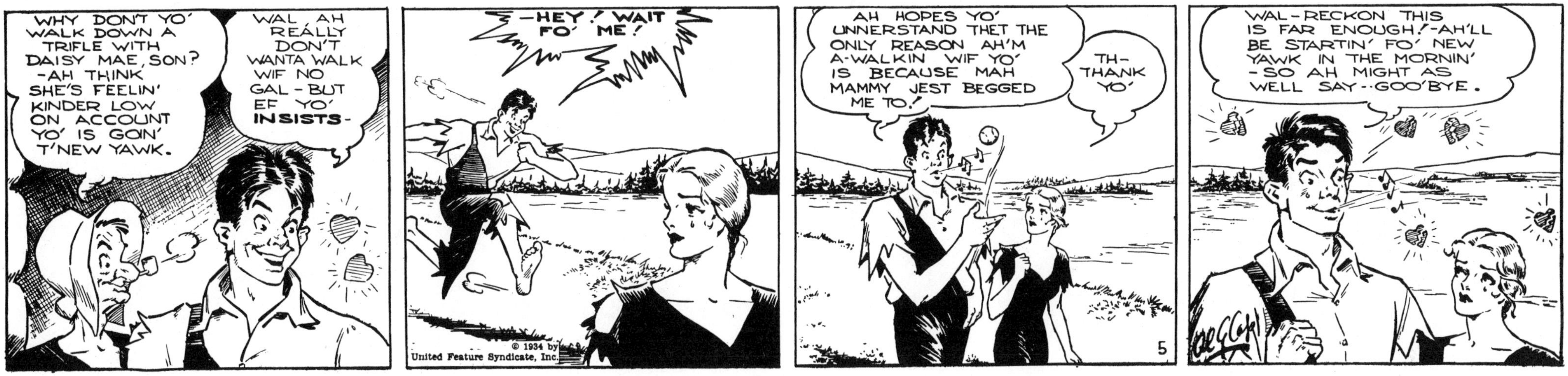
WHY DON'T YO' WALK DOWN A TRIFLE WITH DAISY MAE, SON? -AH THINK SHE'S FEELIN' KINDER LOW ON ACCOUNT YO' IS GOIN' T'NEW YAWK.
WAL AH REALLY DON'T WANTA WALK WIF NO GAL - BUT EF YO' INSISTS-
-HEY! WAIT FO' ME!
© 1934 by United Feature Syndicate, Inc.
AH HOPES YO' UNNERSTAND THET THE ONLY REASON AH'M A-WALKIN WIF YO' IS BECAUSE MAH MAMMY JEST BEGGED ME TO.!
TH-THANK YO'
5
WAL-RECKON THIS IS FAR ENOUGH!-AH'LL BE STARTIN' FO' NEW YAWK IN THE MORNIN' -SO AH MIGHT AS WELL SAY--GOO'BYE.

LI'L ABNER That S'cuses It By Al Capp

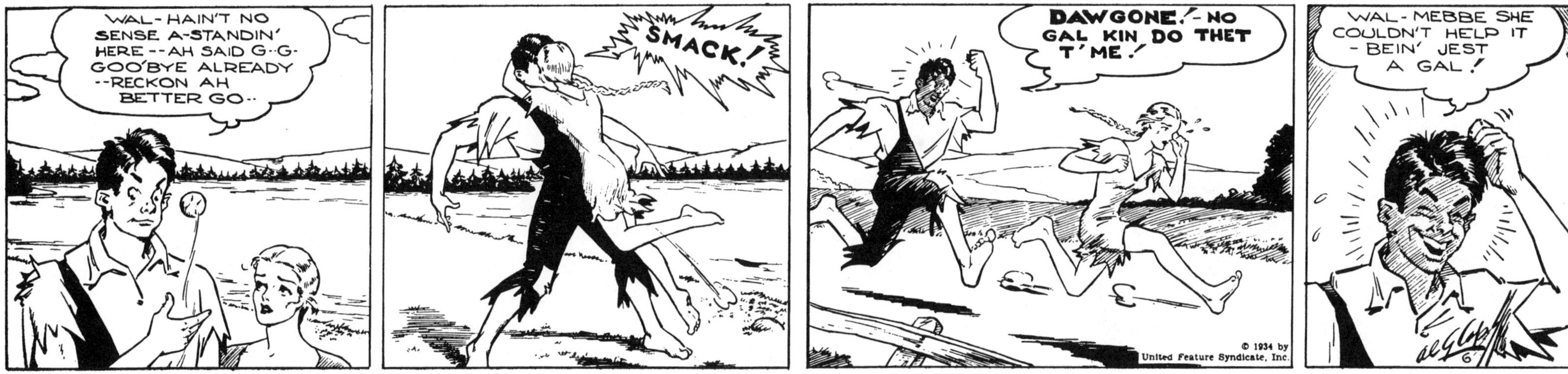
WAL-HAIN'T NO SENSE A-STANDIN' HERE--AH SAID G-G-GOO'BYE ALREADY --RECKON AH BETTER GO--
SMACK!
DAWGONE!-NO GAL KIN DO THET T'ME.!
© 1934 by United Feature Syndicate, Inc.
WAL-MEBBE SHE COULDN'T HELP IT -BEIN' JEST A GAL!
6

LI'L ABNER It Makes a Difference

By Al Capp

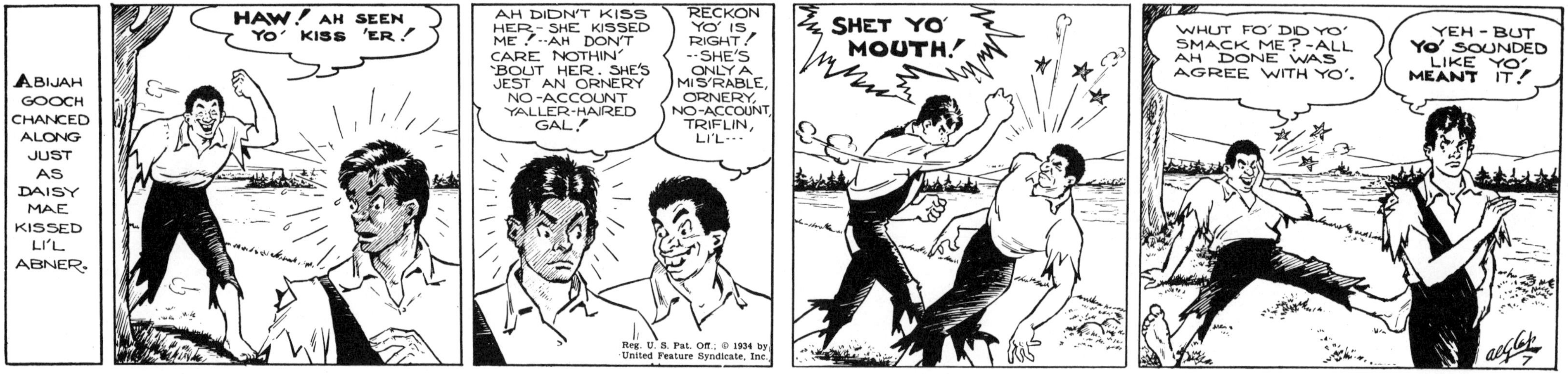
ABIJAH GOOCH CHANCED ALONG JUST AS DAISY MAE KISSED LI'L ABNER.
HAW! AH SEEN YO' KISS 'ER!
AH DIDN'T KISS HER - SHE KISSED ME! --AH DON'T CARE NOTHIN' 'BOUT HER. SHE'S JEST AN ORNERY NO-ACCOUNT YALLER-HAIRED GAL!
RECKON YO' IS RIGHT! --SHE'S ONLY A MIS'RABLE, ORNERY, NO-ACCOUNT, TRIFLIN, LI'L---
Reg. U. S. Pat. Off.; © 1934 by United Feature Syndicate, Inc.
SHET YO' MOUTH!
WHUT FO' DID YO' SMACK ME? - ALL AH DONE WAS AGREE WITH YO'.
YEH - BUT YO' SOUNDED LIKE YO' MEANT IT!
Al Capp
7

LI'L ABNER Off on His Own

By Al Capp

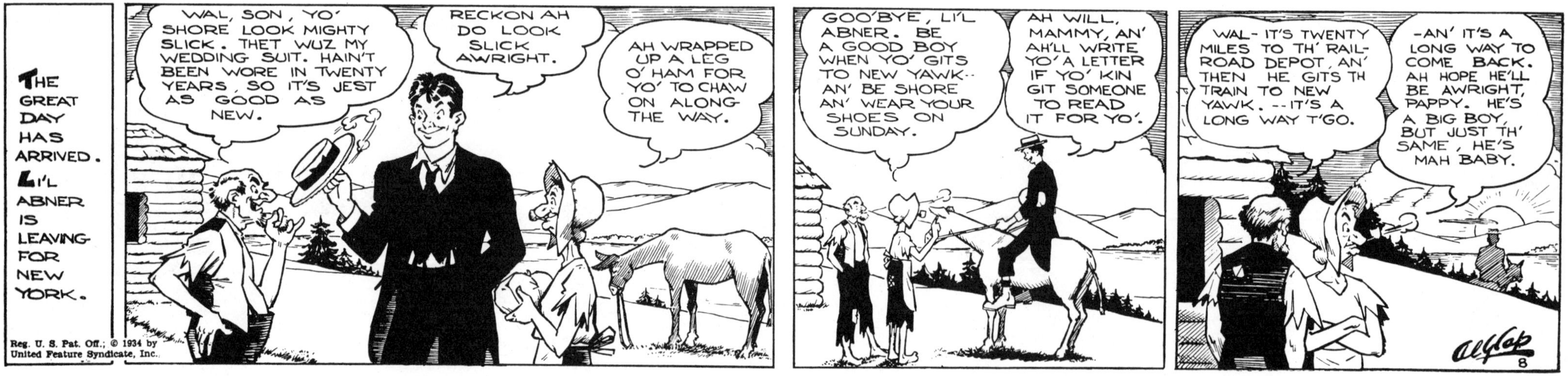
THE GREAT DAY HAS ARRIVED. LI'L ABNER IS LEAVING FOR NEW YORK.
WAL, SON, YO' SHORE LOOK MIGHTY SLICK. THET WUZ MY WEDDING SUIT. HAIN'T BEEN WORE IN TWENTY YEARS, SO IT'S JEST AS GOOD AS NEW.
RECKON AH DO LOOK SLICK AWRIGHT.
AH WRAPPED UP A LEG O' HAM FOR YO' TO CHAW ON ALONG THE WAY.
Reg. U. S. Pat. Off.; © 1934 by United Feature Syndicate, Inc.
GOO'BYE, LI'L ABNER. BE A GOOD BOY WHEN YO' GITS TO NEW YAWK-- AN' BE SHORE AN' WEAR YOUR SHOES ON SUNDAY.
AH WILL, MAMMY, AN' AH'LL WRITE YO' A LETTER IF YO' KIN GIT SOMEONE TO READ IT FOR YO'.
WAL - IT'S TWENTY MILES TO TH' RAIL-ROAD DEPOT, AN' THEN HE GITS TH TRAIN TO NEW YAWK. --IT'S A LONG WAY T'GO.
-AN' IT'S A LONG WAY TO COME BACK. AH HOPE HE'LL BE AWRIGHT, PAPPY. HE'S A BIG BOY, BUT JUST TH' SAME, HE'S MAH BABY.
Al Capp
8

LI'L ABNER Well Laid Plans By Al Capp

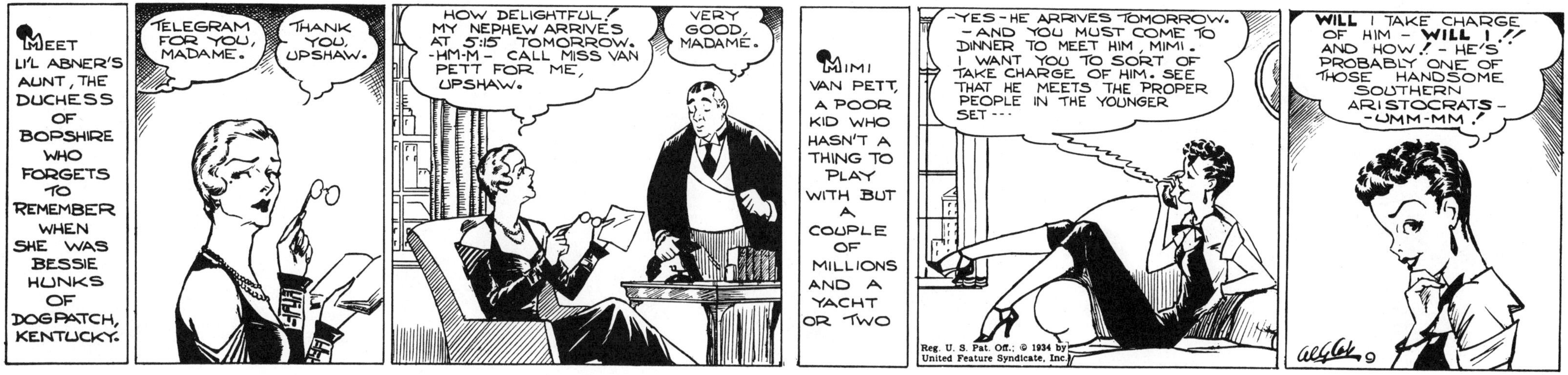
MEET LI'L ABNER'S AUNT, THE DUCHESS OF BOPSHIRE WHO FORGETS TO REMEMBER WHEN SHE WAS BESSIE HUNKS OF DOGPATCH, KENTUCKY.
TELEGRAM FOR YOU, MADAME.
THANK YOU, UPSHAW.
HOW DELIGHTFUL! MY NEPHEW ARRIVES AT 5:15 TOMORROW. -HM-M- CALL MISS VAN PETT FOR ME, UPSHAW.
VERY GOOD, MADAME.
MIMI VAN PETT, A POOR KID WHO HASN'T A THING TO PLAY WITH BUT A COUPLE OF MILLIONS AND A YACHT OR TWO
-YES-HE ARRIVES TOMORROW. -AND YOU MUST COME TO DINNER TO MEET HIM, MIMI. I WANT YOU TO SORT OF TAKE CHARGE OF HIM. SEE THAT HE MEETS THE PROPER PEOPLE IN THE YOUNGER SET---
Reg. U. S. Pat. Off.; © 1934 by United Feature Syndicate, Inc.
WILL I TAKE CHARGE OF HIM - WILL I!!! AND HOW! - HE'S PROBABLY ONE OF THOSE HANDSOME SOUTHERN ARISTOCRATS - -UMM-MM!

LI'L ABNER The Big Town By Al Capp

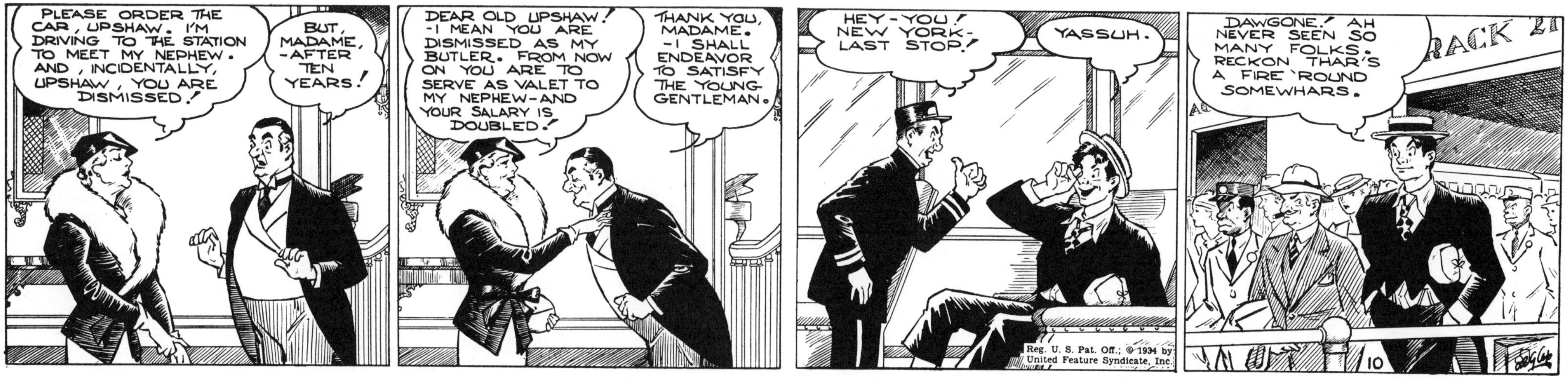
PLEASE ORDER THE CAR, UPSHAW. I'M DRIVING TO THE STATION TO MEET MY NEPHEW. AND, INCIDENTALLY, UPSHAW, YOU ARE DISMISSED!
BUT, MADAME, -AFTER TEN YEARS!
DEAR OLD UPSHAW! -I MEAN YOU ARE DISMISSED AS MY BUTLER. FROM NOW ON YOU ARE TO SERVE AS VALET TO MY NEPHEW-AND YOUR SALARY IS DOUBLED!
THANK YOU, MADAME. -I SHALL ENDEAVOR TO SATISFY THE YOUNG GENTLEMAN.
HEY-YOU! NEW YORK-LAST STOP!
YASSUH.
Reg. U. S. Pat. Off.; © 1934 by United Feature Syndicate, Inc.
DAWGONE! AH NEVER SEEN SO MANY FOLKS. RECKON THAR'S A FIRE 'ROUND SOMEWHARS.

LI'L ABNER Perfect Illusion

By Al Capp

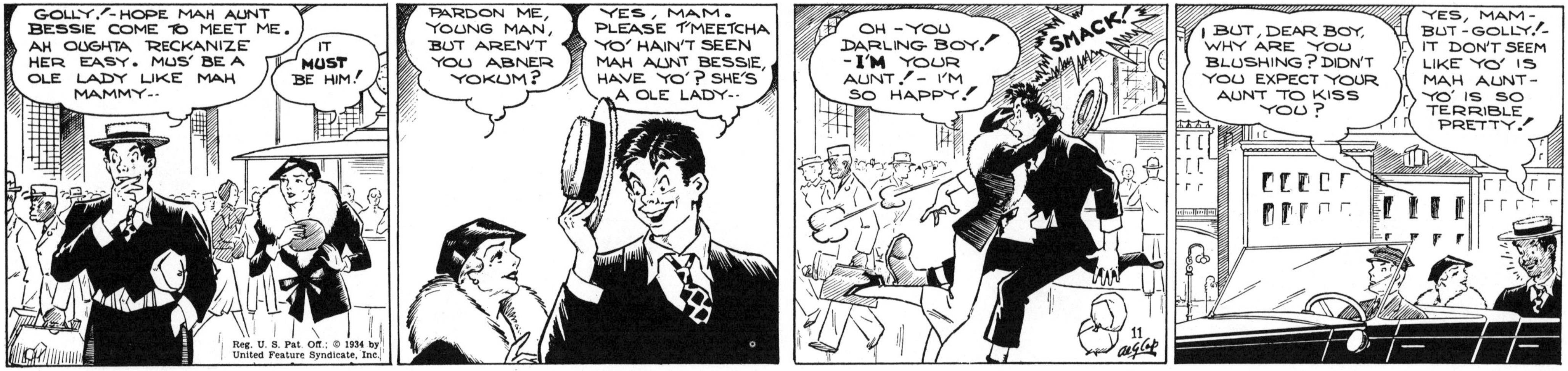

GOLLY.!-HOPE MAH AUNT BESSIE COME TO MEET ME. AH OUGHTA RECKANIZE HER EASY. MUS' BE A OLE LADY LIKE MAH MAMMY--
IT MUST BE HIM!
Reg. U. S. Pat. Off.; © 1934 by United Feature Syndicate, Inc.
PARDON ME, YOUNG MAN, BUT AREN'T YOU ABNER YOKUM?
YES, MAM. PLEASE T'MEETCHA YO' HAIN'T SEEN MAH AUNT BESSIE, HAVE YO'? SHE'S A OLE LADY--
OH-YOU DARLING BOY.! -I'M YOUR AUNT.!- I'M SO HAPPY.!
SMACK!
11
BUT, DEAR BOY, WHY ARE YOU BLUSHING? DIDN'T YOU EXPECT YOUR AUNT TO KISS YOU?
YES, MAM- BUT-GOLLY.!- IT DON'T SEEM LIKE YO' IS MAH AUNT- YO' IS SO TERRIBLE PRETTY.!

LI'L ABNER Getting Acquainted

By Al Capp

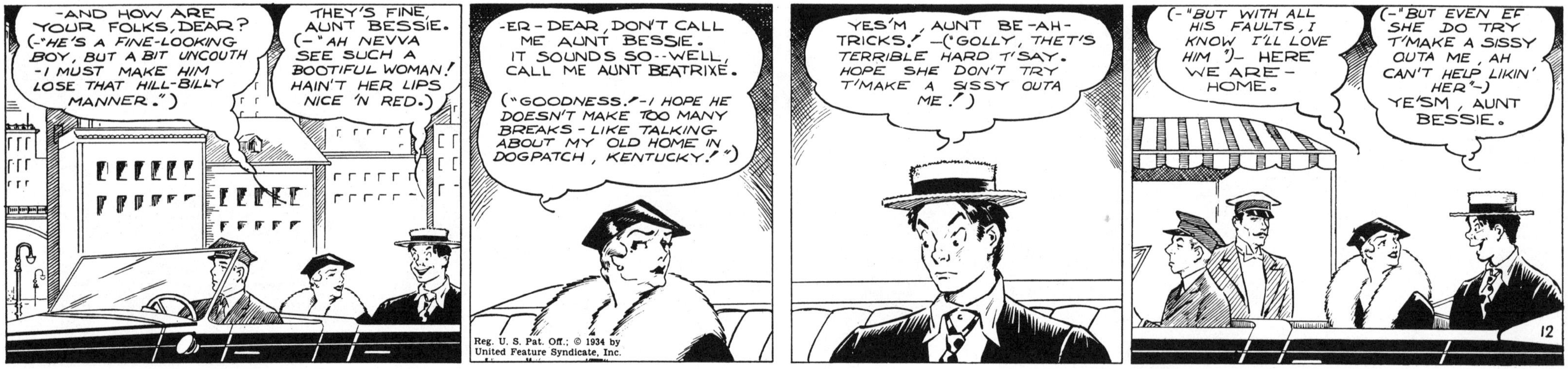

-AND HOW ARE YOUR FOLKS, DEAR? (-"HE'S A FINE-LOOKING BOY, BUT A BIT UNCOUTH -I MUST MAKE HIM LOSE THAT HILL-BILLY MANNER.")
THEY'S FINE, AUNT BESSIE. (-"AH NEVVA SEE SUCH A BOOTIFUL WOMAN! HAIN'T HER LIPS NICE 'N RED.)
-ER-DEAR, DON'T CALL ME AUNT BESSIE. IT SOUNDS SO--WELL, CALL ME AUNT BEATRIXE.
("GOODNESS.!-I HOPE HE DOESN'T MAKE TOO MANY BREAKS-LIKE TALKING ABOUT MY OLD HOME IN DOGPATCH, KENTUCKY.!")
Reg. U. S. Pat. Off.; © 1934 by United Feature Syndicate, Inc.
YES'M, AUNT BE-AH-TRICKS.!-("GOLLY, THET'S TERRIBLE HARD T'SAY. HOPE SHE DON'T TRY T'MAKE A SISSY OUTA ME.!")
(-"BUT WITH ALL HIS FAULTS, I KNOW I'LL LOVE HIM")- HERE WE ARE- HOME.
(-"BUT EVEN EF SHE DO TRY T'MAKE A SISSY OUTA ME, AH CAN'T HELP LIKIN' HER"-) YE'SM, AUNT BESSIE.
12

LI'L ABNER Without Stretching the Truth

By Al Capp

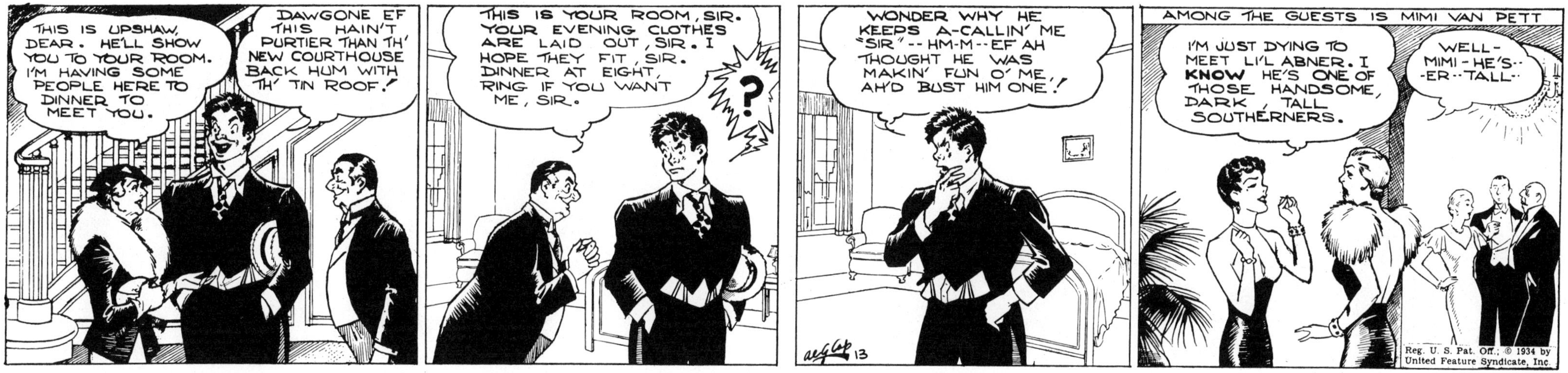
THIS IS UPSHAW, DEAR. HE'LL SHOW YOU TO YOUR ROOM. I'M HAVING SOME PEOPLE HERE TO DINNER TO MEET YOU.
DAWGONE EF THIS HAIN'T PURTIER THAN TH' NEW COURTHOUSE BACK HUM WITH TH' TIN ROOF!
THIS IS YOUR ROOM, SIR. YOUR EVENING CLOTHES ARE LAID OUT, SIR. I HOPE THEY FIT, SIR. DINNER AT EIGHT. RING IF YOU WANT ME, SIR.
?
WONDER WHY HE KEEPS A-CALLIN' ME "SIR"--HM-M--EF AH THOUGHT HE WAS MAKIN' FUN O' ME, AH'D BUST HIM ONE!
AMONG THE GUESTS IS MIMI VAN PETT
I'M JUST DYING TO MEET LI'L ABNER. I KNOW HE'S ONE OF THOSE HANDSOME, DARK, TALL SOUTHERNERS.
WELL-MIMI-HE'S--ER--TALL--
Reg. U. S. Pat. Off.; © 1934 by United Feature Syndicate, Inc.

LI'L ABNER Better and Better

By Al Capp

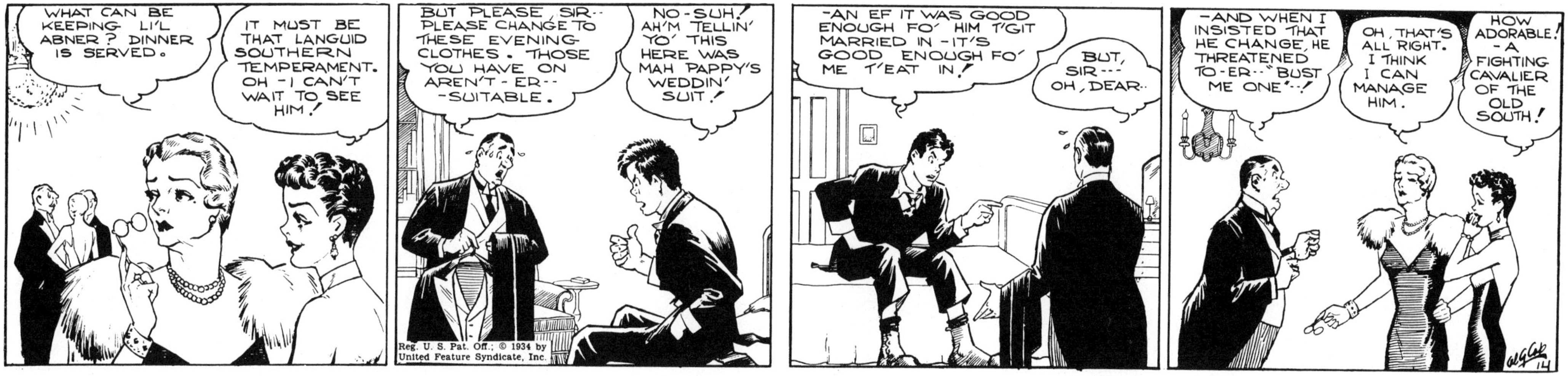
WHAT CAN BE KEEPING LI'L ABNER? DINNER IS SERVED.
IT MUST BE THAT LANGUID SOUTHERN TEMPERAMENT. OH-I CAN'T WAIT TO SEE HIM!
BUT PLEASE, SIR--PLEASE CHANGE TO THESE EVENING CLOTHES. THOSE YOU HAVE ON AREN'T-ER--SUITABLE.
NO-SUH! AH'M TELLIN' YO' THIS HERE WAS MAH PAPPY'S WEDDIN' SUIT!
Reg. U. S. Pat. Off.; © 1934 by United Feature Syndicate, Inc.
-AN EF IT WAS GOOD ENOUGH FO' HIM T'GIT MARRIED IN-IT'S GOOD ENOUGH FO' ME T'EAT IN!
BUT, SIR--- OH, DEAR..
-AND WHEN I INSISTED THAT HE CHANGE, HE THREATENED TO-ER--"BUST ME ONE"--!
OH, THAT'S ALL RIGHT. I THINK I CAN MANAGE HIM.
HOW ADORABLE! -A FIGHTING CAVALIER OF THE OLD SOUTH!

LI'L ABNER A One-Track Mind

By Al Capp

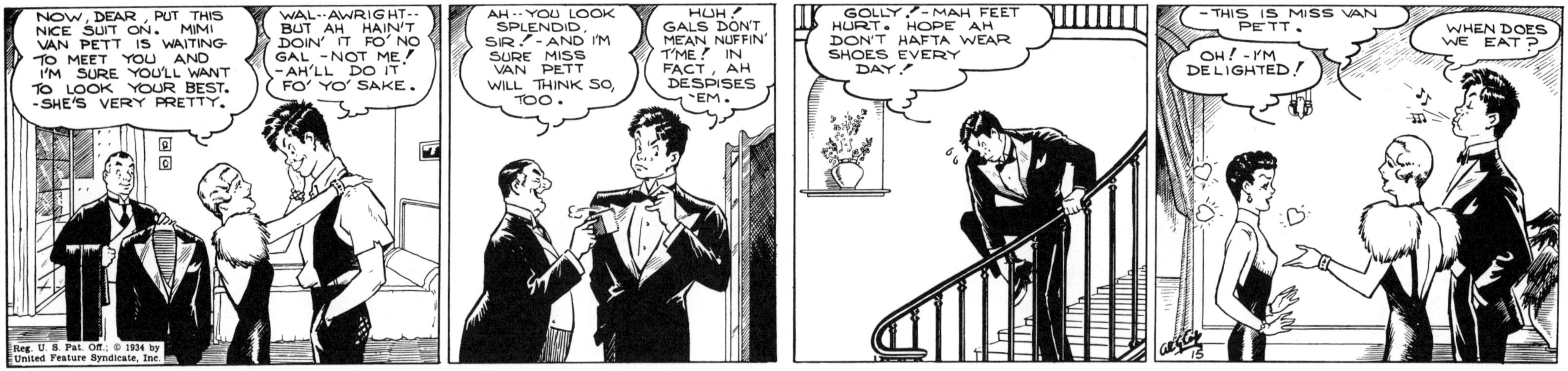

NOW, DEAR, PUT THIS NICE SUIT ON. MIMI VAN PETT IS WAITING TO MEET YOU AND I'M SURE YOU'LL WANT TO LOOK YOUR BEST. -SHE'S VERY PRETTY.
WAL--AWRIGHT--BUT AH HAIN'T DOIN' IT FO' NO GAL -NOT ME! -AH'LL DO IT FO' YO' SAKE.
Reg. U. S. Pat. Off.; © 1934 by United Feature Syndicate, Inc.
AH--YOU LOOK SPLENDID, SIR! -AND I'M SURE MISS VAN PETT WILL THINK SO, TOO.
HUH! GALS DON'T MEAN NUFFIN' T'ME! IN FACT, AH DESPISES 'EM.
GOLLY! -MAH FEET HURT. HOPE AH DON'T HAFTA WEAR SHOES EVERY DAY!
-THIS IS MISS VAN PETT.
OH! -I'M DELIGHTED!
WHEN DOES WE EAT?
15

LI'L ABNER We All Understand One Another

By Al Capp

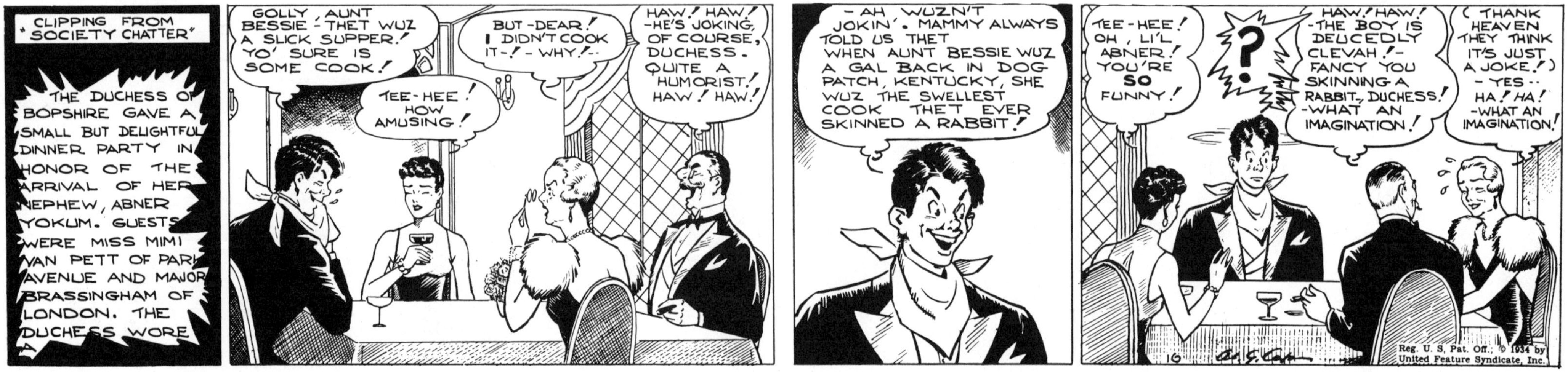

CLIPPING FROM "SOCIETY CHATTER"
THE DUCHESS OF BOPSHIRE GAVE A SMALL BUT DELIGHTFUL DINNER PARTY IN HONOR OF THE ARRIVAL OF HER NEPHEW, ABNER YOKUM. GUESTS WERE MISS MIMI VAN PETT OF PARK AVENUE AND MAJOR BRASSINGHAM OF LONDON. THE DUCHESS WORE A
GOLLY, AUNT BESSIE - THET WUZ A SLICK SUPPER! YO' SURE IS SOME COOK!
TEE-HEE! HOW AMUSING!
BUT-DEAR! I DIDN'T COOK IT-! -WHY!-
HAW! HAW! -HE'S JOKING, OF COURSE, DUCHESS. QUITE A HUMORIST! HAW! HAW!
-AH WUZN'T JOKIN'. MAMMY ALWAYS TOLD US THET WHEN AUNT BESSIE WUZ A GAL BACK IN DOG PATCH, KENTUCKY, SHE WUZ THE SWELLEST COOK THET EVER SKINNED A RABBIT!
TEE-HEE! OH, LI'L ABNER! YOU'RE SO FUNNY!
?
HAW! HAW! -THE BOY IS DEUCEDLY CLEVAH! -FANCY YOU SKINNING A RABBIT, DUCHESS! -WHAT AN IMAGINATION!
(THANK HEAVEN THEY THINK IT'S JUST A JOKE!) -YES--HA! HA! -WHAT AN IMAGINATION!
16
Reg. U. S. Pat. Off.; © 1934 by United Feature Syndicate, Inc.

LI'L ABNER — The Call of the Wild — By Al Capp

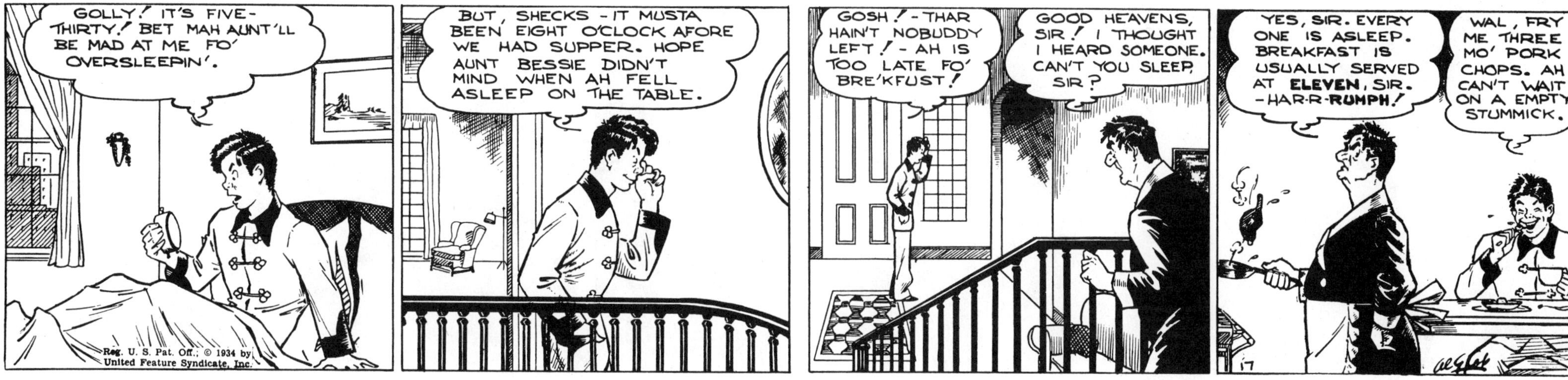

GOLLY! IT'S FIVE-THIRTY! BET MAH AUNT'LL BE MAD AT ME FO' OVERSLEEPIN'.
Reg. U. S. Pat. Off.; © 1934 by United Feature Syndicate, Inc.
BUT, SHECKS - IT MUSTA BEEN EIGHT O'CLOCK AFORE WE HAD SUPPER. HOPE AUNT BESSIE DIDN'T MIND WHEN AH FELL ASLEEP ON THE TABLE.
GOSH! - THAR HAIN'T NOBUDDY LEFT! - AH IS TOO LATE FO' BRE'KFUST!
GOOD HEAVENS, SIR! I THOUGHT I HEARD SOMEONE. CAN'T YOU SLEEP, SIR?
YES, SIR. EVERY ONE IS ASLEEP. BREAKFAST IS USUALLY SERVED AT ELEVEN, SIR. -HAR-R-RUMPH!
WAL, FRY ME THREE MO' PORK CHOPS. AH CAN'T WAIT ON A EMPTY STUMMICK.
17

LI'L ABNER — Won Over — By Al Capp

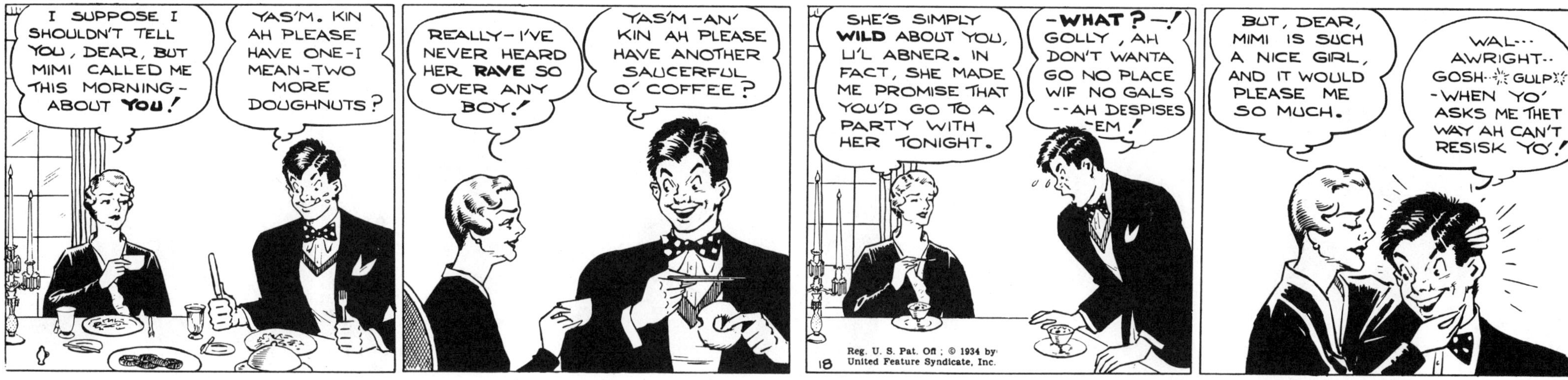

I SUPPOSE I SHOULDN'T TELL YOU, DEAR, BUT MIMI CALLED ME THIS MORNING - ABOUT YOU!
YAS'M. KIN AH PLEASE HAVE ONE-I MEAN-TWO MORE DOUGHNUTS?
REALLY- I'VE NEVER HEARD HER RAVE SO OVER ANY BOY!
YAS'M -AN' KIN AH PLEASE HAVE ANOTHER SAUCERFUL O' COFFEE?
SHE'S SIMPLY WILD ABOUT YOU, LI'L ABNER. IN FACT, SHE MADE ME PROMISE THAT YOU'D GO TO A PARTY WITH HER TONIGHT.
-WHAT? -! GOLLY, AH DON'T WANTA GO NO PLACE WIF NO GALS --AH DESPISES 'EM!
18
Reg. U. S. Pat. Off.; © 1934 by United Feature Syndicate, Inc.
BUT, DEAR, MIMI IS SUCH A NICE GIRL, AND IT WOULD PLEASE ME SO MUCH.
WAL--- AWRIGHT-- GOSH-- GULP - WHEN YO' ASKS ME THET WAY AH CAN'T RESISK YO'!

LI'L ABNER Trouble in the Offing By Al Capp

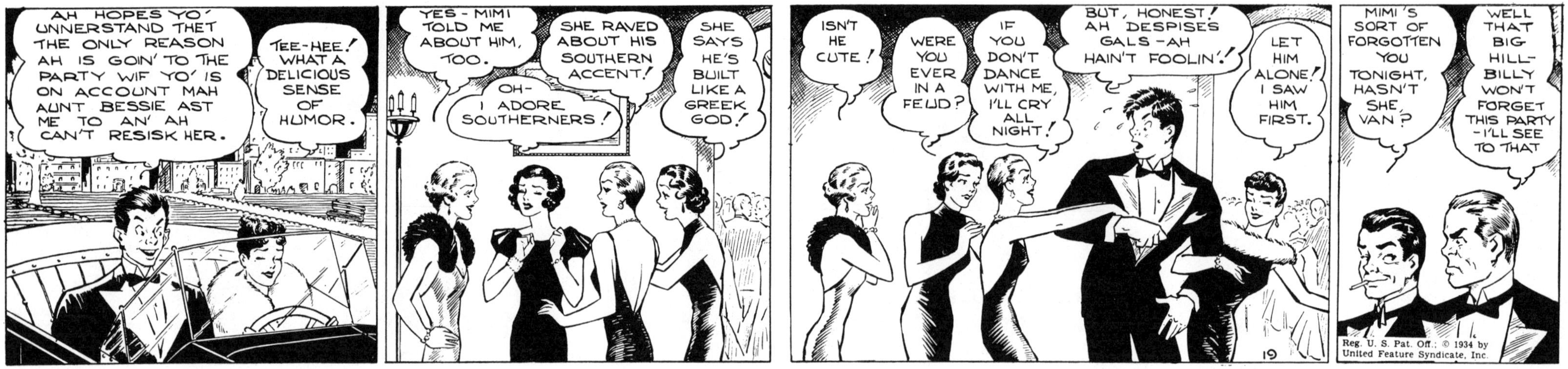
AH HOPES YO' UNNERSTAND THET THE ONLY REASON AH IS GOIN' TO THE PARTY WIF YO' IS ON ACCOUNT MAH AUNT BESSIE AST ME TO AN' AH CAN'T RESISK HER.
TEE-HEE! WHAT A DELICIOUS SENSE OF HUMOR.
YES - MIMI TOLD ME ABOUT HIM, TOO.
OH- I ADORE SOUTHERNERS!
SHE RAVED ABOUT HIS SOUTHERN ACCENT!
SHE SAYS HE'S BUILT LIKE A GREEK GOD!
ISN'T HE CUTE!
WERE YOU EVER IN A FEUD?
IF YOU DON'T DANCE WITH ME, I'LL CRY ALL NIGHT!
BUT, HONEST! AH DESPISES GALS -AH HAIN'T FOOLIN'!
LET HIM ALONE! I SAW HIM FIRST.
19
MIMI'S SORT OF FORGOTTEN YOU TONIGHT, HASN'T SHE, VAN?
WELL THAT BIG HILL-BILLY WON'T FORGET THIS PARTY -I'LL SEE TO THAT
Reg. U. S. Pat. Off.; © 1934 by United Feature Syndicate, Inc.

LI'L ABNER Fightin' Words! By Al Capp

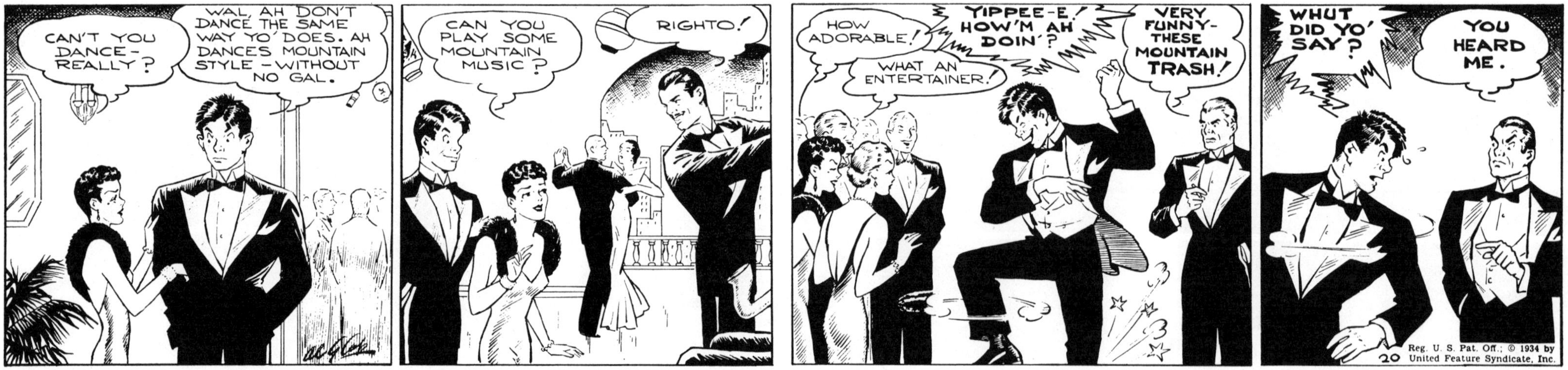
CAN'T YOU DANCE- REALLY?
WAL, AH DON'T DANCE THE SAME WAY YO' DOES. AH DANCES MOUNTAIN STYLE - WITHOUT NO GAL.
CAN YOU PLAY SOME MOUNTAIN MUSIC?
RIGHTO!
HOW ADORABLE!
WHAT AN ENTERTAINER!
YIPPEE-E! HOW'M AH DOIN'?
VERY FUNNY- THESE MOUNTAIN TRASH!
WHUT DID YO' SAY?
YOU HEARD ME.
20
Reg. U. S. Pat. Off.; © 1934 by United Feature Syndicate, Inc.

LI'L ABNER First Blood ! By Al Capp

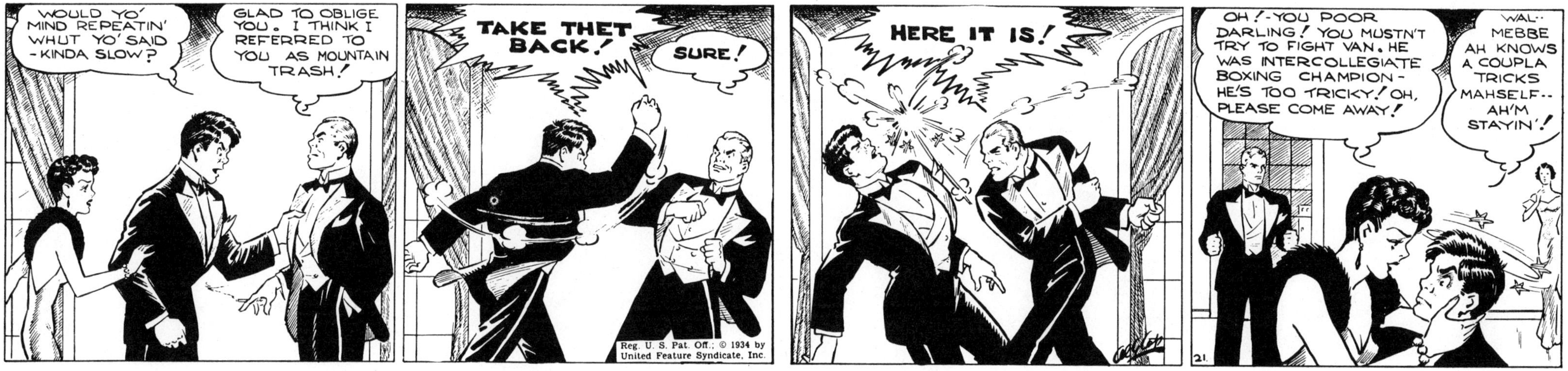

WOULD YO' MIND REPEATIN' WHUT YO' SAID -KINDA SLOW?
GLAD TO OBLIGE YOU. I THINK I REFERRED TO YOU AS MOUNTAIN TRASH!
TAKE THET BACK!
SURE!
Reg. U. S. Pat. Off.; © 1934 by United Feature Syndicate, Inc.
HERE IT IS!
OH!-YOU POOR DARLING! YOU MUSTN'T TRY TO FIGHT VAN. HE WAS INTERCOLLEGIATE BOXING CHAMPION - HE'S TOO TRICKY! OH, PLEASE COME AWAY!
WAL-- MEBBE AH KNOWS A COUPLA TRICKS MAHSELF-- AH'M STAYIN'!
21.

LI'L ABNER —An Out ! By Al Capp

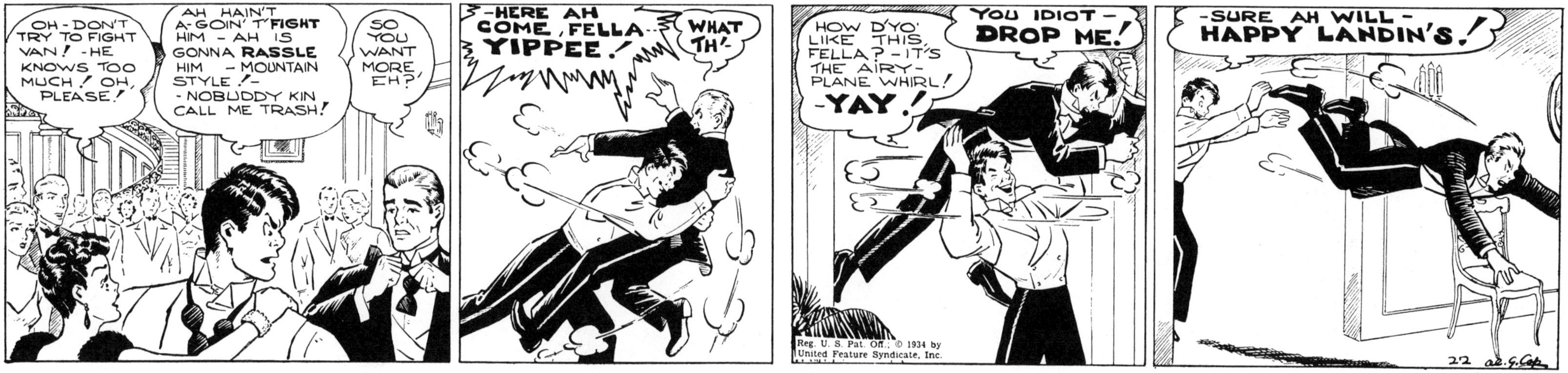

OH - DON'T TRY TO FIGHT VAN! -HE KNOWS TOO MUCH! OH, PLEASE!
AH HAIN'T A-GOIN' T'FIGHT HIM - AH IS GONNA RASSLE HIM - MOUNTAIN STYLE!- - NOBUDDY KIN CALL ME TRASH!
SO YOU WANT MORE, EH?
-HERE AH COME, FELLA-- YIPPEE!
WHAT TH'-
HOW D'YO' LIKE THIS, FELLA? - IT'S THE AIRY-PLANE WHIRL! -YAY!
YOU IDIOT - DROP ME!
Reg. U. S. Pat. Off.; © 1934 by United Feature Syndicate, Inc.
-SURE AH WILL - HAPPY LANDIN'S!
22

LI'L ABNER Not On the Program ! By Al Capp

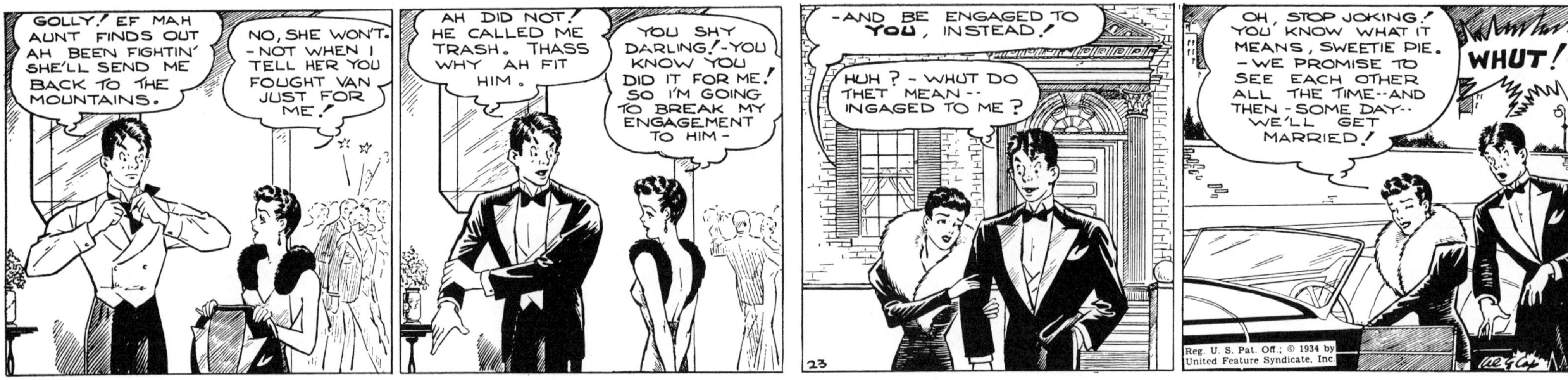

GOLLY! EF MAH AUNT FINDS OUT AH BEEN FIGHTIN' SHE'LL SEND ME BACK TO THE MOUNTAINS.
NO, SHE WON'T. - NOT WHEN I TELL HER YOU FOUGHT VAN JUST FOR ME!
AH DID NOT! HE CALLED ME TRASH. THASS WHY AH FIT HIM.
YOU SHY DARLING! - YOU KNOW YOU DID IT FOR ME! SO I'M GOING TO BREAK MY ENGAGEMENT TO HIM -
- AND BE ENGAGED TO YOU, INSTEAD!
HUH ? - WHUT DO THET MEAN -- INGAGED TO ME ?
23
OH, STOP JOKING! YOU KNOW WHAT IT MEANS, SWEETIE PIE. - WE PROMISE TO SEE EACH OTHER ALL THE TIME -- AND THEN - SOME DAY -- WE'LL GET MARRIED!
WHUT!
Reg. U. S. Pat. Off.; © 1934 by United Feature Syndicate, Inc.

LI'L ABNER Something To Worry About ! By Al Capp

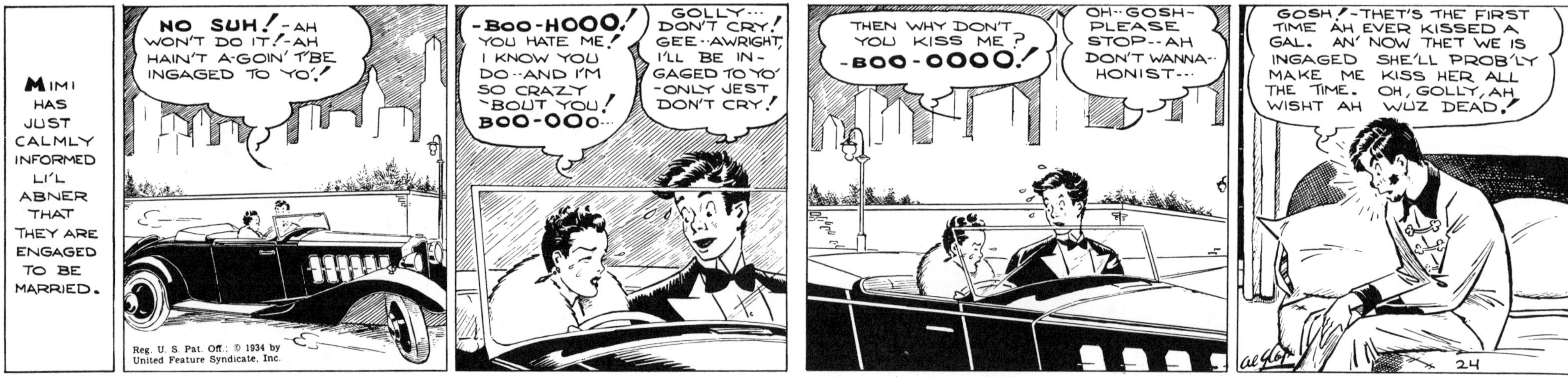

MIMI HAS JUST CALMLY INFORMED LI'L ABNER THAT THEY ARE ENGAGED TO BE MARRIED.
NO SUH! - AH WON'T DO IT! - AH HAIN'T A-GOIN' T'BE INGAGED TO YO'!
Reg. U. S. Pat. Off.; © 1934 by United Feature Syndicate, Inc.
- BOO-HOOO! YOU HATE ME! I KNOW YOU DO -- AND I'M SO CRAZY 'BOUT YOU! BOO-OOo...
GOLLY... DON'T CRY! GEE -- AWRIGHT, I'LL BE IN-GAGED TO YO' - ONLY JEST DON'T CRY!
THEN WHY DON'T YOU KISS ME ? - BOO - OOOO!
OH -- GOSH - PLEASE STOP -- AH DON'T WANNA -- HONIST ---
GOSH! - THET'S THE FIRST TIME AH EVER KISSED A GAL. AN' NOW THET WE IS INGAGED SHE'LL PROB'LY MAKE ME KISS HER ALL THE TIME. OH, GOLLY, AH WISHT AH WUZ DEAD!
24

LI'L ABNER Back Home

By Al Capp

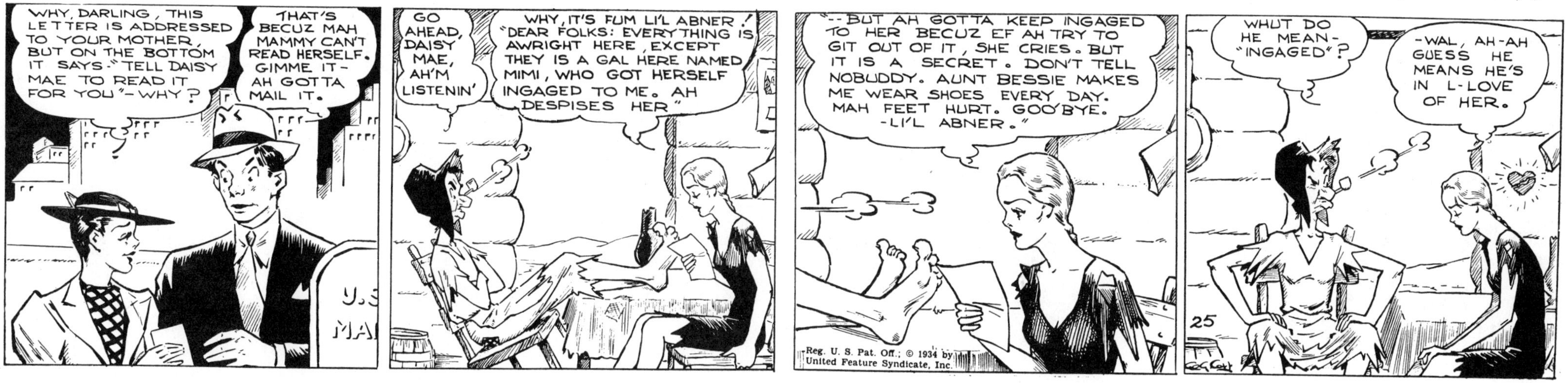

WHY, DARLING, THIS LETTER IS ADDRESSED TO YOUR MOTHER, BUT ON THE BOTTOM IT SAYS-"TELL DAISY MAE TO READ IT FOR YOU"-WHY?
THAT'S BECUZ MAH MAMMY CAN'T READ HERSELF. GIMME IT- AH GOTTA MAIL IT.
U.S. MAI
GO AHEAD, DAISY MAE, AH'M LISTENIN'
WHY, IT'S FUM LI'L ABNER! "DEAR FOLKS: EVERYTHING IS AWRIGHT HERE, EXCEPT THEY IS A GAL HERE NAMED MIMI, WHO GOT HERSELF INGAGED TO ME. AH DESPISES HER"
"--BUT AH GOTTA KEEP INGAGED TO HER BECUZ EF AH TRY TO GIT OUT OF IT, SHE CRIES. BUT IT IS A SECRET. DON'T TELL NOBUDDY. AUNT BESSIE MAKES ME WEAR SHOES EVERY DAY. MAH FEET HURT. GOO'BYE. -LI'L ABNER."
Reg. U. S. Pat. Off.; © 1934 by United Feature Syndicate, Inc.
WHUT DO HE MEAN- "INGAGED"?
-WAL, AH-AH GUESS HE MEANS HE'S IN L-LOVE OF HER.
25

LI'L ABNER When the Cat's Away—

By Al Capp

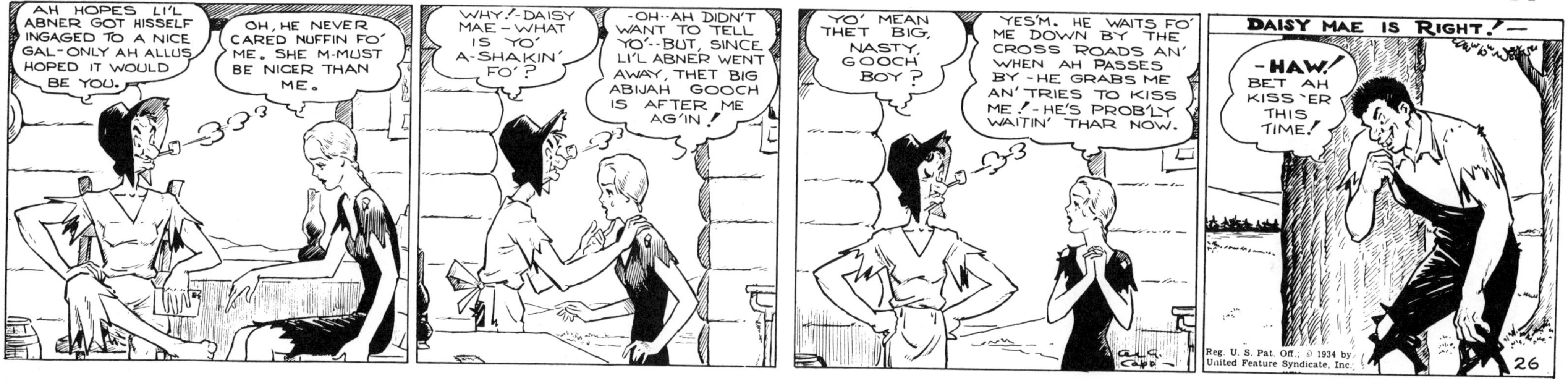

AH HOPES LI'L ABNER GOT HISSELF INGAGED TO A NICE GAL-ONLY AH ALLUS HOPED IT WOULD BE YOU.
OH, HE NEVER CARED NUFFIN FO' ME. SHE M-MUST BE NICER THAN ME.
WHY!-DAISY MAE-WHAT IS YO' A-SHAKIN' FO'?
-OH--AH DIDN'T WANT TO TELL YO'--BUT, SINCE LI'L ABNER WENT AWAY, THET BIG ABIJAH GOOCH IS AFTER ME AG'IN!
YO' MEAN THET BIG, NASTY, GOOCH BOY?
YES'M. HE WAITS FO' ME DOWN BY THE CROSS ROADS AN' WHEN AH PASSES BY-HE GRABS ME AN' TRIES TO KISS ME!-HE'S PROB'LY WAITIN' THAR NOW.
DAISY MAE IS RIGHT!—
-HAW! BET AH KISS 'ER THIS TIME!
Reg. U. S. Pat. Off.; © 1934 by United Feature Syndicate, Inc.
26

LI'L ABNER — Leave It To Mammy! — By Al Capp

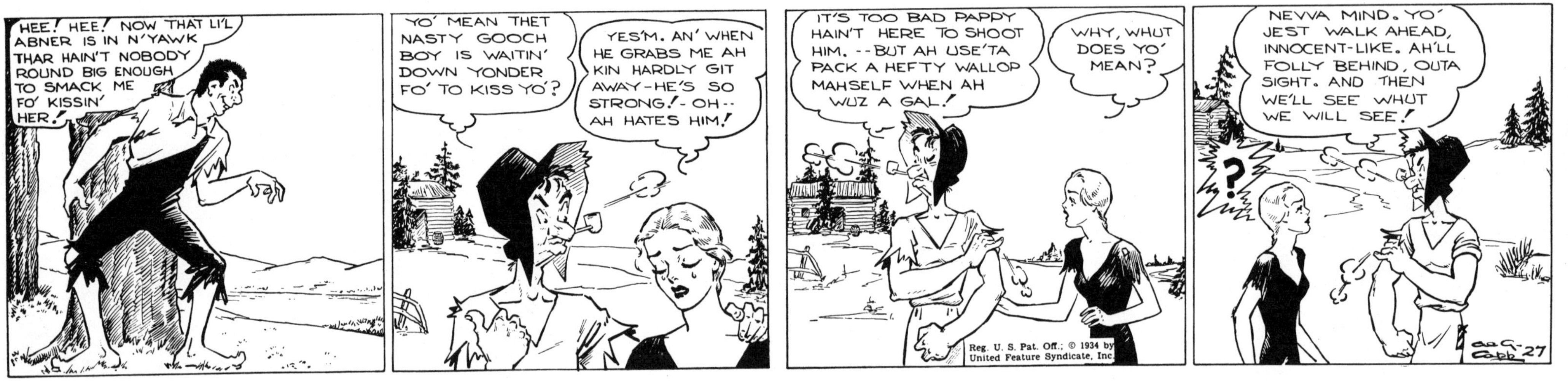

HEE! HEE! NOW THAT LI'L ABNER IS IN N'YAWK THAR HAIN'T NOBODY ROUND BIG ENOUGH TO SMACK ME FO' KISSIN' HER!
YO' MEAN THET NASTY GOOCH BOY IS WAITIN' DOWN YONDER FO' TO KISS YO'?
YES'M. AN' WHEN HE GRABS ME AH KIN HARDLY GIT AWAY-HE'S SO STRONG!-OH-- AH HATES HIM!
IT'S TOO BAD PAPPY HAIN'T HERE TO SHOOT HIM. --BUT AH USE'TA PACK A HEFTY WALLOP MAHSELF WHEN AH WUZ A GAL!
WHY, WHUT DOES YO' MEAN?
Reg. U. S. Pat. Off.; © 1934 by United Feature Syndicate, Inc.
NEVVA MIND. YO' JEST WALK AHEAD, INNOCENT-LIKE. AH'LL FOLLY BEHIND, OUTA SIGHT. AND THEN WE'LL SEE WHUT WE WILL SEE!
?
Capp 27

LI'L ABNER — The War's On! — By Al Capp

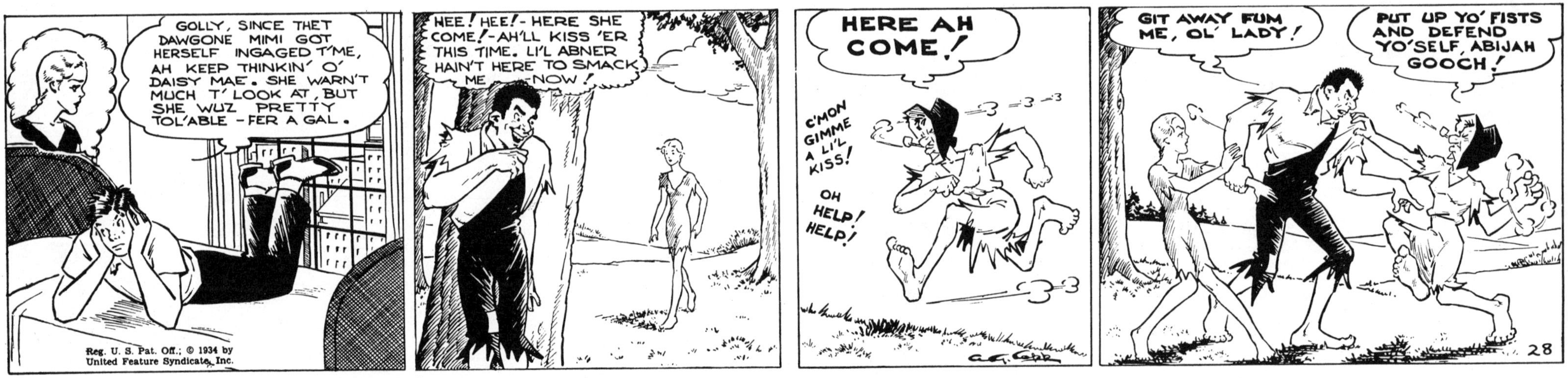

GOLLY, SINCE THET DAWGONE MIMI GOT HERSELF INGAGED T'ME, AH KEEP THINKIN' O' DAISY MAE. SHE WARN'T MUCH T' LOOK AT, BUT SHE WUZ PRETTY TOL'ABLE - FER A GAL.
Reg. U. S. Pat. Off.; © 1934 by United Feature Syndicate, Inc.
HEE! HEE!- HERE SHE COME!- AH'LL KISS 'ER THIS TIME. LI'L ABNER HAIN'T HERE TO SMACK ME --NOW!
HERE AH COME!
C'MON GIMME A LI'L KISS!
OH HELP! HELP!
GIT AWAY FUM ME, OL' LADY!
PUT UP YO' FISTS AND DEFEND YO'SELF, ABIJAH GOOCH!
28

LI'L ABNER Is That So?

By Al Capp

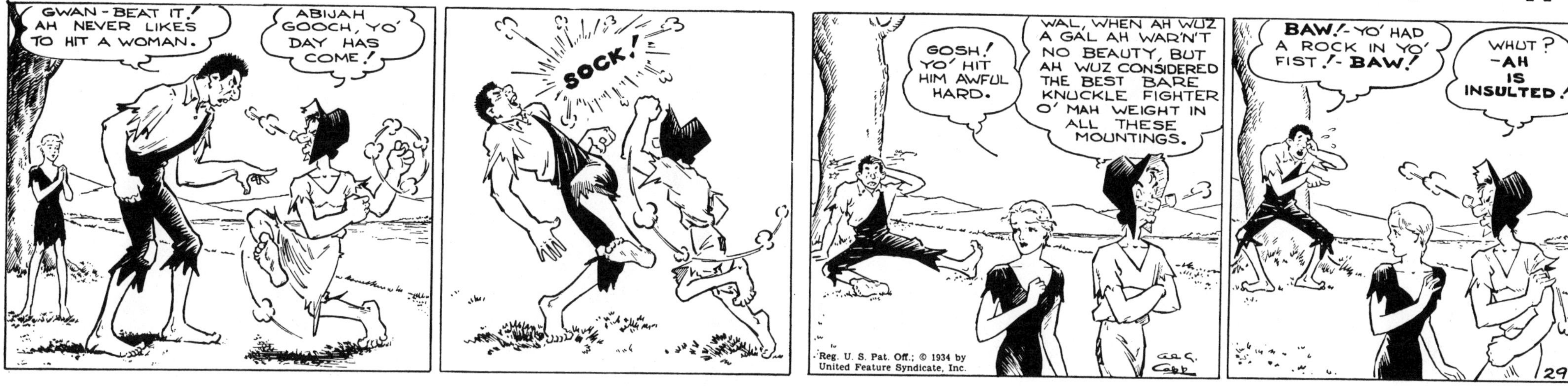

GWAN - BEAT IT! AH NEVER LIKES TO HIT A WOMAN.
ABIJAH GOOCH, YO' DAY HAS COME!
SOCK!
GOSH! YO' HIT HIM AWFUL HARD.
WAL, WHEN AH WUZ A GAL AH WAR'N'T NO BEAUTY, BUT AH WUZ CONSIDERED THE BEST BARE KNUCKLE FIGHTER O' MAH WEIGHT IN ALL THESE MOUNTINGS.
Reg. U. S. Pat. Off.; © 1934 by United Feature Syndicate, Inc.
BAW! - YO' HAD A ROCK IN YO' FIST! - BAW!
WHUT? - AH IS INSULTED!
29

LI'L ABNER What's This?

By Al Capp

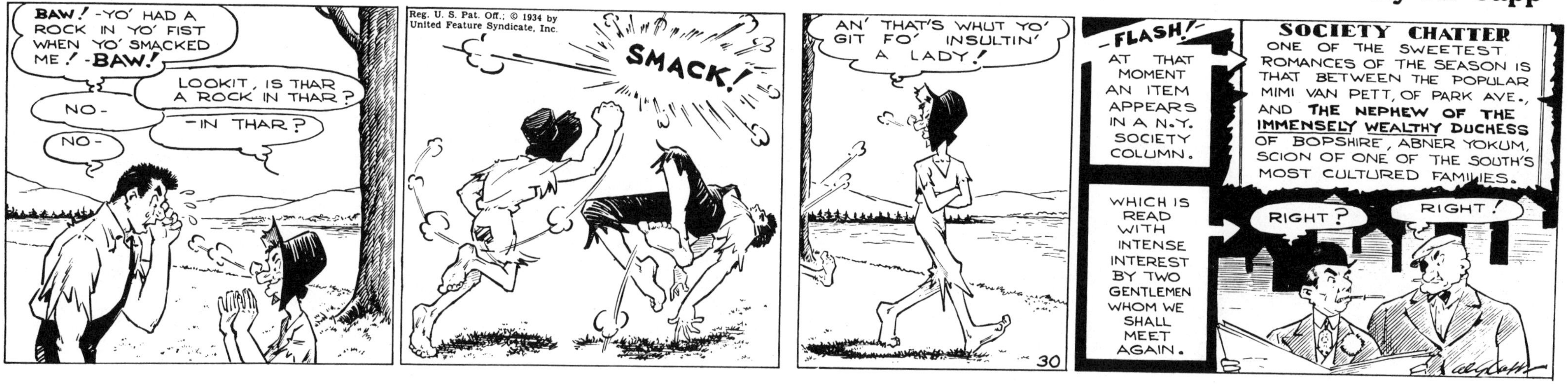

BAW! - YO' HAD A ROCK IN YO' FIST WHEN YO' SMACKED ME! - BAW!
LOOKIT, IS THAR A ROCK IN THAR?
NO-
-IN THAR?
NO-
Reg. U. S. Pat. Off.; © 1934 by United Feature Syndicate, Inc.
SMACK!
AN' THAT'S WHUT YO' GIT FO' INSULTIN' A LADY!
30
-FLASH!-
AT THAT MOMENT AN ITEM APPEARS IN A N.Y. SOCIETY COLUMN.
SOCIETY CHATTER
ONE OF THE SWEETEST ROMANCES OF THE SEASON IS THAT BETWEEN THE POPULAR MIMI VAN PETT, OF PARK AVE., AND THE NEPHEW OF THE IMMENSELY WEALTHY DUCHESS OF BOPSHIRE, ABNER YOKUM, SCION OF ONE OF THE SOUTH'S MOST CULTURED FAMILIES.
WHICH IS READ WITH INTENSE INTEREST BY TWO GENTLEMEN WHOM WE SHALL MEET AGAIN.
RIGHT?
RIGHT!

LI'L ABNER   Quick Action   By Al Capp

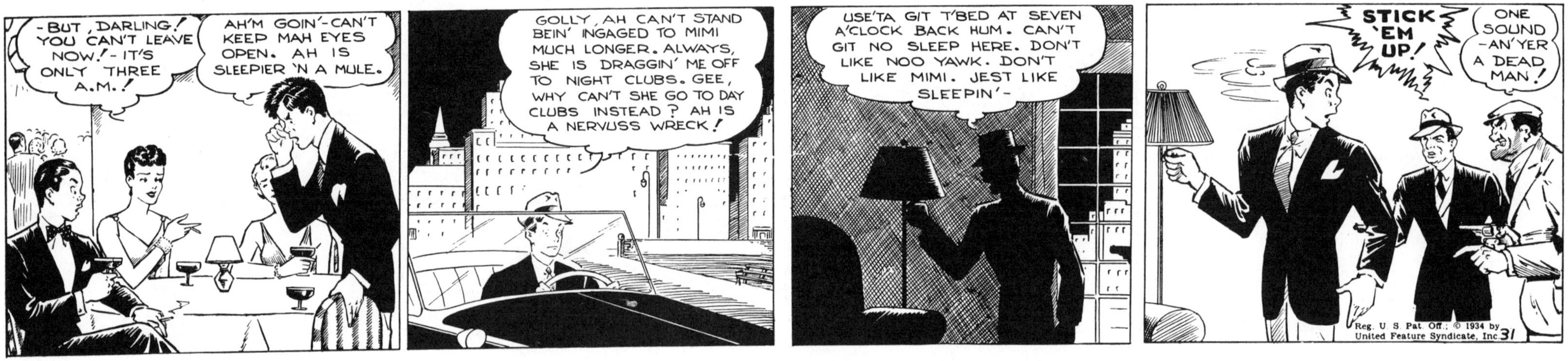

-BUT, DARLING! YOU CAN'T LEAVE NOW!-IT'S ONLY THREE A.M.!
AH'M GOIN'-CAN'T KEEP MAH EYES OPEN. AH IS SLEEPIER 'N A MULE.
GOLLY, AH CAN'T STAND BEIN' INGAGED TO MIMI MUCH LONGER. ALWAYS, SHE IS DRAGGIN' ME OFF TO NIGHT CLUBS. GEE, WHY CAN'T SHE GO TO DAY CLUBS INSTEAD? AH IS A NERVUSS WRECK!
USE'TA GIT T'BED AT SEVEN A'CLOCK BACK HUM. CAN'T GIT NO SLEEP HERE. DON'T LIKE NOO YAWK. DON'T LIKE MIMI. JEST LIKE SLEEPIN'-
STICK 'EM UP!
ONE SOUND -AN'YER A DEAD MAN!
Reg. U S Pat Off.; © 1934 by United Feature Syndicate, Inc
31

LI'L ABNER   He Likes It!   By Al Capp

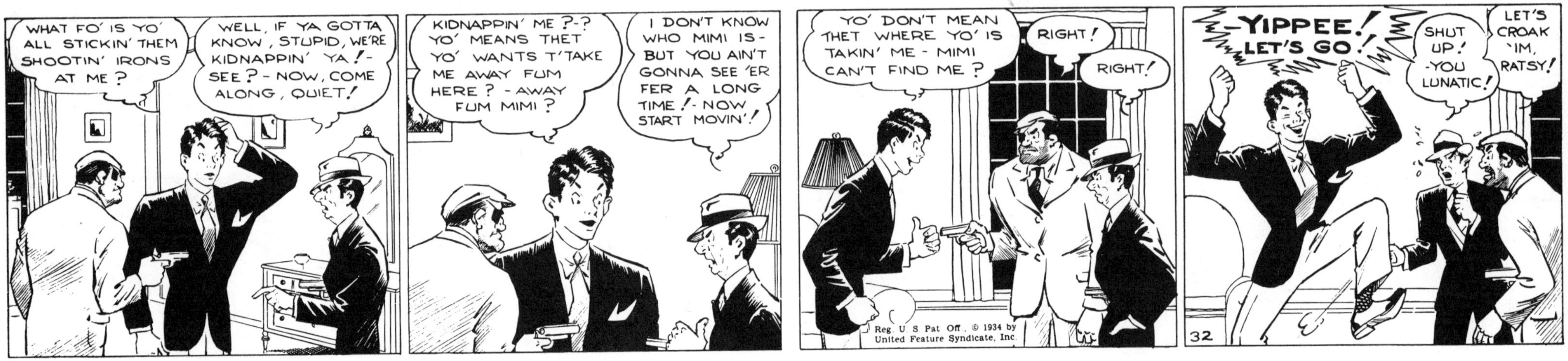

WHAT FO' IS YO' ALL STICKIN' THEM SHOOTIN' IRONS AT ME?
WELL, IF YA GOTTA KNOW, STUPID, WE'RE KIDNAPPIN' YA!-SEE?-NOW, COME ALONG, QUIET!
KIDNAPPIN' ME?-? YO' MEANS THET YO' WANTS T'TAKE ME AWAY FUM HERE?-AWAY FUM MIMI?
I DON'T KNOW WHO MIMI IS-BUT YOU AIN'T GONNA SEE 'ER FER A LONG TIME!-NOW START MOVIN'!
YO' DON'T MEAN THET WHERE YO' IS TAKIN' ME-MIMI CAN'T FIND ME?
RIGHT!
RIGHT!
Reg. U S Pat Off., © 1934 by United Feature Syndicate, Inc.
-YIPPEE! LET'S GO!
SHUT UP! -YOU LUNATIC!
LET'S CROAK 'IM, RATSY!
32

LI'L ABNER Abner Takes A Hand

By Al Capp

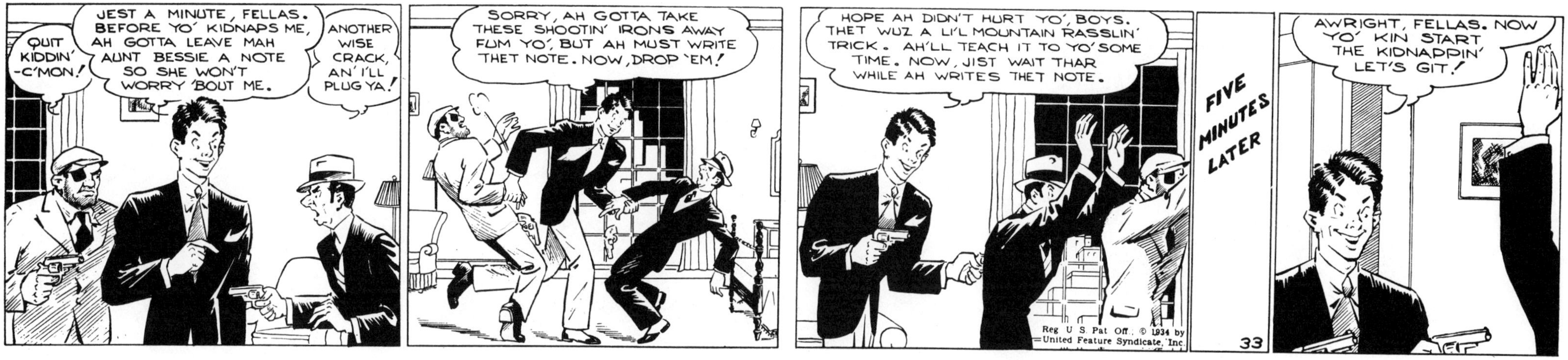
QUIT KIDDIN' -C'MON!
JEST A MINUTE, FELLAS. BEFORE YO' KIDNAPS ME, AH GOTTA LEAVE MAH AUNT BESSIE A NOTE SO SHE WON'T WORRY 'BOUT ME.
ANOTHER WISE CRACK, AN' I'LL PLUG YA!
SORRY, AH GOTTA TAKE THESE SHOOTIN' IRONS AWAY FUM YO', BUT AH MUST WRITE THET NOTE. NOW, DROP 'EM!
HOPE AH DIDN'T HURT YO', BOYS. THET WUZ A LI'L MOUNTAIN RASSLIN' TRICK. AH'LL TEACH IT TO YO' SOME TIME. NOW, JIST WAIT THAR WHILE AH WRITES THET NOTE.
Reg U S Pat Off. © 1934 by United Feature Syndicate, Inc.
FIVE MINUTES LATER
33
AWRIGHT, FELLAS. NOW YO' KIN START THE KIDNAPPIN' LET'S GIT!

LI'L ABNER At Whose Mercy ?

By Al Capp

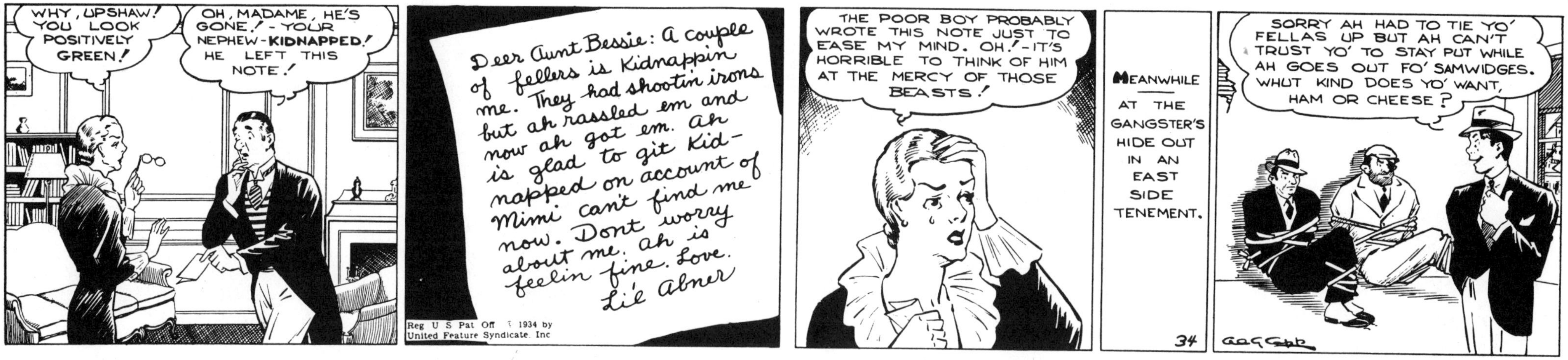
WHY, UPSHAW! YOU LOOK POSITIVELY GREEN!
OH, MADAME, HE'S GONE! - YOUR NEPHEW - KIDNAPPED! HE LEFT THIS NOTE!
Deer Aunt Bessie: A couple of fellers is Kidnappin me. They had shootin irons but ah rassled em and now ah got em. Ah is glad to git Kid-napped on account of Mimi can't find me now. Dont worry about me. Ah is feelin fine. Love. Li'l Abner
Reg U S Pat Off © 1934 by United Feature Syndicate, Inc
THE POOR BOY PROBABLY WROTE THIS NOTE JUST TO EASE MY MIND. OH! - IT'S HORRIBLE TO THINK OF HIM AT THE MERCY OF THOSE BEASTS!
MEANWHILE
AT THE GANGSTER'S HIDE OUT IN AN EAST SIDE TENEMENT.
34
SORRY AH HAD TO TIE YO' FELLAS UP BUT AH CAN'T TRUST YO' TO STAY PUT WHILE AH GOES OUT FO' SAMWIDGES. WHUT KIND DOES YO' WANT, HAM OR CHEESE?

LI'L ABNER The Reception Committee By Al Capp

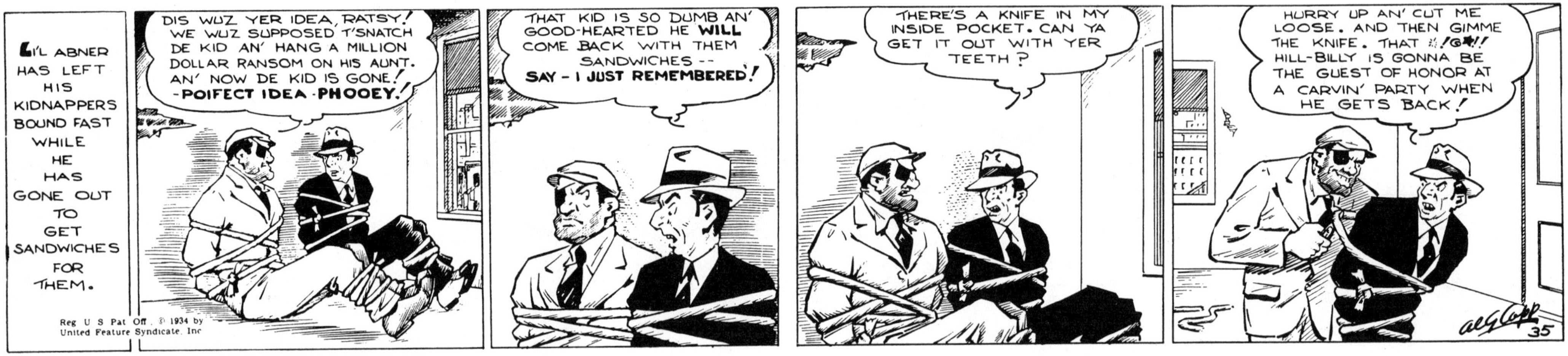
LI'L ABNER HAS LEFT HIS KIDNAPPERS BOUND FAST WHILE HE HAS GONE OUT TO GET SANDWICHES FOR THEM.
Reg U S Pat Off, © 1934 by United Feature Syndicate, Inc
DIS WUZ YER IDEA, RATSY! WE WUZ SUPPOSED T'SNATCH DE KID AN' HANG A MILLION DOLLAR RANSOM ON HIS AUNT. AN' NOW DE KID IS GONE! -POIFECT IDEA-PHOOEY!
THAT KID IS SO DUMB AN' GOOD-HEARTED HE WILL COME BACK WITH THEM SANDWICHES -- SAY - I JUST REMEMBERED!
THERE'S A KNIFE IN MY INSIDE POCKET. CAN YA GET IT OUT WITH YER TEETH?
HURRY UP AN' CUT ME LOOSE. AND THEN GIMME THE KNIFE. THAT !@*!! HILL-BILLY IS GONNA BE THE GUEST OF HONOR AT A CARVIN' PARTY WHEN HE GETS BACK!
Al G. Capp 35

LI'L ABNER Too Bad! By Al Capp

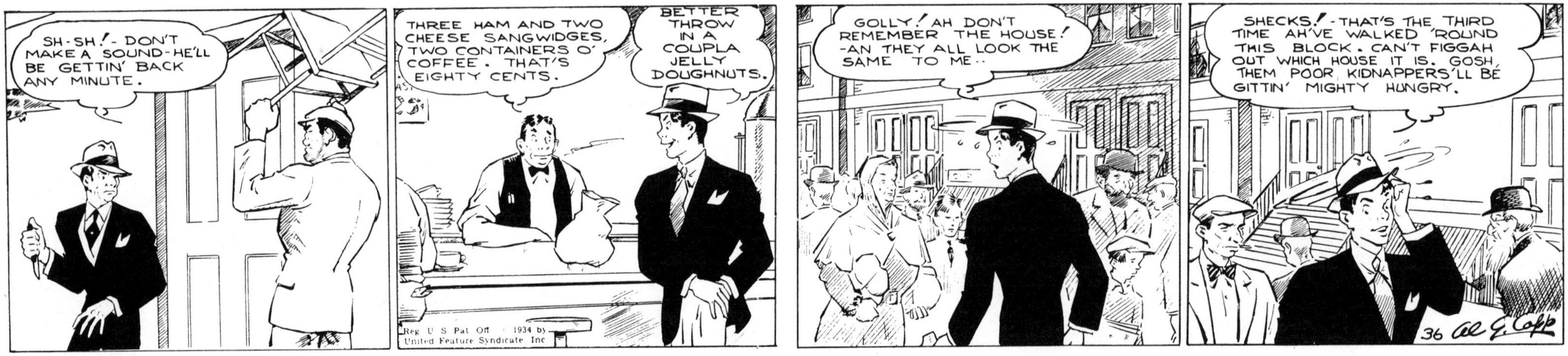
SH-SH! - DON'T MAKE A SOUND - HE'LL BE GETTIN' BACK ANY MINUTE.
THREE HAM AND TWO CHEESE SANGWIDGES, TWO CONTAINERS O' COFFEE. THAT'S EIGHTY CENTS.
BETTER THROW IN A COUPLA JELLY DOUGHNUTS.
Reg U S Pat Off © 1934 by United Feature Syndicate Inc
GOLLY! AH DON'T REMEMBER THE HOUSE! -AN THEY ALL LOOK THE SAME TO ME--
SHECKS! - THAT'S THE THIRD TIME AH'VE WALKED 'ROUND THIS BLOCK. CAN'T FIGGAH OUT WHICH HOUSE IT IS. GOSH, THEM POOR KIDNAPPERS'LL BE GITTIN' MIGHTY HUNGRY.
36 Al G. Capp

LI'L ABNER Where Ignorance Is Bliss By Al Capp

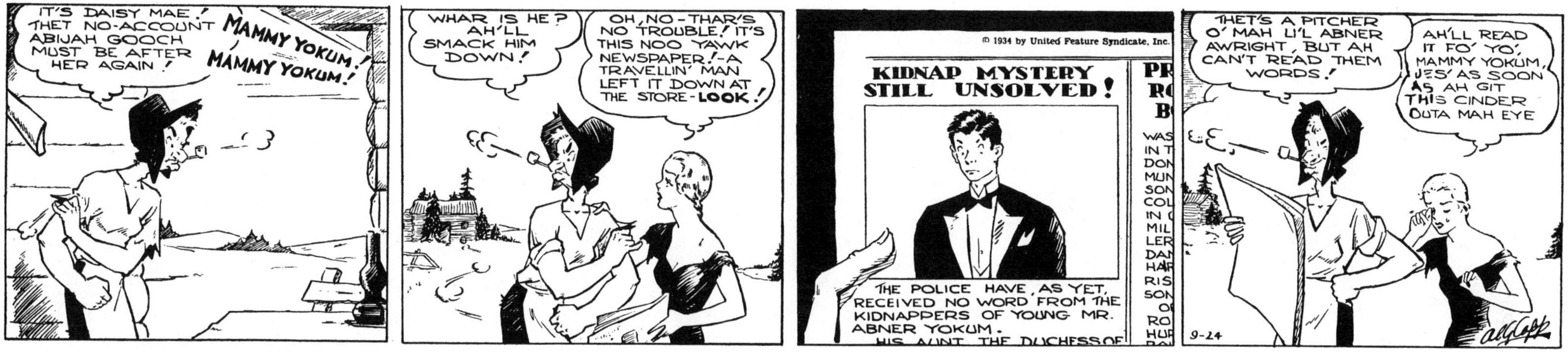

IT'S DAISY MAE! THET NO-ACCOUNT ABIJAH GOOCH MUST BE AFTER HER AGAIN!
MAMMY YOKUM! MAMMY YOKUM!
WHAR IS HE? AH'LL SMACK HIM DOWN!
OH, NO - THAR'S NO TROUBLE! IT'S THIS NOO YAWK NEWSPAPER! - A TRAVELLIN' MAN LEFT IT DOWN AT THE STORE - LOOK!
© 1934 by United Feature Syndicate, Inc.
KIDNAP MYSTERY STILL UNSOLVED!
THE POLICE HAVE, AS YET, RECEIVED NO WORD FROM THE KIDNAPPERS OF YOUNG MR. ABNER YOKUM.
THET'S A PITCHER O' MAH LI'L ABNER AWRIGHT, BUT AH CAN'T READ THEM WORDS!
AH'LL READ IT FO' YO', MAMMY YOKUM, JES' AS SOON AS AH GIT THIS CINDER OUTA MAH EYE
9-24
Al Capp

LI'L ABNER She's A-Comin' From the Mountains! By Al Capp

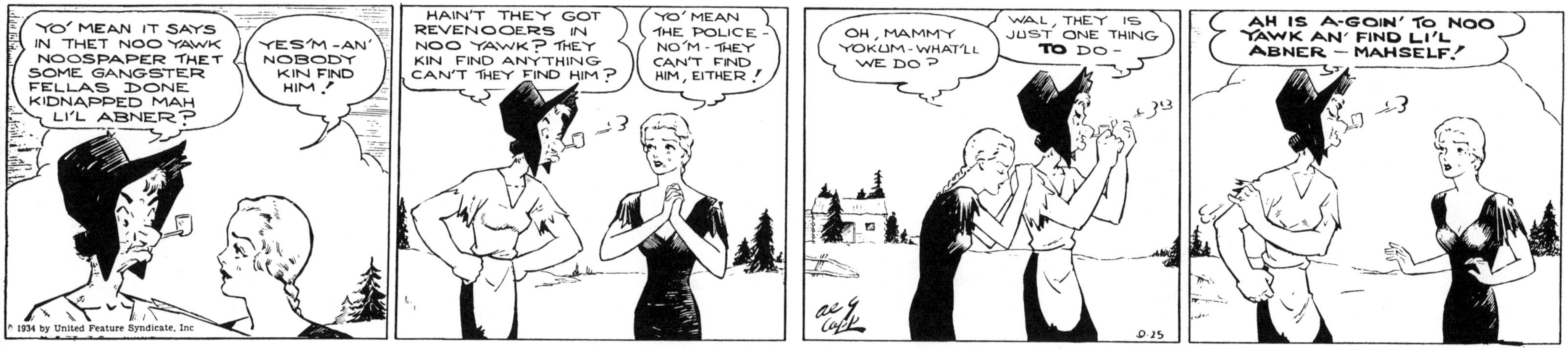

YO' MEAN IT SAYS IN THET NOO YAWK NOOSPAPER THET SOME GANGSTER FELLAS DONE KIDNAPPED MAH LI'L ABNER?
YES'M - AN' NOBODY KIN FIND HIM!
© 1934 by United Feature Syndicate, Inc
HAIN'T THEY GOT REVENOOERS IN NOO YAWK? THEY KIN FIND ANYTHING - CAN'T THEY FIND HIM?
YO' MEAN THE POLICE - NO'M - THEY CAN'T FIND HIM, EITHER!
OH, MAMMY YOKUM - WHAT'LL WE DO?
WAL, THEY IS JUST ONE THING TO DO -
Al Capp
9-25
AH IS A-GOIN' TO NOO YAWK AN' FIND LI'L ABNER - MAHSELF!

LI'L ABNER A Clean Fighter By Al Capp

AW, CAN'T AH COME TO NOO YAWK WITH YO', MAMMY?
NO, PAPPY. YO' GOTTA STAY HOME AN' TEND THE PIGS. HM-M-WONDER EF AH OUGHTER TAKE MAH SHOES ALONG--
© 1934 by United Feature Syndicate, Inc.
RECKON AH WILL! DON'T WANT FOLKS IN NOO YAWK TO THINK WE YOKUMS HAIN'T GOT NO STYLE!-HOW MUCH MONEY IS YO' GOT, PAPPY?
A DOLLAR AN' THIRTY CENTS
AH'LL TAKE IT ALL! IT'S A LOT O' MONEY, BUT AH HEERD NOO YAWK WAS A MIGHTY EXPENSIVE PLACE
HAIN'T YO' BETTER TAKE THIS SHOOTIN' IRON?
NO, PAPPY! WHEN AH FINDS THEM GANGSTER FELLAS WHICH KIDNAPPED MAH LI'L ABNER -AH'LL USE MAH BARE FISKS ON 'EM!
HOT DIGGETTY!
9-26

LI'L ABNER Off to the Big City By Al Capp

GOODBYE, MAMMY. AH HOPES YO' FINDS LI'L ABNER AN' COME HOME QUICK. AH IS GITTIN' LONESOME AWREDDY!
DON'T GIT SEDIMENTAL, PAPPY. AH HATES TO GO MAHSELF, BUT MAH BOY IS IN TROUBLE AN' HE NEEDS HIS MAMMY.
-AN' WHEN YO' FINDS HIM TELL HIM AH WAS A-PRAYIN' FO' HIM - EV'RY NIGHT.
9-27
IT'S TWENTY MILES TO THE RAIL-ROAD STATION
GIT ALONG, SALOMEY! DON'T YO' REELIZE AH GOTTA GIT TO NOO YAWK?
-WHERE THE WEEKLY NEW YORK TRAIN IS JUST PULLING OUT!
HEY, TRAIN - WAIT FO' ME!
1934 by United Feature Syndicate, Inc

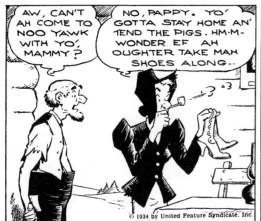

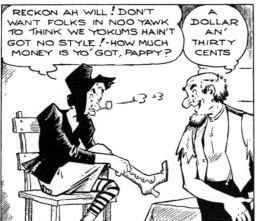

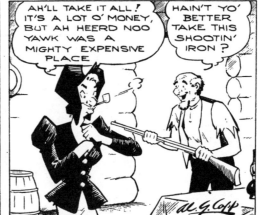

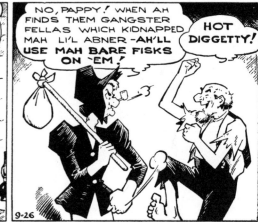

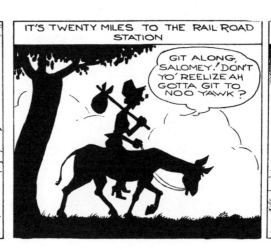

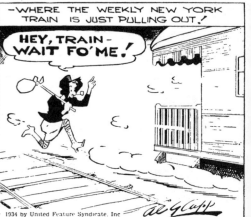

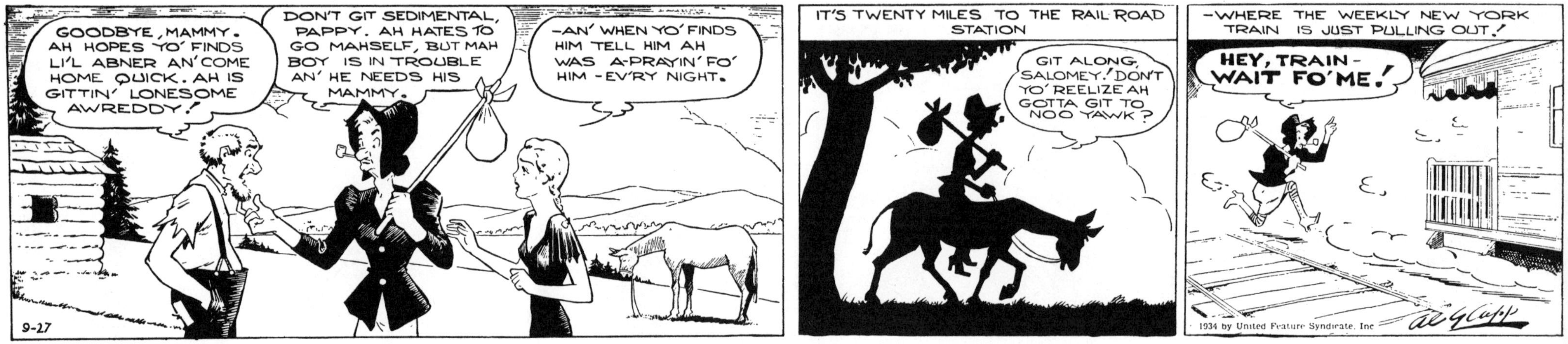

LI'L ABNER You Can't Fool Her Twice By Al Capp

WHEW!-AH JUST KETCHED THIS TRAIN IN TIME! CAN'T FIGGER OUT HOW SHE KIN GO SO FAST WITHOUT NO MULE TO PULL HER!
TICKET, PLEASE
- DON'T WANT NO TICKET! AH ONCE BOUGHT A LOTTERY TICKET FUM A TRAVELLIN' MAN AN' AH DIDN'T WIN NOTHIN', SO AH HAIN'T NEVER GONNA BUY ANOTHER ONE!
LISTEN- IF YOU WON'T BUY A TICKET, I'LL HAVE TO PUT YOU OFF, LADY!
9-28
LEGGO MAH ARM!- MAH LI'L ABNER IS IN TROUBLE IN NOO YAWK -AH GOTTA GIT THERE TO HELP HIM-
C'MON! C'MON!
-AN' THEY HAIN'T NOBODY GONNA STOP ME!
SOCK!
© 1934 by United Feature Syndicate Inc

LI'L ABNER If She Only Knew! By Al Capp

AH'M SORRY AH HAD TO SMACK THET CONDUCTOR BUT HE TRIED TO STOP ME FUM RIDIN' TO NOO YAWK- JUST BECUZ AH WOULDN'T BUY A TICKET! TSK-TSK- NOW, I ASKS YO'- WARN'T HE SILLY?
BRFSK!
-AN' SHE SAYS SHE WON'T BUY A TICKET! -AN' WHEN I TRIES TO PUT HER OFF SHE HAULS OFF AND SOCKS ME! WHAT A WALLOP!
SO I SEE!
SHE CAN'T GET AWAY WITH THAT! C'MON- WE'LL BOTH SNEAK UP BEHIND HER, GRAB HER BY THE ARMS, AND THROW HER OUT!
OKAY! BUT LET'S GET A COUPLA MORE MEN TO HELP US. THAT LITTLE OLD LADY'S GOT A PUNCH LIKE DEMPSEY IN HIS PRIME!
© 1934 by United Feature Syndicate, Inc.
FLASH-
NEW YORK CITY: THE HOME OF LI'L ABNER'S AUNT, THE DUCHESS OF BOPSHIRE
THE POLICE ARE CALLING, MADAME- THEY'VE CAPTURED THE KIDNAPPERS!
BUT THE BOY- WHERE IS HE?
9-29

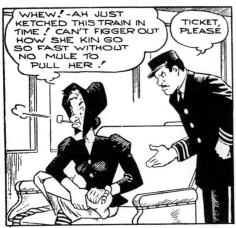

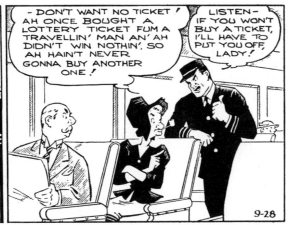

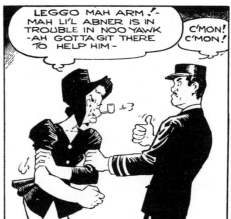

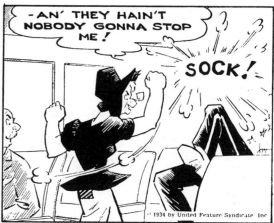

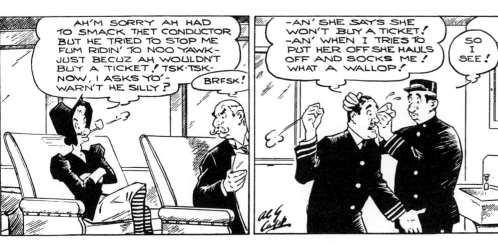

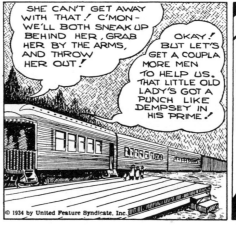

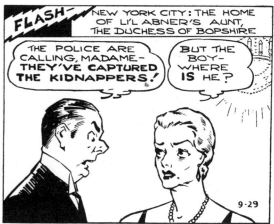

LI'L ABNER Walkin' on the Railroad

By Al Capp

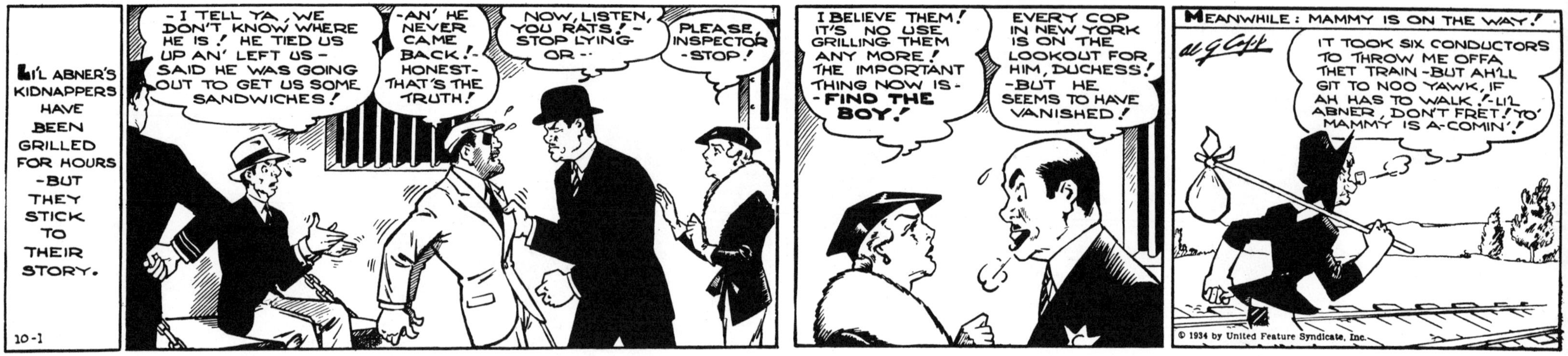
LI'L ABNER'S KIDNAPPERS HAVE BEEN GRILLED FOR HOURS -BUT THEY STICK TO THEIR STORY.
10-1
-I TELL YA, WE DON'T KNOW WHERE HE IS! HE TIED US UP AN' LEFT US - SAID HE WAS GOING OUT TO GET US SOME SANDWICHES!
-AN' HE NEVER CAME BACK!- HONEST- THAT'S THE TRUTH!
NOW, LISTEN, YOU RATS!- STOP LYING- OR --
PLEASE, INSPECTOR -STOP!
I BELIEVE THEM! IT'S NO USE GRILLING THEM ANY MORE! THE IMPORTANT THING NOW IS- -FIND THE BOY!
EVERY COP IN NEW YORK IS ON THE LOOKOUT FOR HIM, DUCHESS! -BUT HE SEEMS TO HAVE VANISHED!
MEANWHILE: MAMMY IS ON THE WAY!
IT TOOK SIX CONDUCTORS TO THROW ME OFFA THET TRAIN -BUT AH'LL GIT TO NOO YAWK, IF AH HAS TO WALK!-LI'L ABNER, DON'T FRET! YO' MAMMY IS A-COMIN'!
© 1934 by United Feature Syndicate, Inc.

LI'L ABNER No Stopping Mammy

By Al Capp

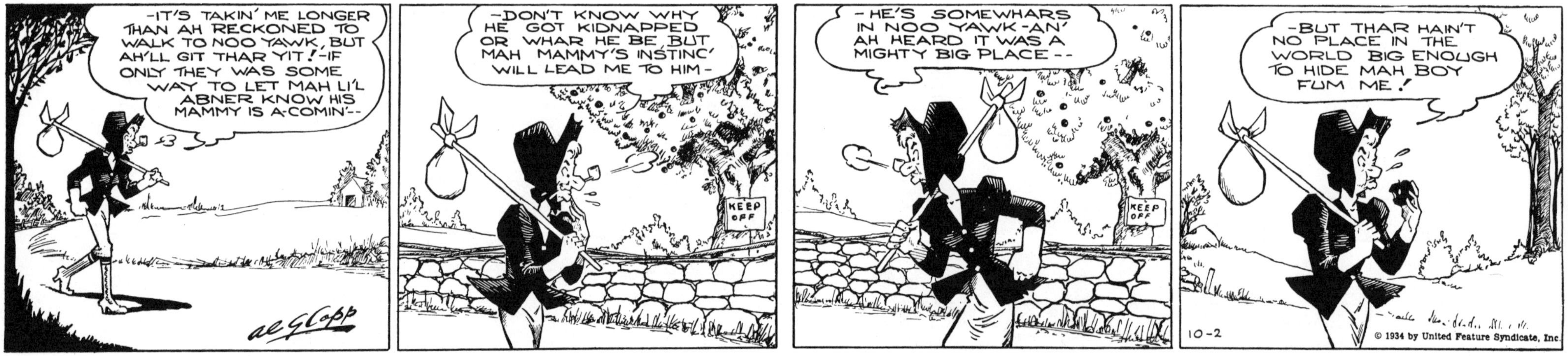
-IT'S TAKIN' ME LONGER THAN AH RECKONED TO WALK TO NOO YAWK, BUT AH'LL GIT THAR YIT!-IF ONLY THEY WAS SOME WAY TO LET MAH LI'L ABNER KNOW HIS MAMMY IS A-COMIN'--
-DON'T KNOW WHY HE GOT KIDNAPPED OR WHAR HE BE, BUT MAH MAMMY'S INSTINC' WILL LEAD ME TO HIM-
KEEP OFF
-HE'S SOMEWHARS IN NOO YAWK-AN' AH HEARD IT WAS A MIGHTY BIG PLACE--
KEEP OFF
-BUT THAR HAIN'T NO PLACE IN THE WORLD BIG ENOUGH TO HIDE MAH BOY FUM ME!
10-2
© 1934 by United Feature Syndicate, Inc.

LI'L ABNER Yo' Cain't Do That ! By Al Capp

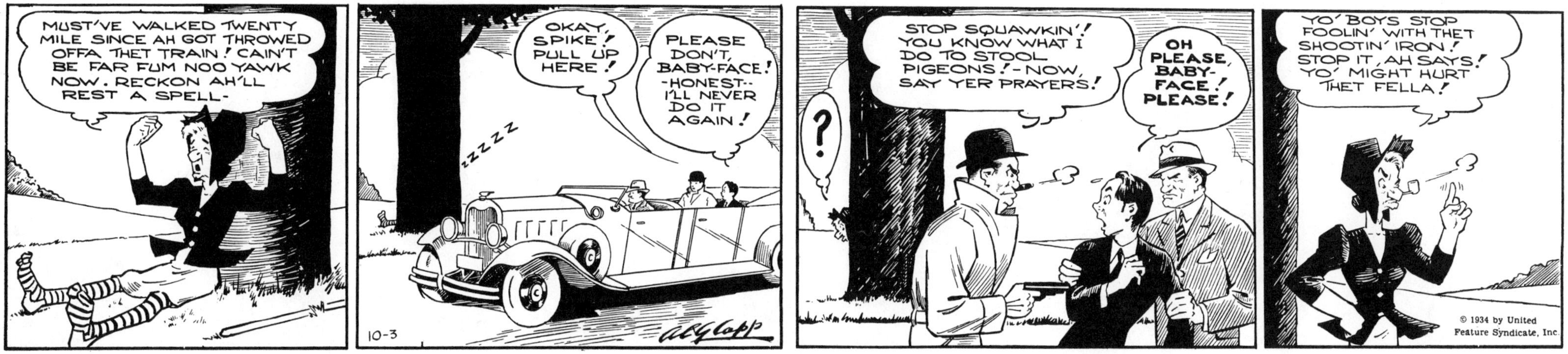

MUST'VE WALKED TWENTY MILE SINCE AH GOT THROWED OFFA THET TRAIN! CAIN'T BE FAR FUM NOO YAWK NOW. RECKON AH'LL REST A SPELL-
OKAY, SPIKE! PULL UP HERE!
PLEASE DON'T, BABY-FACE! -HONEST-- I'LL NEVER DO IT AGAIN!
ZZZZZ
10-3
Al G Capp
STOP SQUAWKIN'! YOU KNOW WHAT I DO TO STOOL PIGEONS!-NOW, SAY YER PRAYERS!
OH PLEASE, BABY-FACE! PLEASE!
?
YO' BOYS STOP FOOLIN' WITH THET SHOOTIN' IRON! STOP IT, AH SAYS! YO' MIGHT HURT THET FELLA!
© 1934 by United Feature Syndicate, Inc.

LI'L ABNER Mammy's Mounting Rasslin' By Al Capp

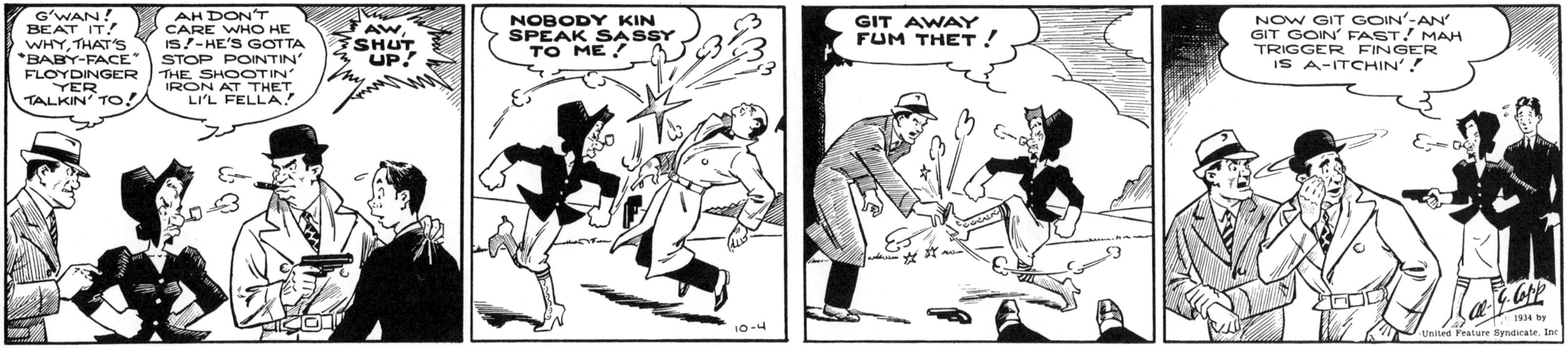

G'WAN! BEAT IT! WHY, THAT'S "BABY-FACE" FLOYDINGER YER TALKIN' TO!
AH DON'T CARE WHO HE IS!-HE'S GOTTA STOP POINTIN' THE SHOOTIN' IRON AT THET LI'L FELLA!
AW, SHUT UP!
NOBODY KIN SPEAK SASSY TO ME!
10-4
GIT AWAY FUM THET!
NOW GIT GOIN'-AN' GIT GOIN' FAST! MAH TRIGGER FINGER IS A-ITCHIN'!
Al G. Capp
1934 by United Feature Syndicate, Inc

LI'L ABNER Favor For Favor

By Al Capp

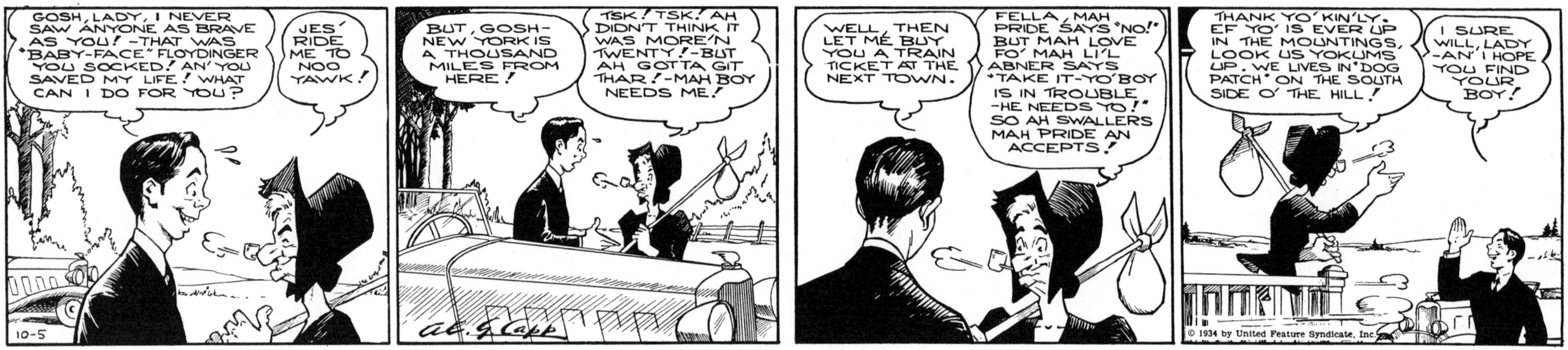
GOSH, LADY, I NEVER SAW ANYONE AS BRAVE AS YOU! -THAT WAS "BABY-FACE" FLOYDINGER YOU SOCKED! AN' YOU SAVED MY LIFE! WHAT CAN I DO FOR YOU?
JES' RIDE ME TO NOO YAWK!
10-5
BUT, GOSH- NEW YORK IS A THOUSAND MILES FROM HERE!
TSK! TSK! AH DIDN'T THINK IT WAS MORE'N TWENTY!-BUT AH GOTTA GIT THAR!-MAH BOY NEEDS ME!
Al. G. Capp
WELL, THEN LET ME BUY YOU A TRAIN TICKET AT THE NEXT TOWN.
FELLA, MAH PRIDE SAYS "NO!" BUT MAH LOVE FO' MAH LI'L ABNER SAYS "TAKE IT-YO' BOY IS IN TROUBLE -HE NEEDS YO!" SO AH SWALLERS MAH PRIDE AN ACCEPTS!
THANK YO' KIN'LY. EF YO' IS EVER UP IN THE MOUNTINGS, LOOK US YOKUMS UP. WE LIVES IN "DOG PATCH" ON THE SOUTH SIDE O' THE HILL!
I SURE WILL, LADY -AN' I HOPE YOU FIND YOUR BOY!
© 1934 by United Feature Syndicate, Inc.

LI'L ABNER "Surprised" Is No Word For It !

By Al Capp

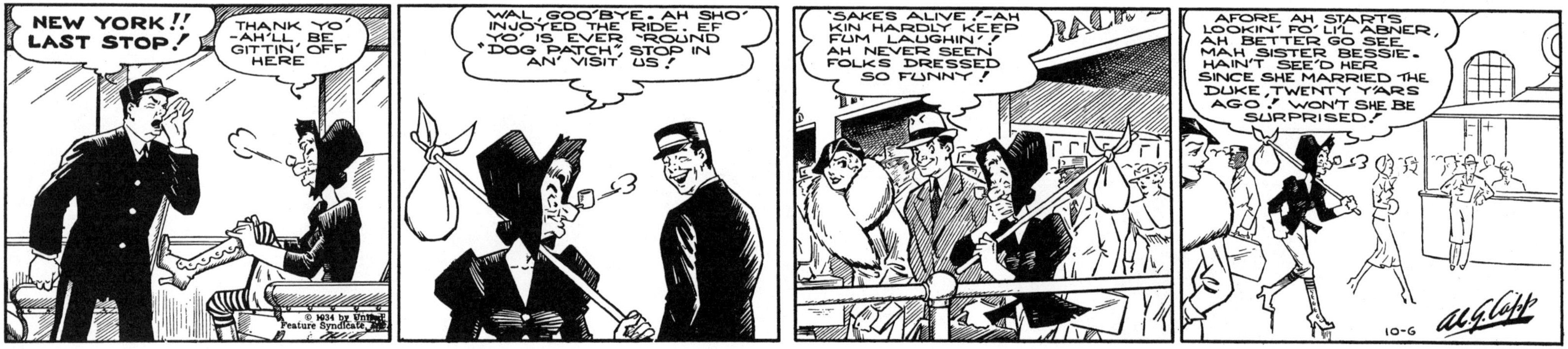
NEW YORK!! LAST STOP!
THANK YO' -AH'LL BE GITTIN' OFF HERE
WAL, GOO'BYE. AH SHO' INJOYED THE RIDE. EF YO' IS EVER 'ROUND "DOG PATCH," STOP IN AN' VISIT US!
'SAKES ALIVE!-AH KIN HARDLY KEEP FUM LAUGHIN'! AH NEVER SEEN FOLKS DRESSED SO FUNNY!
AFORE AH STARTS LOOKIN' FO' LI'L ABNER, AH BETTER GO SEE MAH SISTER BESSIE. HAIN'T SEE'D HER SINCE SHE MARRIED THE DUKE, TWENTY Y'ARS AGO! WON'T SHE BE SURPRISED!
10-6
Al. G. Capp

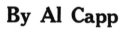

LI'L ABNER Double Error By Al Capp

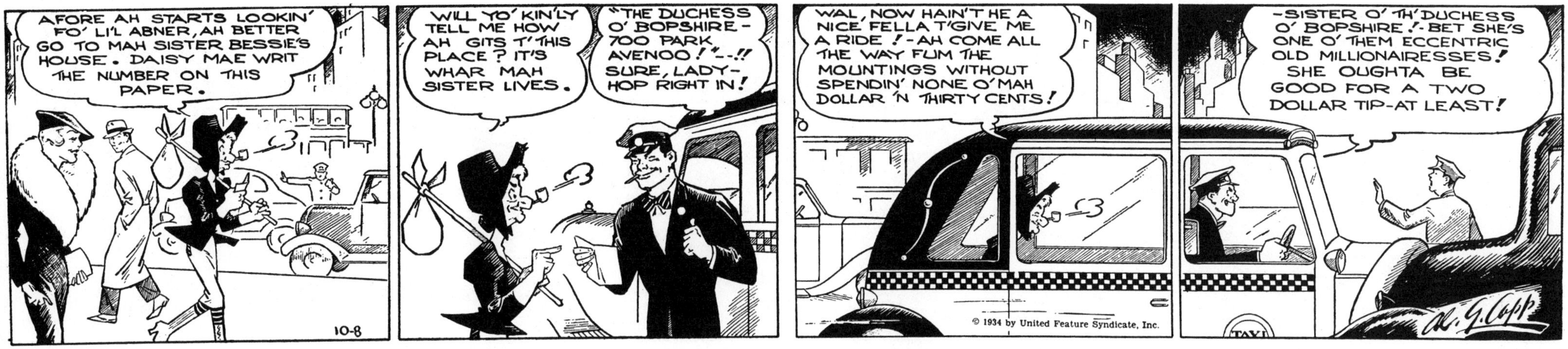
AFORE AH STARTS LOOKIN' FO' LI'L ABNER, AH BETTER GO TO MAH SISTER BESSIE'S HOUSE. DAISY MAE WRIT THE NUMBER ON THIS PAPER.
10-8
WILL YO' KIN'LY TELL ME HOW AH GITS T' THIS PLACE? IT'S WHAR MAH SISTER LIVES.
"THE DUCHESS O' BOPSHIRE - 700 PARK AVENOO!" -- !! SURE, LADY - HOP RIGHT IN!
WAL, NOW HAIN'T HE A NICE FELLA T'GIVE ME A RIDE! - AH COME ALL THE WAY FUM THE MOUNTINGS WITHOUT SPENDIN' NONE O' MAH DOLLAR 'N THIRTY CENTS!
© 1934 by United Feature Syndicate, Inc.
-SISTER O' TH' DUCHESS O' BOPSHIRE! - BET SHE'S ONE O' THEM ECCENTRIC OLD MILLIONAIRESSES! SHE OUGHTA BE GOOD FOR A TWO DOLLAR TIP - AT LEAST!
TAXI

LI'L ABNER Voice From the Mountings By Al Capp

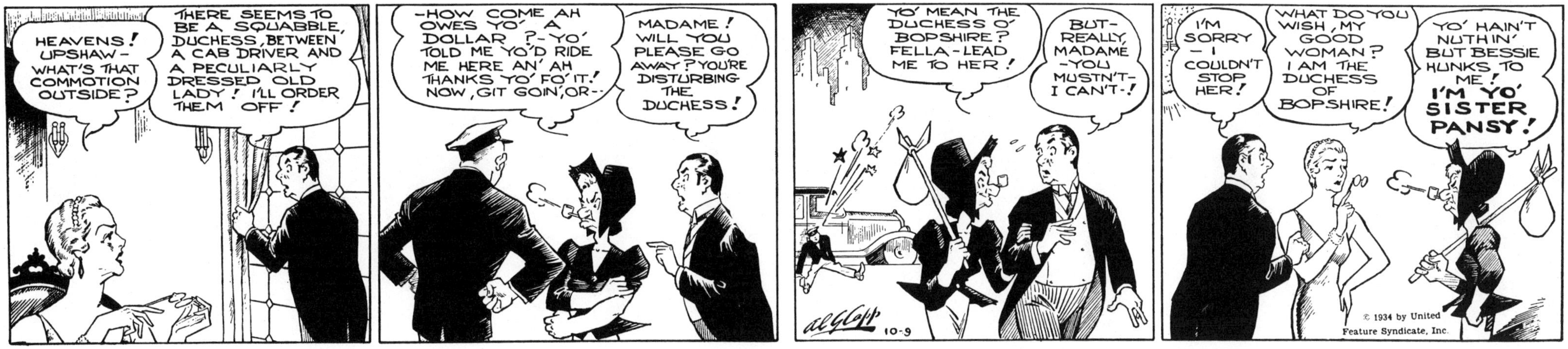
HEAVENS! UPSHAW - WHAT'S THAT COMMOTION OUTSIDE?
THERE SEEMS TO BE A SQUABBLE, DUCHESS, BETWEEN A CAB DRIVER AND A PECULIARLY DRESSED OLD LADY! I'LL ORDER THEM OFF!
-HOW COME AH OWES YO' A DOLLAR? - YO' TOLD ME YO'D RIDE ME HERE AN' AH THANKS YO' FO' IT! NOW, GIT GOIN', OR --
MADAME! WILL YOU PLEASE GO AWAY? YOU'RE DISTURBING THE DUCHESS!
YO' MEAN THE DUCHESS O' BOPSHIRE? FELLA - LEAD ME TO HER!
BUT - REALLY, MADAME - YOU MUSTN'T - I CAN'T -!
10-9
I'M SORRY - I COULDN'T STOP HER!
WHAT DO YOU WISH, MY GOOD WOMAN? I AM THE DUCHESS OF BOPSHIRE!
YO' HAIN'T NUTHIN' BUT BESSIE HUNKS TO ME! I'M YO' SISTER PANSY!
© 1934 by United Feature Syndicate, Inc.

LI'L ABNER Mammy Knows Better By Al Capp

DEAR SISTER PANSY! WHY DIDN'T YOU WRITE THAT YOU WERE COMING TO VISIT ME?
ON ACCOUNT O' AH CAIN'T WRITE! ALSO, AH DIDN'T COME T'VISIT YO'! AH COME TO FIND LI'L ABNER.
© 1934 UNITED FEATURE SYNDICATE, INC.
BUT THE POLICE HAVE SCOURED NEW YORK AND THEY CAN'T FIND HIM! HOW CAN YOU?
AH KIN FIND HIM AWRIGHT- WITHOUT LEAVIN' THIS HOUSE!
10-10
BUT HOW?
BY CONJURIN' UP A VISION! OUR OLD GRAN'MAMMY TEACHED ME HOW TO DO IT AFORE SHE DIED!
Al. G. Capp
CONJURING UP A VISION? - WHY, THAT'S JUST A FOOLISH OLD MOUNTAIN SUPERSTITION!
FOOLISH, IS IT? - WAL, AH'M AGOIN' TO TRY IT! -AN' WE WILL SEE WHAT WE WILL SEE!

LI'L ABNER Mountain Magic By Al Capp

BUT, PANSY-YOU CAN'T FIND LI'L ABNER BY CONJURING UP A VISION OF HIM! - PEOPLE DON'T BELIEVE IN THAT AND MORE!
MEBBE CITY FOLKS DON'T, BUT US MOUNTAIN FOLKS KNOWS BETTER! KIN'LY GIT OUTA HERE. AH IS A-GOIN' TO START!
FUST AH CUTS MAH FINGER AN' MARKS A "X" IN BLOOD ON MAH BROW-
THEN AH REPEATS THE OLD SAYIN' MAH GRAN'MAMMY TEACHED ME - AN' AH WHIRLS AROUN' THREE TIMES-
© 1934 by United Feature Syndicate, Inc.
10-11
THEN AH PUTS OUT THE LIGHT, LAYS STIFF IN BED-AN' WAITS FO' THE VISION!
Al. G. Capp

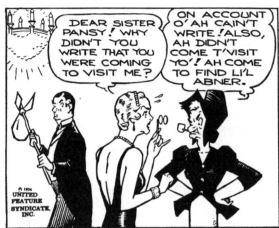

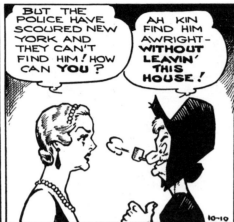

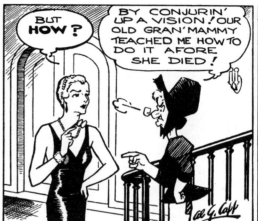

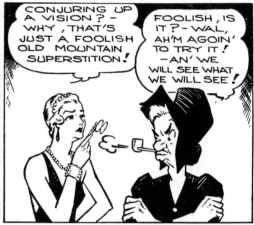

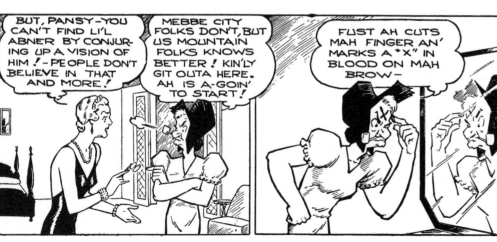

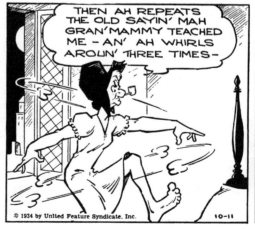

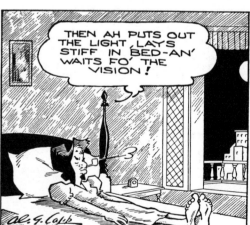

LI'L ABNER The Vision! By Al Capp

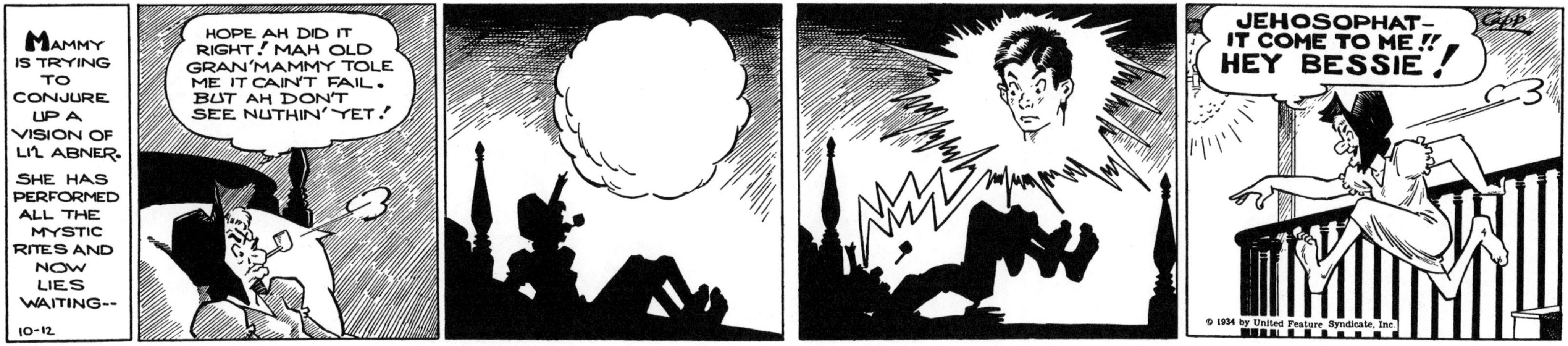

MAMMY IS TRYING TO CONJURE UP A VISION OF LI'L ABNER. SHE HAS PERFORMED ALL THE MYSTIC RITES AND NOW LIES WAITING--
10-12
HOPE AH DID IT RIGHT! MAH OLD GRAN'MAMMY TOLE ME IT CAIN'T FAIL. BUT AH DON'T SEE NUTHIN' YET!
JEHOSOPHAT- IT COME TO ME!! HEY BESSIE!
CAPP
© 1934 by United Feature Syndicate, Inc.

LI'L ABNER Pansy Is No Geranium! By Al Capp

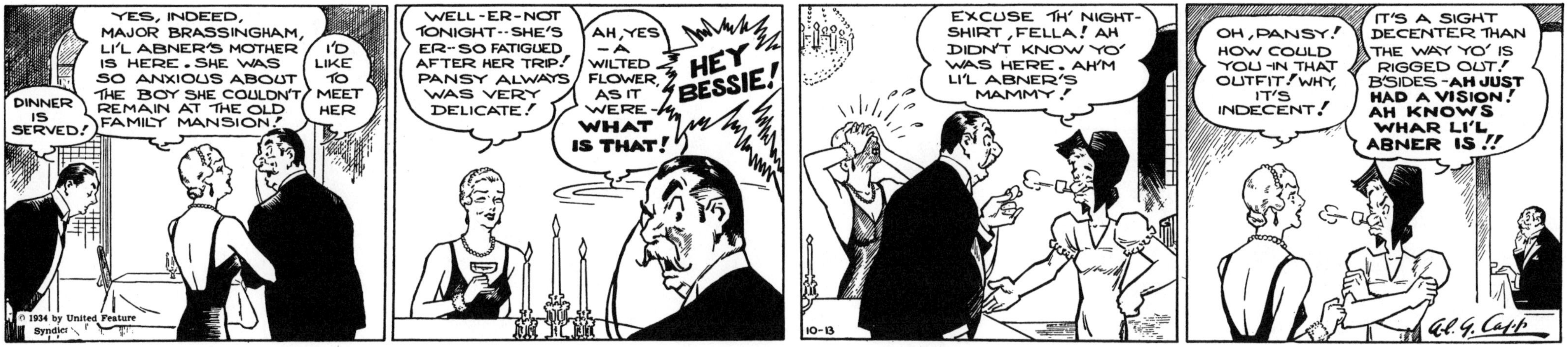

DINNER IS SERVED!
YES, INDEED, MAJOR BRASSINGHAM, LI'L ABNER'S MOTHER IS HERE. SHE WAS SO ANXIOUS ABOUT THE BOY SHE COULDN'T REMAIN AT THE OLD FAMILY MANSION!
I'D LIKE TO MEET HER
© 1934 by United Feature Syndic
WELL-ER-NOT TONIGHT--SHE'S ER--SO FATIGUED AFTER HER TRIP! PANSY ALWAYS WAS VERY DELICATE!
AH, YES -A WILTED FLOWER, AS IT WERE- WHAT IS THAT!
HEY BESSIE!
EXCUSE TH' NIGHT-SHIRT, FELLA! AH DIDN'T KNOW YO' WAS HERE. AH'M LI'L ABNER'S MAMMY!
10-13
OH, PANSY! HOW COULD YOU-IN THAT OUTFIT! WHY, IT'S INDECENT!
IT'S A SIGHT DECENTER THAN THE WAY YO' IS RIGGED OUT! B'SIDES-AH JUST HAD A VISION! AH KNOWS WHAR LI'L ABNER IS!!
Al. G. Capp

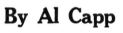

LI'L ABNER — With Just a Vision to Guide Her — By Al Capp

LEGGO O' ME! AH GOTTA GIT GOIN'! AH JEST HAD A VISION! AH KNOWS WHAR LI'L ABNER IS!
PANSY- HAVE YOU GONE MAD? THERE'S NO SUCH THING AS A VISION!
10-15
OH, HAIN'T THAR! - THET JEST SHOWS HOW IGNO-RUNT YO' IS! C'MON- LET'S GIT INTO ONE O' YO' AUTYMOBILES! AH'LL SHOW YO'!!
© 1934 by United Feature Syndicate, Inc.
WHERE TO, MADAME?
STRAIGHT AHEAD -AN' THEN TURN LEFT!
Al Capp
BUT HOW CAN YOU DIRECT US AROUND NEW YORK? YOU DON'T KNOW THE NAME OF A SINGLE STREET HERE!
DON'T HAFTA KNOW NO NAMES! JEST GO WHAR AH TELLS YO'! THE VISION WILL LEAD ME TO MAH BOY!

LI'L ABNER — Re-union In the Kitchen — By Al Capp

INSPIRED BY HER VISION OF LI'L ABNER, MAMMY HAS DIRECTED THE CAR IN A MAD CHASE THROUGH NEW YORK—
STOP RIGHT HERE!!
BUT THIS IS THE ASTOR-GILT CAFE'!
© 1934 by United Feature Syndicate, Inc.
DON'T CARE WHUT IT IS! THE VISION TOLD ME LI'L ABNER WAS RIGHT IN HERE!
BUT, MADAM, YOU CAN'T COME IN HERE! -DRESSED LIKE THAT!
OUTA MAH WAY!
10-16
LI'L ABNER!
MAMMY!
Al. G. Capp

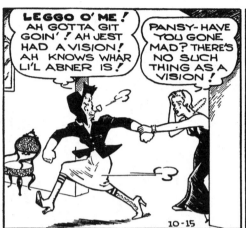

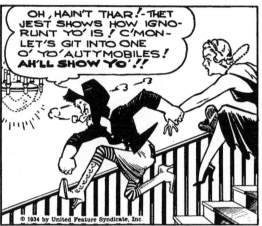

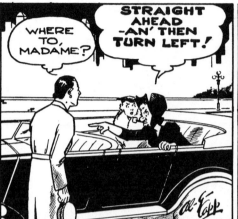

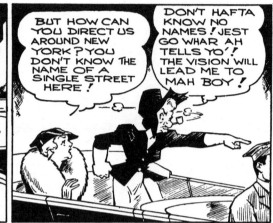

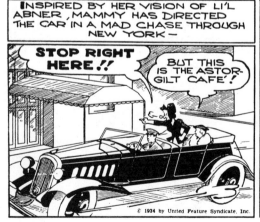

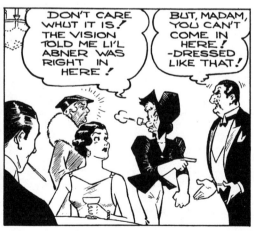

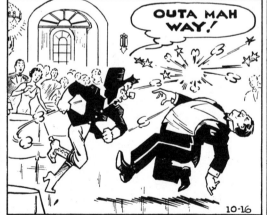

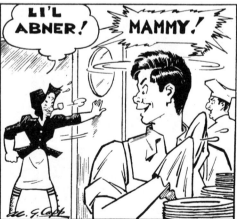

LI'L ABNER — Has He Done Wrong? — By Al Capp

SON, YO' MAMMY IS SHO' GLAD TO SEE YO' AG'IN!
AN' AH IS GLAD TO SEE YO' MAMMY! THET'S SOME SLICK OUTFIT YO' IS GOT ON!
DARLING! WHERE-
HOW IS YO' FEELIN'? DOES YO' FEET STILL HURT FUM WEARIN' SHOES?
MAH FEET FEELS FINE. HOW IS YOURN?
BUT- LI'L ABNER-
I CAN'T BEAR THIS ANY LONGER! WHERE HAVE YOU BEEN?-HOW DID YOU GET HERE?
10-17
THASS RIGHT, SON- AH FO'GOT TO AX YO'- WHAR YO' BEEN ALL THIS TIME?
RIGHT HERE, MAMMY- A-WASHIN' DISHES! GOLLY-AH GOT MAHSELF INTO A TERRIBLE MESS!
WELL, TELL US! TELL US!!
TO-MORROW: LI'L ABNER EXPLAINS
© 1934 by United Feature Syndicate, Inc

LI'L ABNER — A Hero to His Mammy — By Al Capp

LI'L ABNER'S STORY
"WAL, AFTER AH LOST THEM KIDNAPPERS, AH GOT POW'FUL HUNGRY. SO AH COME IN HERE, AN ET 'N ET--
YOUR CHECK IS EXACTLY TEN DOLLARS!
TSK! TSK! ALL AH GOT IS FO'TEEN CENTS.
OH, MY!
-SO AH PROMISED 'EM AH'D STAY HERE AN' WASH DISHES TO PAY FO' THE DINNER. BUT- SHECKS!-EV'RY TIME AH EATS AH OWES 'EM MORE MONEY!-
TWO ROAST DUCKS FOR BREAKFAST! YOU'LL WASH PLENTY MORE DISHES TO PAY FOR THAT!!
YASSUH
-AN' AS A RESULK, AH GOTTA WASH MORE DISHES! AH IS BE'N HERE THREE WEEKS NOW - SLEEPIN' IN THE CELLAR"
-JUST EATIN' AN' WASHIN' DISHES! WHUT A MESS! LOOKS LIKE AH'LL NEVER GIT OUTA HERE!
BUT WHY DIDN'T YOU COME TO ME, DEAR? I'D HAVE PAID IT! OH-HOW DUMB!
DUMB, NUTHIN'! -IT WAS THE YOKUM PRIDE! AH IS PROUD OF YO' SON!
10-18
© 1934 by United Feature Syndicate, Inc

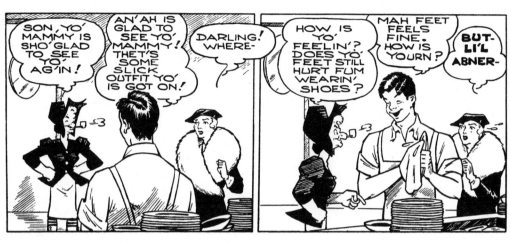

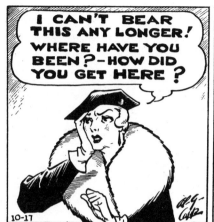

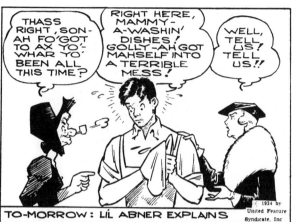

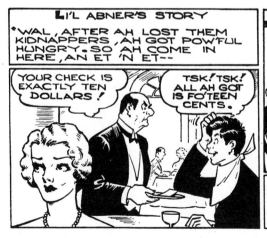

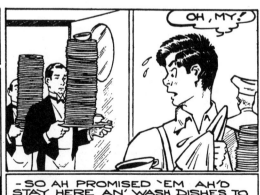

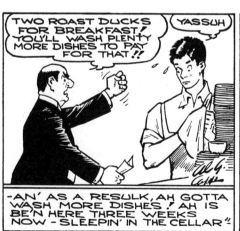

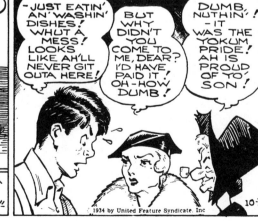

LI'L ABNER Mammy Knows Best By Al Capp

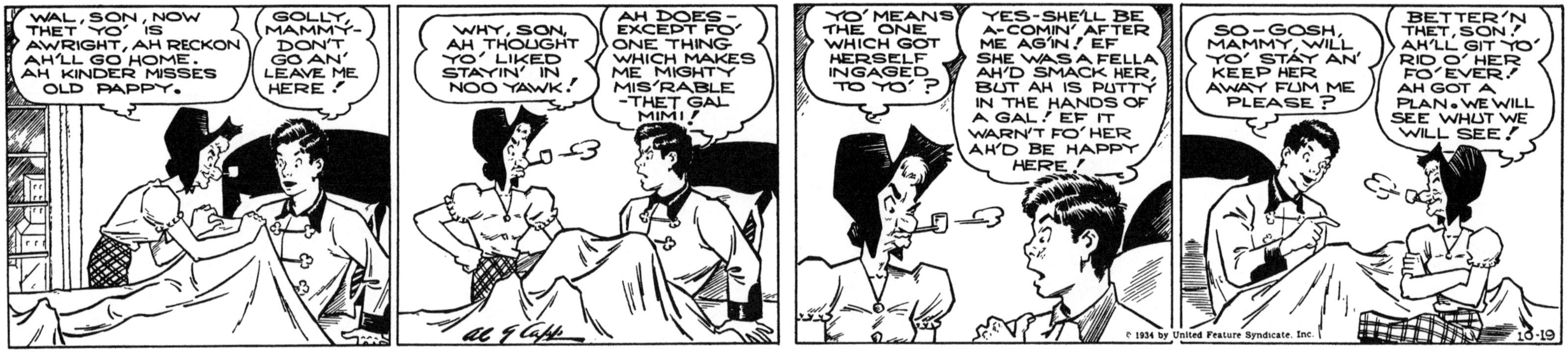

WAL, SON, NOW THET YO' IS AWRIGHT, AH RECKON AH'LL GO HOME. AH KINDER MISSES OLD PAPPY.
GOLLY, MAMMY- DON'T GO AN' LEAVE ME HERE!
WHY, SON, AH THOUGHT YO' LIKED STAYIN' IN NOO YAWK!
AH DOES - EXCEPT FO' ONE THING WHICH MAKES ME MIGHTY MIS'RABLE -THET GAL MIMI!
YO' MEANS THE ONE WHICH GOT HERSELF INGAGED TO YO'?
YES-SHE'LL BE A-COMIN' AFTER ME AG'IN! EF SHE WAS A FELLA AH'D SMACK HER, BUT AH IS PUTTY IN THE HANDS OF A GAL! EF IT WARN'T FO' HER AH'D BE HAPPY HERE!
SO-GOSH, MAMMY, WILL YO' STAY AN' KEEP HER AWAY FUM ME PLEASE?
BETTER'N THET, SON! AH'LL GIT YO' RID O' HER FO'EVER! AH GOT A PLAN. WE WILL SEE WHUT WE WILL SEE!
© 1934 by United Feature Syndicate, Inc.
10-19

LI'L ABNER Folks At Home By Al Capp

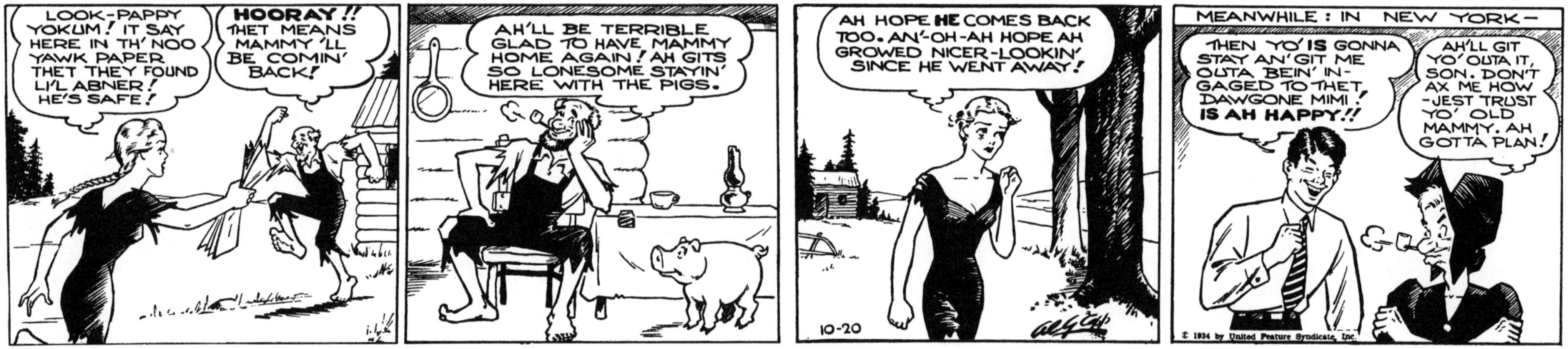

LOOK-PAPPY YOKUM! IT SAY HERE IN TH' NOO YAWK PAPER THET THEY FOUND LI'L ABNER! HE'S SAFE!
HOORAY!! THET MEANS MAMMY'LL BE COMIN' BACK!
AH'LL BE TERRIBLE GLAD TO HAVE MAMMY HOME AGAIN! AH GITS SO LONESOME STAYIN' HERE WITH THE PIGS.
AH HOPE HE COMES BACK TOO. AN'-OH-AH HOPE AH GROWED NICER-LOOKIN' SINCE HE WENT AWAY!
10-20
MEANWHILE: IN NEW YORK-
THEN YO' IS GONNA STAY AN' GIT ME OUTA BEIN' IN-GAGED TO THET DAWGONE MIMI! IS AH HAPPY!!
AH'LL GIT YO' OUTA IT, SON. DON'T AX ME HOW -JEST TRUST YO' OLD MAMMY. AH GOTTA PLAN!
© 1934 by United Feature Syndicate, Inc.

LI'L ABNER **Miss New York!** **By Al Capp**

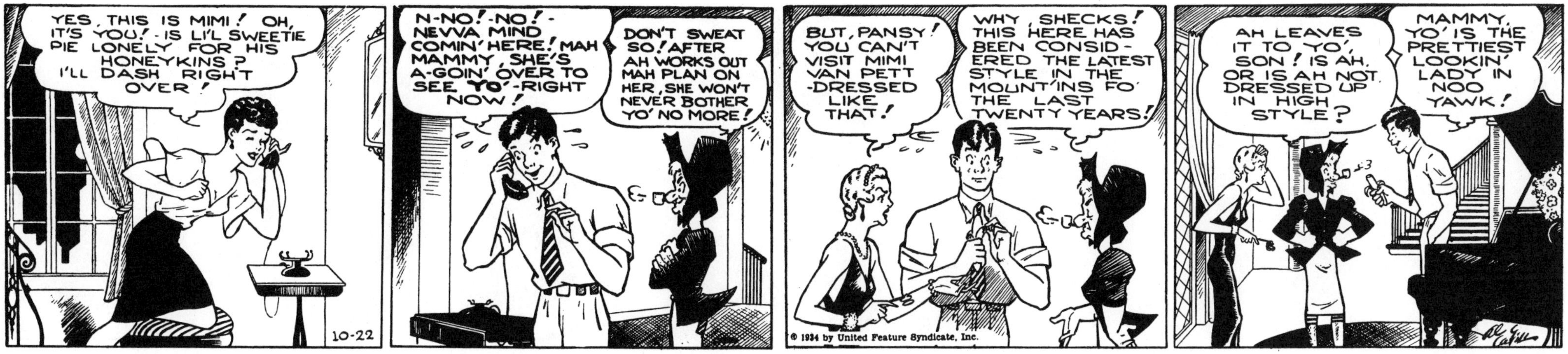
YES, THIS IS MIMI! OH, IT'S YOU! -IS LI'L SWEETIE PIE LONELY FOR HIS HONEYKINS? I'LL DASH RIGHT OVER!
10-22
N-NO!-NO!-NEVVA MIND COMIN' HERE! MAH MAMMY, SHE'S A-GOIN' OVER TO SEE YO'-RIGHT NOW!
DON'T SWEAT SO! AFTER AH WORKS OUT MAH PLAN ON HER, SHE WON'T NEVER BOTHER YO' NO MORE!
BUT, PANSY! YOU CAN'T VISIT MIMI VAN PETT -DRESSED LIKE THAT!
WHY, SHECKS! THIS HERE HAS BEEN CONSID-ERED THE LATEST STYLE IN THE MOUNT'INS FO' THE LAST TWENTY YEARS!
© 1934 by United Feature Syndicate, Inc.
AH LEAVES IT TO YO', SON! IS AH, OR IS AH NOT, DRESSED UP IN HIGH STYLE?
MAMMY, YO' IS THE PRETTIEST LOOKIN' LADY IN NOO YAWK!

LI'L ABNER **The Little Deceiver** **By Al Capp**

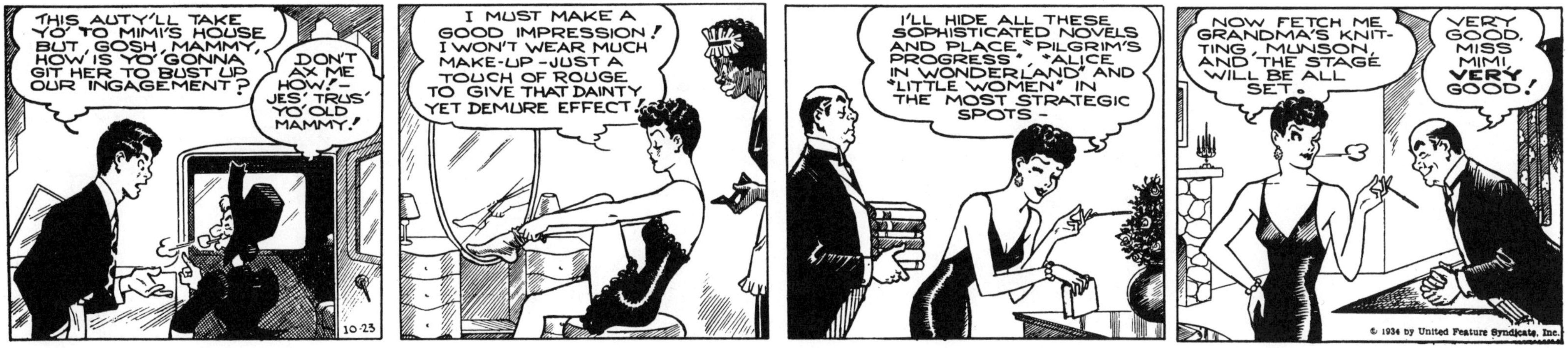
THIS AUTY'LL TAKE YO' TO MIMI'S HOUSE BUT, GOSH, MAMMY, HOW IS YO' GONNA GIT HER TO BUST UP OUR INGAGEMENT?
DON'T AX ME HOW!- JES' TRUS' YO' OLD MAMMY!
10-23
I MUST MAKE A GOOD IMPRESSION! I WON'T WEAR MUCH MAKE-UP -JUST A TOUCH OF ROUGE TO GIVE THAT DAINTY YET DEMURE EFFECT!
I'LL HIDE ALL THESE SOPHISTICATED NOVELS AND PLACE "PILGRIM'S PROGRESS", "ALICE IN WONDERLAND" AND "LITTLE WOMEN" IN THE MOST STRATEGIC SPOTS -
NOW FETCH ME GRANDMA'S KNIT-TING, MUNSON, AND THE STAGE WILL BE ALL SET.
VERY GOOD, MISS MIMI, VERY GOOD!
© 1934 by United Feature Syndicate, Inc.

LI'L ABNER Keep Your Shirt On, Mammy ! **By Al Capp**

MRS. YOKUM!
HOWDY!
OH!
10-24
NOT EXACTLY THE ARISTOCRATIC DOWAGER I EXPECTED – BUT WHAT A QUAINT, GENTLE, ADORABLE OLD THING!
NOW AH SEES WHY LI'L ABNER CAIN'T STAND HER! SHE'S JES' A PRIMPED-UP STICK O' CANDY! AH'LL START WORKIN' OUT MAH PLAN RIGHT NOW!
© 1934 by United Feature Syndicate, Inc.
I'LL TAKE YOUR HAT
THASS FINE. JES' A MINUTE AN' YO' KIN TAKE MAH SHOES, TOO!

LI'L ABNER She Can't Fool Mammy **By Al Capp**

OH, MRS. YOKUM, LI'L ABNER HAS TOLD ME SO MUCH ABOUT YOU! AND YOU'RE EVEN SWEETER THAN HE SAID!
THANK YO' (–"TRYIN' TO GIT ME BY FLATTERY. –THE LI'L STICK O' CANDY!"–)
OH! IF YOU ONLY KNEW HOW I ADORE HIM! IT WAS LOVE AT FIRST SIGHT WITH ME!
YO' DON'T SAY! (–"HE GOT A STUMMICK ACHE THE FUST TIME HE SEEN YO'!"–)
10-25
I KNOW HE LOVES ME, TOO. TEE-HEE! I SUPPOSE HE'S RAVED TO YOU ABOUT ME.
HE RAVED AWRIGHT! (–"MAH PORE BOY! AH NEVER SEEN HIM SO MIS'RABLE SINCE HE HAD THE MEASLES."–)
© 1934 by United Feature Syndicate, Inc.
AND AFTER WE'RE MARRIED I KNOW YOU AND I WILL BE DEAR, DEAR FRIENDS. YOU SEEM SO UNDERSTANDING!
YO' BET AH AM! (–"AH UNNERSTAN'S YO' ONLY TOO WELL, LI'L POISON IVY!"–)

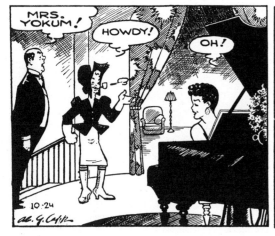

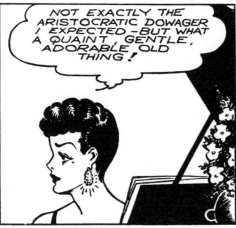

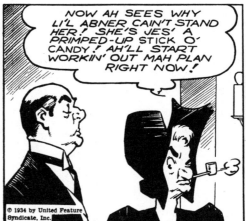

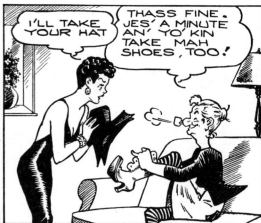

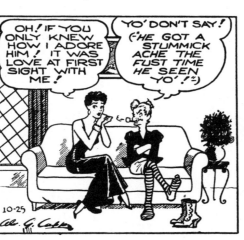

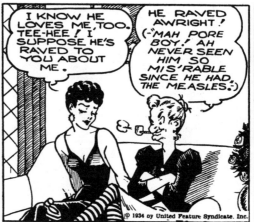

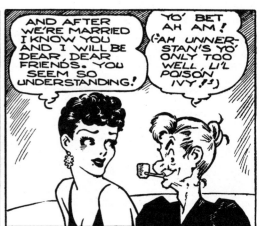

LI'L ABNER The Queen of All the Yokums

By Al Capp

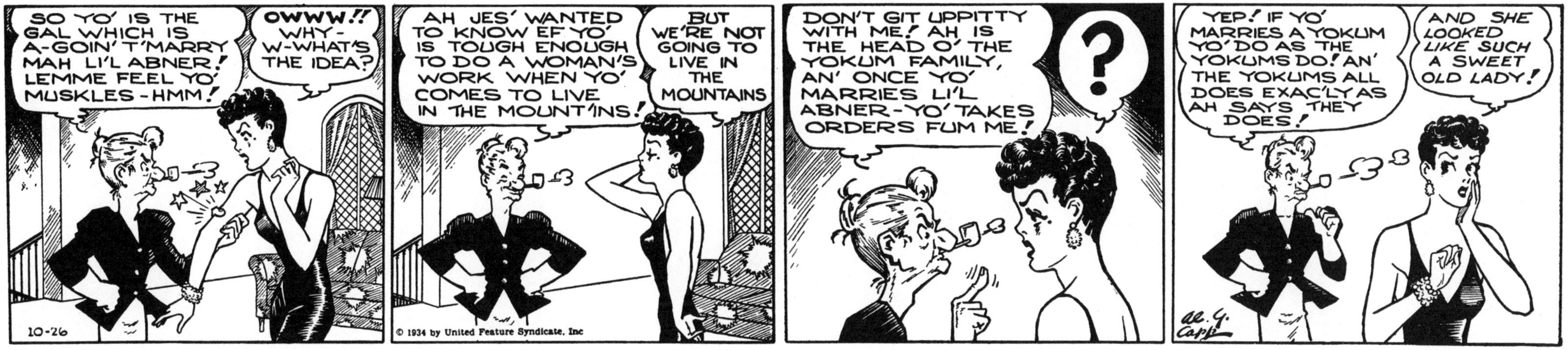

SO YO' IS THE GAL WHICH IS A-GOIN' T'MARRY MAH LI'L ABNER! LEMME FEEL YO' MUSKLES - HMM!
OWWW!! WHY-W-WHAT'S THE IDEA?
10-26
AH JES' WANTED TO KNOW EF YO' IS TOUGH ENOUGH TO DO A WOMAN'S WORK WHEN YO' COMES TO LIVE IN THE MOUNT'INS!
BUT WE'RE NOT GOING TO LIVE IN THE MOUNTAINS
© 1934 by United Feature Syndicate, Inc
DON'T GIT UPPITTY WITH ME! AH IS THE HEAD O' THE YOKUM FAMILY, AN' ONCE YO' MARRIES LI'L ABNER - YO' TAKES ORDERS FUM ME!
?
YEP! IF YO' MARRIES A YOKUM YO' DO AS THE YOKUMS DO! AN' THE YOKUMS ALL DOES EXAC'LY AS AH SAYS THEY DOES!
AND SHE LOOKED LIKE SUCH A SWEET OLD LADY!
Al. G. Capp

LI'L ABNER Can You Take It, Mimi ?

By Al Capp

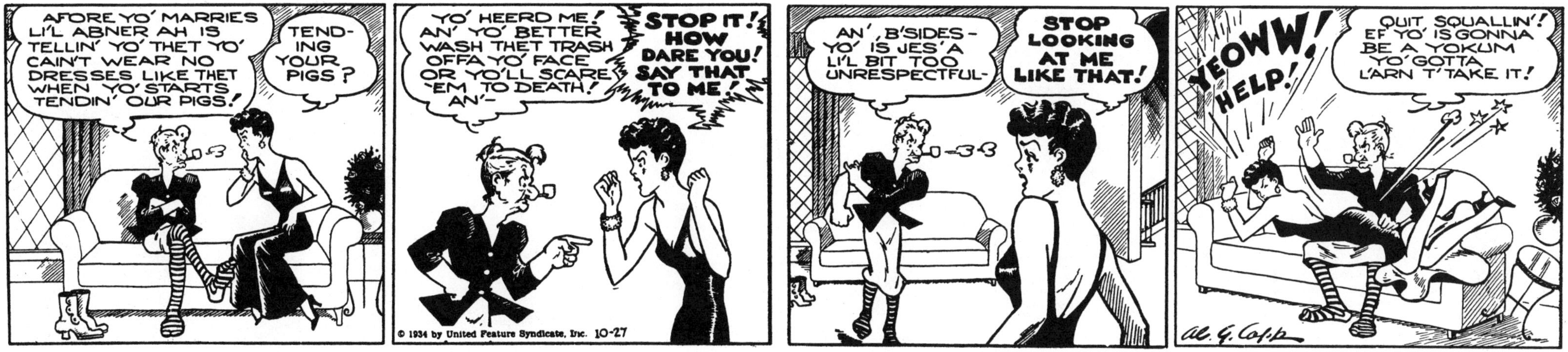

AFORE YO' MARRIES LI'L ABNER AH IS TELLIN' YO' THET YO' CAIN'T WEAR NO DRESSES LIKE THET WHEN YO' STARTS TENDIN' OUR PIGS!
TEND-ING YOUR PIGS?
YO' HEERD ME! AN' YO' BETTER WASH THET TRASH OFFA YO' FACE OR YO'LL SCARE 'EM TO DEATH! AN'-
STOP IT! HOW DARE YOU! SAY THAT TO ME!
© 1934 by United Feature Syndicate, Inc. 10-27
AN', B'SIDES - YO' IS JES' A LI'L BIT TOO UNRESPECTFUL-
STOP LOOKING AT ME LIKE THAT!
YEOWW! HELP!
QUIT SQUALLIN'! EF YO' IS GONNA BE A YOKUM YO' GOTTA L'ARN T'TAKE IT!
Al. G. Capp

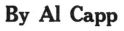

LI'L ABNER Didn't Hurt Mammy By Al Capp

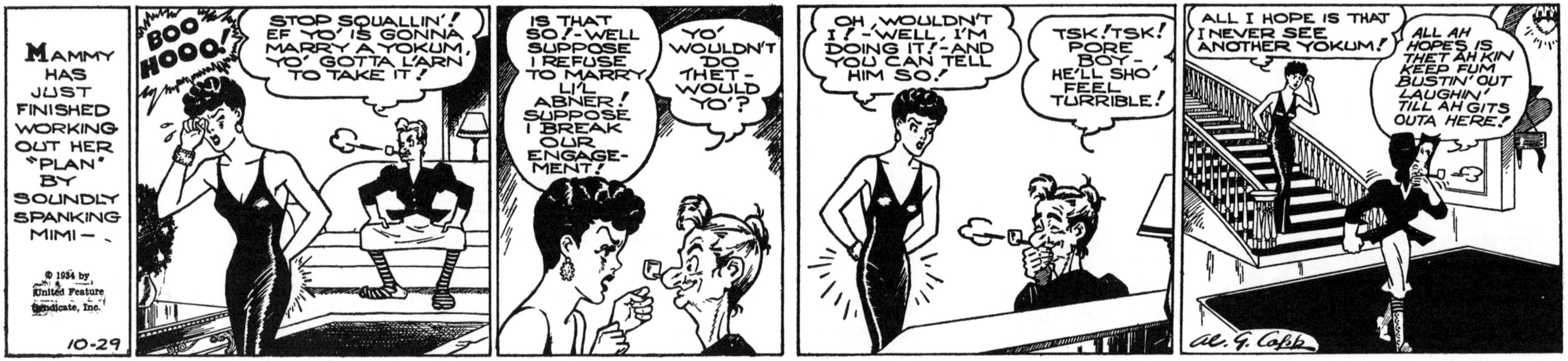

MAMMY HAS JUST FINISHED WORKING OUT HER "PLAN" BY SOUNDLY SPANKING MIMI—.
© 1934 by United Feature Syndicate, Inc.
10-29
BOO HOOO!
STOP SQUALLIN'! EF YO' IS GONNA MARRY A YOKUM, YO' GOTTA L'ARN TO TAKE IT!
IS THAT SO!-WELL SUPPOSE I REFUSE TO MARRY LI'L ABNER! SUPPOSE I BREAK OUR ENGAGE-MENT!
YO' WOULDN'T DO THET-WOULD YO'?
OH, WOULDN'T I!-WELL, I'M DOING IT!-AND YOU CAN TELL HIM SO!
TSK! TSK! PORE BOY-HE'LL SHO' FEEL TURRIBLE!
ALL I HOPE IS THAT I NEVER SEE ANOTHER YOKUM!
ALL AH HOPES IS THET AH KIN KEEP FUM BUSTIN' OUT LAUGHIN' TILL AH GITS OUTA HERE!
Al. G. Capp

LI'L ABNER Mammy's A' Goin' Home By Al Capp

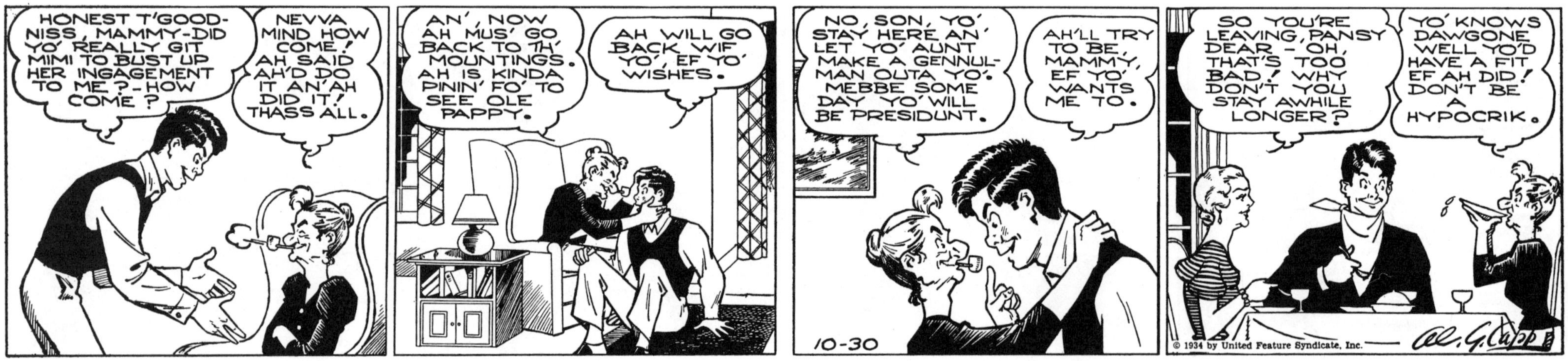

HONEST T'GOOD-NISS, MAMMY-DID YO' REALLY GIT MIMI TO BUST UP HER INGAGEMENT TO ME?-HOW COME?
NEVVA MIND HOW COME! AH SAID AH'D DO IT AN' AH DID IT! THASS ALL.
AN', NOW AH MUS' GO BACK TO TH' MOUNTINGS. AH IS KINDA PININ' FO' TO SEE OLE PAPPY.
AH WILL GO BACK WIF YO', EF YO' WISHES.
NO, SON, YO' STAY HERE AN' LET YO' AUNT MAKE A GENNUL-MAN OUTA YO'. MEBBE SOME DAY YO' WILL BE PRESIDUNT.
AH'LL TRY TO BE, MAMMY, EF YO' WANTS ME TO.
10-30
SO YOU'RE LEAVING, PANSY DEAR - OH, THAT'S TOO BAD! WHY DON'T YOU STAY AWHILE LONGER?
YO' KNOWS DAWGONE WELL YO'D HAVE A FIT EF AH DID! DON'T BE A HYPOCRIK.
© 1934 by United Feature Syndicate, Inc.
Al. G. Capp

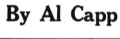

LI'L ABNER Aunty's Eyes

By Al Capp

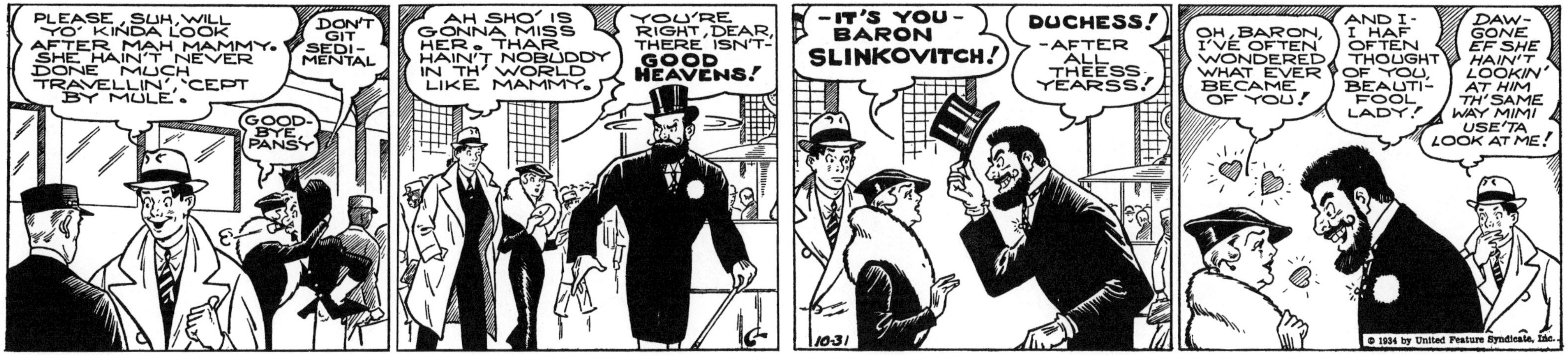

PLEASE, SUH, WILL YO' KINDA LOOK AFTER MAH MAMMY. SHE HAIN'T NEVER DONE MUCH TRAVELLIN', 'CEPT BY MULE.
DON'T GIT SEDI-MENTAL
GOOD-BYE PANSY
AH SHO' IS GONNA MISS HER. THAR HAIN'T NOBUDDY IN TH' WORLD LIKE MAMMY.
YOU'RE RIGHT, DEAR, THERE ISN'T- GOOD HEAVENS!
-IT'S YOU- BARON SLINKOVITCH!
DUCHESS! -AFTER ALL THEESS YEARSS!
10-31
OH, BARON, I'VE OFTEN WONDERED WHAT EVER BECAME OF YOU!
AND I- I HAF OFTEN THOUGHT OF YOU, BEAUTI-FOOL LADY!
DAW-GONE EF SHE HAIN'T LOOKIN' AT HIM TH' SAME WAY MIMI USE'TA LOOK AT ME!
© 1934 by United Feature Syndicate, Inc.

LI'L ABNER Mountain Gallantry

By Al Capp

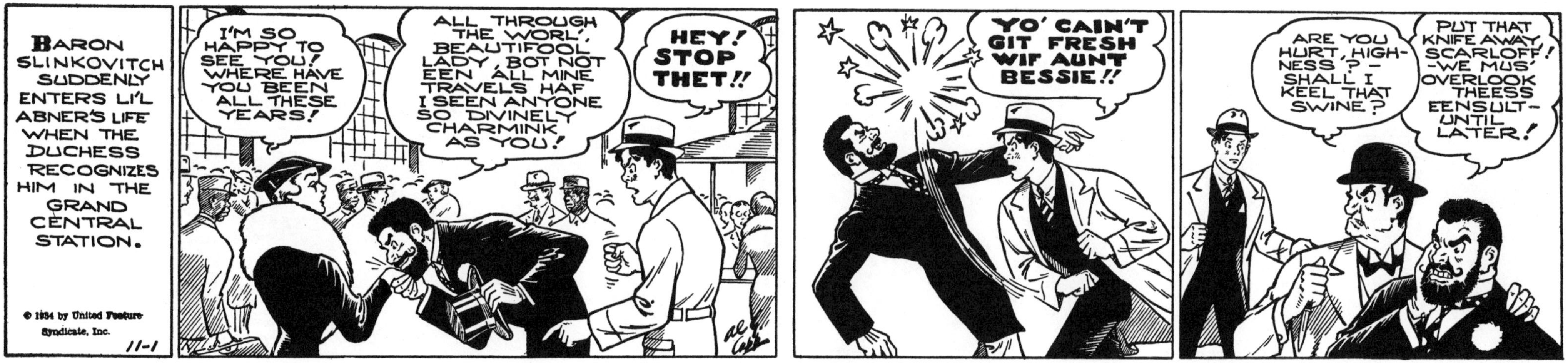

BARON SLINKOVITCH SUDDENLY ENTERS LI'L ABNER'S LIFE WHEN THE DUCHESS RECOGNIZES HIM IN THE GRAND CENTRAL STATION.
© 1934 by United Feature Syndicate, Inc.
11-1
I'M SO HAPPY TO SEE YOU! WHERE HAVE YOU BEEN ALL THESE YEARS!
ALL THROUGH THE WORL', BEAUTIFOOL LADY, BOT NOT EEN ALL MINE TRAVELS HAF I SEEN ANYONE SO DIVINELY CHARMINK AS YOU!
HEY! STOP THET!!
YO' CAIN'T GIT FRESH WIF AUNT BESSIE!!
ARE YOU HURT, HIGH-NESS? - SHALL I KEEL THAT SWINE?
PUT THAT KNIFE AWAY, SCARLOFF! -WE MUS' OVERLOOK THEESS EENSULT- UNTIL LATER!

LI'L ABNER Unlucky Blow

By Al Capp

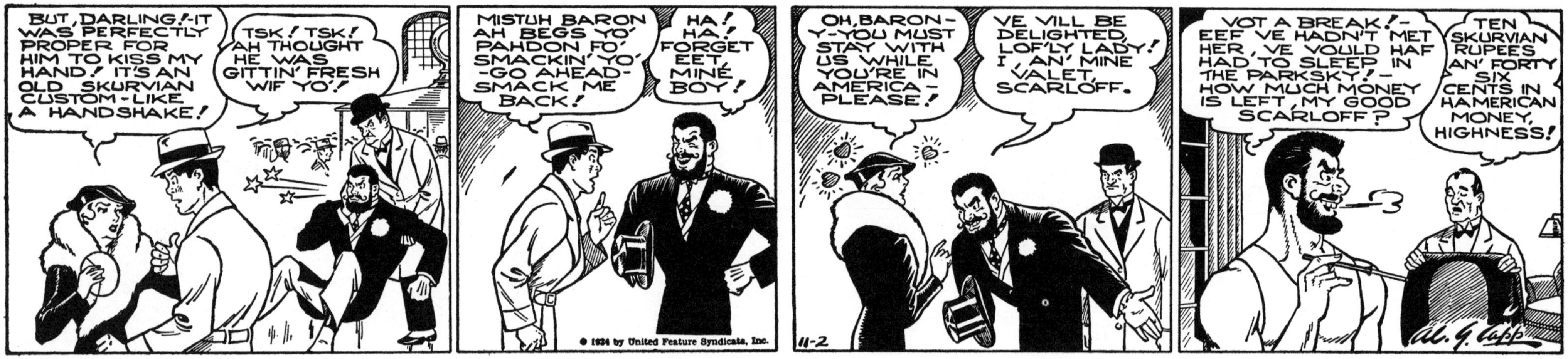
BUT, DARLING!-IT WAS PERFECTLY PROPER FOR HIM TO KISS MY HAND! IT'S AN OLD SKURVIAN CUSTOM-LIKE A HANDSHAKE!
TSK! TSK! AH THOUGHT HE WAS GITTIN' FRESH WIF YO'!
MISTUH BARON AH BEGS YO' PAHDON FO' SMACKIN' YO' -GO AHEAD- SMACK ME BACK!
HA! HA! FORGET EET, MINÉ BOY!
© 1934 by United Feature Syndicate, Inc.
OH, BARON-Y-YOU MUST STAY WITH US WHILE YOU'RE IN AMERICA-PLEASE!
VE VILL BE DELIGHTED, LOF'LY LADY! I, AN' MINE VALET, SCARLOFF.
11-2
VOT A BREAK!-EEF VE HADN'T MET HER, VE VOULD HAF HAD TO SLEEP IN THE PARKSKY!-HOW MUCH MONEY IS LEFT, MY GOOD SCARLOFF?
TEN SKURVIAN RUPEES AN' FORTY SIX CENTS IN HAMERICAN MONEY, HIGHNESS!
Al. G. Capp

LI'L ABNER Funny Custom

By Al Capp

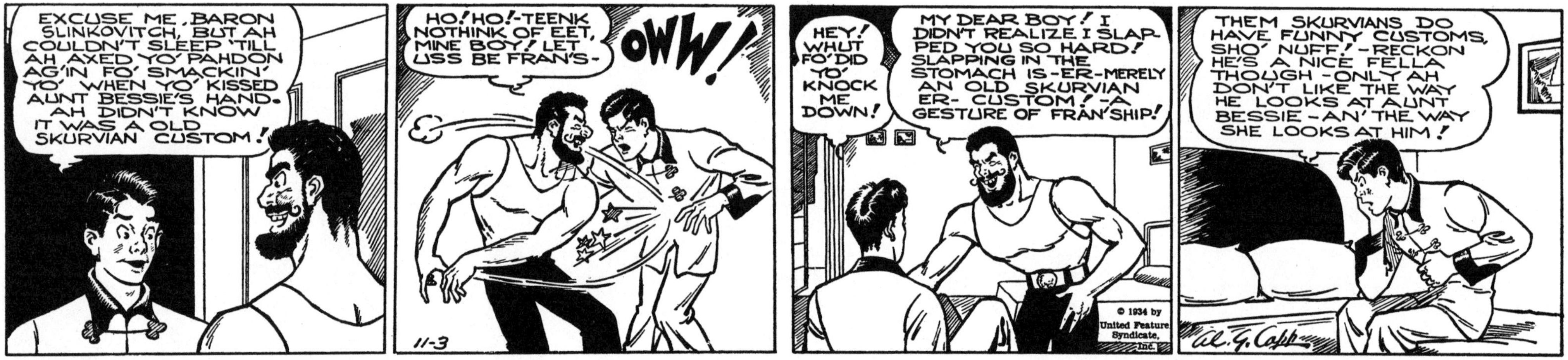
EXCUSE ME, BARON SLINKOVITCH, BUT AH COULDN'T SLEEP 'TILL AH AXED YO' PAHDON AG'IN FO' SMACKIN' YO' WHEN YO' KISSED AUNT BESSIE'S HAND. AH DIDN'T KNOW IT WAS A OLD SKURVIAN CUSTOM!
HO! HO!-TEENK NOTHINK OF EET, MINE BOY! LET USS BE FRAN'S-
OWW!
11-3
HEY! WHUT FO' DID YO' KNOCK ME DOWN!
MY DEAR BOY! I DIDN'T REALIZE I SLAPPED YOU SO HARD! SLAPPING IN THE STOMACH IS-ER-MERELY AN OLD SKURVIAN ER- CUSTOM!-A GESTURE OF FRAN'SHIP!
© 1934 by United Feature Syndicate, Inc.
THEM SKURVIANS DO HAVE FUNNY CUSTOMS, SHO' NUFF!-RECKON HE'S A NICE FELLA THOUGH-ONLY AH DON'T LIKE THE WAY HE LOOKS AT AUNT BESSIE-AN' THE WAY SHE LOOKS AT HIM!
Al. G. Capp

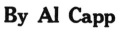

LI'L ABNER — A Serpent in the House

By Al Capp

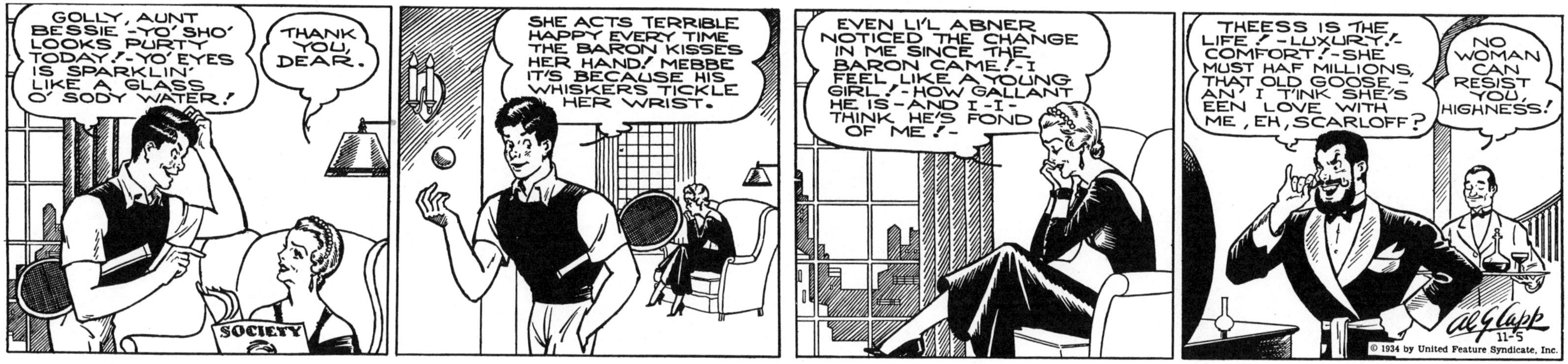
GOLLY, AUNT BESSIE -YO' SHO' LOOKS PURTY TODAY!-YO' EYES IS SPARKLIN' LIKE A GLASS O' SODY WATER!
THANK YOU, DEAR.
SOCIETY
SHE ACTS TERRIBLE HAPPY EVERY TIME THE BARON KISSES HER HAND! MEBBE IT'S BECAUSE HIS WHISKERS TICKLE HER WRIST.
EVEN LI'L ABNER NOTICED THE CHANGE IN ME SINCE THE BARON CAME!-I FEEL LIKE A YOUNG GIRL!-HOW GALLANT HE IS-AND I-I-THINK HE'S FOND OF ME!-
THEESS IS THE LIFE!-LUXURY!-COMFORT!-SHE MUST HAF MILLIONS, THAT OLD GOOSE,-AN' I T'INK SHE'S EEN LOVE WITH ME, EH, SCARLOFF?
NO WOMAN CAN RESIST YOU, HIGHNESS!
Al G Capp
11-5
© 1934 by United Feature Syndicate, Inc.

LI'L ABNER — Object: Matrimony

By Al Capp

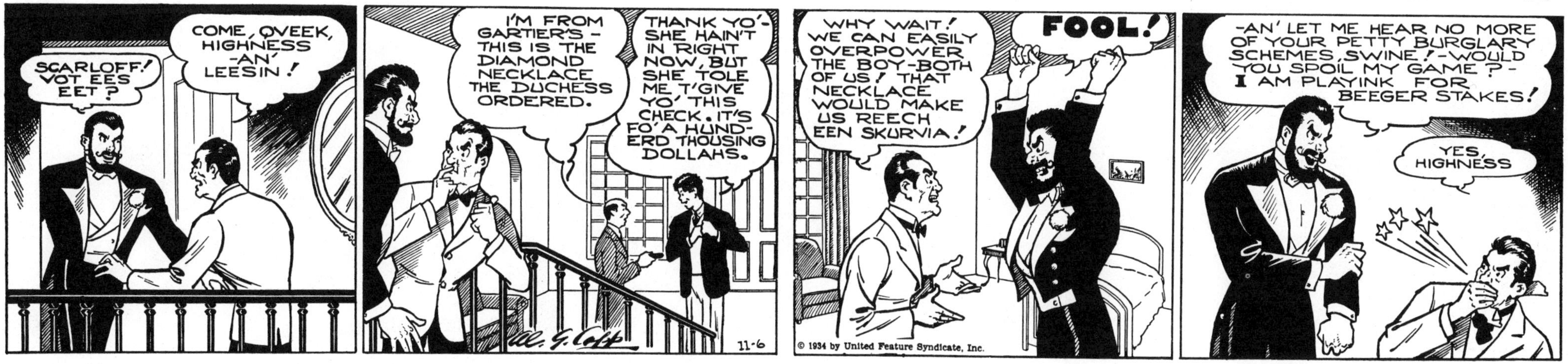
SCARLOFF! VOT EES EET?
COME, QVEEK, HIGHNESS -AN' LEESIN!
I'M FROM GARTIER'S - THIS IS THE DIAMOND NECKLACE THE DUCHESS ORDERED.
THANK YO'-SHE HAIN'T IN RIGHT NOW, BUT SHE TOLE ME T'GIVE YO' THIS CHECK. IT'S FO' A HUND-ERD THOUSING DOLLAHS.
Al. G. Capp
11-6
WHY WAIT! WE CAN EASILY OVERPOWER THE BOY-BOTH OF US! THAT NECKLACE WOULD MAKE US REECH EEN SKURVIA!
FOOL!
© 1934 by United Feature Syndicate, Inc.
-AN' LET ME HEAR NO MORE OF YOUR PETTY BURGLARY SCHEMES, SWINE!-WOULD YOU SPOIL MY GAME?-I AM PLAYINK FOR BEEGER STAKES!
YES, HIGHNESS

LI'L ABNER   Crime Afoot !   By Al Capp

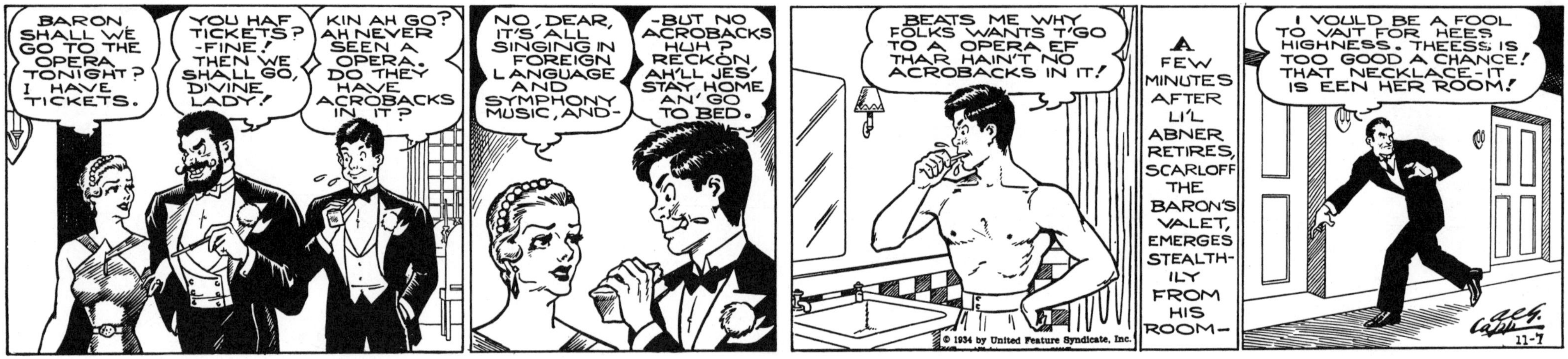

BARON, SHALL WE GO TO THE OPERA TONIGHT? I HAVE TICKETS.
YOU HAF TICKETS? -FINE! THEN WE SHALL GO, DIVINE LADY!
KIN AH GO? AH NEVER SEEN A OPERA. DO THEY HAVE ACROBACKS IN IT?
NO, DEAR, IT'S ALL SINGING IN FOREIGN LANGUAGE AND SYMPHONY MUSIC, AND-
-BUT NO ACROBACKS HUH? RECKON AH'LL JES' STAY HOME AN' GO TO BED.
BEATS ME WHY FOLKS WANTS T'GO TO A OPERA EF THAR HAIN'T NO ACROBACKS IN IT!
© 1934 by United Feature Syndicate, Inc.
A FEW MINUTES AFTER LI'L ABNER RETIRES, SCARLOFF THE BARON'S VALET, EMERGES STEALTH-ILY FROM HIS ROOM-
I VOULD BE A FOOL TO VAIT FOR HEES HIGHNESS. THEESS IS TOO GOOD A CHANCE! THAT NECKLACE-IT IS EEN HER ROOM!
11-7

LI'L ABNER   Thet Hain't No Mouse!   By Al Capp

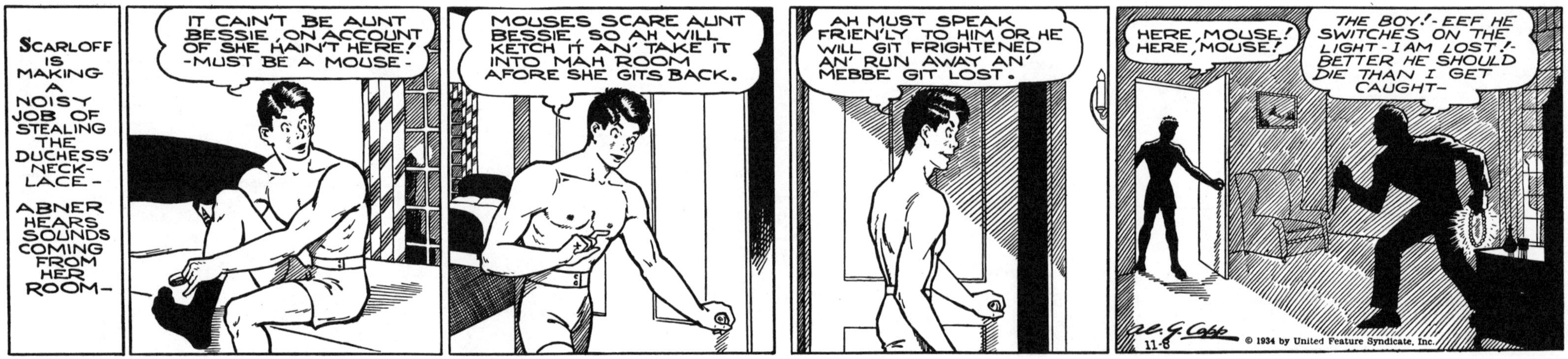

SCARLOFF IS MAKING A NOISY JOB OF STEALING THE DUCHESS' NECK-LACE-
ABNER HEARS SOUNDS COMING FROM HER ROOM-
IT CAIN'T BE AUNT BESSIE, ON ACCOUNT OF SHE HAIN'T HERE! -MUST BE A MOUSE-
MOUSES SCARE AUNT BESSIE, SO AH WILL KETCH IT AN' TAKE IT INTO MAH ROOM AFORE SHE GITS BACK.
AH MUST SPEAK FRIEN'LY TO HIM OR HE WILL GIT FRIGHTENED AN' RUN AWAY AN' MEBBE GIT LOST.
HERE, MOUSE! HERE, MOUSE!
THE BOY!-EEF HE SWITCHES ON THE LIGHT-I AM LOST!-BETTER HE SHOULD DIE THAN I GET CAUGHT-
11-8
© 1934 by United Feature Syndicate, Inc.

LI'L ABNER Talk Fast, Scarloff ! **By Al Capp**

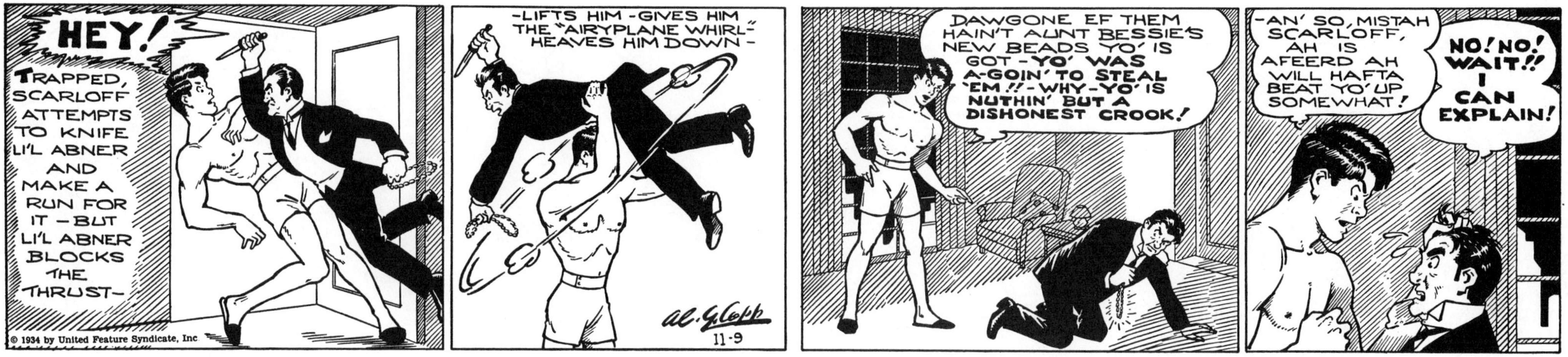
HEY!
TRAPPED, SCARLOFF ATTEMPTS TO KNIFE LI'L ABNER AND MAKE A RUN FOR IT – BUT LI'L ABNER BLOCKS THE THRUST –
© 1934 by United Feature Syndicate, Inc.
– LIFTS HIM – GIVES HIM THE "AIRYPLANE WHIRL" HEAVES HIM DOWN –
Al. G. Capp
11-9
DAWGONE EF THEM HAIN'T AUNT BESSIE'S NEW BEADS YO' IS GOT – YO' WAS A-GOIN' TO STEAL 'EM !! – WHY – YO' IS NUTHIN' BUT A DISHONEST CROOK !
– AN' SO, MISTAH SCARLOFF, AH IS AFEERD AH WILL HAFTA BEAT YO' UP SOMEWHAT !
NO! NO! WAIT!! I CAN EXPLAIN!

LI'L ABNER Hook, Line and Sinker ! **By Al Capp**

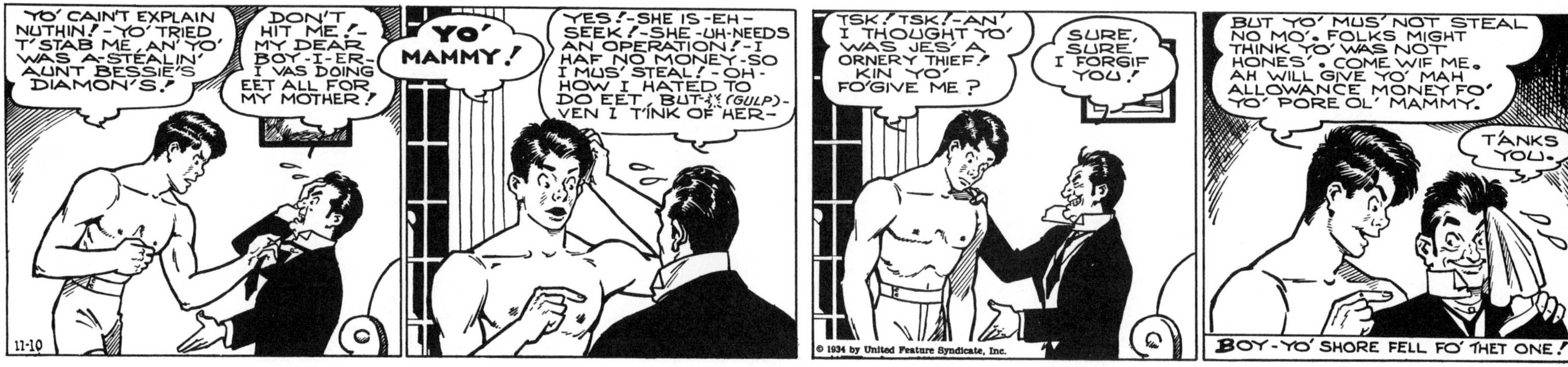
YO' CAIN'T EXPLAIN NUTHIN! – YO' TRIED T' STAB ME, AN' YO' WAS A-STEALIN' AUNT BESSIE'S DIAMON'S!
DON'T HIT ME! – MY DEAR BOY – I – ER – I VAS DOING EET ALL FOR MY MOTHER!
11-10
YO' MAMMY!
YES! – SHE IS – EH – SEEK! – SHE – UH – NEEDS AN OPERATION! – I HAF NO MONEY – SO I MUS' STEAL! – OH – HOW I HATED TO DO EET, BUT – (GULP) – VEN I T'INK OF HER –
TSK! TSK! – AN' I THOUGHT YO' WAS JES' A ORNERY THIEF! KIN YO' FO'GIVE ME ?
SURE, SURE I FORGIF YOU!
© 1934 by United Feature Syndicate, Inc.
BUT YO' MUS' NOT STEAL NO MO'. FOLKS MIGHT THINK YO' WAS NOT HONES'. COME WIF ME. AH WILL GIVE YO' MAH ALLOWANCE MONEY FO' YO' PORE OL' MAMMY.
T'ANKS YOU.
BOY – YO' SHORE FELL FO' THET ONE!

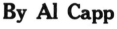

LI'L ABNER Opinions Differ By Al Capp

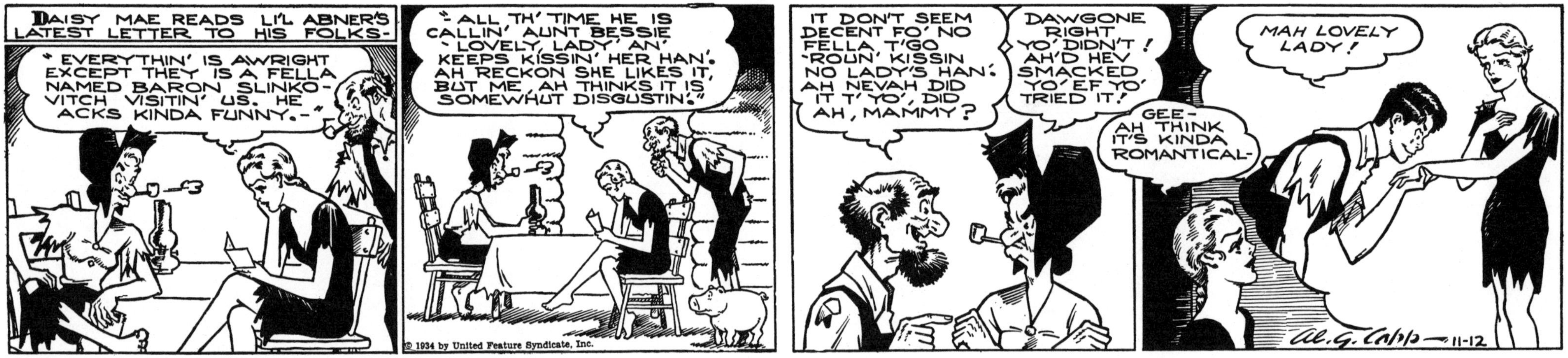
DAISY MAE READS LI'L ABNER'S LATEST LETTER TO HIS FOLKS-
"EVERYTHIN' IS AWRIGHT EXCEPT THEY IS A FELLA NAMED BARON SLINKO-VITCH VISITIN' US. HE ACKS KINDA FUNNY.-
-ALL TH' TIME HE IS CALLIN' AUNT BESSIE 'LOVELY LADY' AN' KEEPS KISSIN' HER HAN'. AH RECKON SHE LIKES IT, BUT ME, AH THINKS IT IS SOMEWHUT DISGUSTIN'."
© 1934 by United Feature Syndicate, Inc.
IT DON'T SEEM DECENT FO' NO FELLA T'GO 'ROUN' KISSIN NO LADY'S HAN'. AH NEVAH DID IT T' YO', DID AH, MAMMY?
DAWGONE RIGHT YO' DIDN'T! AH'D HEV SMACKED YO' EF YO' TRIED IT!
GEE-AH THINK IT'S KINDA ROMANTICAL-
MAH LOVELY LADY!
Al. G. Capp 11-12

LI'L ABNER The Plot Thickens By Al Capp

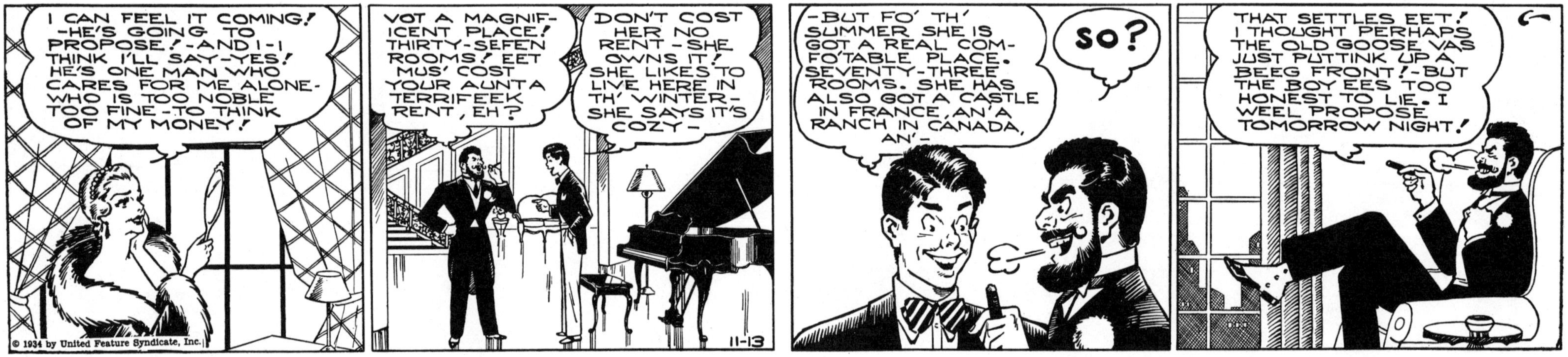
I CAN FEEL IT COMING! -HE'S GOING TO PROPOSE! -AND I-I THINK I'LL SAY-YES! HE'S ONE MAN WHO CARES FOR ME ALONE-WHO IS TOO NOBLE TOO FINE-TO THINK OF MY MONEY!
© 1934 by United Feature Syndicate, Inc.
VOT A MAGNIF-ICENT PLACE! THIRTY-SEFEN ROOMS! EET MUS' COST YOUR AUNTA TERRIFEEK RENT, EH?
DON'T COST HER NO RENT-SHE OWNS IT! SHE LIKES TO LIVE HERE IN TH' WINTER-SHE SAYS IT'S COZY-
11-13
-BUT FO' TH' SUMMER SHE IS GOT A REAL COM-FO'TABLE PLACE. SEVENTY-THREE ROOMS. SHE HAS ALSO GOT A CASTLE IN FRANCE, AN' A RANCH IN CANADA, AN'-
SO?
THAT SETTLES EET! I THOUGHT PERHAPS THE OLD GOOSE VAS JUST PUTTINK UP A BEEG FRONT! -BUT THE BOY EES TOO HONEST TO LIE. I WEEL PROPOSE TOMORROW NIGHT!

LI'L ABNER As Welcome As A Toothache

By Al Capp

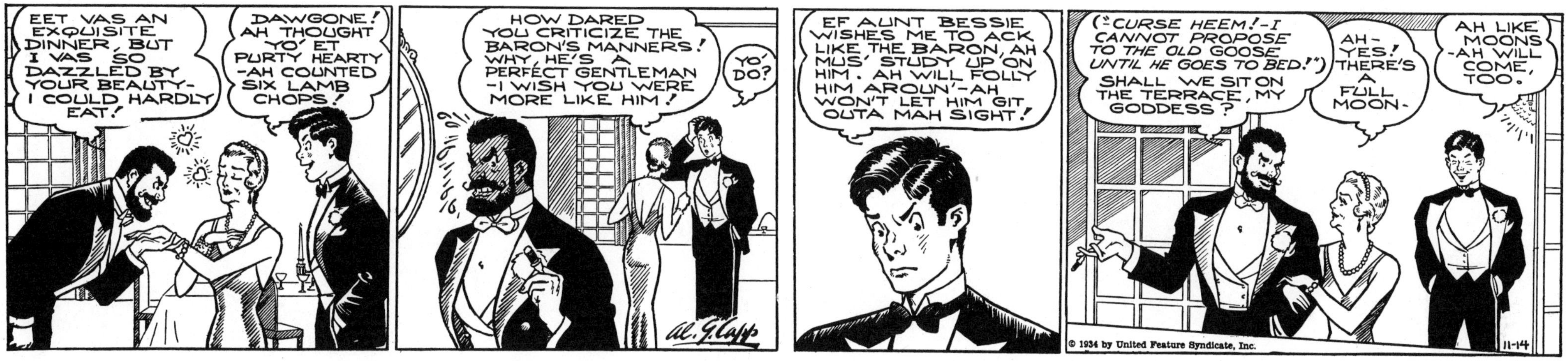

EET VAS AN EXQUISITE DINNER, BUT I VAS SO DAZZLED BY YOUR BEAUTY- I COULD HARDLY EAT!
DAWGONE! AH THOUGHT YO' ET PURTY HEARTY -AH COUNTED SIX LAMB CHOPS!
HOW DARED YOU CRITICIZE THE BARON'S MANNERS! WHY, HE'S A PERFECT GENTLEMAN -I WISH YOU WERE MORE LIKE HIM!
YO' DO?
Al. G. Capp
EF AUNT BESSIE WISHES ME TO ACK LIKE THE BARON, AH MUS' STUDY UP ON HIM. AH WILL FOLLY HIM AROUN'-AH WON'T LET HIM GIT OUTA MAH SIGHT!
("CURSE HEEM!-I CANNOT PROPOSE TO THE OLD GOOSE UNTIL HE GOES TO BED!") SHALL WE SIT ON THE TERRACE, MY GODDESS?
AH-YES! THERE'S A FULL MOON-
AH LIKE MOONS -AH WILL COME, TOO.
© 1934 by United Feature Syndicate, Inc.
11-14

LI'L ABNER Wake Up, Abner!

By Al Capp

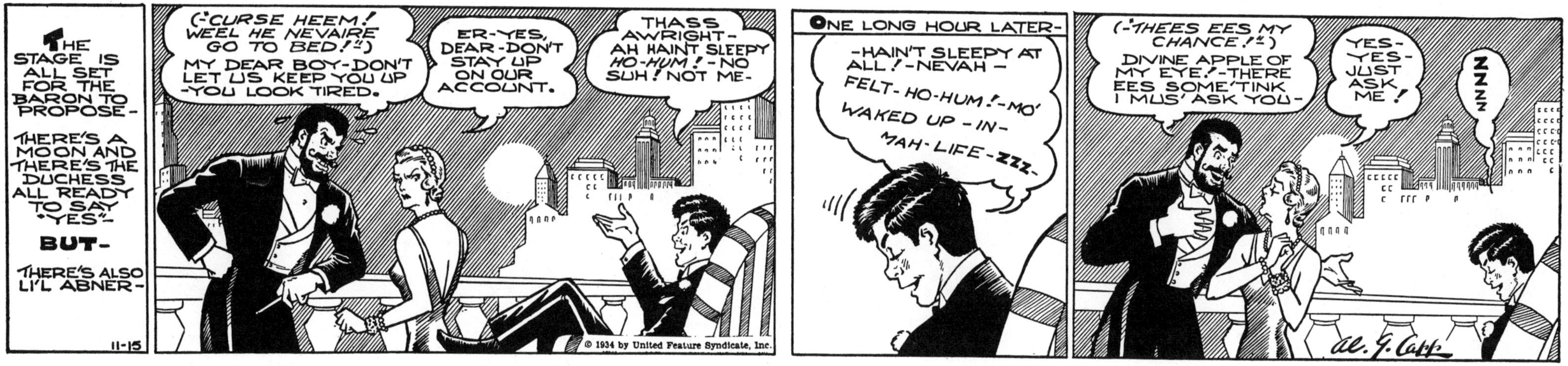

THE STAGE IS ALL SET FOR THE BARON TO PROPOSE-
THERE'S A MOON AND THERE'S THE DUCHESS ALL READY TO SAY "YES"-
BUT-
THERE'S ALSO LI'L ABNER-
11-15
("CURSE HEEM! WEEL HE NEVAIRE GO TO BED!") MY DEAR BOY-DON'T LET US KEEP YOU UP -YOU LOOK TIRED.
ER-YES, DEAR-DON'T STAY UP ON OUR ACCOUNT.
THASS AWRIGHT- AH HAINT SLEEPY HO-HUM!-NO SUH! NOT ME-
© 1934 by United Feature Syndicate, Inc.
ONE LONG HOUR LATER-
-HAIN'T SLEEPY AT ALL!-NEVAH- FELT-HO-HUM!-MO' WAKED UP-IN- MAH-LIFE-ZZZ-
("THEES EES MY CHANCE!") DIVINE APPLE OF MY EYE!-THERE EES SOME'TINK I MUS' ASK YOU-
YES- YES- JUST ASK ME!
ZZZZ
Al. G. Capp

LI'L ABNER A Perfect Gentleman **By Al Capp**

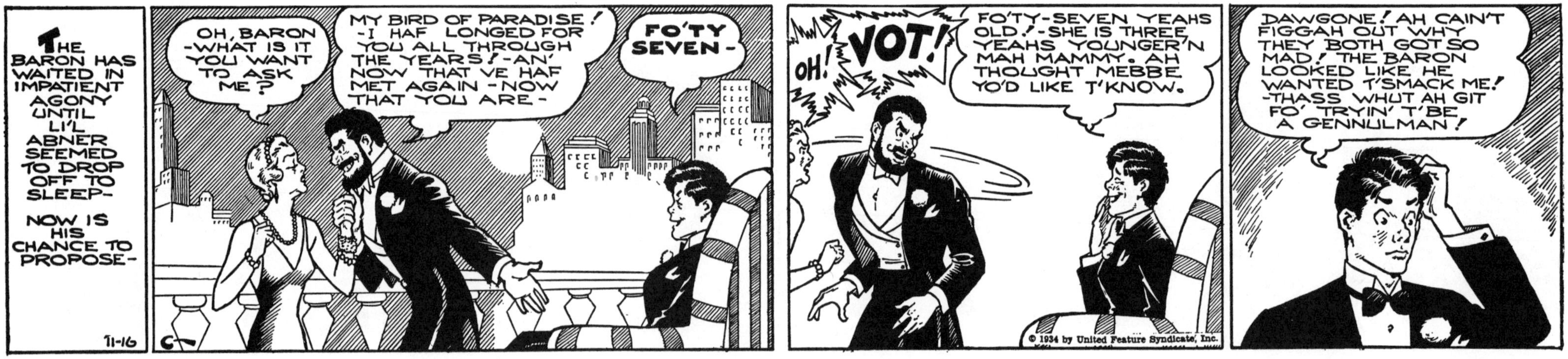
THE BARON HAS WAITED IN IMPATIENT AGONY UNTIL LI'L ABNER SEEMED TO DROP OFF TO SLEEP-
NOW IS HIS CHANCE TO PROPOSE-
11-16
OH, BARON -WHAT IS IT YOU WANT TO ASK ME?
MY BIRD OF PARADISE! -I HAF LONGED FOR YOU ALL THROUGH THE YEARS!-AN' NOW THAT VE HAF MET AGAIN -NOW THAT YOU ARE-
FO'TY SEVEN-
OH!
VOT!
FO'TY-SEVEN YEAHS OLD!-SHE IS THREE YEAHS YOUNGER'N MAH MAMMY. AH THOUGHT MEBBE YO'D LIKE T'KNOW.
© 1934 by United Feature Syndicate, Inc.
DAWGONE! AH CAIN'T FIGGAH OUT WHY THEY BOTH GOT SO MAD! THE BARON LOOKED LIKE HE WANTED T'SMACK ME! -THASS WHUT AH GIT FO' TRYIN' T'BE A GENNULMAN!

LI'L ABNER A Pressing Need **By Al Capp**

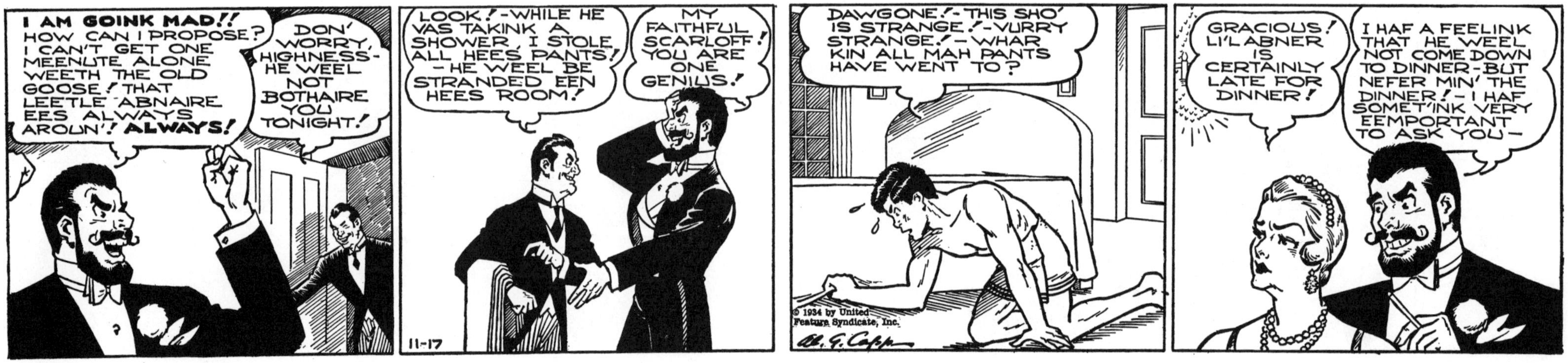
I AM GOINK MAD!! HOW CAN I PROPOSE? I CAN'T GET ONE MEENUTE ALONE WEETH THE OLD GOOSE! THAT LEETLE ABNAIRE EES ALWAYS AROUN'! ALWAYS!
DON' WORRY, HIGHNESS-HE WEEL NOT BOTHAIRE YOU TONIGHT!
LOOK!-WHILE HE VAS TAKINK A SHOWER I STOLE ALL HEES PANTS! -HE WEEL BE STRANDED EEN HEES ROOM!
MY FAITHFUL SCARLOFF! YOU ARE ONE GENIUS!
11-17
DAWGONE!-THIS SHO' IS STRANGE!-VURRY STRANGE!-WHAR KIN ALL MAH PANTS HAVE WENT TO?
© 1934 by United Feature Syndicate, Inc.
Al. G. Capp
GRACIOUS! LI'L ABNER IS CERTAINLY LATE FOR DINNER!
I HAF A FEELINK THAT HE WEEL NOT COME DOWN TO DINNER-BUT NEFER MIN' THE DINNER!-I HAF SOMET'INK VERY EEMPORTANT TO ASK YOU-

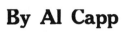

LI'L ABNER Nothing to Get Skeered About By Al Capp

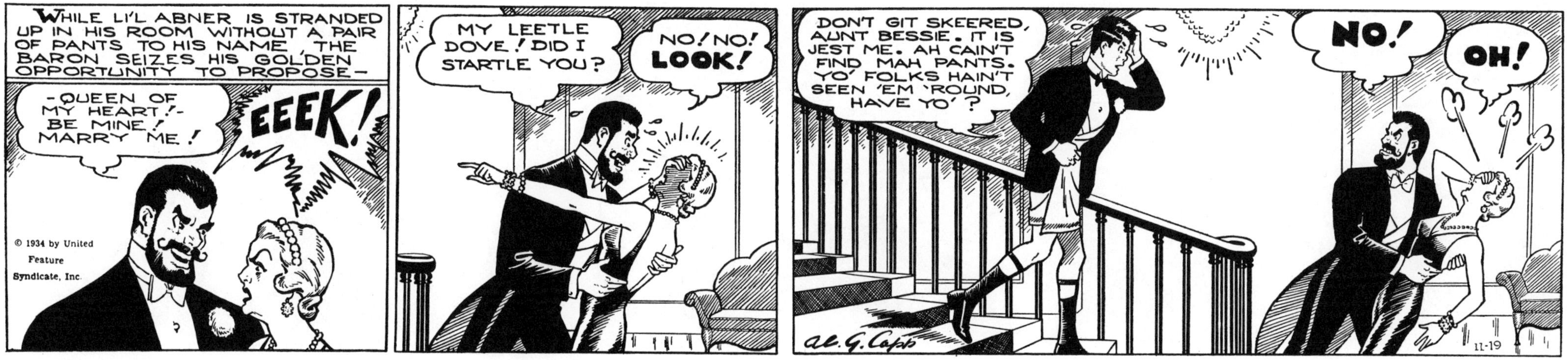

WHILE LI'L ABNER IS STRANDED UP IN HIS ROOM WITHOUT A PAIR OF PANTS TO HIS NAME, THE BARON SEIZES HIS GOLDEN OPPORTUNITY TO PROPOSE–
-QUEEN OF MY HEART!- BE MINE! MARRY ME!
EEEK!
© 1934 by United Feature Syndicate, Inc.
MY LEETLE DOVE! DID I STARTLE YOU?
NO! NO! LOOK!
DON'T GIT SKEERED, AUNT BESSIE. IT IS JEST ME. AH CAIN'T FIND MAH PANTS. YO' FOLKS HAIN'T SEEN 'EM 'ROUND, HAVE YO'?
NO!
OH!
Al. G. Capp
11-19

LI'L ABNER The Chance of A Lifetime By Al Capp

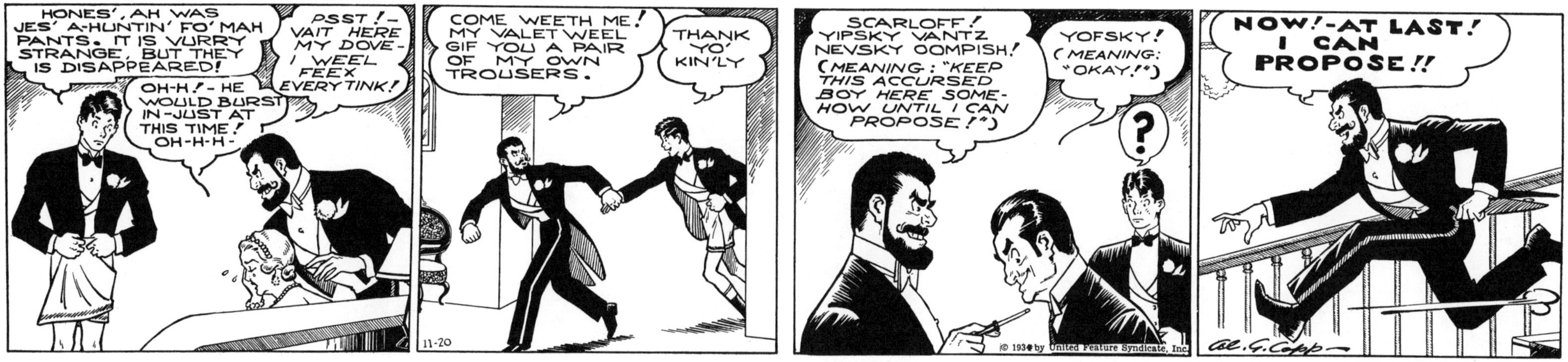

HONES', AH WAS JES' A-HUNTIN' FO' MAH PANTS. IT IS VURRY STRANGE, BUT THEY IS DISAPPEARED!
OH-H!- HE WOULD BURST IN-JUST AT THIS TIME! OH-H-H-
PSST!- VAIT HERE MY DOVE- I WEEL FEEX EVERYTINK!
11-20
COME WEETH ME! MY VALET WEEL GIF YOU A PAIR OF MY OWN TROUSERS.
THANK YO' KIN'LY
SCARLOFF! YIPSKY VANTZ NEVSKY OOMPISH! (MEANING: "KEEP THIS ACCURSED BOY HERE SOME-HOW UNTIL I CAN PROPOSE!")
YOFSKY! (MEANING: "OKAY!")
?
© 1934 by United Feature Syndicate, Inc.
NOW!-AT LAST! I CAN PROPOSE!!
Al. G. Capp

LI'L ABNER Team Work

By Al Capp

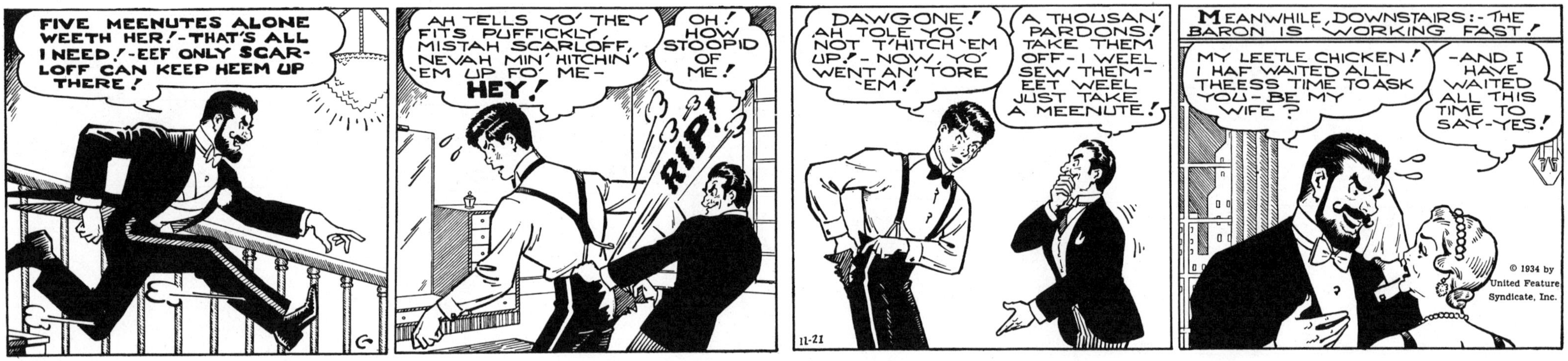

FIVE MEENUTES ALONE WEETH HER!-THAT'S ALL I NEED!-EEF ONLY SCARLOFF CAN KEEP HEEM UP THERE!
AH TELLS YO' THEY FITS PUFFICKLY, MISTAH SCARLOFF, NEVAH MIN' HITCHIN' 'EM UP FO' ME- HEY!
OH! HOW STOOPID OF ME!
RIP!
DAWGONE! AH TOLE YO' NOT T'HITCH 'EM UP!-NOW, YO' WENT AN' TORE 'EM!
A THOUSAN' PARDONS! TAKE THEM OFF-I WEEL SEW THEM-EET WEEL JUST TAKE A MEENUTE!
11-21
MEANWHILE, DOWNSTAIRS:-THE BARON IS WORKING FAST!
MY LEETLE CHICKEN! I HAF WAITED ALL THEESS TIME TO ASK YOU-BE MY WIFE?
-AND I HAVE WAITED ALL THIS TIME TO SAY-YES!
© 1934 by United Feature Syndicate, Inc.

LI'L ABNER Po'k Chops Is Mo' Important

By Al Capp

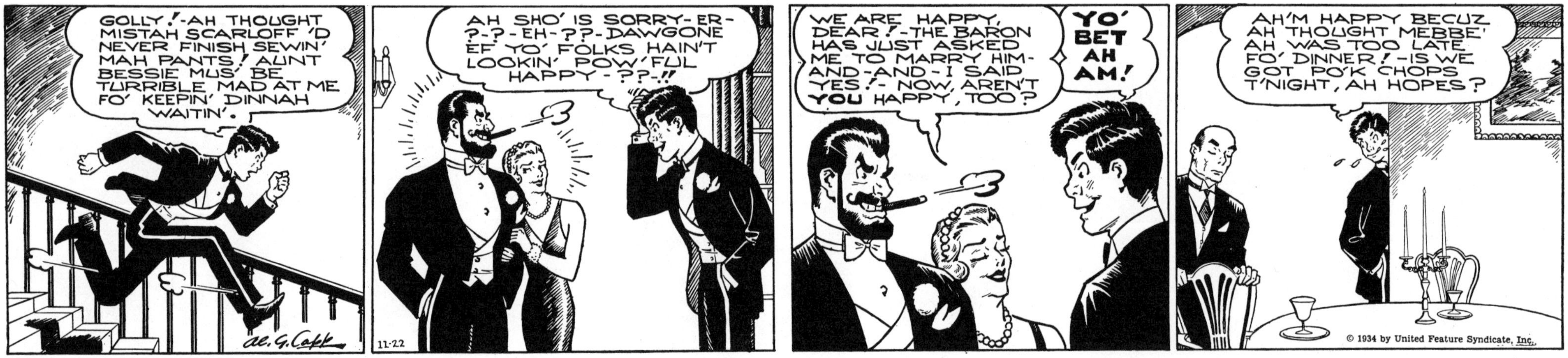

GOLLY!-AH THOUGHT MISTAH SCARLOFF 'D NEVER FINISH SEWIN' MAH PANTS! AUNT BESSIE MUS' BE TURRIBLE MAD AT ME FO' KEEPIN' DINNAH WAITIN'.
Al. G. Capp
AH SHO' IS SORRY-ER-?-?-EH-??-DAWGONE EF YO' FOLKS HAIN'T LOOKIN' POW'FUL HAPPY-??-!!
11-22
WE ARE HAPPY, DEAR!-THE BARON HAS JUST ASKED ME TO MARRY HIM-AND-AND-I SAID YES!-NOW, AREN'T YOU HAPPY, TOO?
YO' BET AH AM!
AH'M HAPPY BECUZ AH THOUGHT MEBBE' AH WAS TOO LATE FO' DINNER!-IS WE GOT PO'K CHOPS T'NIGHT, AH HOPES?
© 1934 by United Feature Syndicate, Inc.

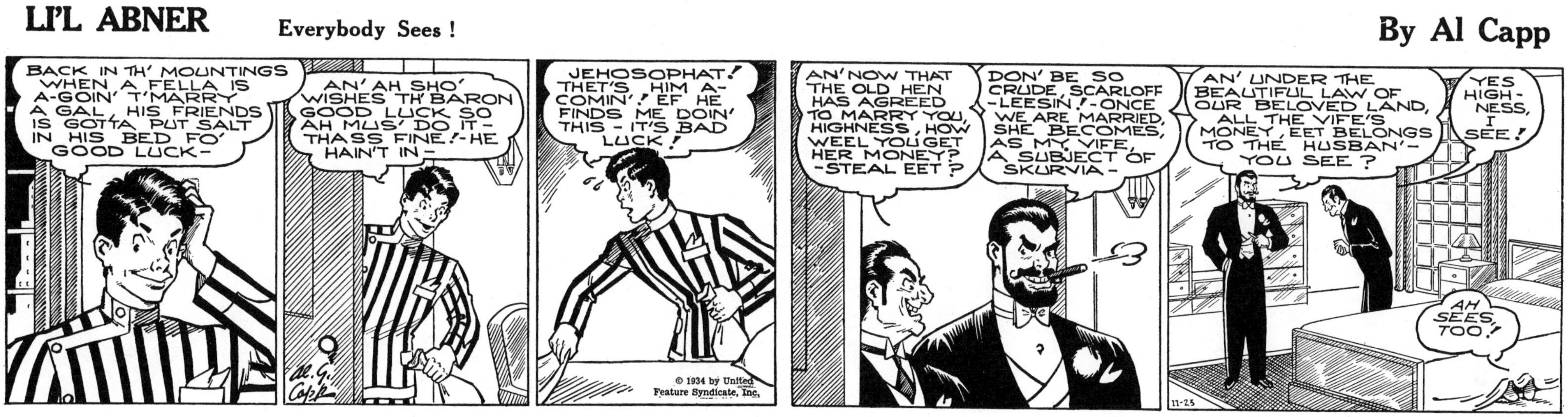
LI'L ABNER
Everybody Sees !
By Al Capp
BACK IN TH' MOUNTINGS WHEN A FELLA IS A-GOIN' T'MARRY A GAL, HIS FRIENDS IS GOTTA PUT SALT IN HIS BED FO' GOOD LUCK—
AN' AH SHO' WISHES TH' BARON GOOD LUCK SO AH MUS' DO IT— THASS FINE!—HE HAIN'T IN—
JEHOSOPHAT! THET'S HIM A-COMIN'! EF HE FINDS ME DOIN' THIS—IT'S BAD LUCK!
© 1934 by United Feature Syndicate, Inc.
AN' NOW THAT THE OLD HEN HAS AGREED TO MARRY YOU, HIGHNESS, HOW WEEL YOU GET HER MONEY? —STEAL EET?
DON' BE SO CRUDE, SCARLOFF —LEESIN!—ONCE WE ARE MARRIED, SHE BECOMES, AS MY VIFE, A SUBJECT OF SKURVIA—
AN' UNDER THE BEAUTIFUL LAW OF OUR BELOVED LAND, ALL THE VIFE'S MONEY, EET BELONGS TO THE HUSBAN'— YOU SEE?
YES HIGHNESS, I SEE!
AH SEES, TOO!
11-23

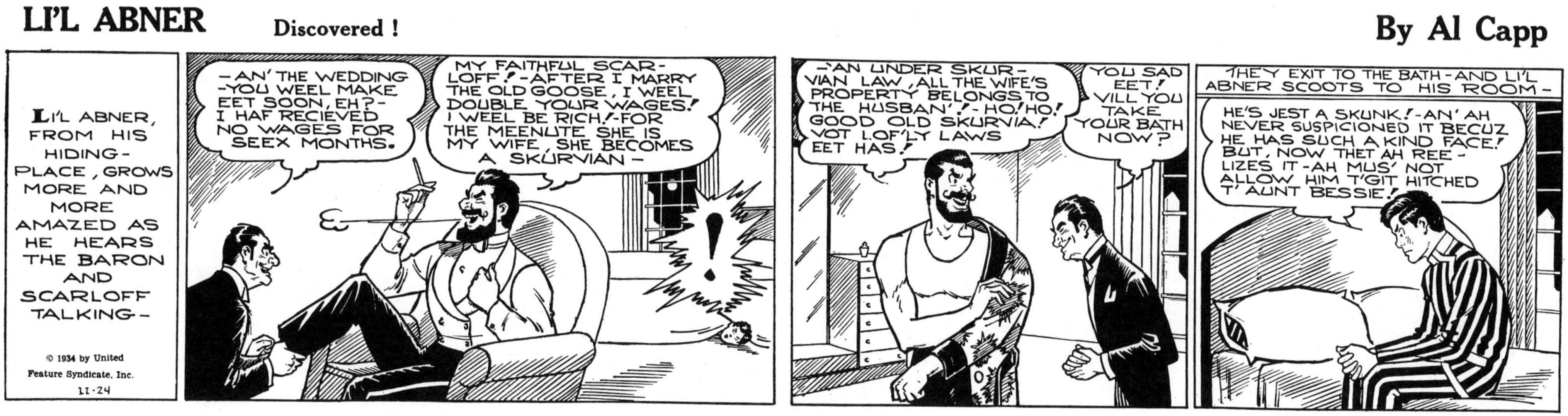
LI'L ABNER
Discovered !
By Al Capp
LI'L ABNER, FROM HIS HIDING-PLACE, GROWS MORE AND MORE AMAZED AS HE HEARS THE BARON AND SCARLOFF TALKING—
© 1934 by United Feature Syndicate, Inc.
11-24
—AN' THE WEDDING —YOU WEEL MAKE EET SOON, EH?— I HAF RECIEVED NO WAGES FOR SEEX MONTHS.
MY FAITHFUL SCARLOFF!—AFTER I MARRY THE OLD GOOSE, I WEEL DOUBLE YOUR WAGES! I WEEL BE RICH!—FOR THE MEENUTE SHE IS MY WIFE, SHE BECOMES A SKURVIAN—
!
—AN UNDER SKURVIAN LAW, ALL THE WIFE'S PROPERTY BELONGS TO THE HUSBAN'!—HO! HO! GOOD OLD SKURVIA! VOT LOF'LY LAWS EET HAS!
YOU SAD EET! VILL YOU TAKE YOUR BATH NOW?
THEY EXIT TO THE BATH—AND LI'L ABNER SCOOTS TO HIS ROOM—
HE'S JEST A SKUNK!—AN' AH NEVER SUSPICIONED IT BECUZ HE HAS SUCH A KIND FACE! BUT, NOW THET AH REE-LIZES IT—AH MUS' NOT ALLOW HIM T'GIT HITCHED T' AUNT BESSIE!

LI'L ABNER Abner Hain't Used to It **By Al Capp**

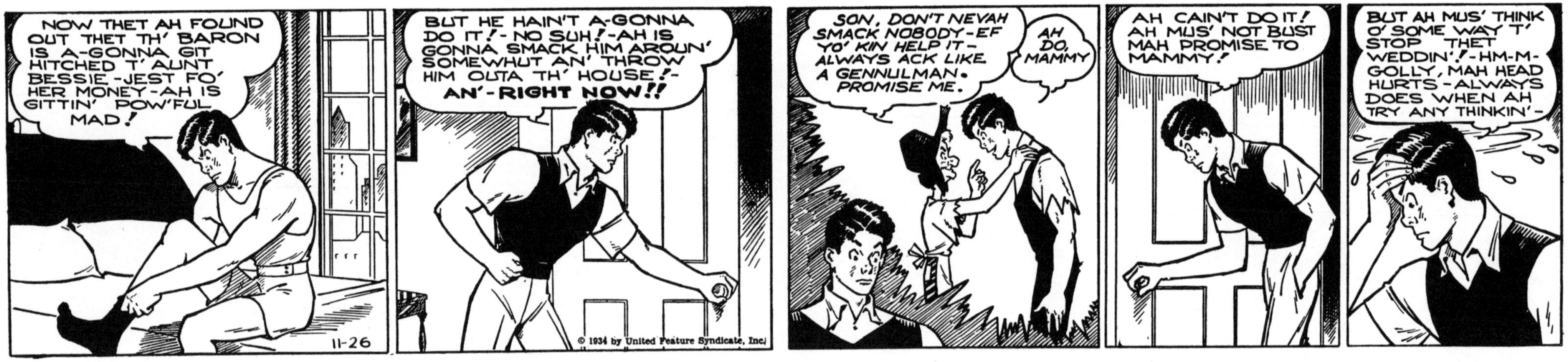
NOW THET AH FOUND OUT THET TH' BARON IS A-GONNA GIT HITCHED T' AUNT BESSIE -JEST FO' HER MONEY-AH IS GITTIN' POW'FUL MAD!
11-26
BUT HE HAIN'T A-GONNA DO IT!- NO SUH!-AH IS GONNA SMACK HIM AROUN' SOMEWHUT AN' THROW HIM OUTA TH' HOUSE!- AN'-RIGHT NOW!!
© 1934 by United Feature Syndicate, Inc.
SON, DON'T NEVAH SMACK NOBODY-EF YO' KIN HELP IT-ALWAYS ACK LIKE A GENNULMAN. PROMISE ME.
AH DO, MAMMY
AH CAIN'T DO IT! AH MUS' NOT BUST MAH PROMISE TO MAMMY!
BUT AH MUS' THINK O' SOME WAY T' STOP THET WEDDIN'!-HM-M-GOLLY, MAH HEAD HURTS-ALWAYS DOES WHEN AH TRY ANY THINKIN'-

LI'L ABNER Looks Bad For Slinkovitch **By Al Capp**

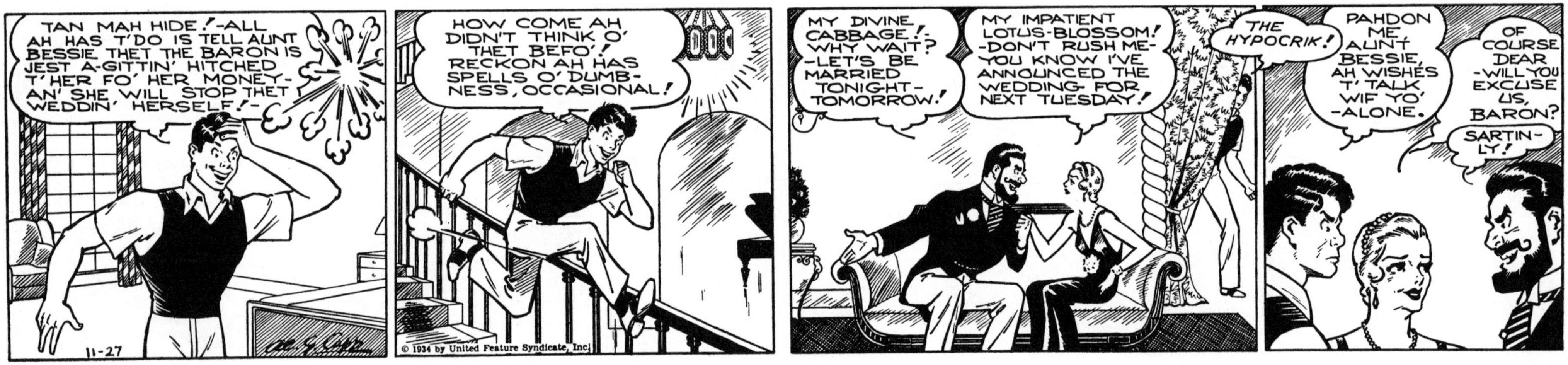
TAN MAH HIDE!-ALL AH HAS T'DO IS TELL AUNT BESSIE THET THE BARON IS JEST A-GITTIN' HITCHED T'HER FO' HER MONEY-AN' SHE WILL STOP THET WEDDIN' HERSELF!-
11-27
HOW COME AH DIDN'T THINK O' THET BEFO'! RECKON AH HAS SPELLS O' DUMB-NESS, OCCASIONAL!
© 1934 by United Feature Syndicate, Inc.
MY DIVINE CABBAGE!-WHY WAIT?-LET'S BE MARRIED TONIGHT-TOMORROW!
MY IMPATIENT LOTUS-BLOSSOM!-DON'T RUSH ME-YOU KNOW I'VE ANNOUNCED THE WEDDING FOR NEXT TUESDAY!
THE HYPOCRIK!
PAHDON ME, AUNT BESSIE, AH WISHES T' TALK WIF YO' -ALONE.
OF COURSE DEAR -WILL YOU EXCUSE US, BARON?
SARTIN-LY!

LI'L ABNER He Hain't Got the Heart **By Al Capp**

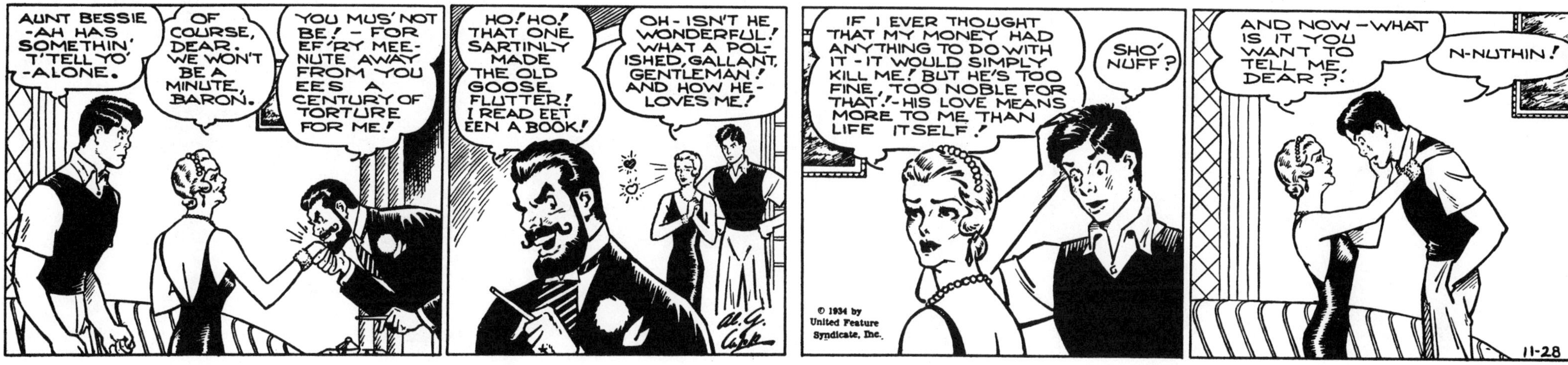
AUNT BESSIE -AH HAS SOMETHIN' T'TELL YO' -ALONE.
OF COURSE, DEAR. WE WON'T BE A MINUTE, BARON.
YOU MUS' NOT BE! - FOR EF'RY MEE-NUTE AWAY FROM YOU EES A CENTURY OF TORTURE FOR ME!
HO! HO! THAT ONE SARTINLY MADE THE OLD GOOSE FLUTTER! I READ EET EEN A BOOK!
OH - ISN'T HE WONDERFUL! WHAT A POL-ISHED, GALLANT, GENTLEMAN! AND HOW HE LOVES ME!
Al. G. Capp
IF I EVER THOUGHT THAT MY MONEY HAD ANYTHING TO DO WITH IT - IT WOULD SIMPLY KILL ME! BUT HE'S TOO FINE, TOO NOBLE FOR THAT! - HIS LOVE MEANS MORE TO ME THAN LIFE ITSELF!
SHO' NUFF?
© 1934 by United Feature Syndicate, Inc.
AND NOW - WHAT IS IT YOU WANT TO TELL ME, DEAR?
N-NUTHIN!
11-28

LI'L ABNER Mammy Unnerstan's **By Al Capp**

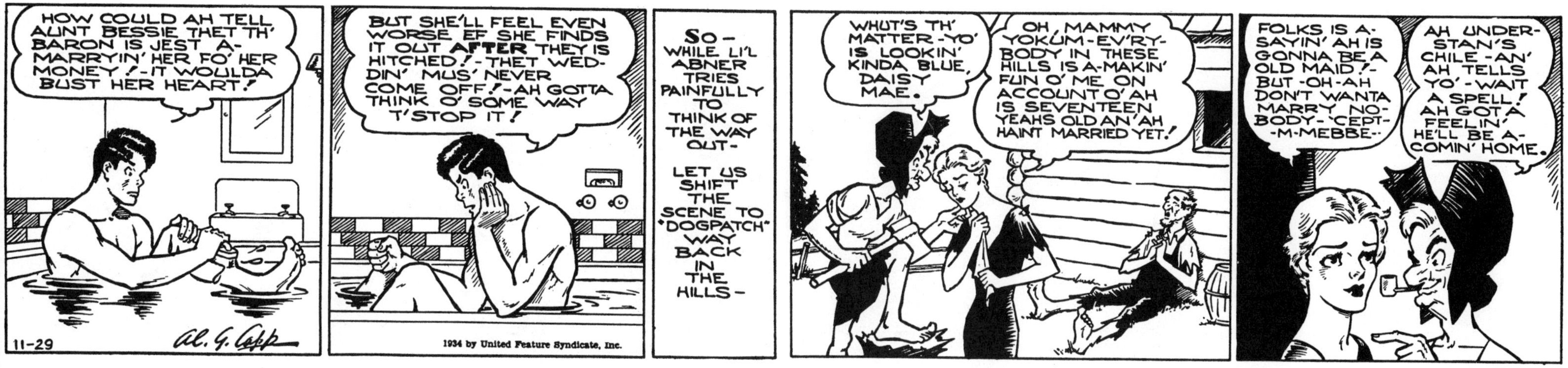
HOW COULD AH TELL AUNT BESSIE THET TH' BARON IS JEST A-MARRYIN' HER FO' HER MONEY! - IT WOULDA BUST HER HEART!
11-29
Al. G. Capp
BUT SHE'LL FEEL EVEN WORSE EF SHE FINDS IT OUT AFTER THEY IS HITCHED! - THET WED-DIN' MUS' NEVER COME OFF! - AH GOTTA THINK O' SOME WAY T'STOP IT!
1934 by United Feature Syndicate, Inc.
SO - WHILE LI'L ABNER TRIES PAINFULLY TO THINK OF THE WAY OUT -
LET US SHIFT THE SCENE TO "DOGPATCH" WAY BACK IN THE HILLS -
WHUT'S TH' MATTER - YO' IS LOOKIN' KINDA BLUE, DAISY MAE.
OH, MAMMY YOKUM - EV'RY-BODY IN THESE HILLS IS A-MAKIN' FUN O' ME ON ACCOUNT O' AH IS SEVENTEEN YEAHS OLD AN' AH HAINT MARRIED YET!
FOLKS IS A-SAYIN' AH IS GONNA BE A OLD MAID! - BUT - OH - AH DON'T WANTA MARRY NO-BODY - 'CEPT- -M-MEBBE--
AH UNDER-STAN'S CHILE - AN' AH TELLS YO' - WAIT A SPELL! AH GOT A FEELIN' HE'LL BE A-COMIN' HOME.

LI'L ABNER Bashful But Honest **By Al Capp**

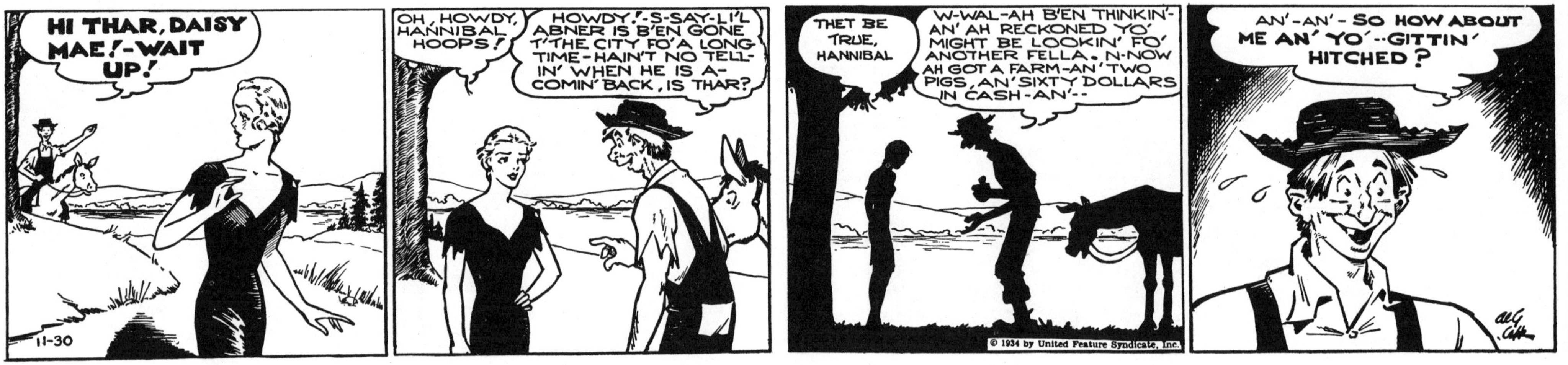

HI THAR, DAISY MAE!-WAIT UP!
11-30
OH, HOWDY, HANNIBAL HOOPS!
HOWDY!-S-SAY-LI'L ABNER IS B'EN GONE T' THE CITY FO' A LONG TIME-HAIN'T NO TELL-IN' WHEN HE IS A-COMIN' BACK, IS THAR?
THET BE TRUE, HANNIBAL
W-WAL-AH B'EN THINKIN'-AN' AH RECKONED YO' MIGHT BE LOOKIN' FO' ANOTHER FELLA. N-NOW AH GOT A FARM-AN' TWO PIGS, AN' SIXTY DOLLARS IN CASH-AN'--
© 1934 by United Feature Syndicate, Inc.
AN'-AN'- SO HOW ABOUT ME AN' YO'--GITTIN' HITCHED?

LI'L ABNER Yes Or No? **By Al Capp**

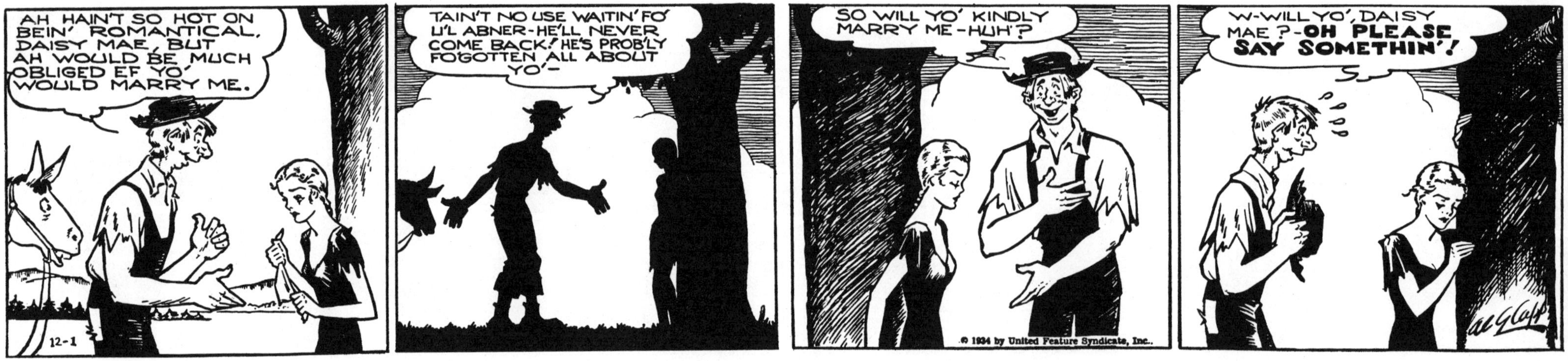

AH HAIN'T SO HOT ON BEIN' ROMANTICAL, DAISY MAE, BUT AH WOULD BE MUCH OBLIGED EF YO' WOULD MARRY ME.
12-1
TAIN'T NO USE WAITIN' FO' LI'L ABNER-HE'LL NEVER COME BACK! HE'S PROB'LY FO'GOTTEN ALL ABOUT YO'-
SO WILL YO' KINDLY MARRY ME-HUH?
© 1934 by United Feature Syndicate, Inc.
W-WILL YO', DAISY MAE?-OH PLEASE SAY SOMETHIN'!

LI'L ABNER
All Or Nothing

By Al Capp

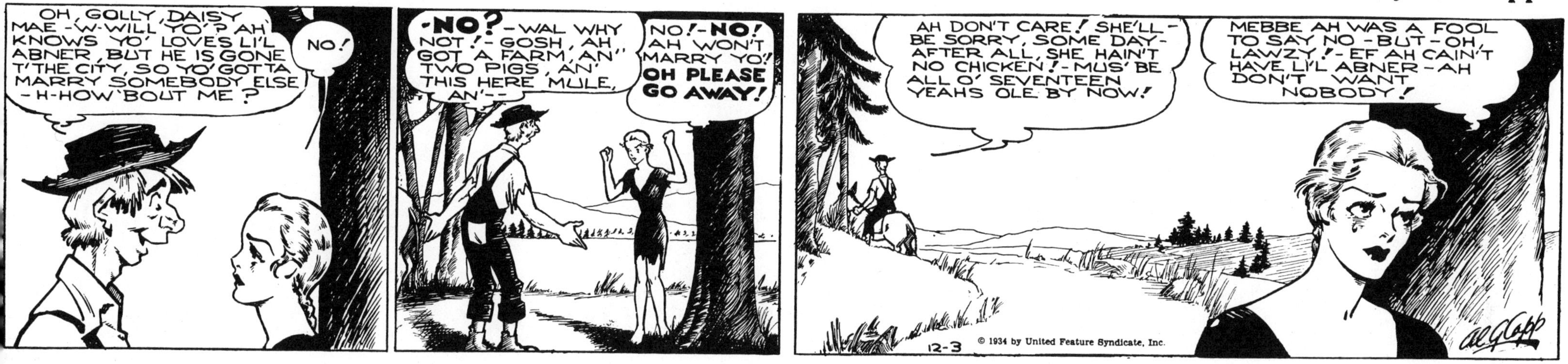

OH, GOLLY, DAISY MAE-W-WILL YO'? AH KNOWS YO' LOVES LI'L ABNER, BUT HE IS GONE T'THE CITY, SO YO' GOTTA MARRY SOMEBODY ELSE -H-HOW 'BOUT ME?
NO!
-NO?-WAL WHY NOT!-GOSH, AH GOT A FARM, AN' TWO PIGS, AN' THIS HERE MULE, AN'--
NO!-NO! AH WON'T MARRY YO'! OH PLEASE GO AWAY!
AH DON'T CARE! SHE'LL BE SORRY, SOME DAY-AFTER ALL, SHE HAIN'T NO CHICKEN!-MUS' BE ALL O' SEVENTEEN YEAHS OLE BY NOW!
MEBBE AH WAS A FOOL TO SAY NO-BUT-OH, LAWZY!-EF AH CAIN'T HAVE LI'L ABNER-AH DON'T WANT NOBODY!
12-3
© 1934 by United Feature Syndicate, Inc.

LI'L ABNER
A Razor?—What Fo'?

By Al Capp

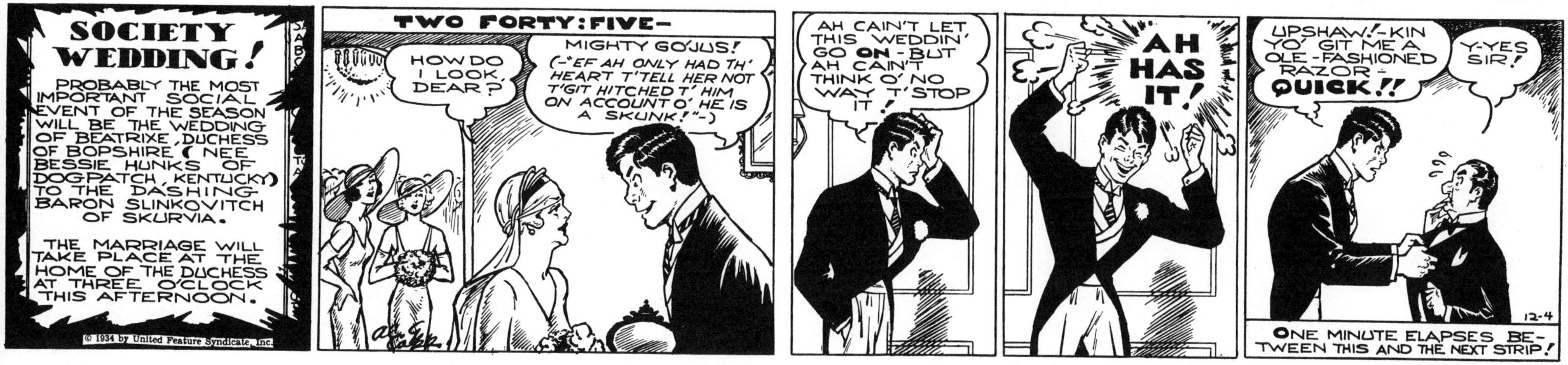

SOCIETY WEDDING!
PROBABLY THE MOST IMPORTANT SOCIAL EVENT OF THE SEASON WILL BE THE WEDDING OF BEATRIXE, DUCHESS OF BOPSHIRE (NEE BESSIE HUNKS OF DOGPATCH, KENTUCKY) TO THE DASHING BARON SLINKOVITCH OF SKURVIA.
THE MARRIAGE WILL TAKE PLACE AT THE HOME OF THE DUCHESS AT THREE O'CLOCK THIS AFTERNOON.
© 1934 by United Feature Syndicate, Inc.
TWO FORTY:FIVE-
HOW DO I LOOK, DEAR?
MIGHTY GO'JUS! (-"EF AH ONLY HAD TH' HEART T'TELL HER NOT T'GIT HITCHED T' HIM ON ACCOUNT O' HE IS A SKUNK!"-)
AH CAIN'T LET THIS WEDDIN' GO ON-BUT AH CAIN'T THINK O' NO WAY T'STOP IT!
AH HAS IT!
UPSHAW!-KIN YO' GIT ME A OLE-FASHIONED RAZOR-QUICK!!
Y-YES SIR!
12-4
ONE MINUTE ELAPSES BETWEEN THIS AND THE NEXT STRIP!

LI'L ABNER Not Quite Ready By Al Capp

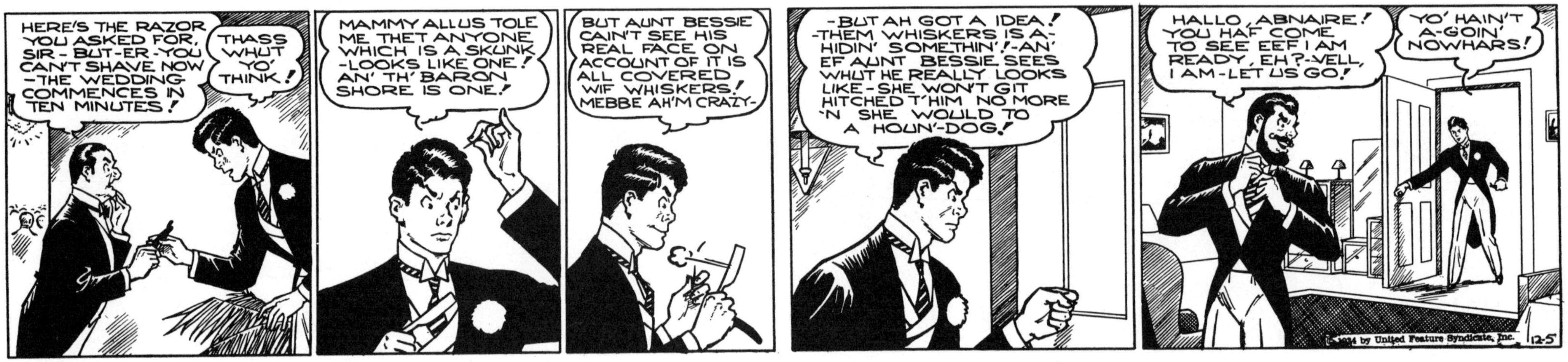
HERE'S THE RAZOR YOU ASKED FOR, SIR - BUT-ER-YOU CAN'T SHAVE NOW -THE WEDDING COMMENCES IN TEN MINUTES!
THASS WHUT YO' THINK!
MAMMY ALLUS TOLE ME THET ANYONE WHICH IS A SKUNK -LOOKS LIKE ONE! AN' TH' BARON SHORE IS ONE!
BUT AUNT BESSIE CAIN'T SEE HIS REAL FACE ON ACCOUNT OF IT IS ALL COVERED WIF WHISKERS! MEBBE AH'M CRAZY-
-BUT AH GOT A IDEA! -THEM WHISKERS IS A-HIDIN' SOMETHIN'!-AN' EF AUNT BESSIE SEES WHUT HE REALLY LOOKS LIKE-SHE WON'T GIT HITCHED T'HIM NO MORE 'N SHE WOULD TO A HOUN'-DOG!
HALLO, ABNAIRE! YOU HAF COME TO SEE EEF I AM READY, EH?-VELL, I AM-LET US GO!
YO' HAIN'T A-GOIN' NOWHARS!
© 1934 by United Feature Syndicate, Inc.
12-5

LI'L ABNER Mountain Merry Go Round By Al Capp

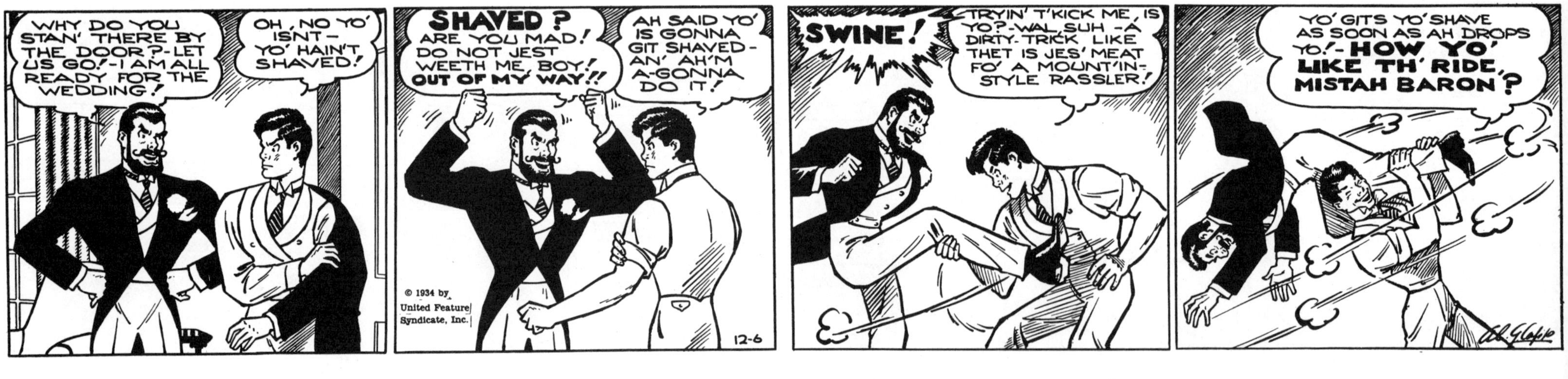
WHY DO YOU STAN' THERE BY THE DOOR?-LET US GO!-I AM ALL READY FOR THE WEDDING!
OH, NO YO' ISN'T - YO' HAIN'T SHAVED!
SHAVED? ARE YOU MAD! DO NOT JEST WEETH ME, BOY! OUT OF MY WAY!!
AH SAID YO' IS GONNA GIT SHAVED - AN' AH'M A-GONNA DO IT!
© 1934 by United Feature Syndicate, Inc.
12-6
SWINE!
TRYIN' T'KICK ME, IS YO?-WAL, SUH -A DIRTY-TRICK LIKE THET IS JES' MEAT FO' A MOUNT'IN-STYLE RASSLER!
YO' GITS YO' SHAVE AS SOON AS AH DROPS YO!-HOW YO' LIKE TH' RIDE, MISTAH BARON?

LI'L ABNER A Close Shave By Al Capp

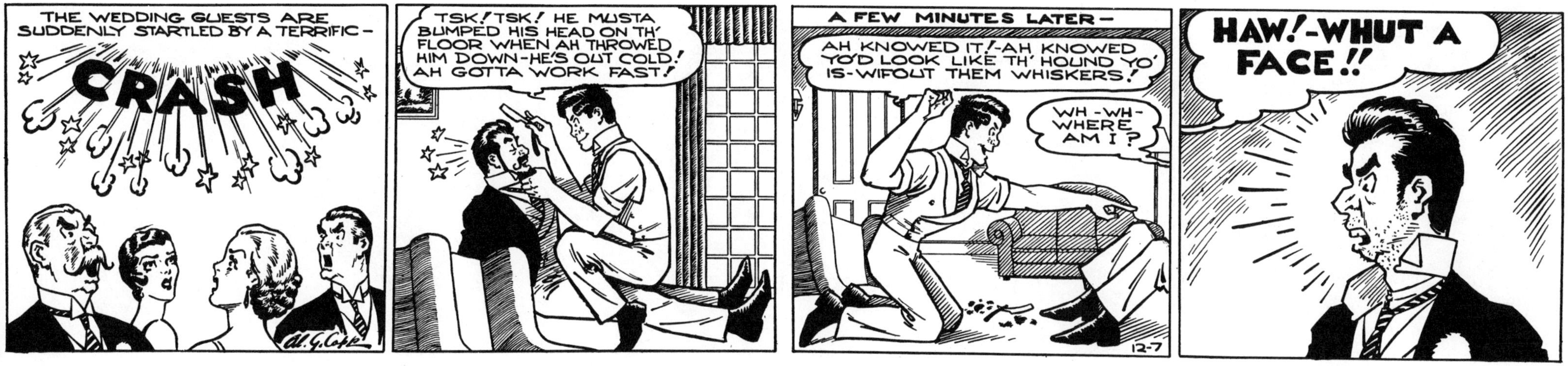
THE WEDDING GUESTS ARE SUDDENLY STARTLED BY A TERRIFIC –
CRASH
TSK! TSK! HE MUSTA BUMPED HIS HEAD ON TH' FLOOR WHEN AH THROWED HIM DOWN – HE'S OUT COLD! AH GOTTA WORK FAST!
A FEW MINUTES LATER –
AH KNOWED IT! – AH KNOWED YO'D LOOK LIKE TH' HOUND YO' IS – WIFOUT THEM WHISKERS!
WH – WH – WHERE AM I ?
12-7
HAW! – WHUT A FACE!!

LI'L ABNER The Ugly Duckling By Al Capp

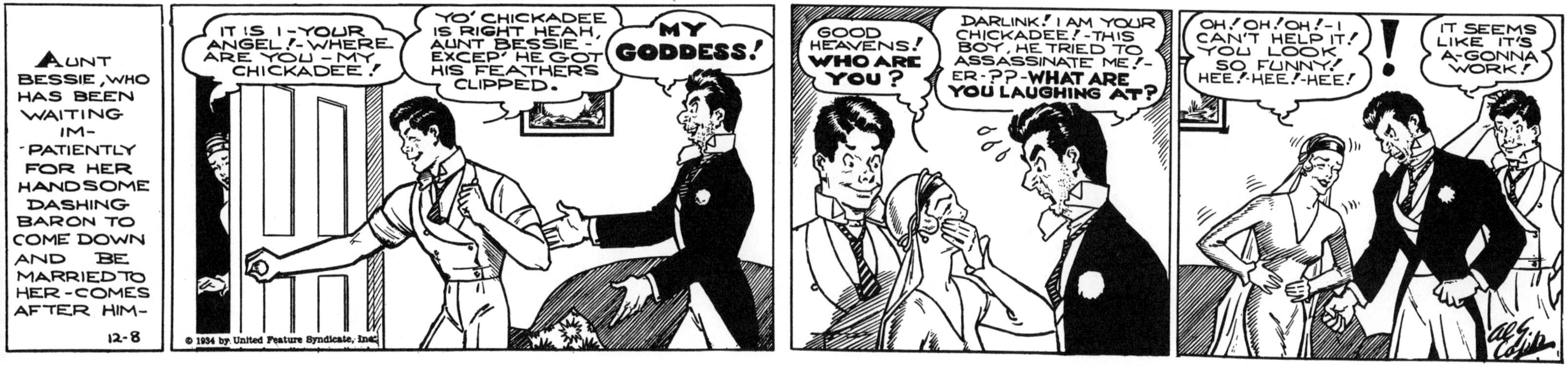
AUNT BESSIE, WHO HAS BEEN WAITING IM-PATIENTLY FOR HER HANDSOME DASHING BARON TO COME DOWN AND BE MARRIED TO HER – COMES AFTER HIM –
12-8
IT IS I – YOUR ANGEL! – WHERE ARE YOU – MY CHICKADEE!
YO' CHICKADEE IS RIGHT HEAH, AUNT BESSIE – EXCEP' HE GOT HIS FEATHERS CLIPPED.
MY GODDESS!
© 1934 by United Feature Syndicate, Inc.
GOOD HEAVENS! WHO ARE YOU ?
DARLINK! I AM YOUR CHICKADEE! – THIS BOY, HE TRIED TO ASSASSINATE ME! – ER – ?? – WHAT ARE YOU LAUGHING AT?
OH! OH! OH! – I CAN'T HELP IT! YOU LOOK SO FUNNY! HEE! – HEE! – HEE!
!
IT SEEMS LIKE IT'S A-GONNA WORK!

LI'L ABNER Go Right Ahead, Abner! By Al Capp

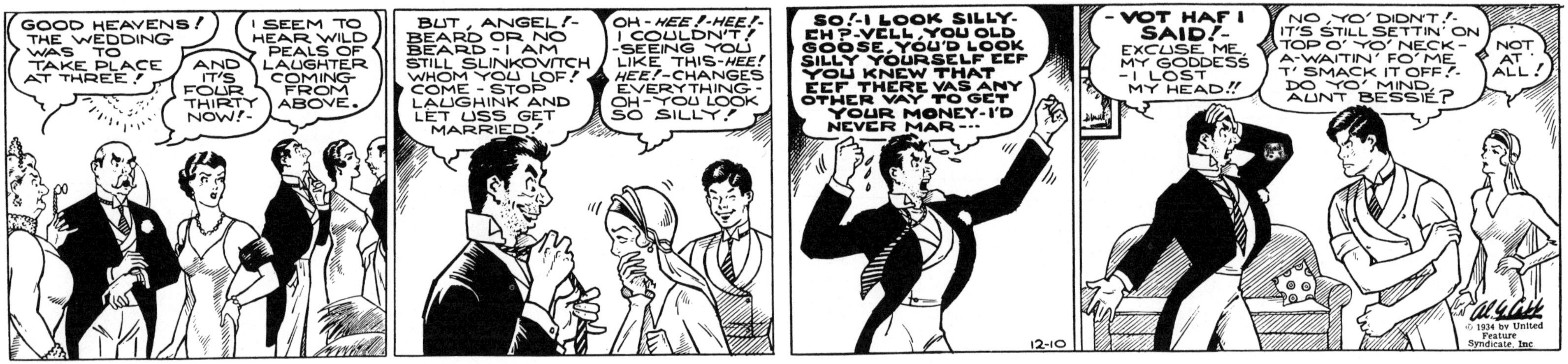
GOOD HEAVENS! THE WEDDING WAS TO TAKE PLACE AT THREE!
AND IT'S FOUR THIRTY NOW!-
I SEEM TO HEAR WILD PEALS OF LAUGHTER COMING FROM ABOVE.
BUT, ANGEL!- BEARD OR NO BEARD - I AM STILL SLINKOVITCH WHOM YOU LOF! COME - STOP LAUGHINK AND LET USS GET MARRIED!
OH - HEE!-HEE!- I COULDN'T! -SEEING YOU LIKE THIS-HEE! HEE!-CHANGES EVERYTHING- OH-YOU LOOK SO SILLY!
SO!-I LOOK SILLY- EH?-VELL, YOU OLD GOOSE, YOU'D LOOK SILLY YOURSELF EEF YOU KNEW THAT EEF THERE VAS ANY OTHER VAY TO GET YOUR MONEY-I'D NEVER MAR---
12-10
-VOT HAF I SAID!- EXCUSE ME, MY GODDESS -I LOST MY HEAD!!
NO, YO' DIDN'T!- IT'S STILL SETTIN' ON TOP O' YO' NECK- A-WAITIN' FO' ME T' SMACK IT OFF!- DO YO' MIND, AUNT BESSIE?
NOT AT ALL!
© 1934 by United Feature Syndicate, Inc

LI'L ABNER Whut Yo' Mean—th' Mountings? By Al Capp

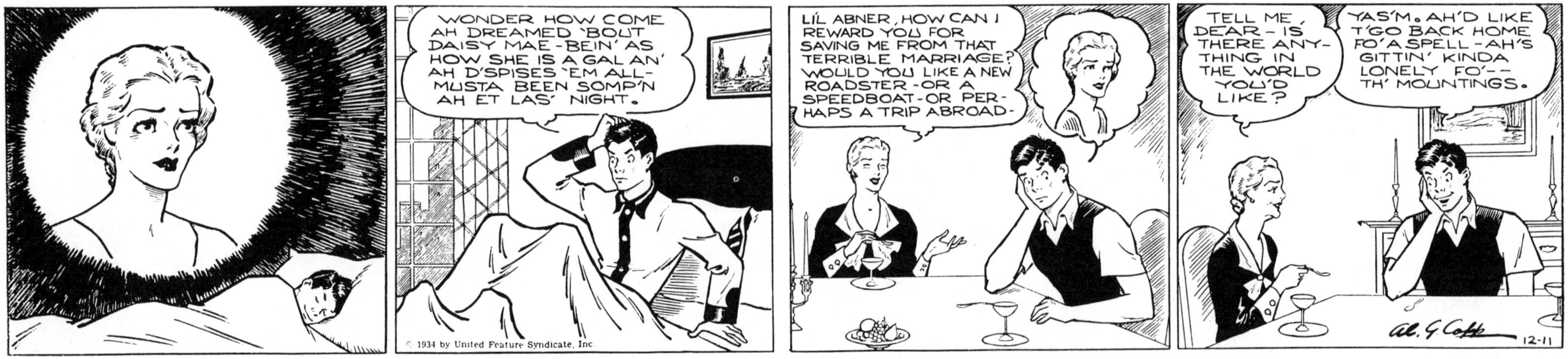
WONDER HOW COME AH DREAMED 'BOUT DAISY MAE-BEIN' AS HOW SHE IS A GAL AN' AH D'SPISES 'EM ALL- MUSTA BEEN SOMP'N AH ET LAS' NIGHT.
© 1934 by United Feature Syndicate, Inc.
LI'L ABNER, HOW CAN I REWARD YOU FOR SAVING ME FROM THAT TERRIBLE MARRIAGE? WOULD YOU LIKE A NEW ROADSTER-OR A SPEEDBOAT-OR PERHAPS A TRIP ABROAD-
TELL ME, DEAR-IS THERE ANYTHING IN THE WORLD YOU'D LIKE?
YAS'M. AH'D LIKE T'GO BACK HOME FO' A SPELL-AH'S GITTIN' KINDA LONELY FO'-- TH' MOUNTINGS.
12-11

LI'L ABNER All Yokums Is Gents By Al Capp

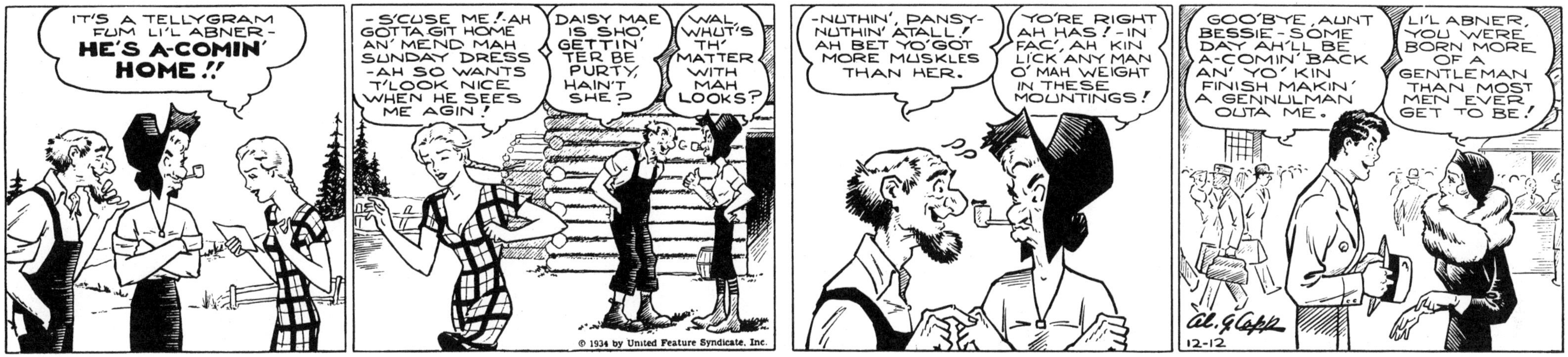

IT'S A TELLYGRAM FUM LI'L ABNER - **HE'S A-COMIN' HOME!!**
-S'CUSE ME! - AH GOTTA GIT HOME AN' MEND MAH SUNDAY DRESS -AH SO WANTS T'LOOK NICE WHEN HE SEES ME AGIN!
DAISY MAE IS SHO' GETTIN' TER BE PURTY, HAIN'T SHE?
WAL, WHUT'S TH' MATTER WITH MAH LOOKS?
© 1934 by United Feature Syndicate, Inc.
-NUTHIN', PANSY- NUTHIN' ATALL! AH BET YO' GOT MORE MUSKLES THAN HER.
YO'RE RIGHT AH HAS! - IN FAC', AH KIN LICK ANY MAN O' MAH WEIGHT IN THESE MOUNTINGS!
GOO'BYE, AUNT BESSIE - SOME DAY AH'LL BE A-COMIN' BACK AN' YO' KIN FINISH MAKIN' A GENNULMAN OUTA ME.
LI'L ABNER, YOU WERE BORN MORE OF A GENTLEMAN THAN MOST MEN EVER GET TO BE!
Al. G. Capp
12-12

LI'L ABNER Nice People—the Scraggs! By Al Capp

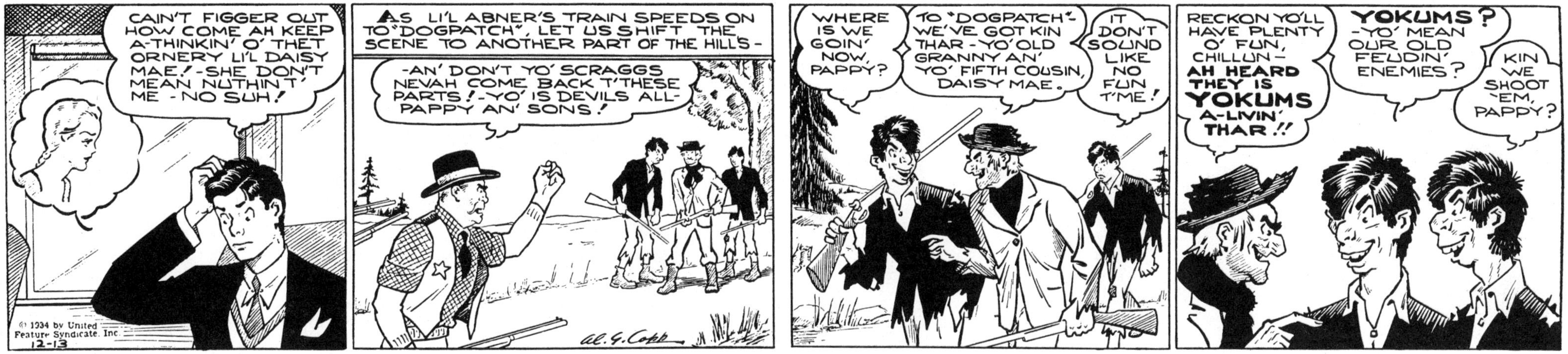

CAIN'T FIGGER OUT HOW COME AH KEEP A-THINKIN' O' THET ORNERY LI'L DAISY MAE! - SHE DON'T MEAN NUTHIN' T' ME - NO SUH!
© 1934 by United Feature Syndicate, Inc
12-13
AS LI'L ABNER'S TRAIN SPEEDS ON TO "DOGPATCH", LET US SHIFT THE SCENE TO ANOTHER PART OF THE HILLS -
-AN' DON'T YO' SCRAGGS NEVAH COME BACK T'THESE PARTS! - YO' IS DEVILS ALL - PAPPY AN' SONS!
Al. G. Capp
WHERE IS WE GOIN' NOW, PAPPY?
TO "DOGPATCH" - WE'VE GOT KIN THAR - YO' OLD GRANNY AN' YO' FIFTH COUSIN, DAISY MAE.
IT DON'T SOUND LIKE NO FUN T'ME!
RECKON YO'LL HAVE PLENTY O' FUN, CHILLUN - **AH HEARD THEY IS YOKUMS A-LIVIN' THAR!!**
YOKUMS? - YO' MEAN OUR OLD FEUDIN' ENEMIES?
KIN WE SHOOT 'EM, PAPPY?

LI'L ABNER Gosh! Hain't She Purty! By Al Capp

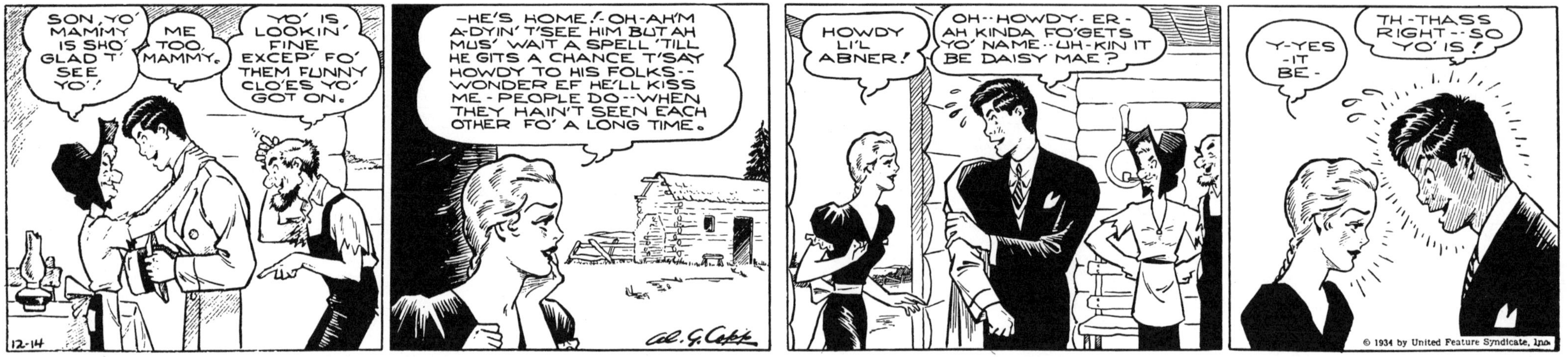

SON, YO' MAMMY IS SHO' GLAD T' SEE YO'!
ME TOO, MAMMY.
YO' IS LOOKIN' FINE EXCEP' FO' THEM FUNNY CLO'ES YO' GOT ON.
12-14
-HE'S HOME!-OH-AH'M A-DYIN' T'SEE HIM BUT AH MUS' WAIT A SPELL 'TILL HE GITS A CHANCE T'SAY HOWDY TO HIS FOLKS--WONDER EF HE'LL KISS ME-PEOPLE DO--WHEN THEY HAIN'T SEEN EACH OTHER FO' A LONG TIME.
Al. G. Capp
HOWDY LI'L ABNER!
OH--HOWDY-ER-AH KINDA FO'GETS YO' NAME--UH-KIN IT BE DAISY MAE?
Y-YES -IT BE-
TH-THASS RIGHT--SO YO' IS!
© 1934 by United Feature Syndicate, Inc.

LI'L ABNER Planning A Jolly Suprise By Al Capp

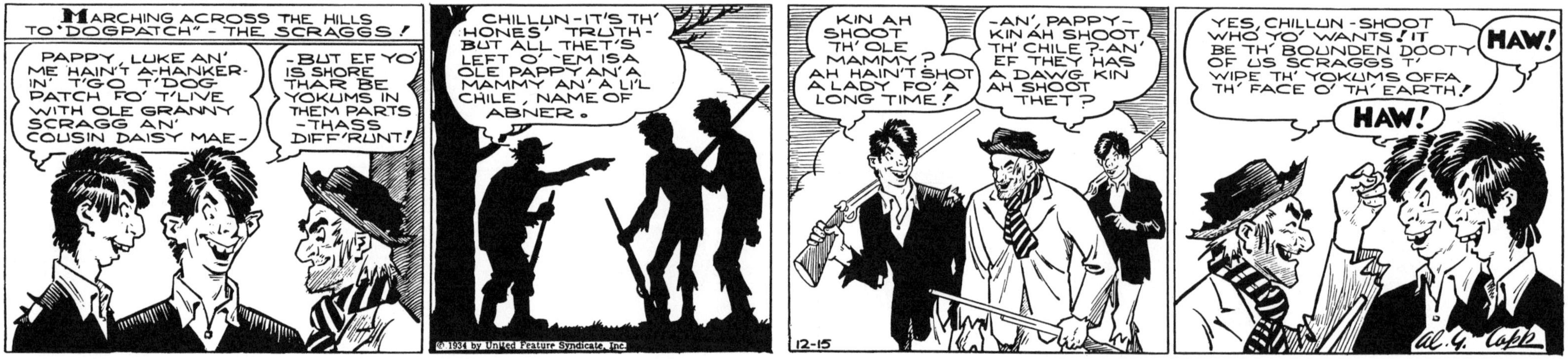

MARCHING ACROSS THE HILLS TO "DOGPATCH" - THE SCRAGGS!
PAPPY, LUKE AN' ME HAIN'T A-HANKER-IN' T'GO T'DOG-PATCH FO' T'LIVE WITH OLE GRANNY SCRAGG AN' COUSIN DAISY MAE-
-BUT EF YO' IS SHORE THAR BE YOKUMS IN THEM PARTS -THASS DIFF'RUNT!
CHILLUN-IT'S TH' HONES' TRUTH-BUT ALL THET'S LEFT O' 'EM IS A OLE PAPPY AN' A MAMMY AN' A LI'L CHILE, NAME OF ABNER.
© 1934 by United Feature Syndicate, Inc.
KIN AH SHOOT TH' OLE MAMMY? AH HAIN'T SHOT A LADY FO' A LONG TIME!
-AN', PAPPY-KIN AH SHOOT TH' CHILE?-AN' EF THEY HAS A DAWG KIN AH SHOOT THET?
12-15
YES, CHILLUN-SHOOT WHO YO' WANTS! IT BE TH' BOUNDEN DOOTY OF US SCRAGGS T' WIPE TH' YOKUMS OFFA TH' FACE O' TH' EARTH!
HAW!
HAW!
Al. G. Capp

LI'L ABNER Yo' Don't Know th' Half o' It, Abner! By Al Capp

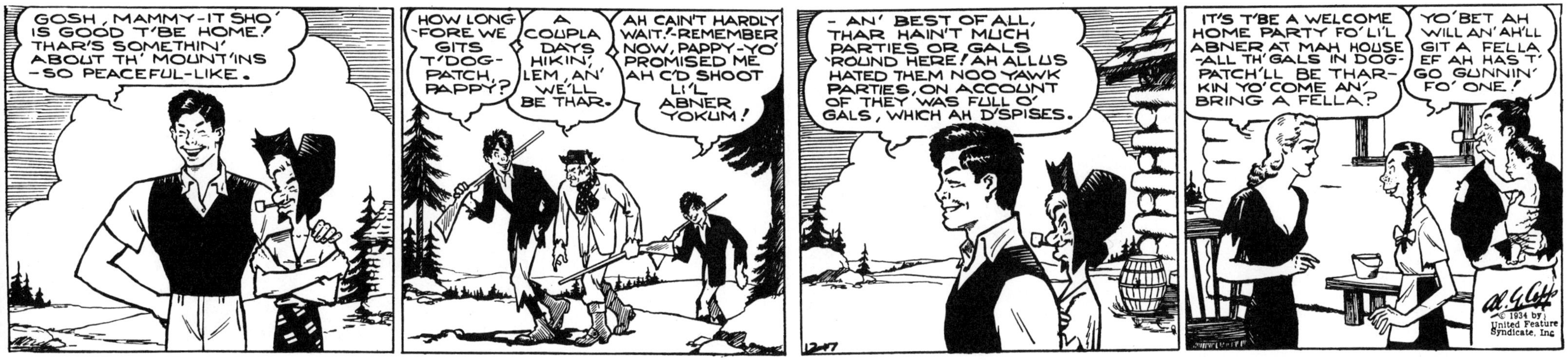

GOSH, MAMMY-IT SHO' IS GOOD T'BE HOME! THAR'S SOMETHIN' ABOUT TH' MOUNT'INS -SO PEACEFUL-LIKE.
HOW LONG 'FORE WE GITS T'DOG-PATCH, PAPPY?
A COUPLA DAYS HIKIN', LEM, AN' WE'LL BE THAR.
AH CAIN'T HARDLY WAIT!-REMEMBER NOW, PAPPY-YO' PROMISED ME AH C'D SHOOT LI'L ABNER YOKUM!
- AN' BEST OF ALL, THAR HAIN'T MUCH PARTIES OR GALS 'ROUND HERE! AH ALLUS HATED THEM NOO YAWK PARTIES, ON ACCOUNT OF THEY WAS FULL O' GALS, WHICH AH D'SPISES.
IT'S T'BE A WELCOME HOME PARTY FO' LI'L ABNER AT MAH HOUSE -ALL TH' GALS IN DOG-PATCH'LL BE THAR-KIN YO' COME AN' BRING A FELLA?
YO' BET AH WILL AN' AH'LL GIT A FELLA EF AH HAS T' GO GUNNIN' FO' ONE!
© 1934 by United Feature Syndicate, Inc

LI'L ABNER He Cain't Fool Mammy By Al Capp

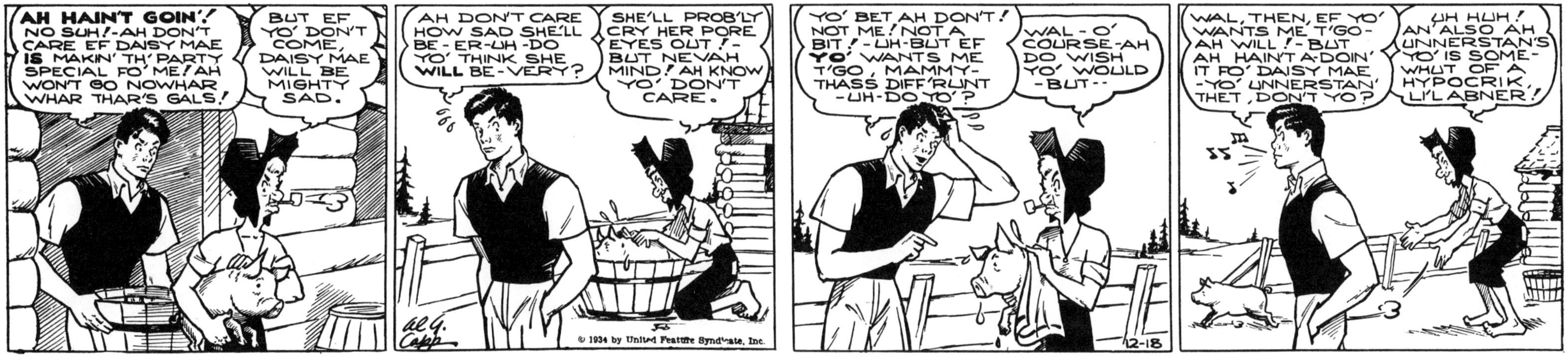

AH HAIN'T GOIN'! NO SUH!-AH DON'T CARE EF DAISY MAE IS MAKIN' TH' PARTY SPECIAL FO' ME! AH WON'T GO NOWHAR WHAR THAR'S GALS!
BUT EF YO' DON'T COME, DAISY MAE WILL BE MIGHTY SAD.
AH DON'T CARE HOW SAD SHE'LL BE-ER-UH-DO YO' THINK SHE WILL BE-VERY?
SHE'LL PROB'LY CRY HER PORE EYES OUT!-BUT NEVAH MIND! AH KNOW YO' DON'T CARE.
© 1934 by United Feature Syndicate, Inc.
YO' BET AH DON'T! NOT ME! NOT A BIT!-UH-BUT EF YO' WANTS ME T'GO, MAMMY-THASS DIFF'RUNT -UH-DO YO'?
WAL-O'COURSE-AH DO WISH YO' WOULD -BUT--
WAL, THEN, EF YO' WANTS ME T'GO-AH WILL!-BUT AH HAIN'T A-DOIN' IT FO' DAISY MAE -YO' UNNERSTAN' THET, DON'T YO?
UH HUH! AN' ALSO AH UNNERSTAN'S YO' IS SOME-WHUT OF A HYPOCRIK, LI'L ABNER!

LI'L ABNER Just A Big Playful Boy **By Al Capp**

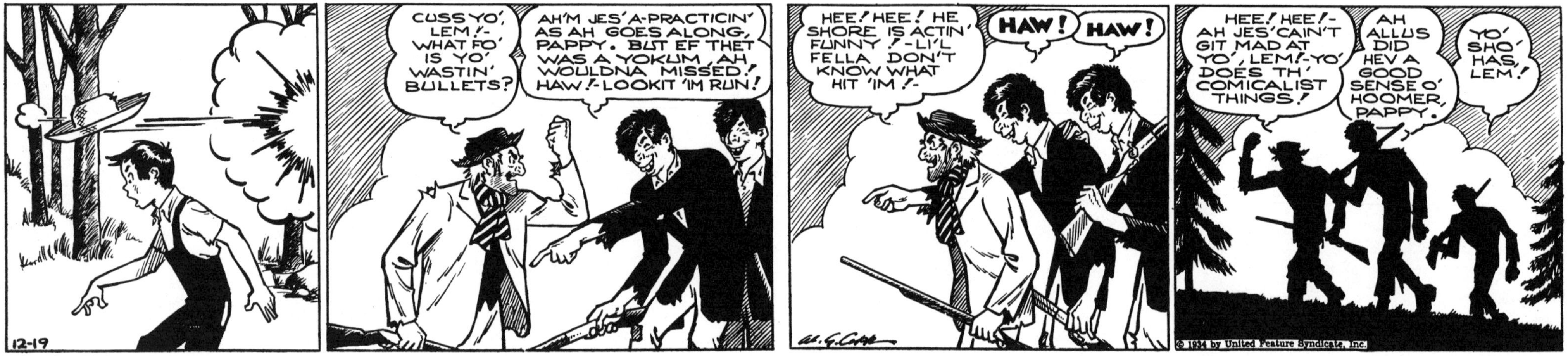
12-19
CUSS YO', LEM!- WHAT FO' IS YO' WASTIN' BULLETS?
AH'M JES' A-PRACTICIN' AS AH GOES ALONG, PAPPY. BUT EF THET WAS A YOKUM, AH WOULDNA MISSED! HAW!- LOOKIT 'IM RUN!
HEE! HEE! HE SHORE IS ACTIN' FUNNY!- LI'L FELLA DON'T KNOW WHAT HIT 'IM!-
HAW!
HAW!
HEE! HEE!- AH JES' CAIN'T GIT MAD AT YO', LEM!- YO' DOES TH' COMICALIST THINGS!
AH ALLUS DID HEV A GOOD SENSE O' HOOMER, PAPPY.
YO' SHO' HAS, LEM!
© 1934 by United Feature Syndicate, Inc.

LI'L ABNER It'll Be A Hot Pahty ! **By Al Capp**

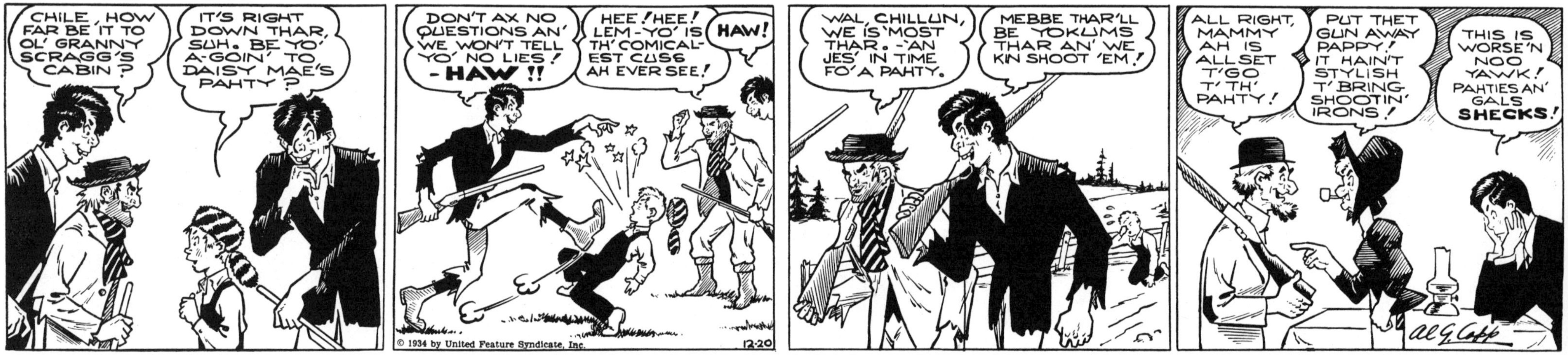
CHILE, HOW FAR BE IT TO OL' GRANNY SCRAGG'S CABIN?
IT'S RIGHT DOWN THAR, SUH. BE YO' A-GOIN' TO DAISY MAE'S PAHTY?
DON'T AX NO QUESTIONS AN' WE WON'T TELL YO' NO LIES! - HAW!!
HEE! HEE! LEM - YO' IS TH' COMICAL-EST CUSS AH EVER SEE!
HAW!
© 1934 by United Feature Syndicate, Inc.
12-20
WAL, CHILLUN, WE IS 'MOST THAR. - AN JES' IN TIME FO' A PAHTY.
MEBBE THAR'LL BE YOKUMS THAR AN' WE KIN SHOOT 'EM!
ALL RIGHT, MAMMY AH IS ALL SET T'GO T' TH' PAHTY!
PUT THET GUN AWAY PAPPY! IT HAIN'T STYLISH T' BRING SHOOTIN' IRONS!
THIS IS WORSE'N NOO YAWK! PAHTIES AN' GALS SHECKS!

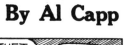

LI'L ABNER

Happy Hain't th' Word !

By Al Capp

-STOP YO' GRUMBLIN' LI'L ABNER! DAISY MAE IS A-GIVIN' THIS PAHTY SPESH-UL FO' YO'. RE-MEMBER, YO' GOT T'ACT LIKE YO' IS INJOYIN' IT!
AWRIGHT, AH'LL ACT LIKE AH IS-BUT AH DON'T HAFTA MEAN IT, DO AH?
Al G. Capp
12-21
THET MUS' BE LI'L ABNER AN' HIS FOLKS -
'PEARS T'ME SHE'S POWFUL STUCK ON HIM!
BANG!
BANG!
© 1934 by United Feature Syndicate, Inc.
GAL! BE THIS TH' SCRAGG SHACK?
YES, SUH-BUT--AH--AH DON'T THINK AH INVITED YO'-ALL!
HEE! HEE! -SHE DON'T THINK SHE INVITED US, CHILLUN!
WE DON'T NEED NO INVITE, GAL-NOT US! HAW!
HAW!! WE IS YO' KIN-FOLK AN' WE IS ALL COME T'LIVE WIF YO'! HAIN'T YO' HAPPY?

LI'L ABNER

A Warm Reception

By Al Capp

SO YO' IS DAISY MAE! WAL, AH'M YO' FIFTH COUSIN ROMEO SCRAGG, AN' THESE IS MAH BOYS, LEM AN' LUKE. WE IS COME T'LIVE WITH YO'.
W-WAL-AH'M SHO' YO' IS ALL W-WELCOME
AH'M GIVIN' A PAHTY.-ALL TH' FOLKS IN DOGPATCH IS HERE. WOULD YO' LIKE TO MEET 'EM?
AH DON'T WANNA MEET NOBODY! -WHAR'S TH' EATS?
AN' IS THAR ANY LIKKER?
© 1934 by United Feature Syndicate, Inc.
HOLD YO' JAWS CHILLUN! TELL ME, COUSIN, BE THAR ANY-ONE HERE BY TH' NAME O' YOKUM?
OH-YO' MEAN LI'L ABNER AN' HIS FOLKS? -THEY'LL BE COMIN' ANY MINUTE.
YOW-EE!!
OH-IS YO' AC-QUAINTED WITH 'EM?
NOT YET, CHILE-BUT WE IS GOIN' OUT T' MEET 'EM!!
Al G. Capp
12-22

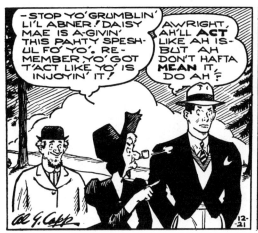

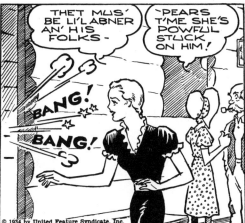

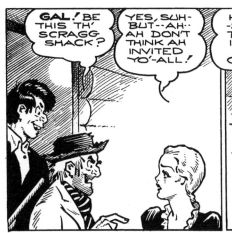

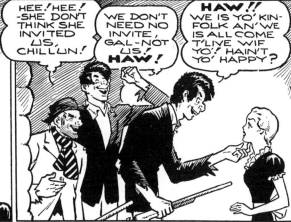

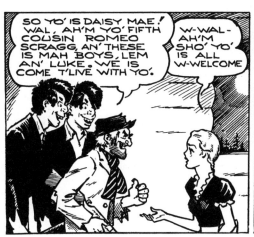

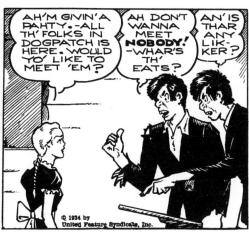

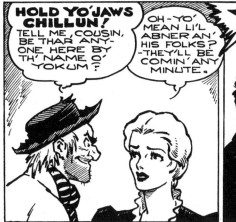

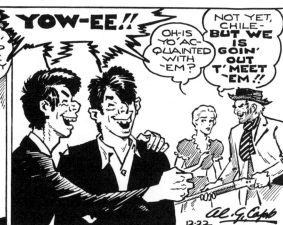

LI'L ABNER The Reception Committee **By Al Capp**

QUICK, COUSIN!- WHICH WAY WILL TH' YOKUMS BE COMIN'?
UP OVER THET THAR HILL!- W-WHUT ARE YO' GONNA DO?
SHOOT 'EM!
HAW!
© 1934 by United Feature Syndicate, Inc.
BUT- WHY? DID THEY EVER DO ANYTHING TO YO'?
NOT EXAC'LY-BUT A HUND'ED YARS AGO TH' YOKUMS AN' US SCRAGGS WAS BLOOD ENEMIES!- WE-ALL THOUGHT ALL TH' YOKUMS WAS KILT OFF -'TILL WE FOUN' OUT ABOUT THIS HERE PART O' TH' FAM'LY!
BUT, THET WAS SO LONG AGO! PLEASE - CAIN'T YO' FO'GIT TH' FEUD?- THESE YOKUMS IS NICE!
GAL- ONLY DEAD YOKUMS IS NICE!
DON'T BOTHER US!
GIT IN TH' HOUSE!
GOSH, MAMMY- MAH FEET HURT! KIN AH TAKE MAH SHOES OFF?
IT HAINT PERLITE T'COME TO A PAHTY WIFOUT NO SHOES. IT'S JES' OVER TH' HILL AN' WE'LL BE THAR.
PAHTIES AN' GALS SHECKS!
12-24

LI'L ABNER Merry Chris'mus Fo' Salomey **By Al Capp**

LET US DROP THE FEUD FOR A MINUTE AND LOOK BACK AT A CHRISTMAS WHEN MAMMY AN' PAPPY WERE YOUNG AND LI'L ABNER WAS A MERE CHILE -
12-25
LI'L ABNER, WHUT DOES YO' WISH MOST FO' YO' CHRIS'MUS DINNAH?
AH WISHES PO'K CHOPS, MAMMY.
© 1934 by United Feature Syndicate, Inc
AWRIGHT, SON! BUT TH' ONLY PO'K CHOPS 'ROUND HERE IS ON' YO' LI'L PIG, SALOMEY.
AH'LL GIT TH' KNIFE!
WH- WHUT IS YO' GONNA DO?
WAL, EF WE IS GONNA HAVE PO'K CHOPS WE GOTTA DO A JOB ON SALOMEY.
OH, MAH GOODNISS! -L-LISSEN, MAMMY- M-MEBBE AH'D JES' AS SOON HAVE PUN'KIN PIE!
AN' A MERRY CHRIS'MUS T' YO'-ALL!
MO' PIE, SALOMEY?

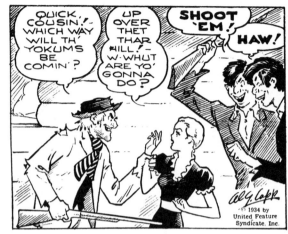

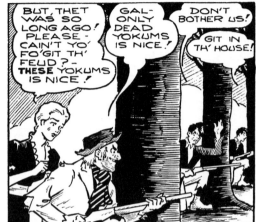

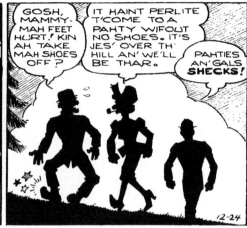

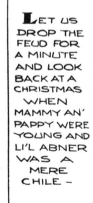

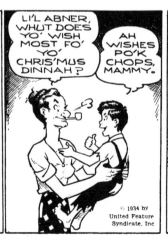

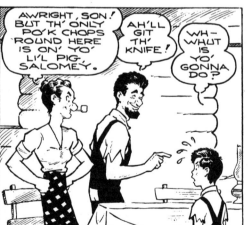

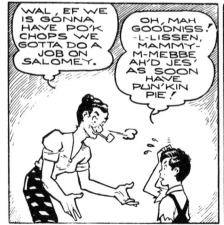

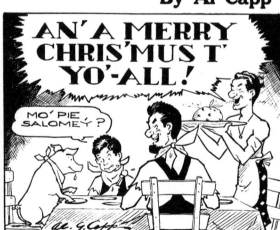

LI'L ABNER Daisy Mae To the Rescue ! By Al Capp

OH, AH BEGS YO'!- DON'T SHOOT 'EM!- THEY'S GOOD FOLKS - EVEN IF THEY IS YOKUMS!
GO 'WAY, CHILE!- -AN' DON'T TRY T'STOP YO' KIN FUM WIPIN' OUT OUR BLOOD EN-EMIES! WHY- WHAR'S YO' PRIDE?
THEY DIDN'T SEE ME!- AH DON'T CARE 'BOUT MAH PRIDE! THEY HAIN'T GONNA HURT LI'L ABNER'S FOLKS - OR HIM!
Al. G. Capp
TAN MAH HIDE EF IT HAIN'T DAISY MAE COME T'MEET US!- IS WE LATE FO' TH' PAHTY?
NO - THAR HAIN'T NO PAHTY- AH- -AH CALLED IT OFF!
© 1934 by United Feature Syndicate, Inc.
YIPPEE-E!!
HUSH, LI'L AB-NER!- WAL, THASS AWRIGHT, CHILE -WE'LL COME OVER AN' VISIT FO' A SPELL, ANY-WAYS -
NO!- NO!- DON'T COME TO MAH HOUSE! PLEASE - OH PLEASE - GO HOME!
12-26

LI'L ABNER No Way T' Treat a Lady By Al Capp

OH, AH BEGS YO'!- DON'T COME T'MAH HOUSE!- TH' PAHTY'S OFF! DON'T AX ME WHY!
IT'S AWRIGHT WIF ME, DAISY MAE. DON'T FEEL BAD. AH DIDN'T WANT T'COME ANYHOW!
KIN AH TAKE MAH SHOES OFF NOW, MAMMY?
?
12-27
DAISY MAE SHO' IS ACTIN' MIGHTY PEE-KOOL-YAR! YO' FOLKS GO HOME. AH IS GONNA FOLLY HER AN' SEE WHUT AH KIN SEE!
Al. G. Capp
THAR'S SOME-ONE A-COMIN' UP TH' HILL, PAPPY! AH CAIN'T TELL WHO 'TIS -
SHOOT 'EM FIRST AN' FIND OUT ARTERWARDS! IT MAY BE A YOKUM!
TAN MAH HIDE!
© 1934 by United Feature Syndicate, Inc

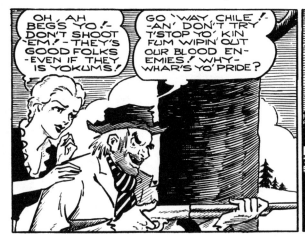

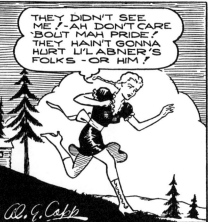

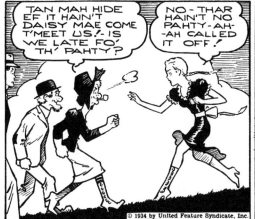

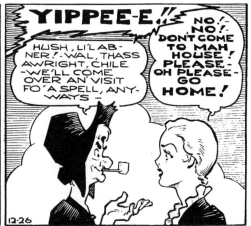

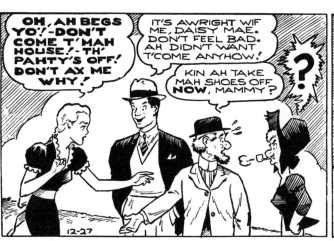

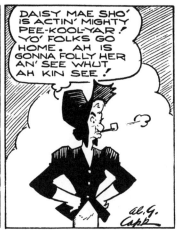

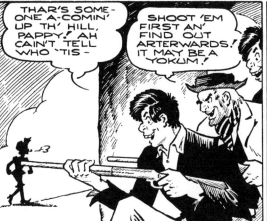

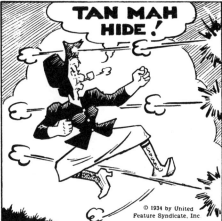

LI'L ABNER Mammy's White Lie By Al Capp

AW, IT'S JES' A LI'L OLE LADY WE B'EN SHOOT-IN' AT, PAPPY!
DAWGONE! AH HOPED IT WAS TH' YOKUMS!
SHE'S A-COMIN' FO' US LICKETY SPLIT!
STOP MESSIN' WIF THEM SHOOT-IN' IRONS, STRANGERS, OR AH'LL SMACK YO' ALL DOWN-!! AN' EF YO' DON'T THINK AH KIN DO IT—
PUT DOWN YO' FISTS, WOMAN! WE THOUGHT YO' WAS A YOKUM!
12-28
WAL, WHUT O' THET?
WHUT O' THET? WHY, WOMAN, WE IS TH' SCRAGGS!- BLOOD-ENEMIES O' TH' YOKUMS FO' A HUND'ED Y'ARS!
-AN' WE IS COME T' WIPE 'EM OUT!
YO' HAIN'T SEEN 'EM 'ROUND HAS YO'?
© 1934 by United Feature Syndicate, Inc.
ME? AH HAIN'T SEEN HIDE NOR HAIR O' 'EM!
Al. G. Capp

LI'L ABNER Lion-Hearted Pappy By Al Capp

TAN MAH HIDE!!
Al. G. Capp
PAPPY!-LI'L ABNER!-AH GOT SOM'THIN' T' TELL YO'- IT'S A-GONNA TAKE ALL YO' COURAGE T' HEAR IT!
- GO AHEAD, TELL US, MAMMY - AH HAIN'T SKEERED O' NUTHIN'!
-AN' YO' KNOWS ME, MAMMY -AH LAUGHS AT DANGER! WHUT IS IT?
TH' SCRAGGS IS HERE!
© 1934 by United Feature Syndicate, Inc.
WH-WHUT'S TH' MATTER, PAPPY?- DID YO' TRIP OVER SOM'THIN'?
HAIN'T NO USE AXIN' HIM, SON -HE CAIN'T ANSWER. GIT SOME WATER - YO' PAPPY HAS FAINTED!!
12-29

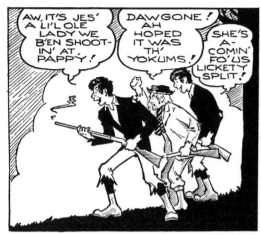

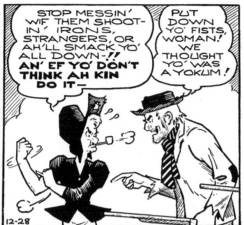

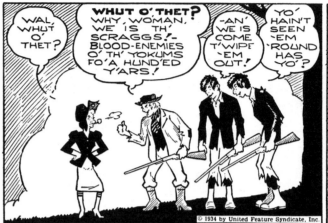

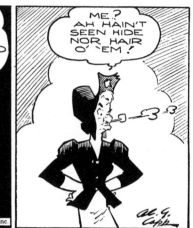

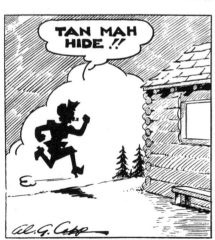

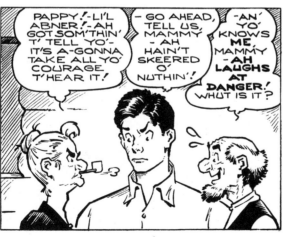

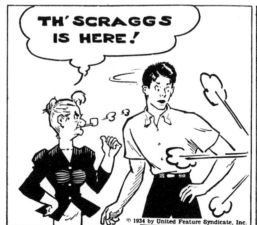

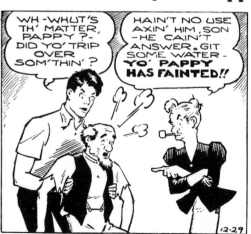

LI'L ABNER

Hyar Come th' Scraggs

By Al Capp

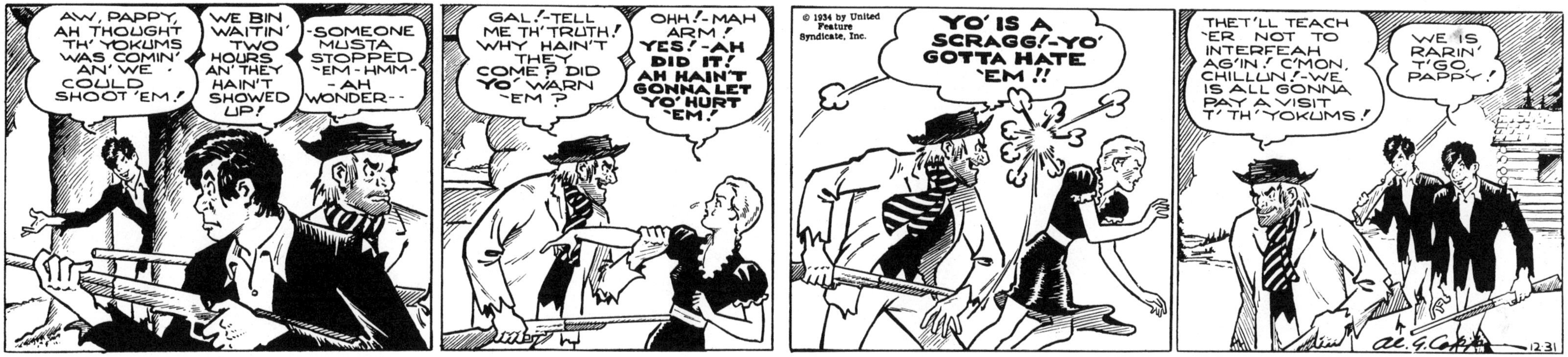

AW, PAPPY, AH THOUGHT TH' YOKUMS WAS COMIN' AN' WE COULD SHOOT 'EM!
WE BIN WAITIN' TWO HOURS AN' THEY HAIN'T SHOWED UP!
-SOMEONE MUSTA STOPPED 'EM-HMM- -AH WONDER--
GAL!-TELL ME TH' TRUTH! WHY HAIN'T THEY COME? DID YO' WARN 'EM?
OHH!-MAH ARM! YES!-AH DID IT! AH HAIN'T GONNA LET YO' HURT 'EM!
© 1934 by United Feature Syndicate, Inc.
YO' IS A SCRAGG!-YO' GOTTA HATE 'EM!!
THET'LL TEACH 'ER NOT TO INTERFEAH AG'IN! C'MON, CHILLUN!-WE IS ALL GONNA PAY A VISIT T' TH' YOKUMS!
WE IS RARIN' T'GO, PAPPY!
Al. G. Capp
12-31

LI'L ABNER

An' th' Same Fum Mistah Capp

By Al Capp

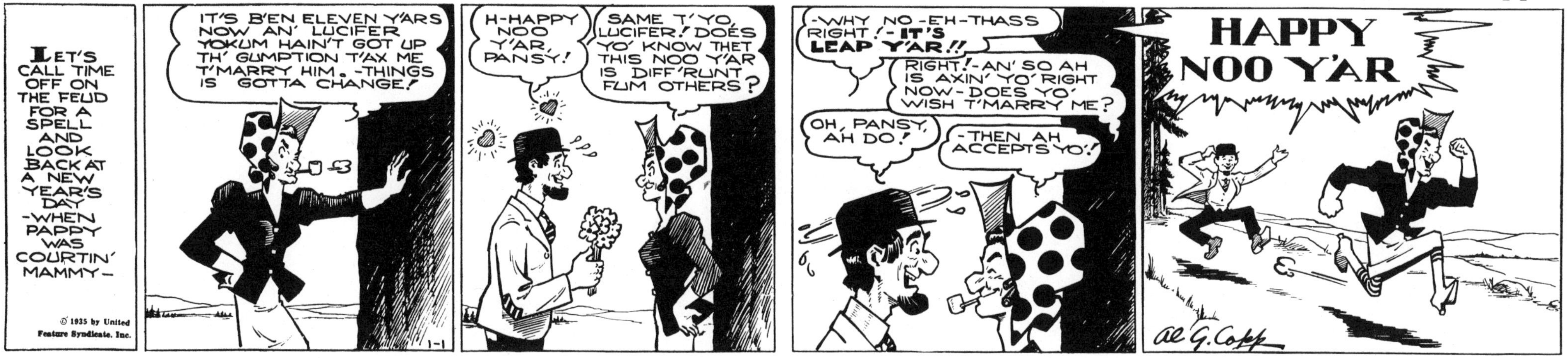

LET'S CALL TIME OFF ON THE FEUD FOR A SPELL AND LOOK BACK AT A NEW YEAR'S DAY -WHEN PAPPY WAS COURTIN' MAMMY-
© 1935 by United Feature Syndicate, Inc.
IT'S B'EN ELEVEN Y'ARS NOW AN' LUCIFER YOKUM HAIN'T GOT UP TH' GUMPTION T'AX ME T'MARRY HIM. -THINGS IS GOTTA CHANGE!
1-1
H-HAPPY NOO Y'AR, PANSY!
SAME T'YO, LUCIFER! DOES YO' KNOW THET THIS NOO Y'AR IS DIFF'RUNT FUM OTHERS?
-WHY NO-EH-THASS RIGHT!-IT'S LEAP Y'AR!!
RIGHT!-AN' SO AH IS AXIN' YO' RIGHT NOW-DOES YO' WISH T'MARRY ME?
OH, PANSY, AH DO!
-THEN AH ACCEPTS YO'!
HAPPY NOO Y'AR
Al G. Capp

LI'L ABNER An' Here Comes Mammy By Al Capp

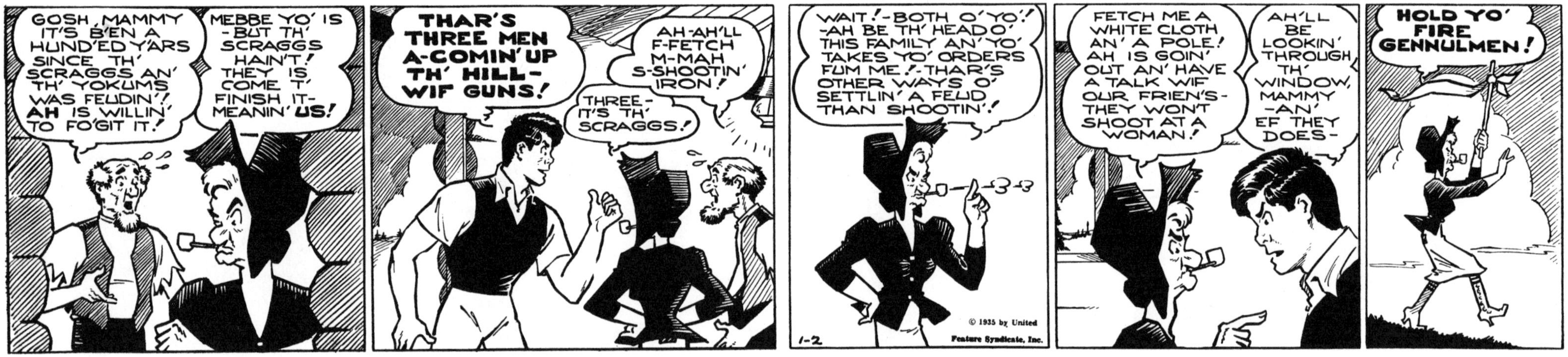

GOSH, MAMMY IT'S B'EN A HUND'ED Y'ARS SINCE TH' SCRAGGS AN' TH' YOKUMS WAS FEUDIN'! AH IS WILLIN' TO FO'GIT IT.'
MEBBE YO' IS - BUT TH' SCRAGGS HAIN'T! THEY IS COME T' FINISH IT - MEANIN' US!
THAR'S THREE MEN A-COMIN' UP TH' HILL - WIF GUNS!
AH-AH'LL F-FETCH M-MAH S-SHOOTIN' IRON!
THREE - IT'S TH' SCRAGGS!
WAIT! - BOTH O' YO'! - AH BE TH' HEAD O' THIS FAMILY AN' YO' TAKES YO' ORDERS FUM ME! - THAR'S OTHER WAYS O' SETTLIN' A FEUD THAN SHOOTIN'!
© 1935 by United Feature Syndicate, Inc.
1-2
FETCH ME A WHITE CLOTH AN' A POLE! AH IS GOIN' OUT AN' HAVE A TALK WIF OUR FRIEN'S - THEY WON'T SHOOT AT A WOMAN!
AH'LL BE LOOKIN' THROUGH TH' WINDOW, MAMMY - AN' EF THEY DOES -
HOLD YO' FIRE GENNULMEN!

LI'L ABNER Yo' Tell 'Em, Mammy By Al Capp

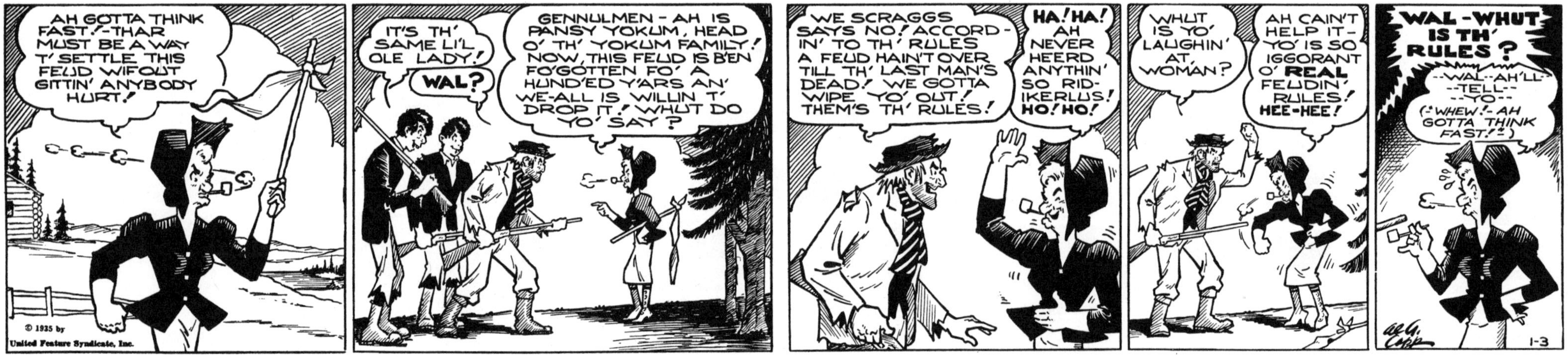

AH GOTTA THINK FAST! - THAR MUST BE A WAY T' SETTLE THIS FEUD WIFOUT GITTIN' ANYBODY HURT!
© 1935 by United Feature Syndicate, Inc.
IT'S TH' SAME LI'L OLE LADY!
WAL?
GENNULMEN - AH IS PANSY YOKUM, HEAD O' TH' YOKUM FAMILY! NOW, THIS FEUD IS B'EN FO'GOTTEN FO' A HUND'ED Y'ARS AN' WE-ALL IS WILLIN T' DROP IT! WHUT DO YO' SAY?
WE SCRAGGS SAYS NO! ACCORD-IN' TO TH' RULES A FEUD HAIN'T OVER TILL TH' LAST MAN'S DEAD! WE GOTTA WIPE YO' OUT! THEM'S TH' RULES!
HA! HA! AH NEVER HEERD ANYTHIN' SO RID-IKERLUS! HO! HO!
WHUT IS YO' LAUGHIN' AT, WOMAN?
AH CAIN'T HELP IT - YO' IS SO IGGORANT O' REAL FEUDIN' RULES! HEE-HEE!
WAL - WHUT IS TH' RULES?
- - WAL - AH'LL - - TELL - - YO' - -
(- WHEW! - AH GOTTA THINK FAST! -)
Al G. Capp
1-3

LI'L ABNER **Rules Is Rules** **By Al Capp**

YO' MEANS T'SAY WE SCRAGGS HAIN'T GOIN' AT THIS FEUD RIGHT?
YO' IS DEAD WRONG! ACC-ORDIN' T' TH' RULES, YO' GOTTA HAVE A BOUND'RY LINE!
BUT THAR HAIN'T NO BOUND'RY LINE!
THEN WE'LL SET ONE AT THIS OLE PINE TREE • EF A YOKUM CROSSES IT-YO' KIN START SHOOTIN' -**BUT NOT BEFORE!**- THET'S A **VERY** IMPO'TANT RULE!
1-4
WELL, MEBBE YO' IS RIGHT - BUT AH'LL BE DAWGONED EF AH EVER HEERD O' THET ONE BEFORE!-
THASS BECUZ YO' IS SO IGGORANT!
AL G. CAPP
AW, PAPPY, CAIN'T WE SHOOT 'ER?
NO, CHILLUN -RULES IS RULES!
-"TAN MAH HIDE! THEY SWALLERED IT!- AN' AH MAKED IT ALL UP OUTA MAH OWN HEAD!-"
© 1935 by United Feature Syndicate, Inc.

LI'L ABNER **Scraggs Is Scraggs** **By Al Capp**

WAL-AH FIXED IT! AH HAD T'LIE MAH HEAD OFF-LAWZY FO'GIVE ME-BUT THAR WON'T BE NO SHOOTIN' -THET IS-EF YO' DON'T PASS TH' OLE PINE TREE!-THET'S TH' BOUND'RY LINE!
WHEW! AM AH GLAD!
IT HAIN'T THET AH'M SCARED, MAMMY-NOT AH! IT'S J-JES' THET AH'M P-PEACEFUL! WHAR'D THEY GO?
BACK TO DAISY MAE'S.
SO THEY'S STAYIN' WIF DAISY MAE! WAL-THEY BETTER BE GOOD T' HER -OR- BOUND'RY OR NOT -AH'LL-
WHY, SON, YO' TOLE ME YO' DIDN'T CARE NOTHIN' 'BOUT HER!
AL G. CAPP
1-5
W-WAL-- AH--AH **DONT!**-- ONLY- YO' SEE-- AH--UH--
MAMMY UNNERSTAN'S, SON, BUT WHUT KIN WE DO?-THIS IS A WAR BETWIXT TH' SCRAGGS AN' TH' YOKUMS - AN' DAISY MAE-SHE'S A SCRAGG!
© 1935 by United Feature Syndicate, Inc.

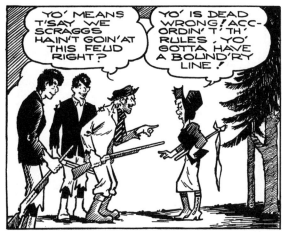

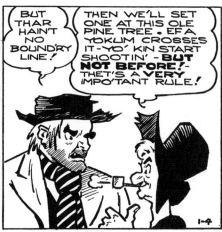

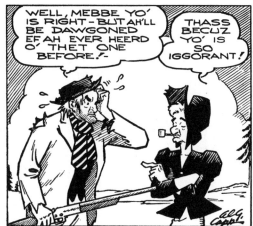

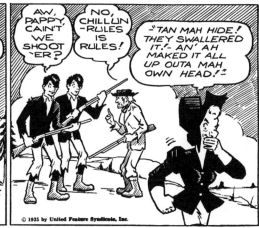

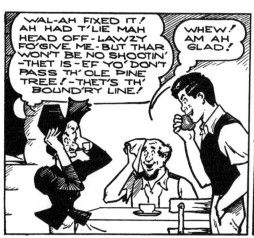

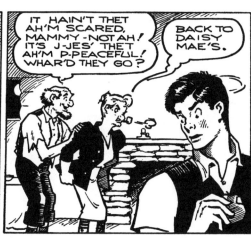

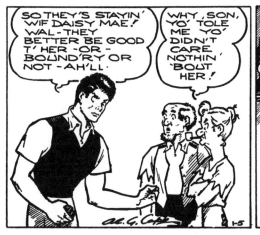

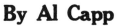

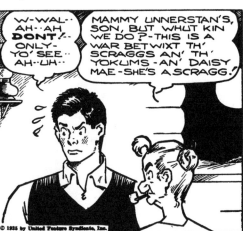

LI'L ABNER Dangerous Curs Ahead By Al Capp

LOOK YONDER, SON, AN' YO' KIN SEE TH' SCRAGGS' GUNS A-POINTIN' THROUGH THET THICKET-A-WAITIN' TO SHOOT TH' FIRST YOKUM THET PASSES TH' OL' PINE TREE!
AH SEEN 'EM, MAMMY-THREE GUNS.
SHECKS, MAMMY! LET ME FIGHT 'EM -AH KIN LICK 'EM ALL!-
-AN', LI'L ABNER, AH WILL LICK YO' EF YO' DON'T KEEP YO' PROMISE T'STAY AWAY FUM THET BOUND'RY LINE!
DAWGONE!-EF IT WASN'T FO' MAMMY AH'D TEAR OVER THAR AN' SMACK 'EM ALL-EVEN EF THEY HAS GOT GUNS -JEHOSOPHAT!!
-AND THERE IS PAPPY-WHO, IN HIS DUMB WAY HAS CLEAN FORGOTTEN ABOUT THE SCRAGGS -CHASING SALOMEY, WHO-IN ITS DUMB WAY-IS HEADING STRAIGHT FOR THE FATAL BOUNDARY LINE!
BUT, SALOMEY -YO GOTTA TAKE YO' BATH!
© 1935 by United Feature Syndicate, Inc.
AL CAPP
1-7

LI'L ABNER Too Late ? By Al Capp

LOOK!-THAR'S PAPPY YOKUM A-CHASIN' HIS PIG-!-HE'S A-COMIN' NEAR TH' BOUND'RY!-KIN WE SHOOT HIM NOW?
NO, CHILLUN -YO' GOTTA WAIT TILL HE PASSES TH' OLD PINE TREE!
-WHILE ABOUT A HUNDRED YARDS THE OTHER SIDE-
PAPPY!
AIM CAREFUL, CHILLUN!-AN' TH' MINUTE HE PASSES TH' BOUND'RY-LET 'IM HAVE IT!
SALOMEY!-COME BACK HERE!-OH, WHY IS YO' SO CONTRARY?
AL CAPP
1-8
© 1935 by United Feature Syndicate, Inc.

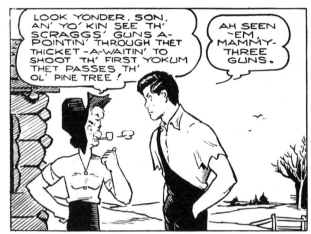

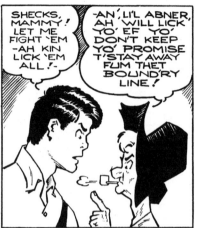

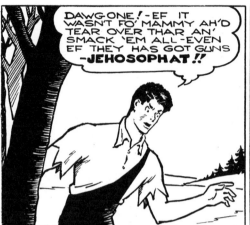

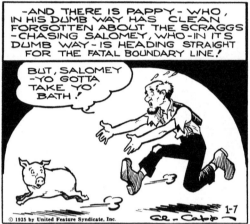

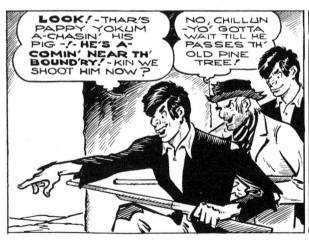

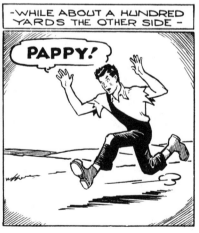

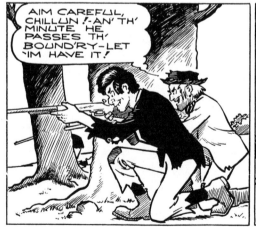

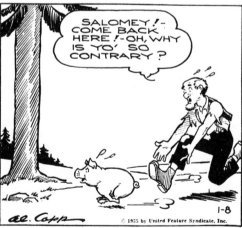

LI'L ABNER Li'l Abner's Inspiration By Al Capp

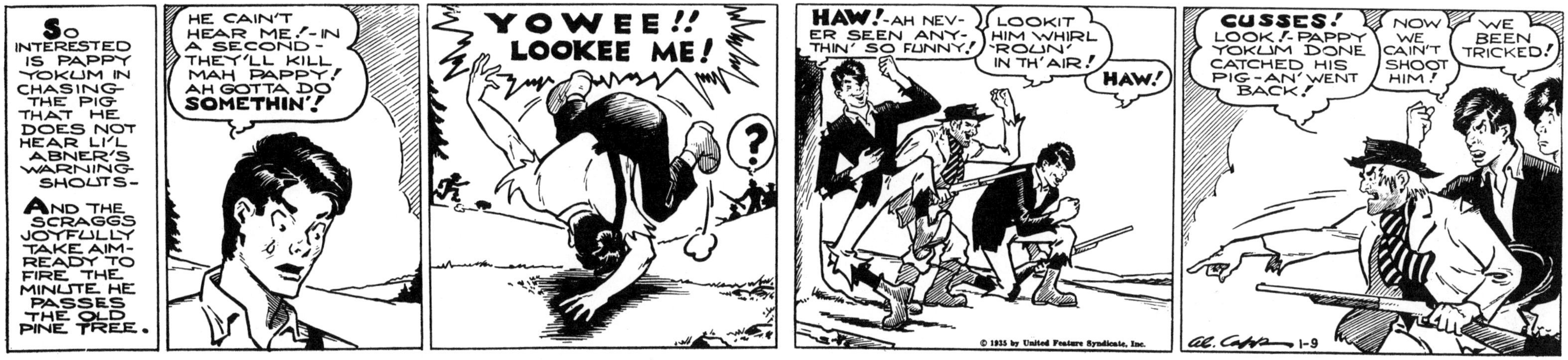

SO INTERESTED IS PAPPY YOKUM IN CHASING THE PIG THAT HE DOES NOT HEAR LI'L ABNER'S WARNING SHOUTS - AND THE SCRAGGS JOYFULLY TAKE AIM - READY TO FIRE THE MINUTE HE PASSES THE OLD PINE TREE.
HE CAIN'T HEAR ME!-IN A SECOND - THEY'LL KILL MAH PAPPY! AH GOTTA DO SOMETHIN'!
YOWEE!! LOOKEE ME!
?
HAW!-AH NEVER SEEN ANYTHIN' SO FUNNY!
LOOKIT HIM WHIRL 'ROUN' IN TH' AIR!
HAW!
© 1935 by United Feature Syndicate, Inc.
CUSSES! LOOK!-PAPPY YOKUM DONE CATCHED HIS PIG-AN' WENT BACK!
NOW WE CAIN'T SHOOT HIM!
WE BEEN TRICKED!
Al. Capp 1-9

LI'L ABNER Gittin' Madder'n Madder! By Al Capp

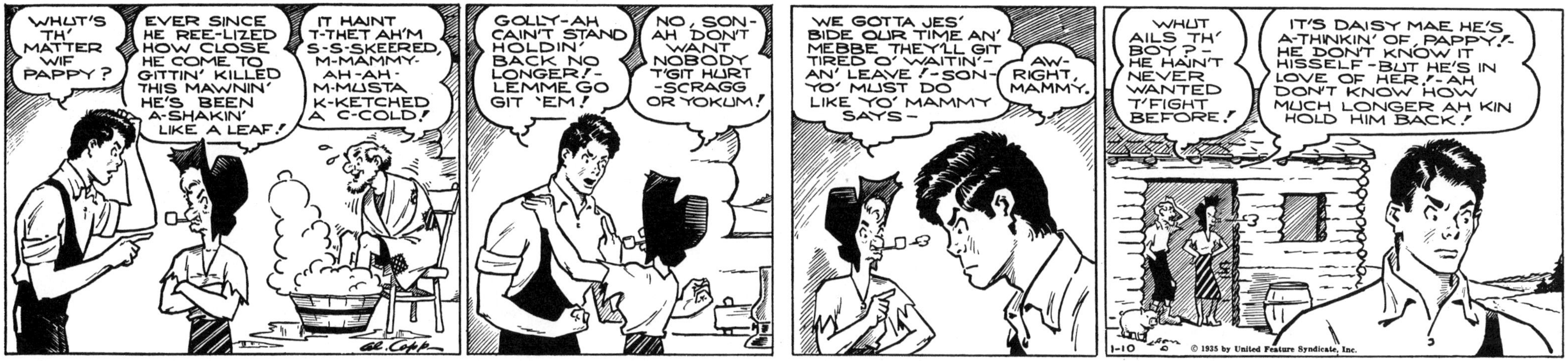

WHUT'S TH' MATTER WIF PAPPY?
EVER SINCE HE REE-LIZED HOW CLOSE HE COME TO GITTIN' KILLED THIS MAWNIN' HE'S BEEN A-SHAKIN' LIKE A LEAF!
IT HAINT T-THET AH'M S-S-SKEERED, M-MAMMY-AH-AH-M-MUSTA K-KETCHED A C-COLD!
Al. Capp
GOLLY-AH CAIN'T STAND HOLDIN' BACK NO LONGER!-LEMME GO GIT 'EM!
NO, SON-AH DON'T WANT NOBODY T'GIT HURT -SCRAGG OR YOKUM!
WE GOTTA JES' BIDE OUR TIME AN' MEBBE THEY'LL GIT TIRED O' WAITIN'-AN' LEAVE!-SON-YO' MUST DO LIKE YO' MAMMY SAYS-
AW-RIGHT, MAMMY.
WHUT AILS TH' BOY?-HE HAIN'T NEVER WANTED T'FIGHT BEFORE!
IT'S DAISY MAE HE'S A-THINKIN' OF, PAPPY!-HE DON'T KNOW IT HISSELF-BUT HE'S IN LOVE OF HER!-AH DON'T KNOW HOW MUCH LONGER AH KIN HOLD HIM BACK!
1-10
© 1935 by United Feature Syndicate, Inc.

LI'L ABNER Don't Fo'get Yo' Promise ! By Al Capp

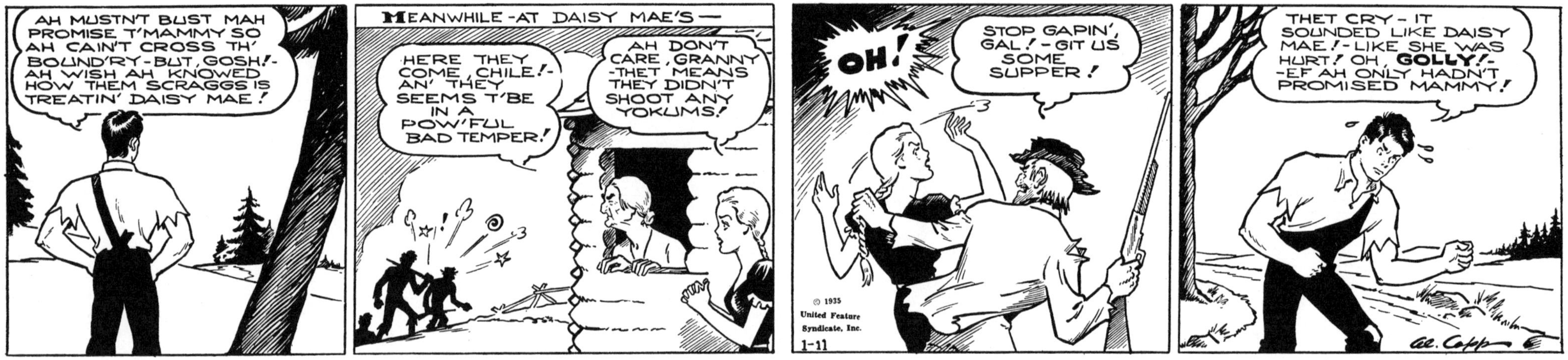
AH MUSTN'T BUST MAH PROMISE T'MAMMY SO AH CAIN'T CROSS TH' BOUND'RY - BUT, GOSH! - AH WISH AH KNOWED HOW THEM SCRAGGS IS TREATIN' DAISY MAE!
MEANWHILE - AT DAISY MAE'S —
HERE THEY COME, CHILE! - AN' THEY SEEMS T'BE IN A POW'FUL BAD TEMPER!
AH DON'T CARE, GRANNY - THET MEANS THEY DIDN'T SHOOT ANY YOKUMS!
OH!
STOP GAPIN', GAL! - GIT US SOME SUPPER!
© 1935 United Feature Syndicate, Inc.
1-11
THET CRY - IT SOUNDED LIKE DAISY MAE! - LIKE SHE WAS HURT! OH, GOLLY! - -EF AH ONLY HADN'T PROMISED MAMMY!
Al. Capp

LI'L ABNER Boy—You're Forgiven ! By Al Capp

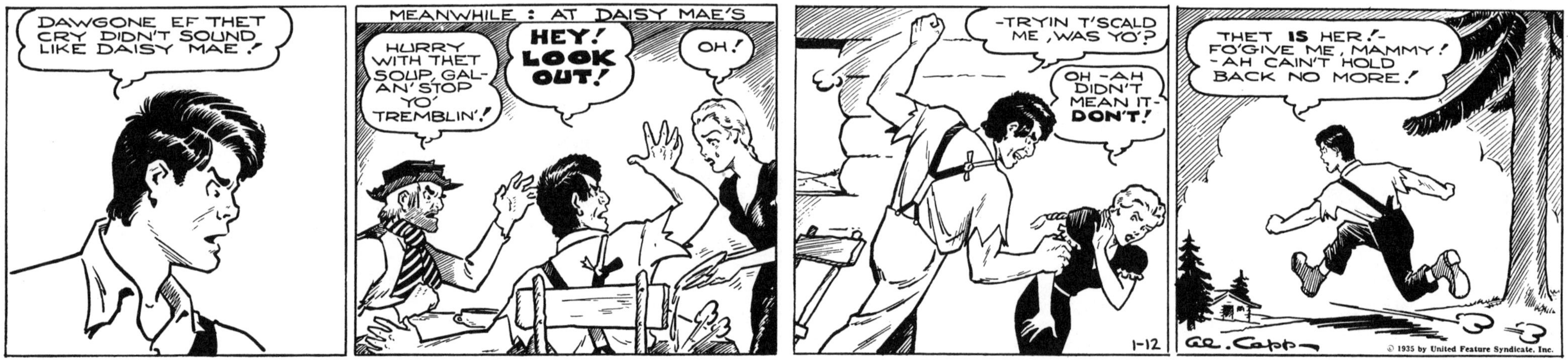
DAWGONE EF THET CRY DIDN'T SOUND LIKE DAISY MAE!
MEANWHILE : AT DAISY MAE'S
HURRY WITH THET SOUP, GAL - AN' STOP YO' TREMBLIN'!
HEY! LOOK OUT!
OH!
-TRYIN T'SCALD ME, WAS YO'?
OH - AH DIDN'T MEAN IT - DON'T!
1-12
THET IS HER! - FO'GIVE ME, MAMMY! - AH CAIN'T HOLD BACK NO MORE!
Al. Capp
© 1935 by United Feature Syndicate, Inc.

LI'L ABNER How Yo' Like That **By Al Capp**

STOP RUNNIN' AWAY! C'MON BACK, GAL!- AH WANTA SMACK YO' AGAIN!
DAW-GONE!
© 1935 by United Feature Syndicate, Inc.
HEY!-WHUT FO' DID YO' DO THET?
ON ACCOUNT YO' BACK WAS FACIN' ME, BUT-
-NOW THET YO' IS TURNED 'ROUND AH CHANGES MAH STYLE!
1-14
CUSS ME, LEM, EF THET DIDN'T SOUND LIKE LUKE A-YELLIN'!-GIT YO' GUN-WE'LL GO OUT AN' SEE!
JES' A ("GLUB") MINUTE, PAPPY-

LI'L ABNER First Blood **By Al Capp**

OH, LI'L ABNER-HURRY! LET'S GIT AWAY BEFO' TH' OTHERS COME OUT AFTER YO'!
NO SUH! AH'S GONNA FINISH THIS FEUD UP RIGHT NOW!-AH B'EN HOLDIN' MAHSELF BACK PLENTY LONG ENOUGH!
BUT TH' OTHERS HAS GUNS-AN' YO' HAINT!-OH PLEASE!-EF YO' WON'T DO IT FO' ME-THINK HOW YO' MAMMY'D FEEL EF YO' GOT KILT!
SHECKS, THASS RIGHT!-RECKON SHE WOULDN'T LIKE IT-LET'S GO!
1-15
LOOK!-THAR'S LUKE ON TH' GROUND-AN' THAR'S DAISY MAE A-RUNNIN' OFF-!-WITH LI'L ABNER YOKUM-HE DONE CROSSED TH' BOUND'RY!
AH GOTTA BEAD ON HIM PAPPY
AH HIT HIM!
YOWEE!
© 1935 by United Feature Syndicate, Inc.

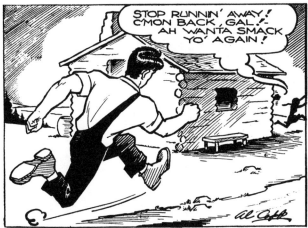

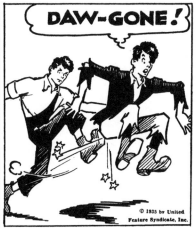

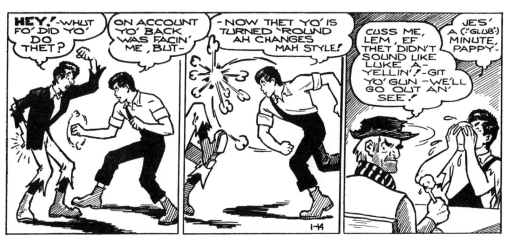

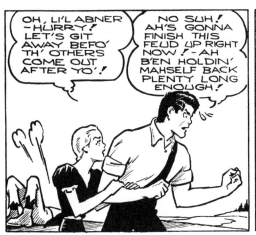

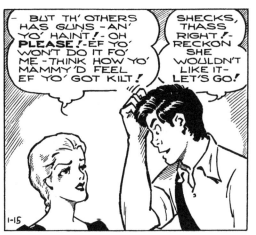

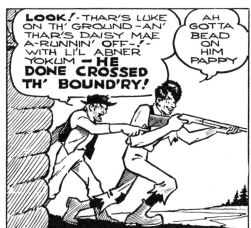

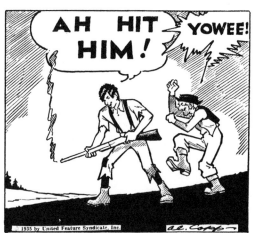

LI'L ABNER Mammy's Gotta Plan By Al Capp

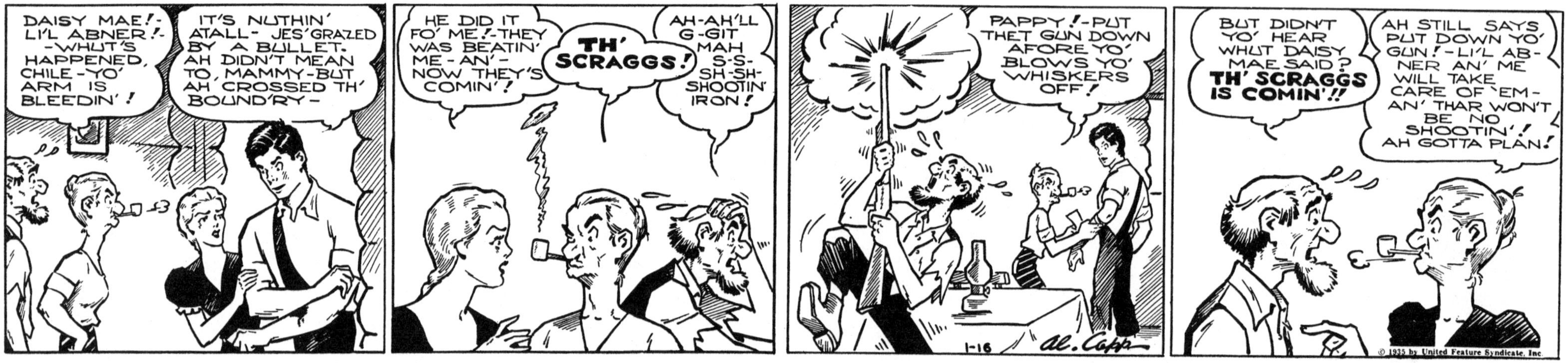
DAISY MAE!- LI'L ABNER!- -WHUT'S HAPPENED, CHILE-YO' ARM IS BLEEDIN'!
IT'S NUTHIN' ATALL- JES' GRAZED BY A BULLET- AH DIDN'T MEAN TO, MAMMY-BUT AH CROSSED TH' BOUND'RY-
HE DID IT FO' ME!-THEY WAS BEATIN' ME-AN'- NOW THEY'S COMIN'!
TH' SCRAGGS!
AH-AH'LL G-GIT MAH S-S-SH-SH-SHOOTIN' IRON!
PAPPY!-PUT THET GUN DOWN AFORE YO' BLOWS YO' WHISKERS OFF!
1-16
Al. Capp
BUT DIDN'T YO' HEAR WHUT DAISY MAE SAID? TH' SCRAGGS IS COMIN'!!
AH STILL SAYS PUT DOWN YO' GUN!-LI'L AB-NER AN' ME WILL TAKE CARE OF 'EM- AN' THAR WON'T BE NO SHOOTIN'! AH GOTTA PLAN!
© 1935 by United Feature Syndicate, Inc.

LI'L ABNER The Plot Begins By Al Capp

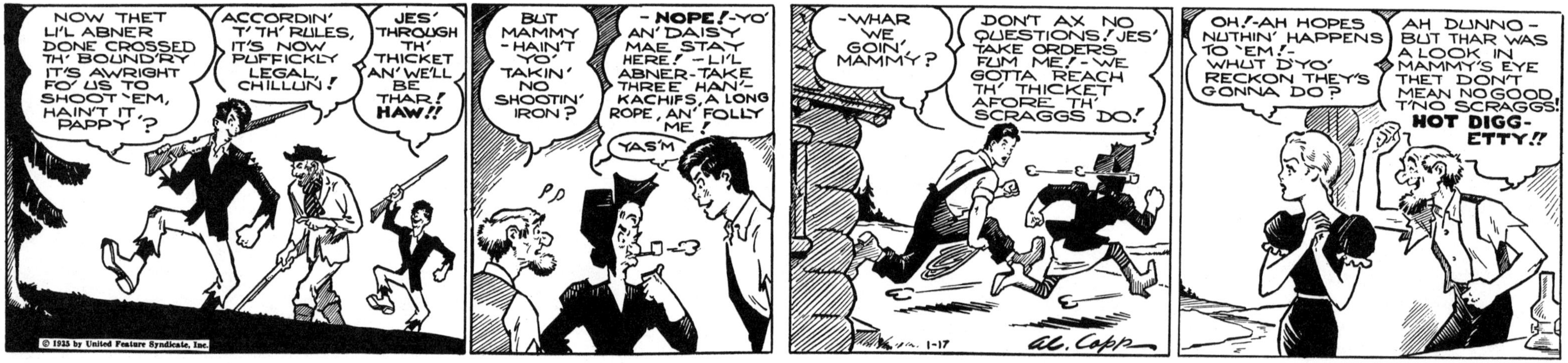
NOW THET LI'L ABNER DONE CROSSED TH' BOUND'RY IT'S AWRIGHT FO' US TO SHOOT 'EM, HAIN'T IT, PAPPY?
ACCORDIN' T' TH' RULES, IT'S NOW PUFFICKLY LEGAL, CHILLUN!
JES' THROUGH TH' THICKET AN' WE'LL BE THAR! HAW!!
© 1935 by United Feature Syndicate, Inc.
BUT MAMMY -HAIN'T YO' TAKIN' NO SHOOTIN' IRON?
-NOPE!-YO' AN' DAISY MAE STAY HERE!-LI'L ABNER-TAKE THREE HAN-KACHIFS, A LONG ROPE, AN' FOLLY ME!
YAS'M
-WHAR WE GOIN', MAMMY?
DON'T AX NO QUESTIONS! JES' TAKE ORDERS FUM ME!-WE GOTTA REACH TH' THICKET AFORE TH' SCRAGGS DO!
1-17
Al. Capp
OH!-AH HOPES NUTHIN' HAPPENS TO 'EM!- WHUT D'YO' RECKON THEY'S GONNA DO?
AH DUNNO- BUT THAR WAS A LOOK IN MAMMY'S EYE THET DON'T MEAN NO GOOD T'NO SCRAGGS! HOT DIGG-ETTY!!

LI'L ABNER Into the Trap

By Al Capp

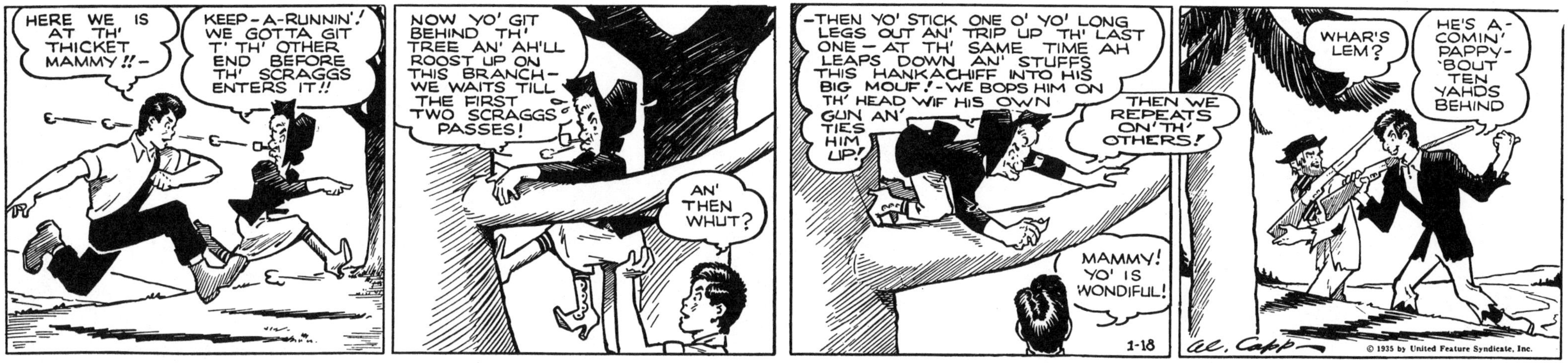

HERE WE IS AT TH' THICKET MAMMY!! –
KEEP-A-RUNNIN'! WE GOTTA GIT T' TH' OTHER END BEFORE TH' SCRAGGS ENTERS IT!!
NOW YO' GIT BEHIND TH' TREE AN' AH'LL ROOST UP ON THIS BRANCH – WE WAITS TILL THE FIRST TWO SCRAGGS PASSES!
AN' THEN WHUT?
–THEN YO' STICK ONE O' YO' LONG LEGS OUT AN' TRIP UP TH' LAST ONE – AT TH' SAME TIME AH LEAPS DOWN AN' STUFFS THIS HANKACHIFF INTO HIS BIG MOUF! – WE BOPS HIM ON TH' HEAD WIF HIS OWN GUN AN' TIES HIM UP!
THEN WE REPEATS ON TH' OTHERS!
MAMMY! YO' IS WONDIFUL!
1-18
WHAR'S LEM?
HE'S A-COMIN' PAPPY – 'BOUT TEN YAHDS BEHIND
Al. Capp
© 1935 by United Feature Syndicate, Inc.

LI'L ABNER Thar's Still Two T'Go

By Al Capp

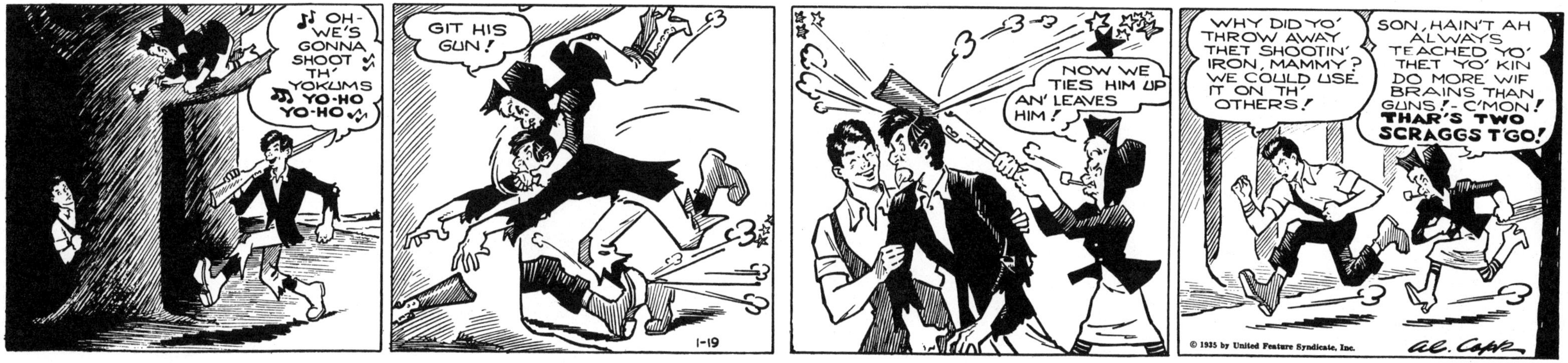

OH – WE'S GONNA SHOOT TH' YOKUMS YO-HO YO-HO
GIT HIS GUN!
1-19
NOW WE TIES HIM UP AN' LEAVES HIM!
WHY DID YO' THROW AWAY THET SHOOTIN' IRON, MAMMY? WE COULD USE IT ON TH' OTHERS!
SON, HAIN'T AH ALWAYS TEACHED YO' THET YO' KIN DO MORE WIF BRAINS THAN GUNS! – C'MON! THAR'S TWO SCRAGGS T'GO!
© 1935 by United Feature Syndicate, Inc.
Al. Capp

LI'L ABNER No Pleasure For the Scraggs By Al Capp

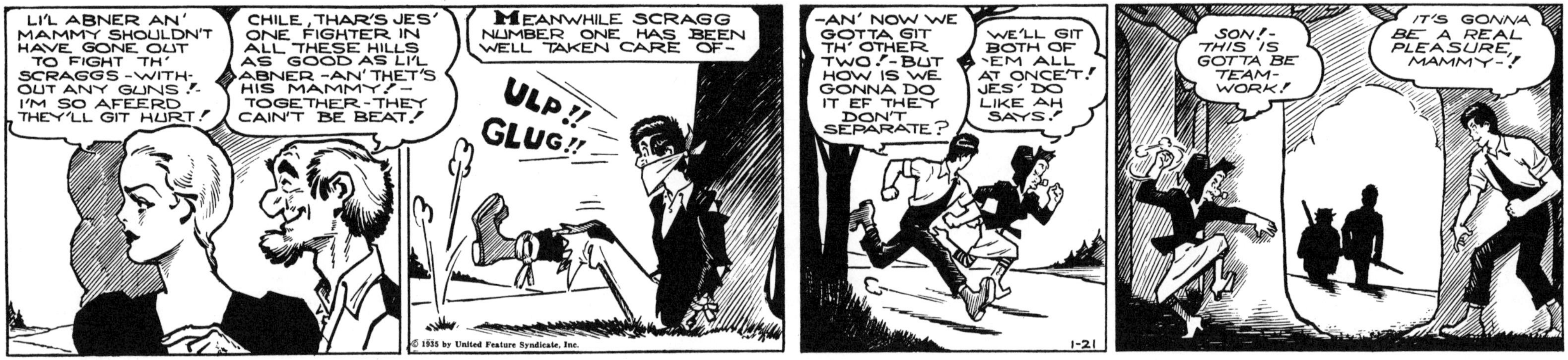

LI'L ABNER AN' MAMMY SHOULDN'T HAVE GONE OUT TO FIGHT TH' SCRAGGS - WITH-OUT ANY GUNS!- I'M SO AFEERD THEY'LL GIT HURT!
CHILE, THAR'S JES' ONE FIGHTER IN ALL THESE HILLS AS GOOD AS LI'L ABNER - AN' THET'S HIS MAMMY!- TOGETHER - THEY CAIN'T BE BEAT!
MEANWHILE SCRAGG NUMBER ONE HAS BEEN WELL TAKEN CARE OF-
ULP!! GLUG!!
© 1935 by United Feature Syndicate, Inc.
-AN' NOW WE GOTTA GIT TH' OTHER TWO!- BUT HOW IS WE GONNA DO IT EF THEY DON'T SEPARATE?
WE'LL GIT BOTH OF 'EM ALL AT ONCE'T! JES' DO LIKE AH SAYS!
1-21
SON!- THIS IS GOTTA BE TEAM-WORK!
IT'S GONNA BE A REAL PLEASURE, MAMMY-!

LI'L ABNER A Clean Victory By Al Capp

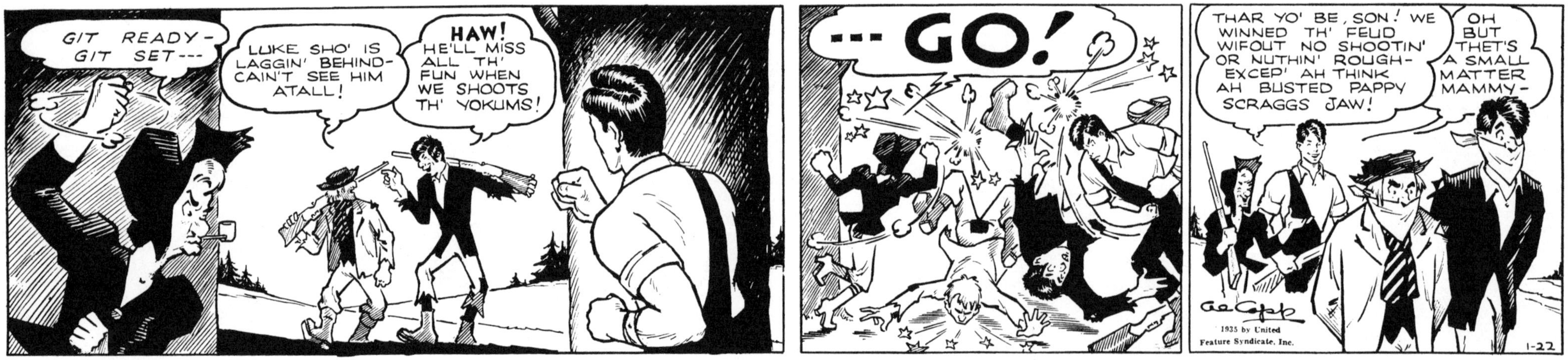

GIT READY- GIT SET---
LUKE SHO' IS LAGGIN' BEHIND- CAIN'T SEE HIM ATALL!
HAW! HE'LL MISS ALL TH' FUN WHEN WE SHOOTS TH' YOKUMS!
--- GO!
THAR YO' BE, SON! WE WINNED TH' FEUD WIFOUT NO SHOOTIN' OR NUTHIN' ROUGH- EXCEP' AH THINK AH BUSTED PAPPY SCRAGGS JAW!
OH BUT THET'S A SMALL MATTER MAMMY-
Al Capp
1935 by United Feature Syndicate, Inc.
1-22

LI'L ABNER So Long, Boys! By Al Capp

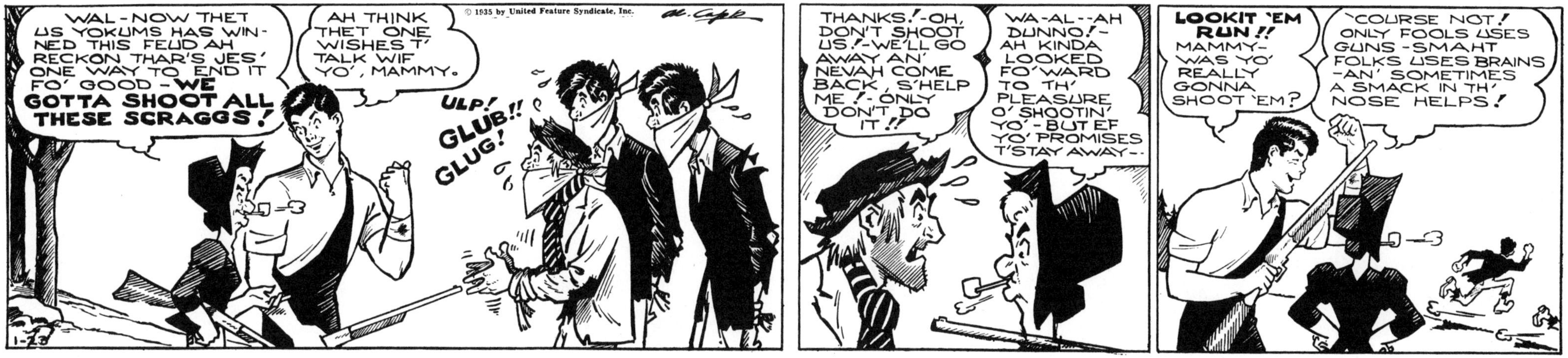

WAL - NOW THET US YOKUMS HAS WIN-NED THIS FEUD AH RECKON THAR'S JES' ONE WAY TO END IT FO' GOOD - **WE GOTTA SHOOT ALL THESE SCRAGGS!**
AH THINK THET ONE WISHES T' TALK WIF YO', MAMMY.
ULP!! GLUB!! GLUG!
© 1935 by United Feature Syndicate, Inc.
Al Capp
1-23
THANKS! - OH, DON'T SHOOT US! - WE'LL GO AWAY AN' NEVAH COME BACK, S'HELP ME! - ONLY DON'T DO IT!!
WA-AL - - AH DUNNO! - AH KINDA LOOKED FO'WARD TO TH' PLEASURE O' SHOOTIN' YO' - BUT EF YO' PROMISES T'STAY AWAY - -
LOOKIT 'EM RUN!! MAMMY - WAS YO' REALLY GONNA SHOOT 'EM?
'COURSE NOT! ONLY FOOLS USES GUNS - SMAHT FOLKS USES BRAINS - AN' SOMETIMES A SMACK IN TH' NOSE HELPS!

LI'L ABNER A Fast Worker By Al Capp

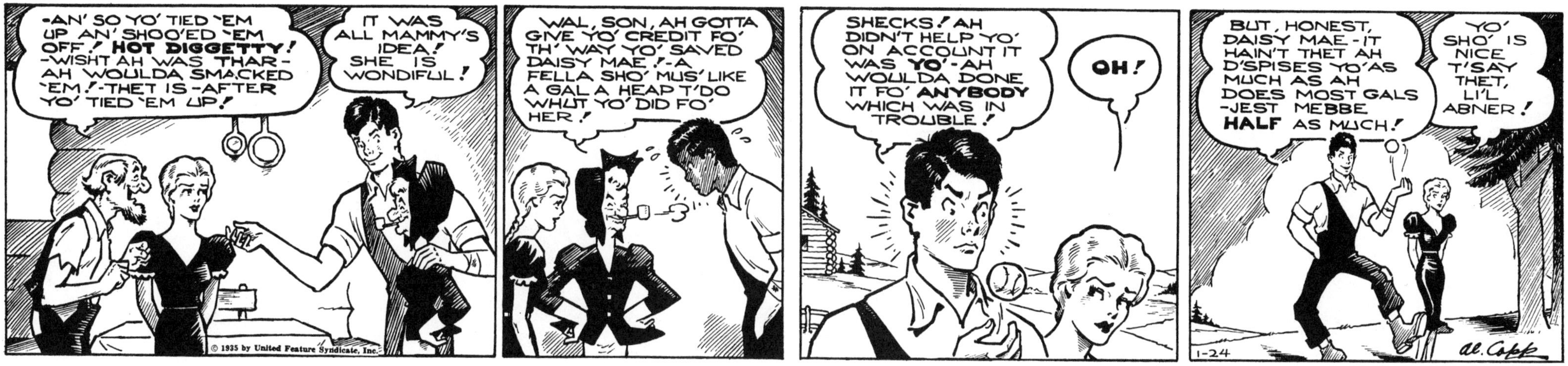

- AN' SO YO' TIED 'EM UP AN' SHOO'ED 'EM OFF! **HOT DIGGETTY!** - WISHT AH WAS THAR - AH WOULDA SMACKED 'EM! - THET IS - AFTER YO' TIED 'EM UP!
IT WAS ALL MAMMY'S IDEA! SHE IS WONDIFUL!
© 1935 by United Feature Syndicate, Inc.
WAL, SON, AH GOTTA GIVE YO' CREDIT FO' TH' WAY YO' SAVED DAISY MAE! - A FELLA SHO' MUS' LIKE A GAL A HEAP T'DO WHUT YO' DID FO' HER!
SHECKS! AH DIDN'T HELP YO' ON ACCOUNT IT WAS **YO'** - AH WOULDA DONE IT FO' **ANYBODY** WHICH WAS IN TROUBLE!
OH!
BUT, HONEST, DAISY MAE - IT HAIN'T THET AH D'SPISES YO' AS MUCH AS AH DOES MOST GALS - JEST MEBBE **HALF** AS MUCH!
YO' SHO' IS NICE T'SAY THET, LI'L ABNER!
1-24
Al Capp

LI'L ABNER Can't Yo' See, Abner ? By Al Capp

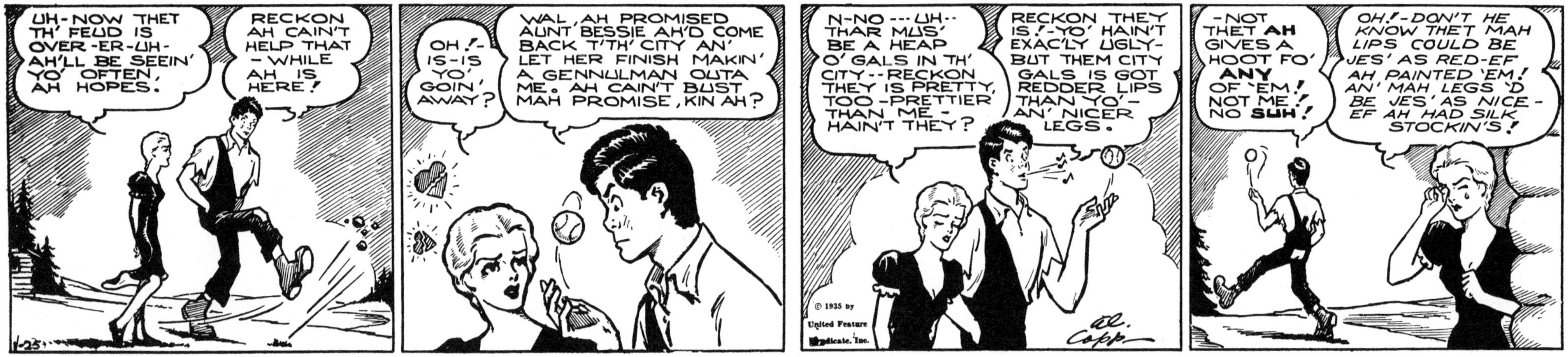
UH-NOW THET TH' FEUD IS OVER-ER-UH-AH'LL BE SEEIN' YO' OFTEN, AH HOPES.
RECKON AH CAIN'T HELP THAT -WHILE AH IS HERE!
1-25
OH!-IS-IS YO' GOIN' AWAY?
WAL, AH PROMISED AUNT BESSIE AH'D COME BACK T'TH' CITY AN' LET HER FINISH MAKIN' A GENNULMAN OUTA ME. AH CAIN'T BUST MAH PROMISE, KIN AH?
N-NO---UH--THAR MUS' BE A HEAP O' GALS IN TH' CITY--RECKON THEY IS PRETTY, TOO-PRETTIER THAN ME-HAIN'T THEY?
RECKON THEY IS!-YO' HAIN'T EXAC'LY UGLY-BUT THEM CITY GALS IS GOT REDDER LIPS THAN YO'-AN' NICER LEGS.
© 1935 by United Feature Syndicate, Inc.
AL CAPP
-NOT THET AH GIVES A HOOT FO' ANY OF 'EM! NOT ME! NO SUH!
OH!-DON'T HE KNOW THET MAH LIPS COULD BE JES' AS RED-EF AH PAINTED 'EM! AN' MAH LEGS 'D BE JES' AS NICE-EF AH HAD SILK STOCKIN'S!

LI'L ABNER Meet "Marryin' Sam" By Al Capp

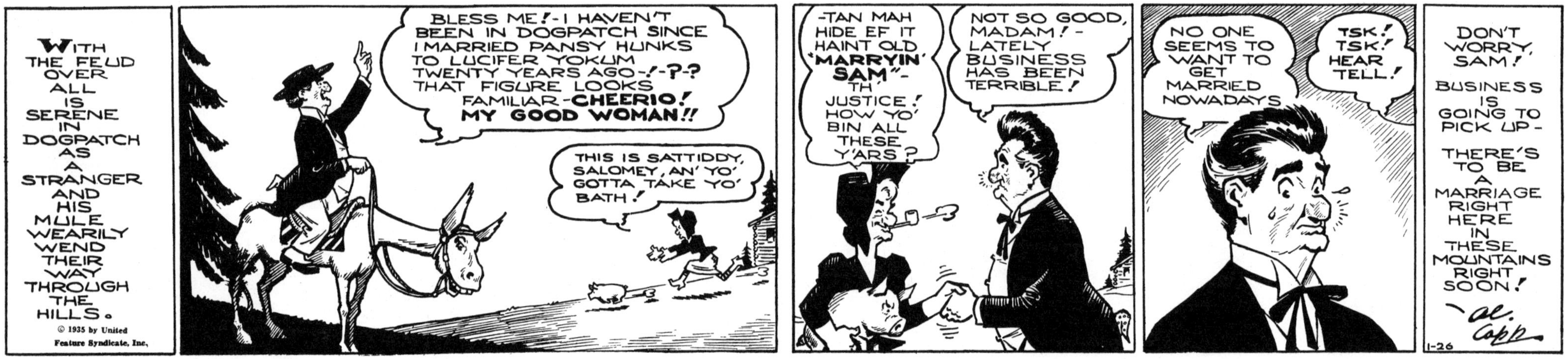
WITH THE FEUD OVER ALL IS SERENE IN DOGPATCH AS A STRANGER AND HIS MULE WEARILY WEND THEIR WAY THROUGH THE HILLS.
© 1935 by United Feature Syndicate, Inc.
BLESS ME!-I HAVEN'T BEEN IN DOGPATCH SINCE I MARRIED PANSY HUNKS TO LUCIFER YOKUM TWENTY YEARS AGO-!-?-? THAT FIGURE LOOKS FAMILIAR-CHEERIO! MY GOOD WOMAN!!
THIS IS SATTIDDY, SALOMEY, AN' YO' GOTTA TAKE YO' BATH!
-TAN MAH HIDE EF IT HAINT OLD "MARRYIN' SAM"-TH' JUSTICE! HOW YO' BIN ALL THESE Y'ARS?
NOT SO GOOD, MADAM!-LATELY BUSINESS HAS BEEN TERRIBLE!
NO ONE SEEMS TO WANT TO GET MARRIED NOWADAYS
TSK! TSK! HEAR TELL!
DON'T WORRY, SAM! BUSINESS IS GOING TO PICK UP-THERE'S TO BE A MARRIAGE RIGHT HERE IN THESE MOUNTAINS RIGHT SOON!
AL CAPP
1-26

LI'L ABNER

More About "Marryin' Sam"

By Al Capp

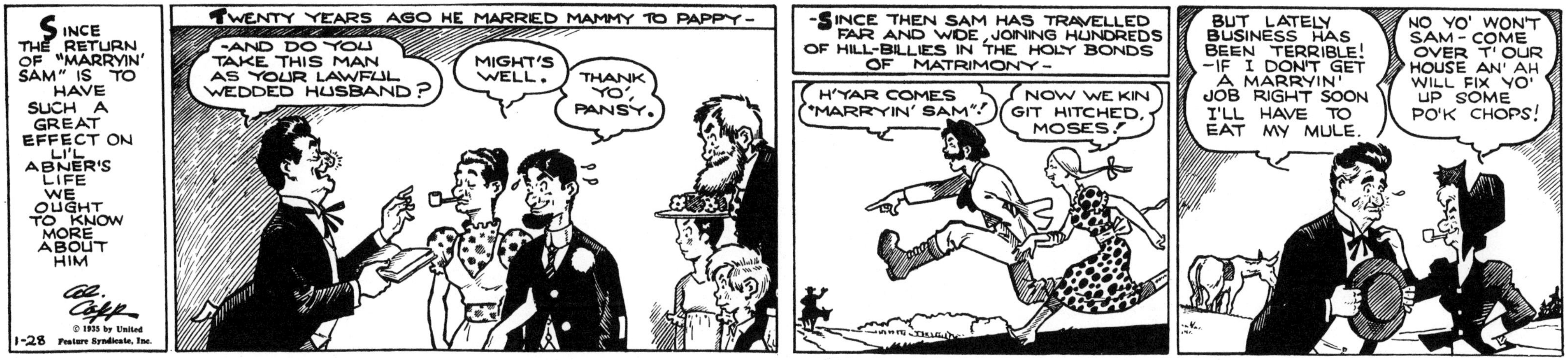
SINCE THE RETURN OF "MARRYIN' SAM" IS TO HAVE SUCH A GREAT EFFECT ON LI'L ABNER'S LIFE WE OUGHT TO KNOW MORE ABOUT HIM
Al. Capp
© 1935 by United Feature Syndicate, Inc.
1-28
TWENTY YEARS AGO HE MARRIED MAMMY TO PAPPY-
-AND DO YOU TAKE THIS MAN AS YOUR LAWFUL WEDDED HUSBAND?
MIGHT'S WELL.
THANK YO', PANSY.
-SINCE THEN SAM HAS TRAVELLED FAR AND WIDE, JOINING HUNDREDS OF HILL-BILLIES IN THE HOLY BONDS OF MATRIMONY-
H'YAR COMES "MARRYIN' SAM"!
NOW WE KIN GIT HITCHED, MOSES!
BUT LATELY BUSINESS HAS BEEN TERRIBLE! -IF I DON'T GET A MARRYIN' JOB RIGHT SOON I'LL HAVE TO EAT MY MULE.
NO YO' WON'T SAM - COME OVER T' OUR HOUSE AN' AH WILL FIX YO' UP SOME PO'K CHOPS!

LI'L ABNER

Dishonorable Intentions

By Al Capp

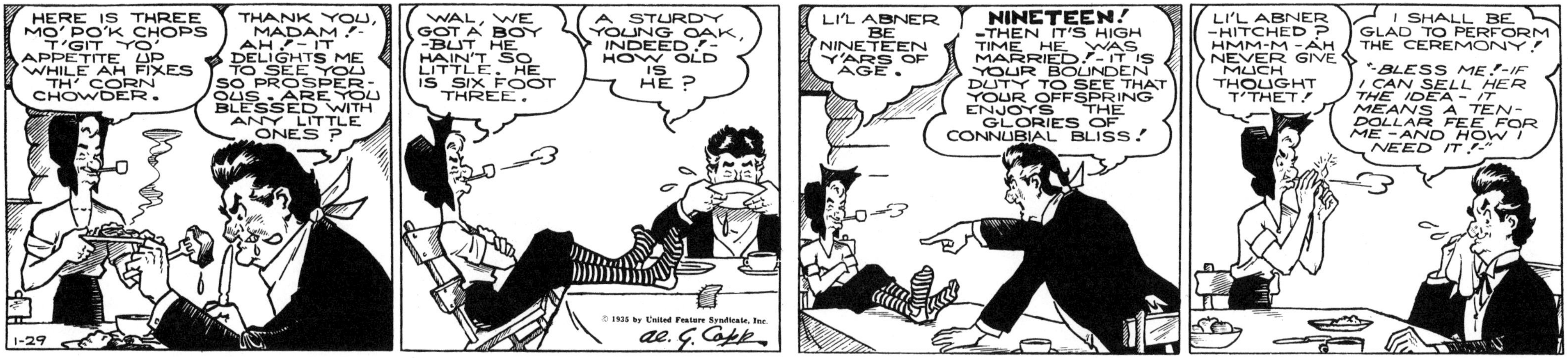
HERE IS THREE MO' PO'K CHOPS T'GIT YO' APPETITE UP WHILE AH FIXES TH' CORN CHOWDER.
THANK YOU, MADAM!- AH!- IT DELIGHTS ME TO SEE YOU SO PROSPER-OUS. ARE YOU BLESSED WITH ANY LITTLE ONES?
1-29
WAL, WE GOT A BOY -BUT HE HAIN'T SO LITTLE. HE IS SIX FOOT THREE.
A STURDY YOUNG OAK, INDEED!- HOW OLD IS HE?
© 1935 by United Feature Syndicate, Inc.
Al. G. Capp
LI'L ABNER BE NINETEEN Y'ARS OF AGE.
NINETEEN! -THEN IT'S HIGH TIME HE WAS MARRIED!- IT IS YOUR BOUNDEN DUTY TO SEE THAT YOUR OFFSPRING ENJOYS THE GLORIES OF CONNUBIAL BLISS!
LI'L ABNER -HITCHED? HMM-M -AH NEVER GIVE MUCH THOUGHT T'THET!
I SHALL BE GLAD TO PERFORM THE CEREMONY!
"-BLESS ME!- IF I CAN SELL HER THE IDEA - IT MEANS A TEN-DOLLAR FEE FOR ME - AND HOW I NEED IT!-"

LI'L ABNER A Soft Prospect By Al Capp

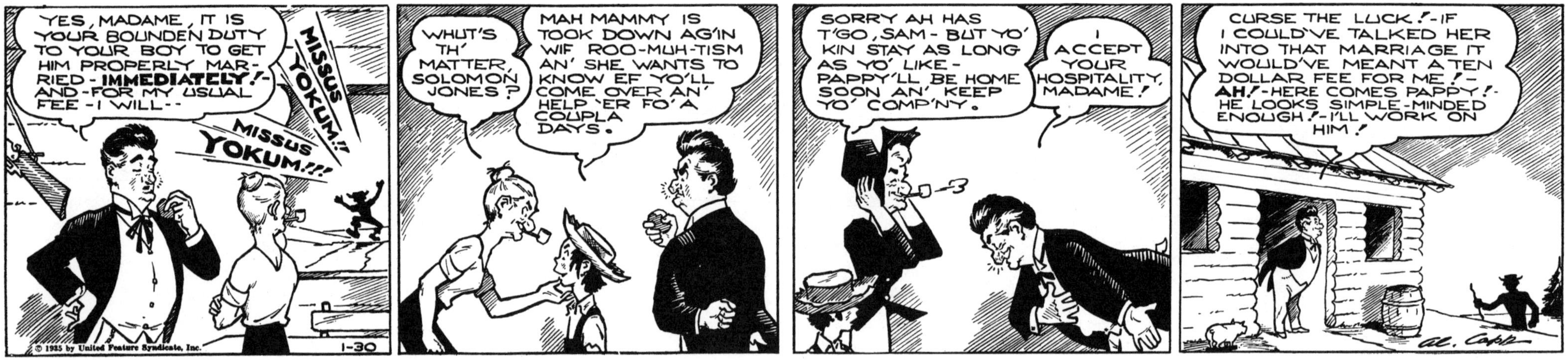

YES, MADAME, IT IS YOUR BOUNDEN DUTY TO YOUR BOY TO GET HIM PROPERLY MARRIED - IMMEDIATELY!- AND-FOR MY USUAL FEE - I WILL--
MISSUS YOKUM!!
MISSUS YOKUM!!!
© 1935 by United Feature Syndicate, Inc.
1-30
WHUT'S TH' MATTER, SOLOMON JONES?
MAH MAMMY IS TOOK DOWN AG'IN WIF ROO-MUH-TISM AN' SHE WANTS TO KNOW EF YO'LL COME OVER AN' HELP 'ER FO' A COUPLA DAYS.
SORRY AH HAS T'GO, SAM - BUT YO' KIN STAY AS LONG AS YO' LIKE - PAPPY'LL BE HOME SOON AN' KEEP YO' COMP'NY.
I ACCEPT YOUR HOSPITALITY, MADAME!
CURSE THE LUCK!- IF I COULD'VE TALKED HER INTO THAT MARRIAGE IT WOULD'VE MEANT A TEN DOLLAR FEE FOR ME!- AH!- HERE COMES PAPPY!- HE LOOKS SIMPLE-MINDED ENOUGH!- I'LL WORK ON HIM!
Al Capp

LI'L ABNER All Set To Go By Al Capp

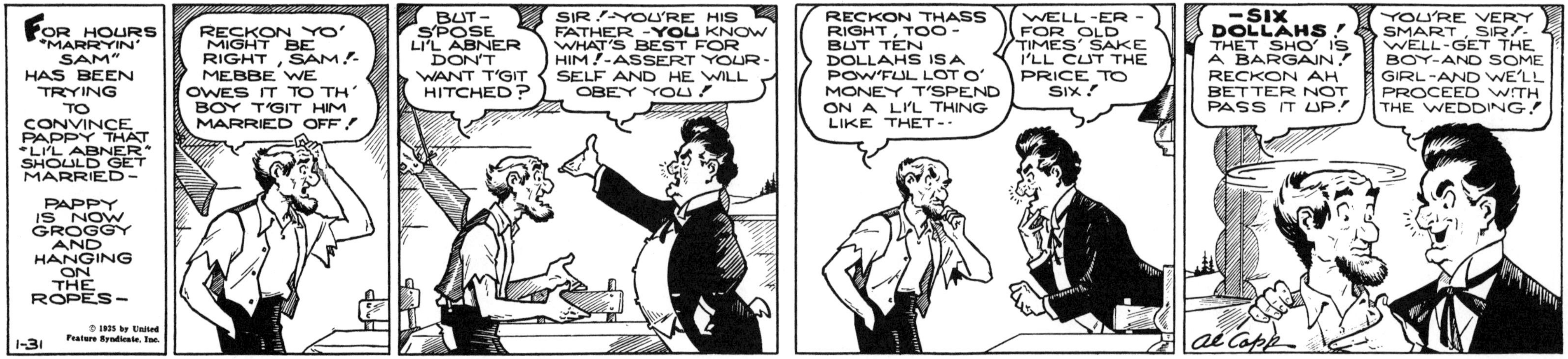

FOR HOURS "MARRYIN' SAM" HAS BEEN TRYING TO CONVINCE PAPPY THAT "LI'L ABNER" SHOULD GET MARRIED-
PAPPY IS NOW GROGGY AND HANGING ON THE ROPES-
© 1935 by United Feature Syndicate, Inc.
1-31
RECKON YO' MIGHT BE RIGHT, SAM!- MEBBE WE OWES IT TO TH' BOY T'GIT HIM MARRIED OFF!
BUT- S'POSE LI'L ABNER DON'T WANT T'GIT HITCHED?
SIR!- YOU'RE HIS FATHER - YOU KNOW WHAT'S BEST FOR HIM!- ASSERT YOURSELF AND HE WILL OBEY YOU!
RECKON THASS RIGHT, TOO- BUT TEN DOLLAHS IS A POW'FUL LOT O' MONEY T'SPEND ON A LI'L THING LIKE THET--
WELL-ER- FOR OLD TIMES' SAKE I'LL CUT THE PRICE TO SIX!
-SIX DOLLAHS! THET SHO' IS A BARGAIN! RECKON AH BETTER NOT PASS IT UP!
YOU'RE VERY SMART, SIR!- WELL-GET THE BOY-AND SOME GIRL-AND WE'LL PROCEED WITH THE WEDDING!
Al Capp

LI'L ABNER For Pappy's Sake

By Al Capp

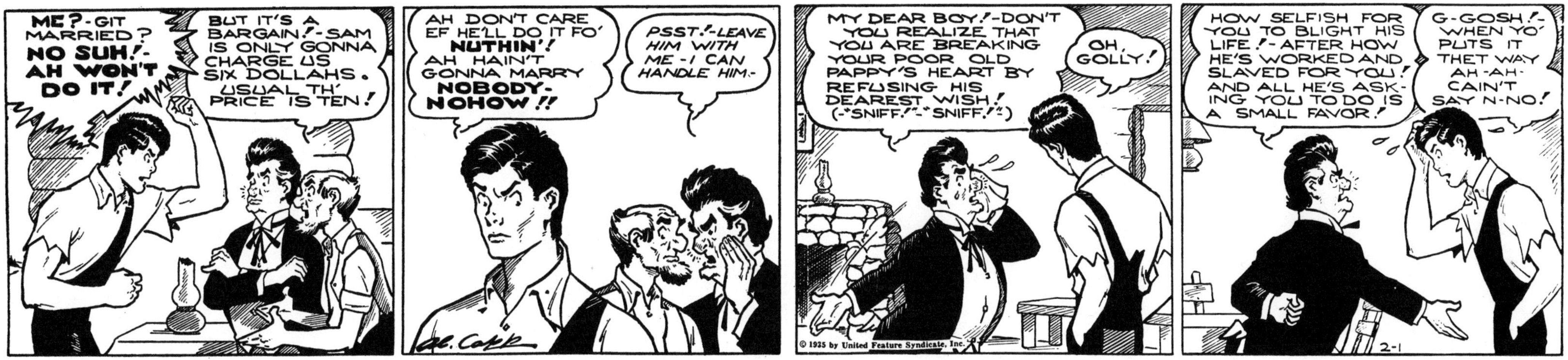
ME?-GIT MARRIED? NO SUH!-AH WON'T DO IT!
BUT IT'S A BARGAIN!-SAM IS ONLY GONNA CHARGE US SIX DOLLAHS. USUAL TH' PRICE IS TEN!
AH DON'T CARE EF HE'LL DO IT FO' NUTHIN'! AH HAIN'T GONNA MARRY NOBODY-NOHOW!!
PSST!-LEAVE HIM WITH ME-I CAN HANDLE HIM.-
Al. Capp
MY DEAR BOY!-DON'T YOU REALIZE THAT YOU ARE BREAKING YOUR POOR OLD PAPPY'S HEART BY REFUSING HIS DEAREST WISH! (-*SNIFF!*-*SNIFF!*-)
OH, GOLLY!
© 1935 by United Feature Syndicate, Inc.
HOW SELFISH FOR YOU TO BLIGHT HIS LIFE!-AFTER HOW HE'S WORKED AND SLAVED FOR YOU! AND ALL HE'S ASKING YOU TO DO IS A SMALL FAVOR!
G-GOSH!-WHEN YO' PUTS IT THET WAY AH-AH-CAIN'T SAY N-NO!
2-1

LI'L ABNER Now Thar's No Way Out

By Al Capp

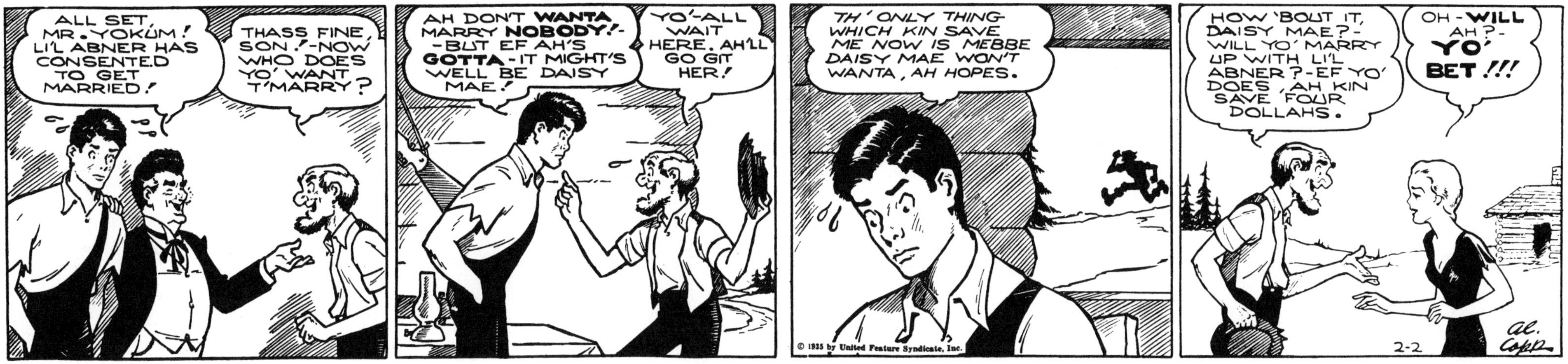
ALL SET, MR. YOKUM! LI'L ABNER HAS CONSENTED TO GET MARRIED!
THASS FINE, SON!-NOW WHO DOES YO' WANT T'MARRY?
AH DON'T WANTA MARRY NOBODY!--BUT EF AH'S GOTTA-IT MIGHT'S WELL BE DAISY MAE!
YO'-ALL WAIT HERE. AH'LL GO GIT HER!
TH' ONLY THING WHICH KIN SAVE ME NOW IS MEBBE DAISY MAE WON'T WANTA, AH HOPES.
© 1935 by United Feature Syndicate, Inc.
HOW 'BOUT IT, DAISY MAE?-WILL YO' MARRY UP WITH LI'L ABNER?-EF YO' DOES, AH KIN SAVE FOUR DOLLAHS.
OH-WILL AH?-YO' BET!!!
2-2
Al. Capp

LI'L ABNER The Happy Bridegroom **By Al Capp**

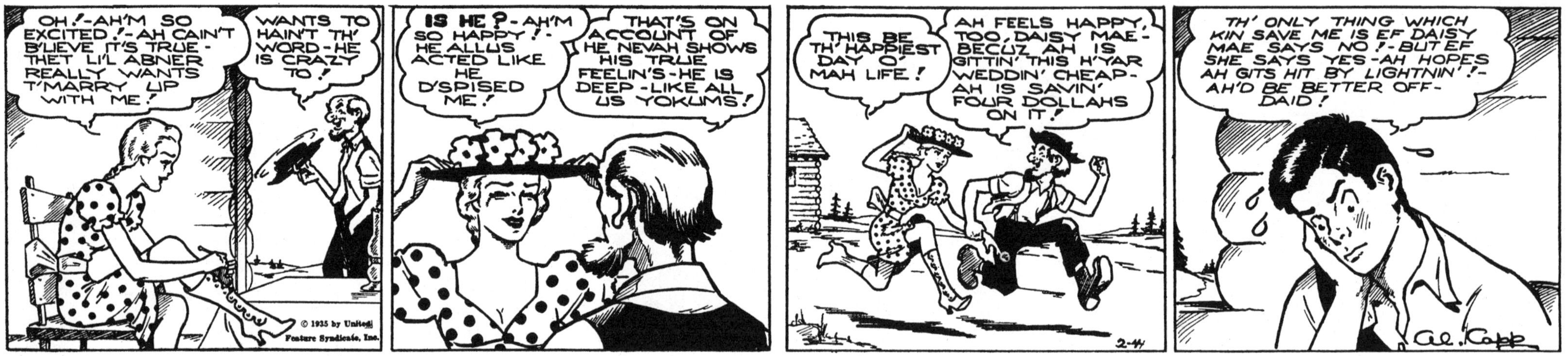

OH!-AH'M SO EXCITED!-AH CAIN'T B'LIEVE IT'S TRUE-THET LI'L ABNER REALLY WANTS T'MARRY UP WITH ME!
WANTS TO HAIN'T TH' WORD-HE IS CRAZY TO!
© 1935 by United Feature Syndicate, Inc.
IS HE?-AH'M SO HAPPY!-HE ALLUS ACTED LIKE HE D'SPISED ME!
THAT'S ON ACCOUNT OF HE NEVAH SHOWS HIS TRUE FEELIN'S-HE IS DEEP-LIKE ALL US YOKUMS!
THIS BE TH' HAPPIEST DAY O' MAH LIFE!
AH FEELS HAPPY, TOO, DAISY MAE-BECUZ AH IS GITTIN' THIS H'YAR WEDDIN' CHEAP-AH IS SAVIN' FOUR DOLLAHS ON IT!
2-4
TH' ONLY THING WHICH KIN SAVE ME IS EF DAISY MAE SAYS NO!-BUT EF SHE SAYS YES-AH HOPES AH GITS HIT BY LIGHTNIN'!-AH'D BE BETTER OFF-DAID!
Al. Capp

LI'L ABNER All Hope Is Lost! **By Al Capp**

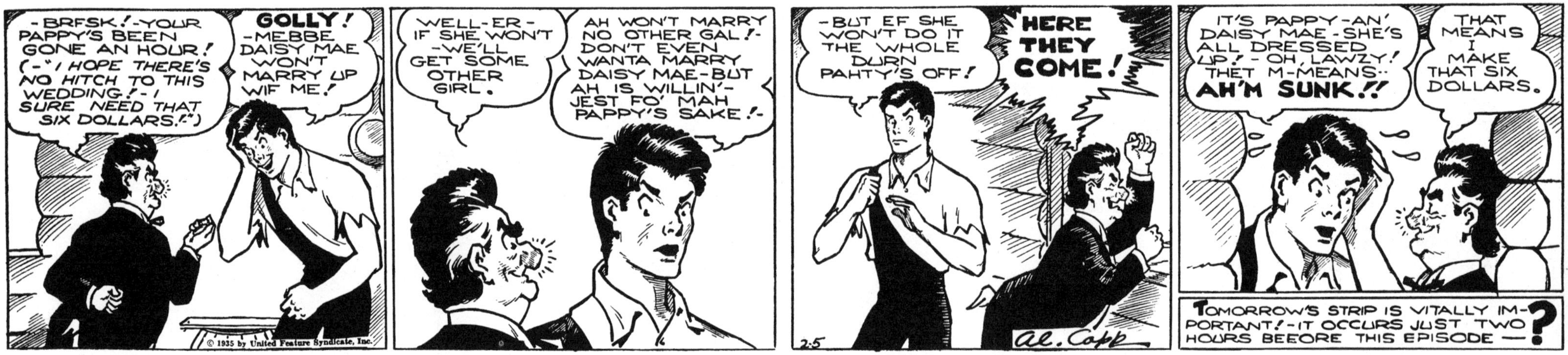

-BRFSK!-YOUR PAPPY'S BEEN GONE AN HOUR! (-"I HOPE THERE'S NO HITCH TO THIS WEDDING!-I SURE NEED THAT SIX DOLLARS!")
GOLLY!-MEBBE DAISY MAE WON'T MARRY UP WIF ME!
© 1935 by United Feature Syndicate, Inc.
WELL-ER-IF SHE WON'T-WE'LL GET SOME OTHER GIRL.
AH WON'T MARRY NO OTHER GAL!-DON'T EVEN WANTA MARRY DAISY MAE-BUT AH IS WILLIN'-JEST FO' MAH PAPPY'S SAKE!-
-BUT EF SHE WON'T DO IT THE WHOLE DURN PAHTY'S OFF!
HERE THEY COME!
2-5
Al. Capp
IT'S PAPPY-AN' DAISY MAE-SHE'S ALL DRESSED UP!-OH, LAWZY! THET M-MEANS-- AH'M SUNK!!
THAT MEANS I MAKE THAT SIX DOLLARS.
TOMORROW'S STRIP IS VITALLY IMPORTANT!-IT OCCURS JUST TWO HOURS BEEORE THIS EPISODE—?

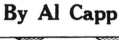

LI'L ABNER **Mammy Gits A Certain Feelin'** **By Al Capp**

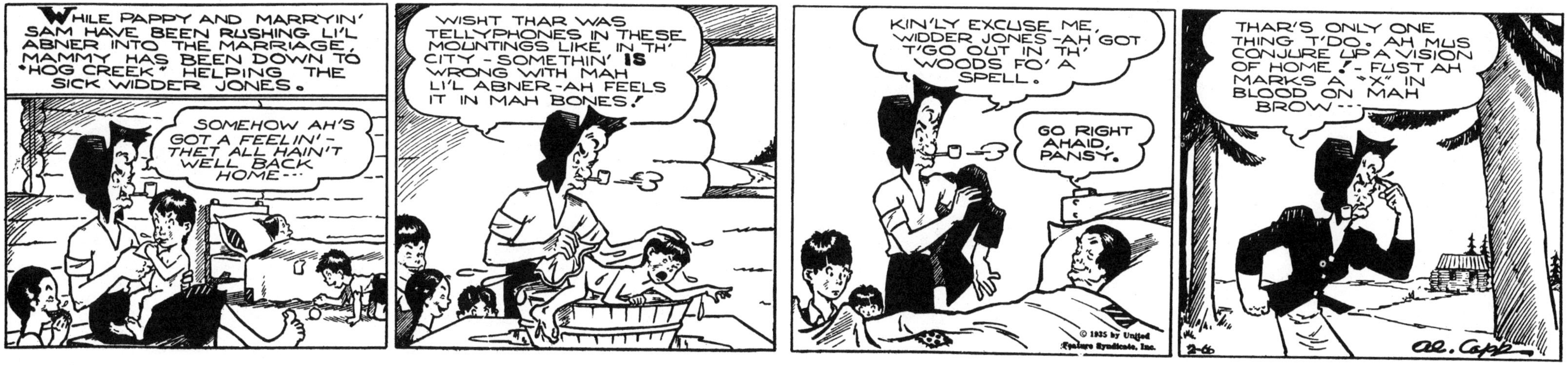

WHILE PAPPY AND MARRYIN' SAM HAVE BEEN RUSHING LI'L ABNER INTO THE MARRIAGE, MAMMY HAS BEEN DOWN TO "HOG CREEK" HELPING THE SICK WIDDER JONES.
SOMEHOW AH'S GOT A FEELIN' - THET ALL HAIN'T WELL BACK HOME---
WISHT THAR WAS TELLYPHONES IN THESE MOUNTINGS LIKE IN TH' CITY - SOMETHIN' IS WRONG WITH MAH LI'L ABNER - AH FEELS IT IN MAH BONES!
KIN'LY EXCUSE ME, WIDDER JONES - AH GOT T'GO OUT IN TH' WOODS FO' A SPELL.
GO RIGHT AHAID, PANSY.
© 1935 by United Feature Syndicate, Inc.
THAR'S ONLY ONE THING T'DO. AH MUS CONJURE UP A VISION OF HOME! - FUST AH MARKS A "X" IN BLOOD ON MAH BROW---
2-6
Al. Capp

LI'L ABNER **Mammy Swings Into Action** **By Al Capp**

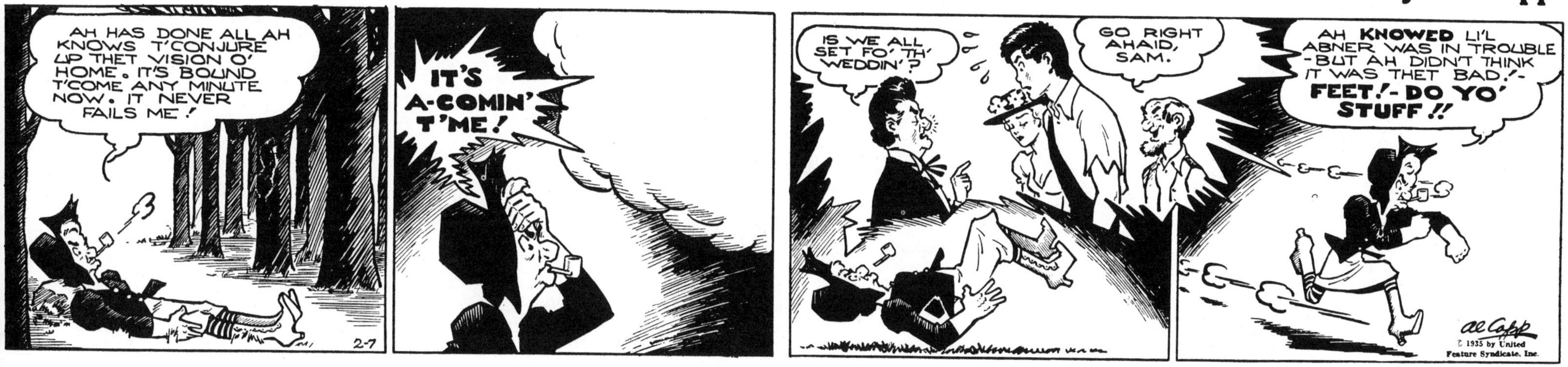

AH HAS DONE ALL AH KNOWS T'CONJURE UP THET VISION O' HOME. IT'S BOUND T'COME ANY MINUTE NOW. IT NEVER FAILS ME!
2-7
IT'S A-COMIN' T'ME!
IS WE ALL SET FO' TH' WEDDIN'?
GO RIGHT AHAID, SAM.
AH KNOWED LI'L ABNER WAS IN TROUBLE - BUT AH DIDN'T THINK IT WAS THET BAD! - FEET! - DO YO' STUFF!!
Al Capp
© 1935 by United Feature Syndicate, Inc.

LI'L ABNER Sam Tries To Pull A Fast One **By Al Capp**

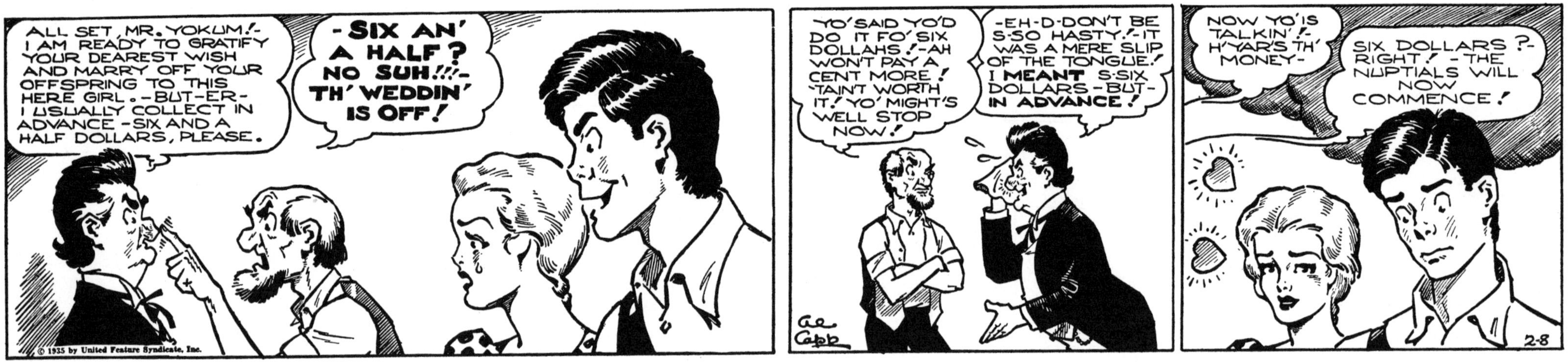
ALL SET, MR. YOKUM!- I AM READY TO GRATIFY YOUR DEAREST WISH AND MARRY OFF YOUR OFFSPRING TO THIS HERE GIRL.-BUT-ER- I USUALLY COLLECT IN ADVANCE -SIX AND A HALF DOLLARS, PLEASE.
-SIX AN' A HALF? NO SUH!!!- TH' WEDDIN' IS OFF!
© 1935 by United Feature Syndicate, Inc.
YO' SAID YO'D DO IT FO' SIX DOLLAHS!-AH WON'T PAY A CENT MORE! 'TAIN'T WORTH IT! YO' MIGHT'S WELL STOP NOW!
-EH-D-DON'T BE S-SO HASTY!-IT WAS A MERE SLIP OF THE TONGUE! I MEANT S-SIX DOLLARS-BUT- IN ADVANCE!
AL CAPP
NOW YO'IS TALKIN'!- H'YAR'S TH' MONEY-
SIX DOLLARS?- RIGHT! -THE NUPTIALS WILL NOW COMMENCE!
2-8

LI'L ABNER The Unexpected Guest **By Al Capp**

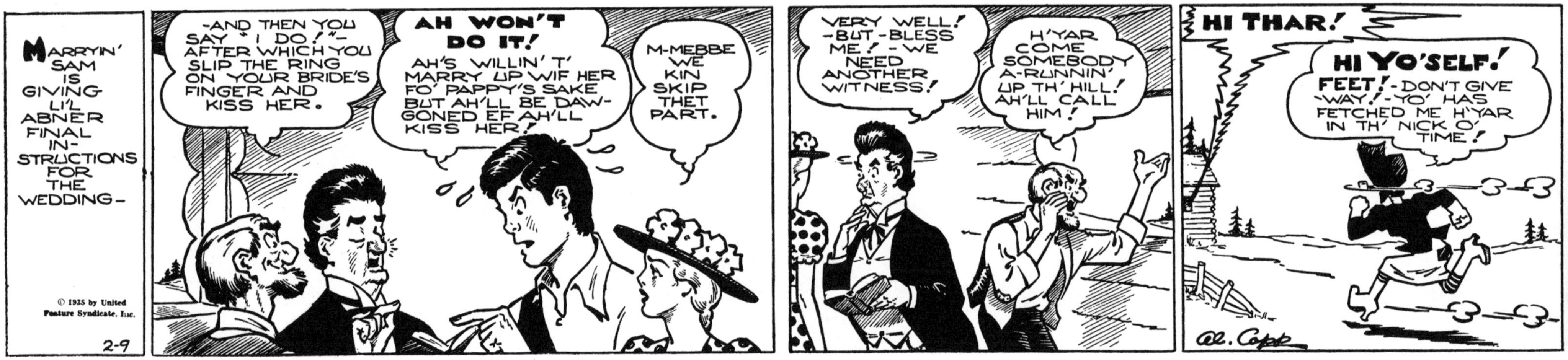
MARRYIN' SAM IS GIVING LI'L ABNER FINAL IN-STRUCTIONS FOR THE WEDDING-
© 1935 by United Feature Syndicate, Inc.
2-9
-AND THEN YOU SAY "I DO!"- AFTER WHICH YOU SLIP THE RING ON YOUR BRIDE'S FINGER AND KISS HER.
AH WON'T DO IT! AH'S WILLIN' T' MARRY UP WIF HER FO' PAPPY'S SAKE BUT AH'LL BE DAW-GONED EF AH'LL KISS HER!
M-MEBBE WE KIN SKIP THET PART.
VERY WELL! -BUT-BLESS ME!-WE NEED ANOTHER WITNESS!
H'YAR COME SOMEBODY A-RUNNIN' UP TH' HILL! AH'LL CALL HIM!
HI THAR!
HI YO'SELF! FEET!-DON'T GIVE -WAY!-YO' HAS FETCHED ME H'YAR IN TH' NICK O' TIME!
AL. CAPP

LI'L ABNER You Cain't Put Sam Down By Al Capp

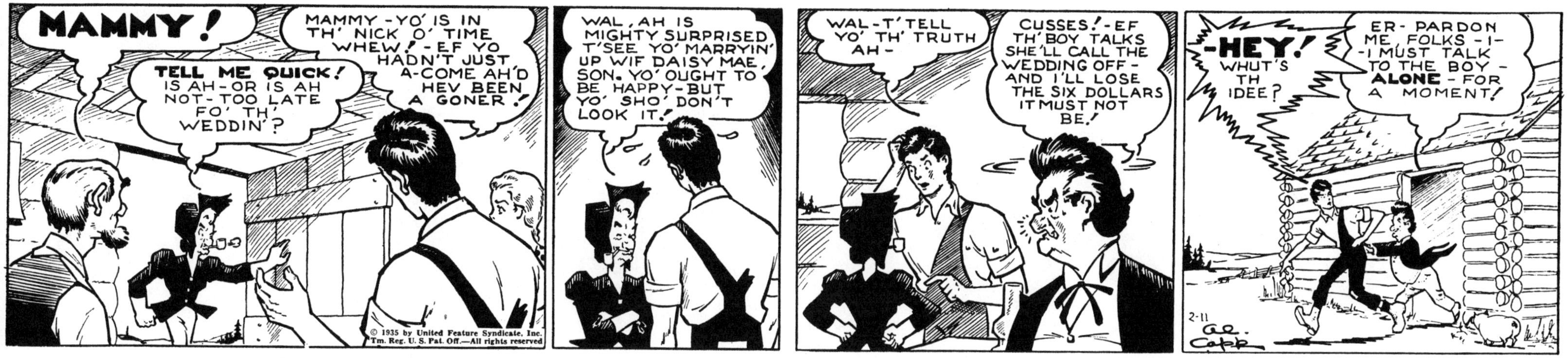
MAMMY!
TELL ME QUICK! IS AH-OR IS AH NOT-TOO LATE FO' TH' WEDDIN'?
MAMMY-YO' IS IN TH' NICK O' TIME WHEW!-EF YO HADN'T JUST A-COME AH'D HEV BEEN A GONER!
© 1935 by United Feature Syndicate, Inc. Tm. Reg. U. S. Pat. Off.—All rights reserved
WAL, AH IS MIGHTY SURPRISED T'SEE YO' MARRYIN' UP WIF DAISY MAE, SON. YO' OUGHT TO BE HAPPY-BUT YO' SHO' DON'T LOOK IT!
WAL-T'TELL YO' TH' TRUTH AH-
CUSSES!-EF TH' BOY TALKS SHE'LL CALL THE WEDDING OFF-AND I'LL LOSE THE SIX DOLLARS IT MUST NOT BE!
-HEY! WHUT'S TH IDEE?
ER-PARDON ME, FOLKS-I--I MUST TALK TO THE BOY-ALONE-FOR A MOMENT!
2-11
Al Capp

LI'L ABNER The Spider and the Fly By Al Capp

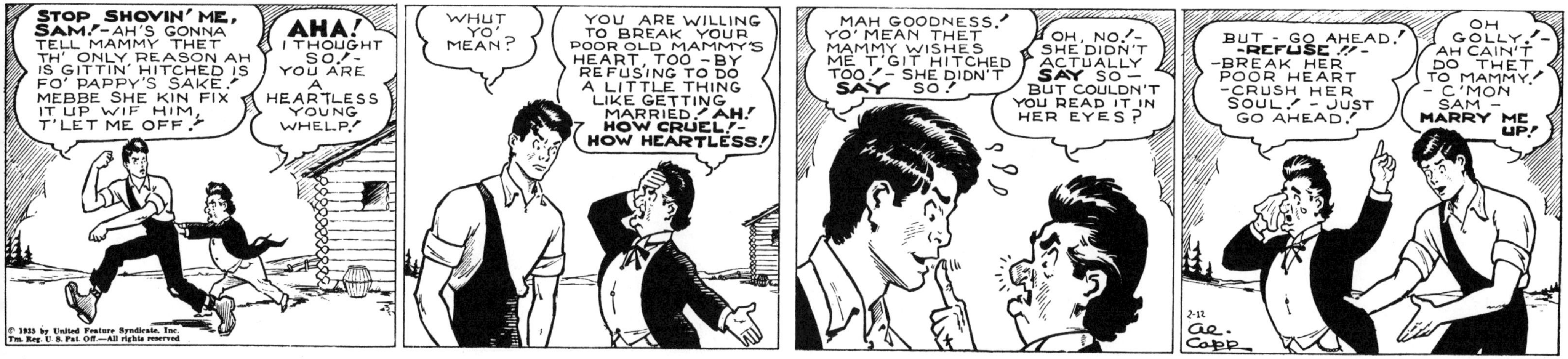
STOP SHOVIN' ME, SAM!-AH'S GONNA TELL MAMMY THET TH' ONLY REASON AH IS GITTIN' HITCHED IS FO' PAPPY'S SAKE!-MEBBE SHE KIN FIX IT UP WIF HIM, T'LET ME OFF!
AHA! I THOUGHT SO!-YOU ARE A HEARTLESS YOUNG WHELP!
© 1935 by United Feature Syndicate, Inc. Tm. Reg. U. S. Pat. Off.—All rights reserved
WHUT YO' MEAN?
YOU ARE WILLING TO BREAK YOUR POOR OLD MAMMY'S HEART, TOO-BY REFUSING TO DO A LITTLE THING LIKE GETTING MARRIED! AH! HOW CRUEL!-HOW HEARTLESS!
MAH GOODNESS! YO' MEAN THET MAMMY WISHES ME T'GIT HITCHED TOO!-SHE DIDN'T SAY SO!
OH, NO!-SHE DIDN'T ACTUALLY SAY SO-BUT COULDN'T YOU READ IT IN HER EYES?
BUT-GO AHEAD! -REFUSE!!- -BREAK HER POOR HEART -CRUSH HER SOUL!-JUST GO AHEAD!
OH GOLLY!-AH CAIN'T DO THET TO MAMMY!-C'MON SAM-MARRY ME UP!
2-12
Al Capp

LI'L ABNER Like A Lamb To the Slaughter By Al Capp

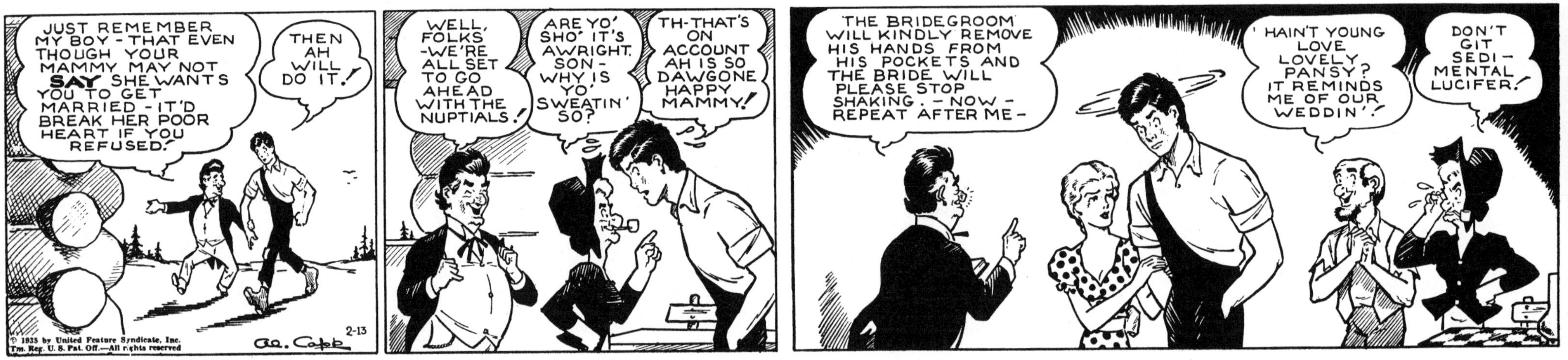

JUST REMEMBER MY BOY - THAT EVEN THOUGH YOUR MAMMY MAY NOT SAY SHE WANTS YOU TO GET MARRIED - IT'D BREAK HER POOR HEART IF YOU REFUSED!
THEN AH WILL DO IT!
© 1935 by United Feature Syndicate, Inc. Tm. Reg. U. S. Pat. Off.—All rights reserved
AL CAPP
2-13
WELL, FOLKS -WE'RE ALL SET TO GO AHEAD WITH THE NUPTIALS!
ARE YO' SHO' IT'S AWRIGHT, SON - WHY IS YO' SWEATIN' SO?
TH-THAT'S ON ACCOUNT AH IS SO DAWGONE HAPPY MAMMY!
THE BRIDEGROOM WILL KINDLY REMOVE HIS HANDS FROM HIS POCKETS AND THE BRIDE WILL PLEASE STOP SHAKING. - NOW - REPEAT AFTER ME -
HAIN'T YOUNG LOVE LOVELY, PANSY? IT REMINDS ME OF OUR WEDDIN'!
DON'T GIT SEDI-MENTAL LUCIFER!

LI'L ABNER Some People Might Like It By Al Capp

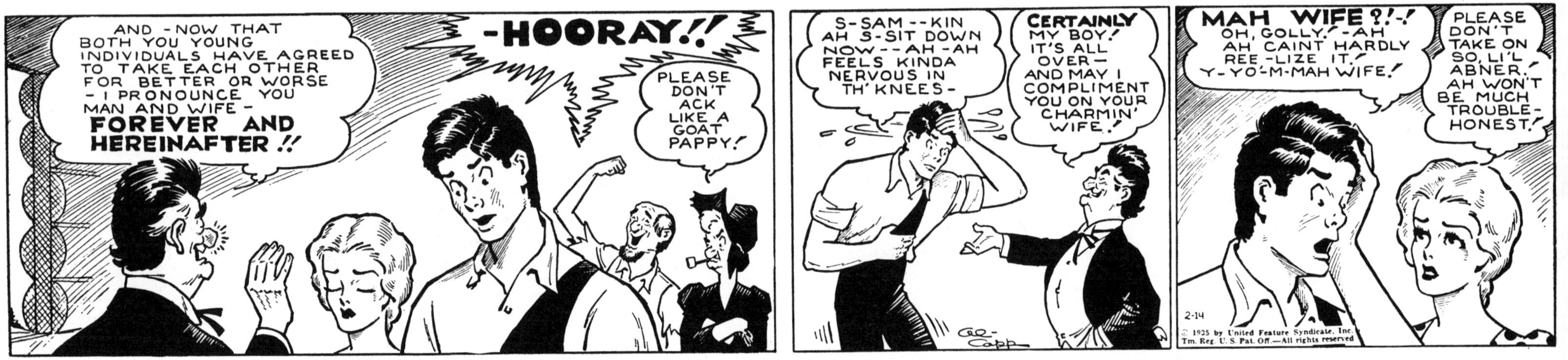

AND - NOW THAT BOTH YOU YOUNG INDIVIDUALS HAVE AGREED TO TAKE EACH OTHER FOR BETTER OR WORSE - I PRONOUNCE YOU MAN AND WIFE - FOREVER AND HEREINAFTER!!
-HOORAY!!
PLEASE DON'T ACK LIKE A GOAT PAPPY!
S-SAM--KIN AH S-SIT DOWN NOW--AH-AH FEELS KINDA NERVOUS IN TH' KNEES-
CERTAINLY MY BOY! IT'S ALL OVER - AND MAY I COMPLIMENT YOU ON YOUR CHARMIN' WIFE!
AL CAPP
MAH WIFE?!-! OH, GOLLY! -AH AH CAINT HARDLY REE-LIZE IT! Y-YO'-M-MAH WIFE!
PLEASE DON'T TAKE ON SO, LI'L ABNER! AH WON'T BE MUCH TROUBLE-HONEST!
2-14
© 1935 by United Feature Syndicate, Inc. Tm. Reg. U. S. Pat. Off.—All rights reserved

LI'L ABNER Something's Up ! ? By Al Capp

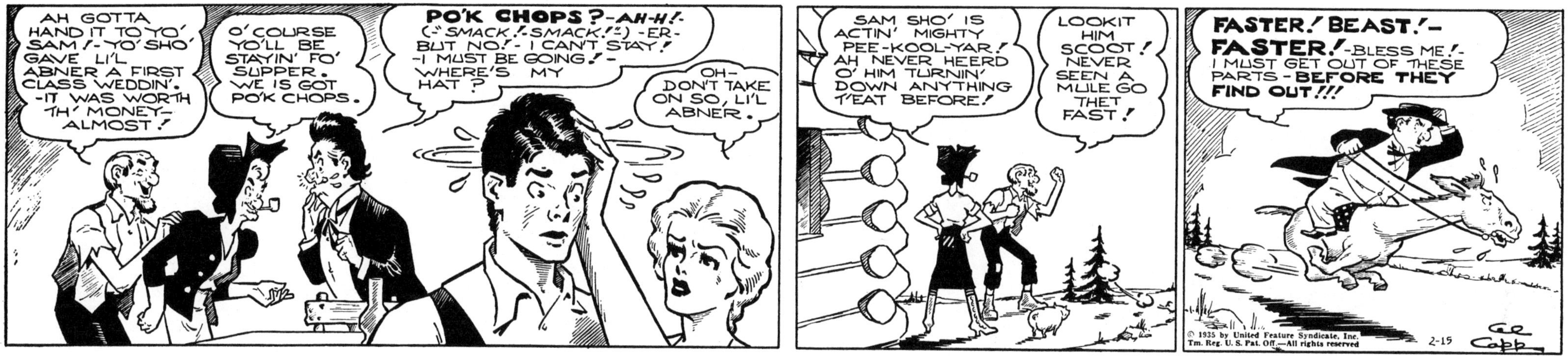

AH GOTTA HAND IT TO YO' SAM !- YO' SHO' GAVE LI'L ABNER A FIRST CLASS WEDDIN'. -IT WAS WORTH TH' MONEY- ALMOST !
O' COURSE YO'LL BE STAYIN' FO' SUPPER. WE IS GOT PO'K CHOPS.
PO'K CHOPS ?-AH-H !- (-" SMACK !- SMACK !"-) -ER- BUT NO !- I CAN'T STAY ! -I MUST BE GOING !- WHERE'S MY HAT ?
OH- DON'T TAKE ON SO, LI'L ABNER.
SAM SHO' IS ACTIN' MIGHTY PEE-KOOL-YAR ! AH NEVER HEERD O' HIM TURNIN' DOWN ANYTHING T'EAT BEFORE !
LOOKIT HIM SCOOT ! NEVER SEEN A MULE GO THET FAST !
FASTER ! BEAST !- FASTER !- BLESS ME !- I MUST GET OUT OF THESE PARTS - BEFORE THEY FIND OUT !!!
© 1935 by United Feature Syndicate, Inc. Tm. Reg. U. S. Pat. Off.—All rights reserved
2-15
Al Capp

LI'L ABNER Maybe It Warn't A Bargain By Al Capp

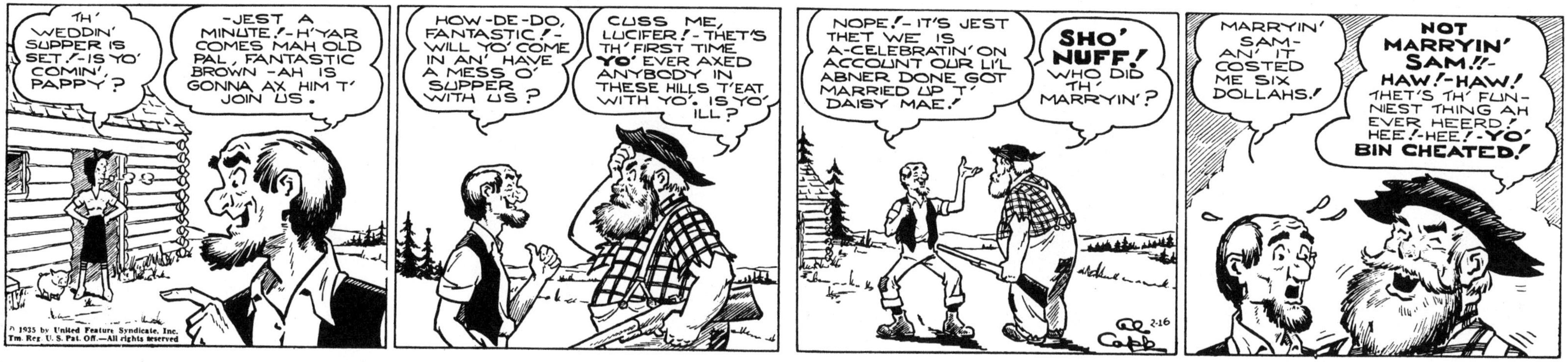

TH' WEDDIN' SUPPER IS SET !- IS YO' COMIN', PAPPY ?
-JEST A MINUTE !- H'YAR COMES MAH OLD PAL, FANTASTIC BROWN - AH IS GONNA AX HIM T' JOIN US.
© 1935 by United Feature Syndicate, Inc. Tm. Reg. U. S. Pat. Off.—All rights reserved
HOW-DE-DO, FANTASTIC !- WILL YO' COME IN AN' HAVE A MESS O' SUPPER WITH US ?
CUSS ME, LUCIFER !- THET'S TH' FIRST TIME YO' EVER AXED ANYBODY IN THESE HILLS T'EAT WITH YO'. IS YO' ILL ?
NOPE !- IT'S JEST THET WE IS A-CELEBRATIN' ON ACCOUNT OUR LI'L ABNER DONE GOT MARRIED UP T' DAISY MAE.
SHO' NUFF ! WHO DID TH' MARRYIN' ?
2-16
Al Capp
MARRYIN' SAM- AN' IT COSTED ME SIX DOLLAHS.
NOT MARRYIN' SAM !!- HAW !- HAW ! THET'S TH' FUN- NIEST THING AH EVER HEERD ! HEE !- HEE !- YO' BIN CHEATED !

LI'L ABNER A Swell Wedding Present By Al Capp

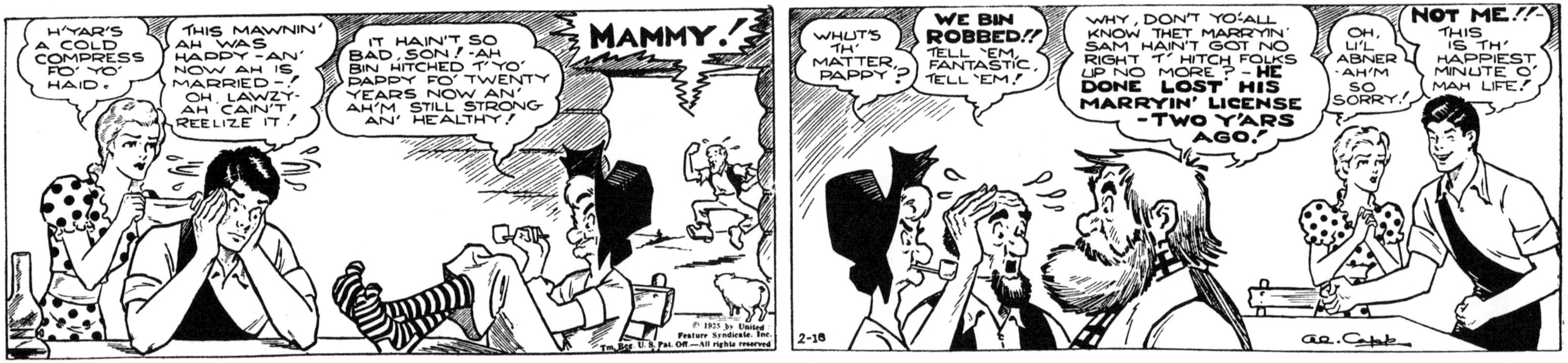

H'YAR'S A COLD COMPRESS FO' YO' HAID.
THIS MAWNIN' AH WAS HAPPY - AN' NOW AH IS MARRIED - ! OH, LAWZY - AH CAIN'T REELIZE IT!
IT HAIN'T SO BAD, SON! - AH BIN HITCHED T' YO' PAPPY FO' TWENTY YEARS NOW AN' AH'M STILL STRONG AN' HEALTHY!
MAMMY!
© 1935 by United Feature Syndicate, Inc. Tm. Reg. U. S. Pat. Off.—All rights reserved
WHUT'S TH' MATTER, PAPPY?
WE BIN ROBBED!! TELL 'EM, FANTASTIC, TELL 'EM!
WHY, DON'T YO'-ALL KNOW THET MARRYIN' SAM HAIN'T GOT NO RIGHT T' HITCH FOLKS UP NO MORE? - HE DONE LOST HIS MARRYIN' LICENSE - TWO Y'ARS AGO!
OH, LI'L ABNER - AH'M SO SORRY!
NOT ME!! - THIS IS TH' HAPPIEST MINUTE O' MAH LIFE!
2-18
AL. CAPP

LI'L ABNER Is Ah—Oh Is Ah Haint ? By Al Capp

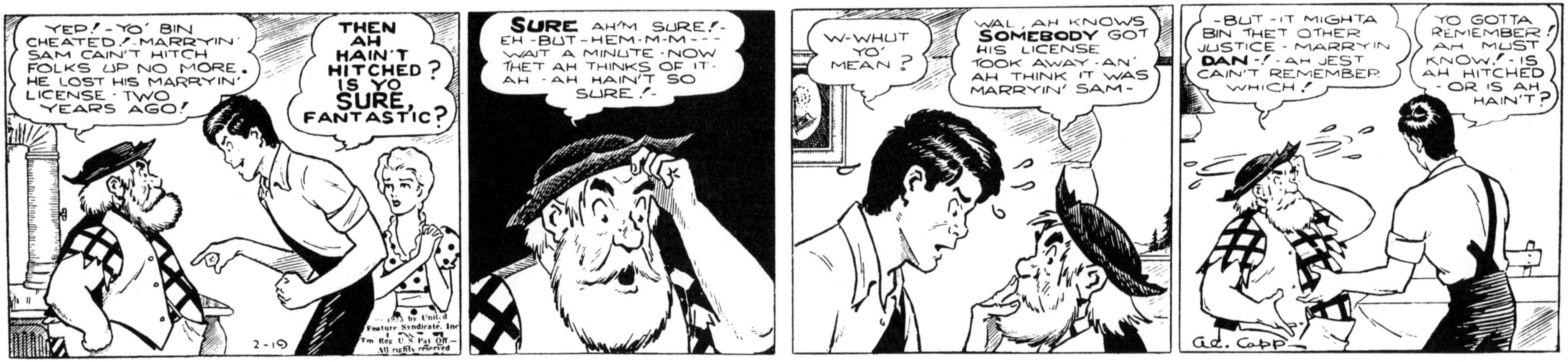

YEP! - YO' BIN CHEATED! - MARRYIN' SAM CAIN'T HITCH FOLKS UP NO MORE. HE LOST HIS MARRYIN' LICENSE - TWO YEARS AGO!
THEN AH HAIN'T HITCHED? IS YO SURE, FANTASTIC?
2-19
© 1935 by United Feature Syndicate, Inc Tm Reg U S Pat Off.— All rights reserved
SURE AH'M SURE! - EH - BUT - HEM - M - M - - - WAIT A MINUTE - NOW THET AH THINKS OF IT - AH - AH HAIN'T SO SURE! -
W-WHUT YO' MEAN?
WAL, AH KNOWS SOMEBODY GOT HIS LICENSE TOOK AWAY - AN' AH THINK IT WAS MARRYIN' SAM -
- BUT - IT MIGHTA BIN THET OTHER JUSTICE - MARRYIN DAN - ! - AH JEST CAIN'T REMEMBER WHICH!
YO GOTTA REMEMBER! AH MUST KNOW! - IS AH HITCHED - OR IS AH HAIN'T?
AL. CAPP

LI'L ABNER His Weakest Point By Al Capp

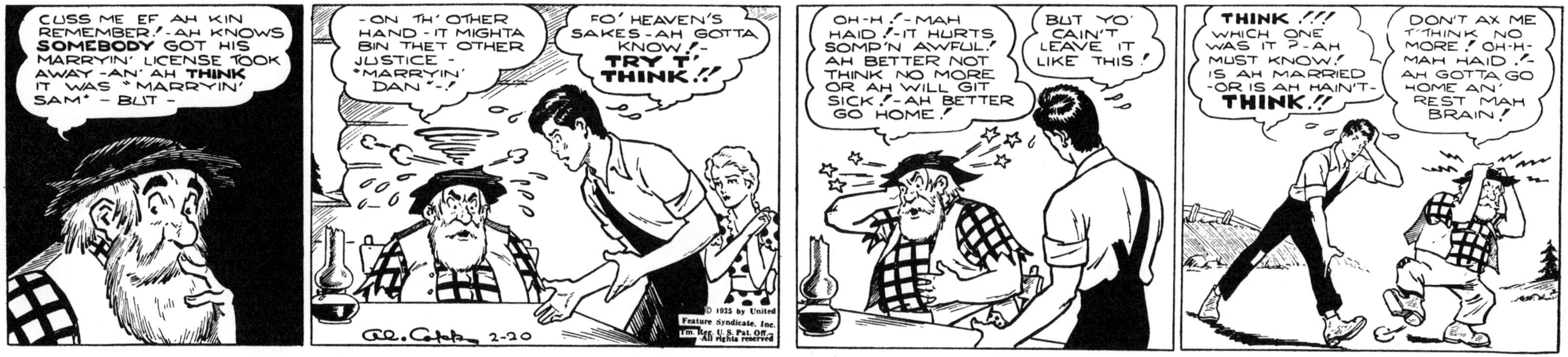

CUSS ME EF AH KIN REMEMBER!-AH KNOWS **SOMEBODY** GOT HIS MARRYIN' LICENSE TOOK AWAY-AN' AH **THINK** IT WAS "MARRYIN' SAM" - BUT -
-ON TH' OTHER HAND-IT MIGHTA BIN THET OTHER JUSTICE - "MARRYIN' DAN"-!
FO' HEAVEN'S SAKES-AH GOTTA KNOW!- **TRY T' THINK!!**
2-20
© 1935 by United Feature Syndicate, Inc. Tm. Reg. U. S. Pat. Off.—All rights reserved
OH-H!-MAH HAID!-IT HURTS SOMP'N AWFUL! AH BETTER NOT THINK NO MORE OR AH WILL GIT SICK!-AH BETTER GO HOME!
BUT YO' CAIN'T LEAVE IT LIKE THIS!
THINK!!! WHICH ONE WAS IT?-AH MUST KNOW! IS AH MARRIED -OR IS AH HAIN'T- **THINK!!**
DON'T AX ME T'THINK NO MORE! OH-H-MAH HAID!-AH GOTTA GO HOME AN' REST MAH BRAIN!

LI'L ABNER Bridegroom Or Bachelor? By Al Capp

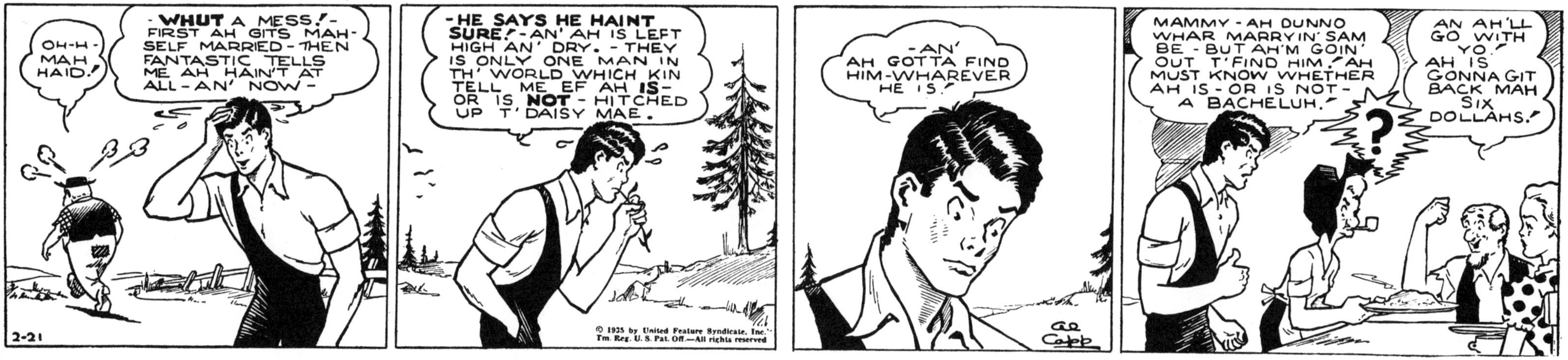

OH-H-MAH HAID!
-**WHUT** A MESS!-FIRST AH GITS MAH-SELF MARRIED-THEN FANTASTIC TELLS ME AH HAIN'T AT ALL-AN' NOW-
2-21
-**HE SAYS HE HAINT SURE!**-AN' AH IS LEFT HIGH AN' DRY.-THEY IS ONLY ONE MAN IN TH' WORLD WHICH KIN TELL ME EF AH **IS**-OR IS **NOT**-HITCHED UP T' DAISY MAE.
© 1935 by United Feature Syndicate, Inc. Tm. Reg. U. S. Pat. Off.—All rights reserved
-AN' AH GOTTA FIND HIM-WHAREVER HE IS!
Al Capp
MAMMY-AH DUNNO WHAR MARRYIN' SAM BE-BUT AH'M GOIN' OUT T'FIND HIM! AH MUST KNOW WHETHER AH IS-OR IS NOT-A BACHELUH!
?
AN AH'LL GO WITH YO'! AH IS GONNA GIT BACK MAH SIX DOLLAHS!

LI'L ABNER Yo' Cain't Fool Him Twice! By Al Capp

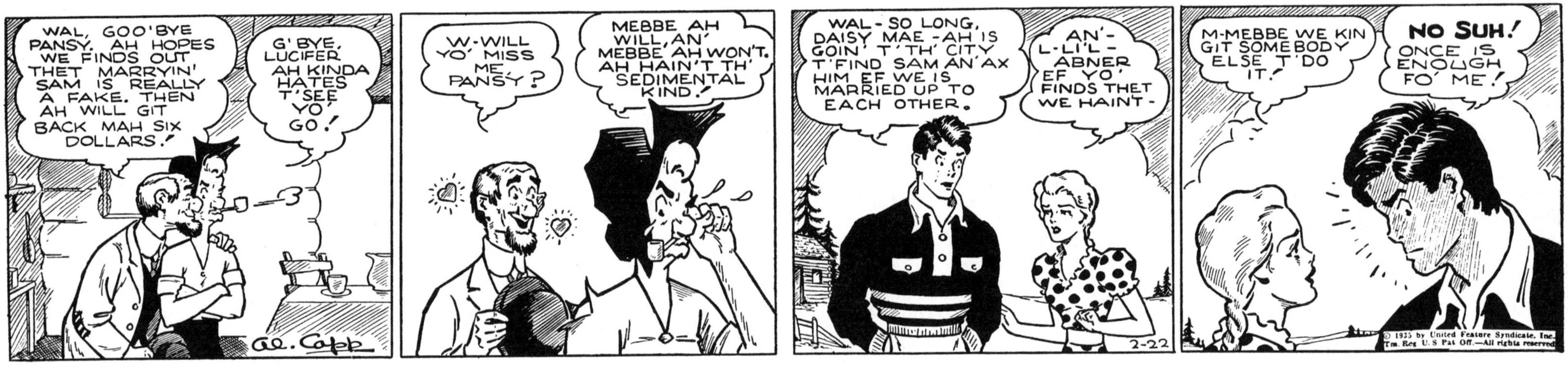

WAL, GOO'BYE PANSY. AH HOPES WE FINDS OUT THET MARRYIN' SAM IS REALLY A FAKE. THEN AH WILL GIT BACK MAH SIX DOLLARS!
G'BYE, LUCIFER. AH KINDA HATES T'SEE YO' GO!
AL CAPP
W-WILL YO' MISS ME, PANSY?
MEBBE AH WILL, AN' MEBBE AH WON'T. AH HAIN'T TH' SEDIMENTAL KIND!
WAL-SO LONG, DAISY MAE-AH IS GOIN' T' TH' CITY T'FIND SAM AN' AX HIM EF WE IS MARRIED UP TO EACH OTHER.
AN'-L-LI'L-ABNER EF YO' FINDS THET WE HAIN'T-
2-22
M-MEBBE WE KIN GIT SOMEBODY ELSE T'DO IT!
NO SUH! ONCE IS ENOUGH FO' ME!
© 1935 by United Feature Syndicate, Inc. Tm. Reg. U. S. Pat. Off.—All rights reserved

LI'L ABNER Two Minds With But A Single Thought! By Al Capp

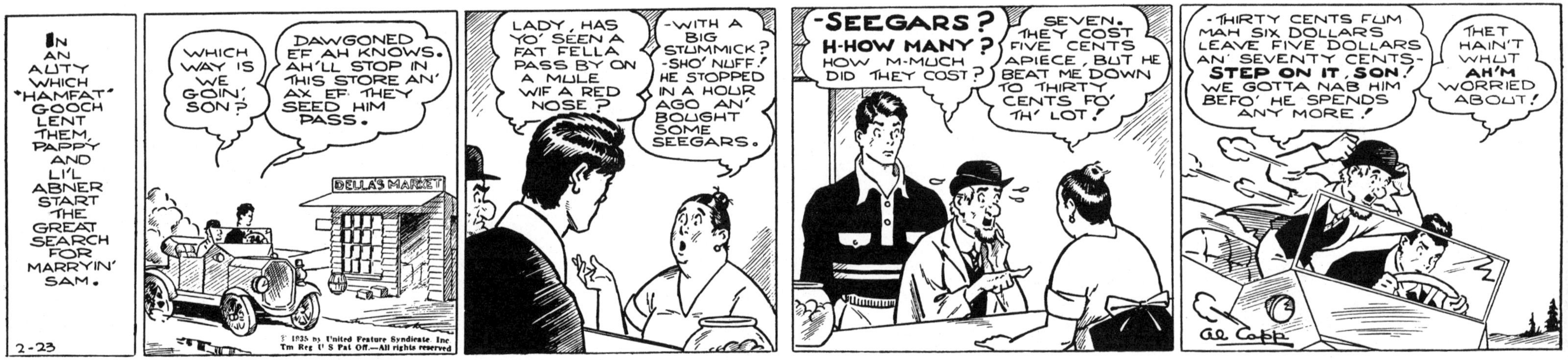

IN AN AUTY WHICH "HAMFAT" GOOCH LENT THEM, PAPPY AND LI'L ABNER START THE GREAT SEARCH FOR MARRYIN' SAM.
2-23
WHICH WAY IS WE GOIN', SON?
DAWGONED EF AH KNOWS. AH'LL STOP IN THIS STORE AN' AX EF THEY SEED HIM PASS.
DELLA'S MARKET
© 1935 by United Feature Syndicate, Inc. Tm Reg U S Pat Off.—All rights reserved
LADY, HAS YO' SEEN A FAT FELLA PASS BY ON A MULE WIF A RED NOSE?
-WITH A BIG STUMMICK? -SHO' NUFF! HE STOPPED IN A HOUR AGO AN' BOUGHT SOME SEEGARS.
-SEEGARS? H-HOW MANY? HOW M-MUCH DID THEY COST?
SEVEN. THEY COST FIVE CENTS APIECE, BUT HE BEAT ME DOWN TO THIRTY CENTS FO' TH' LOT!
-THIRTY CENTS FUM MAH SIX DOLLARS LEAVE FIVE DOLLARS AN' SEVENTY CENTS- STEP ON IT, SON! WE GOTTA NAB HIM BEFO' HE SPENDS ANY MORE!
THET HAIN'T WHUT AH'M WORRIED ABOUT!
AL CAPP

LI'L ABNER Mammy Knows Men

By Al Capp

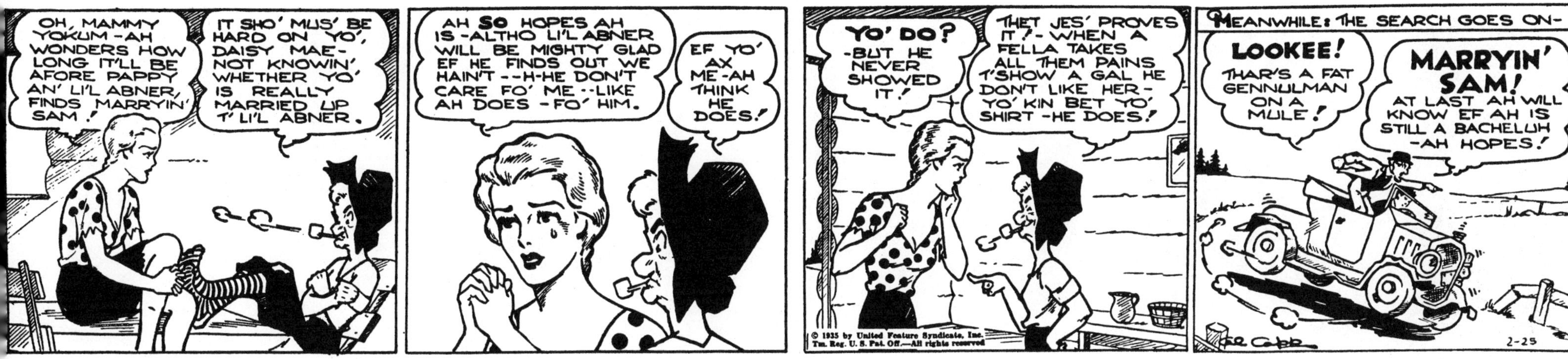

OH, MAMMY YOKUM - AH WONDERS HOW LONG IT'LL BE AFORE PAPPY AN' LI'L ABNER FINDS MARRYIN' SAM!
IT SHO' MUS' BE HARD ON YO', DAISY MAE - NOT KNOWIN' WHETHER YO' IS REALLY MARRIED UP T' LI'L ABNER.
AH SO HOPES AH IS - ALTHO LI'L ABNER WILL BE MIGHTY GLAD EF HE FINDS OUT WE HAIN'T - - H-HE DON'T CARE FO' ME - - LIKE AH DOES - FO' HIM.
EF YO' AX ME - AH THINK HE DOES!
YO' DO? - BUT HE NEVER SHOWED IT!
THET JES' PROVES IT! - WHEN A FELLA TAKES ALL THEM PAINS T'SHOW A GAL HE DON'T LIKE HER - YO' KIN BET YO' SHIRT - HE DOES!
© 1935 by United Feature Syndicate, Inc. Tm. Reg. U. S. Pat. Off.—All rights reserved
MEANWHILE: THE SEARCH GOES ON -
LOOKEE! THAR'S A FAT GENNULMAN ON A MULE!
MARRYIN' SAM! AT LAST AH WILL KNOW EF AH IS STILL A BACHELUH - AH HOPES!
Al Capp
2-25

LI'L ABNER Public Enemies!

By Al Capp

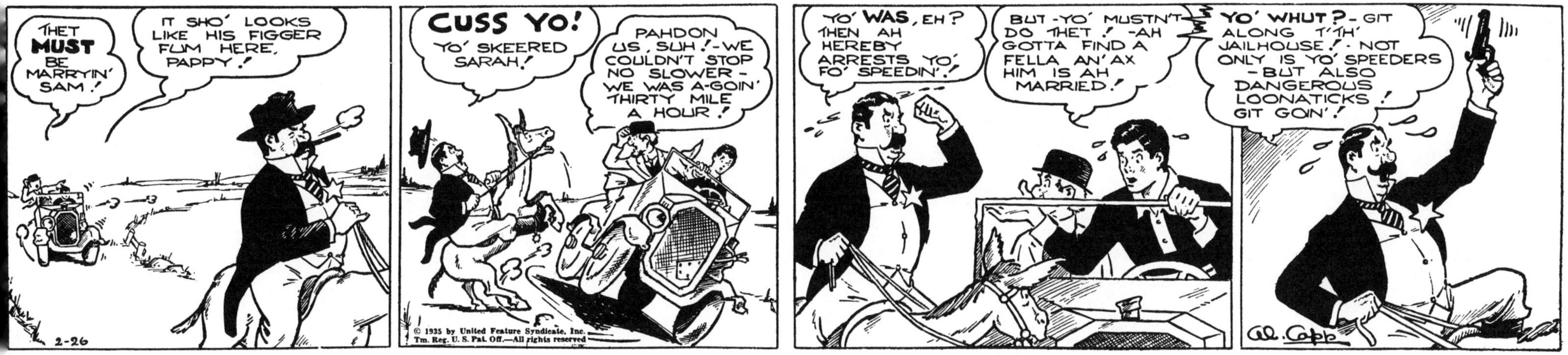

THET MUST BE MARRYIN' SAM!
IT SHO' LOOKS LIKE HIS FIGGER FUM HERE, PAPPY!
2-26
CUSS YO! YO' SKEERED SARAH!
PAHDON US, SUH! - WE COULDN'T STOP NO SLOWER - WE WAS A-GOIN' THIRTY MILE A HOUR!
© 1935 by United Feature Syndicate, Inc. Tm. Reg. U. S. Pat. Off.—All rights reserved
YO' WAS, EH? THEN AH HEREBY ARRESTS YO' FO' SPEEDIN'!
BUT - YO' MUSTN'T DO THET! - AH GOTTA FIND A FELLA AN' AX HIM IS AH MARRIED!
YO' WHUT? - GIT ALONG T' TH' JAILHOUSE! - NOT ONLY IS YO' SPEEDERS - BUT ALSO DANGEROUS LOONATICKS! GIT GOIN'!
Al Capp

LI'L ABNER It's A Small World By Al Capp

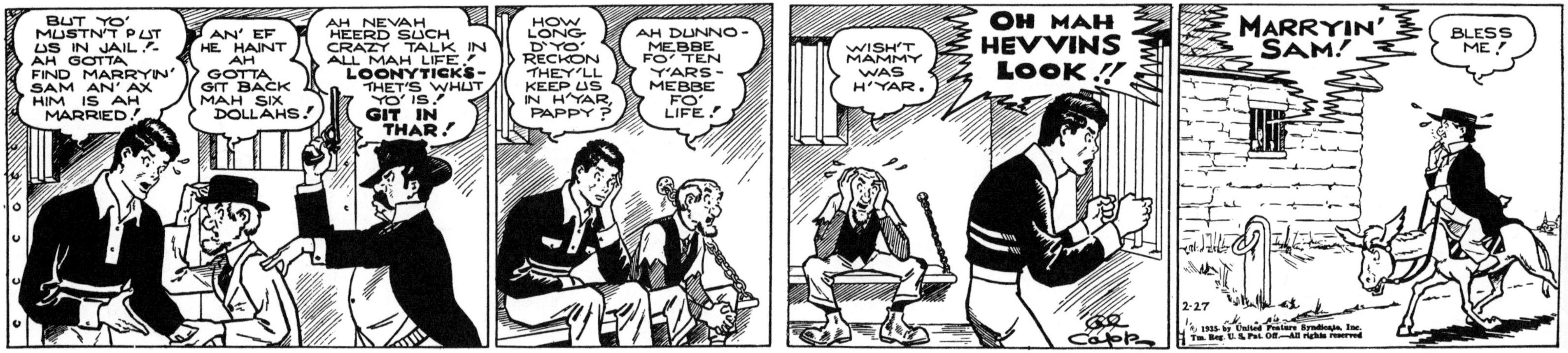

BUT YO' MUSTN'T PUT US IN JAIL!- AH GOTTA FIND MARRYIN' SAM AN' AX HIM IS AH MARRIED!
AN' EF HE HAINT AH GOTTA GIT BACK MAH SIX DOLLAHS!
AH NEVAH HEERD SUCH CRAZY TALK IN ALL MAH LIFE! LOONYTICKS- THET'S WHUT YO' IS! GIT IN THAR!
HOW LONG D'YO' RECKON THEY'LL KEEP US IN H'YAR, PAPPY?
AH DUNNO- MEBBE FO' TEN Y'ARS- MEBBE FO' LIFE!
WISH'T MAMMY WAS H'YAR.
OH MAH HEVVINS LOOK!!
MARRYIN' SAM!
BLESS ME!
2-27
Al Capp
© 1935 by United Feature Syndicate, Inc. Tm. Reg. U. S. Pat. Off.—All rights reserved

LI'L ABNER A Dark Outlook By Al Capp

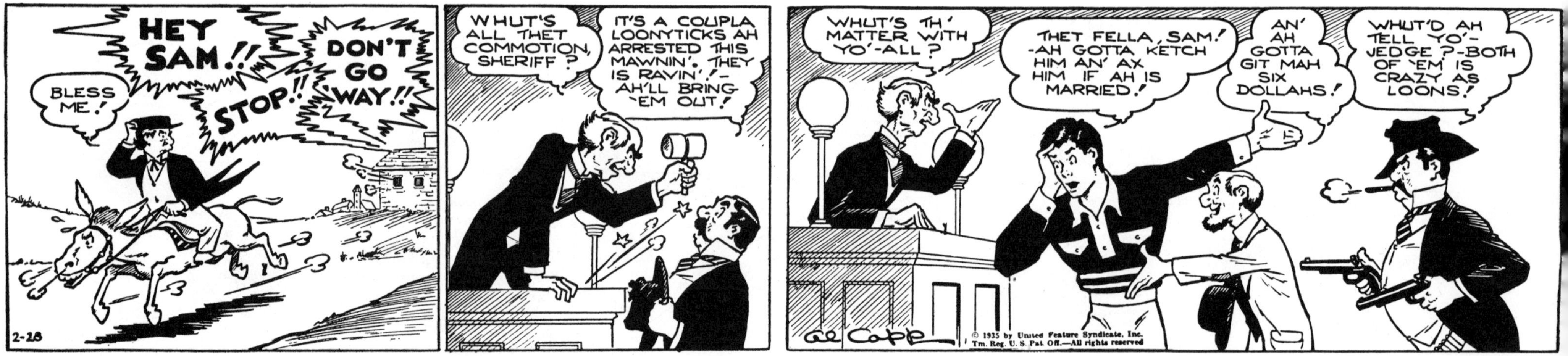

HEY SAM.!!
STOP!!
DON'T GO 'WAY!!
BLESS ME!
2-28
WHUT'S ALL THET COMMOTION, SHERIFF?
IT'S A COUPLA LOONYTICKS AH ARRESTED THIS MAWNIN'. THEY IS RAVIN'!- AH'LL BRING 'EM OUT!
WHUT'S TH' MATTER WITH YO'-ALL?
THET FELLA, SAM! -AH GOTTA KETCH HIM AN' AX HIM IF AH IS MARRIED!
AN' AH GOTTA GIT MAH SIX DOLLAHS!
WHUT'D AH TELL YO'- JEDGE?-BOTH OF 'EM IS CRAZY AS LOONS!
Al Capp
© 1935 by United Feature Syndicate, Inc. Tm. Reg. U. S. Pat. Off.—All rights reserved

LI'L ABNER — Haint It A Small World? — By Al Capp

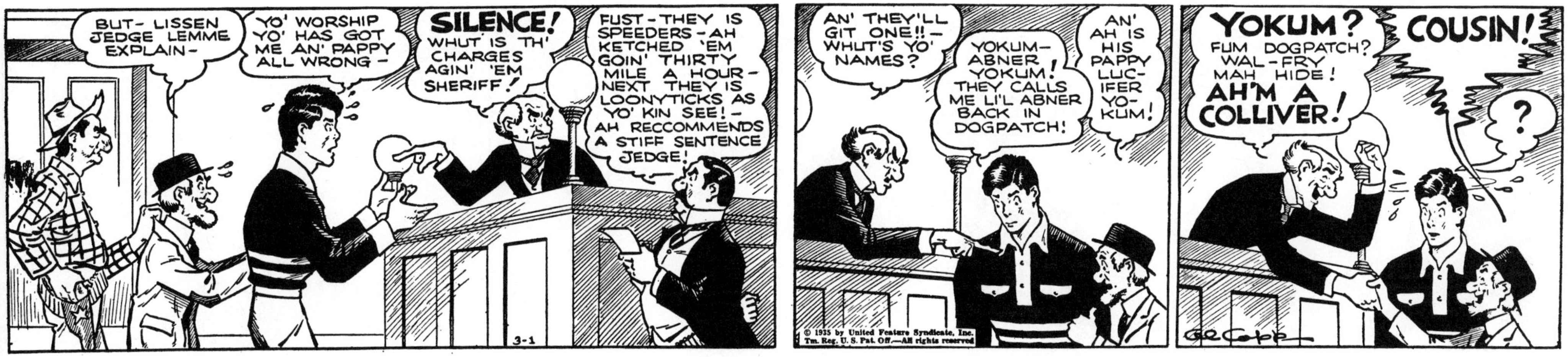

BUT- LISSEN JEDGE LEMME EXPLAIN-
YO' WORSHIP YO' HAS GOT ME AN' PAPPY ALL WRONG -
SILENCE! WHUT IS TH' CHARGES AGIN' 'EM SHERIFF!
FUST - THEY IS SPEEDERS - AH KETCHED 'EM GOIN' THIRTY MILE A HOUR - NEXT THEY IS LOONYTICKS AS YO' KIN SEE! - AH RECCOMMENDS A STIFF SENTENCE JEDGE!
3-1
AN' THEY'LL GIT ONE!! - WHUT'S YO' NAMES?
YOKUM - ABNER YOKUM! THEY CALLS ME LI'L ABNER BACK IN DOGPATCH!
AN' AH IS HIS PAPPY LUCIFER YOKUM!
© 1935 by United Feature Syndicate, Inc. Tm. Reg. U. S. Pat. Off.—All rights reserved
YOKUM? FUM DOGPATCH? WAL - FRY MAH HIDE! AH'M A COLLIVER!
COUSIN!
?

LI'L ABNER — Alias Marryin' Sam — By Al Capp

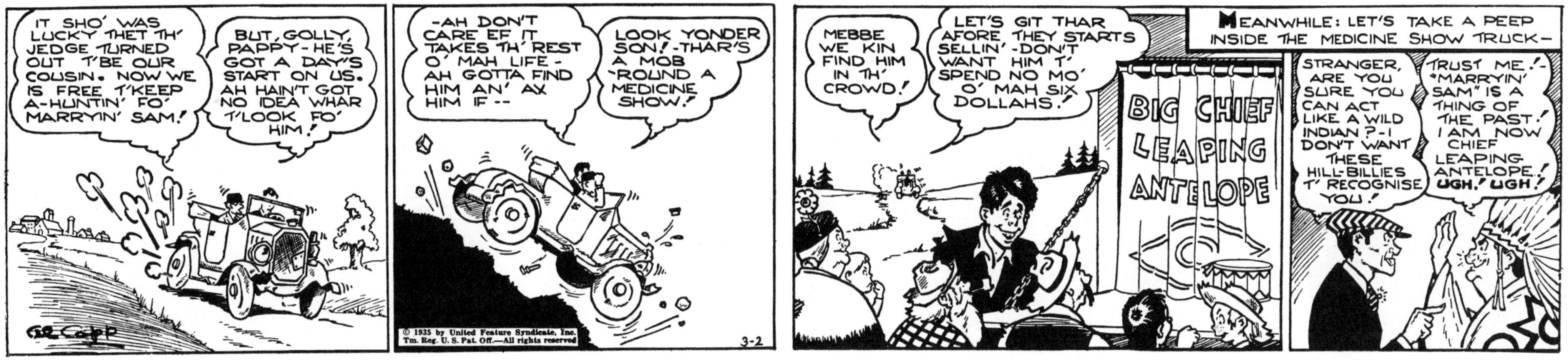

IT SHO' WAS LUCKY THET TH' JEDGE TURNED OUT T'BE OUR COUSIN. NOW WE IS FREE T'KEEP A-HUNTIN' FO' MARRYIN' SAM!
BUT, GOLLY, PAPPY - HE'S GOT A DAY'S START ON US. AH HAIN'T GOT NO IDEA WHAR T'LOOK FO' HIM!
-AH DON'T CARE EF IT TAKES TH' REST O' MAH LIFE - AH GOTTA FIND HIM AN' AX HIM IF --
LOOK YONDER SON! - THAR'S A MOB 'ROUND A MEDICINE SHOW!
© 1935 by United Feature Syndicate, Inc. Tm. Reg. U. S. Pat. Off.—All rights reserved
3-2
MEBBE WE KIN FIND HIM IN TH' CROWD!
LET'S GIT THAR AFORE THEY STARTS SELLIN' - DON'T WANT HIM T' SPEND NO MO' O' MAH SIX DOLLAHS!
BIG CHIEF LEAPING ANTELOPE
MEANWHILE: LET'S TAKE A PEEP INSIDE THE MEDICINE SHOW TRUCK -
STRANGER, ARE YOU SURE YOU CAN ACT LIKE A WILD INDIAN? - I DON'T WANT THESE HILL-BILLIES T' RECOGNISE YOU!
TRUST ME! - "MARRYIN' SAM" IS A THING OF THE PAST! I AM NOW CHIEF LEAPING ANTELOPE! UGH! UGH!

LI'L ABNER Stick Around, Abner **By Al Capp**

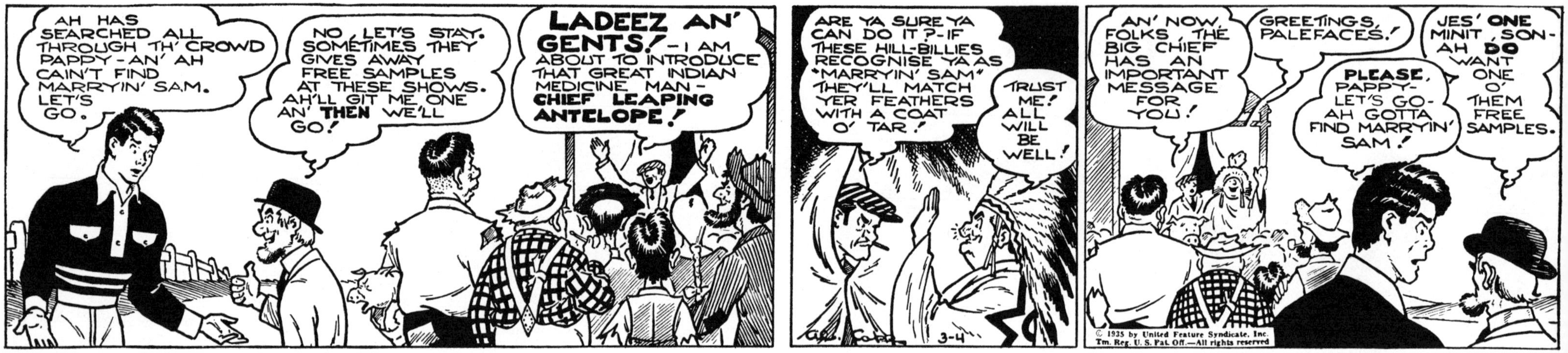

AH HAS SEARCHED ALL THROUGH TH' CROWD PAPPY - AN' AH CAIN'T FIND MARRYIN' SAM. LET'S GO.
NO, LET'S STAY. SOMETIMES THEY GIVES AWAY FREE SAMPLES AT THESE SHOWS. AH'LL GIT ME ONE AN' THEN WE'LL GO!
LADEEZ AN' GENTS! - I AM ABOUT TO INTRODUCE THAT GREAT INDIAN MEDICINE MAN - CHIEF LEAPING ANTELOPE!
ARE YA SURE YA CAN DO IT ? - IF THESE HILL-BILLIES RECOGNISE YA AS "MARRYIN' SAM" THEY'LL MATCH YER FEATHERS WITH A COAT O' TAR!
TRUST ME! ALL WILL BE WELL!
3-4
AN' NOW, FOLKS, THE BIG CHIEF HAS AN IMPORTANT MESSAGE FOR YOU!
GREETINGS, PALEFACES!
PLEASE, PAPPY - LET'S GO - AH GOTTA FIND MARRYIN' SAM!
JES' ONE MINIT, SON - AH DO WANT ONE O' THEM FREE SAMPLES.
© 1935 by United Feature Syndicate, Inc. Tm. Reg. U. S. Pat. Off.—All rights reserved

LI'L ABNER Pappy Sees Red! **By Al Capp**

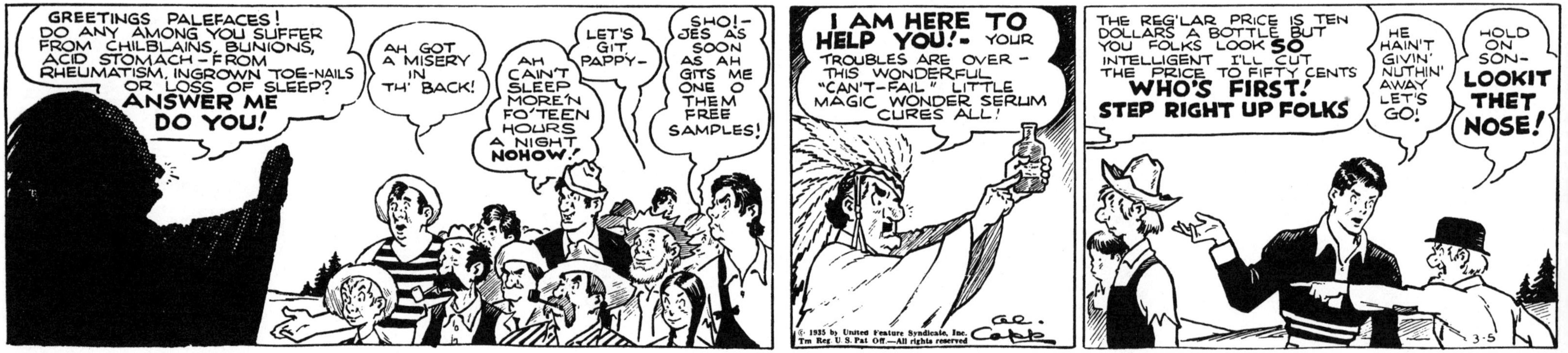

GREETINGS PALEFACES! DO ANY AMONG YOU SUFFER FROM CHILBLAINS, BUNIONS, ACID STOMACH - FROM RHEUMATISM, INGROWN TOE-NAILS OR LOSS OF SLEEP? ANSWER ME DO YOU!
AH GOT A MISERY IN TH' BACK!
AH CAIN'T SLEEP MORE'N FO'TEEN HOURS A NIGHT NOHOW!
LET'S GIT, PAPPY -
SHO! - JES AS SOON AS AH GITS ME ONE O THEM FREE SAMPLES!
I AM HERE TO HELP YOU! - YOUR TROUBLES ARE OVER - THIS WONDERFUL "CAN'T-FAIL" LITTLE MAGIC WONDER SERUM CURES ALL!
© 1935 by United Feature Syndicate, Inc. Tm Reg. U.S. Pat Off.—All rights reserved
THE REG'LAR PRICE IS TEN DOLLARS A BOTTLE BUT YOU FOLKS LOOK SO INTELLIGENT I'LL CUT THE PRICE TO FIFTY CENTS WHO'S FIRST! STEP RIGHT UP FOLKS
HE HAIN'T GIVIN' NUTHIN' AWAY LET'S GO!
HOLD ON SON - LOOKIT THET NOSE!
3-5

LI'L ABNER Lost By A Nose

By Al Capp

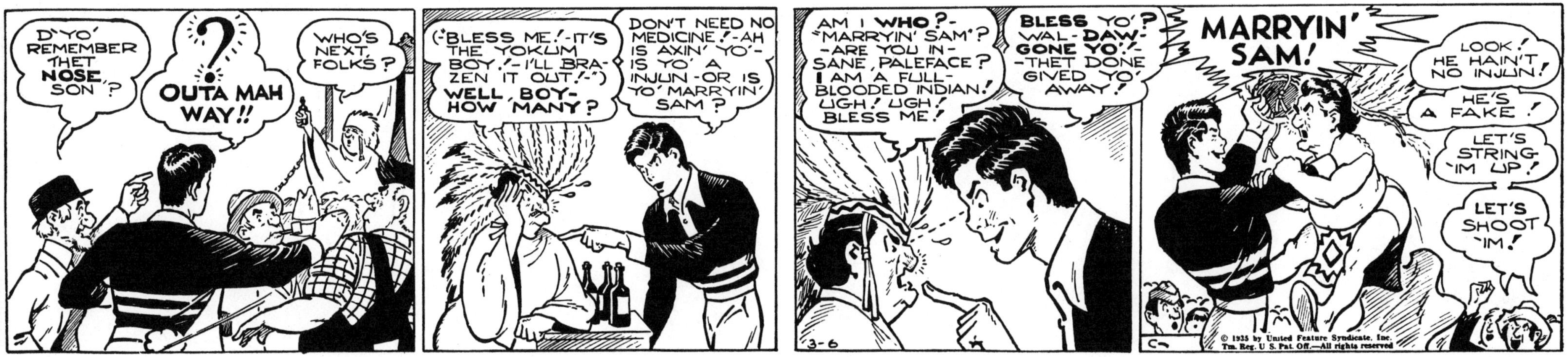
D'YO' REMEMBER THET NOSE, SON'?
?
OUTA MAH WAY!!
WHO'S NEXT, FOLKS?
(-'BLESS ME!'-IT'S THE YOKUM BOY!-I'LL BRAZEN IT OUT!-")
WELL, BOY-HOW MANY?
DON'T NEED NO MEDICINE!-AH IS AXIN' YO'-IS YO' A INJUN-OR IS YO' MARRYIN' SAM?
AM I WHO?-"MARRYIN' SAM"?-ARE YOU IN-SANE, PALEFACE? I AM A FULL-BLOODED INDIAN! UGH! UGH! BLESS ME!
BLESS YO'? WAL-DAW-GONE YO'!-THET DONE GIVED YO' AWAY!
MARRYIN' SAM!
LOOK! HE HAIN'T NO INJUN!
HE'S A FAKE!
LET'S STRING 'IM UP!
LET'S SHOOT 'IM!
3-6
© 1935 by United Feature Syndicate, Inc. Tm. Reg. U. S. Pat. Off.—All rights reserved

LI'L ABNER Crime Doesn't Pay

By Al Capp

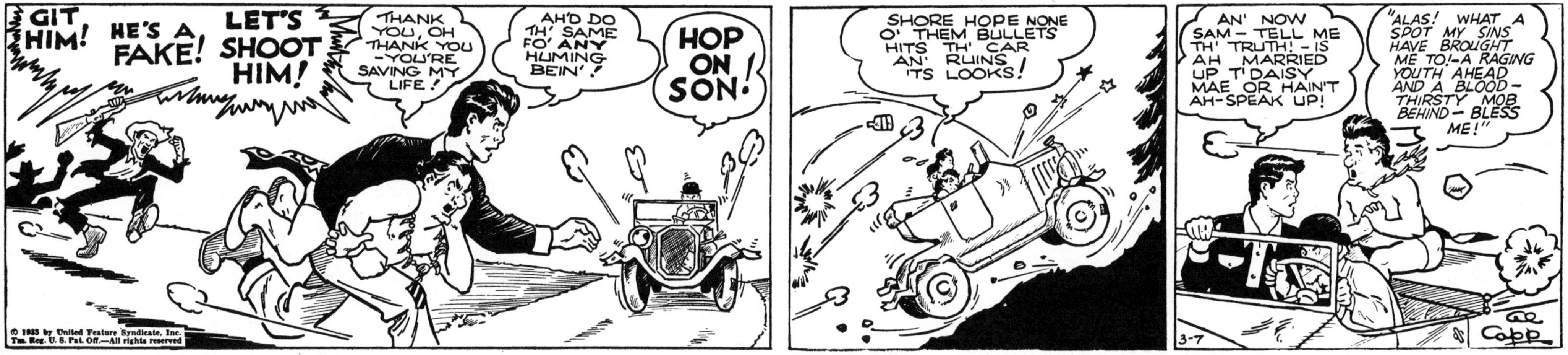
GIT HIM!
HE'S A FAKE!
LET'S SHOOT HIM!
THANK YOU, OH THANK YOU -YOU'RE SAVING MY LIFE!
AH'D DO TH' SAME FO' ANY HUMING BEIN'!
HOP ON SON!
© 1935 by United Feature Syndicate, Inc. Tm. Reg. U. S. Pat. Off.—All rights reserved
SHORE HOPE NONE O' THEM BULLETS HITS TH' CAR AN' RUINS ITS LOOKS!
AN' NOW SAM - TELL ME TH' TRUTH! - IS AH MARRIED UP T'DAISY MAE OR HAIN'T AH-SPEAK UP!
"ALAS! WHAT A SPOT MY SINS HAVE BROUGHT ME TO!-A RAGING YOUTH AHEAD AND A BLOOD-THIRSTY MOB BEHIND-BLESS ME!"
3-7
Capp

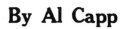

LI'L ABNER A Repentant Sinner By Al Capp

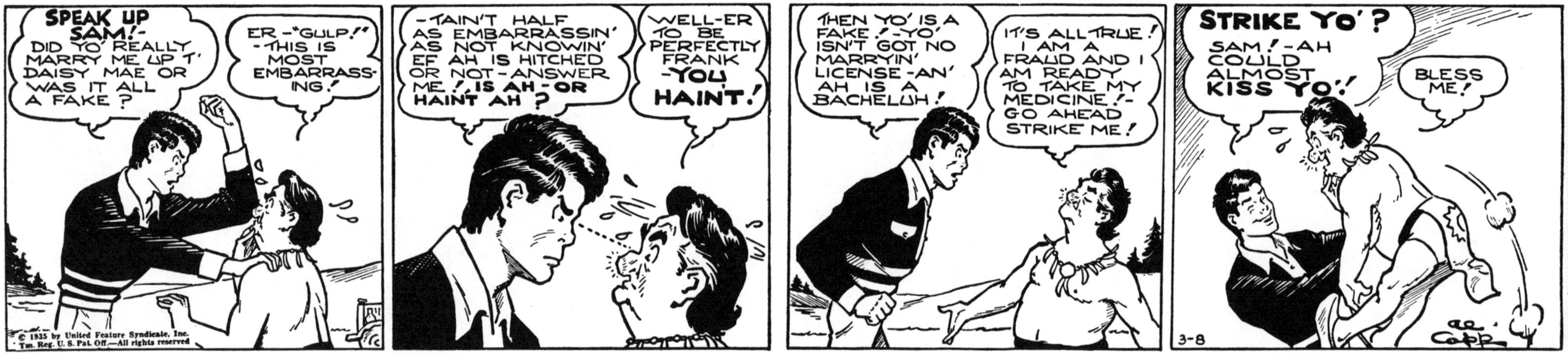

SPEAK UP SAM!- DID YO' REALLY MARRY ME UP T' DAISY MAE OR WAS IT ALL A FAKE ?
ER -"GULP!" -THIS IS MOST EMBARRASS-ING.!
© 1935 by United Feature Syndicate, Inc. Tm. Reg. U. S. Pat. Off.—All rights reserved
-TAIN'T HALF AS EMBARRASSIN' AS NOT KNOWIN' EF AH IS HITCHED OR NOT-ANSWER ME!, IS AH-OR HAINT AH ?
WELL-ER TO BE PERFECTLY FRANK -YOU HAIN'T.!
THEN YO' IS A FAKE.!-YO' ISN'T GOT NO MARRYIN' LICENSE-AN' AH IS A BACHELUH!
IT'S ALL TRUE! I AM A FRAUD AND I AM READY TO TAKE MY MEDICINE.!- GO AHEAD STRIKE ME!
STRIKE YO' ? SAM!-AH COULD ALMOST KISS YO'!
BLESS ME!
3-8

LI'L ABNER Boy—Is Yo' Sho' Yo' Is? By Al Capp

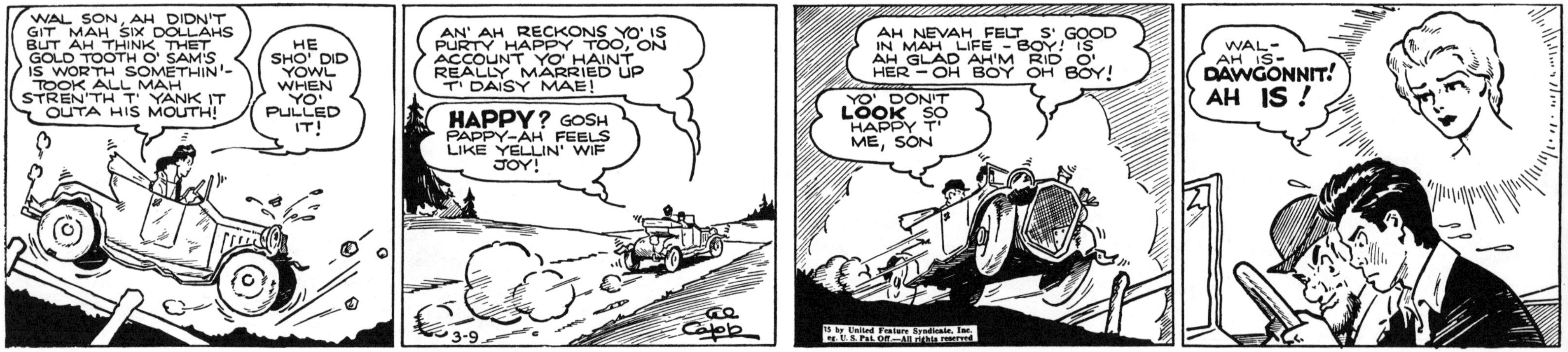

WAL SON, AH DIDN'T GIT MAH SIX DOLLAHS BUT AH THINK THET GOLD TOOTH O' SAM'S IS WORTH SOMETHIN'- TOOK ALL MAH STREN'TH T' YANK IT OUTA HIS MOUTH!
HE SHO' DID YOWL WHEN YO' PULLED IT!
AN' AH RECKONS YO' IS PURTY HAPPY TOO, ON ACCOUNT YO' HAINT REALLY MARRIED UP T' DAISY MAE!
HAPPY? GOSH PAPPY-AH FEELS LIKE YELLIN' WIF JOY!
3-9
AH NEVAH FELT S' GOOD IN MAH LIFE - BOY! IS AH GLAD AH'M RID O' HER - OH BOY OH BOY!
YO' DON'T LOOK SO HAPPY T' ME, SON
'35 by United Feature Syndicate, Inc. eg. U. S. Pat. Off.—All rights reserved
WAL- AH IS- DAWGONNIT! AH IS!

LI'L ABNER Happy Hain't the Word! By Al Capp

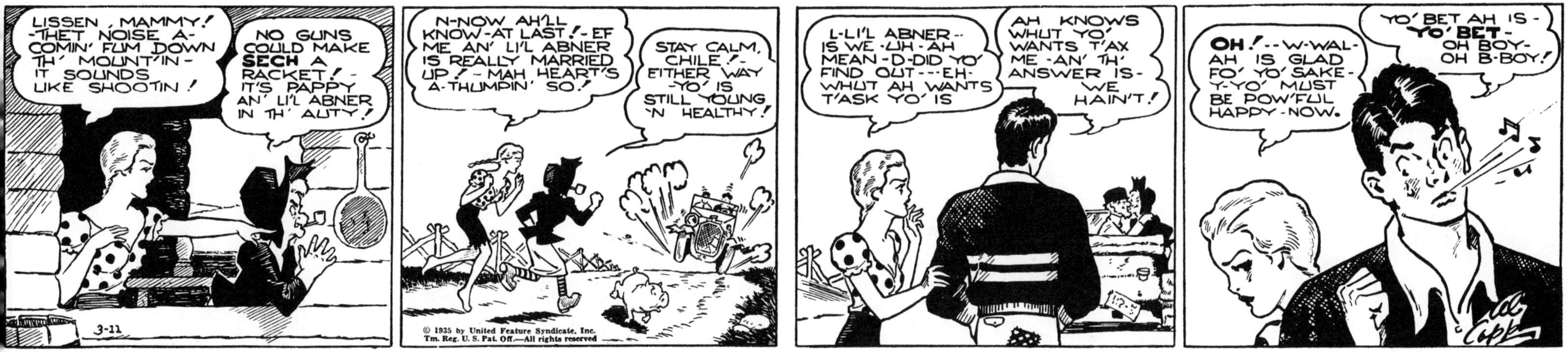

LISSEN, MAMMY! -THET NOISE A-COMIN' FUM DOWN TH' MOUNT'IN - IT SOUNDS LIKE SHOOTIN!
NO GUNS COULD MAKE SECH A RACKET! - IT'S PAPPY AN' LI'L ABNER IN TH' AUTY!
3-11
N-NOW AH'LL KNOW-AT LAST! - EF ME AN' LI'L ABNER IS REALLY MARRIED UP! - MAH HEART'S A-THUMPIN' SO!
STAY CALM, CHILE! - EITHER WAY -YO' IS STILL YOUNG 'N HEALTHY!
© 1935 by United Feature Syndicate, Inc. Tm. Reg. U. S. Pat. Off.—All rights reserved
L-LI'L ABNER-- IS WE-UH-AH MEAN-D-DID YO' FIND OUT---EH- WHUT AH WANTS T'ASK YO' IS
AH KNOWS WHUT YO' WANTS T'AX ME-AN' TH' ANSWER IS- WE HAIN'T!
OH! -- W-WAL- AH IS GLAD FO' YO' SAKE-Y-YO' MUST BE POW'FUL HAPPY-NOW.
YO' BET AH IS - YO' BET - OH BOY- OH B-BOY!
Al Capp

LI'L ABNER A Woman of Experience By Al Capp

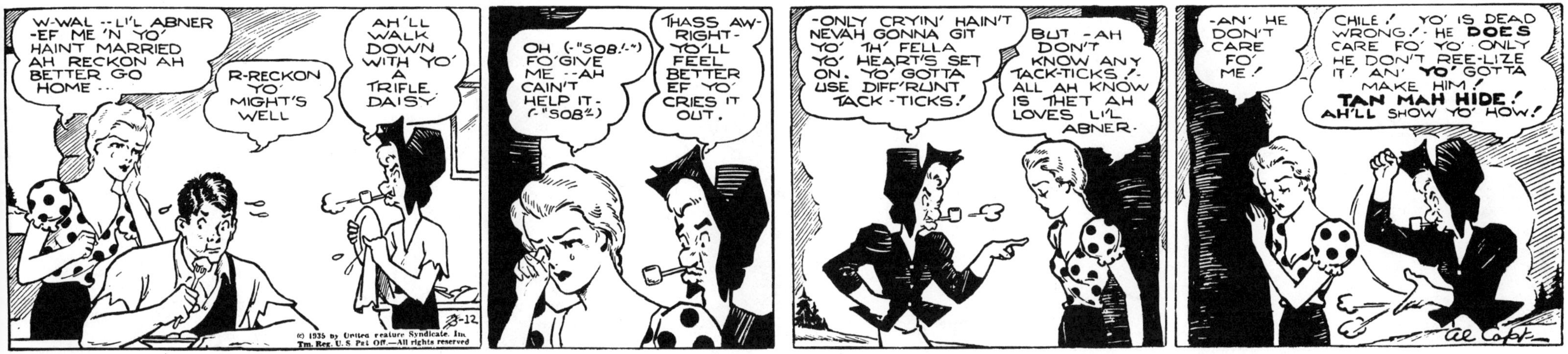

W-WAL --LI'L ABNER -EF ME 'N YO' HAINT MARRIED AH RECKON AH BETTER GO HOME --
R-RECKON YO' MIGHT'S WELL
AH'LL WALK DOWN WITH YO' A TRIFLE DAISY
3-12
(c) 1935 by United Feature Syndicate, Inc Tm. Reg. U. S. Pat. Off.—All rights reserved
OH (-"SOB!-") FO'GIVE ME --AH CAIN'T HELP IT- (-"SOB!-")
THASS AW-RIGHT- YO'LL FEEL BETTER EF YO' CRIES IT OUT.
-ONLY CRYIN' HAIN'T NEVAH GONNA GIT YO' TH' FELLA YO' HEART'S SET ON. YO' GOTTA USE DIFF'RUNT TACK-TICKS!
BUT -AH DON'T KNOW ANY TACK-TICKS! - ALL AH KNOW IS THET AH LOVES LI'L ABNER-
-AN' HE DON'T CARE FO' ME!
CHILE! YO' IS DEAD WRONG! - HE DOES CARE FO' YO' ONLY HE DON'T REE-LIZE IT! AN' YO' GOTTA MAKE HIM! TAN MAH HIDE! AH'LL SHOW YO' HOW!
Al Capp

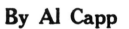

LI'L ABNER Take It From Mammy! By Al Capp

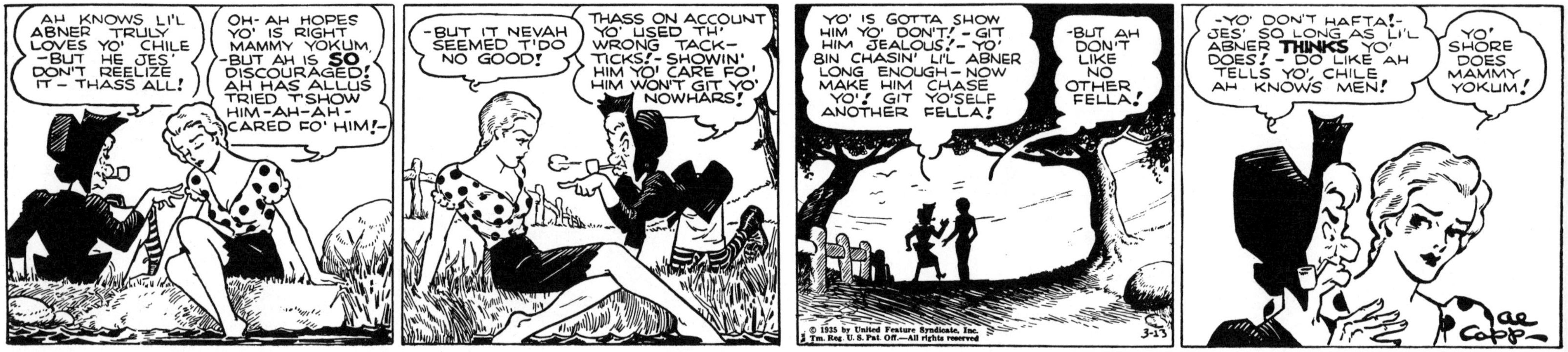
AH KNOWS LI'L ABNER TRULY LOVES YO' CHILE —BUT HE JES' DON'T REELIZE IT — THASS ALL!
OH- AH HOPES YO' IS RIGHT MAMMY YOKUM. -BUT AH IS SO DISCOURAGED! AH HAS ALLUS TRIED T'SHOW HIM-AH-AH- CARED FO' HIM!—
-BUT IT NEVAH SEEMED T'DO NO GOOD!
THASS ON ACCOUNT YO' USED TH' WRONG TACK-TICKS!- SHOWIN' HIM YO' CARE FO' HIM WON'T GIT YO' NOWHARS!
YO' IS GOTTA SHOW HIM YO' DON'T! - GIT HIM JEALOUS!- YO' BIN CHASIN' LI'L ABNER LONG ENOUGH - NOW MAKE HIM CHASE YO'! GIT YO'SELF ANOTHER FELLA!
-BUT AH DON'T LIKE NO OTHER FELLA!
© 1935 by United Feature Syndicate, Inc. Tm. Reg. U. S. Pat. Off.—All rights reserved
3-13
-YO' DON'T HAFTA!- JES' SO LONG AS LI'L ABNER THINKS YO' DOES! - DO LIKE AH TELLS YO', CHILE AH KNOWS MEN!
YO' SHORE DOES MAMMY YOKUM!
Al Capp

LI'L ABNER Take Me!—I'm Yourn! By Al Capp

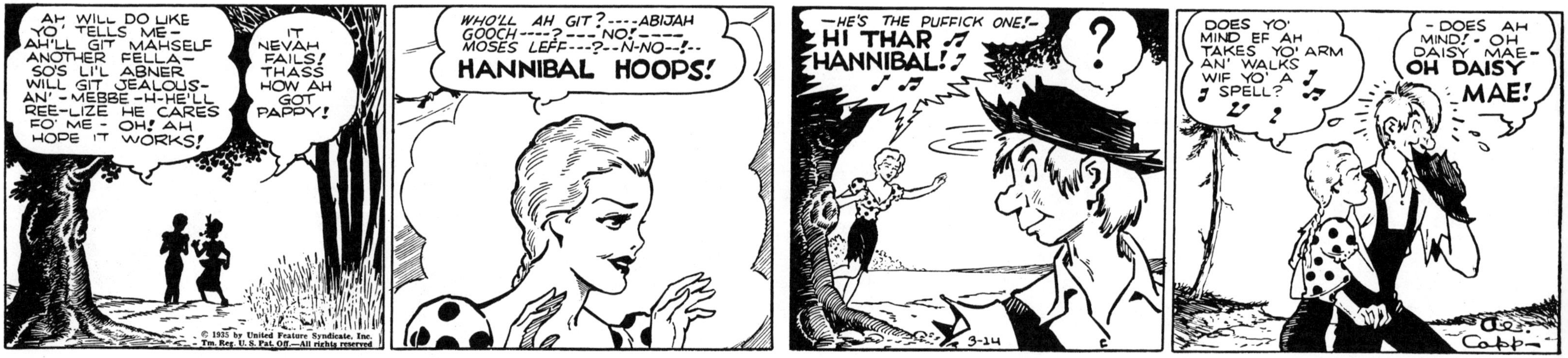
AH WILL DO LIKE YO' TELLS ME- AH'LL GIT MAHSELF ANOTHER FELLA- SO'S LI'L ABNER WILL GIT JEALOUS- AN' - MEBBE -H-HE'LL REE-LIZE HE CARES FO' ME - OH! AH HOPE IT WORKS!
IT NEVAH FAILS! THASS HOW AH GOT PAPPY!
© 1935 by United Feature Syndicate, Inc. Tm. Reg. U. S. Pat. Off.—All rights reserved
WHO'LL AH GIT?----ABIJAH GOOCH----?---NO!----- MOSES LEFF---?--N-NO--!-- HANNIBAL HOOPS!
—HE'S THE PUFFICK ONE!—
HI THAR HANNIBAL!
?
3-14
DOES YO' MIND EF AH TAKES YO' ARM AN' WALKS WIF YO' A SPELL?
- DOES AH MIND! - OH DAISY MAE- OH DAISY MAE!
Al Capp

LI'L ABNER No Effect! By Al Capp

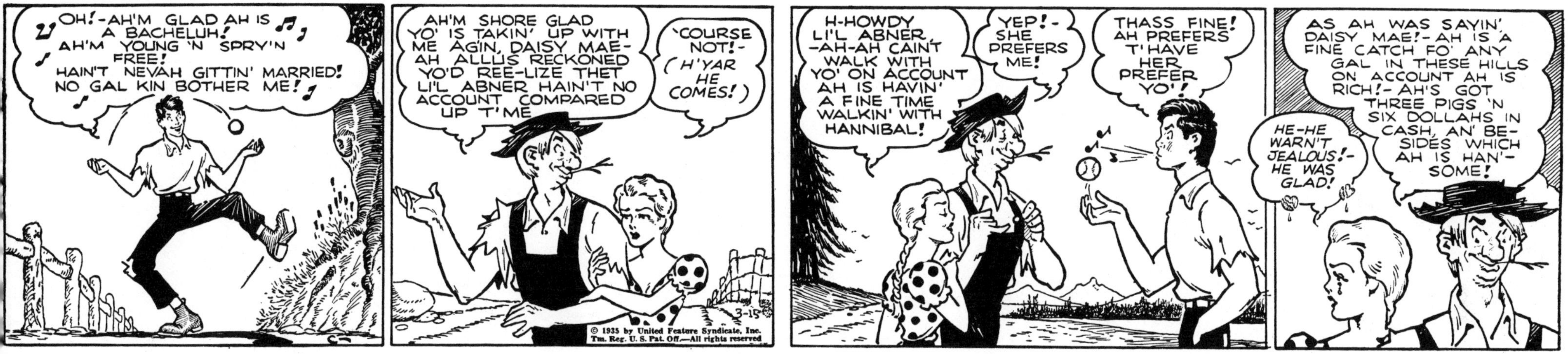

OH!-AH'M GLAD AH IS A BACHELUH! AH'M YOUNG 'N SPRY'N FREE! HAIN'T NEVAH GITTIN' MARRIED! NO GAL KIN BOTHER ME!
AH'M SHORE GLAD YO' IS TAKIN' UP WITH ME AGIN, DAISY MAE- AH ALLUS RECKONED YO'D REE-LIZE THET LI'L ABNER HAIN'T NO ACCOUNT COMPARED UP T'ME
'COURSE NOT!- (H'YAR HE COMES!)
3-15
© 1935 by United Feature Syndicate, Inc. Tm. Reg. U. S. Pat. Off.—All rights reserved
H-HOWDY LI'L ABNER, -AH-AH CAIN'T WALK WITH YO' ON ACCOUNT AH IS HAVIN' A FINE TIME WALKIN' WITH HANNIBAL!
YEP!-SHE PREFERS ME!
THASS FINE! AH PREFERS T'HAVE HER PREFER YO'!
AS AH WAS SAYIN', DAISY MAE!-AH IS A FINE CATCH FO' ANY GAL IN THESE HILLS ON ACCOUNT AH IS RICH!-AH'S GOT THREE PIGS 'N SIX DOLLAHS IN CASH, AN' BE-SIDES WHICH AH IS HAN'-SOME!
HE-HE WARN'T JEALOUS!-HE WAS GLAD!

LI'L ABNER He Don't Care—Much! By Al Capp

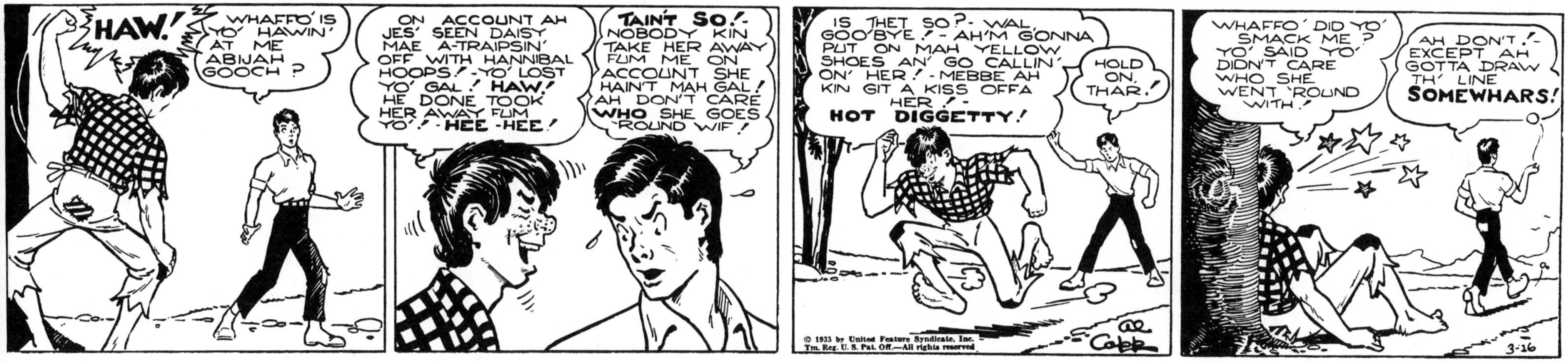

HAW!
WHAFFO' IS YO' HAWIN' AT ME ABIJAH GOOCH ?
ON ACCOUNT AH JES' SEEN DAISY MAE A-TRAIPSIN' OFF WITH HANNIBAL HOOPS!-YO' LOST YO' GAL! HAW! HE DONE TOOK HER AWAY FUM YO'!-HEE-HEE!
TAIN'T SO!-NOBODY KIN TAKE HER AWAY FUM ME ON ACCOUNT SHE HAIN'T MAH GAL! AH DON'T CARE WHO SHE GOES 'ROUND WIF!
IS THET SO?-WAL, GOO'BYE!-AH'M GONNA PUT ON MAH YELLOW SHOES AN' GO CALLIN' ON' HER!-MEBBE AH KIN GIT A KISS OFFA HER!-
HOT DIGGETTY!
HOLD ON, THAR!
© 1935 by United Feature Syndicate, Inc. Tm. Reg. U. S. Pat. Off.—All rights reserved
WHAFFO' DID YO' SMACK ME? YO' SAID YO' DIDN'T CARE WHO SHE WENT 'ROUND WITH!
AH DON'T!-EXCEPT AH GOTTA DRAW TH' LINE SOMEWHARS!
3-16

LI'L ABNER The Symptoms Are the Same By Al Capp

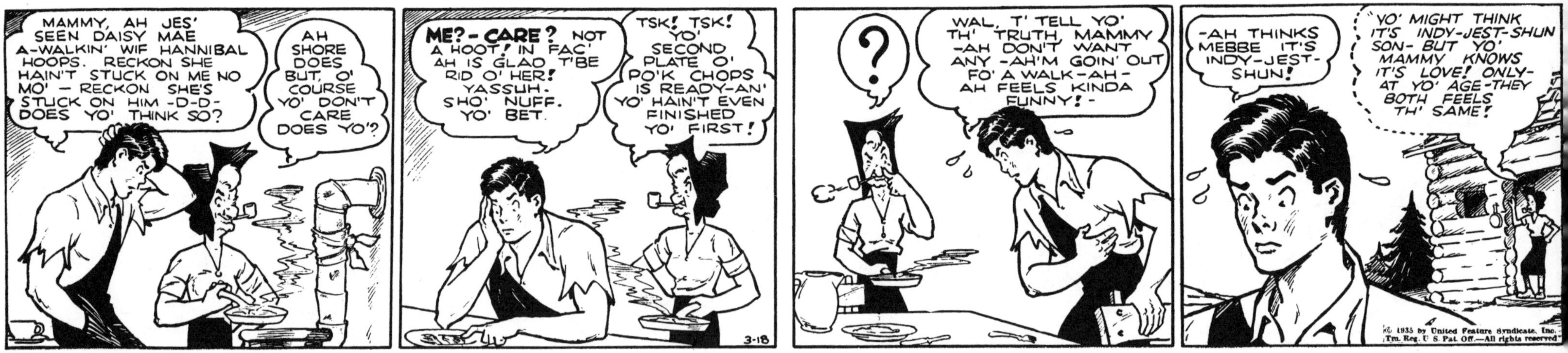

MAMMY, AH JES' SEEN DAISY MAE A-WALKIN' WIF HANNIBAL HOOPS. RECKON SHE HAIN'T STUCK ON ME NO MO' — RECKON SHE'S STUCK ON HIM -D-D-DOES YO' THINK SO?
AH SHORE DOES BUT, O' COURSE YO' DON'T CARE DOES YO'?
ME?- CARE? NOT A HOOT! IN FAC' AH IS GLAD T'BE RID O' HER! YASSUH- SHO' NUFF. YO' BET.
TSK! TSK! YO' SECOND PLATE O' PO'K CHOPS IS READY-AN' YO' HAIN'T EVEN FINISHED YO' FIRST!
3-18
?
WAL, T' TELL YO' TH' TRUTH, MAMMY -AH DON'T WANT ANY -AH'M GOIN' OUT FO' A WALK-AH-AH FEELS KINDA FUNNY!-
-AH THINKS MEBBE IT'S INDY-JEST-SHUN!
YO' MIGHT THINK IT'S INDY-JEST-SHUN SON- BUT YO' MAMMY KNOWS IT'S LOVE! ONLY- AT YO' AGE-THEY BOTH FEELS TH' SAME!
© 1935 by United Feature Syndicate, Inc. Tm. Reg. U S. Pat. Off.—All rights reserved

LI'L ABNER A Pee-koolyar Feelin' By Al Capp

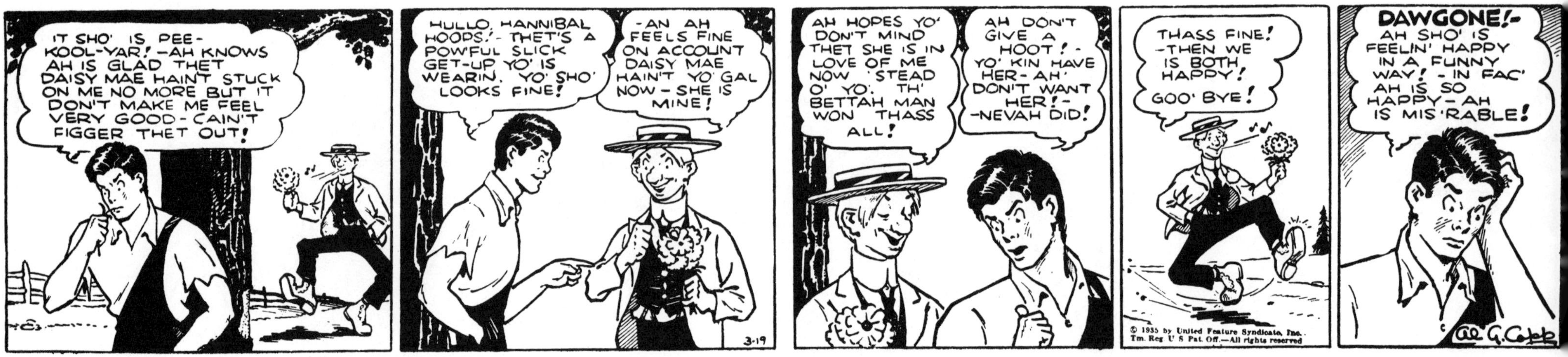

IT SHO' IS PEE-KOOL-YAR! -AH KNOWS AH IS GLAD THET DAISY MAE HAIN'T STUCK ON ME NO MORE BUT IT DON'T MAKE ME FEEL VERY GOOD- CAIN'T FIGGER THET OUT!
HULLO, HANNIBAL HOOPS!- THET'S A POW'FUL SLICK GET-UP YO' IS WEARIN. YO' SHO' LOOKS FINE!
-AN AH FEELS FINE ON ACCOUNT DAISY MAE HAIN'T YO' GAL NOW - SHE IS MINE!
3-19
AH HOPES YO' DON'T MIND THET SHE IS IN LOVE OF ME NOW 'STEAD O' YO'. TH' BETTAH MAN WON THASS ALL!
AH DON'T GIVE A HOOT!- YO' KIN HAVE HER- AH' DON'T WANT HER!- -NEVAH DID!
THASS FINE! -THEN WE IS BOTH HAPPY!
GOO' BYE!
© 1935 by United Feature Syndicate, Inc. Tm. Reg. U S Pat. Off.—All rights reserved
DAWGONE!- AH SHO' IS FEELIN' HAPPY IN A FUNNY WAY! - IN FAC' AH IS SO HAPPY- AH IS MIS'RABLE!

LI'L ABNER A Mountain Don Juan

By Al Capp

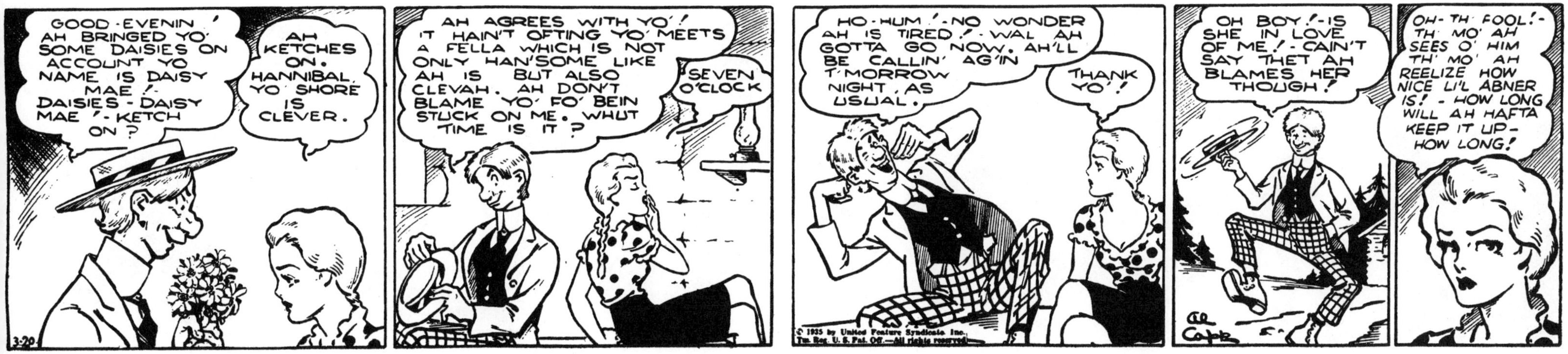
GOOD-EVENIN'! AH BRINGED YO' SOME DAISIES ON ACCOUNT YO NAME IS DAISY MAE!- DAISIES - DAISY MAE!- KETCH ON?
AH KETCHES ON. HANNIBAL, YO' SHORE IS CLEVER.
AH AGREES WITH YO'! IT HAIN'T OFTING YO' MEETS A FELLA WHICH IS NOT ONLY HAN'SOME LIKE AH IS BUT ALSO CLEVAH. AH DON'T BLAME YO' FO' BEIN STUCK ON ME. WHUT TIME IS IT?
SEVEN O'CLOCK
HO-HUM!-NO WONDER AH IS TIRED!-WAL AH GOTTA GO NOW. AH'LL BE CALLIN' AG'IN T'MORROW NIGHT, AS USUAL.
THANK YO'!
© 1935 by United Feature Syndicate Inc. Tm. Reg. U. S. Pat. Off.—All rights reserved
OH BOY!-IS SHE IN LOVE OF ME!-CAIN'T SAY THET AH BLAMES HER THOUGH!
AL CAPP
OH-TH' FOOL!-TH' MO' AH SEES O' HIM TH' MO' AH REELIZE HOW NICE LI'L ABNER IS!-HOW LONG WILL AH HAFTA KEEP IT UP-HOW LONG!

LI'L ABNER A Fast Worker

By Al Capp

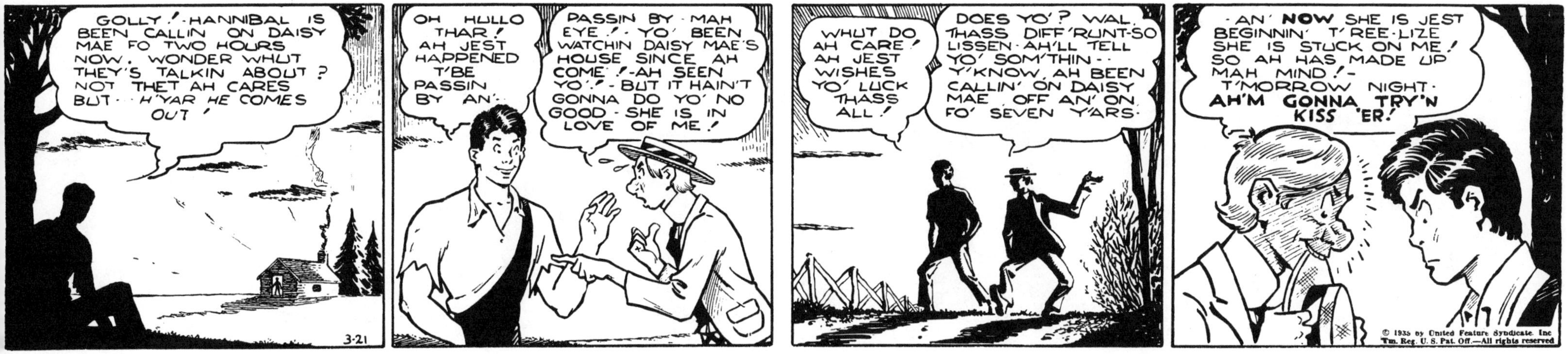
GOLLY!-HANNIBAL IS BEEN CALLIN ON DAISY MAE FO TWO HOURS NOW. WONDER WHUT THEY'S TALKIN ABOUT? NOT THET AH CARES BUT- H'YAR HE COMES OUT!
OH HULLO THAR! AH JEST HAPPENED T'BE PASSIN BY AN'-
PASSIN BY-MAH EYE!-YO' BEEN WATCHIN DAISY MAE'S HOUSE SINCE AH COME!-AH SEEN YO'!-BUT IT HAIN'T GONNA DO YO' NO GOOD-SHE IS IN LOVE OF ME!
WHUT DO AH CARE! AH JEST WISHES YO' LUCK THASS ALL!
DOES YO'? WAL THASS DIFF'RUNT-SO LISSEN-AH'LL TELL YO' SOM'THIN--Y'KNOW, AH BEEN CALLIN' ON DAISY MAE OFF AN' ON FO' SEVEN Y'ARS-
-AN' NOW SHE IS JEST BEGINNIN' T'REE-LIZE SHE IS STUCK ON ME! SO AH HAS MADE UP MAH MIND!-T'MORROW NIGHT-AH'M GONNA TRY'N KISS 'ER!
© 1935 by United Feature Syndicate Inc Tm. Reg. U. S. Pat. Off.—All rights reserved

LI'L ABNER Kidding Himself

By Al Capp

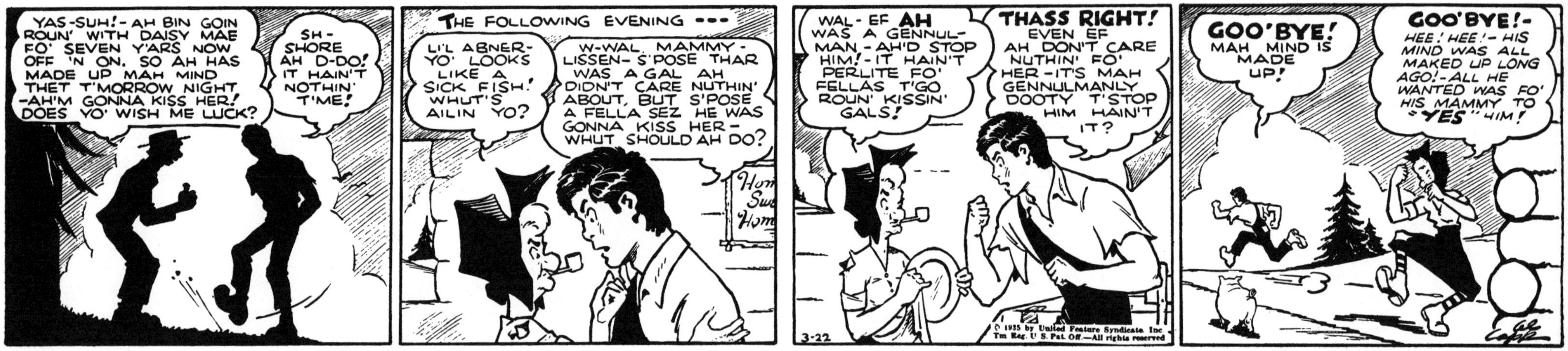

YAS-SUH!-AH BIN GOIN ROUN' WITH DAISY MAE FO' SEVEN Y'ARS NOW OFF 'N ON. SO AH HAS MADE UP MAH MIND THET T'MORROW NIGHT -AH'M GONNA KISS HER! DOES YO' WISH ME LUCK?
SH-SHORE AH D-DO! IT HAIN'T NOTHIN' T'ME!
THE FOLLOWING EVENING ---
LI'L ABNER-YO' LOOKS LIKE A SICK FISH! WHUT'S AILIN YO?
W-WAL, MAMMY-LISSEN-S'POSE THAR WAS A GAL AH DIDN'T CARE NUTHIN' ABOUT, BUT S'POSE A FELLA SEZ HE WAS GONNA KISS HER-WHUT SHOULD AH DO?
WAL-EF AH WAS A GENNULMAN-AH'D STOP HIM!-IT HAIN'T PERLITE FO' FELLAS T'GO ROUN' KISSIN' GALS!
THASS RIGHT! EVEN EF AH DON'T CARE NUTHIN' FO' HER-IT'S MAH GENNULMANLY DOOTY T'STOP HIM HAIN'T IT?
3-22
© 1935 by United Feature Syndicate, Inc. Tm. Reg. U.S. Pat. Off.—All rights reserved
GOO'BYE! MAH MIND IS MADE UP!
GOO'BYE!-HEE! HEE!-HIS MIND WAS ALL MAKED UP LONG AGO!-ALL HE WANTED WAS FO' HIS MAMMY TO "YES" HIM!
Al Capp

LI'L ABNER No Protection Needed

By Al Capp

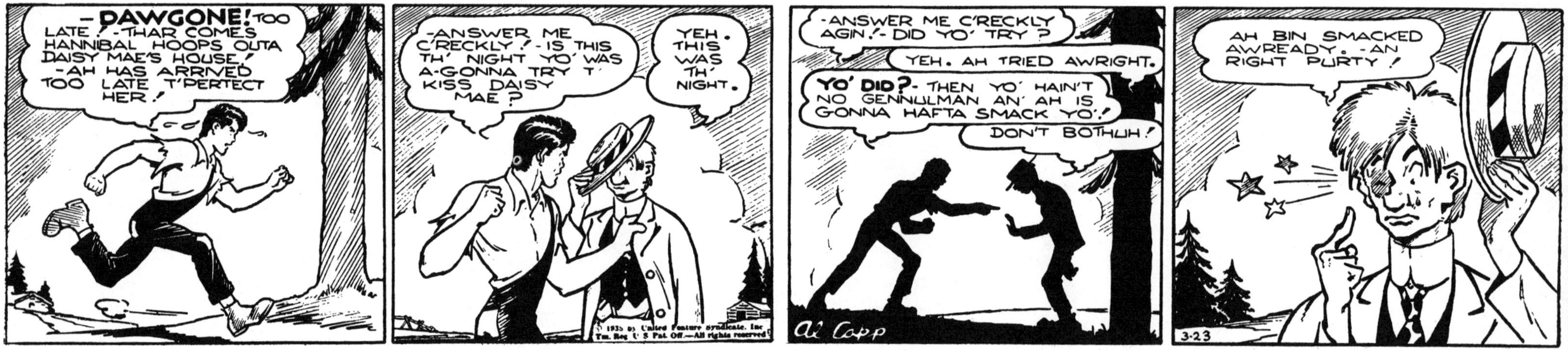

-DAWGONE! TOO LATE!-THAR COMES HANNIBAL HOOPS OUTA DAISY MAE'S HOUSE! -AH HAS ARRIVED TOO LATE T'PERTECT HER!
-ANSWER ME C'RECKLY!-IS THIS TH' NIGHT YO' WAS A-GONNA TRY T' KISS DAISY MAE?
YEH. THIS WAS TH' NIGHT.
© 1935 by United Feature Syndicate, Inc. Tm. Reg. U.S. Pat. Off.—All rights reserved
-ANSWER ME C'RECKLY AGIN!-DID YO' TRY?
YEH. AH TRIED AWRIGHT.
YO' DID?-THEN YO' HAIN'T NO GENNULMAN AN' AH IS GONNA HAFTA SMACK YO'!
DON'T BOTHUH!
Al Capp
AH BIN SMACKED AWREADY.-AN RIGHT PURTY!
3-23

LI'L ABNER Daisy Mae Understands By Al Capp

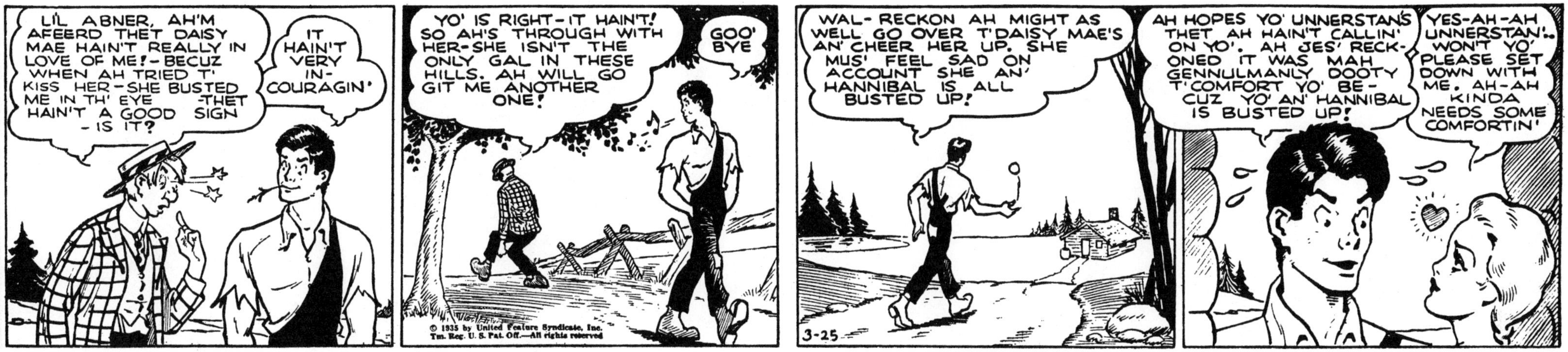

LI'L ABNER, AH'M AFEERD THET DAISY MAE HAIN'T REALLY IN LOVE OF ME! - BECUZ WHEN AH TRIED T' KISS HER - SHE BUSTED ME IN TH' EYE -THET HAIN'T A GOOD SIGN - IS IT?
IT HAIN'T VERY IN-COURAGIN'
YO' IS RIGHT - IT HAIN'T! SO AH'S THROUGH WITH HER - SHE ISN'T THE ONLY GAL IN THESE HILLS. AH WILL GO GIT ME ANOTHER ONE!
GOO' BYE
© 1935 by United Feature Syndicate, Inc. Tm. Reg. U. S. Pat. Off.—All rights reserved
WAL - RECKON AH MIGHT AS WELL GO OVER T'DAISY MAE'S AN' CHEER HER UP. SHE MUS' FEEL SAD ON ACCOUNT SHE AN' HANNIBAL IS ALL BUSTED UP!
3-25
AH HOPES YO' UNNERSTAN'S THET AH HAIN'T CALLIN' ON YO'. AH JES' RECK-ONED IT WAS MAH GENNULMANLY DOOTY T'COMFORT YO' BE-CUZ YO' AN' HANNIBAL IS BUSTED UP!
YES-AH-AH UNNERSTAN'.- WON'T YO' PLEASE SET DOWN WITH ME. AH-AH KINDA NEEDS SOME COMFORTIN'

LI'L ABNER His Bounden Duty By Al Capp

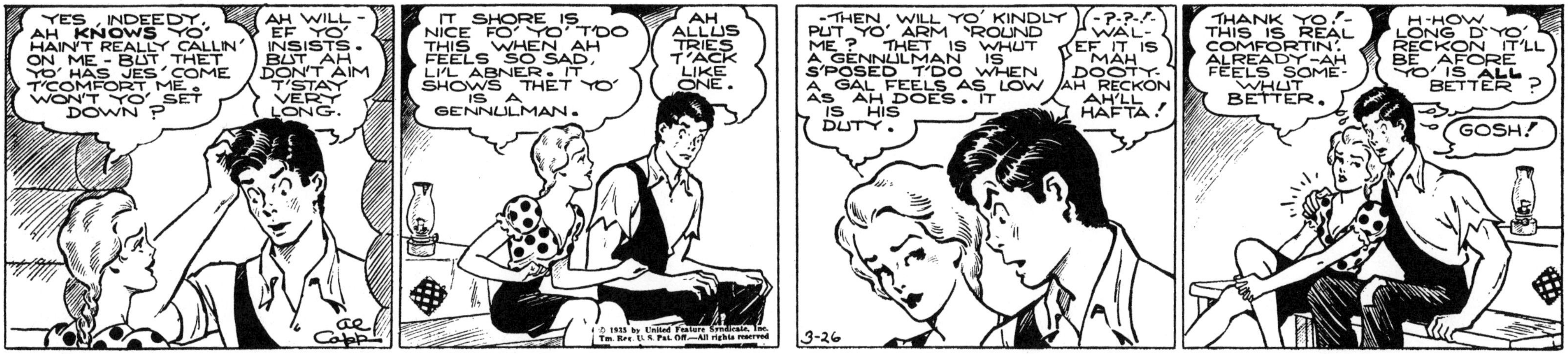

YES, INDEEDY. AH KNOWS YO' HAIN'T REALLY CALLIN' ON ME - BUT THET YO' HAS JES' COME T'COMFORT ME. WON'T YO' SET DOWN?
AH WILL - EF YO' INSISTS. BUT AH DON'T AIM T'STAY VERY LONG.
Al Capp
IT SHORE IS NICE FO' YO' T'DO THIS WHEN AH FEELS SO SAD, LI'L ABNER. IT SHOWS THET YO' IS A GENNULMAN.
AH ALLUS TRIES T'ACK LIKE ONE.
© 1935 by United Feature Syndicate, Inc. Tm. Reg. U. S. Pat. Off.—All rights reserved
-THEN, WILL YO' KINDLY PUT YO' ARM 'ROUND ME? THET IS WHUT A GENNULMAN IS S'POSED T'DO WHEN A GAL FEELS AS LOW AS AH DOES. IT IS HIS DUTY.
-?-?-!- WAL- EF IT IS MAH DOOTY- AH RECKON AH'LL HAFTA!
3-26
THANK YO'!- THIS IS REAL COMFORTIN'. ALREADY - AH FEELS SOME-WHUT BETTER.
H-HOW LONG D'YO' RECKON IT'LL BE AFORE YO' IS ALL BETTER?
GOSH!

LI'L ABNER It Won't Be Long Now By Al Capp

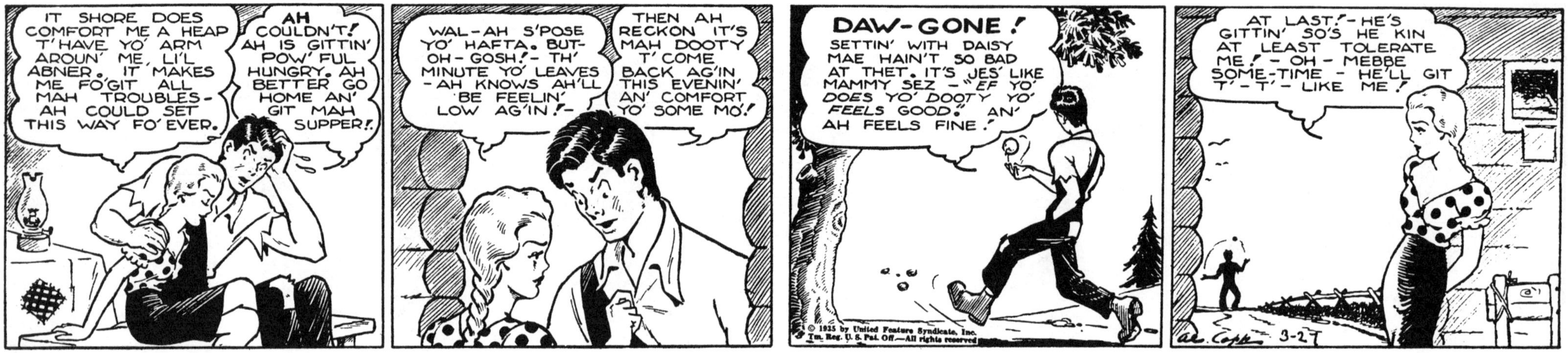

IT SHORE DOES COMFORT ME A HEAP T'HAVE YO' ARM AROUN' ME, LI'L ABNER. IT MAKES ME FO'GIT ALL MAH TROUBLES - AH COULD SET THIS WAY FO' EVER.
AH COULDN'T! AH IS GITTIN' POW'FUL HUNGRY. AH BETTER GO HOME AN' GIT MAH SUPPER!
WAL-AH S'POSE YO' HAFTA. BUT- OH-GOSH!- TH' MINUTE YO' LEAVES -AH KNOWS AH'LL BE FEELIN' LOW AG'IN!-
THEN AH RECKON IT'S MAH DOOTY T'COME BACK AG'IN THIS EVENIN' AN' COMFORT YO' SOME MO'!
DAW-GONE! SETTIN' WITH DAISY MAE HAIN'T SO BAD AT THET. IT'S JES' LIKE MAMMY SEZ - "EF YO' DOES YO' DOOTY YO' FEELS GOOD!" AN' AH FEELS FINE.
© 1935 by United Feature Syndicate, Inc. Tm. Reg. U. S. Pat. Off.—All rights reserved
AT LAST!- HE'S GITTIN' SO'S HE KIN AT LEAST TOLERATE ME! - OH - MEBBE SOME-TIME - HE'LL GIT T'-T'- LIKE ME!
Al Capp 3-27

LI'L ABNER The Mysterious Stranger By Al Capp

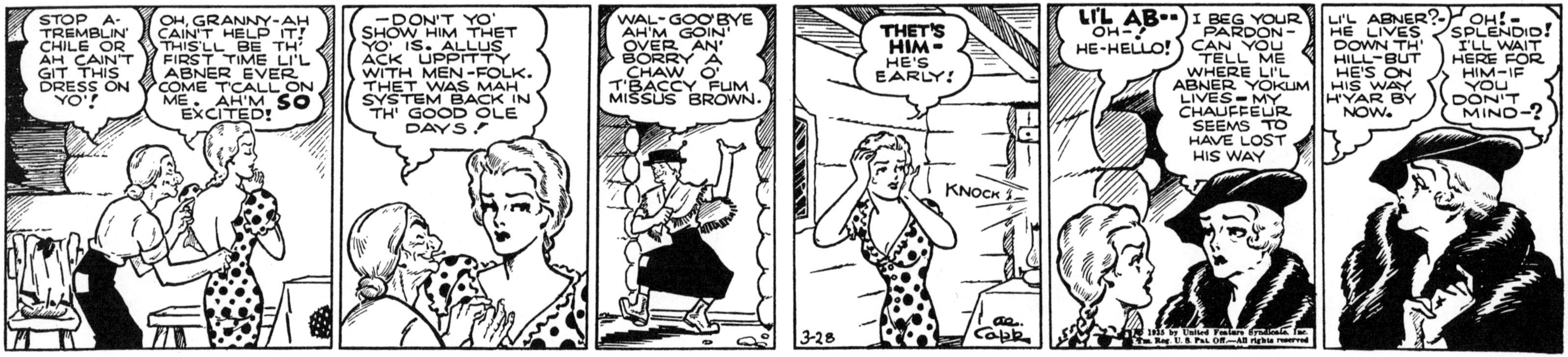

STOP A-TREMBLIN' CHILE OR AH CAIN'T GIT THIS DRESS ON YO'!
OH, GRANNY-AH CAIN'T HELP IT! THIS'LL BE TH' FIRST TIME LI'L ABNER EVER COME T'CALL ON ME. AH'M SO EXCITED!
-DON'T YO' SHOW HIM THET YO' IS. ALLUS ACK UPPITTY WITH MEN-FOLK. THET WAS MAH SYSTEM BACK IN TH' GOOD OLE DAYS!
WAL-GOO'BYE AH'M GOIN' OVER AN' BORRY A CHAW O' T'BACCY FUM MISSUS BROWN.
THET'S HIM- HE'S EARLY!
KNOCK!
3-28
Al Capp
LI'L AB-- OH-! HE-HELLO!
I BEG YOUR PARDON - CAN YOU TELL ME WHERE LI'L ABNER YOKUM LIVES - MY CHAUFFEUR SEEMS TO HAVE LOST HIS WAY
© 1935 by United Feature Syndicate, Inc. Tm. Reg. U. S. Pat. Off.—All rights reserved
LI'L ABNER?- HE LIVES DOWN TH' HILL-BUT HE'S ON HIS WAY H'YAR BY NOW.
OH!- SPLENDID! I'LL WAIT HERE FOR HIM-IF YOU DON'T MIND-?

LI'L ABNER A Heartbreak For Daisy Mae By Al Capp

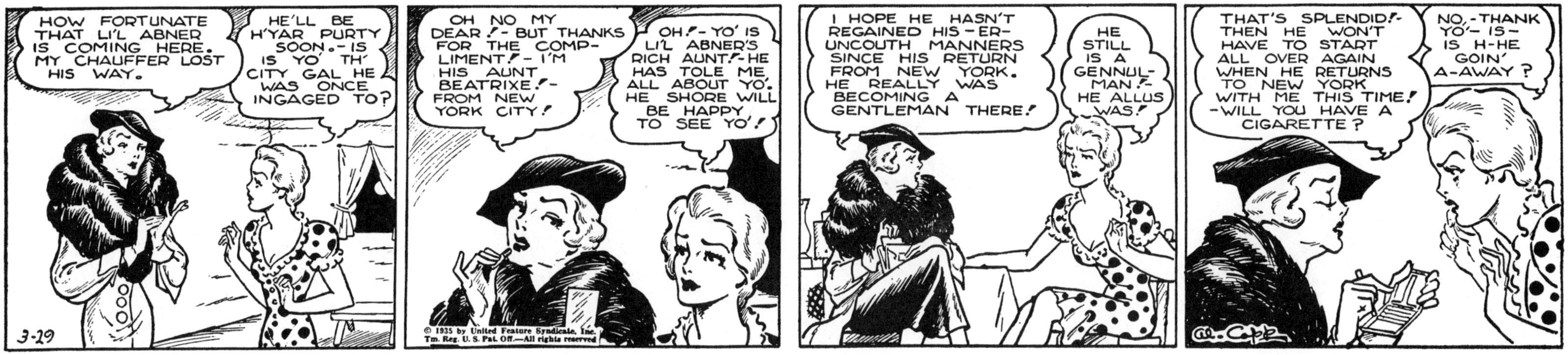
HOW FORTUNATE THAT LI'L ABNER IS COMING HERE. MY CHAUFFER LOST HIS WAY.
HE'LL BE H'YAR PURTY SOON.-IS IS YO' TH' CITY GAL HE WAS ONCE INGAGED TO?
3-29
OH NO MY DEAR!-BUT THANKS FOR THE COMPLIMENT!-I'M HIS AUNT BEATRIXE!-FROM NEW YORK CITY!
OH!-YO' IS LI'L ABNER'S RICH AUNT!-HE HAS TOLE ME ALL ABOUT YO'. HE SHORE WILL BE HAPPY TO SEE YO'!
© 1935 by United Feature Syndicate, Inc. Tm. Reg. U. S. Pat. Off.—All rights reserved
I HOPE HE HASN'T REGAINED HIS-ER-UNCOUTH MANNERS SINCE HIS RETURN FROM NEW YORK. HE REALLY WAS BECOMING A GENTLEMAN THERE!
HE STILL IS A GENNUL-MAN!-HE ALLUS WAS!
THAT'S SPLENDID!-THEN HE WON'T HAVE TO START ALL OVER AGAIN WHEN HE RETURNS TO NEW YORK WITH ME THIS TIME!-WILL YOU HAVE A CIGARETTE?
NO,-THANK YO'-IS-IS H-HE GOIN' A-AWAY?
Al Capp

LI'L ABNER Yo' Is Bustin' Her Heart, Aunt Bessie! By Al Capp

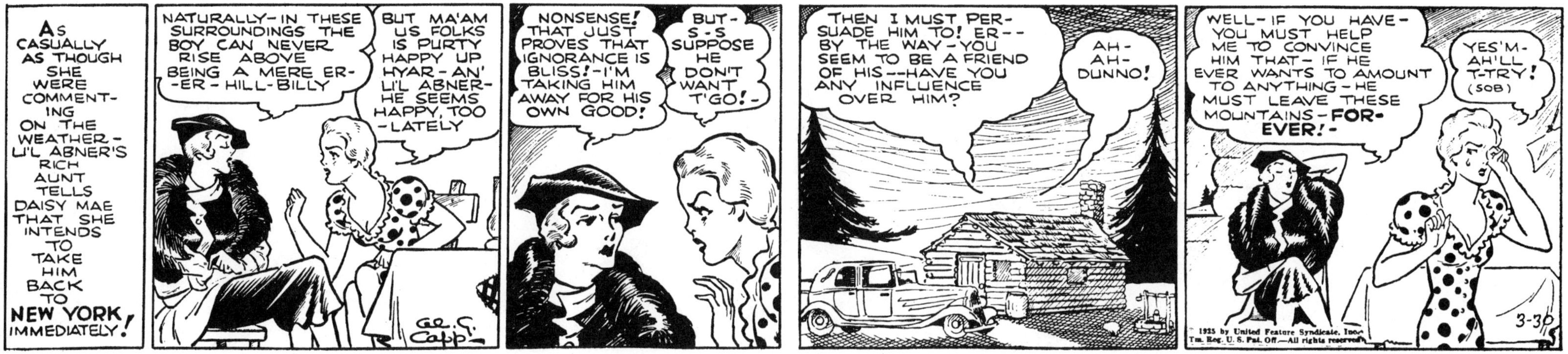
AS CASUALLY AS THOUGH SHE WERE COMMENTING ON THE WEATHER-LI'L ABNER'S RICH AUNT TELLS DAISY MAE THAT SHE INTENDS TO TAKE HIM BACK TO NEW YORK IMMEDIATELY!
NATURALLY-IN THESE SURROUNDINGS THE BOY CAN NEVER RISE ABOVE BEING A MERE ER--ER-HILL-BILLY
BUT MA'AM US FOLKS IS PURTY HAPPY UP HYAR-AN' LI'L ABNER-HE SEEMS HAPPY, TOO-LATELY
Al G. Capp
NONSENSE! THAT JUST PROVES THAT IGNORANCE IS BLISS!-I'M TAKING HIM AWAY FOR HIS OWN GOOD!
BUT-S-S SUPPOSE HE DON'T WANT T'GO!-
THEN I MUST PERSUADE HIM TO! ER--BY THE WAY-YOU SEEM TO BE A FRIEND OF HIS--HAVE YOU ANY INFLUENCE OVER HIM?
AH-AH-DUNNO!
WELL-IF YOU HAVE-YOU MUST HELP ME TO CONVINCE HIM THAT-IF HE EVER WANTS TO AMOUNT TO ANYTHING-HE MUST LEAVE THESE MOUNTAINS-FOR-EVER!-
YES'M-AH'LL T-TRY! (SOB)
1935 by United Feature Syndicate, Inc. Tm. Reg. U. S. Pat. Off.—All rights reserved
3-30

LI'L ABNER

Love Is Like That!

By Al Capp

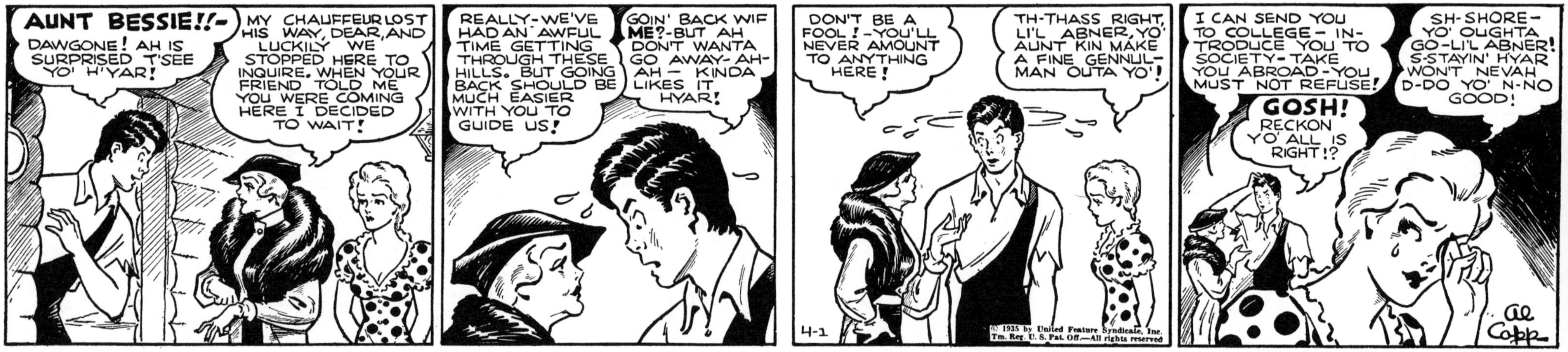
AUNT BESSIE!!- DAWGONE! AH IS SURPRISED T'SEE YO' H'YAR!
MY CHAUFFEUR LOST HIS WAY, DEAR, AND LUCKILY WE STOPPED HERE TO INQUIRE. WHEN YOUR FRIEND TOLD ME YOU WERE COMING HERE I DECIDED TO WAIT!
REALLY-WE'VE HAD AN AWFUL TIME GETTING THROUGH THESE HILLS. BUT GOING BACK SHOULD BE MUCH EASIER WITH YOU TO GUIDE US!
GOIN' BACK WIF ME?-BUT AH DON'T WANTA GO AWAY-AH-AH- KINDA LIKES IT HYAR!
DON'T BE A FOOL!-YOU'LL NEVER AMOUNT TO ANYTHING HERE!
TH-THASS RIGHT, LI'L ABNER, YO' AUNT KIN MAKE A FINE GENNUL-MAN OUTA YO'!
4-1
© 1935 by United Feature Syndicate, Inc. Tm. Reg. U. S. Pat. Off.—All rights reserved
I CAN SEND YOU TO COLLEGE - INTRODUCE YOU TO SOCIETY - TAKE YOU ABROAD - YOU MUST NOT REFUSE!
SH-SHORE- YO' OUGHTA GO-LI'L ABNER! S-STAYIN' HYAR WON'T NEVAH D-DO YO' N-NO GOOD!
GOSH! RECKON YO' ALL IS RIGHT!?
al Capp

LI'L ABNER

The Greatest Sacrifice

By Al Capp

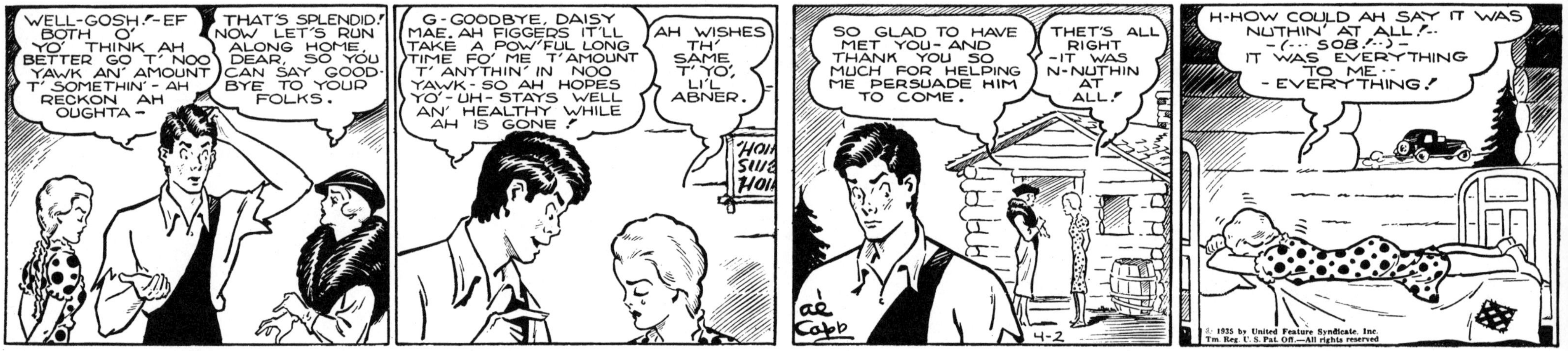
WELL-GOSH!-EF BOTH O' YO' THINK AH BETTER GO T' NOO YAWK AN' AMOUNT T' SOMETHIN'-AH RECKON AH OUGHTA-
THAT'S SPLENDID! NOW LET'S RUN ALONG HOME, DEAR, SO YOU CAN SAY GOOD-BYE TO YOUR FOLKS.
G-GOODBYE, DAISY MAE. AH FIGGERS IT'LL TAKE A POW'FUL LONG TIME FO' ME T'AMOUNT T' ANYTHIN' IN NOO YAWK-SO AH HOPES YO'-UH-STAYS WELL AN' HEALTHY WHILE AH IS GONE!
AH WISHES TH' SAME T' YO', LI'L ABNER.
SO GLAD TO HAVE MET YOU- AND THANK YOU SO MUCH FOR HELPING ME PERSUADE HIM TO COME.
THET'S ALL RIGHT -IT WAS N-NUTHIN AT ALL!
al Capp
4-2
H-HOW COULD AH SAY IT WAS NUTHIN' AT ALL!- -(...SOB!...)- IT WAS EVERYTHING TO ME-- -EVERYTHING!
© 1935 by United Feature Syndicate, Inc. Tm. Reg. U. S. Pat. Off.—All rights reserved

LI'L ABNER Daisy Mae's A Sticker By Al Capp

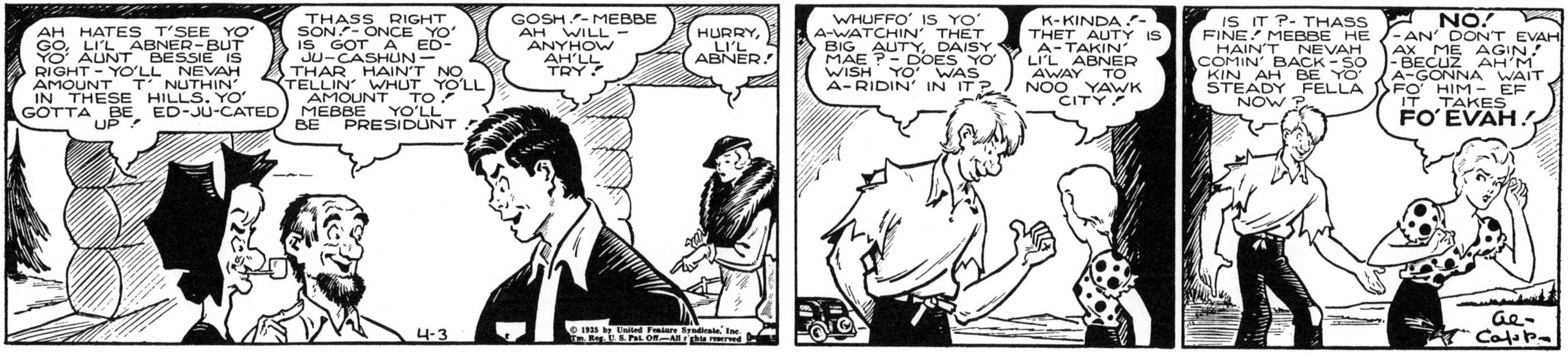
AH HATES T'SEE YO' GO, LI'L ABNER-BUT YO' AUNT BESSIE IS RIGHT-YO'LL NEVAH AMOUNT T' NUTHIN' IN THESE HILLS. YO' GOTTA BE ED-JU-CATED UP!
THASS RIGHT SON!-ONCE YO' IS GOT A ED-JU-CASHUN-THAR HAIN'T NO TELLIN' WHUT YO'LL AMOUNT TO! MEBBE YO'LL BE PRESIDUNT!
GOSH!-MEBBE AH WILL-ANYHOW AH'LL TRY!
HURRY, LI'L ABNER!
4-3
© 1935 by United Feature Syndicate, Inc. Tm. Reg. U. S. Pat. Off.—All rights reserved
WHUFFO' IS YO' A-WATCHIN' THET BIG AUTY, DAISY MAE?-DOES YO' WISH YO' WAS A-RIDIN' IN IT?
K-KINDA!-THET AUTY IS A-TAKIN' LI'L ABNER AWAY TO NOO YAWK CITY!
IS IT?-THASS FINE! MEBBE HE HAIN'T NEVAH COMIN' BACK-SO KIN AH BE YO' STEADY FELLA NOW?
NO!-AN' DON'T EVAH AX ME AGIN!-BECUZ AH'M A-GONNA WAIT FO' HIM-EF IT TAKES FO'EVAH!

LI'L ABNER Who Is He? By Al Capp

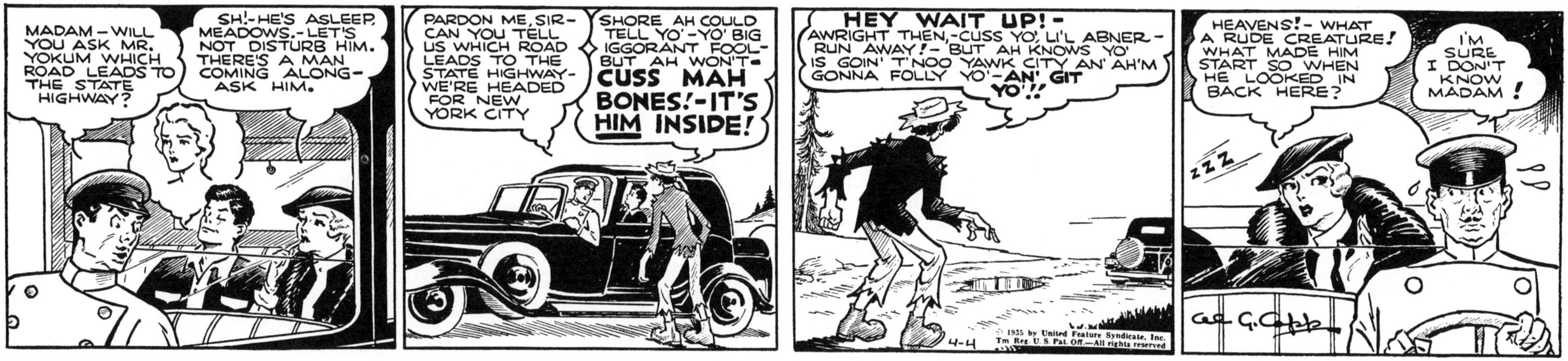
MADAM-WILL YOU ASK MR. YOKUM WHICH ROAD LEADS TO THE STATE HIGHWAY?
SH!-HE'S ASLEEP, MEADOWS.-LET'S NOT DISTURB HIM. THERE'S A MAN COMING ALONG-ASK HIM.
PARDON ME, SIR-CAN YOU TELL US WHICH ROAD LEADS TO THE STATE HIGHWAY-WE'RE HEADED FOR NEW YORK CITY
SHORE AH COULD TELL YO'-YO' BIG IGGORANT FOOL-BUT AH WON'T-CUSS MAH BONES!-IT'S HIM INSIDE!
HEY WAIT UP!-AWRIGHT THEN,-CUSS YO', LI'L ABNER-RUN AWAY!-BUT AH KNOWS YO' IS GOIN' T'NOO YAWK CITY AN' AH'M GONNA FOLLY YO'-AN' GIT YO'!!
4-4
© 1935 by United Feature Syndicate, Inc. Tm Reg. U. S. Pat. Off.—All rights reserved
HEAVENS!-WHAT A RUDE CREATURE! WHAT MADE HIM START SO WHEN HE LOOKED IN BACK HERE?
I'M SURE I DON'T KNOW MADAM!
ZZZ

LI'L ABNER Trailin' Abner **By Al Capp**

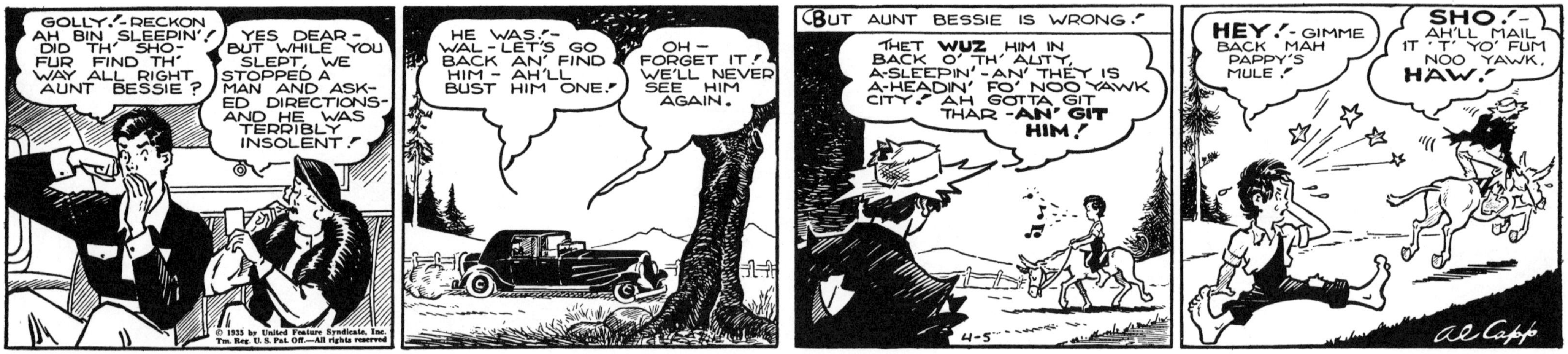
GOLLY!-RECKON AH BIN SLEEPIN'! DID TH' SHO-FUR FIND TH' WAY ALL RIGHT AUNT BESSIE?
YES DEAR-BUT WHILE YOU SLEPT, WE STOPPED A MAN AND ASKED DIRECTIONS-AND HE WAS TERRIBLY INSOLENT!
© 1935 by United Feature Syndicate, Inc. Tm. Reg. U. S. Pat. Off.—All rights reserved
HE WAS!-WAL-LET'S GO BACK AN' FIND HIM-AH'LL BUST HIM ONE!
OH-FORGET IT! WE'LL NEVER SEE HIM AGAIN.
BUT AUNT BESSIE IS WRONG!
THET WUZ HIM IN BACK O' TH' AUTY, A-SLEEPIN'-AN' THEY IS A-HEADIN' FO' NOO YAWK CITY! AH GOTTA GIT THAR-AN' GIT HIM!
4-5
HEY!-GIMME BACK MAH PAPPY'S MULE!
SHO!-AH'LL MAIL IT 'T' YO' FUM NOO YAWK. HAW!
Al Capp

LI'L ABNER Hot On Abner's Trail! **By Al Capp**

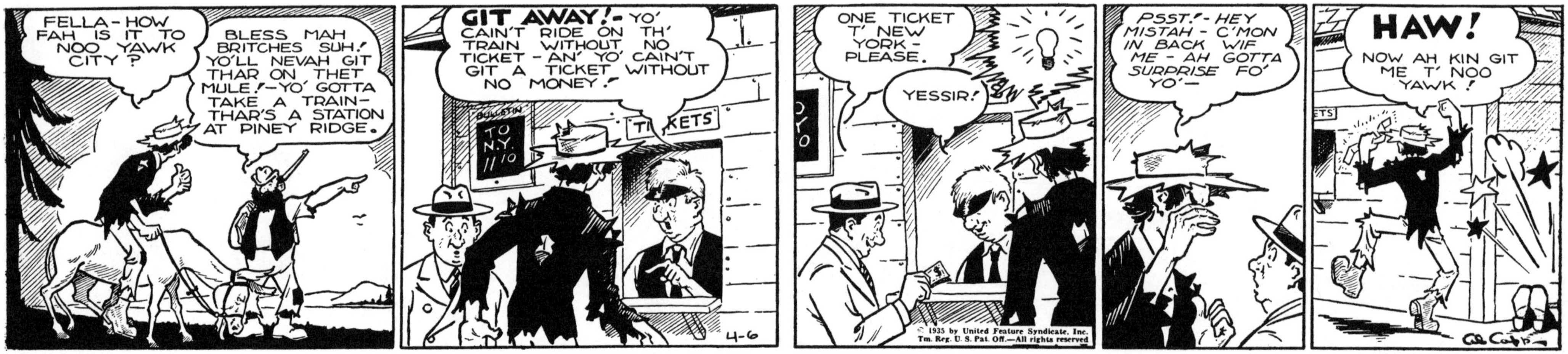
FELLA-HOW FAH IS IT TO NOO YAWK CITY?
BLESS MAH BRITCHES SUH! YO'LL NEVAH GIT THAR ON THET MULE!-YO' GOTTA TAKE A TRAIN-THAR'S A STATION AT PINEY RIDGE.
GIT AWAY!-YO' CAIN'T RIDE ON TH' TRAIN WITHOUT NO TICKET-AN' YO' CAIN'T GIT A TICKET WITHOUT NO MONEY!
TO N.Y. 11.10
TICKETS
4-6
ONE TICKET T' NEW YORK-PLEASE.
YESSIR!
© 1935 by United Feature Syndicate, Inc. Tm. Reg. U. S. Pat. Off.—All rights reserved
PSST!-HEY MISTAH-C'MON IN BACK WIF ME-AH GOTTA SURPRISE FO' YO'-
HAW!
NOW AH KIN GIT ME T' NOO YAWK!
Al Capp

LI'L ABNER — A Real Pal — By Al Capp

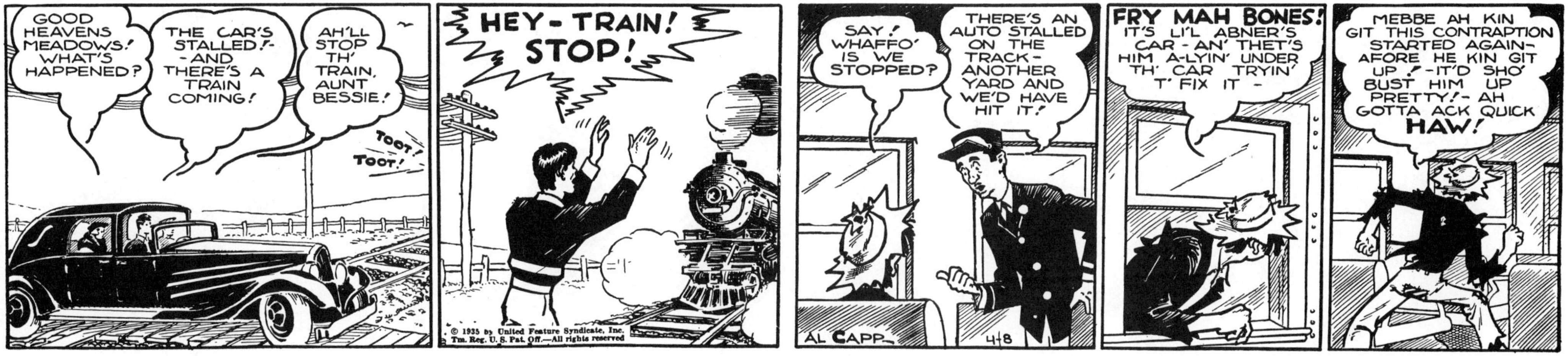
GOOD HEAVENS MEADOWS! WHAT'S HAPPENED?
THE CAR'S STALLED! - AND THERE'S A TRAIN COMING!
AH'LL STOP TH' TRAIN, AUNT BESSIE!
TOOT! TOOT!
HEY - TRAIN! STOP!
© 1935 by United Feature Syndicate, Inc. Tm. Reg. U. S. Pat. Off.—All rights reserved
SAY! WHAFFO' IS WE STOPPED?
THERE'S AN AUTO STALLED ON THE TRACK - ANOTHER YARD AND WE'D HAVE HIT IT!
AL CAPP
4-8
FRY MAH BONES! IT'S LI'L ABNER'S CAR - AN' THET'S HIM A-LYIN' UNDER TH' CAR TRYIN' T' FIX IT -
MEBBE AH KIN GIT THIS CONTRAPTION STARTED AGAIN - AFORE HE KIN GIT UP! - IT'D SHO' BUST HIM UP PRETTY! - AH GOTTA ACK QUICK HAW!

LI'L ABNER — A Quick Education — By Al Capp

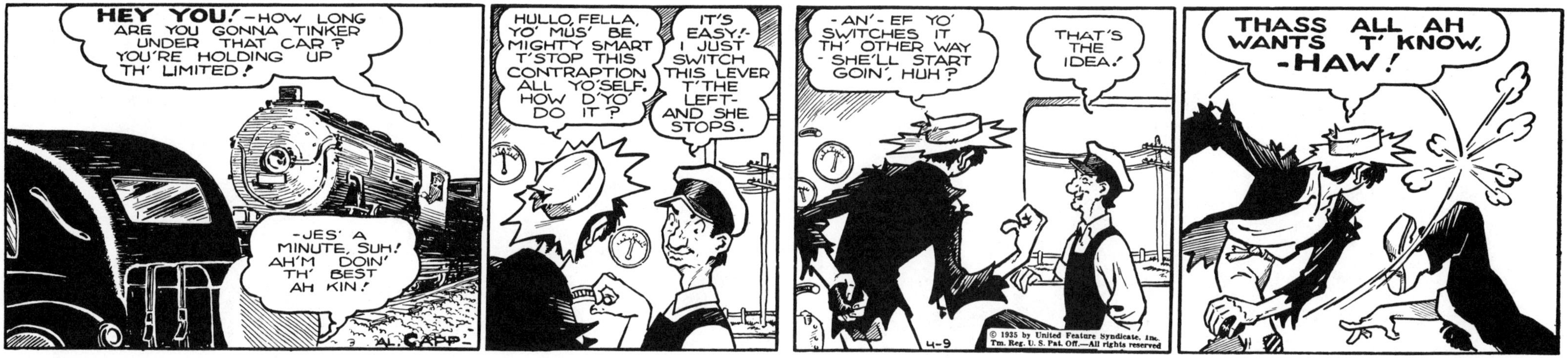
HEY YOU! - HOW LONG ARE YOU GONNA TINKER UNDER THAT CAR? YOU'RE HOLDING UP TH' LIMITED!
- JES' A MINUTE, SUH! AH'M DOIN' TH' BEST AH KIN!
AL CAPP
HULLO, FELLA, YO' MUS' BE MIGHTY SMART T'STOP THIS CONTRAPTION ALL YO'SELF. HOW D'YO' DO IT?
IT'S EASY! - I JUST SWITCH THIS LEVER T'THE LEFT - AND SHE STOPS.
- AN' - EF YO' SWITCHES IT TH' OTHER WAY - SHE'LL START GOIN', HUH?
THAT'S THE IDEA!
4-9
© 1935 by United Feature Syndicate, Inc. Tm. Reg. U. S. Pat. Off.—All rights reserved
THASS ALL AH WANTS T' KNOW, - HAW!

LI'L ABNER Caught Short By Al Capp

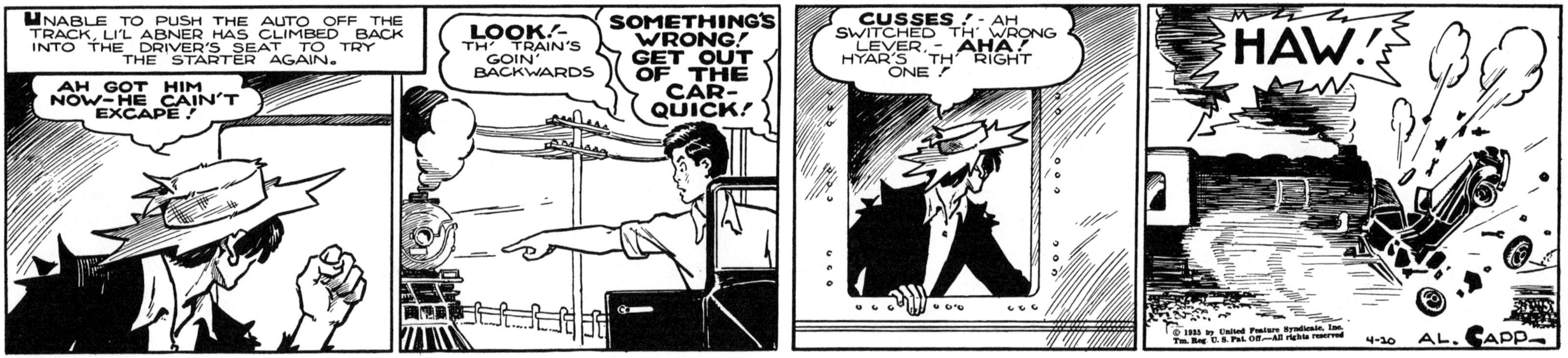
UNABLE TO PUSH THE AUTO OFF THE TRACK, LI'L ABNER HAS CLIMBED BACK INTO THE DRIVER'S SEAT TO TRY THE STARTER AGAIN.
AH GOT HIM NOW—HE CAIN'T ESCAPE!
LOOK!— TH' TRAIN'S GOIN' BACKWARDS
SOMETHING'S WRONG! GET OUT OF THE CAR— QUICK!
CUSSES!—AH SWITCHED TH' WRONG LEVER,—AHA! HYAR'S TH' RIGHT ONE!
HAW!
© 1935 by United Feature Syndicate, Inc. Tm. Reg. U. S. Pat. Off.—All rights reserved
4-10
AL. CAPP

LI'L ABNER A Jolly Trip in Store By Al Capp

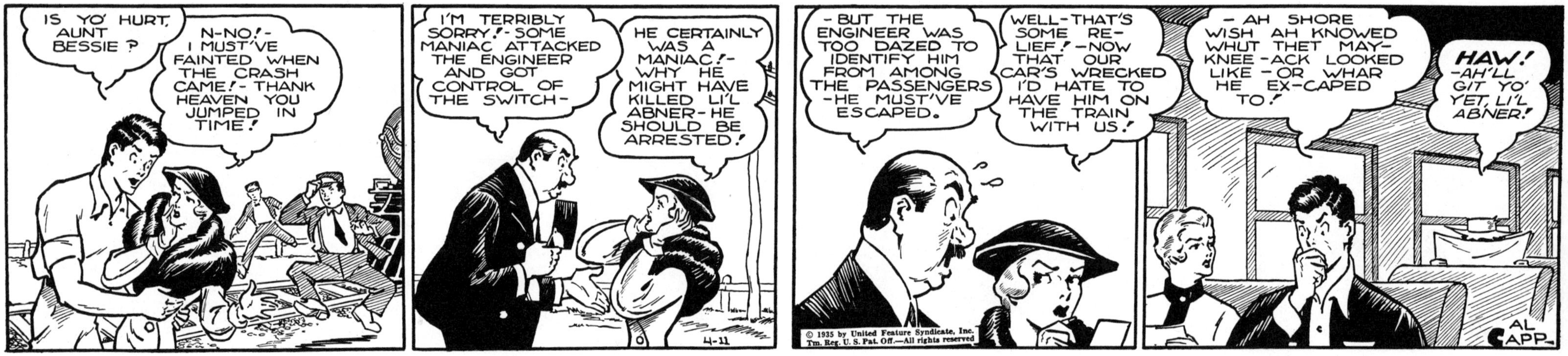
IS YO' HURT, AUNT BESSIE?
N-NO!— I MUST'VE FAINTED WHEN THE CRASH CAME!—THANK HEAVEN YOU JUMPED IN TIME!
I'M TERRIBLY SORRY!—SOME MANIAC ATTACKED THE ENGINEER AND GOT CONTROL OF THE SWITCH—
HE CERTAINLY WAS A MANIAC!—WHY HE MIGHT HAVE KILLED LI'L ABNER—HE SHOULD BE ARRESTED!
4-11
—BUT THE ENGINEER WAS TOO DAZED TO IDENTIFY HIM FROM AMONG THE PASSENGERS—HE MUST'VE ESCAPED.
WELL—THAT'S SOME RE-LIEF!—NOW THAT OUR CAR'S WRECKED I'D HATE TO HAVE HIM ON THE TRAIN WITH US!
© 1935 by United Feature Syndicate, Inc. Tm. Reg. U. S. Pat. Off.—All rights reserved
—AH SHORE WISH AH KNOWED WHUT THET MAY-KNEE-ACK LOOKED LIKE—OR WHAR HE EX-CAPED TO!
HAW! —AH'LL GIT YO' YET, LI'L ABNER!
AL CAPP

LI'L ABNER Meet Mr. Bashmugg By Al Capp

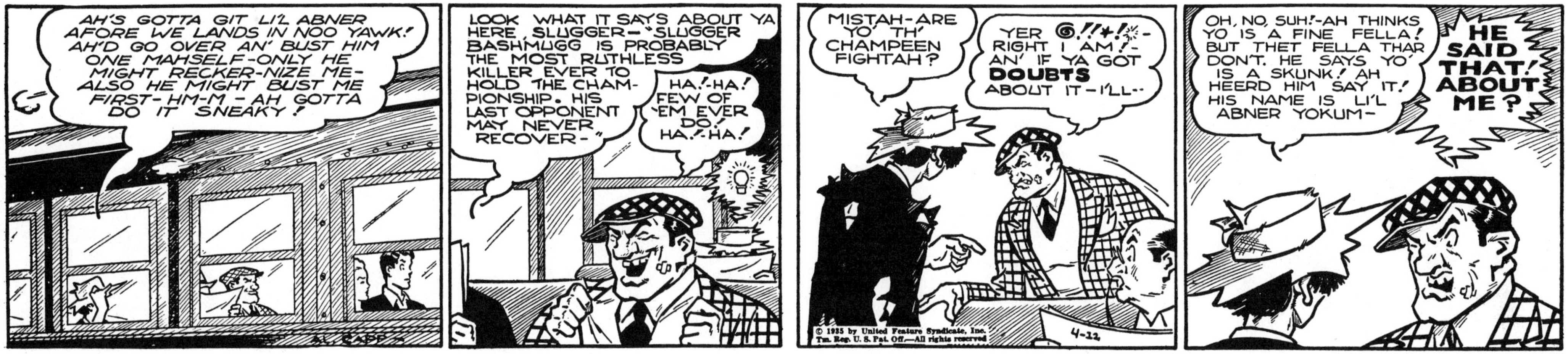

AH'S GOTTA GIT LI'L ABNER AFORE WE LANDS IN NOO YAWK! AH'D GO OVER AN' BUST HIM ONE MAHSELF-ONLY HE MIGHT RECKER-NIZE ME-ALSO HE MIGHT BUST ME FIRST-HM-M-AH GOTTA DO IT SNEAKY!
AL CAPP
LOOK WHAT IT SAYS ABOUT YA HERE, SLUGGER-"SLUGGER BASHMUGG IS PROBABLY THE MOST RUTHLESS KILLER EVER TO HOLD THE CHAMPIONSHIP. HIS LAST OPPONENT MAY NEVER RECOVER-"
HA!-HA! FEW OF 'EM EVER DO! HA!-HA!
MISTAH-ARE YO' TH' CHAMPEEN FIGHTAH?
YER @!!+!- RIGHT I AM!-AN' IF YA GOT DOUBTS ABOUT IT-I'LL--
© 1935 by United Feature Syndicate, Inc. Tm. Reg. U. S. Pat. Off.—All rights reserved
4-22
OH, NO, SUH!-AH THINKS YO' IS A FINE FELLA! BUT THET FELLA THAR DON'T. HE SAYS YO' IS A SKUNK! AH HEERD HIM SAY IT! HIS NAME IS LI'L ABNER YOKUM-
HE SAID THAT! ABOUT ME?

LI'L ABNER Invitation To A Slaughter By Al Capp

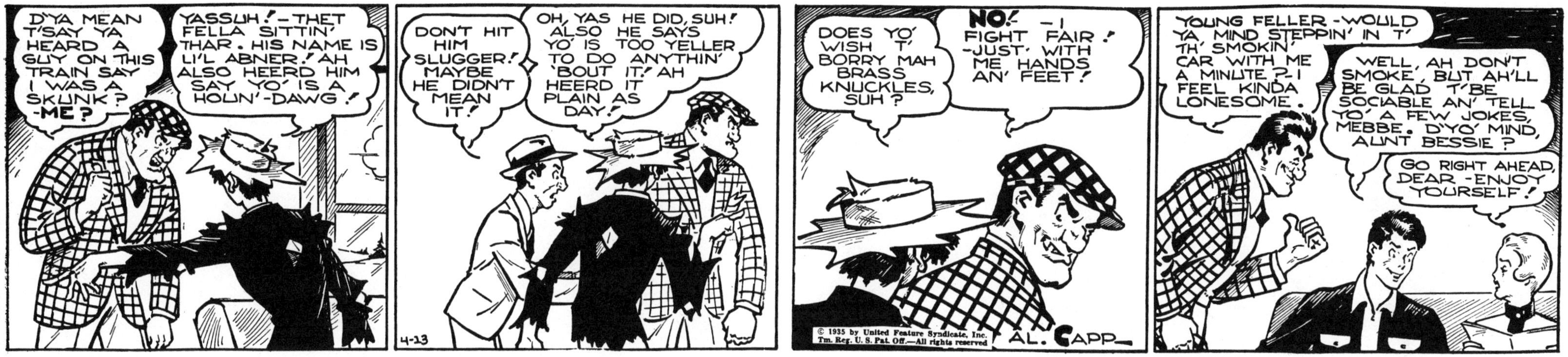

D'YA MEAN T'SAY YA HEARD A GUY ON THIS TRAIN SAY I WAS A SKUNK? -ME?
YASSUH!-THET FELLA SITTIN' THAR. HIS NAME IS LI'L ABNER! AH ALSO HEERD HIM SAY YO' IS A HOUN'-DAWG!
DON'T HIT HIM SLUGGER! MAYBE HE DIDN'T MEAN IT!
OH, YAS HE DID, SUH! ALSO HE SAYS YO' IS TOO YELLER TO DO ANYTHIN' 'BOUT IT! AH HEERD IT PLAIN AS DAY!
4-23
DOES YO' WISH T' BORRY MAH BRASS KNUCKLES, SUH?
NO!-I FIGHT FAIR!-JUST WITH ME HANDS AN' FEET!
© 1935 by United Feature Syndicate, Inc. Tm. Reg. U. S. Pat. Off.—All rights reserved
AL. CAPP
YOUNG FELLER-WOULD YA MIND STEPPIN' IN T' TH' SMOKIN' CAR WITH ME A MINUTE?-I FEEL KINDA LONESOME.
WELL, AH DON'T SMOKE, BUT AH'LL BE GLAD T'BE SOCIABLE AN' TELL YO' A FEW JOKES, MEBBE. D'YO' MIND, AUNT BESSIE?
GO RIGHT AHEAD, DEAR-ENJOY YOURSELF!

LI'L ABNER Glad To Oblige ! By Al Capp

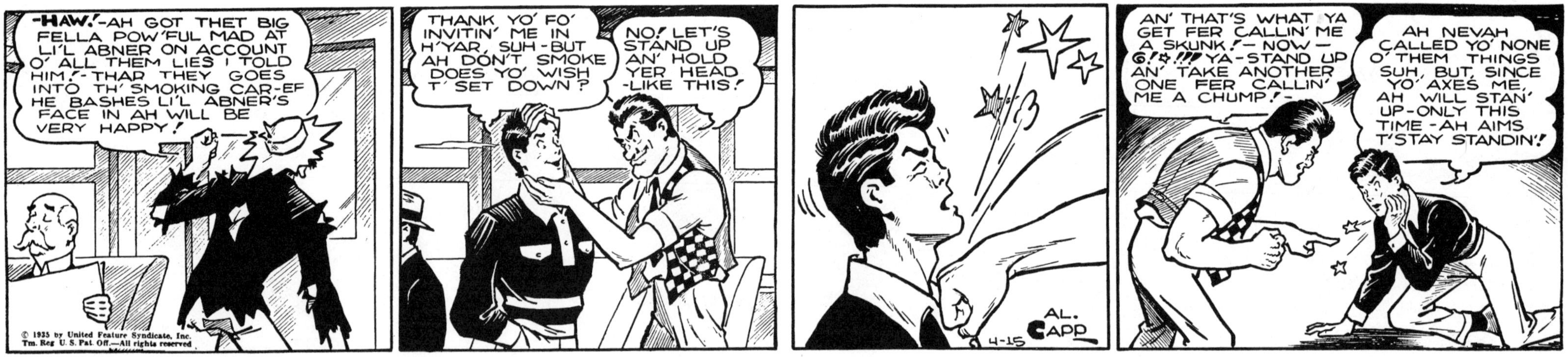

-HAW!-AH GOT THET BIG FELLA POW'FUL MAD AT LI'L ABNER ON ACCOUNT O' ALL THEM LIES I TOLD HIM!-THAR THEY GOES INTO TH' SMOKING CAR-EF HE BASHES LI'L ABNER'S FACE IN AH WILL BE VERY HAPPY!
© 1935 by United Feature Syndicate, Inc. Tm. Reg U. S. Pat. Off.—All rights reserved
THANK YO' FO' INVITIN' ME IN H'YAR, SUH-BUT AH DON'T SMOKE DOES YO' WISH T' SET DOWN?
NO! LET'S STAND UP AN' HOLD YER HEAD -LIKE THIS!
AL. CAPP 4-15
AN' THAT'S WHAT YA GET FER CALLIN' ME A SKUNK!-NOW-G!☆!!! YA-STAND UP AN' TAKE ANOTHER ONE FER CALLIN' ME A CHUMP!-
AH NEVAH CALLED YO' NONE O' THEM THINGS SUH, BUT, SINCE YO' AXES ME, AH WILL STAN' UP-ONLY THIS TIME-AH AIMS T'STAY STANDIN'!

LI'L ABNER A Chip Off the Old Block By Al Capp

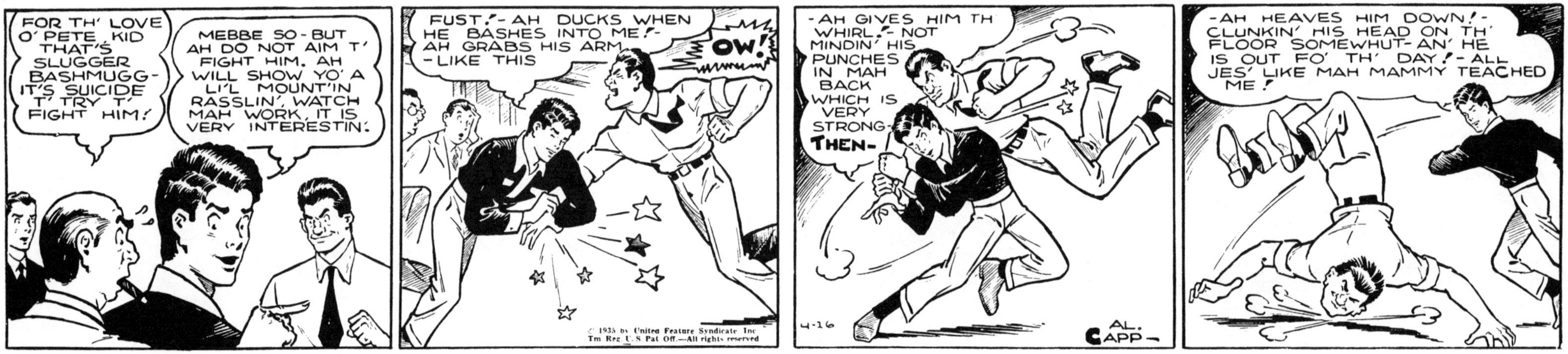

FOR TH' LOVE O' PETE, KID THAT'S SLUGGER BASHMUGG-IT'S SUICIDE T' TRY T' FIGHT HIM!
MEBBE SO-BUT AH DO NOT AIM T' FIGHT HIM. AH WILL SHOW YO' A LI'L MOUNT'IN RASSLIN', WATCH MAH WORK, IT IS VERY INTERESTIN'.
FUST!-AH DUCKS WHEN HE BASHES INTO ME!-AH GRABS HIS ARM -LIKE THIS
OW!
© 1935 by United Feature Syndicate Inc Tm Reg U S Pat Off.—All rights reserved
-AH GIVES HIM TH WHIRL!-NOT MINDIN' HIS PUNCHES IN MAH BACK WHICH IS VERY STRONG-THEN-
4-16 AL. CAPP
-AH HEAVES HIM DOWN!-CLUNKIN' HIS HEAD ON TH' FLOOR SOMEWHUT-AN' HE IS OUT FO' TH' DAY!-ALL JES' LIKE MAH MAMMY TEACHED ME!

LI'L ABNER Too Late ! By Al Capp

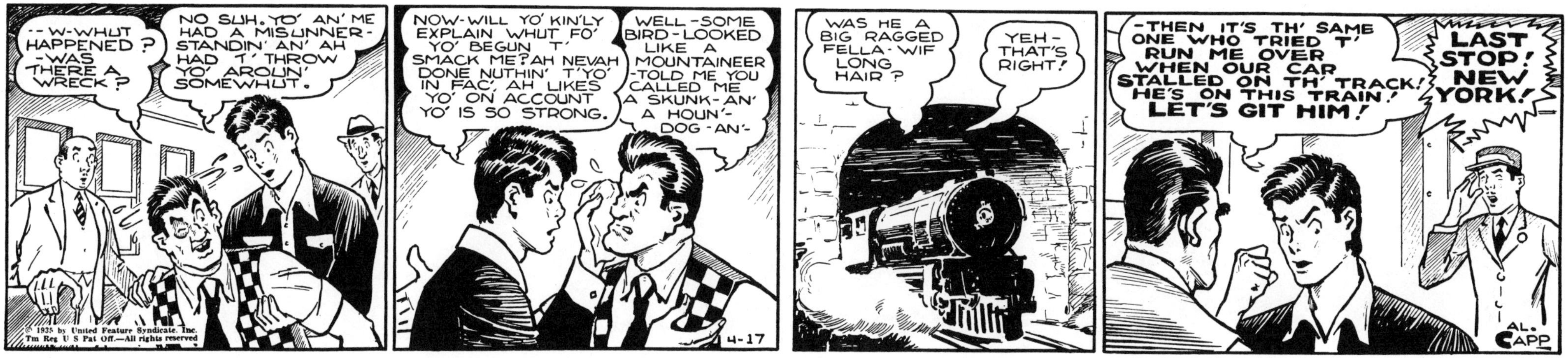

-- W-WHUT HAPPENED ? -WAS THERE A WRECK ?
NO SUH. YO' AN' ME HAD A MISUNNER-STANDIN' AN' AH HAD T' THROW YO' AROUN' SOMEWHUT.
© 1935 by United Feature Syndicate, Inc. Tm Reg U S Pat Off.—All rights reserved
NOW-WILL YO' KIN'LY EXPLAIN WHUT FO' YO' BEGUN T' SMACK ME? AH NEVAH DONE NUTHIN' T'YO' IN FAC', AH LIKES YO' ON ACCOUNT YO' IS SO STRONG.
WELL-SOME BIRD-LOOKED LIKE A MOUNTAINEER -TOLD ME YOU CALLED ME A SKUNK-AN' A HOUN'-DOG-AN'-
4-17
WAS HE A BIG RAGGED FELLA-WIF LONG HAIR ?
YEH-THAT'S RIGHT!
-THEN IT'S TH' SAME ONE WHO TRIED T' RUN ME OVER WHEN OUR CAR STALLED ON TH' TRACK! HE'S ON THIS TRAIN! LET'S GIT HIM!
LAST STOP! NEW YORK!
AL. CAPP

LI'L ABNER A Clever Plan By Al Capp

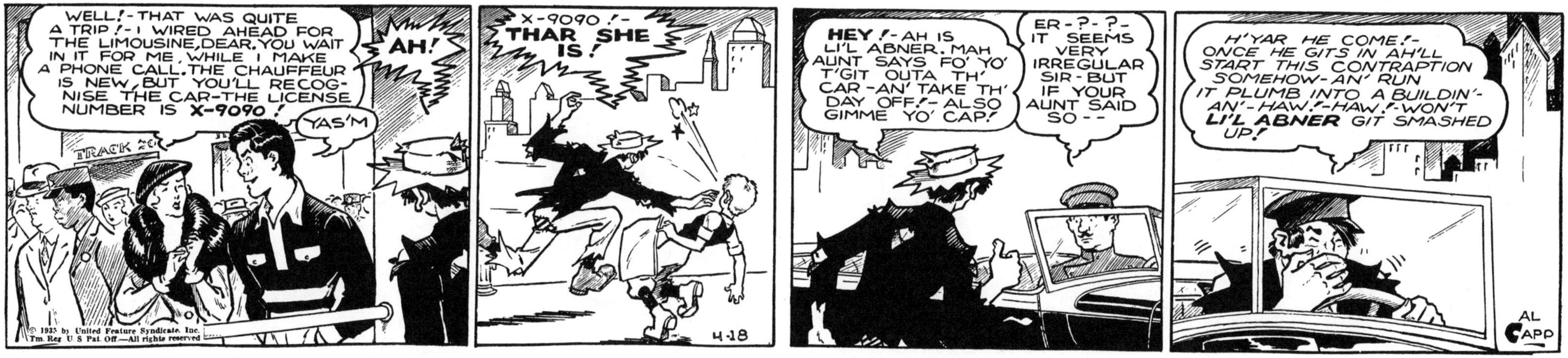

WELL!-THAT WAS QUITE A TRIP!-I WIRED AHEAD FOR THE LIMOUSINE, DEAR. YOU WAIT IN IT FOR ME, WHILE I MAKE A PHONE CALL. THE CHAUFFEUR IS NEW, BUT YOU'LL RECOGNISE THE CAR-THE LICENSE NUMBER IS X-9090 !
YAS'M
AH!
TRACK 20
© 1935 by United Feature Syndicate, Inc. Tm Reg U S Pat Off.—All rights reserved
X-9090 !- THAR SHE IS!
4-18
HEY!-AH IS LI'L ABNER. MAH AUNT SAYS FO' YO' T'GIT OUTA TH' CAR-AN' TAKE TH' DAY OFF!-ALSO GIMME YO' CAP!
ER-?-?-IT SEEMS VERY IRREGULAR SIR-BUT IF YOUR AUNT SAID SO--
H'YAR HE COME!-ONCE HE GITS IN AH'LL START THIS CONTRAPTION SOMEHOW-AN' RUN IT PLUMB INTO A BUILDIN'-AN'-HAW!-HAW!-WON'T LI'L ABNER GIT SMASHED UP!
AL CAPP

LI'L ABNER
When Yokum Meets Scragg

By Al Capp

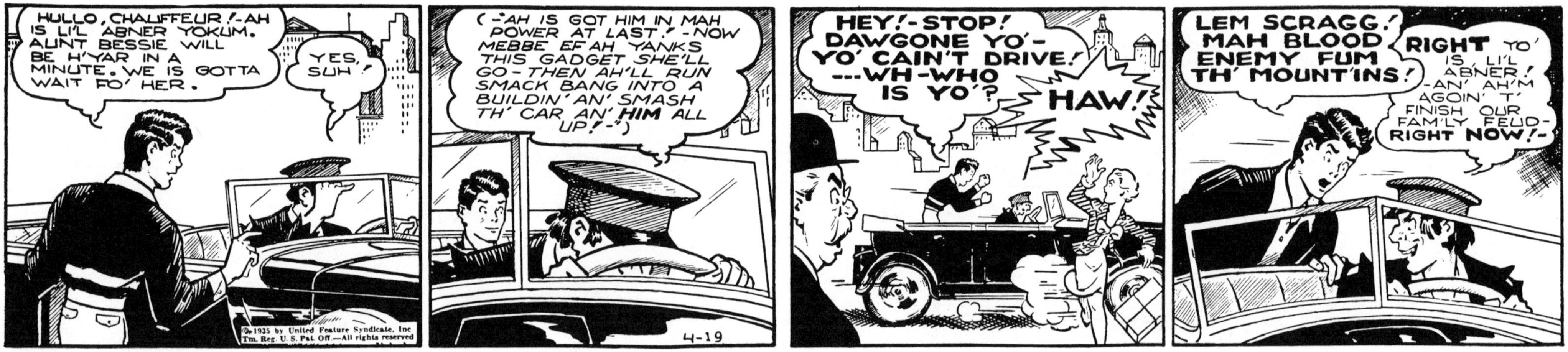
HULLO, CHAUFFEUR!-AH IS LI'L ABNER YOKUM. AUNT BESSIE WILL BE H'YAR IN A MINUTE. WE IS GOTTA WAIT FO' HER.
YES, SUH!
© 1935 by United Feature Syndicate, Inc. Tm. Reg. U. S. Pat. Off.—All rights reserved
(-"AH IS GOT HIM IN MAH POWER AT LAST!" -NOW MEBBE EF AH YANKS THIS GADGET SHE'LL GO-THEN AH'LL RUN SMACK BANG INTO A BUILDIN' AN' SMASH TH' CAR AN' **HIM** ALL UP!-")
4-19
HEY!-STOP! DAWGONE YO'-YO' CAIN'T DRIVE! ---WH-WHO IS YO'?
HAW!
LEM SCRAGG! MAH BLOOD ENEMY FUM TH' MOUNT'INS!
RIGHT YO' IS, LI'L ABNER! -AN' AH'M AGOIN' T' FINISH OUR FAM'LY FEUD-**RIGHT NOW!**-

LI'L ABNER
No Such Luck !

By Al Capp

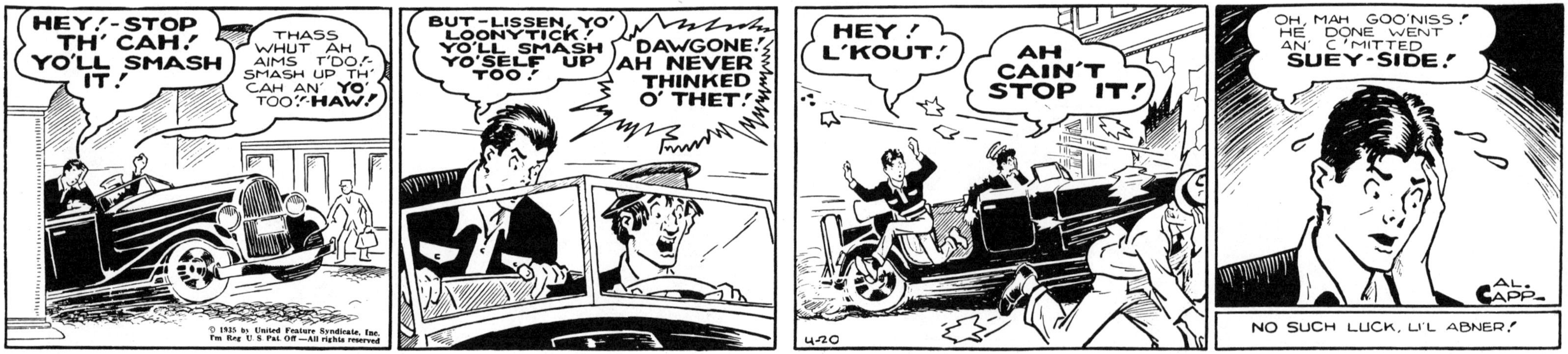
HEY!-STOP TH' CAH! YO'LL SMASH IT!
THASS WHUT AH AIMS T'DO!-SMASH UP TH' CAH AN' **YO'** TOO!-**HAW!**
© 1935 by United Feature Syndicate, Inc. Tm Reg U. S. Pat. Off.—All rights reserved
BUT-LISSEN, YO' LOONYTICK! YO'LL SMASH YO'SELF UP TOO!
DAWGONE! AH NEVER THINKED O' THET!
HEY! L'KOUT!
AH CAIN'T STOP IT!
4-20
OH, MAH GOO'NISS! HE DONE WENT AN' C'MITTED **SUEY-SIDE!**
AL. CAPP
NO SUCH LUCK, LI'L ABNER!

LI'L ABNER — Nevah Heerd o' Such a Animal — By Al Capp

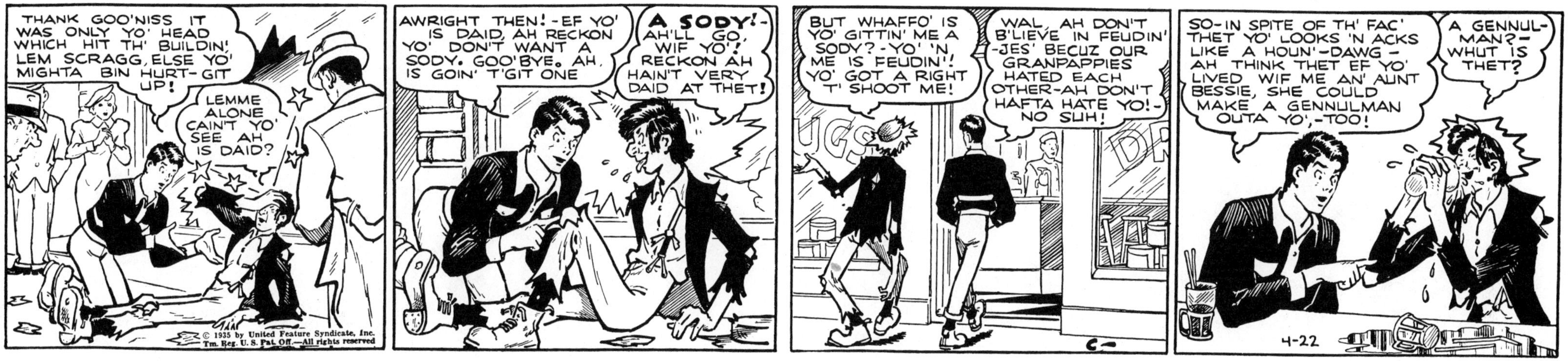

THANK GOO'NISS IT WAS ONLY YO' HEAD WHICH HIT TH' BUILDIN'! LEM SCRAGG, ELSE YO' MIGHTA BIN HURT- GIT UP!
LEMME ALONE CAIN'T YO' SEE AH IS DAID?
© 1935 by United Feature Syndicate, Inc. Tm. Reg. U. S. Pat. Off.—All rights reserved
AWRIGHT THEN! -EF YO' IS DAID, AH RECKON YO' DON'T WANT A SODY. GOO'BYE. AH IS GOIN' T'GIT ONE
A SODY! - AH'LL GO, WIF YO'! RECKON AH HAIN'T VERY DAID AT THET!
BUT WHAFFO' IS YO' GITTIN' ME A SODY? - YO' 'N ME IS FEUDIN'! YO' GOT A RIGHT T' SHOOT ME!
WAL, AH DON'T B'LIEVE IN FEUDIN' -JES' BECUZ OUR GRANPAPPIES HATED EACH OTHER-AH DON'T HAFTA HATE YO! - NO SUH!
SO- IN SPITE OF TH' FAC' THET YO' LOOKS 'N ACKS LIKE A HOUN'-DAWG - AH THINK THET EF YO' LIVED WIF ME AN' AUNT BESSIE, SHE COULD MAKE A GENNULMAN OUTA YO', -TOO!
A GENNUL-MAN? - WHUT IS THET?
4-22

LI'L ABNER — Hain't Had No Experience — By Al Capp

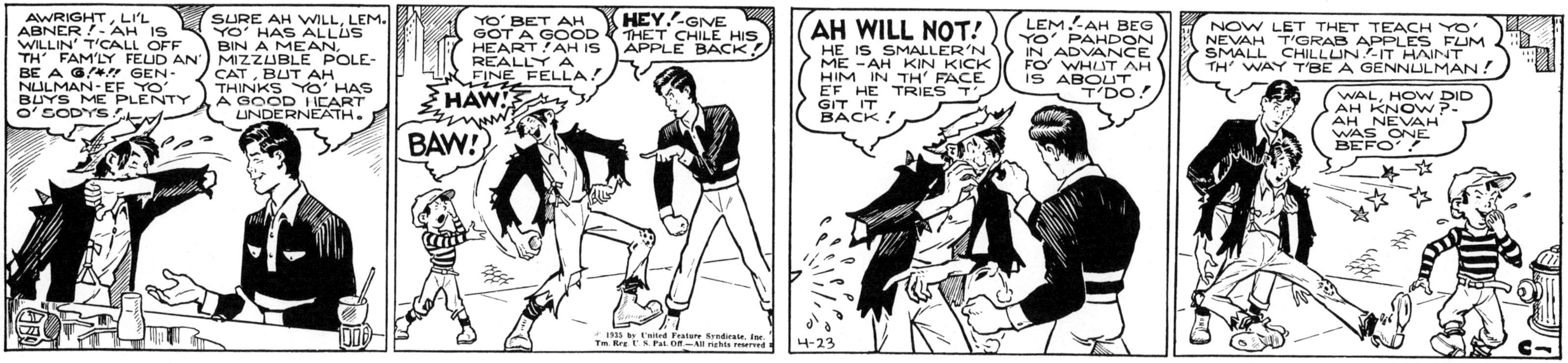

AWRIGHT, LI'L ABNER! - AH IS WILLIN' T'CALL OFF TH' FAM'LY FEUD AN' BE A @!*!! GEN-NULMAN-EF YO' BUYS ME PLENTY O' SODYS!
SURE AH WILL, LEM. YO' HAS ALLUS BIN A MEAN, MIZZUBLE POLE-CAT, BUT AH THINKS YO' HAS A GOOD HEART UNDERNEATH.
YO' BET AH GOT A GOOD HEART! AH IS REALLY A FINE FELLA!
HEY! - GIVE THET CHILE HIS APPLE BACK!
HAW!
BAW!
© 1935 by United Feature Syndicate, Inc. Tm. Reg. U. S. Pat. Off.—All rights reserved
AH WILL NOT! HE IS SMALLER'N ME - AH KIN KICK HIM IN TH' FACE EF HE TRIES T' GIT IT BACK!
LEM! - AH BEG YO' PAHDON IN ADVANCE FO' WHUT AH IS ABOUT T'DO!
4-23
NOW LET THET TEACH YO' NEVAH T'GRAB APPLES FUM SMALL CHILLUN! - IT HAINT TH' WAY T'BE A GENNULMAN!
WAL, HOW DID AH KNOW? - AH NEVAH WAS ONE BEFO'!

LI'L ABNER — He Could If He Tried — By Al Capp

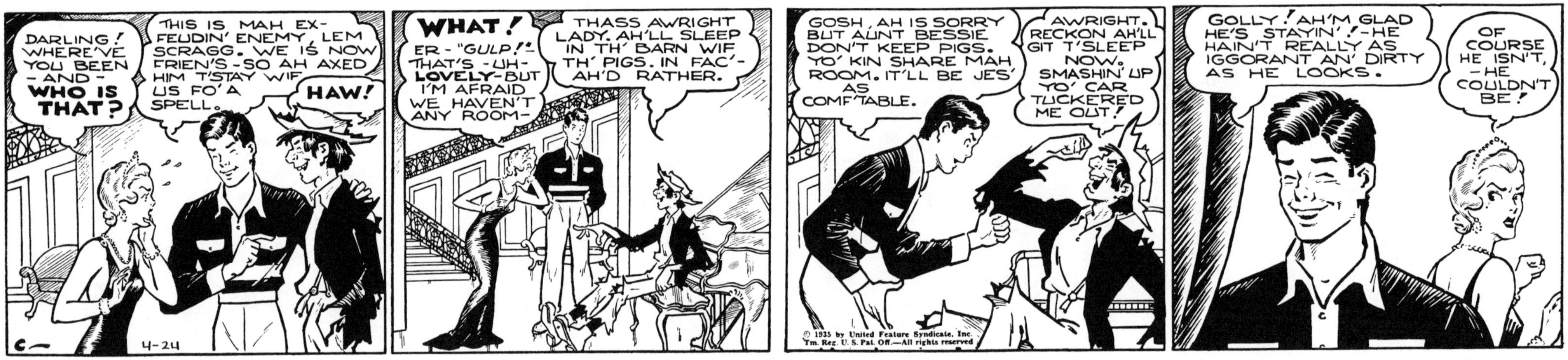

DARLING! WHERE'VE YOU BEEN - AND - WHO IS THAT?
THIS IS MAH EX-FEUDIN' ENEMY, LEM SCRAGG. WE IS NOW FRIEN'S - SO AH AXED HIM T'STAY WIF US FO'A SPELL.
HAW!
4-24
WHAT! ER - "GULP!" - THAT'S - UH - LOVELY - BUT I'M AFRAID WE HAVEN'T ANY ROOM -
THASS AWRIGHT LADY. AH'LL SLEEP IN TH' BARN WIF TH' PIGS. IN FAC' - AH'D RATHER.
GOSH, AH IS SORRY BUT AUNT BESSIE DON'T KEEP PIGS. YO' KIN SHARE MAH ROOM. IT'LL BE JES' AS COMF'TABLE.
AWRIGHT. RECKON AH'LL GIT T'SLEEP NOW. SMASHIN' UP YO' CAR TUCKERED ME OUT!
© 1935 by United Feature Syndicate, Inc. Tm. Reg. U. S. Pat. Off.—All rights reserved
GOLLY! AH'M GLAD HE'S STAYIN'! - HE HAIN'T REALLY AS IGGORANT AN' DIRTY AS HE LOOKS.
OF COURSE HE ISN'T, - HE COULDN'T BE!

LI'L ABNER — A Gentleman of the Old School — By Al Capp

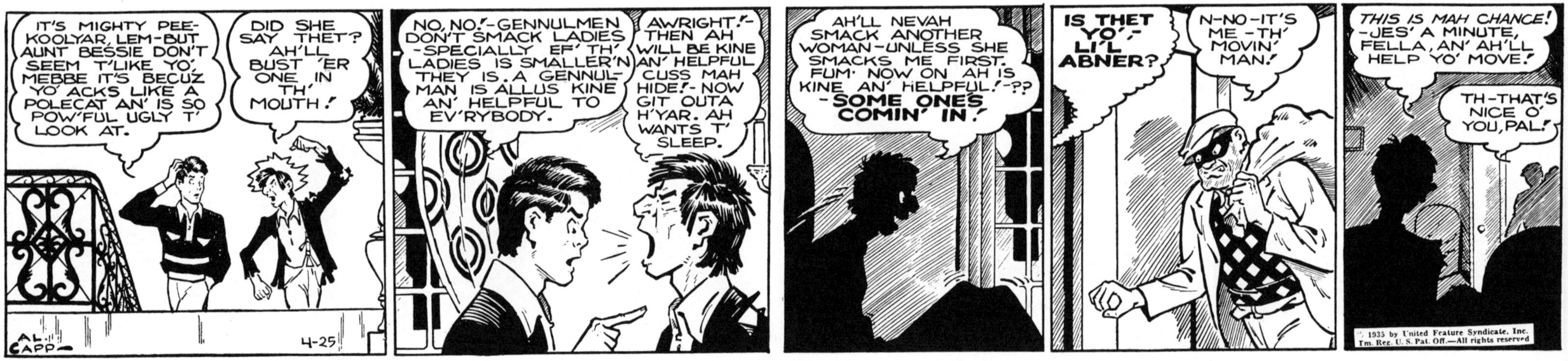

IT'S MIGHTY PEE-KOOLYAR, LEM - BUT AUNT BESSIE DON'T SEEM T'LIKE YO'. MEBBE IT'S BECUZ YO' ACKS LIKE A POLECAT AN' IS SO POW'FUL UGLY T' LOOK AT.
DID SHE SAY THET? AH'LL BUST 'ER ONE IN TH' MOUTH!
AL CAPP
4-25
NO, NO! - GENNULMEN DON'T SMACK LADIES - SPECIALLY EF' TH' LADIES IS SMALLER'N THEY IS. A GENNUL-MAN IS ALLUS KINE AN' HELPFUL TO EV'RYBODY.
AWRIGHT! - THEN AH WILL BE KINE AN' HELPFUL. CUSS MAH HIDE! - NOW GIT OUTA H'YAR. AH WANTS T' SLEEP.
AH'LL NEVAH SMACK ANOTHER WOMAN - UNLESS SHE SMACKS ME FIRST. FUM NOW ON AH IS KINE AN' HELPFUL! - ?? - SOME ONE'S COMIN' IN!
IS THET YO', LI'L ABNER?
N-NO - IT'S ME - TH' MOVIN' MAN!
THIS IS MAH CHANCE! - JES' A MINUTE, FELLA, AN' AH'LL HELP YO' MOVE!
TH-THAT'S NICE O' YOU, PAL!
© 1935 by United Feature Syndicate, Inc. Tm. Reg. U. S. Pat. Off.—All rights reserved

LI'L ABNER Look Out, Li'l Abner **By Al Capp**

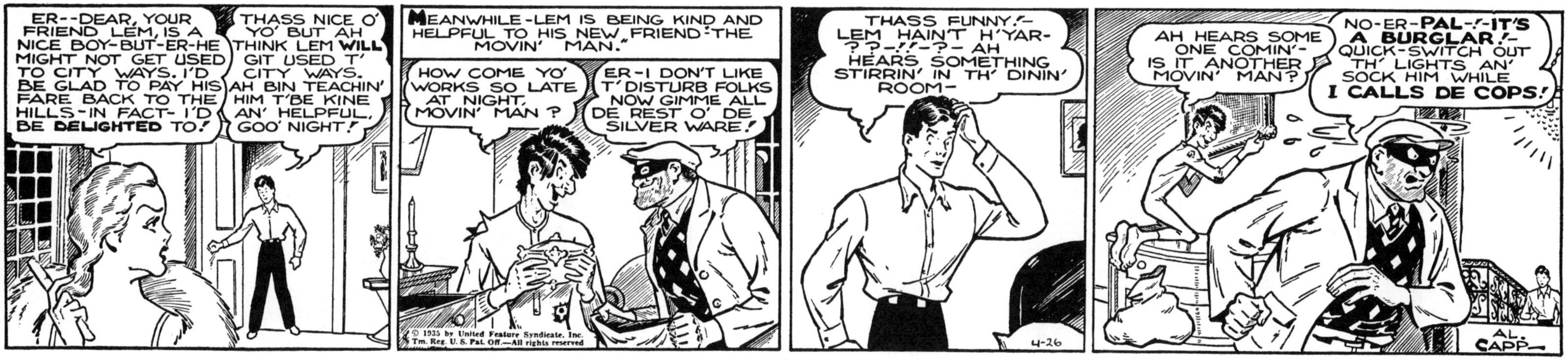
ER--DEAR, YOUR FRIEND LEM, IS A NICE BOY-BUT-ER-HE MIGHT NOT GET USED TO CITY WAYS. I'D BE GLAD TO PAY HIS FARE BACK TO THE HILLS-IN FACT- I'D BE DELIGHTED TO!
THASS NICE O' YO' BUT AH THINK LEM WILL GIT USED T' CITY WAYS. AH BIN TEACHIN' HIM T'BE KINE AN' HELPFUL. GOO' NIGHT!
MEANWHILE-LEM IS BEING KIND AND HELPFUL TO HIS NEW "FRIEND"-THE MOVIN' MAN."
HOW COME YO' WORKS SO LATE AT NIGHT, MOVIN' MAN ?
ER-I DON'T LIKE T' DISTURB FOLKS NOW GIMME ALL DE REST O' DE SILVER WARE!
© 1935 by United Feature Syndicate, Inc. Tm. Reg. U. S. Pat. Off.—All rights reserved
THASS FUNNY!-LEM HAIN'T H'YAR-??-!!-?- AH HEARS SOMETHING STIRRIN' IN TH' DININ' ROOM-
4-26
AH HEARS SOME ONE COMIN'- IS IT ANOTHER MOVIN' MAN?
NO-ER-PAL-!-IT'S A BURGLAR!- QUICK-SWITCH OUT TH' LIGHTS AN' SOCK HIM WHILE I CALLS DE COPS!
AL. CAPP

LI'L ABNER A Joke on th' Movin' Man **By Al Capp**

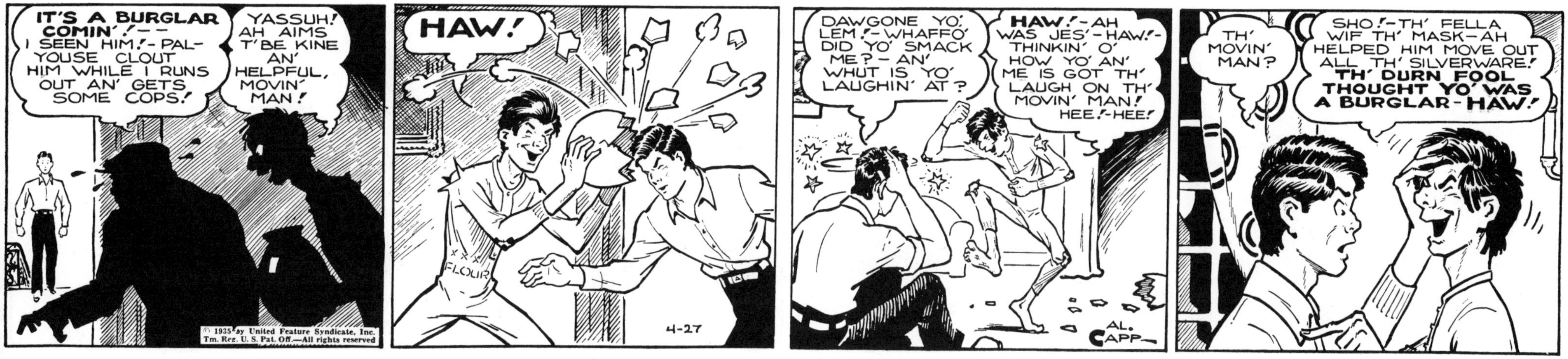
IT'S A BURGLAR COMIN'!-- I SEEN HIM!-PAL- YOUSE CLOUT HIM WHILE I RUNS OUT AN' GETS SOME COPS!
YASSUH! AH AIMS T'BE KINE AN' HELPFUL, MOVIN' MAN!
© 1935 by United Feature Syndicate, Inc. Tm. Reg. U. S. Pat. Off.—All rights reserved
HAW!
FLOUR
4-27
DAWGONE YO', LEM!-WHAFFO' DID YO' SMACK ME?-AN' WHUT IS YO' LAUGHIN' AT?
HAW!-AH WAS JES'-HAW!-THINKIN' O' HOW YO' AN' ME IS GOT TH' LAUGH ON TH' MOVIN' MAN! HEE!-HEE!
AL. CAPP
TH' MOVIN' MAN?
SHO!-TH' FELLA WIF TH' MASK-AH HELPED HIM MOVE OUT ALL TH' SILVERWARE! TH' DURN FOOL THOUGHT YO' WAS A BURGLAR-HAW!

LI'L ABNER Don't Be Too Sure! By Al Capp

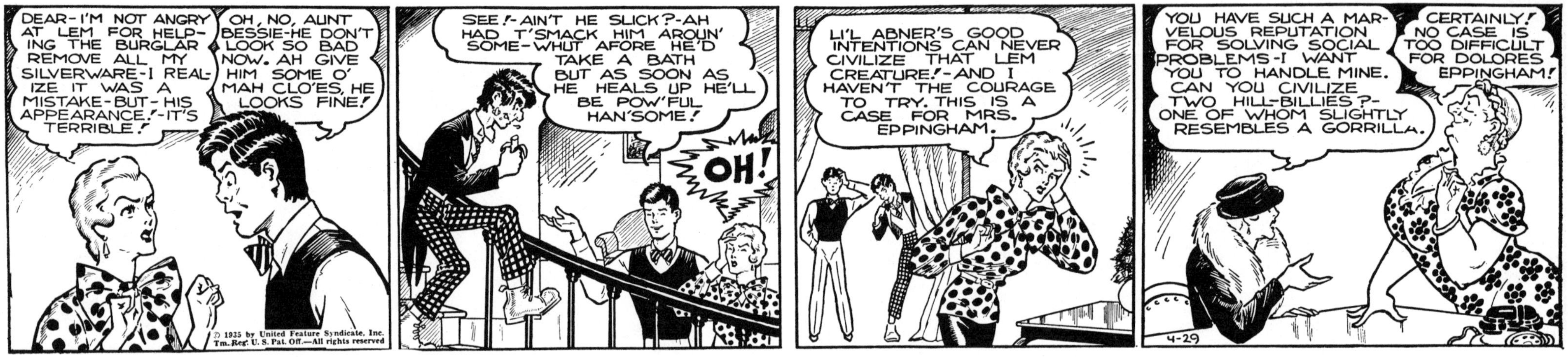

DEAR-I'M NOT ANGRY AT LEM FOR HELPING THE BURGLAR REMOVE ALL MY SILVERWARE-I REALIZE IT WAS A MISTAKE-BUT-HIS APPEARANCE!-IT'S TERRIBLE!
OH, NO, AUNT BESSIE-HE DON'T LOOK SO BAD NOW. AH GIVE HIM SOME O' MAH CLO'ES, HE LOOKS FINE!
© 1935 by United Feature Syndicate, Inc. Tm. Reg. U. S. Pat. Off.—All rights reserved
SEE!-AIN'T HE SLICK?-AH HAD T'SMACK HIM AROUN' SOME-WHUT AFORE HE'D TAKE A BATH BUT AS SOON AS HE HEALS UP HE'LL BE POW'FUL HAN'SOME!
OH!
LI'L ABNER'S GOOD INTENTIONS CAN NEVER CIVILIZE THAT LEM CREATURE!-AND I HAVEN'T THE COURAGE TO TRY. THIS IS A CASE FOR MRS. EPPINGHAM.
YOU HAVE SUCH A MARVELOUS REPUTATION FOR SOLVING SOCIAL PROBLEMS-I WANT YOU TO HANDLE MINE. CAN YOU CIVILIZE TWO HILL-BILLIES?-ONE OF WHOM SLIGHTLY RESEMBLES A GORRILLA.
CERTAINLY! NO CASE IS TOO DIFFICULT FOR DOLORES EPPINGHAM!
4-29

LI'L ABNER A Gentleman of the Old School By Al Capp

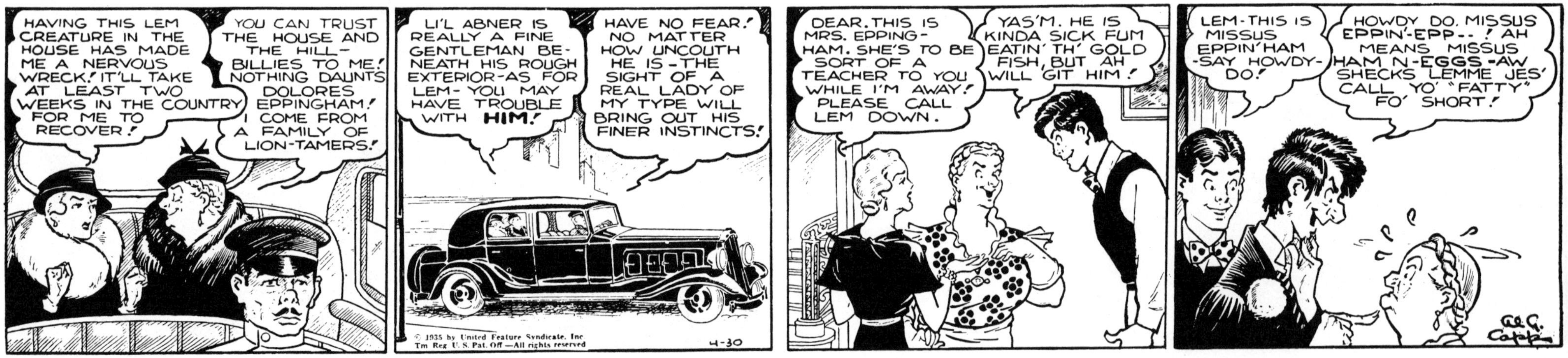

HAVING THIS LEM CREATURE IN THE HOUSE HAS MADE ME A NERVOUS WRECK! IT'LL TAKE AT LEAST TWO WEEKS IN THE COUNTRY FOR ME TO RECOVER!
YOU CAN TRUST THE HOUSE AND THE HILL-BILLIES TO ME! NOTHING DAUNTS DOLORES EPPINGHAM! I COME FROM A FAMILY OF LION-TAMERS!
LI'L ABNER IS REALLY A FINE GENTLEMAN BENEATH HIS ROUGH EXTERIOR-AS FOR LEM-YOU MAY HAVE TROUBLE WITH HIM!
HAVE NO FEAR! NO MATTER HOW UNCOUTH HE IS-THE SIGHT OF A REAL LADY OF MY TYPE WILL BRING OUT HIS FINER INSTINCTS!
© 1935 by United Feature Syndicate, Inc. Tm Reg. U. S. Pat. Off.—All rights reserved
4-30
DEAR. THIS IS MRS. EPPINGHAM. SHE'S TO BE SORT OF A TEACHER TO YOU WHILE I'M AWAY! PLEASE CALL LEM DOWN.
YAS'M. HE IS KINDA SICK FUM EATIN' TH' GOLD FISH, BUT AH WILL GIT HIM!
LEM-THIS IS MISSUS EPPIN'HAM-SAY HOWDY-DO!
HOWDY DO, MISSUS EPPIN'-EPP--! AH MEANS MISSUS HAM N-EGGS-AW SHECKS LEMME JES' CALL YO' "FATTY" FO' SHORT!
Al G. Capp

LI'L ABNER

It Don't Make Sense To Lem !

By Al Capp

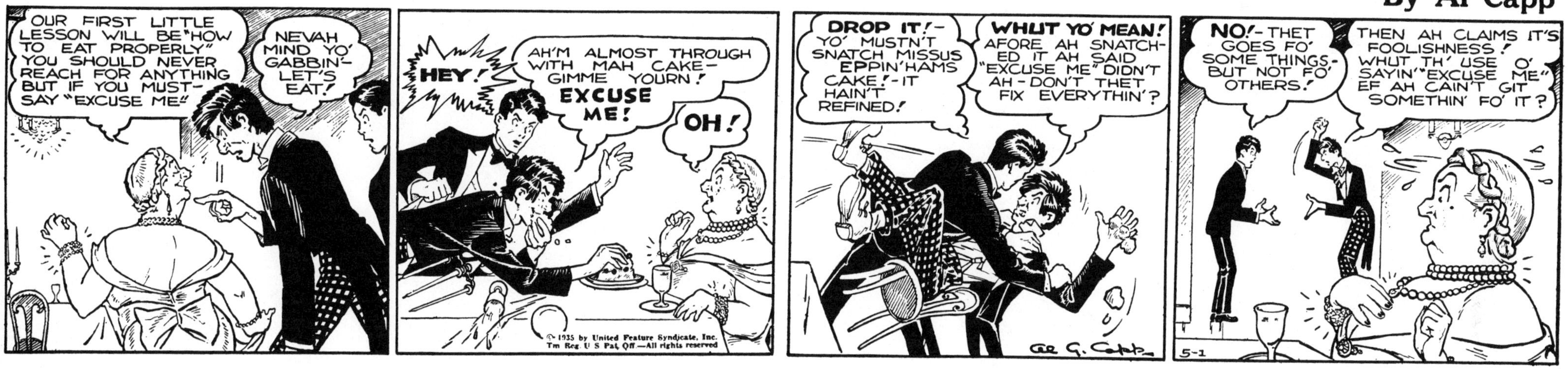
OUR FIRST LITTLE LESSON WILL BE "HOW TO EAT PROPERLY" YOU SHOULD NEVER REACH FOR ANYTHING BUT IF YOU MUST- SAY "EXCUSE ME"
NEVAH MIND YO' GABBIN'- LET'S EAT!
HEY!
AH'M ALMOST THROUGH WITH MAH CAKE- GIMME YOURN! EXCUSE ME!
OH!
© 1935 by United Feature Syndicate, Inc. Tm Reg. U S Pat. Off.—All rights reserved
DROP IT!- YO' MUSTN'T SNATCH MISSUS EPPIN'HAMS CAKE!- IT HAIN'T REFINED!
WHUT YO' MEAN! AFORE AH SNATCHED IT AH SAID "EXCUSE ME" DIDN'T AH - DON'T THET FIX EVERYTHIN'?
AL G. CAPP
NO!- THET GOES FO' SOME THINGS- BUT NOT FO' OTHERS!
THEN AH CLAIMS IT'S FOOLISHNESS! WHUT TH' USE O' SAYIN' "EXCUSE ME" EF AH CAIN'T GIT SOMETHIN' FO' IT?
5-1

LI'L ABNER

A Pushover

By Al Capp

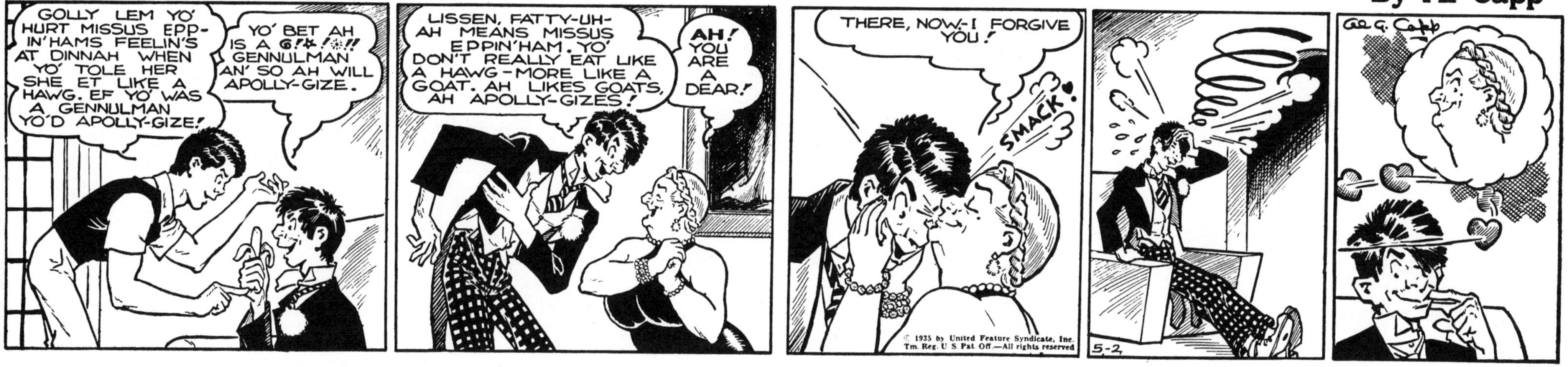
GOLLY LEM YO' HURT MISSUS EPPIN'HAMS FEELIN'S AT DINNAH WHEN YO' TOLE HER SHE ET LIKE A HAWG. EF YO' WAS A GENNULMAN YO'D APOLLY-GIZE!
YO' BET AH IS A @!*!*!! GENNULMAN AN' SO AH WILL APOLLY-GIZE.
LISSEN, FATTY-UH-AH MEANS MISSUS EPPIN'HAM. YO' DON'T REALLY EAT LIKE A HAWG - MORE LIKE A GOAT. AH LIKES GOATS, AH APOLLY-GIZES!
AH! YOU ARE A DEAR!
THERE, NOW- I FORGIVE YOU!
SMACK!
© 1935 by United Feature Syndicate, Inc. Tm. Reg. U S Pat. Off.—All rights reserved
5-2
AL G. CAPP

LI'L ABNER The Object of His Affections

By Al Capp

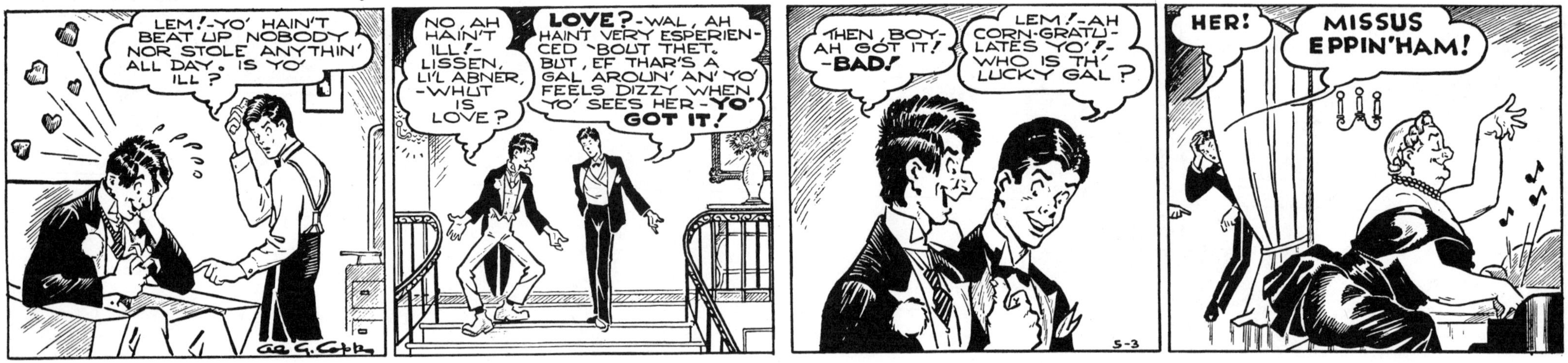
LEM!-YO' HAIN'T BEAT UP NOBODY NOR STOLE ANYTHIN' ALL DAY. IS YO' ILL?
NO, AH HAIN'T ILL!- LISSEN, LI'L ABNER, -WHUT IS LOVE?
LOVE?-WAL, AH HAIN'T VERY ESPERIENCED 'BOUT THET. BUT, EF THAR'S A GAL AROUN' AN' YO' FEELS DIZZY WHEN YO' SEES HER-YO' GOT IT!
THEN, BOY- AH GOT IT! -BAD!
LEM!-AH CORN-GRATULATES YO'!- WHO IS TH' LUCKY GAL?
HER!
MISSUS EPPIN'HAM!

LI'L ABNER Too Shy

By Al Capp

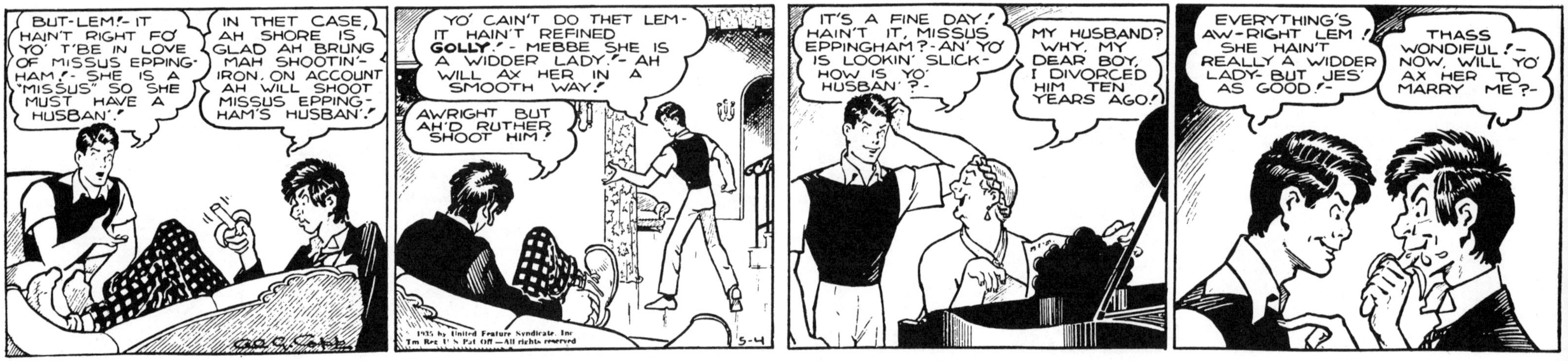
BUT-LEM!- IT HAIN'T RIGHT FO' YO' T'BE IN LOVE OF MISSUS EPPINGHAM!- SHE IS A "MISSUS" SO SHE MUST HAVE A HUSBAN'!
IN THET CASE, AH SHORE IS GLAD AH BRUNG MAH SHOOTIN'-IRON, ON ACCOUNT AH WILL SHOOT MISSUS EPPINGHAM'S HUSBAN'!
YO' CAIN'T DO THET LEM- IT HAIN'T REFINED GOLLY!- MEBBE SHE IS A WIDDER LADY!- AH WILL AX HER IN A SMOOTH WAY!
AWRIGHT BUT AH'D RUTHER SHOOT HIM!
IT'S A FINE DAY! HAIN'T IT, MISSUS EPPINGHAM?-AN' YO' IS LOOKIN' SLICK- HOW IS YO' HUSBAN'?-
MY HUSBAND? WHY, MY DEAR BOY, I DIVORCED HIM TEN YEARS AGO!
EVERYTHING'S AW-RIGHT LEM! SHE HAIN'T REALLY A WIDDER LADY- BUT JES' AS GOOD!-
THASS WONDIFUL!- NOW, WILL YO' AX HER TO MARRY ME?-

LI'L ABNER Love In Bloom By Al Capp

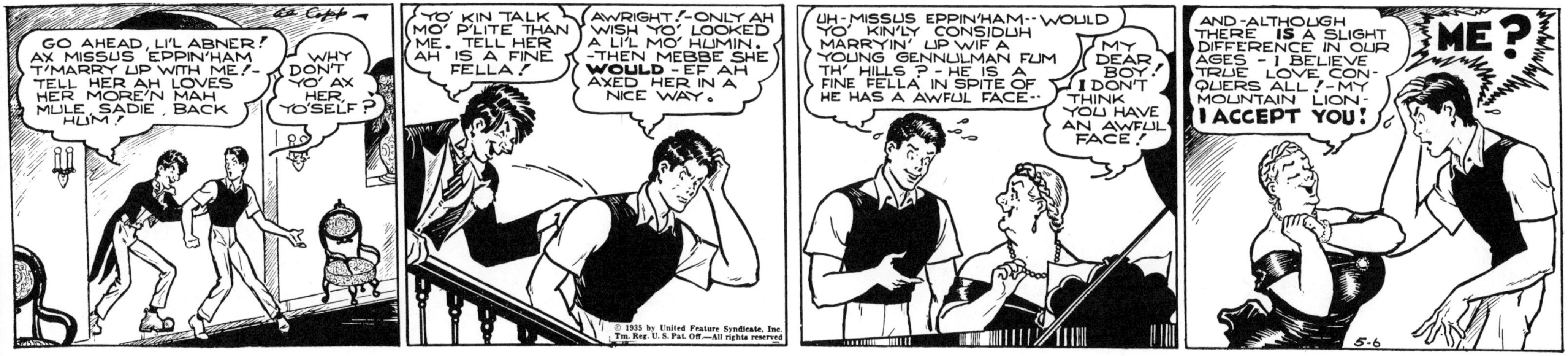
Al Capp
GO AHEAD, LI'L ABNER! AX MISSUS EPPIN'HAM T'MARRY UP WITH ME!- TELL HER AH LOVES HER MORE'N MAH MULE, SADIE, BACK HUM!
WHY DON'T YO' AX HER, YO'SELF?
YO' KIN TALK MO' P'LITE THAN ME. TELL HER AH IS A FINE FELLA!
AWRIGHT!-ONLY AH WISH YO' LOOKED A LI'L MO' HUMIN. -THEN MEBBE SHE WOULD-EF AH AXED HER IN A NICE WAY.
© 1935 by United Feature Syndicate, Inc. Tm. Reg. U. S. Pat. Off.—All rights reserved
UH-MISSUS EPPIN'HAM--WOULD YO' KIN'LY CONSIDUH MARRYIN' UP WIF A YOUNG GENNULMAN FUM TH' HILLS?-HE IS A FINE FELLA IN SPITE OF HE HAS A AWFUL FACE--
MY DEAR BOY! I DON'T THINK YOU HAVE AN AWFUL FACE!
AND-ALTHOUGH THERE IS A SLIGHT DIFFERENCE IN OUR AGES - I BELIEVE TRUE LOVE CONQUERS ALL!-MY MOUNTAIN LION- I ACCEPT YOU!
ME?
5-6

LI'L ABNER Love's Labor Lost By Al Capp

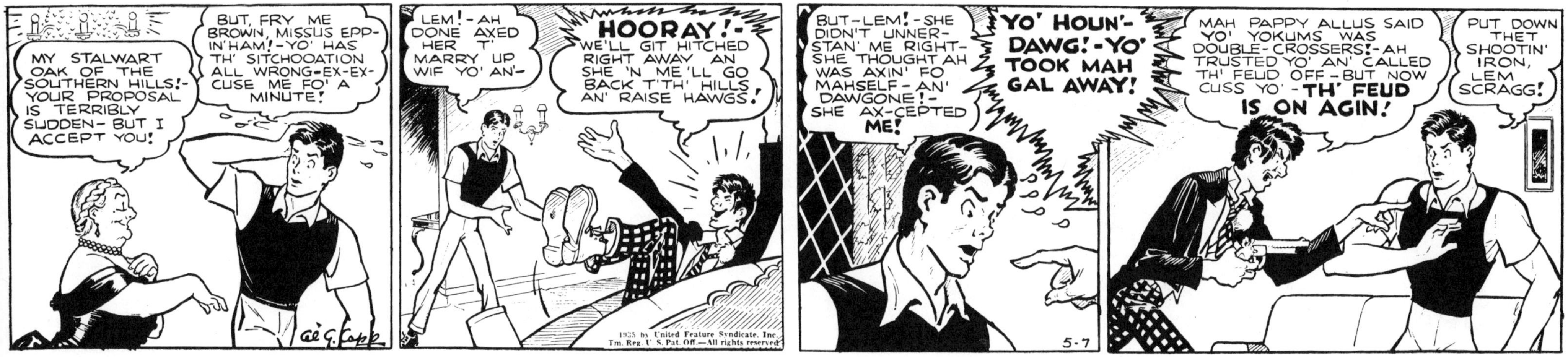
MY STALWART OAK OF THE SOUTHERN HILLS!- YOUR PROPOSAL IS TERRIBLY SUDDEN- BUT I ACCEPT YOU!
BUT, FRY ME BROWN, MISSUS EPPIN'HAM!-YO' HAS TH' SITCHOOATION ALL WRONG-EX-EXCUSE ME FO' A MINUTE!
Al G. Capp
LEM!-AH DONE AXED HER T' MARRY UP WIF YO' AN'-
HOORAY!- WE'LL GIT HITCHED RIGHT AWAY AN SHE 'N ME'LL GO BACK T'TH' HILLS AN' RAISE HAWGS.
1935 by United Feature Syndicate, Inc. Tm. Reg. U. S. Pat. Off.—All rights reserved
BUT-LEM!-SHE DIDN'T UNNERSTAN' ME RIGHT- SHE THOUGHT AH WAS AXIN' FO MAHSELF-AN' DAWGONE!- SHE AX-CEPTED ME!
YO' HOUN'-DAWG!-YO' TOOK MAH GAL AWAY!
5-7
MAH PAPPY ALLUS SAID YO' YOKUMS WAS DOUBLE-CROSSERS!-AH TRUSTED YO' AN' CALLED TH' FEUD OFF-BUT NOW CUSS YO'-TH' FEUD IS ON AGIN!
PUT DOWN THET SHOOTIN' IRON, LEM SCRAGG!

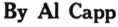

LI'L ABNER The Woman In the Case **By Al Capp**

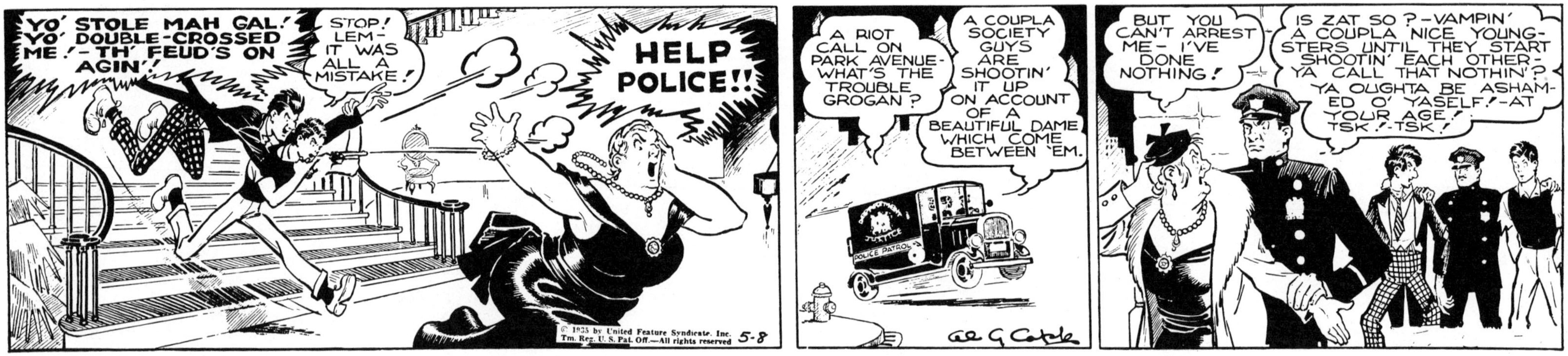
YO' STOLE MAH GAL! YO' DOUBLE-CROSSED ME!-TH' FEUD'S ON AGIN'!
STOP! LEM- IT WAS ALL A MISTAKE!
HELP POLICE!!
© 1935 by United Feature Syndicate, Inc. Tm. Reg. U. S. Pat. Off.—All rights reserved
5-8
A RIOT CALL ON PARK AVENUE- WHAT'S THE TROUBLE GROGAN?
A COUPLA SOCIETY GUYS ARE SHOOTIN' IT UP ON ACCOUNT OF A BEAUTIFUL DAME WHICH COME BETWEEN 'EM.
POLICE PATROL
BUT YOU CAN'T ARREST ME- I'VE DONE NOTHING!
IS ZAT SO?-VAMPIN' A COUPLA NICE YOUNGSTERS UNTIL THEY START SHOOTIN' EACH OTHER- YA CALL THAT NOTHIN'? YA OUGHTA BE ASHAMED O' YASELF!-AT YOUR AGE!-TSK!-TSK!

LI'L ABNER Aunt Bessie to the Rescue **By Al Capp**

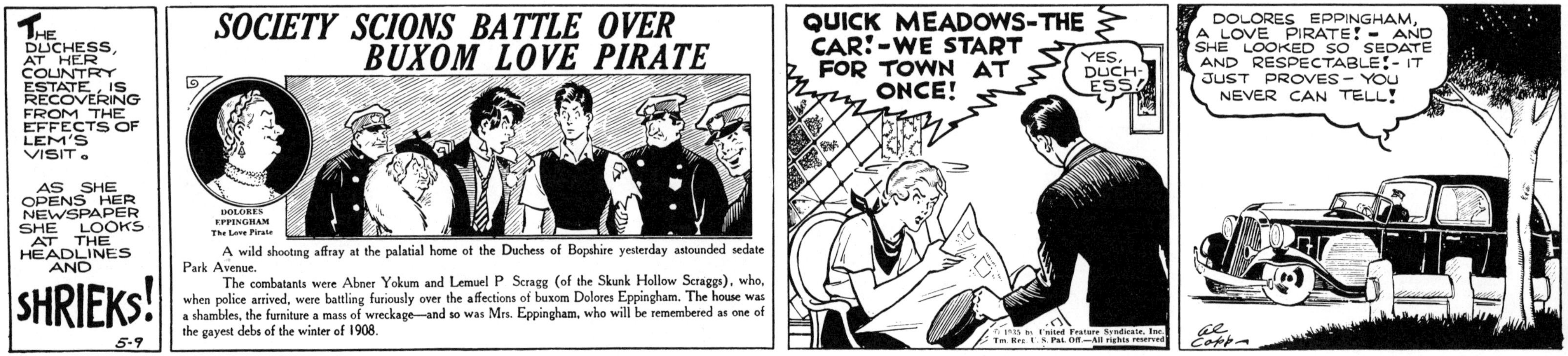
THE DUCHESS, AT HER COUNTRY ESTATE, IS RECOVERING FROM THE EFFECTS OF LEM'S VISIT.
AS SHE OPENS HER NEWSPAPER SHE LOOKS AT THE HEADLINES AND
SHRIEKS!
5-9
SOCIETY SCIONS BATTLE OVER BUXOM LOVE PIRATE
DOLORES EPPINGHAM
The Love Pirate
A wild shooting affray at the palatial home of the Duchess of Bopshire yesterday astounded sedate Park Avenue.
The combatants were Abner Yokum and Lemuel P. Scragg (of the Skunk Hollow Scraggs), who, when police arrived, were battling furiously over the affections of buxom Dolores Eppingham. The house was a shambles, the furniture a mass of wreckage—and so was Mrs. Eppingham, who will be remembered as one of the gayest debs of the winter of 1908.
QUICK MEADOWS-THE CAR!-WE START FOR TOWN AT ONCE!
YES, DUCHESS.
© 1935 by United Feature Syndicate, Inc. Tm. Reg. U. S. Pat. Off.—All rights reserved
DOLORES EPPINGHAM, A LOVE PIRATE!- AND SHE LOOKED SO SEDATE AND RESPECTABLE!- IT JUST PROVES- YOU NEVER CAN TELL!

LI'L ABNER The Price of Folly **By Al Capp**

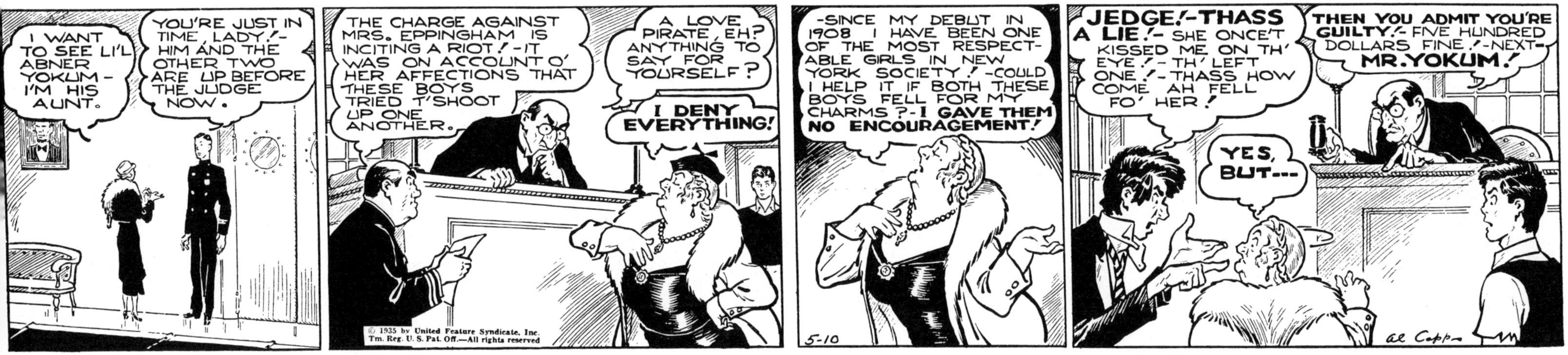
I WANT TO SEE LI'L ABNER YOKUM - I'M HIS AUNT.
YOU'RE JUST IN TIME, LADY!- HIM AND THE OTHER TWO ARE UP BEFORE THE JUDGE NOW.
THE CHARGE AGAINST MRS. EPPINGHAM IS INCITING A RIOT!-IT WAS ON ACCOUNT O' HER AFFECTIONS THAT THESE BOYS TRIED T'SHOOT UP ONE ANOTHER.
A LOVE PIRATE, EH? ANYTHING TO SAY FOR YOURSELF?
I DENY EVERYTHING!
© 1935 by United Feature Syndicate, Inc. Tm. Reg. U. S. Pat. Off.—All rights reserved
-SINCE MY DEBUT IN 1908 I HAVE BEEN ONE OF THE MOST RESPECTABLE GIRLS IN NEW YORK SOCIETY!-COULD I HELP IT IF BOTH THESE BOYS FELL FOR MY CHARMS?-I GAVE THEM NO ENCOURAGEMENT!
5-10
JEDGE!-THASS A LIE!- SHE ONCE'T KISSED ME ON TH' EYE!-TH' LEFT ONE!-THASS HOW COME AH FELL FO' HER!
YES, BUT---
THEN YOU ADMIT YOU'RE GUILTY!-FIVE HUNDRED DOLLARS FINE!-NEXT- MR. YOKUM!
Al Capp

LI'L ABNER A Gentleman and A Scholar **By Al Capp**

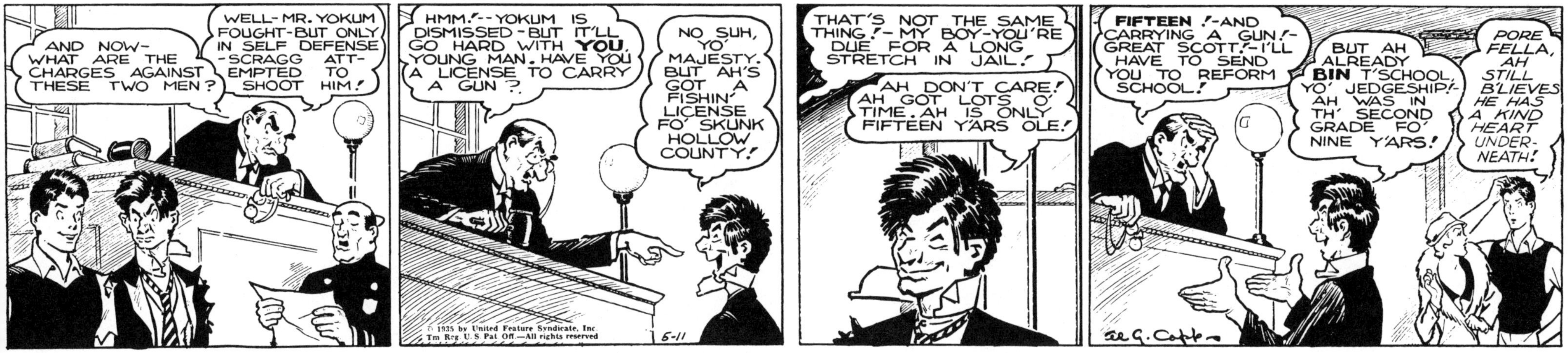
AND NOW-WHAT ARE THE CHARGES AGAINST THESE TWO MEN?
WELL-MR. YOKUM FOUGHT-BUT ONLY IN SELF DEFENSE -SCRAGG ATTEMPTED TO SHOOT HIM!
HMM!--YOKUM IS DISMISSED-BUT IT'LL GO HARD WITH YOU, YOUNG MAN. HAVE YOU A LICENSE TO CARRY A GUN?
NO SUH, YO' MAJESTY. BUT AH'S GOT A FISHIN' LICENSE FO' SKUNK HOLLOW COUNTY!
© 1935 by United Feature Syndicate, Inc. Tm Reg U. S. Pat Off.—All rights reserved
5-11
THAT'S NOT THE SAME THING!-MY BOY-YOU'RE DUE FOR A LONG STRETCH IN JAIL!
AH DON'T CARE! AH GOT LOTS O' TIME. AH IS ONLY FIFTEEN Y'ARS OLE!
FIFTEEN!-AND CARRYING A GUN!- GREAT SCOTT!-I'LL HAVE TO SEND YOU TO REFORM SCHOOL!
BUT AH ALREADY BIN T'SCHOOL, YO' JEDGESHIP!-AH WAS IN TH' SECOND GRADE FO' NINE Y'ARS!
PORE FELLA, AH STILL B'LIEVES HE HAS A KIND HEART UNDERNEATH!
Al G. Capp

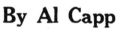

LI'L ABNER   Willing To Wait   By Al Capp

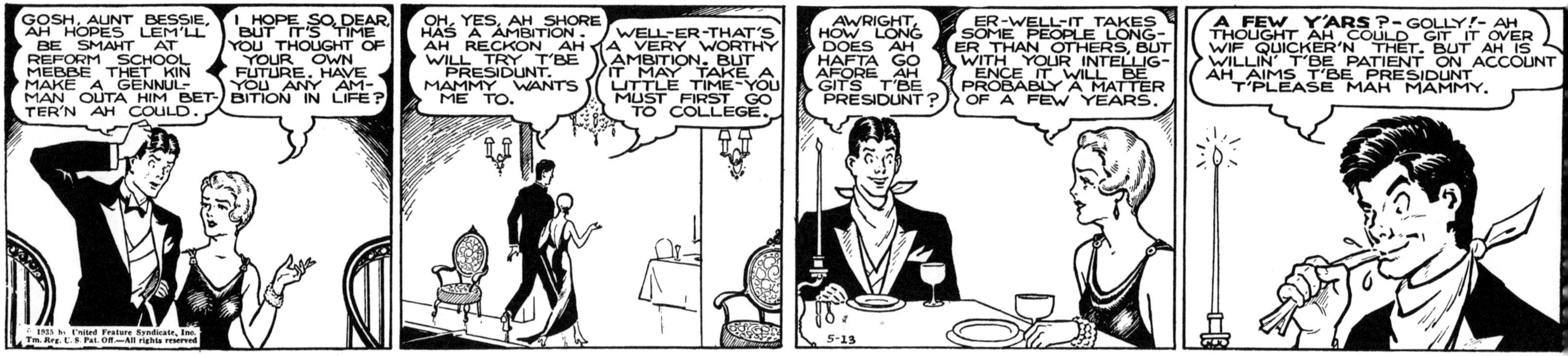
GOSH, AUNT BESSIE, AH HOPES LEM'LL BE SMAHT AT REFORM SCHOOL MEBBE THET KIN MAKE A GENNUL-MAN OUTA HIM BET-TER'N AH COULD.
I HOPE SO, DEAR, BUT IT'S TIME YOU THOUGHT OF YOUR OWN FUTURE. HAVE YOU ANY AM-BITION IN LIFE?
© 1935 by United Feature Syndicate, Inc. Tm. Reg. U. S. Pat. Off.—All rights reserved
OH, YES, AH SHORE HAS A AMBITION. AH RECKON AH WILL TRY T'BE PRESIDUNT. MAMMY WANTS ME TO.
WELL-ER-THAT'S A VERY WORTHY AMBITION. BUT IT MAY TAKE A LITTLE TIME-YOU MUST FIRST GO TO COLLEGE.
AWRIGHT, HOW LONG DOES AH HAFTA GO AFORE AH GITS T'BE PRESIDUNT?
ER-WELL-IT TAKES SOME PEOPLE LONG-ER THAN OTHERS, BUT WITH YOUR INTELLIG-ENCE IT WILL BE PROBABLY A MATTER OF A FEW YEARS.
5-13
A FEW Y'ARS? - GOLLY! - AH THOUGHT AH COULD GIT IT OVER WIF QUICKER'N THET. BUT AH IS WILLIN' T'BE PATIENT ON ACCOUNT AH AIMS T'BE PRESIDUNT T'PLEASE MAH MAMMY.

LI'L ABNER   Jes' Stay as Sweet as You Are   By Al Capp

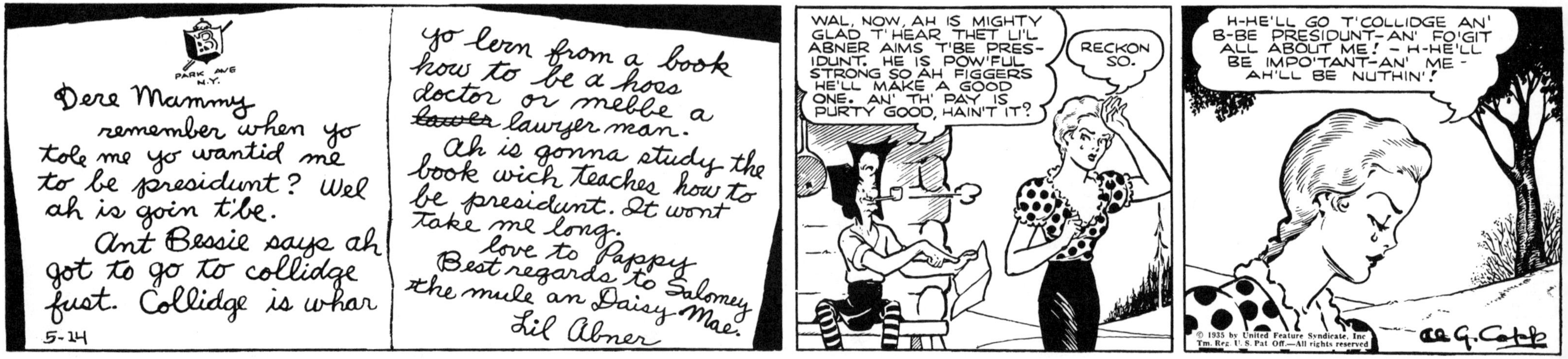
PARK AVE N.Y.
Dere Mammy
remember when yo tole me yo wantid me to be president? Wel ah is goin t'be.
Ant Bessie says ah got to go to collidge fust. Collidge is whar
5-14
yo lern from a book how to be a hoss doctor or mebbe a lawer lawyer man.
Ah is gonna study the book wich teaches how to be presidunt. It wont take me long.
love to Pappy
Best regards to Salomey the mule an Daisy Mae.
Lil Abner
WAL, NOW, AH IS MIGHTY GLAD T'HEAR THET LI'L ABNER AIMS T'BE PRES-IDUNT. HE IS POW'FUL STRONG SO AH FIGGERS HE'LL MAKE A GOOD ONE. AN' TH' PAY IS PURTY GOOD, HAIN'T IT?
RECKON SO.
H-HE'LL GO T'COLLIDGE AN' B-BE PRESIDUNT-AN' FO'GIT ALL ABOUT ME! - H-HE'LL BE IMPO'TANT-AN' ME - AH'LL BE NUTHIN'!
© 1935 by United Feature Syndicate, Inc. Tm. Reg. U. S. Pat. Off.—All rights reserved
Al G. Capp

LI'L ABNER Abner's Gonna Be Rich ? By Al Capp

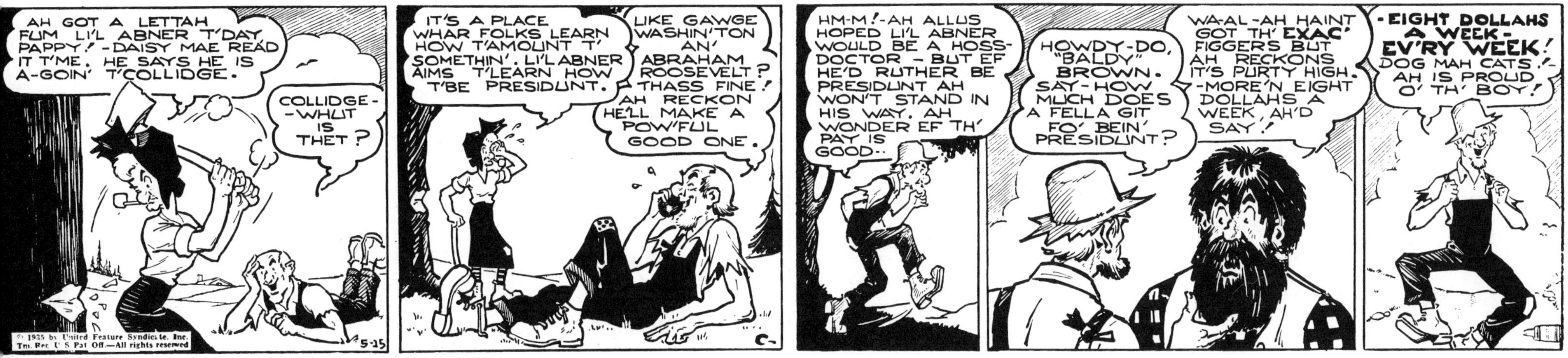
AH GOT A LETTAH FUM LI'L ABNER T'DAY, PAPPY! -DAISY MAE READ IT T'ME. HE SAYS HE IS A-GOIN' T'COLLIDGE.
COLLIDGE--WHUT IS THET?
© 1935 by United Feature Syndicate, Inc. Tm. Reg. U S Pat Off.—All rights reserved
5-15
IT'S A PLACE WHAR FOLKS LEARN HOW T'AMOUNT T' SOMETHIN'. LI'L ABNER AIMS T'LEARN HOW T'BE PRESIDUNT.
LIKE GAWGE WASHIN'TON AN' ABRAHAM ROOSEVELT? THASS FINE! AH RECKON HE'LL MAKE A POW'FUL GOOD ONE.
HM-M!-AH ALLUS HOPED LI'L ABNER WOULD BE A HOSS-DOCTOR - BUT EF HE'D RUTHER BE PRESIDUNT AH WON'T STAND IN HIS WAY. AH WONDER EF TH' PAY IS GOOD--
HOWDY-DO, "BALDY" BROWN. SAY-HOW MUCH DOES A FELLA GIT FO' BEIN' PRESIDUNT?
WA-AL-AH HAINT GOT TH' EXAC' FIGGERS BUT AH RECKONS IT'S PURTY HIGH. -MORE'N EIGHT DOLLAHS A WEEK, AH'D SAY!
-EIGHT DOLLAHS A WEEK- EV'RY WEEK! DOG MAH CATS!- AH IS PROUD O' TH' BOY!

LI'L ABNER Abner Aims High By Al Capp

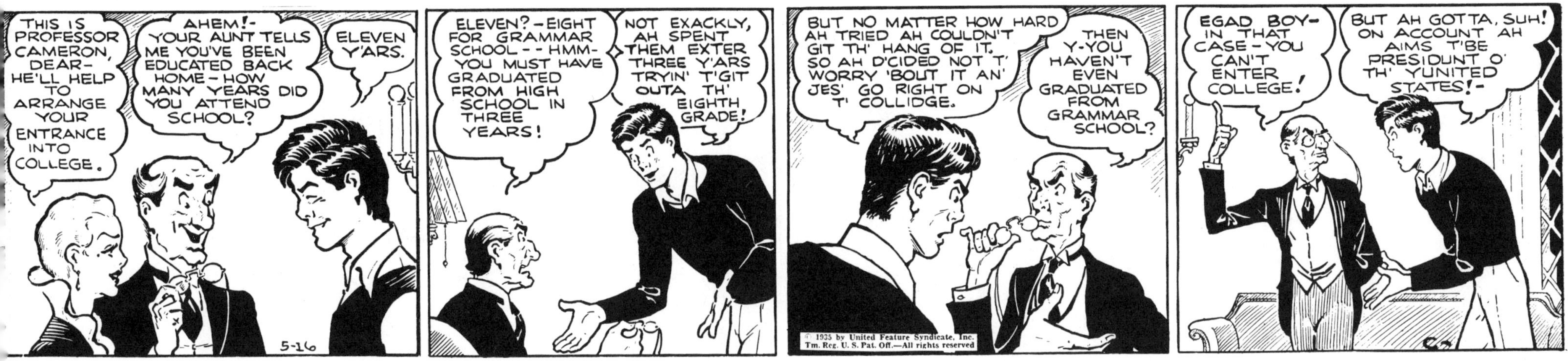
THIS IS PROFESSOR CAMERON, DEAR- HE'LL HELP TO ARRANGE YOUR ENTRANCE INTO COLLEGE.
AHEM!- YOUR AUNT TELLS ME YOU'VE BEEN EDUCATED BACK HOME-HOW MANY YEARS DID YOU ATTEND SCHOOL?
ELEVEN Y'ARS.
5-16
ELEVEN?-EIGHT FOR GRAMMAR SCHOOL--HMM- YOU MUST HAVE GRADUATED FROM HIGH SCHOOL IN THREE YEARS!
NOT EXACKLY, AH SPENT THEM EXTER THREE Y'ARS TRYIN' T'GIT OUTA TH' EIGHTH GRADE!
BUT NO MATTER HOW HARD AH TRIED AH COULDN'T GIT TH' HANG OF IT. SO AH D'CIDED NOT T' WORRY 'BOUT IT AN' JES' GO RIGHT ON T' COLLIDGE.
THEN Y-YOU HAVEN'T EVEN GRADUATED FROM GRAMMAR SCHOOL?
© 1935 by United Feature Syndicate, Inc. Tm. Reg. U. S. Pat. Off.—All rights reserved
EGAD BOY- IN THAT CASE-YOU CAN'T ENTER COLLEGE!
BUT AH GOTTA, SUH! ON ACCOUNT AH AIMS T'BE PRESIDUNT O' TH' YUNITED STATES!-

LI'L ABNER Danger Ahead ? By Al Capp

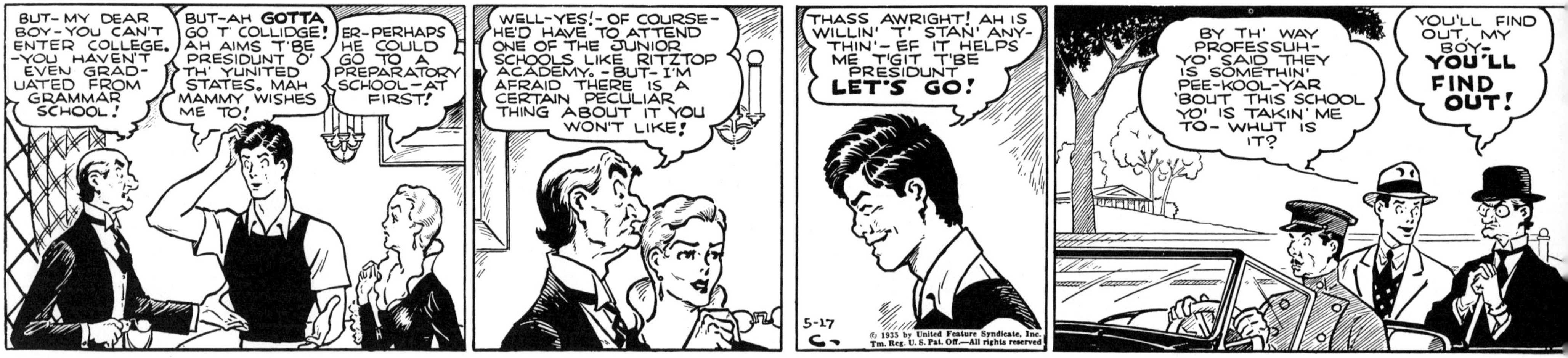
BUT-MY DEAR BOY-YOU CAN'T ENTER COLLEGE. -YOU HAVEN'T EVEN GRADUATED FROM GRAMMAR SCHOOL!
BUT-AH GOTTA GO T' COLLIDGE! AH AIMS T'BE PRESIDUNT O' TH' YUNITED STATES. MAH MAMMY WISHES ME TO!
ER-PERHAPS HE COULD GO TO A PREPARATORY SCHOOL-AT FIRST!
WELL-YES!-OF COURSE-HE'D HAVE TO ATTEND ONE OF THE JUNIOR SCHOOLS LIKE RITZTOP ACADEMY.-BUT-I'M AFRAID THERE IS A CERTAIN PECULIAR THING ABOUT IT YOU WON'T LIKE!
THASS AWRIGHT! AH IS WILLIN' T' STAN' ANYTHIN'-EF IT HELPS ME T'GIT T'BE PRESIDUNT LET'S GO!
5-17
© 1935 by United Feature Syndicate, Inc. Tm. Reg. U. S. Pat. Off.—All rights reserved
BY TH' WAY PROFESSUH-YO' SAID THEY IS SOMETHIN' PEE-KOOL-YAR 'BOUT THIS SCHOOL YO' IS TAKIN' ME TO-WHUT IS IT?
YOU'LL FIND OUT, MY BOY-YOU'LL FIND OUT!

LI'L ABNER Bound To Rise By Al Capp

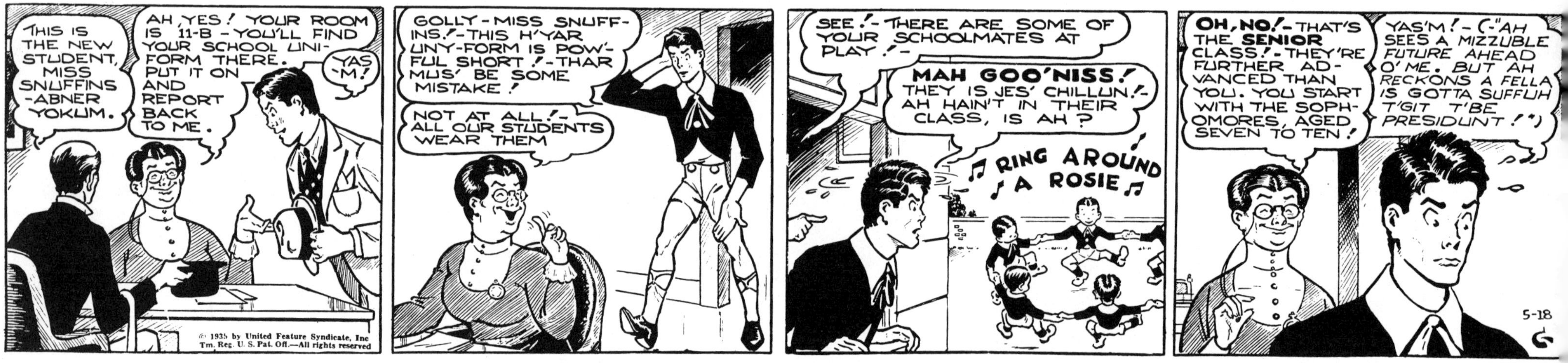
THIS IS THE NEW STUDENT, MISS SNUFFINS -ABNER YOKUM.
AH YES! YOUR ROOM IS 11-B -YOU'LL FIND YOUR SCHOOL UNIFORM THERE. PUT IT ON AND REPORT BACK TO ME.
YAS-M!
© 1935 by United Feature Syndicate, Inc Tm. Reg. U. S. Pat. Off.—All rights reserved
GOLLY-MISS SNUFFINS!-THIS H'YAR UNY-FORM IS POW'FUL SHORT!-THAR MUS' BE SOME MISTAKE!
NOT AT ALL!-ALL OUR STUDENTS WEAR THEM
SEE!-THERE ARE SOME OF YOUR SCHOOLMATES AT PLAY!-
MAH GOO'NISS! THEY IS JES' CHILLUN!-AH HAIN'T IN THEIR CLASS, IS AH?
RING AROUND A ROSIE
OH, NO!-THAT'S THE SENIOR CLASS!-THEY'RE FURTHER ADVANCED THAN YOU. YOU START WITH THE SOPHOMORES, AGED SEVEN TO TEN!
YAS'M!-(-"AH SEES A MIZZUBLE FUTURE AHEAD O'ME. BUT AH RECKONS A FELLA IS GOTTA SUFFUH T'GIT T'BE PRESIDUNT!")
5-18

LI'L ABNER Do Or Die By Al Capp

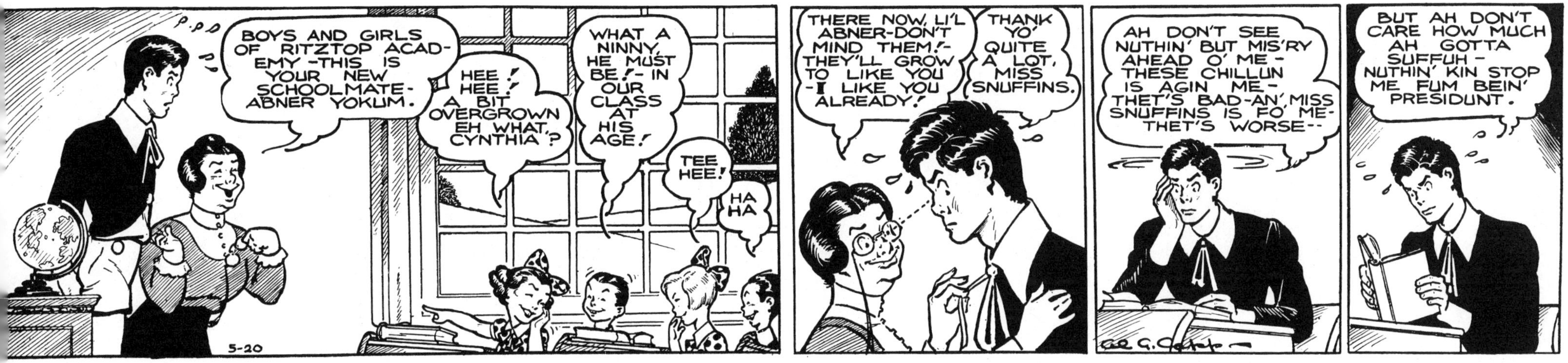
BOYS AND GIRLS OF RITZTOP ACADEMY -THIS IS YOUR NEW SCHOOLMATE-ABNER YOKUM.
HEE! HEE! A BIT OVERGROWN EH WHAT, CYNTHIA?
WHAT A NINNY, HE MUST BE!- IN OUR CLASS AT HIS AGE!
TEE HEE!
HA HA
5-20
THERE NOW, LI'L ABNER-DON'T MIND THEM!- THEY'LL GROW TO LIKE YOU -I LIKE YOU ALREADY!
THANK YO' QUITE A LOT, MISS SNUFFINS.
AH DON'T SEE NUTHIN' BUT MIS'RY AHEAD O' ME - THESE CHILLUN IS AGIN ME- THET'S BAD-AN' MISS SNUFFINS IS FO' ME- THET'S WORSE--
BUT AH DON'T CARE HOW MUCH AH GOTTA SUFFUH - NUTHIN' KIN STOP ME FUM BEIN' PRESIDUNT.

LI'L ABNER A Friend In Need By Al Capp

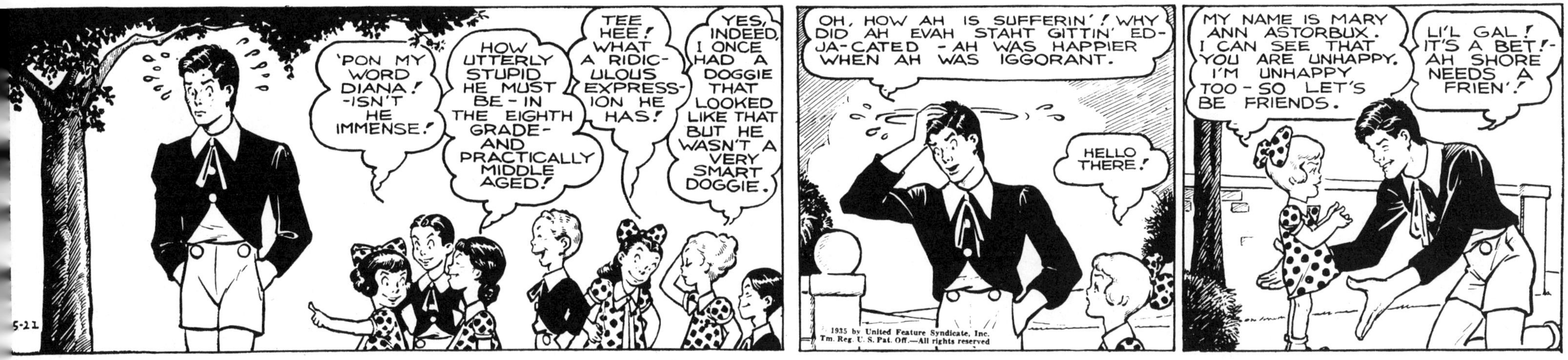
'PON MY WORD DIANA! -ISN'T HE IMMENSE!
HOW UTTERLY STUPID HE MUST BE - IN THE EIGHTH GRADE- AND PRACTICALLY MIDDLE AGED!
TEE HEE! WHAT A RIDICULOUS EXPRESSION HE HAS!
YES, INDEED, I ONCE HAD A DOGGIE THAT LOOKED LIKE THAT BUT HE WASN'T A VERY SMART DOGGIE.
5-21
OH, HOW AH IS SUFFERIN'! WHY DID AH EVAH STAHT GITTIN' EDJA-CATED -AH WAS HAPPIER WHEN AH WAS IGGORANT.
HELLO THERE!
1935 by United Feature Syndicate, Inc. Tm. Reg. U. S. Pat. Off.—All rights reserved
MY NAME IS MARY ANN ASTORBUX. I CAN SEE THAT YOU ARE UNHAPPY. I'M UNHAPPY TOO - SO LET'S BE FRIENDS.
LI'L GAL! IT'S A BET!- AH SHORE NEEDS A FRIEN'!

LI'L ABNER A Well-Known Woman By Al Capp

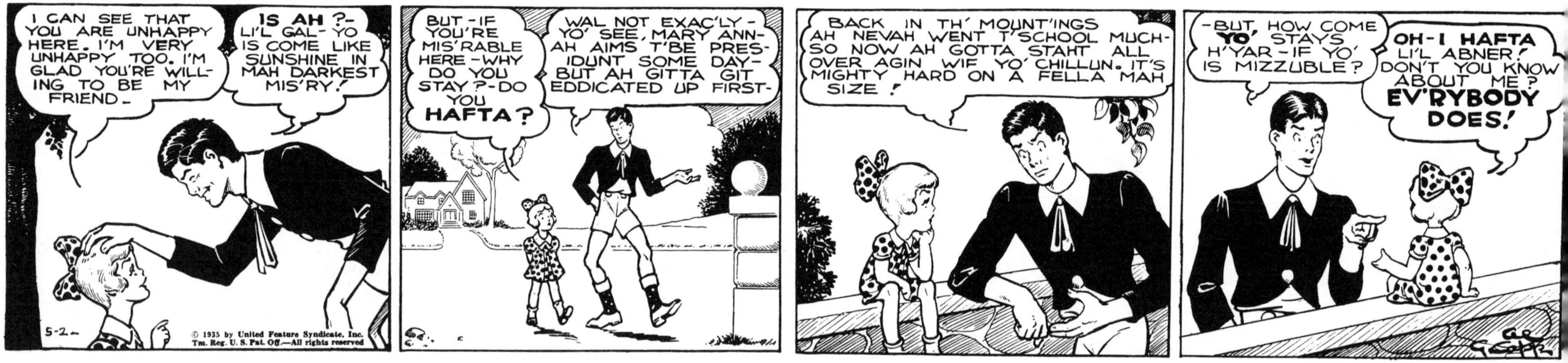
I CAN SEE THAT YOU ARE UNHAPPY HERE. I'M VERY UNHAPPY TOO. I'M GLAD YOU'RE WILLING TO BE MY FRIEND.
IS AH ?- LI'L GAL- YO IS COME LIKE SUNSHINE IN MAH DARKEST MIS'RY!
5-2
© 1935 by United Feature Syndicate, Inc. Tm. Reg. U. S. Pat. Off.—All rights reserved
BUT - IF YOU'RE MIS'RABLE HERE - WHY DO YOU STAY ?- DO YOU HAFTA ?
WAL NOT EXAC'LY - YO' SEE, MARY ANN - AH AIMS T'BE PRES-IDUNT SOME DAY - BUT AH GITTA GIT EDDICATED UP FIRST -
BACK IN TH' MOUNT'INGS AH NEVAH WENT T'SCHOOL MUCH - SO NOW AH GOTTA STAHT ALL OVER AGIN WIF YO' CHILLUN. IT'S MIGHTY HARD ON A FELLA MAH SIZE!
- BUT, HOW COME YO' STAYS H'YAR - IF YO' IS MIZZUBLE ?
OH - I HAFTA LI'L ABNER! DON'T YOU KNOW ABOUT ME ? EV'RYBODY DOES!

LI'L ABNER A Woman of Mystery By Al Capp

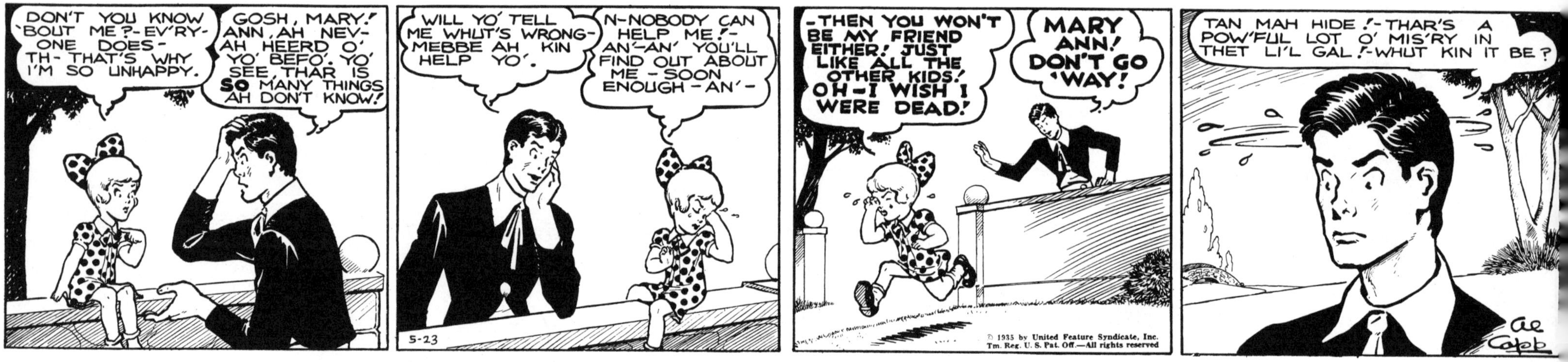
DON'T YOU KNOW 'BOUT ME ?- EV'RY-ONE DOES - TH- THAT'S WHY I'M SO UNHAPPY.
GOSH, MARY ANN, AH NEV-AH HEERD O' YO' BEFO'. YO' SEE, THAR IS SO MANY THINGS AH DON'T KNOW!
WILL YO' TELL ME WHUT'S WRONG - MEBBE AH KIN HELP YO'.
N-NOBODY CAN HELP ME!- AN'-AN' YOU'LL FIND OUT ABOUT ME - SOON ENOUGH - AN' -
5-23
- THEN YOU WON'T BE MY FRIEND EITHER! JUST LIKE ALL THE OTHER KIDS! OH - I WISH I WERE DEAD!
MARY ANN! DON'T GO 'WAY!
© 1935 by United Feature Syndicate, Inc. Tm. Reg. U. S. Pat. Off.—All rights reserved
TAN MAH HIDE!- THAR'S A POW'FUL LOT O' MIS'RY IN THET LI'L GAL!- WHUT KIN IT BE ?

LI'L ABNER Jealousy **By Al Capp**

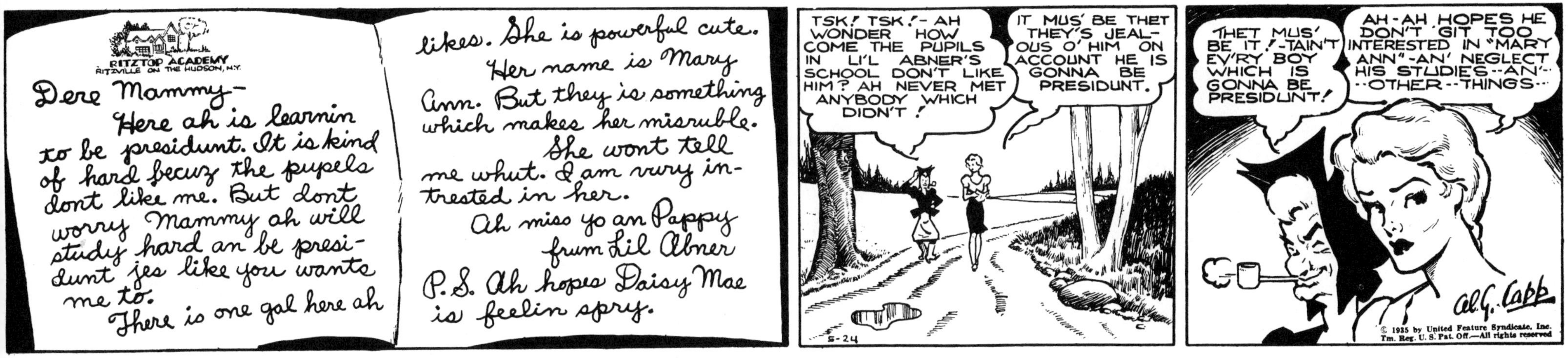
RITZTOP ACADEMY
RITZVILLE ON THE HUDSON, N.Y.
Dere Mammy—
Here ah is learnin to be presidunt. It is kind of hard becuz the pupels dont like me. But dont worry Mammy ah will study hard an be presidunt jes like you wants me to.
There is one gal here ah likes. She is powerful cute.
Her name is Mary Ann. But they is something which makes her misruble.
She wont tell me whut. I am vury intrested in her.
Ah miss yo an Pappy
frum Lil Abner
P.S. Ah hopes Daisy Mae is feelin spry.
TSK! TSK!—AH WONDER HOW COME THE PUPILS IN LI'L ABNER'S SCHOOL DON'T LIKE HIM? AH NEVER MET ANYBODY WHICH DIDN'T!
IT MUS' BE THET THEY'S JEALOUS O' HIM ON ACCOUNT HE IS GONNA BE PRESIDUNT.
5-24
THET MUS' BE IT!—TAIN'T EV'RY BOY WHICH IS GONNA BE PRESIDUNT!
AH-AH HOPES HE DON'T GIT TOO INTERESTED IN "MARY ANN"—AN' NEGLECT HIS STUDIES—AN'—OTHER—THINGS—
Al G. Capp
© 1935 by United Feature Syndicate, Inc. Tm. Reg. U. S. Pat. Off.—All rights reserved

LI'L ABNER Mary Ann's Secret **By Al Capp**

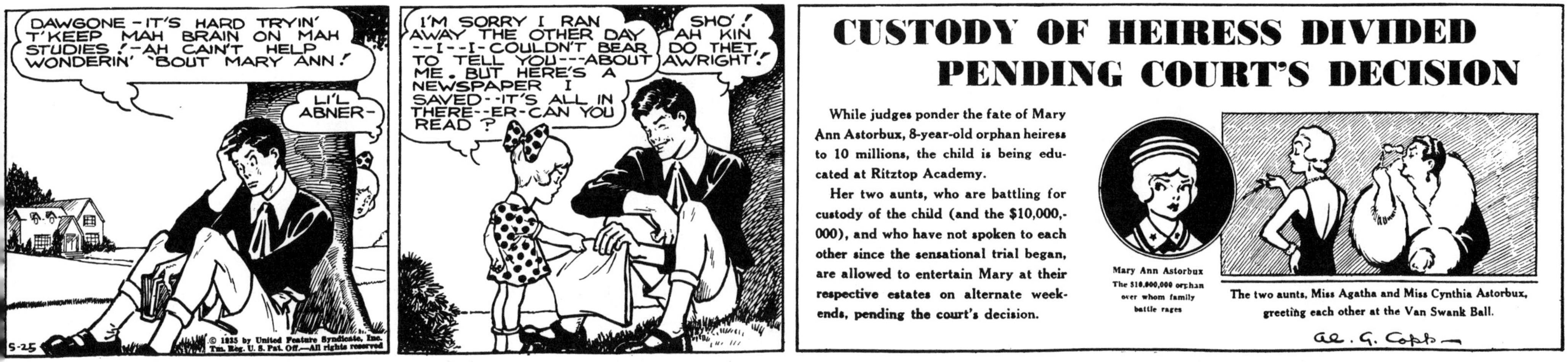
DAWGONE—IT'S HARD TRYIN' T'KEEP MAH BRAIN ON MAH STUDIES!—AH CAIN'T HELP WONDERIN' 'BOUT MARY ANN!
LI'L ABNER—
5-25
© 1935 by United Feature Syndicate, Inc. Tm. Reg. U. S. Pat. Off.—All rights reserved
I'M SORRY I RAN AWAY THE OTHER DAY—I—I—COULDN'T BEAR TO TELL YOU—ABOUT ME. BUT HERE'S A NEWSPAPER I SAVED—IT'S ALL IN THERE—ER—CAN YOU READ?
SHO'! AH KIN DO THET, AWRIGHT!
CUSTODY OF HEIRESS DIVIDED PENDING COURT'S DECISION
While judges ponder the fate of Mary Ann Astorbux, 8-year-old orphan heiress to 10 millions, the child is being educated at Ritztop Academy.
Her two aunts, who are battling for custody of the child (and the $10,000,000), and who have not spoken to each other since the sensational trial began, are allowed to entertain Mary at their respective estates on alternate weekends, pending the court's decision.
Mary Ann Astorbux
The $10,000,000 orphan over whom family battle rages
The two aunts, Miss Agatha and Miss Cynthia Astorbux, greeting each other at the Van Swank Ball.
Al. G. Capp

LI'L ABNER A Friend In Need By Al Capp

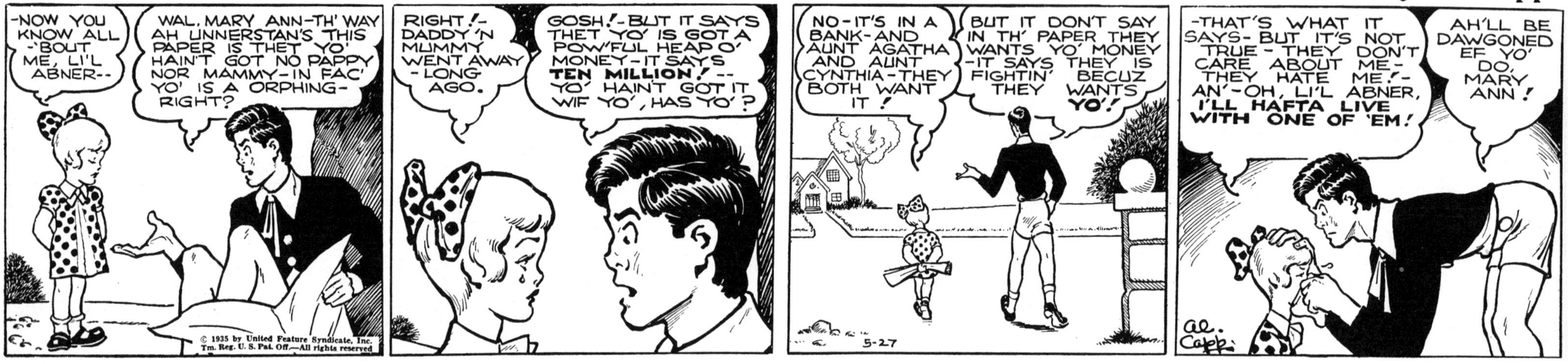
-NOW YOU KNOW ALL -'BOUT ME, LI'L ABNER--
WAL, MARY ANN-TH' WAY AH UNNERSTAN'S THIS PAPER IS THET YO' HAIN'T GOT NO PAPPY NOR MAMMY-IN FAC' YO' IS A ORPHING-RIGHT?
© 1935 by United Feature Syndicate, Inc. Tm. Reg. U. S. Pat. Off.—All rights reserved
RIGHT!-DADDY 'N MUMMY WENT AWAY -LONG AGO.
GOSH!-BUT IT SAYS THET YO' IS GOT A POW'FUL HEAP O' MONEY-IT SAYS TEN MILLION!--YO' HAIN'T GOT IT WIF YO', HAS YO'?
NO-IT'S IN A BANK-AND AUNT AGATHA AND AUNT CYNTHIA-THEY BOTH WANT IT!
BUT IT DON'T SAY IN TH' PAPER THEY WANTS YO' MONEY -IT SAYS THEY IS FIGHTIN' BECUZ THEY WANTS YO'!
5-27
-THAT'S WHAT IT SAYS-BUT IT'S NOT TRUE-THEY DON'T CARE ABOUT ME-THEY HATE ME!-AN'-OH, LI'L ABNER, I'LL HAFTA LIVE WITH ONE OF 'EM!
AH'LL BE DAWGONED EF YO' DO, MARY ANN!
AL CAPP

LI'L ABNER It Looks Pee-kool-yar ! By Al Capp

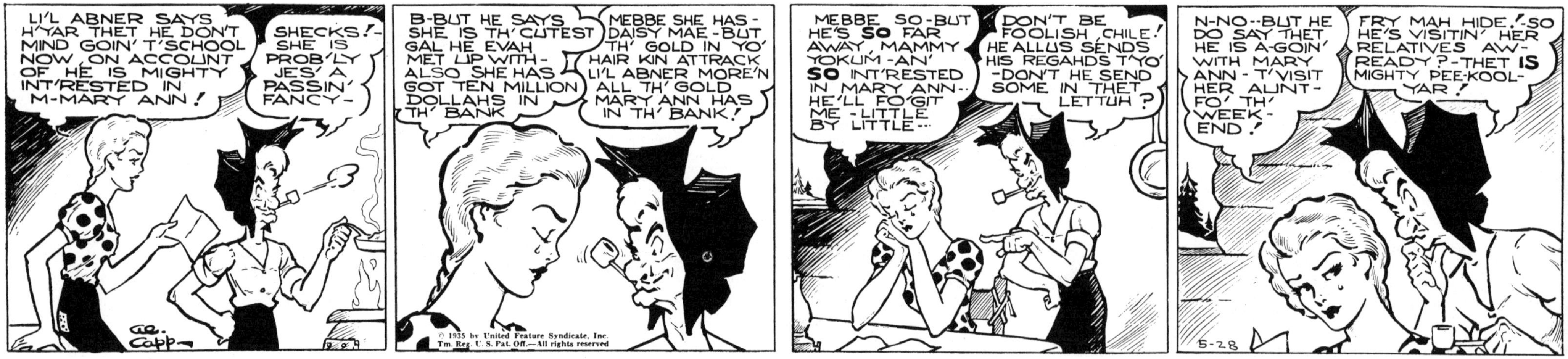
LI'L ABNER SAYS H'YAR THET HE DON'T MIND GOIN' T'SCHOOL NOW ON ACCOUNT OF HE IS MIGHTY INT'RESTED IN M-MARY ANN!
SHECKS!-SHE IS PROB'LY JES' A PASSIN' FANCY-
AL CAPP
B-BUT HE SAYS SHE IS TH' CUTEST GAL HE EVAH MET UP WITH-ALSO SHE HAS GOT TEN MILLION DOLLAHS IN TH' BANK
MEBBE SHE HAS-DAISY MAE-BUT TH' GOLD IN YO' HAIR KIN ATTRACK LI'L ABNER MORE'N ALL TH' GOLD MARY ANN HAS IN TH' BANK!
© 1935 by United Feature Syndicate, Inc. Tm. Reg. U. S. Pat. Off.—All rights reserved
MEBBE SO-BUT HE'S SO FAR AWAY, MAMMY YOKUM-AN' SO INT'RESTED IN MARY ANN--HE'LL FO'GIT ME-LITTLE BY LITTLE--
DON'T BE FOOLISH, CHILE! HE ALLUS SENDS HIS REGAHDS T'YO' -DON'T HE SEND SOME IN THET LETTUH?
N-NO--BUT HE DO SAY THET HE IS A-GOIN' WITH MARY ANN-T'VISIT HER AUNT-FO' TH' WEEK-END!
FRY MAH HIDE!-SO HE'S VISITIN' HER RELATIVES AW-READY?-THET IS MIGHTY PEE-KOOL-YAR!
5-28

LI'L ABNER Second Choice By Al Capp

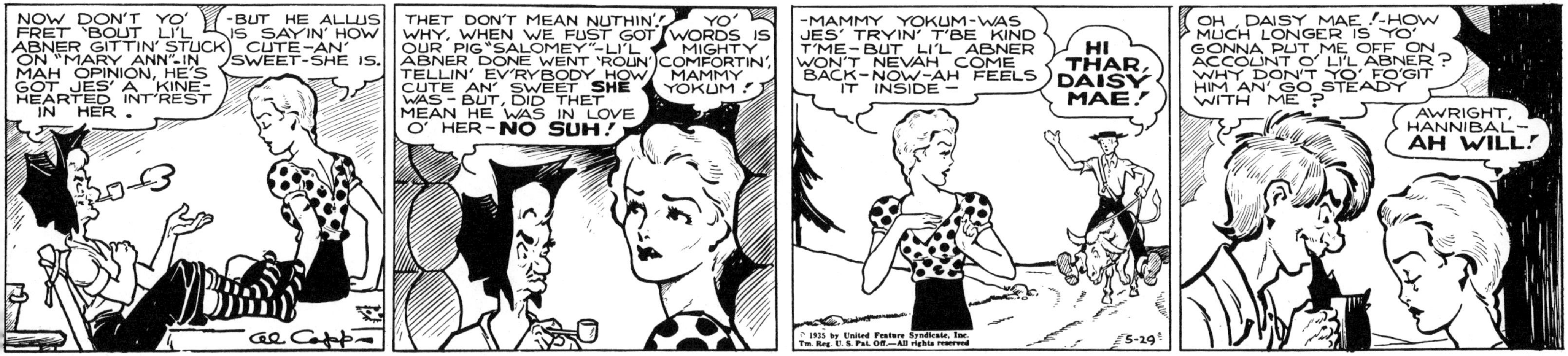
NOW DON'T YO' FRET 'BOUT LI'L ABNER GITTIN' STUCK ON "MARY ANN"-IN MAH OPINION, HE'S GOT JES' A KINE-HEARTED INT'REST IN HER.
-BUT HE ALLUS IS SAYIN' HOW CUTE-AN' SWEET-SHE IS.
THET DON'T MEAN NUTHIN'!-WHY, WHEN WE FUST GOT OUR PIG "SALOMEY"-LI'L ABNER DONE WENT 'ROUN' TELLIN' EV'RYBODY HOW CUTE AN' SWEET **SHE** WAS-BUT, DID THET MEAN HE WAS IN LOVE O' HER-**NO SUH!**
YO' WORDS IS MIGHTY COMFORTIN', MAMMY YOKUM!
-MAMMY YOKUM-WAS JES' TRYIN' T'BE KIND T'ME-BUT LI'L ABNER WON'T NEVAH COME BACK-NOW-AH FEELS IT INSIDE-
HI THAR, DAISY MAE!
© 1935 by United Feature Syndicate, Inc. Tm. Reg. U. S. Pat. Off.—All rights reserved
5-29
OH, DAISY MAE!-HOW MUCH LONGER IS YO' GONNA PUT ME OFF ON ACCOUNT O' LI'L ABNER? WHY DON'T YO' FO'GIT HIM AN' GO STEADY WITH ME?
AWRIGHT, HANNIBAL-**AH WILL!**

LI'L ABNER Cynical Cynthia By Al Capp

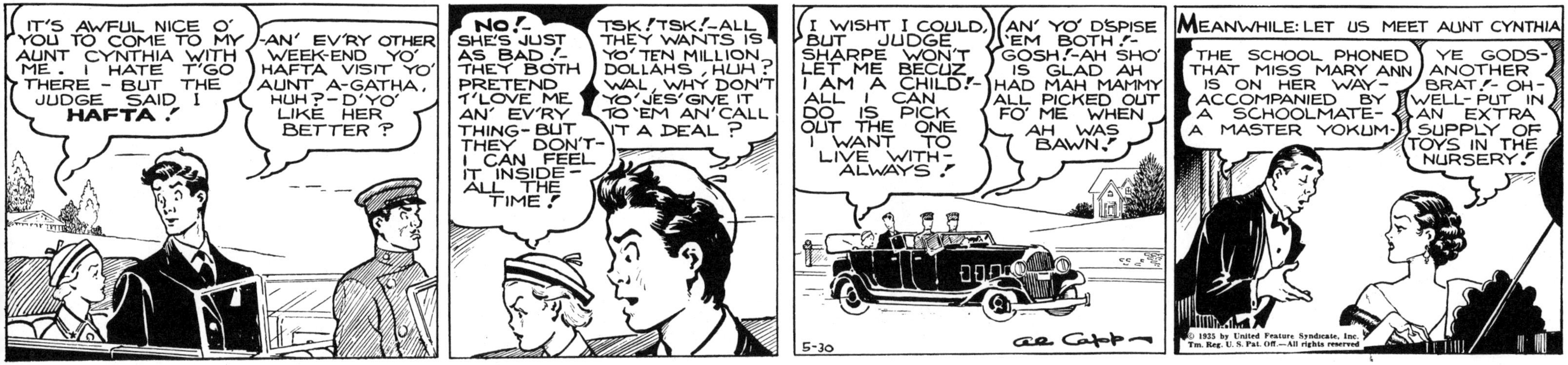
IT'S AWFUL NICE O' YOU TO COME TO MY AUNT CYNTHIA WITH ME. I HATE T'GO THERE-BUT THE JUDGE SAID I **HAFTA!**
-AN' EV'RY OTHER WEEK-END YO' HAFTA VISIT YO' AUNT A-GATHA, HUH?-D'YO' LIKE HER BETTER?
NO!-SHE'S JUST AS BAD!-THEY BOTH PRETEND T'LOVE ME AN' EV'RY THING-BUT THEY DON'T-I CAN FEEL IT INSIDE-ALL THE TIME!
TSK! TSK!-ALL THEY WANTS IS YO' TEN MILLION DOLLAHS, HUH? WAL, WHY DON'T YO' JES' GIVE IT TO 'EM AN' CALL IT A DEAL?
I WISHT I COULD, BUT JUDGE SHARPE WON'T LET ME BECUZ I AM A CHILD!-ALL I CAN DO IS PICK OUT THE ONE I WANT TO LIVE WITH-ALWAYS!
AN' YO' D'SPISE 'EM BOTH!-GOSH!-AH SHO' IS GLAD AH HAD MAH MAMMY ALL PICKED OUT FO' ME WHEN AH WAS BAWN!
5-30
MEANWHILE: LET US MEET AUNT CYNTHIA
THE SCHOOL PHONED THAT MISS MARY ANN IS ON HER WAY-ACCOMPANIED BY A SCHOOLMATE-A MASTER YOKUM-
YE GODS-ANOTHER BRAT!-OH-WELL-PUT IN AN EXTRA SUPPLY OF TOYS IN THE NURSERY!
© 1935 by United Feature Syndicate, Inc. Tm. Reg. U. S. Pat. Off.—All rights reserved

LI'L ABNER — Rehearsing Her Lines — By Al Capp

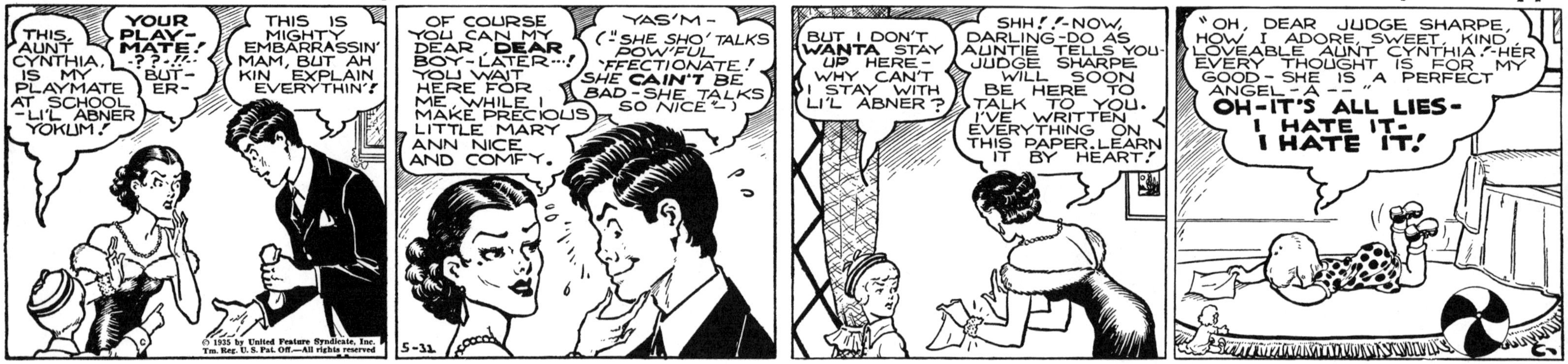

THIS, AUNT CYNTHIA, IS MY PLAYMATE AT SCHOOL -LI'L ABNER YOKUM!
YOUR PLAY-MATE!-??-!!-BUT-ER-
THIS IS MIGHTY EMBARRASSIN' MAM, BUT AH KIN EXPLAIN EVERYTHIN'!
© 1935 by United Feature Syndicate, Inc. Tm. Reg. U. S. Pat. Off.—All rights reserved
OF COURSE YOU CAN MY DEAR, DEAR BOY-LATER...! YOU WAIT HERE FOR ME, WHILE I MAKE PRECIOUS LITTLE MARY ANN NICE AND COMFY.
YAS'M-("SHE SHO' TALKS POW'FUL 'FFECTIONATE! SHE CAIN'T BE BAD-SHE TALKS SO NICE"-)
5-31
BUT I DON'T WANTA STAY UP HERE-WHY CAN'T I STAY WITH LI'L ABNER?
SHH!!-NOW, DARLING-DO AS AUNTIE TELLS YOU-JUDGE SHARPE WILL SOON BE HERE TO TALK TO YOU. I'VE WRITTEN EVERYTHING ON THIS PAPER. LEARN IT BY HEART!
"OH, DEAR JUDGE SHARPE, HOW I ADORE SWEET, KIND, LOVEABLE AUNT CYNTHIA!-HER EVERY THOUGHT IS FOR MY GOOD-SHE IS A PERFECT ANGEL-A --"
OH-IT'S ALL LIES-I HATE IT-I HATE IT!

LI'L ABNER — A Great Judge of Character — By Al Capp

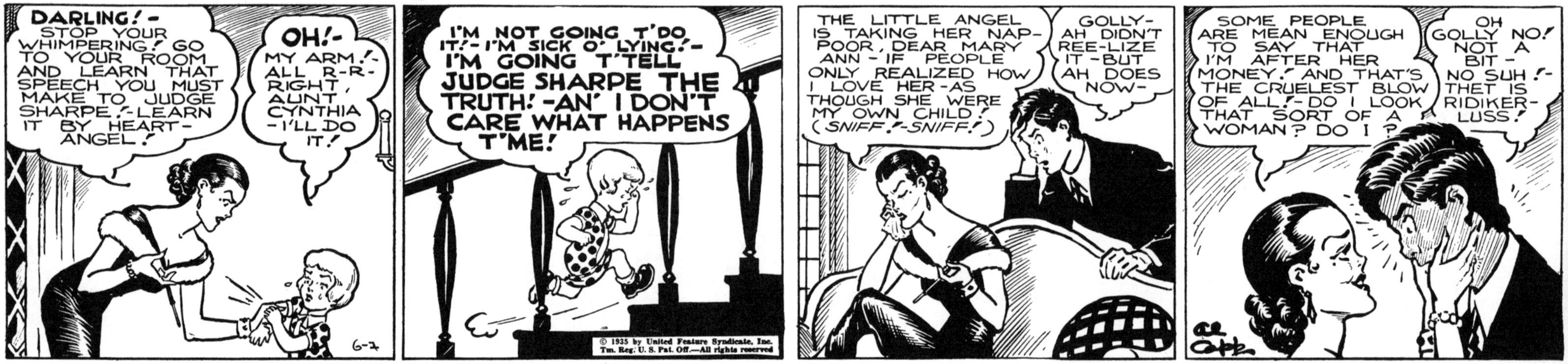

DARLING!-STOP YOUR WHIMPERING! GO TO YOUR ROOM AND LEARN THAT SPEECH YOU MUST MAKE TO JUDGE SHARPE!-LEARN IT BY HEART-ANGEL!
OH!-MY ARM!-ALL R-R-RIGHT, AUNT CYNTHIA -I'LL DO IT!
6-7
I'M NOT GOING T'DO IT!-I'M SICK O' LYING!-I'M GOING T'TELL JUDGE SHARPE THE TRUTH!-AN' I DON'T CARE WHAT HAPPENS T'ME!
© 1935 by United Feature Syndicate, Inc. Tm. Reg. U. S. Pat. Off.—All rights reserved
THE LITTLE ANGEL IS TAKING HER NAP-POOR, DEAR MARY ANN-IF PEOPLE ONLY REALIZED HOW I LOVE HER-AS THOUGH SHE WERE MY OWN CHILD! (SNIFF!-SNIFF!)
GOLLY-AH DIDN'T REE-LIZE IT-BUT AH DOES NOW-
SOME PEOPLE ARE MEAN ENOUGH TO SAY THAT I'M AFTER HER MONEY! AND THAT'S THE CRUELEST BLOW OF ALL!-DO I LOOK THAT SORT OF A WOMAN? DO I?
OH GOLLY NO! NOT A BIT-NO SUH!-THET IS RIDIKER-LUSS!

LI'L ABNER **Easy Mark** **By Al Capp**

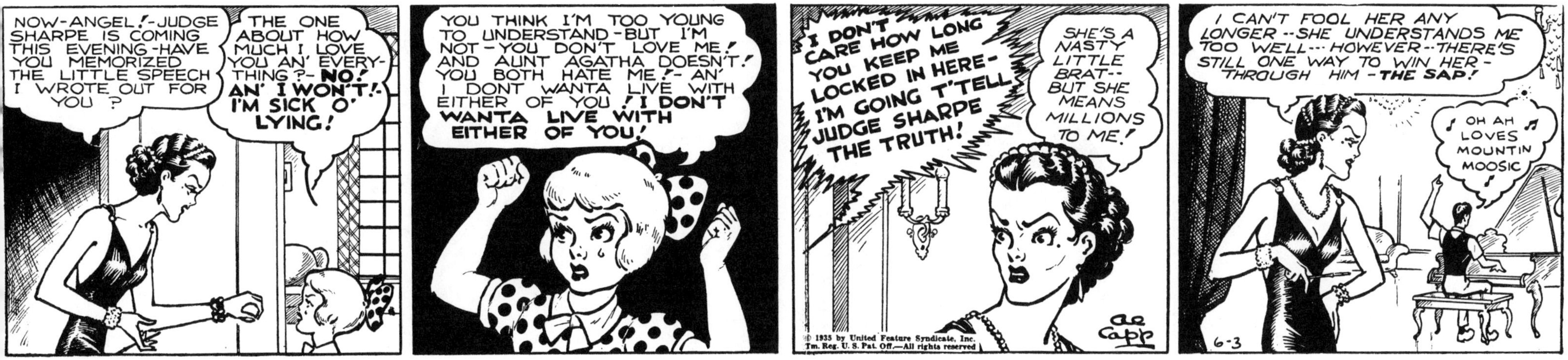
NOW-ANGEL!-JUDGE SHARPE IS COMING THIS EVENING-HAVE YOU MEMORIZED THE LITTLE SPEECH I WROTE OUT FOR YOU?
THE ONE ABOUT HOW MUCH I LOVE YOU AN' EVERYTHING?- NO! AN' I WON'T!- I'M SICK O' LYING!
YOU THINK I'M TOO YOUNG TO UNDERSTAND-BUT I'M NOT-YOU DON'T LOVE ME! AND AUNT AGATHA DOESN'T! YOU BOTH HATE ME!-AN' I DONT WANTA LIVE WITH EITHER OF YOU! I DON'T WANTA LIVE WITH EITHER OF YOU!
I DON'T CARE HOW LONG YOU KEEP ME LOCKED IN HERE- I'M GOING T'TELL JUDGE SHARPE THE TRUTH!
SHE'S A NASTY LITTLE BRAT-- BUT SHE MEANS MILLIONS TO ME!
© 1935 by United Feature Syndicate, Inc. Tm. Reg. U. S. Pat. Off.—All rights reserved
AL CAPP
I CAN'T FOOL HER ANY LONGER--SHE UNDERSTANDS ME TOO WELL---HOWEVER--THERE'S STILL ONE WAY TO WIN HER- THROUGH HIM -THE SAP!
OH AH LOVES MOUNTIN MOOSIC
6-3

LI'L ABNER **A Keen Judge of Character** **By Al Capp**

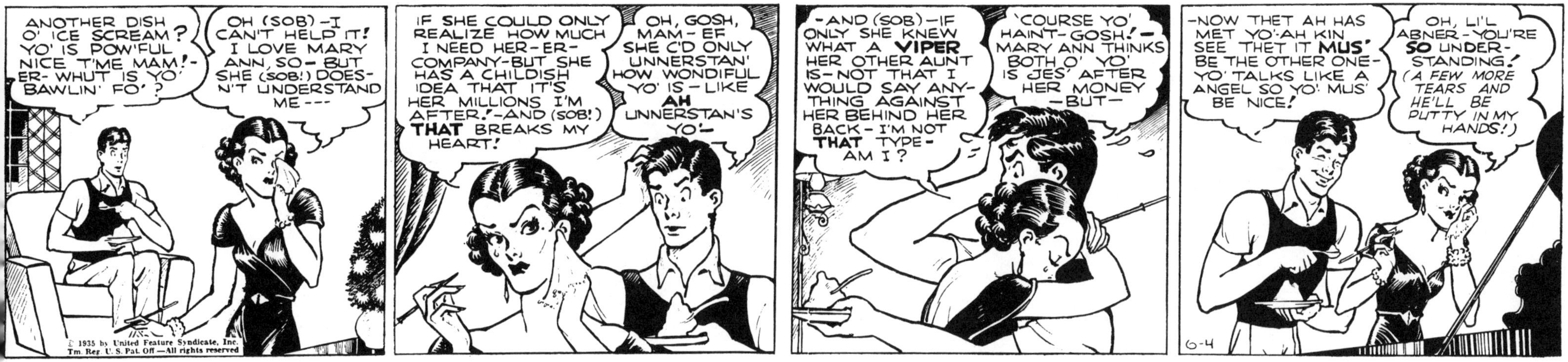
ANOTHER DISH O' ICE SCREAM? YO' IS POW'FUL NICE T'ME MAM!- ER- WHUT IS YO' BAWLIN' FO'?
OH (SOB)-I CAN'T HELP IT! I LOVE MARY ANN, SO- BUT SHE (SOB!) DOESN'T UNDERSTAND ME---
© 1935 by United Feature Syndicate, Inc. Tm. Reg. U. S. Pat. Off.—All rights reserved
IF SHE COULD ONLY REALIZE HOW MUCH I NEED HER-ER- COMPANY-BUT SHE HAS A CHILDISH IDEA THAT IT'S HER MILLIONS I'M AFTER!-AND (SOB!) THAT BREAKS MY HEART!
OH, GOSH, MAM-EF SHE C'D ONLY UNNERSTAN' HOW WONDIFUL YO' IS-LIKE AH UNNERSTAN'S YO'-
-AND (SOB)-IF ONLY SHE KNEW WHAT A VIPER HER OTHER AUNT IS-NOT THAT I WOULD SAY ANYTHING AGAINST HER BEHIND HER BACK-I'M NOT THAT TYPE- AM I?
'COURSE YO' HAINT-GOSH!-MARY ANN THINKS BOTH O' YO' IS JES' AFTER HER MONEY -BUT-
-NOW THET AH HAS MET YO'-AH KIN SEE THET IT MUS' BE THE OTHER ONE- YO' TALKS LIKE A ANGEL SO YO' MUS' BE NICE!
OH, LI'L ABNER-YOU'RE SO UNDERSTANDING! (A FEW MORE TEARS AND HE'LL BE PUTTY IN MY HANDS!)
6-4

LI'L ABNER Advice Is Cheap **By Al Capp**

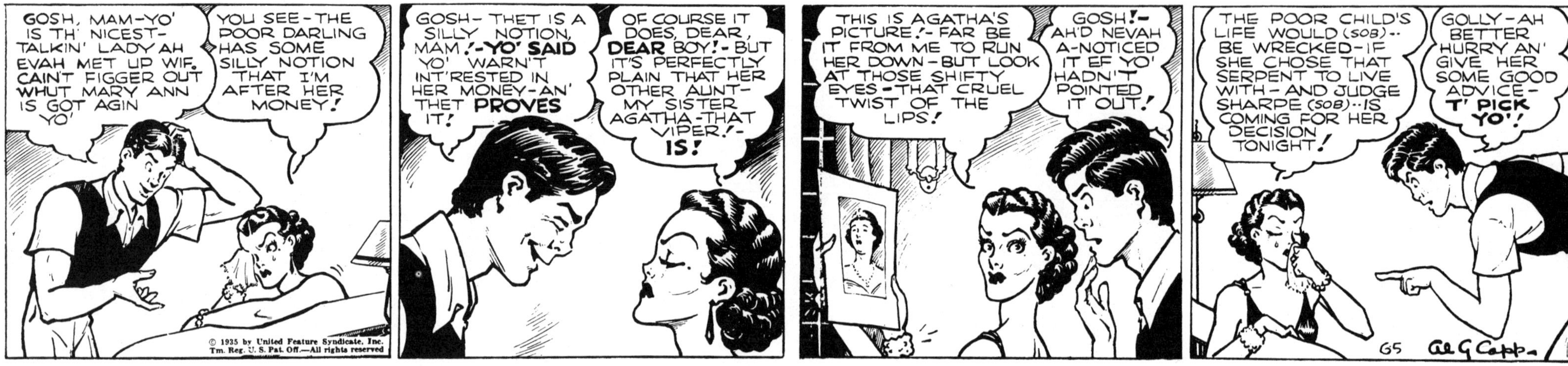
GOSH, MAM-YO' IS TH' NICEST-TALKIN' LADY AH EVAH MET UP WIF. CAIN'T FIGGER OUT WHUT MARY ANN IS GOT AGIN YO'
YOU SEE-THE POOR DARLING HAS SOME SILLY NOTION THAT I'M AFTER HER MONEY!
© 1935 by United Feature Syndicate, Inc. Tm. Reg. U. S. Pat. Off.—All rights reserved
GOSH-THET IS A SILLY NOTION, MAM!-YO' SAID YO' WARN'T INT'RESTED IN HER MONEY-AN' THET PROVES IT!
OF COURSE IT DOES, DEAR, DEAR BOY!-BUT IT'S PERFECTLY PLAIN THAT HER OTHER AUNT-MY SISTER AGATHA-THAT VIPER!-IS!
THIS IS AGATHA'S PICTURE!-FAR BE IT FROM ME TO RUN HER DOWN-BUT LOOK AT THOSE SHIFTY EYES-THAT CRUEL TWIST OF THE LIPS!
GOSH!-AH'D NEVAH A-NOTICED IT EF YO' HADN'T POINTED IT OUT!
THE POOR CHILD'S LIFE WOULD (SOB)..BE WRECKED-IF SHE CHOSE THAT SERPENT TO LIVE WITH-AND JUDGE SHARPE (SOB)..IS COMING FOR HER DECISION TONIGHT!
GOLLY-AH BETTER HURRY AN' GIVE HER SOME GOOD ADVICE-T' PICK YO'!
6-5
Al G Capp

LI'L ABNER Good Intentions **By Al Capp**

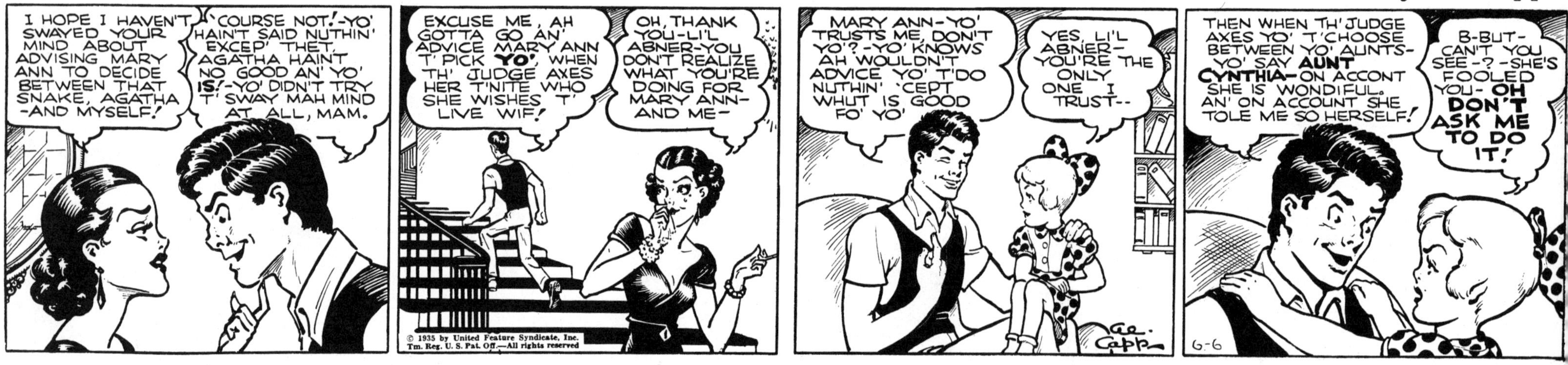
I HOPE I HAVEN'T SWAYED YOUR MIND ABOUT ADVISING MARY ANN TO DECIDE BETWEEN THAT SNAKE, AGATHA -AND MYSELF!
'COURSE NOT!-YO' HAIN'T SAID NUTHIN' EXCEP' THET, AGATHA HAINT NO GOOD AN' YO' IS!-YO' DIDN'T TRY T' SWAY MAH MIND AT ALL, MAM.
EXCUSE ME, AH GOTTA GO AN' ADVICE MARY ANN T' PICK YO', WHEN TH' JUDGE AXES HER T'NITE WHO SHE WISHES T' LIVE WIF!
OH, THANK YOU-LI'L ABNER-YOU DON'T REALIZE WHAT YOU'RE DOING FOR MARY ANN-AND ME-
© 1935 by United Feature Syndicate, Inc. Tm. Reg. U. S. Pat. Off.—All rights reserved
MARY ANN-YO' TRUSTS ME, DON'T YO'?-YO' KNOWS AH WOULDN'T ADVICE YO' T'DO NUTHIN' 'CEPT WHUT IS GOOD FO' YO'
YES, LI'L ABNER-YOU'RE THE ONLY ONE I TRUST--
Al Capp
THEN WHEN TH' JUDGE AXES YO' T'CHOOSE BETWEEN YO' AUNTS-YO' SAY AUNT CYNTHIA-ON ACCOUNT SHE IS WONDIFUL. AN' ON ACCOUNT SHE TOLE ME SO HERSELF!
B-BUT-CAN'T YOU SEE-?-SHE'S FOOLED YOU-OH DON'T ASK ME TO DO IT!
6-6

LI'L ABNER A Wolf In Sheep's Clothing **By Al Capp**

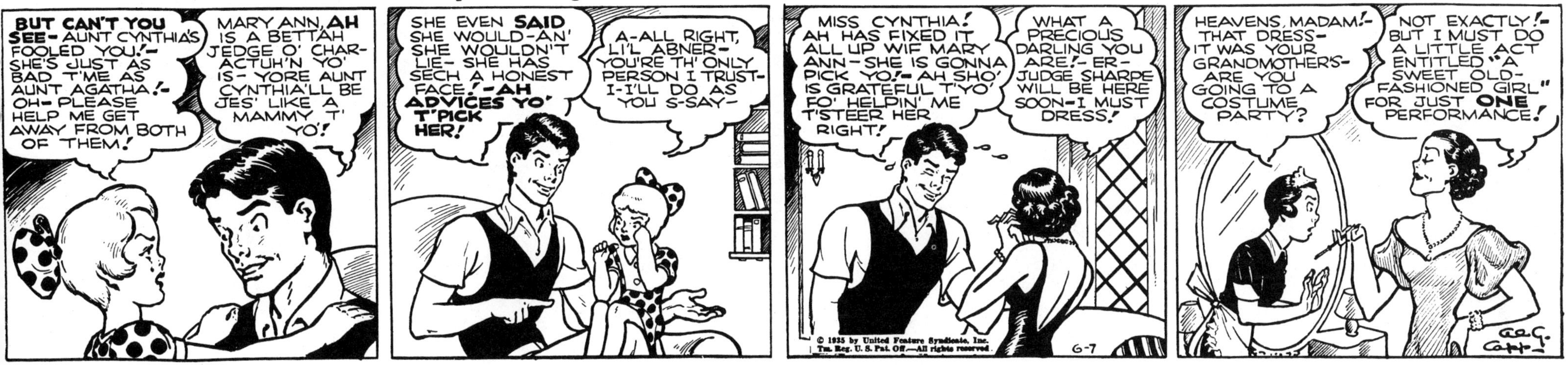

BUT CAN'T YOU SEE- AUNT CYNTHIA'S FOOLED YOU!- SHE'S JUST AS BAD T'ME AS AUNT AGATHA!- OH- PLEASE HELP ME GET AWAY FROM BOTH OF THEM!
MARY ANN, AH IS A BETTAH JEDGE O' CHAR-ACTUH'N YO' IS- YORE AUNT CYNTHIA'LL BE JES' LIKE A MAMMY T' YO'!
SHE EVEN SAID SHE WOULD-AN' SHE WOULDN'T LIE- SHE HAS SECH A HONEST FACE!-AH ADVICES YO' T'PICK HER!
A-ALL RIGHT, LI'L ABNER- YOU'RE TH' ONLY PERSON I TRUST- I-I'LL DO AS YOU S-SAY-
MISS CYNTHIA! AH HAS FIXED IT ALL UP WIF MARY ANN- SHE IS GONNA PICK YO!- AH SHO' IS GRATEFUL T'YO' FO' HELPIN' ME T'STEER HER RIGHT!
WHAT A PRECIOUS DARLING YOU ARE!- ER- JUDGE SHARPE WILL BE HERE SOON- I MUST DRESS!
© 1935 by United Feature Syndicate, Inc. Tm. Reg. U. S. Pat. Off.—All rights reserved
6-7
HEAVENS, MADAM!- THAT DRESS- IT WAS YOUR GRANDMOTHER'S- ARE YOU GOING TO A COSTUME PARTY?
NOT EXACTLY!- BUT I MUST DO A LITTLE ACT ENTITLED "A SWEET OLD-FASHIONED GIRL" FOR JUST ONE PERFORMANCE!

LI'L ABNER Adorably Dumb **By Al Capp**

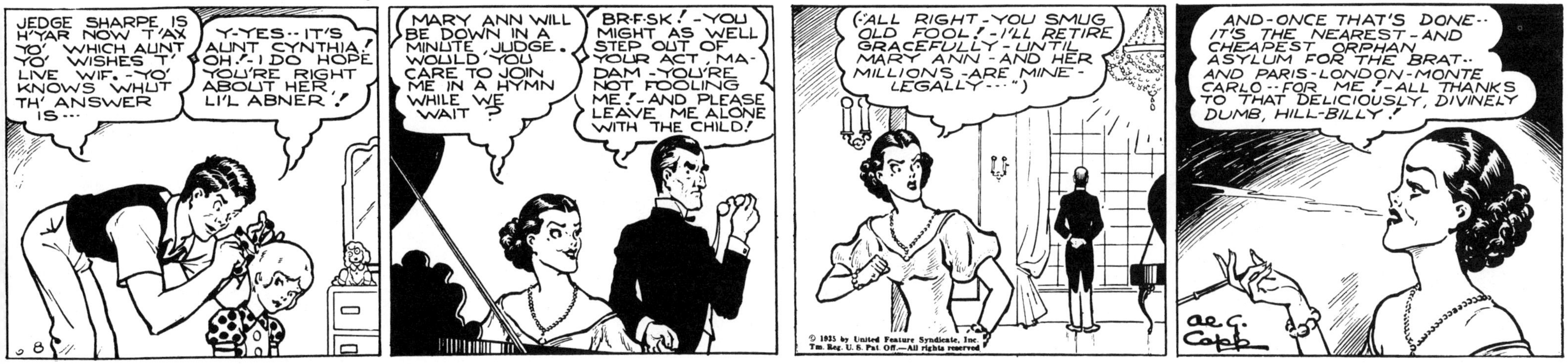

JEDGE SHARPE IS H'YAR NOW T'AX YO' WHICH AUNT YO' WISHES T' LIVE WIF. -YO' KNOWS WHUT TH' ANSWER IS---
Y-YES-- IT'S AUNT CYNTHIA! OH!- I DO HOPE YOU'RE RIGHT ABOUT HER, LI'L ABNER!
MARY ANN WILL BE DOWN IN A MINUTE, JUDGE. WOULD YOU CARE TO JOIN ME IN A HYMN WHILE WE WAIT?
BR-F-SK! - YOU MIGHT AS WELL STEP OUT OF YOUR ACT, MADAM - YOU'RE NOT FOOLING ME!- AND PLEASE LEAVE ME ALONE WITH THE CHILD!
("ALL RIGHT - YOU SMUG OLD FOOL!- I'LL RETIRE GRACEFULLY - UNTIL MARY ANN - AND HER MILLIONS - ARE MINE - LEGALLY---")
© 1935 by United Feature Syndicate, Inc. Tm. Reg. U. S. Pat. Off.—All rights reserved
AND-ONCE THAT'S DONE-- IT'S THE NEAREST - AND CHEAPEST ORPHAN ASYLUM FOR THE BRAT-- AND PARIS-LONDON-MONTE CARLO -- FOR ME!- ALL THANKS TO THAT DELICIOUSLY, DIVINELY DUMB, HILL-BILLY!

LI'L ABNER Good Old Snipes By Al Capp

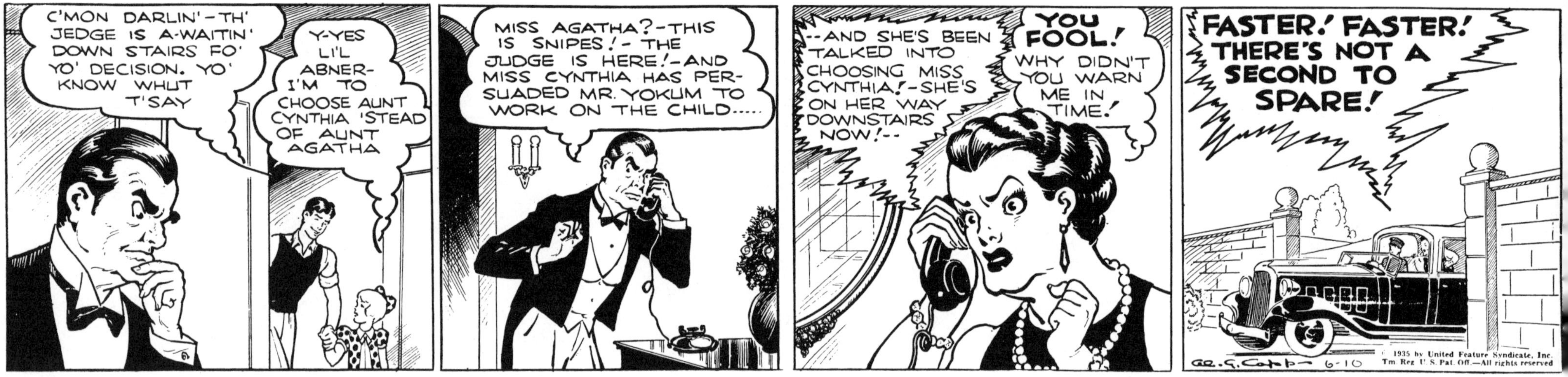
C'MON DARLIN'-TH' JEDGE IS A-WAITIN' DOWN STAIRS FO' YO' DECISION. YO' KNOW WHUT T'SAY
Y-YES LI'L ABNER-I'M TO CHOOSE AUNT CYNTHIA 'STEAD OF AUNT AGATHA
MISS AGATHA?-THIS IS SNIPES!-THE JUDGE IS HERE!-AND MISS CYNTHIA HAS PERSUADED MR. YOKUM TO WORK ON THE CHILD....
--AND SHE'S BEEN TALKED INTO CHOOSING MISS CYNTHIA!-SHE'S ON HER WAY DOWNSTAIRS NOW!--
YOU FOOL! WHY DIDN'T YOU WARN ME IN TIME!
FASTER! FASTER! THERE'S NOT A SECOND TO SPARE!
Al G. Capp 6-10
© 1935 by United Feature Syndicate, Inc. Tm Reg U.S. Pat. Off.—All rights reserved

LI'L ABNER The Uninvited Guest By Al Capp

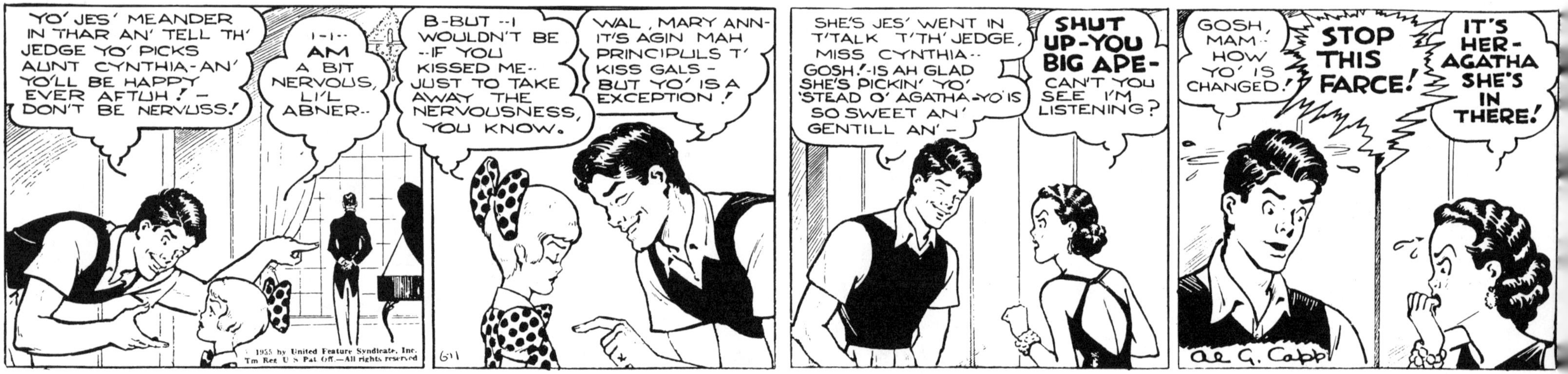
YO' JES' MEANDER IN THAR AN' TELL TH' JEDGE YO' PICKS AUNT CYNTHIA-AN' YO'LL BE HAPPY EVER AFTUH!-DON'T BE NERVUSS!
I-I-I-AM A BIT NERVOUS, LI'L ABNER--
B-BUT--I WOULDN'T BE--IF YOU KISSED ME--JUST TO TAKE AWAY THE NERVOUSNESS, YOU KNOW.
WAL, MARY ANN IT'S AGIN MAH PRINCIPULS T' KISS GALS-BUT YO' IS A EXCEPTION!
© 1935 by United Feature Syndicate, Inc. Tm Reg U.S. Pat. Off.—All rights reserved
6-11
SHE'S JES' WENT IN T'TALK T'TH' JEDGE, MISS CYNTHIA--GOSH!-IS AH GLAD SHE'S PICKIN' YO' 'STEAD O' AGATHA-YO'IS SO SWEET AN' GENTILL AN'-
SHUT UP-YOU BIG APE-CAN'T YOU SEE I'M LISTENING?
GOSH, MAM! HOW YO' IS CHANGED!
STOP THIS FARCE!
IT'S HER-AGATHA SHE'S IN THERE!
Al G. Capp

LI'L ABNER When Ladies Meet **By Al Capp**

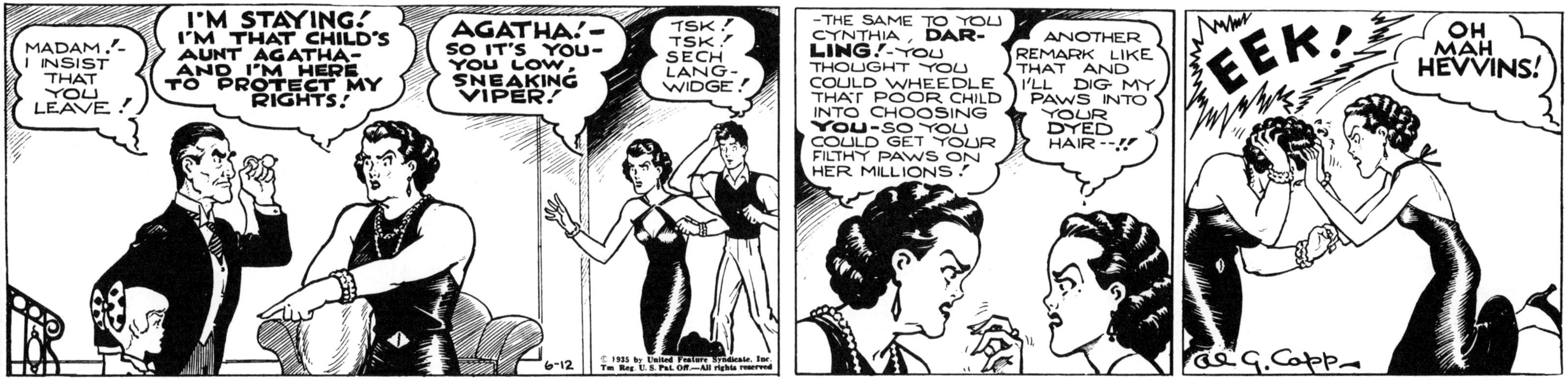

MADAM!- I INSIST THAT YOU LEAVE!
I'M STAYING! I'M THAT CHILD'S AUNT AGATHA- AND I'M HERE TO PROTECT MY RIGHTS!
AGATHA!- SO IT'S YOU- YOU LOW, SNEAKING VIPER!
TSK! TSK! SECH LANG-WIDGE!
6-12
© 1935 by United Feature Syndicate, Inc. Tm Reg. U. S. Pat. Off.—All rights reserved
-THE SAME TO YOU CYNTHIA, DAR-LING!-YOU THOUGHT YOU COULD WHEEDLE THAT POOR CHILD INTO CHOOSING YOU-SO YOU COULD GET YOUR FILTHY PAWS ON HER MILLIONS!
ANOTHER REMARK LIKE THAT AND I'LL DIG MY PAWS INTO YOUR DYED HAIR--!!
EEK!
OH MAH HEVVINS!
Al G. Capp

LI'L ABNER Innocent Bystander Injured **By Al Capp**

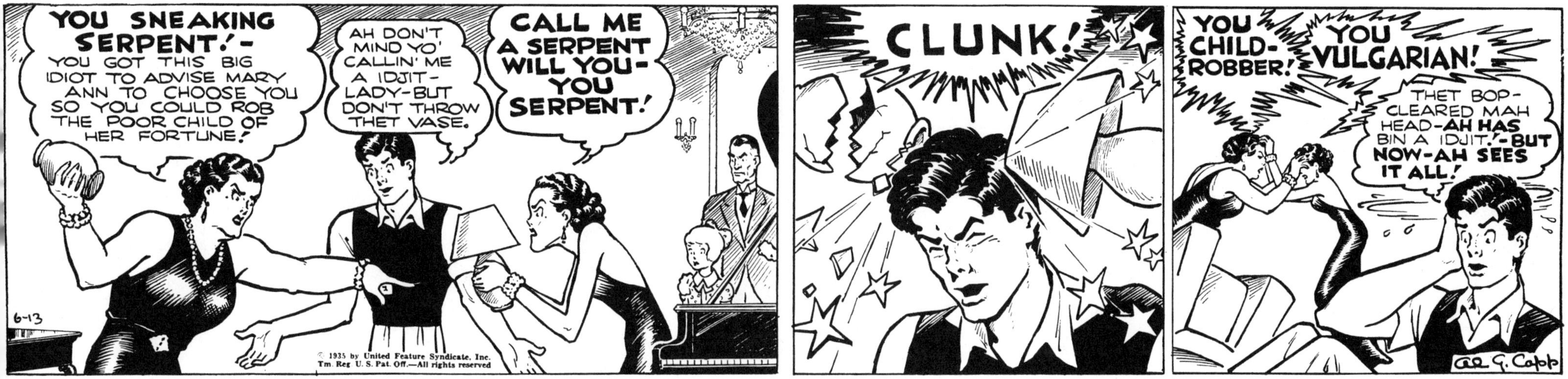

YOU SNEAKING SERPENT!- YOU GOT THIS BIG IDIOT TO ADVISE MARY ANN TO CHOOSE YOU SO YOU COULD ROB THE POOR CHILD OF HER FORTUNE!
AH DON'T MIND YO' CALLIN' ME A IDJIT- LADY-BUT DON'T THROW THET VASE.
CALL ME A SERPENT WILL YOU- YOU SERPENT!
6-13
© 1935 by United Feature Syndicate, Inc. Tm. Reg U. S. Pat. Off.—All rights reserved
CLUNK!
YOU CHILD-ROBBER!
YOU VULGARIAN!
THET BOP- CLEARED MAH HEAD-AH HAS BIN A IDJIT!-BUT NOW-AH SEES IT ALL!
Al G. Capp

LI'L ABNER The Compromise By Al Capp

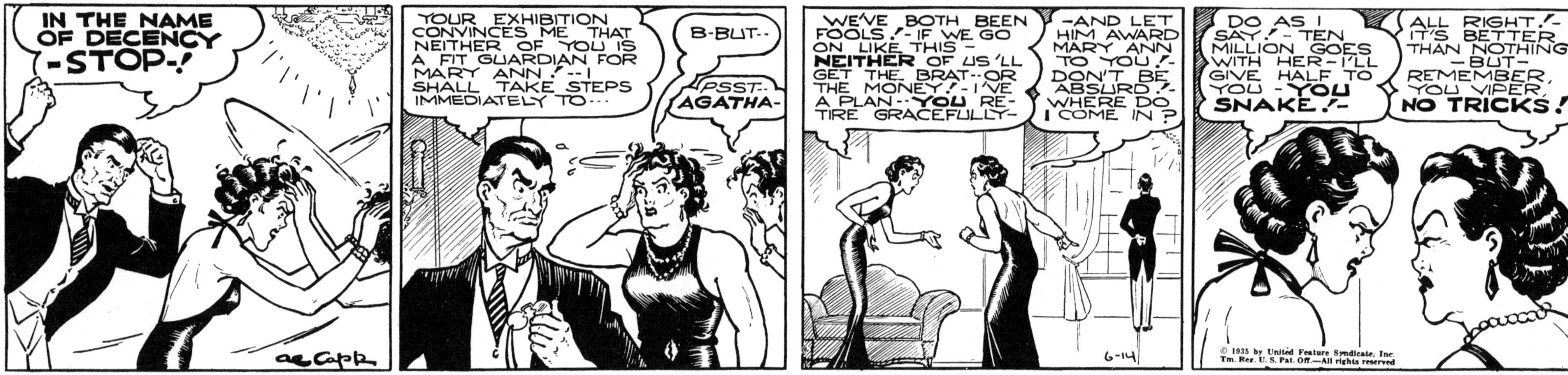
IN THE NAME OF DECENCY -STOP-!
YOUR EXHIBITION CONVINCES ME THAT NEITHER OF YOU IS A FIT GUARDIAN FOR MARY ANN!--I SHALL TAKE STEPS IMMEDIATELY TO---
B-BUT--
PSST- AGATHA-
WE'VE BOTH BEEN FOOLS!-IF WE GO ON LIKE THIS-NEITHER OF US'LL GET THE BRAT--OR THE MONEY!-I'VE A PLAN--YOU RE-TIRE GRACEFULLY-
-AND LET HIM AWARD MARY ANN TO YOU!-
DON'T BE ABSURD!-WHERE DO I COME IN?
DO AS I SAY!-TEN MILLION GOES WITH HER-I'LL GIVE HALF TO YOU-YOU SNAKE!-
ALL RIGHT!-IT'S BETTER THAN NOTHING-BUT-REMEMBER, YOU VIPER, NO TRICKS!
AL CAPP
6-14
© 1935 by United Feature Syndicate, Inc. Tm. Reg. U. S. Pat. Off.—All rights reserved

LI'L ABNER Absent Without Leave By Al Capp

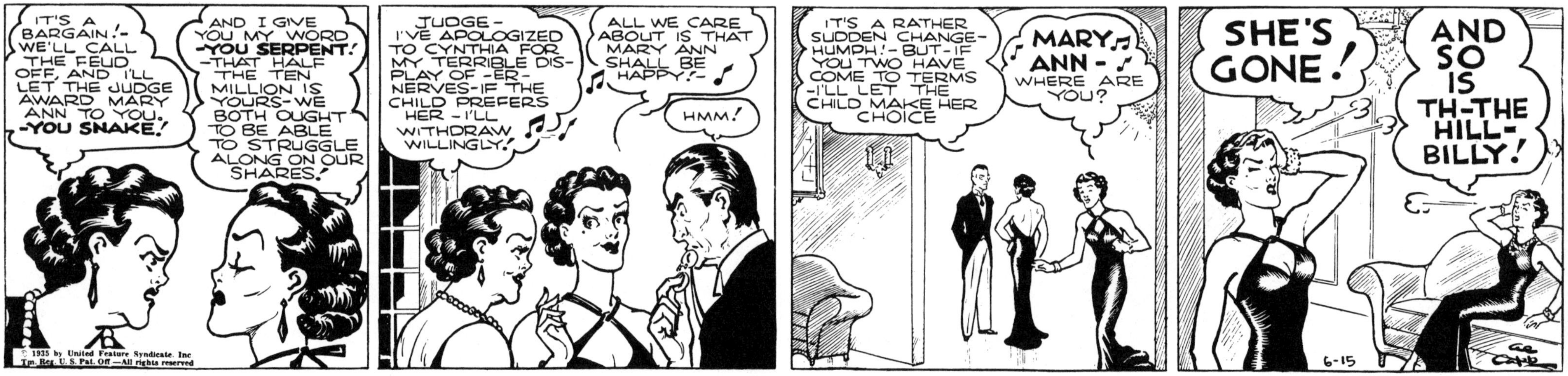
IT'S A BARGAIN!-WE'LL CALL THE FEUD OFF, AND I'LL LET THE JUDGE AWARD MARY ANN TO YOU. -YOU SNAKE!
AND I GIVE YOU MY WORD -YOU SERPENT!-THAT HALF THE TEN MILLION IS YOURS-WE BOTH OUGHT TO BE ABLE TO STRUGGLE ALONG ON OUR SHARES!
© 1935 by United Feature Syndicate, Inc Tm. Reg. U. S. Pat. Off.—All rights reserved
JUDGE-I'VE APOLOGIZED TO CYNTHIA FOR MY TERRIBLE DIS-PLAY OF -ER-NERVES-IF THE CHILD PREFERS HER-I'LL WITHDRAW WILLINGLY!
ALL WE CARE ABOUT IS THAT MARY ANN SHALL BE HAPPY!-
HMM!
IT'S A RATHER SUDDEN CHANGE-HUMPH!-BUT-IF YOU TWO HAVE COME TO TERMS-I'LL LET THE CHILD MAKE HER CHOICE
MARY ANN-WHERE ARE YOU?
SHE'S GONE!
AND SO IS TH-THE HILL-BILLY!
6-15
AL CAPP

LI'L ABNER — Gone But Not Forgotten — By Al Capp

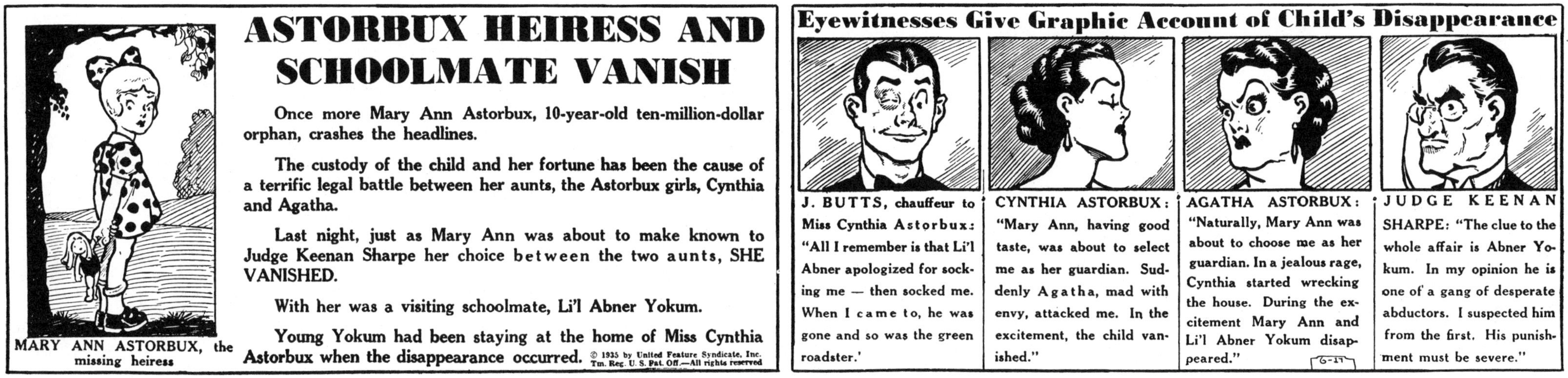
ASTORBUX HEIRESS AND SCHOOLMATE VANISH
Once more Mary Ann Astorbux, 10-year-old ten-million-dollar orphan, crashes the headlines.
The custody of the child and her fortune has been the cause of a terrific legal battle between her aunts, the Astorbux girls, Cynthia and Agatha.
Last night, just as Mary Ann was about to make known to Judge Keenan Sharpe her choice between the two aunts, SHE VANISHED.
With her was a visiting schoolmate, Li'l Abner Yokum.
Young Yokum had been staying at the home of Miss Cynthia Astorbux when the disappearance occurred.
MARY ANN ASTORBUX, the missing heiress
© 1935 by United Feature Syndicate, Inc. Tm. Reg. U. S. Pat. Off.—All rights reserved
Eyewitnesses Give Graphic Account of Child's Disappearance
J. BUTTS, chauffeur to Miss Cynthia Astorbux: "All I remember is that Li'l Abner apologized for socking me — then socked me. When I came to, he was gone and so was the green roadster.'
CYNTHIA ASTORBUX: "Mary Ann, having good taste, was about to select me as her guardian. Suddenly Agatha, mad with envy, attacked me. In the excitement, the child vanished."
AGATHA ASTORBUX: "Naturally, Mary Ann was about to choose me as her guardian. In a jealous rage, Cynthia started wrecking the house. During the excitement Mary Ann and Li'l Abner Yokum disappeared."
6-17
JUDGE KEENAN SHARPE: "The clue to the whole affair is Abner Yokum. In my opinion he is one of a gang of desperate abductors. I suspected him from the first. His punishment must be severe."

LI'L ABNER — Don't Leave Thet Chile ! — By Al Capp

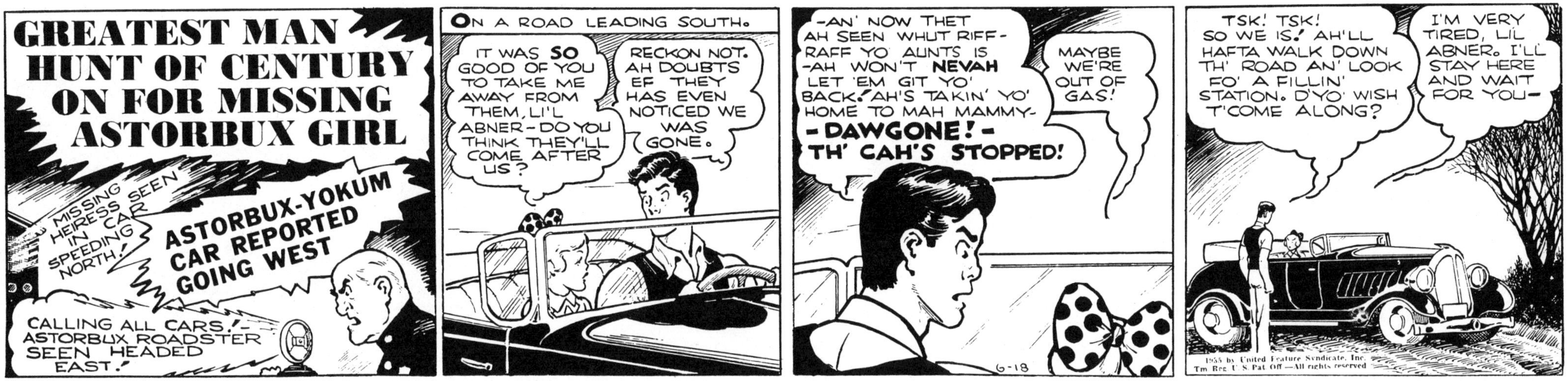
GREATEST MAN HUNT OF CENTURY ON FOR MISSING ASTORBUX GIRL
MISSING HEIRESS SEEN IN CAR SPEEDING NORTH!
ASTORBUX-YOKUM CAR REPORTED GOING WEST
CALLING ALL CARS!— ASTORBUX ROADSTER SEEN HEADED EAST!
ON A ROAD LEADING SOUTH.
IT WAS SO GOOD OF YOU TO TAKE ME AWAY FROM THEM, LI'L ABNER - DO YOU THINK THEY'LL COME AFTER US?
RECKON NOT. AH DOUBTS EF THEY HAS EVEN NOTICED WE WAS GONE.
-AN' NOW THET AH SEEN WHUT RIFF-RAFF YO' AUNTS IS -AH WON'T NEVAH LET 'EM GIT YO' BACK! AH'S TAKIN' YO' HOME TO MAH MAMMY- -DAWGONE!- TH' CAH'S STOPPED!
MAYBE WE'RE OUT OF GAS!
6-18
TSK! TSK! SO WE IS! AH'LL HAFTA WALK DOWN TH' ROAD AN' LOOK FO' A FILLIN' STATION. D'YO' WISH T'COME ALONG?
I'M VERY TIRED, LI'L ABNER. I'LL STAY HERE AND WAIT FOR YOU—
1935 by United Feature Syndicate, Inc. Tm Reg U S Pat Off—All rights reserved

LI'L ABNER   A Desperate Character   By Al Capp

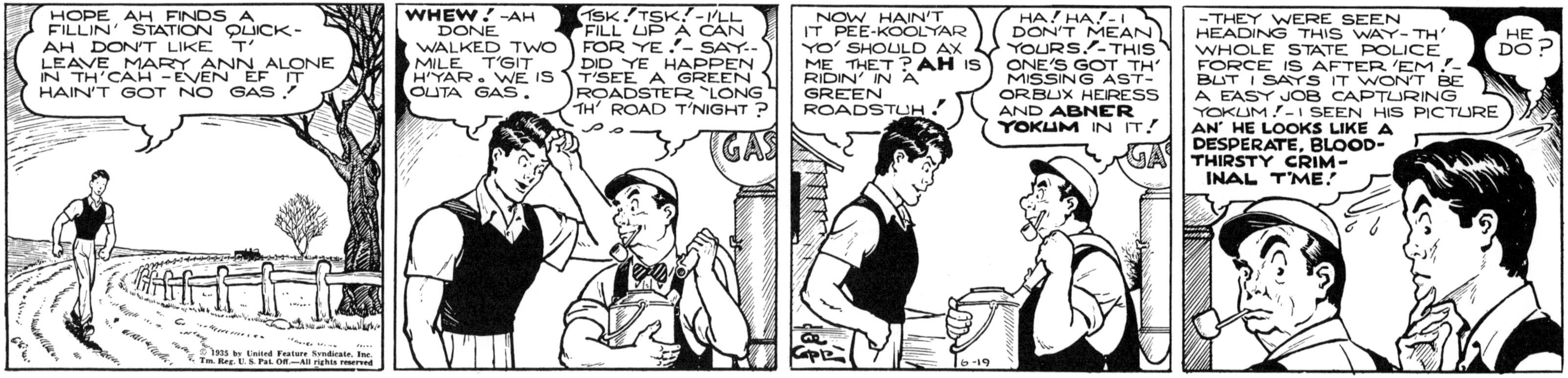
HOPE AH FINDS A FILLIN' STATION QUICK- AH DON'T LIKE T' LEAVE MARY ANN ALONE IN TH' CAH - EVEN EF IT HAIN'T GOT NO GAS!
© 1935 by United Feature Syndicate, Inc. Tm. Reg. U. S. Pat. Off.—All rights reserved
WHEW! -AH DONE WALKED TWO MILE T'GIT H'YAR. WE IS OUTA GAS.
TSK! TSK! - I'LL FILL UP A CAN FOR YE! - SAY - DID YE HAPPEN T'SEE A GREEN ROADSTER 'LONG TH' ROAD T'NIGHT?
GAS
NOW HAIN'T IT PEE-KOOLYAR YO' SHOULD AX ME THET? AH IS RIDIN' IN A GREEN ROADSTUH!
HA! HA! - I DON'T MEAN YOURS! - THIS ONE'S GOT TH' MISSING ASTORBUX HEIRESS AND ABNER YOKUM IN IT!
6-19
-THEY WERE SEEN HEADING THIS WAY- TH' WHOLE STATE POLICE FORCE IS AFTER 'EM! - BUT I SAYS IT WON'T BE A EASY JOB CAPTURING YOKUM! - I SEEN HIS PICTURE AN' HE LOOKS LIKE A DESPERATE, BLOOD-THIRSTY CRIMINAL T'ME!
HE DO?

LI'L ABNER   Lost, Strayed or Stolen?   By Al Capp

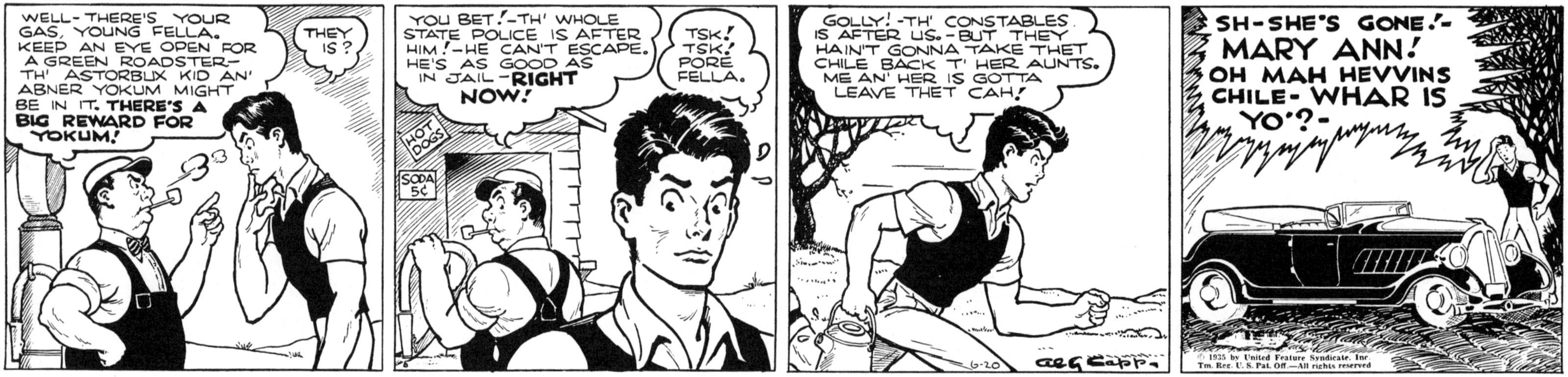
WELL- THERE'S YOUR GAS, YOUNG FELLA. KEEP AN EYE OPEN FOR A GREEN ROADSTER- TH' ASTORBUX KID AN' ABNER YOKUM MIGHT BE IN IT. THERE'S A BIG REWARD FOR YOKUM!
THEY IS?
YOU BET! - TH' WHOLE STATE POLICE IS AFTER HIM! - HE CAN'T ESCAPE. HE'S AS GOOD AS IN JAIL - RIGHT NOW!
TSK! TSK! PORE FELLA.
HOT DOGS
SODA 5¢
GOLLY! - TH' CONSTABLES IS AFTER US. - BUT THEY HAIN'T GONNA TAKE THET CHILE BACK T' HER AUNTS. ME AN' HER IS GOTTA LEAVE THET CAH!
6-20
SH-SHE'S GONE! - MARY ANN! OH MAH HEVVINS CHILE- WHAR IS YO'? -
© 1935 by United Feature Syndicate, Inc. Tm. Reg. U. S. Pat. Off.—All rights reserved

LI'L ABNER Li'l Sister Abner By Al Capp

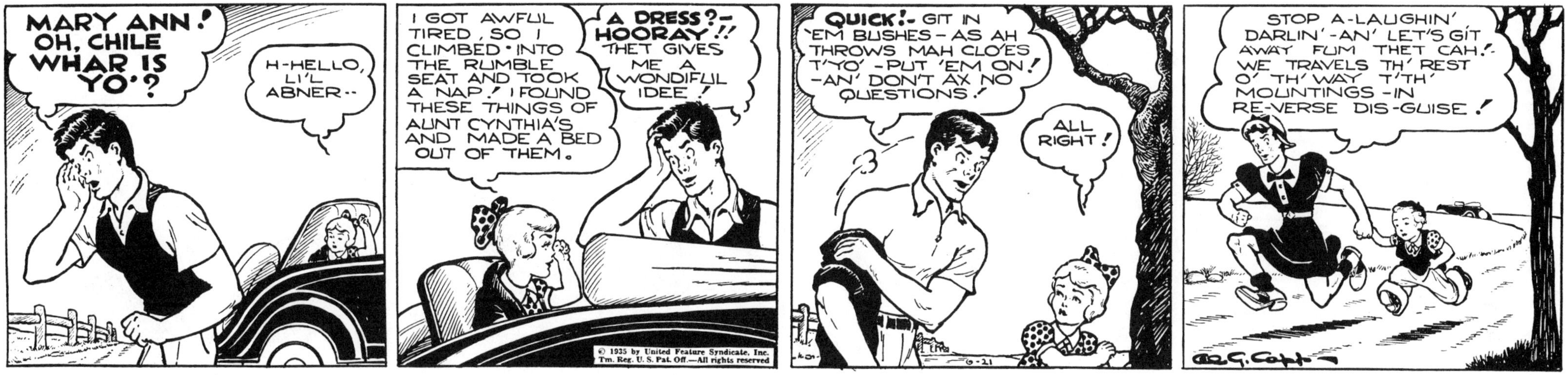

MARY ANN! OH, CHILE WHAR IS YO'?
H-HELLO, LI'L ABNER--
I GOT AWFUL TIRED, SO I CLIMBED INTO THE RUMBLE SEAT AND TOOK A NAP! I FOUND THESE THINGS OF AUNT CYNTHIA'S AND MADE A BED OUT OF THEM.
A DRESS?— HOORAY!! THET GIVES ME A WONDIFUL IDEE!
© 1935 by United Feature Syndicate, Inc. Tm. Reg. U. S. Pat. Off.—All rights reserved
QUICK!- GIT IN 'EM BUSHES – AS AH THROWS MAH CLO'ES T'YO' – PUT 'EM ON! –AN' DON'T AX NO QUESTIONS!
ALL RIGHT!
6-21
STOP A-LAUGHIN' DARLIN' – AN' LET'S GIT AWAY FUM THET CAH!- WE TRAVELS TH' REST O' TH' WAY T'TH' MOUNTINGS – IN RE-VERSE DIS-GUISE!
AL G. CAPP

LI'L ABNER His First Conquest By Al Capp

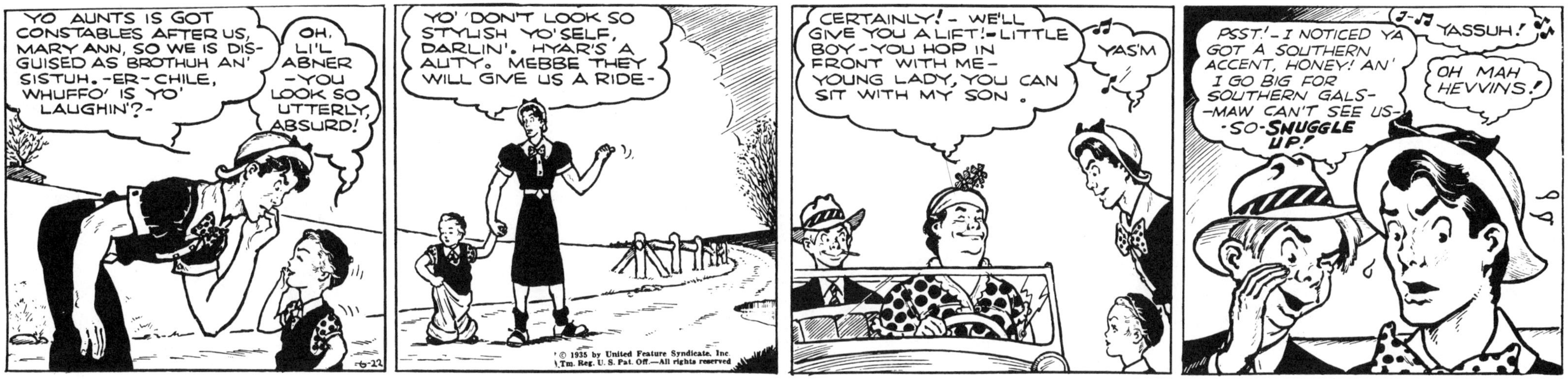

YO AUNTS IS GOT CONSTABLES AFTER US, MARY ANN, SO WE IS DIS-GUISED AS BROTHUH AN' SISTUH. –ER– CHILE, WHUFFO' IS YO' LAUGHIN'?-
OH, LI'L ABNER –YOU LOOK SO UTTERLY ABSURD!
6-22
YO' DON'T LOOK SO STYLISH YO'SELF, DARLIN'. HYAR'S A AUTY. MEBBE THEY WILL GIVE US A RIDE-
© 1935 by United Feature Syndicate, Inc. Tm. Reg. U. S. Pat. Off.—All rights reserved
CERTAINLY! – WE'LL GIVE YOU A LIFT! – LITTLE BOY – YOU HOP IN FRONT WITH ME – YOUNG LADY, YOU CAN SIT WITH MY SON.
YAS'M
PSST! – I NOTICED YA GOT A SOUTHERN ACCENT, HONEY! AN' I GO BIG FOR SOUTHERN GALS- –MAW CAN'T SEE US- –SO- SNUGGLE UP!
YASSUH!
OH MAH HEVVINS!

LI'L ABNER An Old-Fashioned Gal By Al Capp

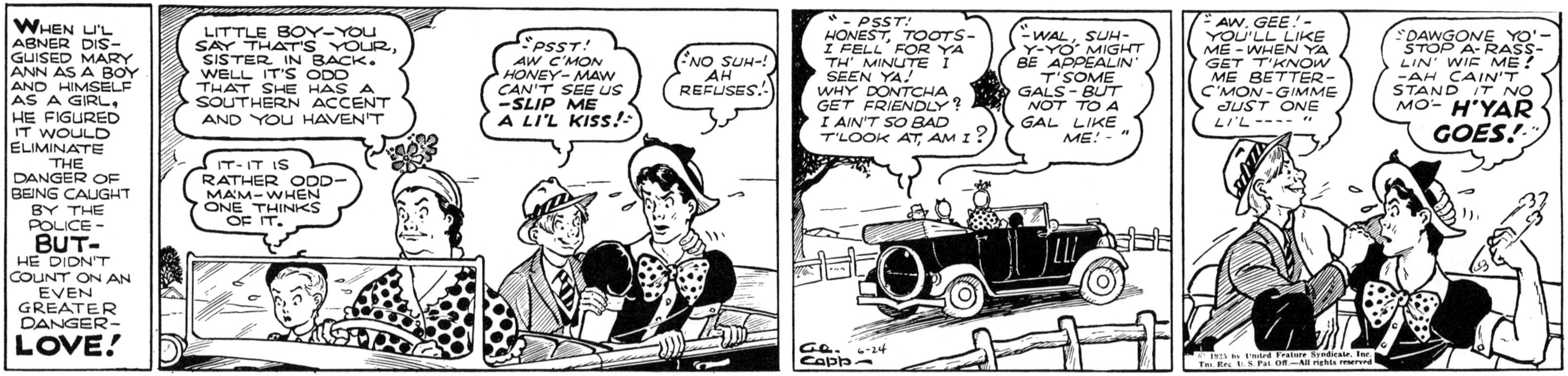

WHEN LI'L ABNER DISGUISED MARY ANN AS A BOY AND HIMSELF AS A GIRL, HE FIGURED IT WOULD ELIMINATE THE DANGER OF BEING CAUGHT BY THE POLICE- BUT- HE DIDN'T COUNT ON AN EVEN GREATER DANGER- LOVE!
LITTLE BOY-YOU SAY THAT'S YOUR SISTER IN BACK. WELL IT'S ODD THAT SHE HAS A SOUTHERN ACCENT AND YOU HAVEN'T
IT-IT IS RATHER ODD-MA'M-WHEN ONE THINKS OF IT.
"PSST! AW C'MON HONEY-MAW CAN'T SEE US -SLIP ME A LI'L KISS!-
"NO SUH-! AH REFUSES!-
"-PSST! HONEST, TOOTS- I FELL FOR YA TH' MINUTE I SEEN YA! WHY DONTCHA GET FRIENDLY? I AIN'T SO BAD T'LOOK AT, AM I?
"-WAL, SUH- Y-YO' MIGHT BE APPEALIN' T'SOME GALS-BUT NOT TO A GAL LIKE ME!-"
"-AW, GEE!- YOU'LL LIKE ME-WHEN YA GET T'KNOW ME BETTER- C'MON-GIMME JUST ONE LI'L ----"
"DAWGONE YO'- STOP A-RASSLIN' WIF ME! -AH CAIN'T STAND IT NO MO'- H'YAR GOES!-"
Al Capp 6-24

LI'L ABNER The Beginning of the End By Al Capp

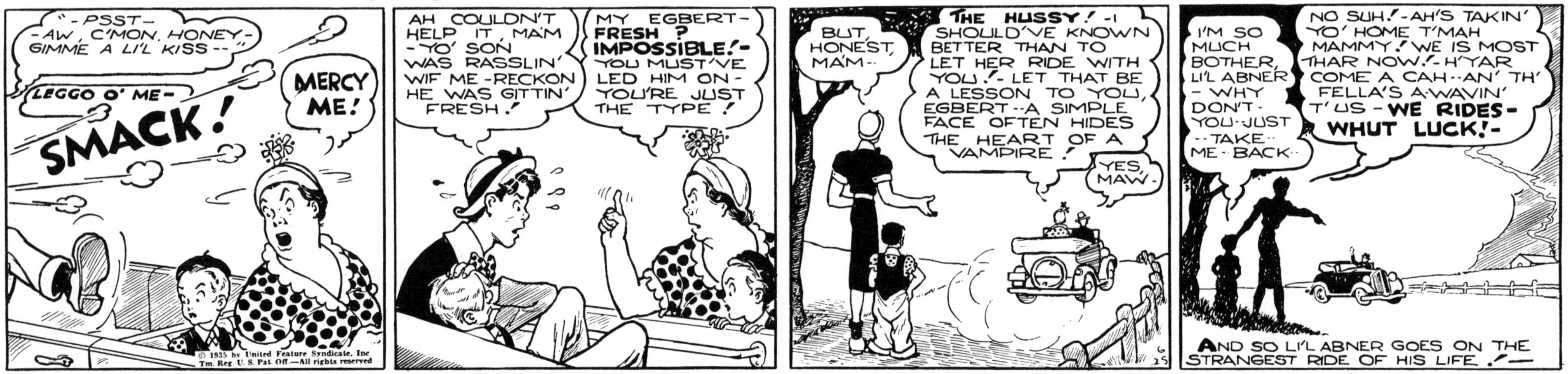

"-PSST- -AW, C'MON, HONEY- GIMME A LI'L KISS--"
LEGGO O' ME-
SMACK!
MERCY ME!
AH COULDN'T HELP IT, MA'M -YO' SON WAS RASSLIN' WIF ME-RECKON HE WAS GITTIN' FRESH!
MY EGBERT- FRESH? IMPOSSIBLE!- YOU MUST'VE LED HIM ON- YOU'RE JUST THE TYPE!
BUT, HONEST, MA'M--
THE HUSSY!-I SHOULD'VE KNOWN BETTER THAN TO LET HER RIDE WITH YOU!-LET THAT BE A LESSON TO YOU, EGBERT--A SIMPLE FACE OFTEN HIDES THE HEART OF A VAMPIRE!
YES, MAW-
6 25
I'M SO MUCH BOTHER, LI'L ABNER - WHY DON'T YOU-JUST --TAKE-- ME--BACK--
NO SUH!-AH'S TAKIN' YO' HOME T'MAH MAMMY! WE IS MOST THAR NOW!-H'YAR COME A CAH--AN' TH' FELLA'S A-WAVIN' T'US-WE RIDES- WHUT LUCK!-
AND SO LI'L ABNER GOES ON THE STRANGEST RIDE OF HIS LIFE!-

LI'L ABNER A Disinterested Viewpoint **By Al Capp**

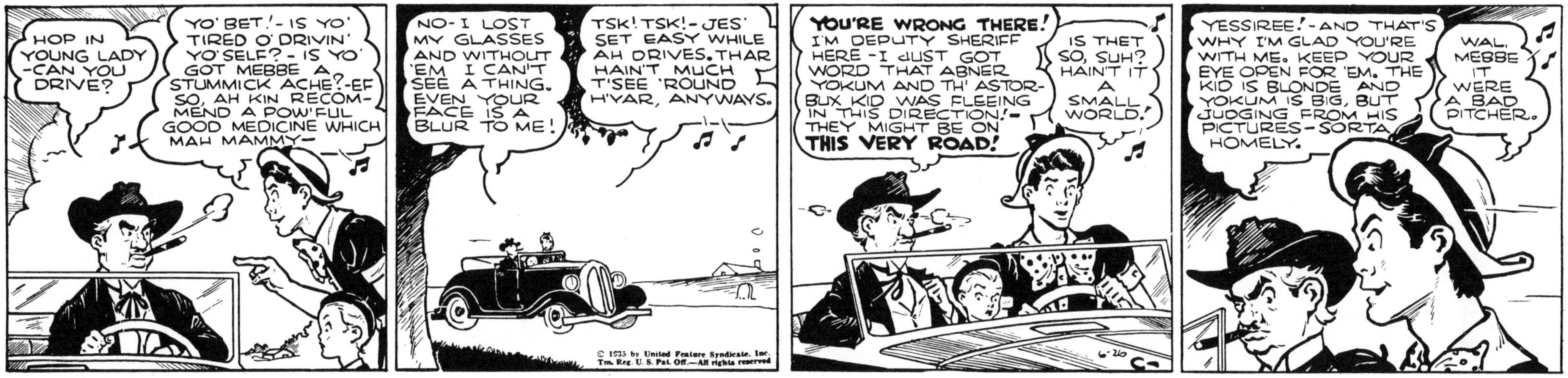

HOP IN YOUNG LADY -CAN YOU DRIVE?
YO' BET!-IS YO' TIRED O' DRIVIN' YO'SELF?-IS YO' GOT MEBBE A STUMMICK ACHE?-EF SO, AH KIN RECOMMEND A POW'FUL GOOD MEDICINE WHICH MAH MAMMY—
NO-I LOST MY GLASSES AND WITHOUT 'EM I CAN'T SEE A THING. EVEN YOUR FACE IS A BLUR TO ME!
TSK! TSK!-JES' SET EASY WHILE AH DRIVES. THAR HAIN'T MUCH T'SEE 'ROUND H'YAR, ANYWAYS.
© 1935 by United Feature Syndicate, Inc. Tm. Reg. U. S. Pat. Off.—All rights reserved
YOU'RE WRONG THERE! I'M DEPUTY SHERIFF HERE-I JUST GOT WORD THAT ABNER YOKUM AND TH' ASTORBUX KID WAS FLEEING IN THIS DIRECTION!-THEY MIGHT BE ON THIS VERY ROAD!
IS THET SO, SUH? HAIN'T IT A SMALL WORLD!
6-26
YESSIREE!-AND THAT'S WHY I'M GLAD YOU'RE WITH ME. KEEP YOUR EYE OPEN FOR 'EM. THE KID IS BLONDE AND YOKUM IS BIG, BUT JUDGING FROM HIS PICTURES-SORTA HOMELY.
WAL, MEBBE IT WERE A BAD PITCHER.

LI'L ABNER A Woman's Intuition **By Al Capp**

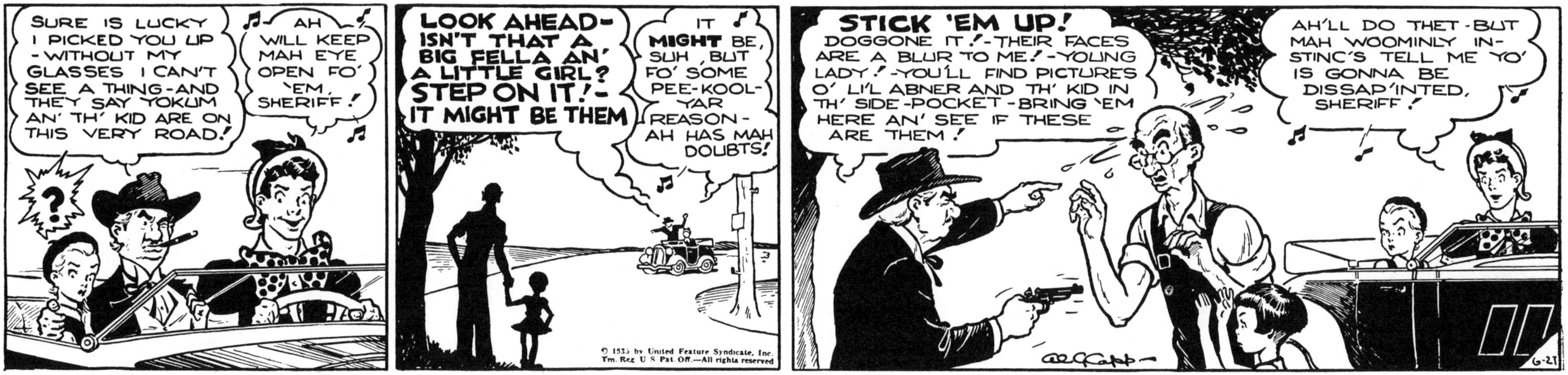

SURE IS LUCKY I PICKED YOU UP -WITHOUT MY GLASSES I CAN'T SEE A THING-AND THEY SAY YOKUM AN' TH' KID ARE ON THIS VERY ROAD!
AH WILL KEEP MAH EYE OPEN FO' 'EM, SHERIFF!
?
LOOK AHEAD-ISN'T THAT A BIG FELLA AN' A LITTLE GIRL? STEP ON IT!-IT MIGHT BE THEM
IT MIGHT BE, SUH, BUT FO' SOME PEE-KOOL-YAR REASON-AH HAS MAH DOUBTS!
© 1935 by United Feature Syndicate, Inc. Tm. Reg. U. S. Pat. Off.—All rights reserved
STICK 'EM UP! DOGGONE IT!-THEIR FACES ARE A BLUR TO ME!-YOUNG LADY!-YOU'LL FIND PICTURES O' LI'L ABNER AND TH' KID IN TH' SIDE-POCKET-BRING 'EM HERE AN' SEE IF THESE ARE THEM!
AH'LL DO THET-BUT MAH WOOMINLY INSTINC'S TELL ME YO' IS GONNA BE DISSAP'INTED, SHERIFF!
6-27

LI'L ABNER A Helping Hand By Al Capp

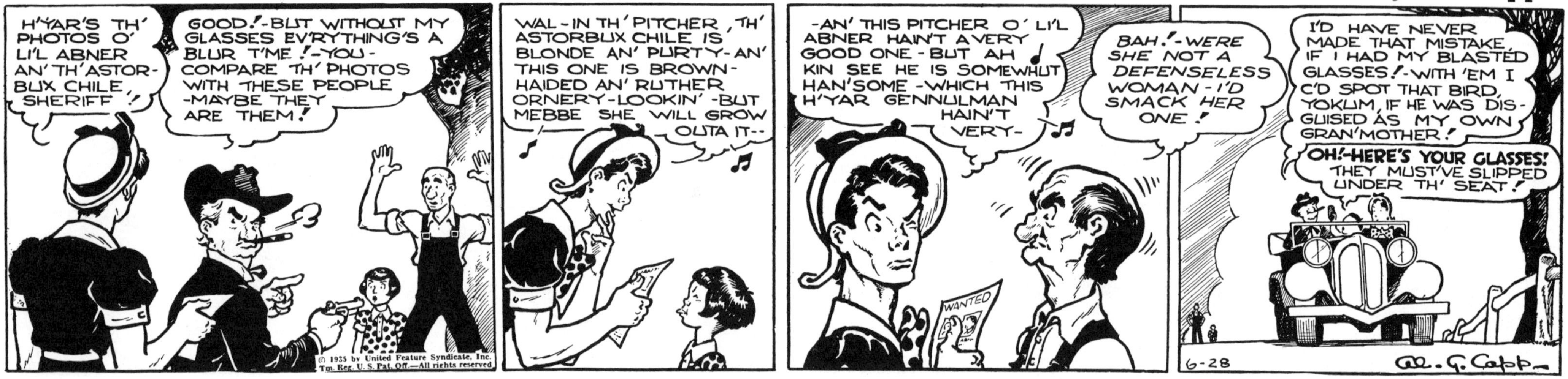

H'YAR'S TH' PHOTOS O' LI'L ABNER AN' TH' ASTORBUX CHILE, SHERIFF !
GOOD!-BUT WITHOUT MY GLASSES EV'RY'THING'S A BLUR T'ME !-YOU-COMPARE TH' PHOTOS WITH THESE PEOPLE -MAYBE THEY ARE THEM !
© 1935 by United Feature Syndicate, Inc. Tm. Reg. U. S. Pat. Off.—All rights reserved
WAL-IN TH' PITCHER, TH' ASTORBUX CHILE IS BLONDE AN' PURTY-AN' THIS ONE IS BROWN-HAIDED AN' RUTHER ORNERY-LOOKIN' -BUT MEBBE SHE WILL GROW OUTA IT--
-AN' THIS PITCHER O' LI'L ABNER HAIN'T A VERY GOOD ONE - BUT AH KIN SEE HE IS SOMEWHUT HAN'SOME - WHICH THIS H'YAR GENNULMAN HAIN'T VERY-
WANTED
BAH!-WERE SHE NOT A DEFENSELESS WOMAN - I'D SMACK HER ONE !
I'D HAVE NEVER MADE THAT MISTAKE, IF I HAD MY BLASTED GLASSES!-WITH 'EM I C'D SPOT THAT BIRD, YOKUM, IF HE WAS DISGUISED AS MY OWN GRAN'MOTHER!
OH!-HERE'S YOUR GLASSES! THEY MUST'VE SLIPPED UNDER TH' SEAT!
6-28
AL. G. CAPP

LI'L ABNER An Old Perkins' Custom By Al Capp

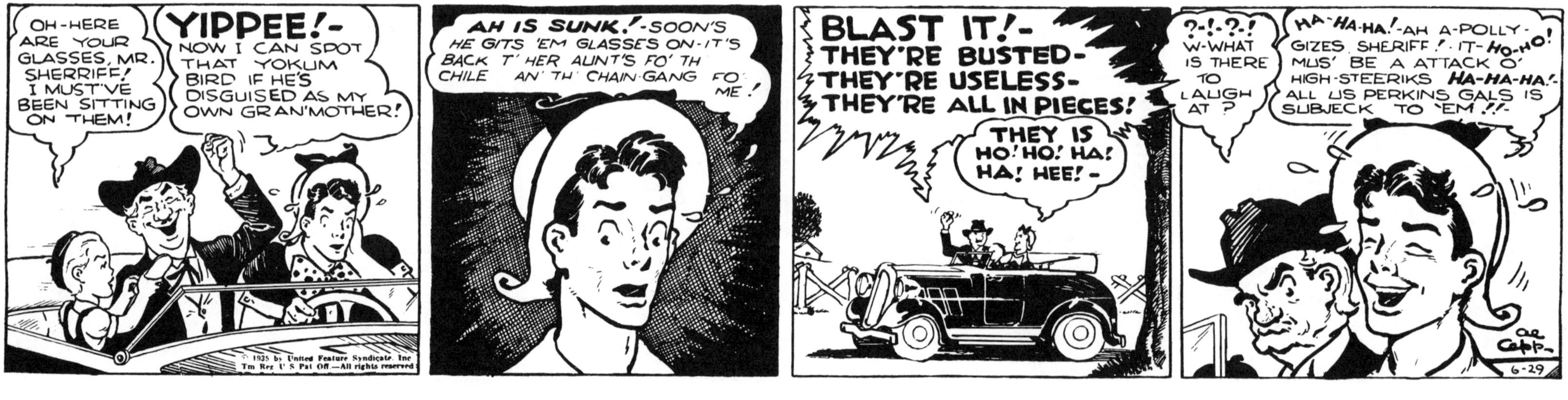

OH-HERE ARE YOUR GLASSES, MR. SHERRIFF! I MUST'VE BEEN SITTING ON THEM!
YIPPEE!- NOW I CAN SPOT THAT YOKUM BIRD IF HE'S DISGUISED AS MY OWN GRAN'MOTHER!
© 1935 by United Feature Syndicate, Inc Tm Reg U S Pat Off—All rights reserved
AH IS SUNK!-SOON'S HE GITS 'EM GLASSES ON-IT'S BACK T' HER AUNT'S FO' TH CHILE AN' TH CHAIN-GANG FO' ME!
BLAST IT!- THEY'RE BUSTED- THEY'RE USELESS- THEY'RE ALL IN PIECES!
THEY IS HO! HO! HA! HA! HEE!-
?-!-?-! W-WHAT IS THERE TO LAUGH AT ?
HA-HA-HA!-AH A-POLLY-GIZES SHERIFF!-IT-HO-HO! MUS' BE A ATTACK O' HIGH-STEERIKS HA-HA-HA!- ALL US PERKINS GALS IS SUBJECK TO 'EM!!-
AL CAPP
6-29

LI'L ABNER Mammy Wants Him Right By Al Capp

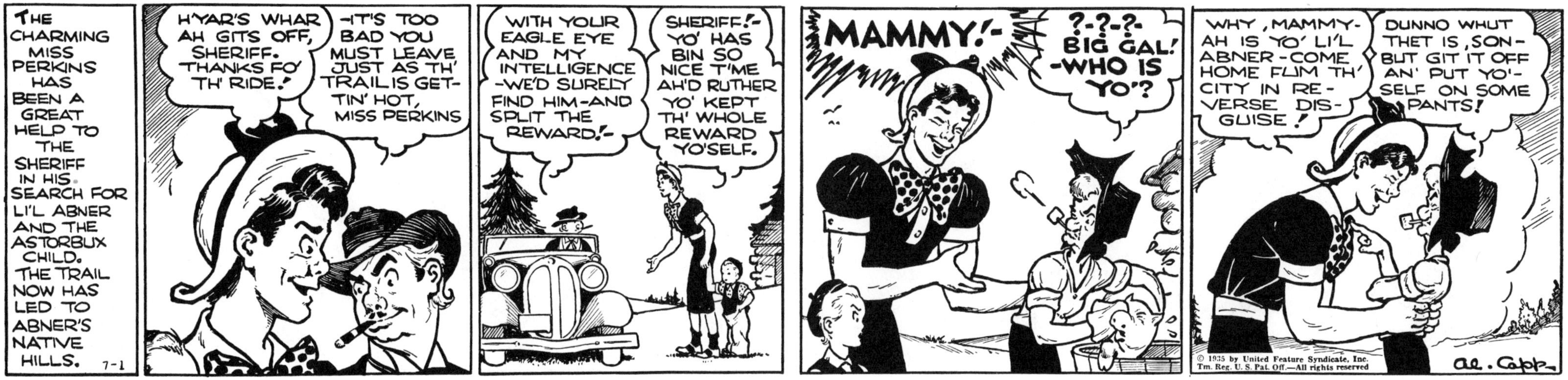
THE CHARMING MISS PERKINS HAS BEEN A GREAT HELP TO THE SHERIFF IN HIS SEARCH FOR LI'L ABNER AND THE ASTORBUX CHILD. THE TRAIL NOW HAS LED TO ABNER'S NATIVE HILLS.
7-1
H'YAR'S WHAR AH GITS OFF, SHERIFF. THANKS FO' TH' RIDE.!
-IT'S TOO BAD YOU MUST LEAVE JUST AS TH' TRAIL IS GETTIN' HOT, MISS PERKINS
WITH YOUR EAGLE EYE AND MY INTELLIGENCE -WE'D SURELY FIND HIM-AND SPLIT THE REWARD!-
SHERIFF!- YO' HAS BIN SO NICE T'ME AH'D RUTHER YO' KEPT TH' WHOLE REWARD YO'SELF.
MAMMY!-
?-?-?- BIG GAL! -WHO IS YO'?
WHY, MAMMY- AH IS YO' LI'L ABNER-COME HOME FUM TH' CITY IN REVERSE DISGUISE!
DUNNO WHUT THET IS, SON- BUT GIT IT OFF AN' PUT YO'SELF ON SOME PANTS!
© 1935 by United Feature Syndicate, Inc. Tm. Reg. U. S. Pat. Off.—All rights reserved
AL CAPP

LI'L ABNER Mammy Swings Into Action By Al Capp

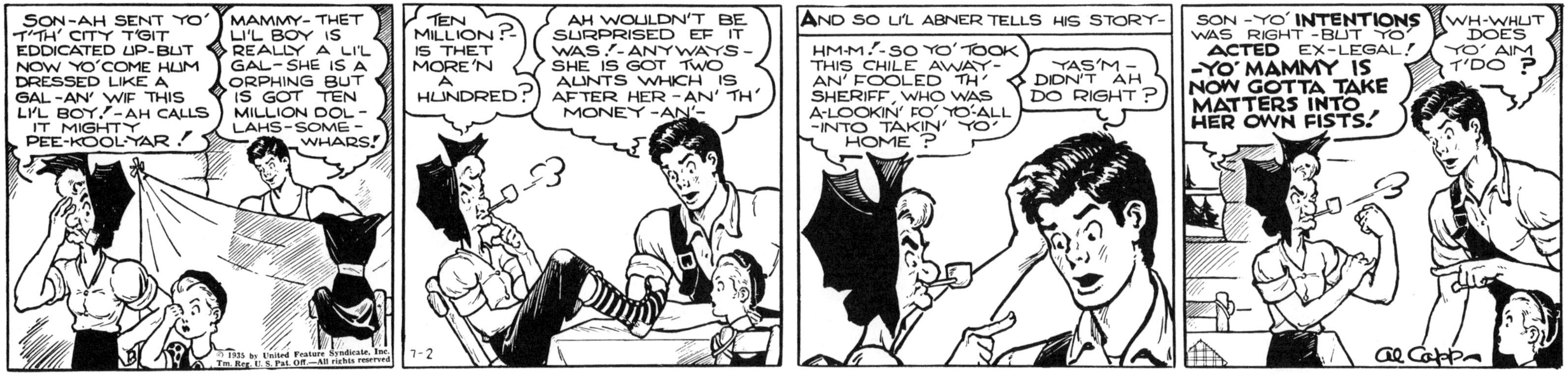
SON-AH SENT YO' T'TH' CITY T'GIT EDDICATED UP-BUT NOW YO' COME HUM DRESSED LIKE A GAL-AN' WIF THIS LI'L BOY!-AH CALLS IT MIGHTY PEE-KOOL-YAR!
MAMMY- THET LI'L BOY IS REALLY A LI'L GAL-SHE IS A ORPHING BUT IS GOT TEN MILLION DOLLAHS-SOMEWHARS!
© 1935 by United Feature Syndicate, Inc. Tm. Reg. U. S. Pat. Off.—All rights reserved
TEN MILLION?- IS THET MORE'N A HUNDRED?
AH WOULDN'T BE SURPRISED EF IT WAS!-ANYWAYS- SHE IS GOT TWO AUNTS WHICH IS AFTER HER-AN' TH' MONEY-AN'-
7-2
AND SO LI'L ABNER TELLS HIS STORY-
HM-M!-SO YO' TOOK THIS CHILE AWAY- AN' FOOLED TH' SHERIFF, WHO WAS A-LOOKIN' FO' YO'-ALL -INTO TAKIN' YO' HOME?
YAS'M- DIDN'T AH DO RIGHT?
SON -YO' INTENTIONS WAS RIGHT -BUT YO' ACTED EX-LEGAL! -YO' MAMMY IS NOW GOTTA TAKE MATTERS INTO HER OWN FISTS!
WH-WHUT DOES YO' AIM T'DO?
AL CAPP

LI'L ABNER The Enemy Arrives By Al Capp

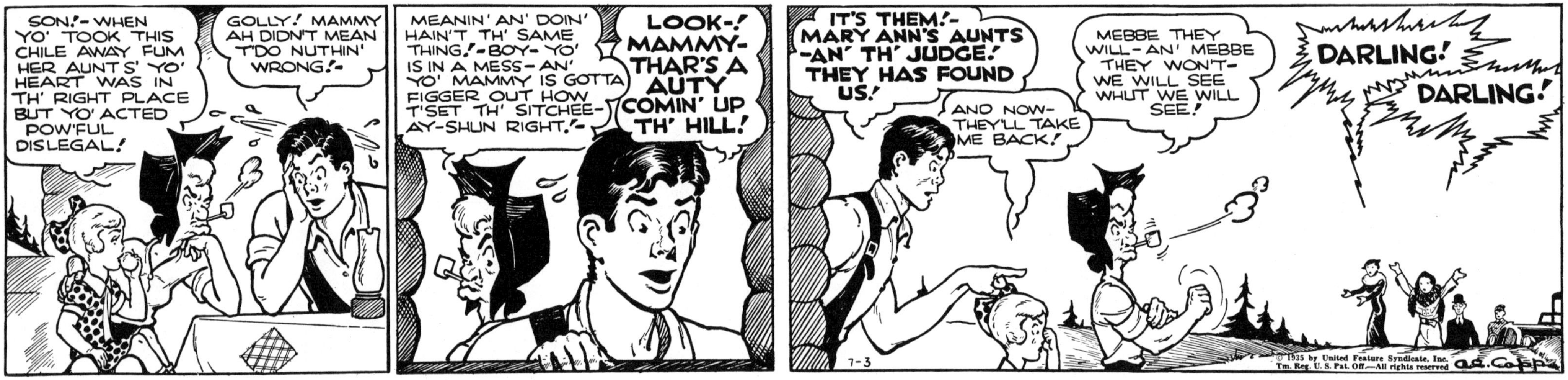

SON!- WHEN YO' TOOK THIS CHILE AWAY FUM HER AUNT S' YO' HEART WAS IN TH' RIGHT PLACE BUT YO' ACTED POW'FUL DISLEGAL!
GOLLY! MAMMY AH DIDN'T MEAN T'DO NUTHIN' WRONG!-
MEANIN' AN' DOIN' HAIN'T TH' SAME THING!- BOY- YO' IS IN A MESS- AN' YO' MAMMY IS GOTTA FIGGER OUT HOW T'SET TH' SITCHEE-AY-SHUN RIGHT!-
LOOK-! MAMMY- THAR'S A AUTY COMIN' UP TH' HILL!
IT'S THEM!- MARY ANN'S AUNTS -AN' TH' JUDGE! THEY HAS FOUND US!
AND NOW- THEY'LL TAKE ME BACK!
MEBBE THEY WILL- AN' MEBBE THEY WON'T- WE WILL SEE WHUT WE WILL SEE!
DARLING!
DARLING!
7-3
© 1935 by United Feature Syndicate, Inc. Tm. Reg. U. S. Pat. Off.—All rights reserved

LI'L ABNER They Can't Fool Mammy By Al Capp

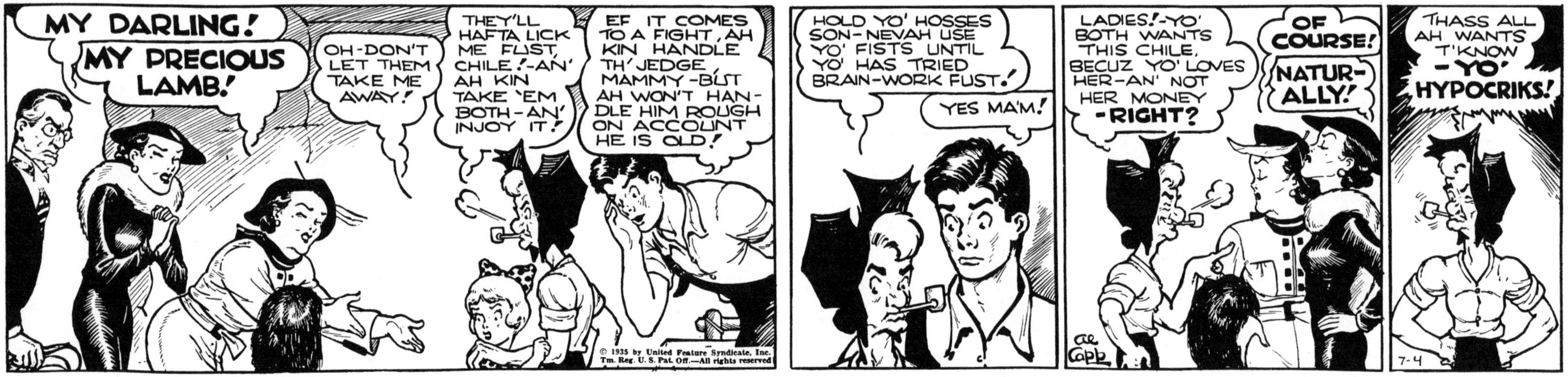

MY DARLING!
MY PRECIOUS LAMB!
OH-DON'T LET THEM TAKE ME AWAY!
THEY'LL HAFTA LICK ME FUST, CHILE!-AN' AH KIN TAKE 'EM BOTH-AN' INJOY IT!
EF IT COMES TO A FIGHT, AH KIN HANDLE TH' JEDGE, MAMMY-BUT AH WON'T HANDLE HIM ROUGH ON ACCOUNT HE IS OLD!
© 1935 by United Feature Syndicate, Inc. Tm. Reg. U. S. Pat. Off.—All rights reserved
HOLD YO' HOSSES SON-NEVAH USE YO' FISTS UNTIL YO' HAS TRIED BRAIN-WORK FUST!
YES MA'M!
LADIES!-YO' BOTH WANTS THIS CHILE, BECUZ YO' LOVES HER-AN' NOT HER MONEY -RIGHT?
OF COURSE!
NATUR-ALLY!
THASS ALL AH WANTS T'KNOW -YO' HYPOCRIKS!
7-4

LI'L ABNER Any Takers ? By Al Capp

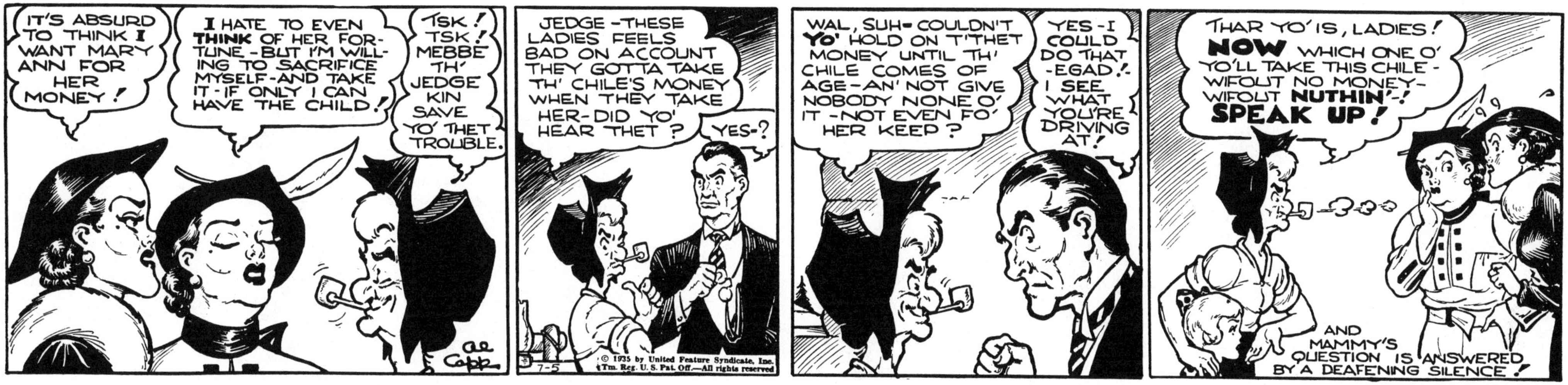
IT'S ABSURD TO THINK I WANT MARY ANN FOR HER MONEY!
I HATE TO EVEN THINK OF HER FORTUNE - BUT I'M WILLING TO SACRIFICE MYSELF - AND TAKE IT - IF ONLY I CAN HAVE THE CHILD!
TSK! TSK! MEBBE TH' JEDGE KIN SAVE YO' THET TROUBLE.
AL CAPP
JEDGE - THESE LADIES FEELS BAD ON ACCOUNT THEY GOTTA TAKE TH' CHILE'S MONEY WHEN THEY TAKE HER - DID YO' HEAR THET?
YES-?
7-5
© 1935 by United Feature Syndicate, Inc. Tm. Reg. U. S. Pat. Off.—All rights reserved
WAL, SUH - COULDN'T YO' HOLD ON T'THET MONEY UNTIL TH' CHILE COMES OF AGE - AN' NOT GIVE NOBODY NONE O' IT - NOT EVEN FO' HER KEEP?
YES - I COULD DO THAT - EGAD! - I SEE WHAT YOU'RE DRIVING AT!
THAR YO' IS, LADIES! NOW WHICH ONE O' YO'LL TAKE THIS CHILE - WIFOUT NO MONEY - WIFOUT NUTHIN'-! SPEAK UP!
AND MAMMY'S QUESTION IS ANSWERED BY A DEAFENING SILENCE!

LI'L ABNER Her Unsuppressed Desire By Al Capp

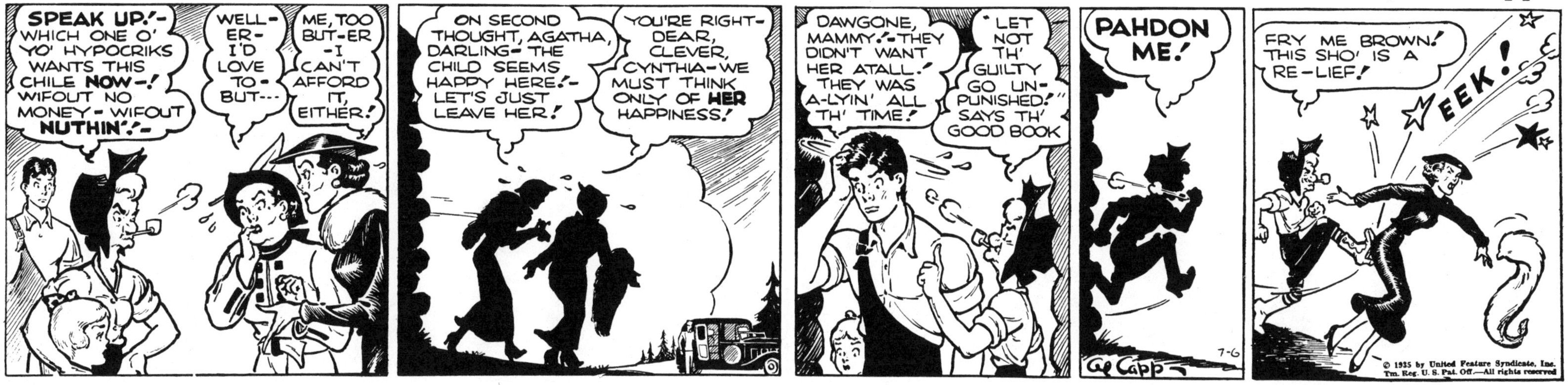
SPEAK UP!- WHICH ONE O' YO' HYPOCRIKS WANTS THIS CHILE NOW-! WIFOUT NO MONEY - WIFOUT NUTHIN'!-
WELL-ER- I'D LOVE TO - BUT---
ME, TOO BUT-ER - I CAN'T AFFORD IT, EITHER!
ON SECOND THOUGHT, AGATHA, DARLING - THE CHILD SEEMS HAPPY HERE! - LET'S JUST LEAVE HER!
YOU'RE RIGHT - DEAR, CLEVER, CYNTHIA - WE MUST THINK ONLY OF HER HAPPINESS!
DAWGONE, MAMMY! - THEY DIDN'T WANT HER ATALL! THEY WAS A-LYIN' ALL TH' TIME!
"LET NOT TH' GUILTY GO UNPUNISHED!" SAYS TH' GOOD BOOK
PAHDON ME!
AL CAPP
7-6
FRY ME BROWN! THIS SHO' IS A RE-LIEF!
EEK!
© 1935 by United Feature Syndicate, Inc. Tm. Reg. U. S. Pat. Off.—All rights reserved

LI'L ABNER Which One ? By Al Capp

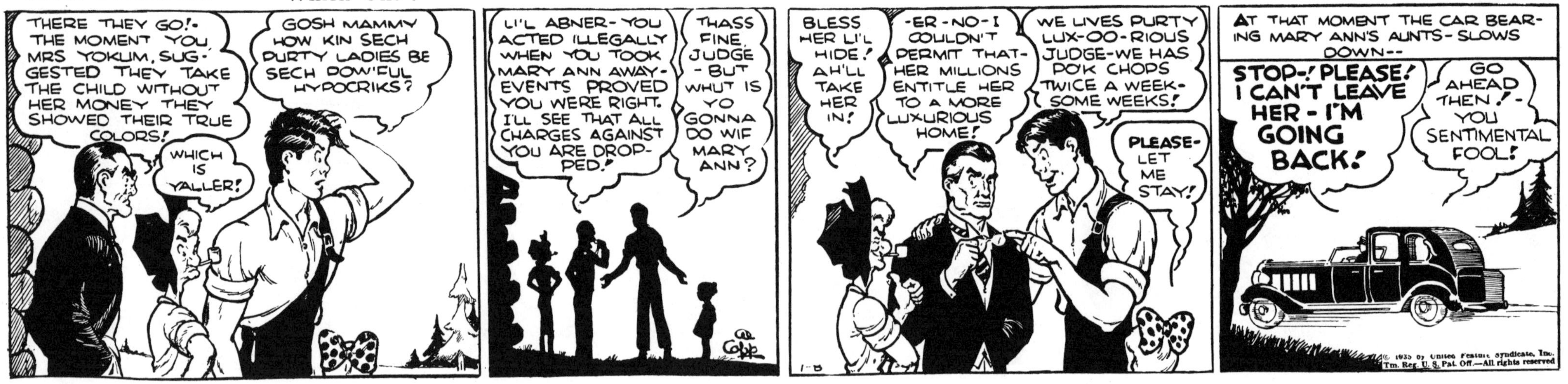
THERE THEY GO!- THE MOMENT YOU, MRS YOKUM, SUG-GESTED THEY TAKE THE CHILD WITHOUT HER MONEY THEY SHOWED THEIR TRUE COLORS!
GOSH MAMMY HOW KIN SECH PURTY LADIES BE SECH POW'FUL HYPOCRIKS?
WHICH IS YALLER!
LI'L ABNER- YOU ACTED ILLEGALLY WHEN YOU TOOK MARY ANN AWAY- EVENTS PROVED YOU WERE RIGHT. I'LL SEE THAT ALL CHARGES AGAINST YOU ARE DROP-PED.!
THASS FINE, JUDGE - BUT WHUT IS YO GONNA DO WIF MARY ANN?
BLESS HER LI'L HIDE! AH'LL TAKE HER IN!
-ER-NO-I COULDN'T PERMIT THAT- HER MILLIONS ENTITLE HER TO A MORE LUXURIOUS HOME!
WE LIVES PURTY LUX-OO-RIOUS JUDGE-WE HAS PO'K CHOPS TWICE A WEEK- SOME WEEKS!
PLEASE- LET ME STAY!
AT THAT MOMENT THE CAR BEARING MARY ANN'S AUNTS- SLOWS DOWN--
STOP-! PLEASE! I CAN'T LEAVE HER - I'M GOING BACK!
GO AHEAD THEN!- YOU SENTIMENTAL FOOL!
© 1935 by United Feature Syndicate, Inc. Tm. Reg. U. S. Pat. Off.—All rights reserved

LI'L ABNER Mammy Has Her Doubts By Al Capp

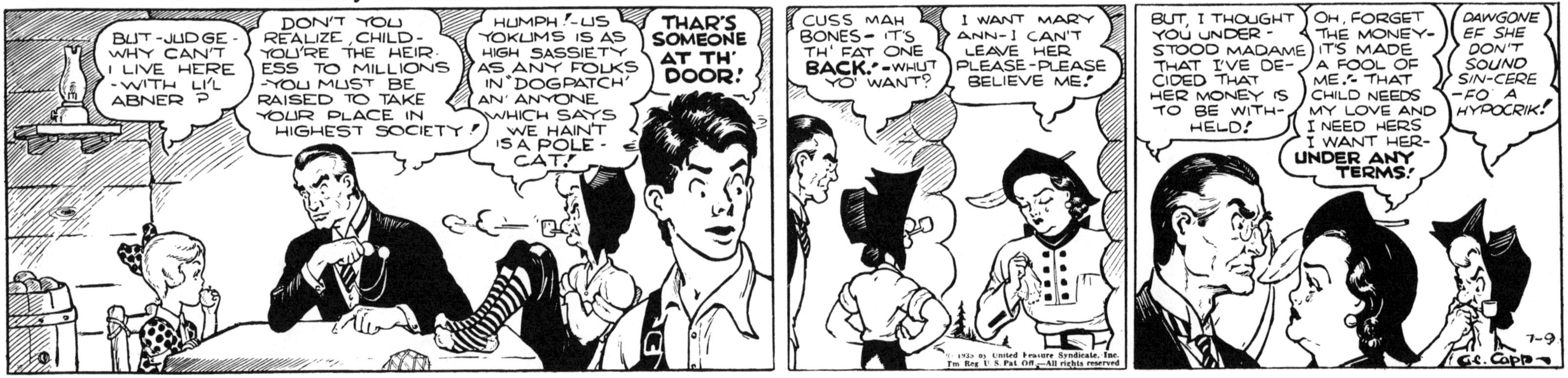
BUT-JUDGE- WHY CAN'T I LIVE HERE -WITH LI'L ABNER?
DON'T YOU REALIZE, CHILD- YOU'RE THE HEIR-ESS TO MILLIONS -YOU MUST BE RAISED TO TAKE YOUR PLACE IN HIGHEST SOCIETY!
HUMPH!-US YOKUMS IS AS HIGH SASSIETY AS ANY FOLKS IN "DOGPATCH" AN' ANYONE WHICH SAYS WE HAIN'T IS A POLE-CAT!
THAR'S SOMEONE AT TH' DOOR!
CUSS MAH BONES- IT'S TH' FAT ONE BACK!-WHUT YO' WANT?
I WANT MARY ANN-I CAN'T LEAVE HER PLEASE-PLEASE BELIEVE ME!
BUT, I THOUGHT YOU UNDER-STOOD MADAME THAT I'VE DE-CIDED THAT HER MONEY IS TO BE WITH-HELD!
OH, FORGET THE MONEY- IT'S MADE A FOOL OF ME!- THAT CHILD NEEDS MY LOVE AND I NEED HERS I WANT HER- UNDER ANY TERMS!
DAWGONE EF SHE DON'T SOUND SIN-CERE -FO' A HYPOCRIK!
© 1935 by United Feature Syndicate, Inc. Tm Reg U S Pat Off—All rights reserved

LI'L ABNER It's Up To Mary Ann By Al Capp

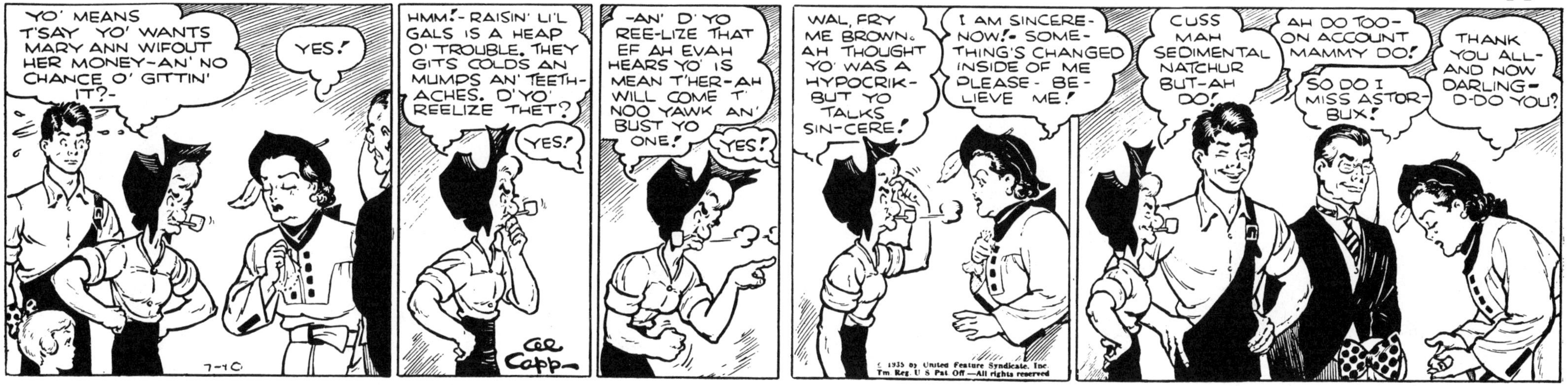
YO' MEANS T'SAY YO' WANTS MARY ANN WIFOUT HER MONEY-AN' NO CHANCE O' GITTIN' IT?-
YES!
7-10
HMM!-RAISIN' LI'L GALS IS A HEAP O' TROUBLE. THEY GITS COLDS AN MUMPS AN' TEETH-ACHES. D'YO' REELIZE THET?
YES!
AL CAPP
-AN' D' YO REE-LIZE THAT EF AH EVAH HEARS YO' IS MEAN T'HER-AH WILL COME T' NOO YAWK AN' BUST YO ONE!
YES!
WAL, FRY ME BROWN. AH THOUGHT YO' WAS A HYPOCRIK-BUT YO TALKS SIN-CERE!
I AM SINCERE-NOW!-SOMETHING'S CHANGED INSIDE OF ME PLEASE-BELIEVE ME!
© 1935 by United Feature Syndicate, Inc. Tm Reg. U S Pat. Off.—All rights reserved
CUSS MAH SEDIMENTAL NATCHUR BUT-AH DO!
AH DO TOO-ON ACCOUNT MAMMY DO!
SO DO I MISS ASTOR-BUX!
THANK YOU ALL-AND NOW DARLING-D-DO YOU?

LI'L ABNER Thet's Nice-Lookin' Trouble, Boy By Al Capp

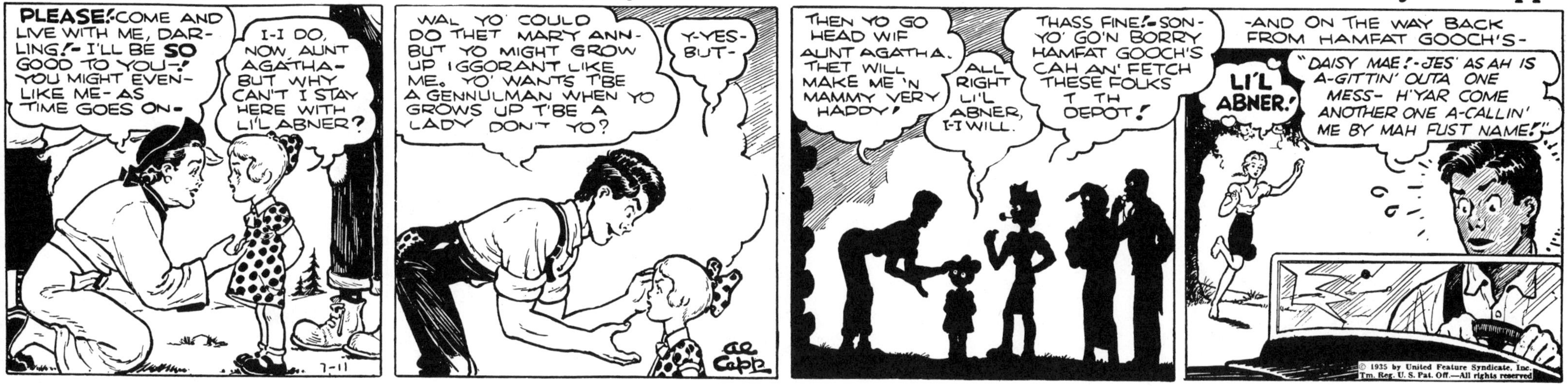
PLEASE!-COME AND LIVE WITH ME, DARLING!-I'LL BE SO GOOD TO YOU-! YOU MIGHT EVEN-LIKE ME-AS TIME GOES ON-
I-I DO, NOW, AUNT AGATHA-BUT WHY CAN'T I STAY HERE WITH LI'L ABNER?
7-11
WAL YO' COULD DO THET MARY ANN-BUT YO MIGHT GROW UP IGGORANT LIKE ME. YO' WANTS T'BE A GENNULMAN WHEN YO GROWS UP T'BE A LADY DON'T YO?
Y-YES-BUT-
AL CAPP
THEN YO GO HEAD WIF AUNT AGATHA. THET WILL MAKE ME 'N MAMMY VERY HAPPY!
ALL RIGHT LI'L ABNER, I-I WILL.
THASS FINE!-SON-YO' GO'N BORRY HAMFAT GOOCH'S CAH AN' FETCH THESE FOLKS T TH DEPOT!
-AND ON THE WAY BACK FROM HAMFAT GOOCH'S-
LI'L ABNER!
"DAISY MAE!-JES' AS AH IS A-GITTIN' OUTA ONE MESS-H'YAR COME ANOTHER ONE A-CALLIN' ME BY MAH FUST NAME!"
© 1935 by United Feature Syndicate, Inc. Tm. Reg. U. S. Pat. Off.—All rights reserved

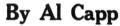

LI'L ABNER Nevah Mind, Boy! By Al Capp

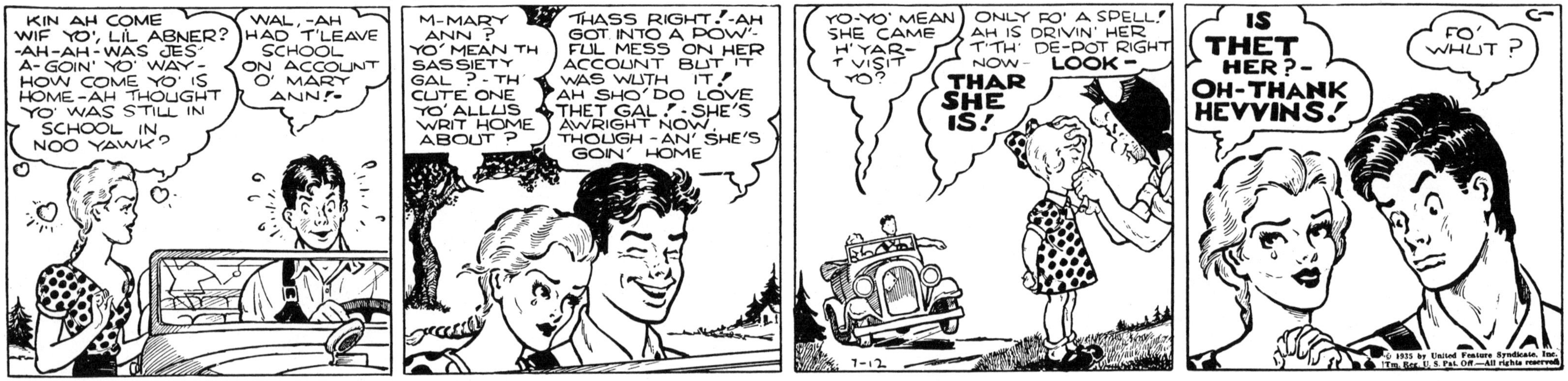

KIN AH COME WIF YO', LI'L ABNER? -AH-AH-WAS JES' A-GOIN' YO' WAY- HOW COME YO' IS HOME-AH THOUGHT YO' WAS STILL IN SCHOOL IN NOO YAWK?
WAL,-AH HAD T'LEAVE SCHOOL ON ACCOUNT O' MARY ANN!-
M-MARY ANN? YO' MEAN TH SASSIETY GAL?-TH' CUTE ONE YO' ALLUS WRIT HOME ABOUT?
THASS RIGHT!-AH GOT INTO A POW'-FUL MESS ON HER ACCOUNT BUT IT WAS WUTH IT! AH SHO' DO LOVE THET GAL!-SHE'S AWRIGHT NOW, THOUGH-AN' SHE'S GOIN' HOME
YO-YO' MEAN SHE CAME H'YAR-T VISIT YO?
ONLY FO' A SPELL! AH IS DRIVIN' HER T'TH' DE-POT RIGHT NOW- LOOK-
THAR SHE IS!
7-12
IS THET HER?-OH-THANK HEVVINS!
FO' WHUT?
© 1935 by United Feature Syndicate, Inc. Tm. Reg. U. S. Pat. Off.—All rights reserved

LI'L ABNER A Busted Romance By Al Capp

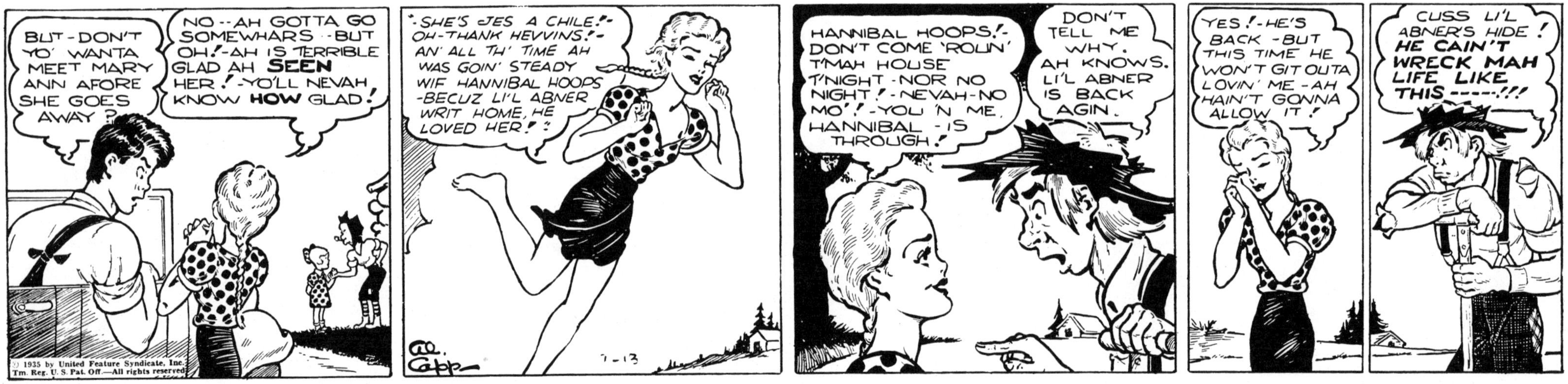

BUT-DON'T YO' WANTA MEET MARY ANN AFORE SHE GOES AWAY?
NO--AH GOTTA GO SOMEWHARS -BUT OH!-AH IS TERRIBLE GLAD AH SEEN HER!-YO'LL NEVAH KNOW HOW GLAD!
© 1935 by United Feature Syndicate, Inc. Tm. Reg. U. S. Pat. Off.—All rights reserved
SHE'S JES A CHILE!-OH-THANK HEVVINS!-AN' ALL TH' TIME AH WAS GOIN' STEADY WIF HANNIBAL HOOPS -BECUZ LI'L ABNER WRIT HOME, HE LOVED HER!
Al Capp
7-13
HANNIBAL HOOPS!-DON'T COME 'ROUN' T'MAH HOUSE T'NIGHT-NOR NO NIGHT!-NEVAH-NO MO'!-YOU 'N ME, HANNIBAL-IS THROUGH!
DON'T TELL ME WHY. AH KNOWS. LI'L ABNER IS BACK AGIN.
YES!-HE'S BACK-BUT THIS TIME HE WON'T GIT OUTA LOVIN' ME-AH HAIN'T GONNA ALLOW IT!
CUSS LI'L ABNER'S HIDE! HE CAIN'T WRECK MAH LIFE LIKE THIS-----!!!

LI'L ABNER A Sure-Cure **By Al Capp**

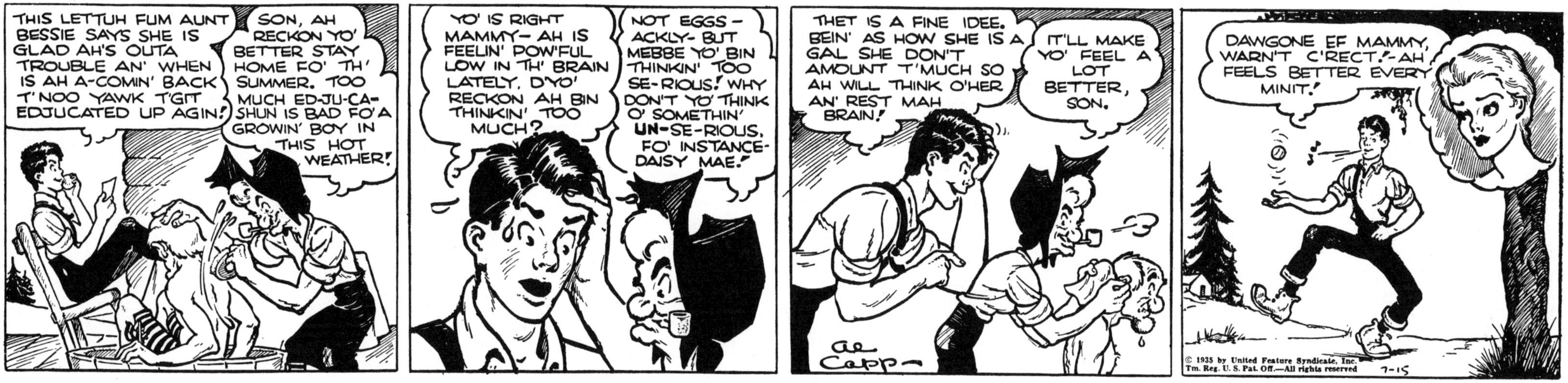
THIS LETTUH FUM AUNT BESSIE SAYS SHE IS GLAD AH'S OUTA TROUBLE AN' WHEN IS AH A-COMIN' BACK T'NOO YAWK T'GIT EDJUCATED UP AGIN!
SON, AH RECKON YO' BETTER STAY HOME FO' TH' SUMMER. TOO MUCH ED-JU-CA-SHUN IS BAD FO'A GROWIN' BOY IN THIS HOT WEATHER!
YO' IS RIGHT MAMMY— AH IS FEELIN' POW'FUL LOW IN TH' BRAIN LATELY. D'YO' RECKON AH BIN THINKIN' TOO MUCH?
NOT EGGS-ACKLY- BUT MEBBE YO' BIN THINKIN' TOO SE-RIOUS! WHY DON'T YO' THINK O' SOMETHIN' UN-SE-RIOUS. FO' INSTANCE- DAISY MAE!
THET IS A FINE IDEE. BEIN' AS HOW SHE IS A GAL SHE DON'T AMOUNT T'MUCH SO AH WILL THINK O'HER AN' REST MAH BRAIN!
IT'LL MAKE YO' FEEL A LOT BETTER, SON.
Al Capp
DAWGONE EF MAMMY WARN'T C'RECT!- AH FEELS BETTER EVERY MINIT!
© 1935 by United Feature Syndicate, Inc. Tm. Reg. U. S. Pat. Off.—All rights reserved
7-15

LI'L ABNER The Snake in the Grass **By Al Capp**

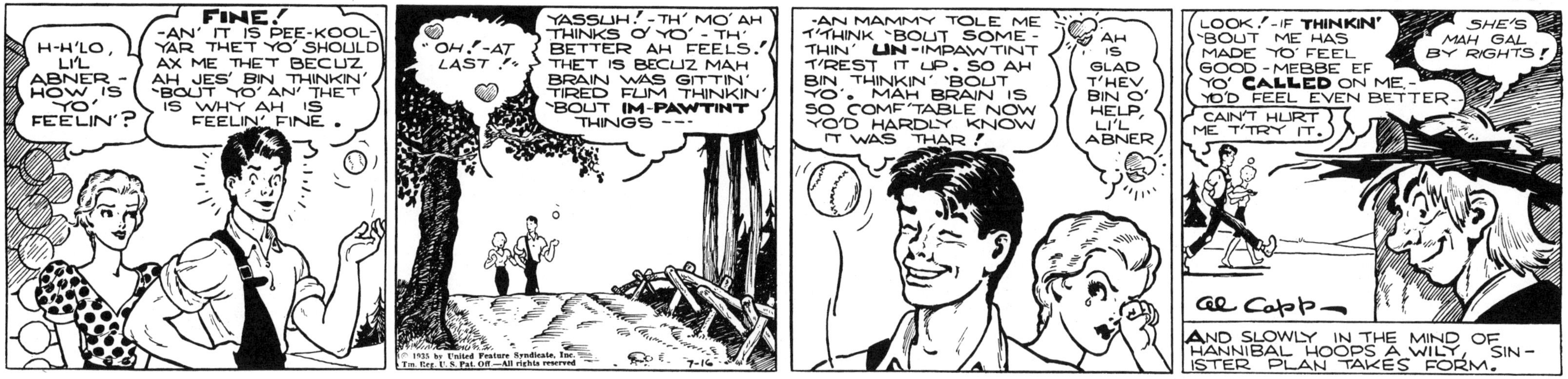
H-H'LO, LI'L ABNER - HOW IS YO' FEELIN'?
FINE! -AN' IT IS PEE-KOOL-YAR THET YO' SHOULD AX ME THET BECUZ AH JES' BIN THINKIN' 'BOUT YO' AN' THET IS WHY AH IS FEELIN' FINE.
"OH!-AT LAST!"
YASSUH!-TH' MO' AH THINKS O' YO' - TH' BETTER AH FEELS! THET IS BECUZ MAH BRAIN WAS GITTIN' TIRED FUM THINKIN' 'BOUT IM-PAWTINT THINGS ---
© 1935 by United Feature Syndicate, Inc. Tm. Reg. U. S. Pat. Off.—All rights reserved
7-16
-AN MAMMY TOLE ME T'THINK 'BOUT SOME-THIN' UN-IMPAWTINT T'REST IT UP. SO AH BIN THINKIN' 'BOUT YO'. MAH BRAIN IS SO COMF'TABLE NOW YO'D HARDLY KNOW IT WAS THAR!
AH IS GLAD T'HEV BIN O' HELP, LI'L ABNER
LOOK!-IF THINKIN' 'BOUT ME HAS MADE YO' FEEL GOOD-MEBBE EF YO' CALLED ON ME,-YO'D FEEL EVEN BETTER--
CAIN'T HURT ME T'TRY IT.
SHE'S MAH GAL BY RIGHTS!
Al Capp
AND SLOWLY IN THE MIND OF HANNIBAL HOOPS A WILY, SIN-ISTER PLAN TAKES FORM.

LI'L ABNER The Bad Loser By Al Capp

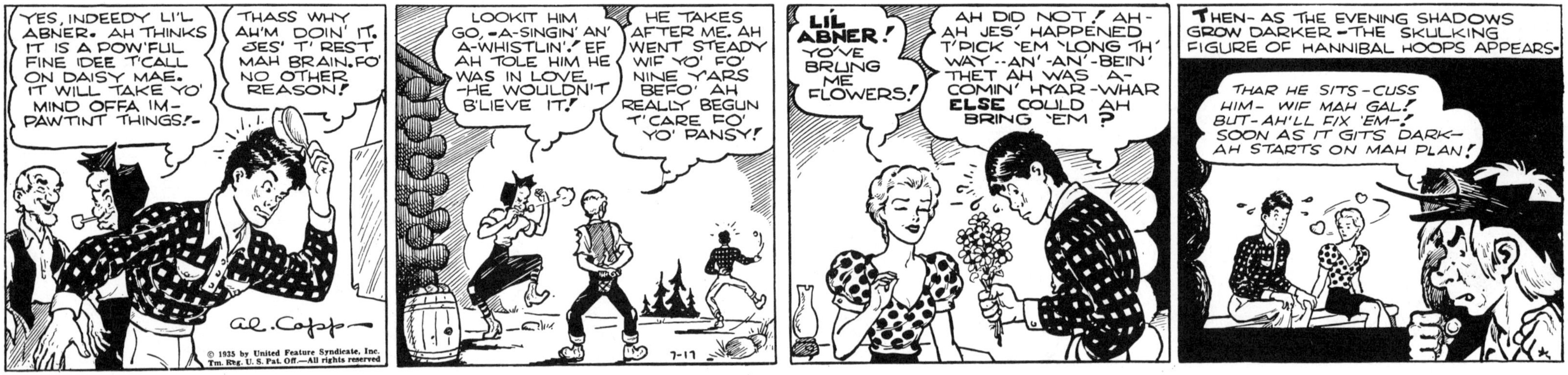

YES, INDEEDY LI'L ABNER. AH THINKS IT IS A POW'FUL FINE IDEE T'CALL ON DAISY MAE. IT WILL TAKE YO' MIND OFFA IM-PAWTINT THINGS!-
THASS WHY AH'M DOIN' IT. JES' T' REST MAH BRAIN. FO' NO OTHER REASON!
Al. Capp
© 1935 by United Feature Syndicate, Inc. Tm. Reg. U. S. Pat. Off.—All rights reserved
LOOKIT HIM GO, -A-SINGIN' AN' A-WHISTLIN'! EF AH TOLE HIM HE WAS IN LOVE -HE WOULDN'T B'LIEVE IT!
HE TAKES AFTER ME. AH WENT STEADY WIF YO' FO' NINE Y'ARS BEFO' AH REALLY BEGUN T'CARE FO' YO' PANSY!
7-17
LI'L ABNER! YO'VE BRUNG ME FLOWERS!
AH DID NOT! AH-AH JES' HAPPENED T'PICK 'EM 'LONG TH' WAY--AN'-AN'-BEIN' THET AH WAS A-COMIN' HYAR-WHAR ELSE COULD AH BRING 'EM?
THEN- AS THE EVENING SHADOWS GROW DARKER - THE SKULKING FIGURE OF HANNIBAL HOOPS APPEARS-
THAR HE SITS-CUSS HIM- WIF MAH GAL! BUT-AH'LL FIX 'EM-! SOON AS IT GITS DARK- AH STARTS ON MAH PLAN!

LI'L ABNER A Ed-ju-cated Gal By Al Capp

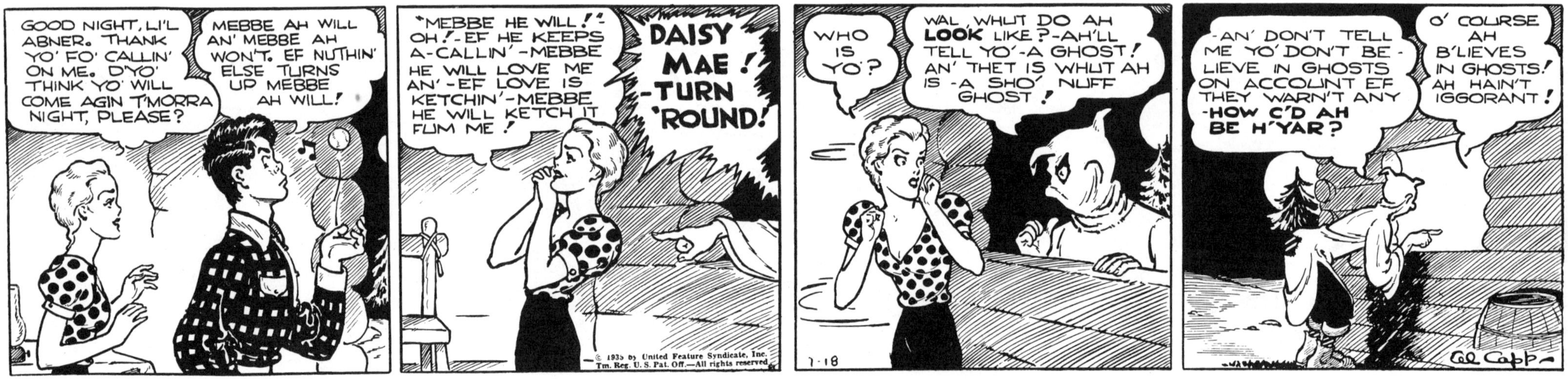

GOOD NIGHT, LI'L ABNER. THANK YO' FO' CALLIN' ON ME. D'YO' THINK YO' WILL COME AGIN T'MORRA NIGHT, PLEASE?
MEBBE AH WILL AN' MEBBE AH WON'T. EF NUTHIN' ELSE TURNS UP MEBBE AH WILL!
"MEBBE HE WILL!"- OH!-EF HE KEEPS A-CALLIN'-MEBBE HE WILL LOVE ME AN'-EF LOVE IS KETCHIN'-MEBBE HE WILL KETCH IT FUM ME!
DAISY MAE! -TURN 'ROUND!
© 1935 by United Feature Syndicate, Inc. Tm. Reg. U. S. Pat. Off.—All rights reserved
7-18
WHO IS YO'?
WAL, WHUT DO AH LOOK LIKE?-AH'LL TELL YO'-A GHOST! AN' THET IS WHUT AH IS-A SHO' NUFF GHOST!
-AN' DON'T TELL ME YO' DON'T BE-LIEVE IN GHOSTS ON ACCOUNT EF THEY WARN'T ANY -HOW C'D AH BE H'YAR?
O' COURSE AH B'LIEVES IN GHOSTS! AH HAIN'T IGGORANT!
Al Capp

LI'L ABNER — Ghosts Don't Lie — By Al Capp

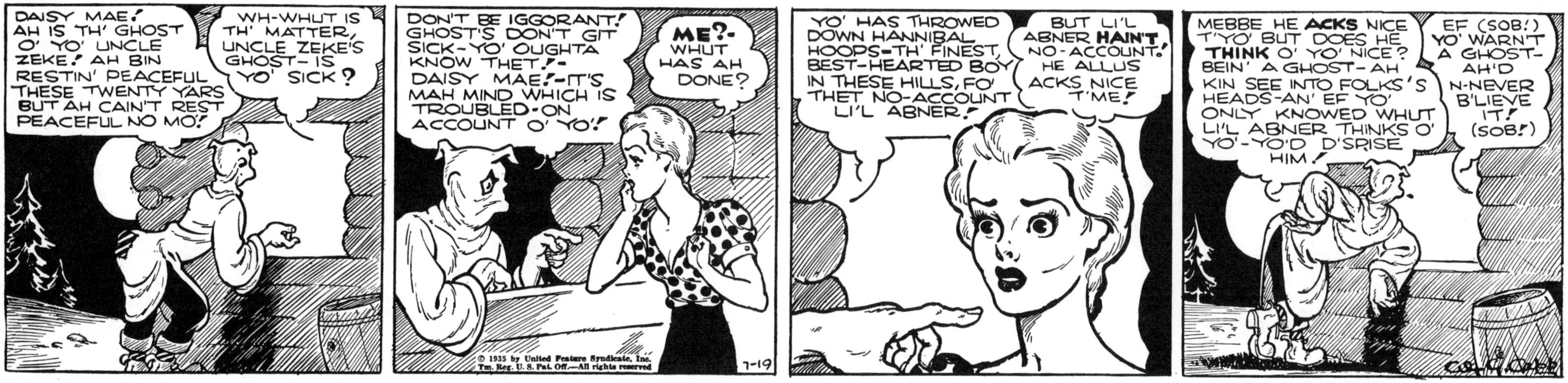

DAISY MAE! AH IS TH' GHOST O' YO' UNCLE ZEKE! AH BIN RESTIN' PEACEFUL THESE TWENTY YARS BUT AH CAIN'T REST PEACEFUL NO MO'!
WH-WHUT IS TH' MATTER, UNCLE ZEKE'S GHOST- IS YO' SICK?
DON'T BE IGGORANT! GHOST'S DON'T GIT SICK-YO' OUGHTA KNOW THET!- DAISY MAE!-IT'S MAH MIND WHICH IS TROUBLED-ON ACCOUNT O' YO'!
ME?- WHUT HAS AH DONE?
© 1935 by United Feature Syndicate, Inc. Tm. Reg. U. S. Pat. Off.—All rights reserved
7-19
YO' HAS THROWED DOWN HANNIBAL HOOPS-TH' FINEST, BEST-HEARTED BOY IN THESE HILLS, FO' THET NO-ACCOUNT LI'L ABNER!
BUT LI'L ABNER HAIN'T NO-ACCOUNT! HE ALLUS ACKS NICE T'ME!
MEBBE HE ACKS NICE T'YO' BUT DOES HE THINK O' YO' NICE? BEIN' A GHOST-AH KIN SEE INTO FOLKS'S HEADS-AN' EF YO' ONLY KNOWED WHUT LI'L ABNER THINKS O' YO'-YO'D D'SPISE HIM!
EF (SOB!) YO' WARN'T A GHOST- AH'D N-NEVER B'LIEVE IT! (SOB!)

LI'L ABNER — The Awful Truth — By Al Capp

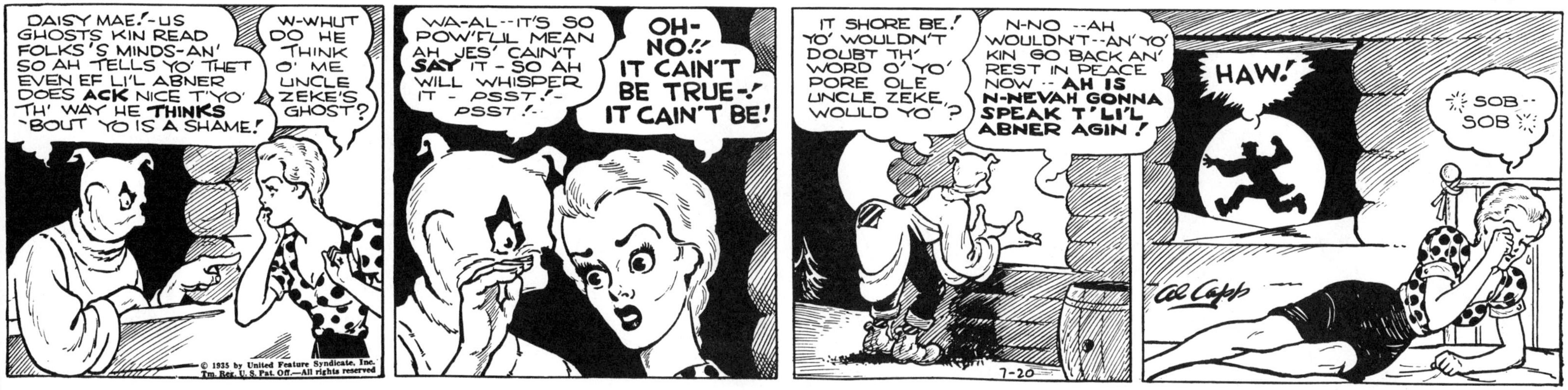

DAISY MAE!-US GHOSTS KIN READ FOLKS'S MINDS-AN' SO AH TELLS YO' THET EVEN EF LI'L ABNER DOES ACK NICE T'YO' TH' WAY HE THINKS 'BOUT YO IS A SHAME!
W-WHUT DO HE THINK O' ME UNCLE ZEKE'S GHOST?
© 1935 by United Feature Syndicate, Inc. Tm. Reg. U. S. Pat. Off.—All rights reserved
WA-AL--IT'S SO POW'FUL MEAN AH JES' CAIN'T SAY IT - SO AH WILL WHISPER IT - PSST!- PSST!-
OH-NO!! IT CAIN'T BE TRUE-! IT CAIN'T BE!
IT SHORE BE! YO' WOULDN'T DOUBT TH' WORD O' YO' PORE OLE UNCLE ZEKE, WOULD YO'?
N-NO --AH WOULDN'T--AN' YO' KIN GO BACK AN' REST IN PEACE NOW -- AH IS N-NEVAH GONNA SPEAK T' LI'L ABNER AGIN!
7-20
HAW!
SOB -- SOB
Al Capp

LI'L ABNER The Curse of Culture By Al Capp

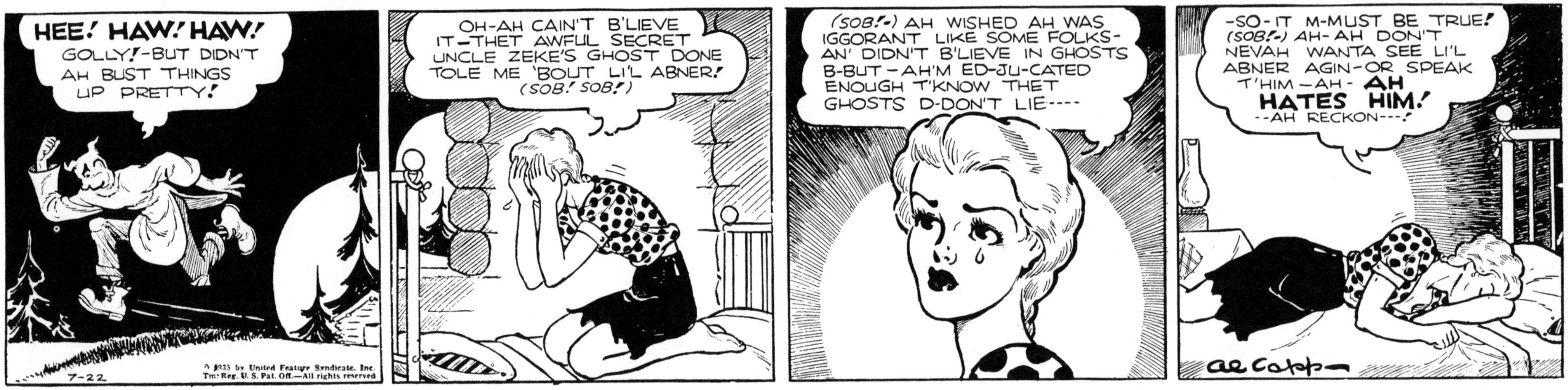
HEE! HAW! HAW! GOLLY!-BUT DIDN'T AH BUST THINGS UP PRETTY!
7-22
© 1935 by United Feature Syndicate, Inc. Tm Reg. U. S. Pat. Off.—All rights reserved
OH-AH CAIN'T B'LIEVE IT-THET AWFUL SECRET UNCLE ZEKE'S GHOST DONE TOLE ME 'BOUT LI'L ABNER! (SOB! SOB!)
(SOB!-) AH WISHED AH WAS IGGORANT LIKE SOME FOLKS-AN' DIDN'T B'LIEVE IN GHOSTS B-BUT-AH'M ED-JU-CATED ENOUGH T'KNOW THET GHOSTS D-DON'T LIE----
-SO-IT M-MUST BE TRUE! (SOB!-) AH-AH DON'T NEVAH WANTA SEE LI'L ABNER AGIN-OR SPEAK T'HIM-AH- AH HATES HIM! --AH RECKON---!
AL CAPP

LI'L ABNER Anything Might Happen By Al Capp

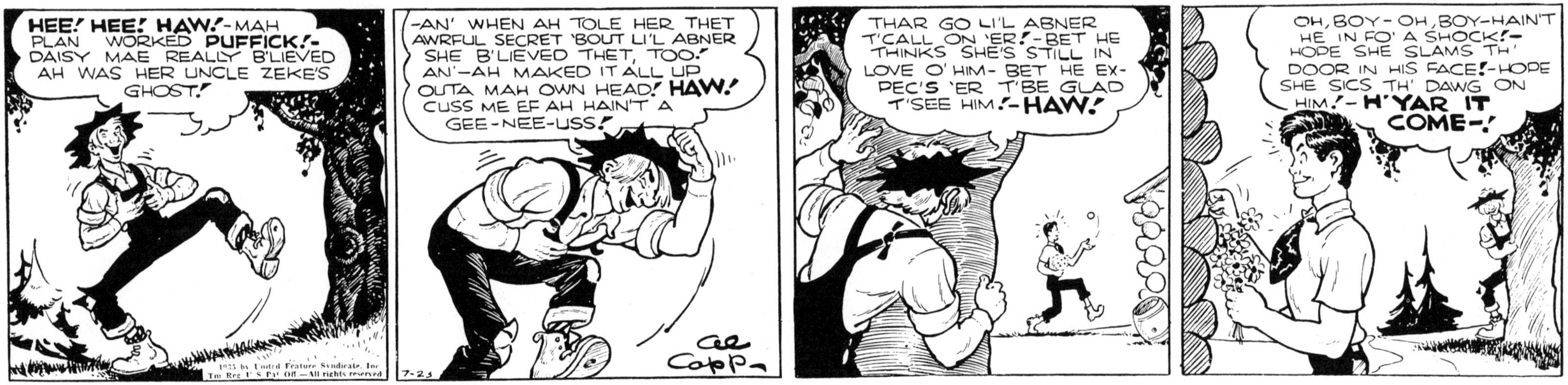
HEE! HEE! HAW!-MAH PLAN WORKED PUFFICK!-DAISY MAE REALLY B'LIEVED AH WAS HER UNCLE ZEKE'S GHOST!
© 1935 by United Feature Syndicate, Inc. Tm Reg. U. S. Pat. Off.—All rights reserved
-AN' WHEN AH TOLE HER THET AWRFUL SECRET 'BOUT LI'L ABNER SHE B'LIEVED THET, TOO! AN'-AH MAKED IT ALL UP OUTA MAH OWN HEAD! HAW! CUSS ME EF AH HAIN'T A GEE-NEE-USS!
7-23
AL CAPP
THAR GO LI'L ABNER T'CALL ON 'ER!-BET HE THINKS SHE'S STILL IN LOVE O' HIM- BET HE EX-PEC'S 'ER T'BE GLAD T'SEE HIM!-HAW!
OH, BOY-OH, BOY-HAIN'T HE IN FO' A SHOCK!-HOPE SHE SLAMS TH' DOOR IN HIS FACE!-HOPE SHE SICS TH' DAWG ON HIM!-H'YAR IT COME-!

LI'L ABNER Is Everybody Happy? By Al Capp

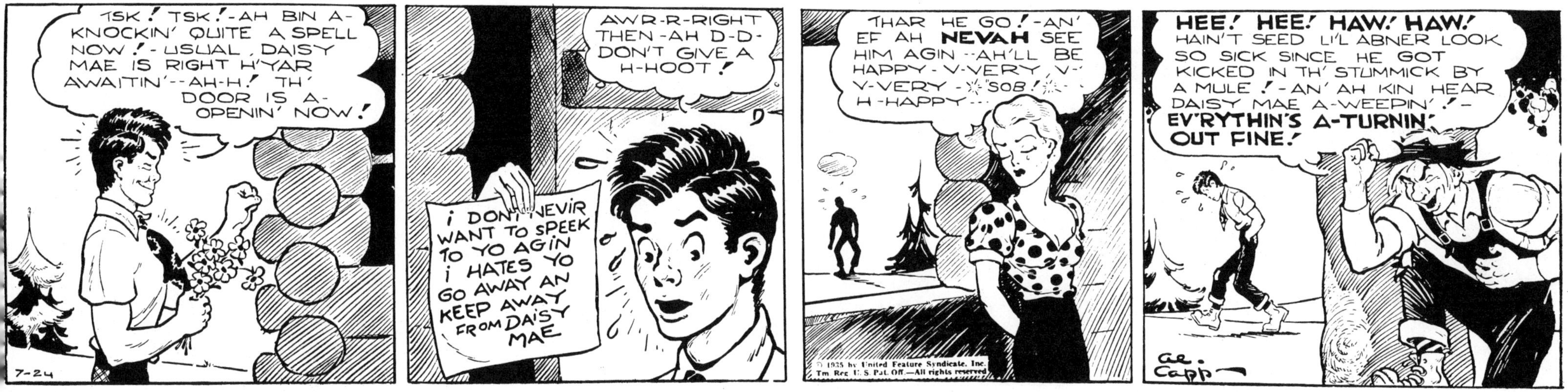
TSK! TSK!-AH BIN A-KNOCKIN' QUITE A SPELL NOW!-USUAL, DAISY MAE IS RIGHT H'YAR AWAITIN'--AH-H! TH' DOOR IS A-OPENIN' NOW!
7-24
AWR-R-RIGHT THEN-AH D-D-DON'T GIVE A H-HOOT!
i DONT NEVIR WANT TO SPEEK TO YO AGIN i HATES YO GO AWAY AN KEEP AWAY FROM DAISY MAE
THAR HE GO!-AN' EF AH NEVAH SEE HIM AGIN--AH'LL BE HAPPY-V-VERY, V-V-VERY-SOB!-H-HAPPY---
© 1935 by United Feature Syndicate, Inc. Tm Reg. U.S. Pat. Off.—All rights reserved
HEE! HEE! HAW! HAW! HAIN'T SEED LI'L ABNER LOOK SO SICK SINCE HE GOT KICKED IN TH' STUMMICK BY A MULE!-AN' AH KIN HEAR DAISY MAE A-WEEPIN'!-EV'RYTHIN'S A-TURNIN' OUT FINE!
Al Capp

LI'L ABNER Mammy Swings Into Action By Al Capp

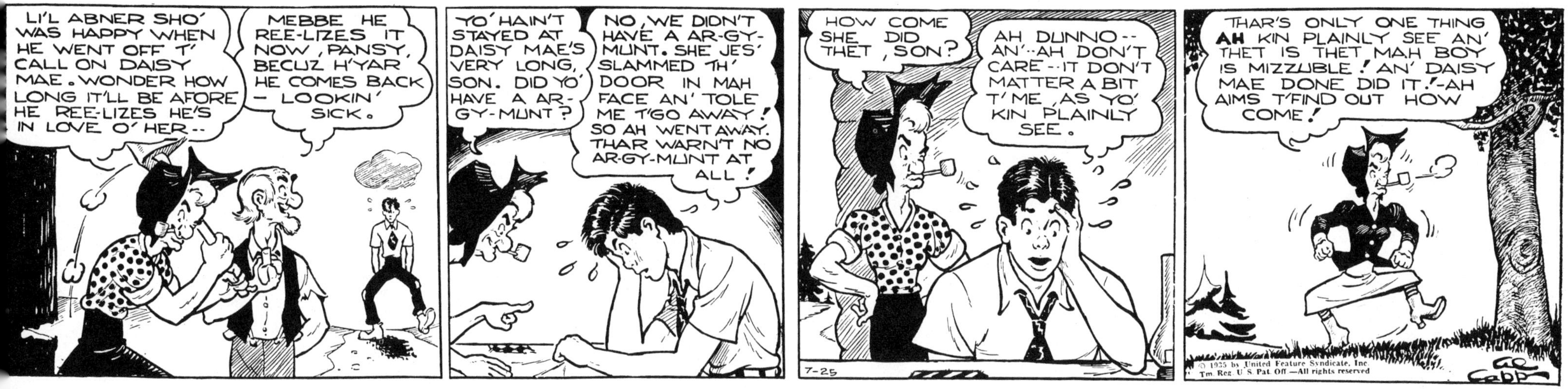
LI'L ABNER SHO' WAS HAPPY WHEN HE WENT OFF T' CALL ON DAISY MAE. WONDER HOW LONG IT'LL BE AFORE HE REE-LIZES HE'S IN LOVE O' HER--
MEBBE HE REE-LIZES IT NOW, PANSY, BECUZ H'YAR HE COMES BACK - LOOKIN' SICK.
YO' HAIN'T STAYED AT DAISY MAE'S VERY LONG, SON. DID YO' HAVE A AR-GY-MUNT?
NO, WE DIDN'T HAVE A AR-GY-MUNT. SHE JES' SLAMMED TH' DOOR IN MAH FACE AN' TOLE ME T'GO AWAY! SO AH WENT AWAY. THAR WARN'T NO AR-GY-MUNT AT ALL!
HOW COME SHE DID THET, SON?
AH DUNNO--AN'--AH DON'T CARE--IT DON'T MATTER A BIT T'ME, AS YO' KIN PLAINLY SEE.
7-25
THAR'S ONLY ONE THING AH KIN PLAINLY SEE AN' THET IS THET MAH BOY IS MIZZUBLE! AN' DAISY MAE DONE DID IT!-AH AIMS T'FIND OUT HOW COME!
© 1935 by United Feature Syndicate, Inc. Tm Reg. U.S. Pat. Off.—All rights reserved
Al Capp

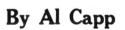

LI'L ABNER

Yo' Cain't Rely On Uncle Zeke !

By Al Capp

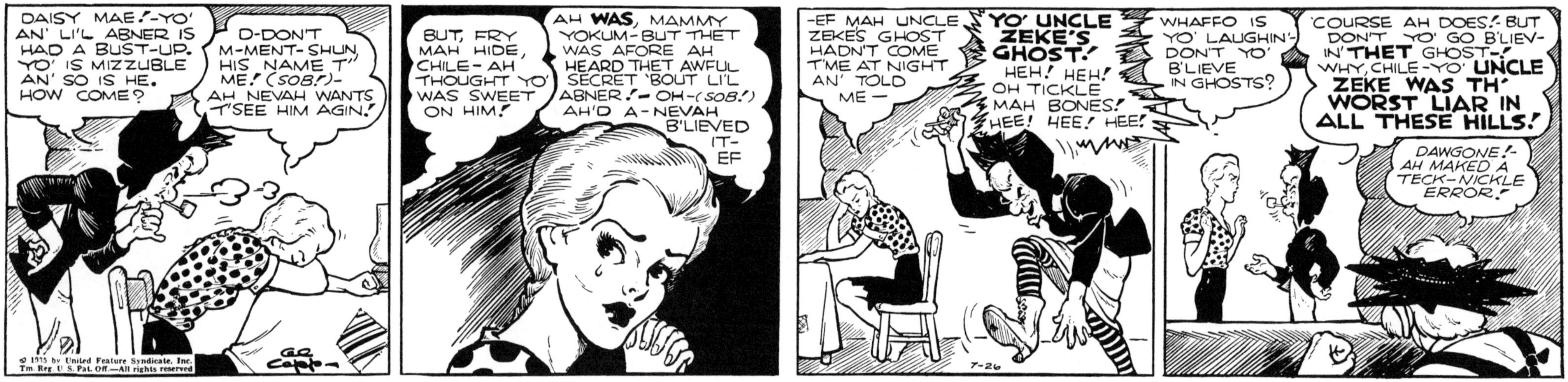

DAISY MAE!-YO' AN' LI'L ABNER IS HAD A BUST-UP. YO' IS MIZZUBLE AN' SO IS HE. HOW COME?
D-DON'T M-MENT-SHUN HIS NAME T' ME! (SOB!)- AH NEVAH WANTS T'SEE HIM AGIN!
© 1935 by United Feature Syndicate, Inc. Tm. Reg. U.S. Pat. Off.—All rights reserved
AL CAPP
BUT, FRY MAH HIDE, CHILE-AH THOUGHT YO' WAS SWEET ON HIM!
AH WAS, MAMMY YOKUM-BUT THET WAS AFORE AH HEARD THET AWFUL SECRET 'BOUT LI'L ABNER!- OH-(SOB!) AH'D A-NEVAH B'LIEVED IT-EF
-EF MAH UNCLE ZEKE'S GHOST HADN'T COME T'ME AT NIGHT AN' TOLD ME—
YO' UNCLE ZEKE'S GHOST! HEH! HEH! OH TICKLE MAH BONES! HEE! HEE! HEE!
7-26
WHAFFO IS YO' LAUGHIN'- DON'T YO' B'LIEVE IN GHOSTS?
'COURSE AH DOES!- BUT DON'T YO' GO B'LIEV-IN' THET GHOST-! WHY, CHILE-YO' UNCLE ZEKE WAS TH' WORST LIAR IN ALL THESE HILLS!
DAWGONE!- AH MAKED A TECK-NICKLE ERROR!

LI'L ABNER

All Is Forgiven

By Al Capp

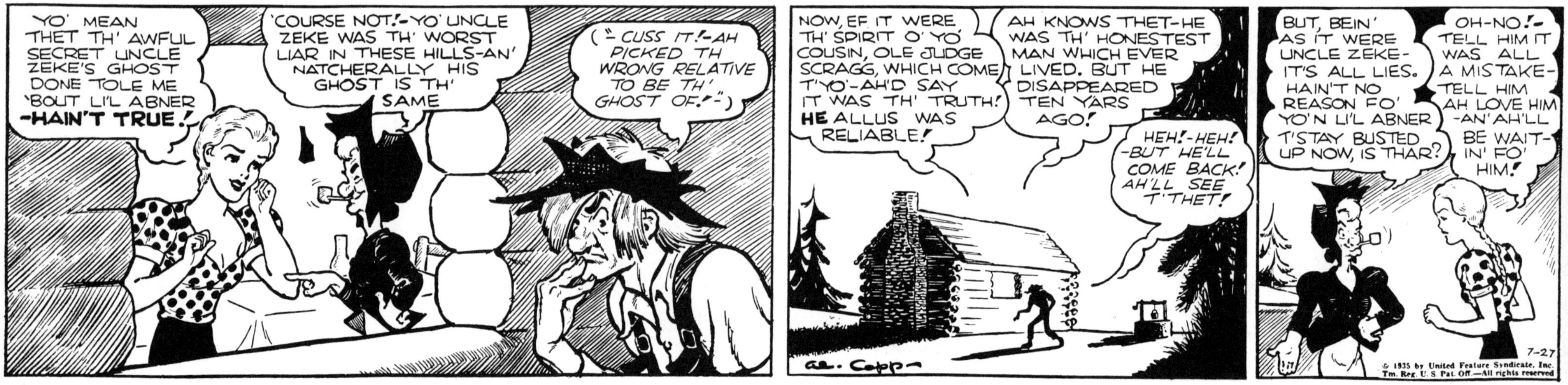

YO' MEAN THET TH' AWFUL SECRET UNCLE ZEKE'S GHOST DONE TOLE ME 'BOUT LI'L ABNER -HAIN'T TRUE!
'COURSE NOT!-YO' UNCLE ZEKE WAS TH' WORST LIAR IN THESE HILLS-AN' NATCHERALLY HIS GHOST IS TH' SAME
("CUSS IT!-AH PICKED TH WRONG RELATIVE TO BE TH' GHOST OF!-")
NOW, EF IT WERE TH' SPIRIT O' YO' COUSIN, OLE JUDGE SCRAGG, WHICH COME T'YO'-AH'D SAY IT WAS TH' TRUTH! HE ALLUS WAS RELIABLE!
AH KNOWS THET-HE WAS TH' HONESTEST MAN WHICH EVER LIVED. BUT HE DISAPPEARED TEN YARS AGO!
HEH!-HEH! -BUT HE'LL COME BACK! AH'LL SEE T'THET!
AL. CAPP
BUT, BEIN' AS IT WERE UNCLE ZEKE- IT'S ALL LIES. HAIN'T NO REASON FO' YO'N LI'L ABNER T'STAY BUSTED UP NOW, IS THAR?
OH-NO!- TELL HIM IT WAS ALL A MISTAKE- TELL HIM AH LOVE HIM -AN' AH'LL BE WAIT-IN' FO' HIM!
7-27
© 1935 by United Feature Syndicate, Inc. Tm. Reg. U.S. Pat. Off.—All rights reserved

LI'L ABNER Positive Proof By Al Capp

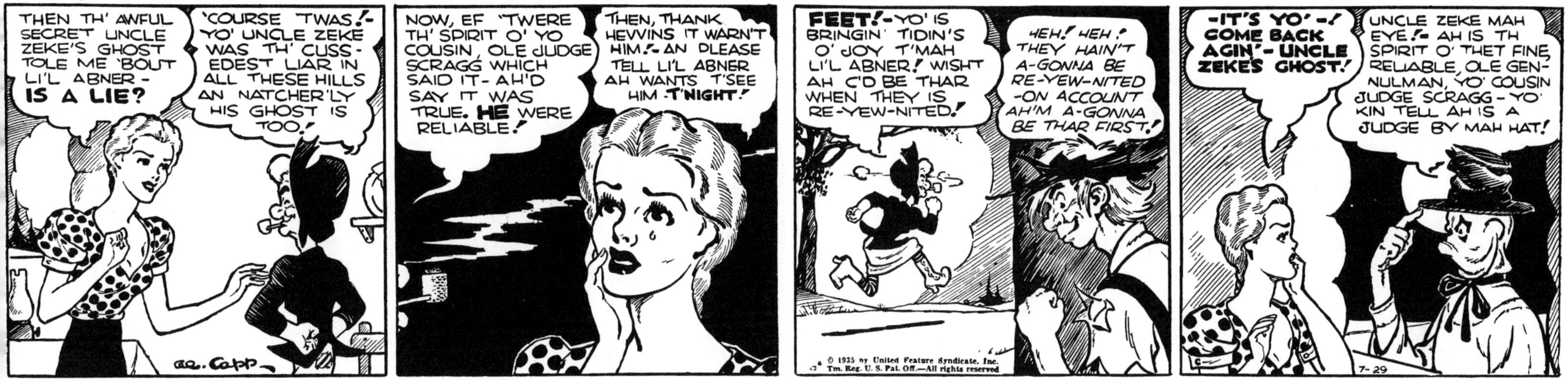

THEN TH' AWFUL SECRET UNCLE ZEKE'S GHOST TOLE ME 'BOUT LI'L ABNER - **IS A LIE?**
'COURSE TWAS!- YO' UNCLE ZEKE WAS TH' CUSS-EDEST LIAR IN ALL THESE HILLS AN NATCHER'LY HIS GHOST IS TOO!
AL CAPP
NOW, EF 'TWERE TH' SPIRIT O' YO COUSIN, OLE JUDGE SCRAGG WHICH SAID IT- AH'D SAY IT WAS TRUE. **HE** WERE RELIABLE!
THEN, THANK HEVVINS IT WARN'T HIM!- AN PLEASE TELL LI'L ABNER AH WANTS T'SEE HIM -**T'NIGHT!**
FEET!-YO' IS BRINGIN' TIDIN'S O' JOY T'MAH LI'L ABNER! WISHT AH C'D BE THAR WHEN THEY IS RE-YEW-NITED!
HEH! HEH! THEY HAIN'T A-GONNA BE RE-YEW-NITED -ON ACCOUNT AH'M A-GONNA BE THAR FIRST!
© 1935 by United Feature Syndicate, Inc. Tm. Reg. U. S. Pat. Off.—All rights reserved
-IT'S YO'-! COME BACK AGIN'- UNCLE ZEKE'S GHOST!
UNCLE ZEKE MAH EYE!- AH IS TH SPIRIT O' THET FINE, RELIABLE, OLE GEN-NULMAN, YO' COUSIN JUDGE SCRAGG - YO' KIN TELL AH IS A JUDGE BY MAH HAT!
7-29

LI'L ABNER The Real McCoy By Al Capp

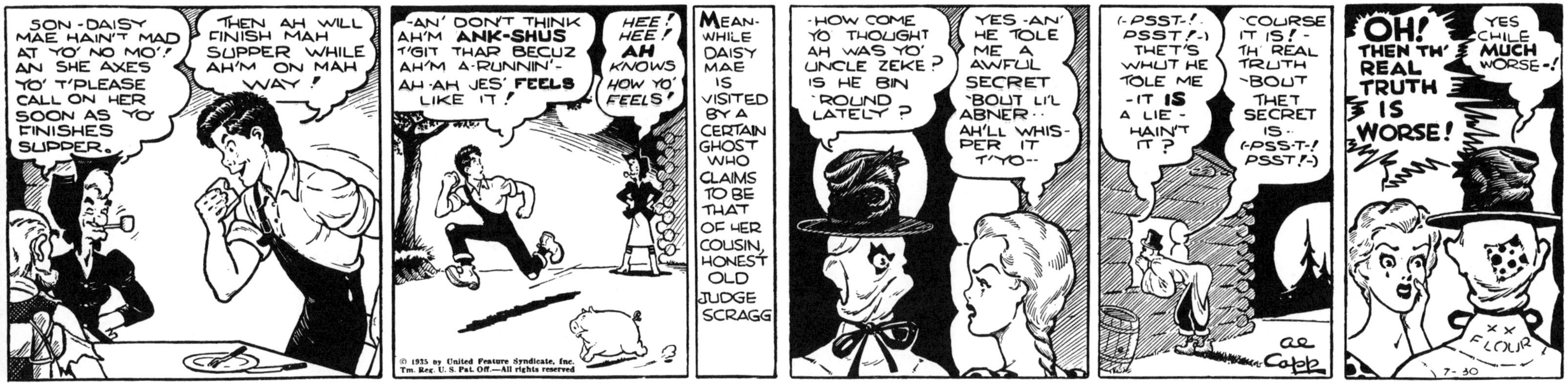

SON-DAISY MAE HAIN'T MAD AT YO' NO MO'! AN SHE AXES YO' T'PLEASE CALL ON HER SOON AS YO' FINISHES SUPPER.
THEN AH WILL FINISH MAH SUPPER WHILE AH'M ON MAH WAY!
-AN' DON'T THINK AH'M **ANK-SHUS** T'GIT THAR BECUZ AH'M A-RUNNIN'- AH-AH JES' **FEELS** LIKE IT!
HEE! HEE! **AH** KNOWS HOW YO' FEELS!
© 1935 by United Feature Syndicate, Inc. Tm. Reg. U. S. Pat. Off.—All rights reserved
MEANWHILE DAISY MAE IS VISITED BY A CERTAIN GHOST WHO CLAIMS TO BE THAT OF HER COUSIN, HONEST OLD JUDGE SCRAGG
-HOW COME YO THOUGHT AH WAS YO' UNCLE ZEKE? IS HE BIN 'ROUND LATELY?
YES-AN' HE TOLE ME A AWFUL SECRET 'BOUT LI'L ABNER-- AH'LL WHIS-PER IT T'YO--
(-PSST-! PSST!-) THET'S WHUT HE TOLE ME -IT **IS** A LIE- HAIN'T IT?
'COURSE IT IS!- TH' REAL TRUTH 'BOUT THET SECRET IS-- (-PSS-T-! PSST!-)
AL CAPP
OH! THEN TH' REAL TRUTH IS WORSE!
YES CHILE **MUCH** WORSE-!
XX FLOUR
7-30

LI'L ABNER Warm Welcome Waiting ! By Al Capp

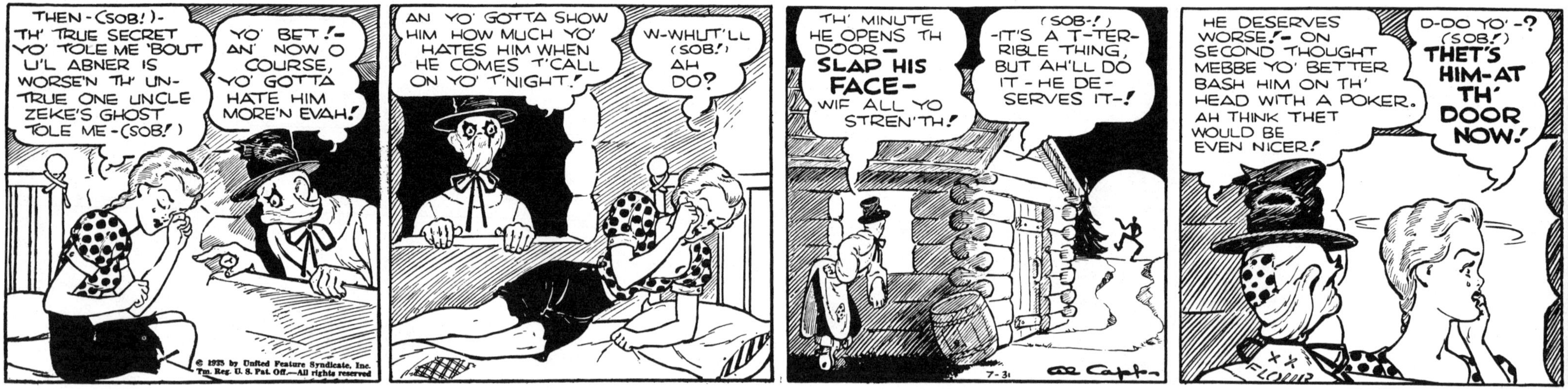

THEN-(SOB!)- TH' TRUE SECRET YO' TOLE ME 'BOUT LI'L ABNER IS WORSE'N TH' UN-TRUE ONE UNCLE ZEKE'S GHOST TOLE ME-(SOB!)
YO' BET!- AN' NOW O COURSE, YO' GOTTA HATE HIM MORE'N EVAH!
© 1935 by United Feature Syndicate, Inc. Tm. Reg. U. S. Pat. Off.—All rights reserved
AN YO' GOTTA SHOW HIM HOW MUCH YO' HATES HIM WHEN HE COMES T'CALL ON YO' T'NIGHT!
W-WHUT'LL (SOB!) AH DO?
TH' MINUTE HE OPENS TH DOOR- SLAP HIS FACE- WIF ALL YO STREN'TH!
(SOB-!) -IT'S A T-TER-RIBLE THING, BUT AH'LL DO IT-HE DE-SERVES IT-!
7-31
HE DESERVES WORSE!- ON SECOND THOUGHT MEBBE YO' BETTER BASH HIM ON TH' HEAD WITH A POKER. AH THINK THET WOULD BE EVEN NICER!
D-DO YO'-? (SOB!) THET'S HIM-AT TH' DOOR NOW!

LI'L ABNER Gals Is Pee-koolyar By Al Capp

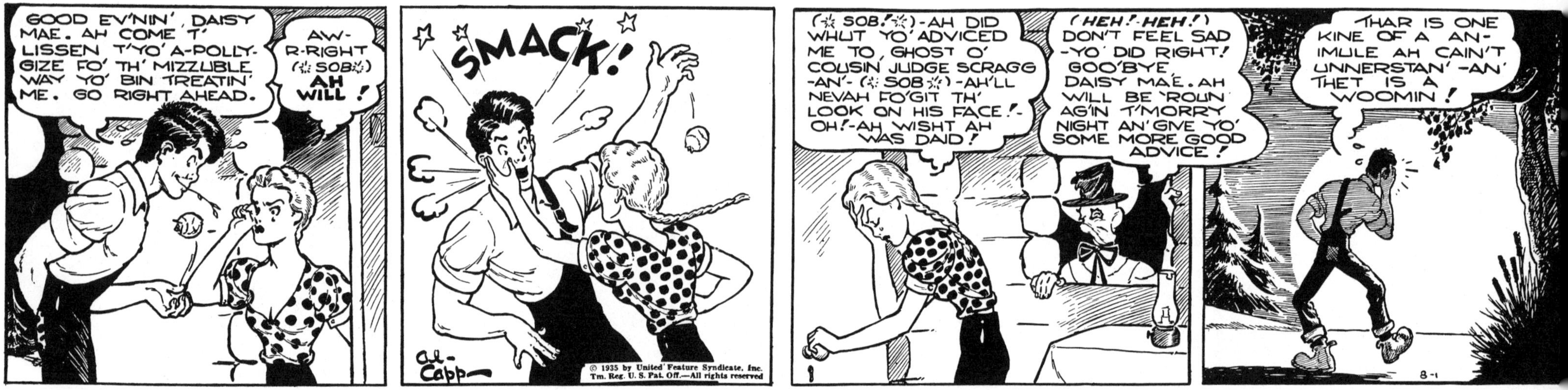

GOOD EV'NIN', DAISY MAE. AH COME T' LISSEN T'YO' A-POLLY-GIZE FO' TH' MIZZUBLE WAY YO' BIN TREATIN' ME. GO RIGHT AHEAD.
AW-R-RIGHT (SOB) AH WILL!
SMACK!
© 1935 by United Feature Syndicate, Inc. Tm. Reg. U. S. Pat. Off.—All rights reserved
(SOB!)-AH DID WHUT YO' ADVICED ME TO, GHOST O' COUSIN JUDGE SCRAGG -AN'-(SOB)-AH'LL NEVAH FO'GIT TH' LOOK ON HIS FACE!- OH!-AH WISHT AH WAS DAID!
(HEH!-HEH!) DON'T FEEL SAD -YO' DID RIGHT! GOO'BYE DAISY MAE. AH WILL BE 'ROUN' AG'IN T'MORRY NIGHT AN' GIVE YO' SOME MORE GOOD ADVICE!
THAR IS ONE KINE OF A AN-IMULE AH CAIN'T UNNERSTAN' -AN' THET IS A WOOMIN!
8-1

LI'L ABNER Sounds Pee-koolyar By Al Capp

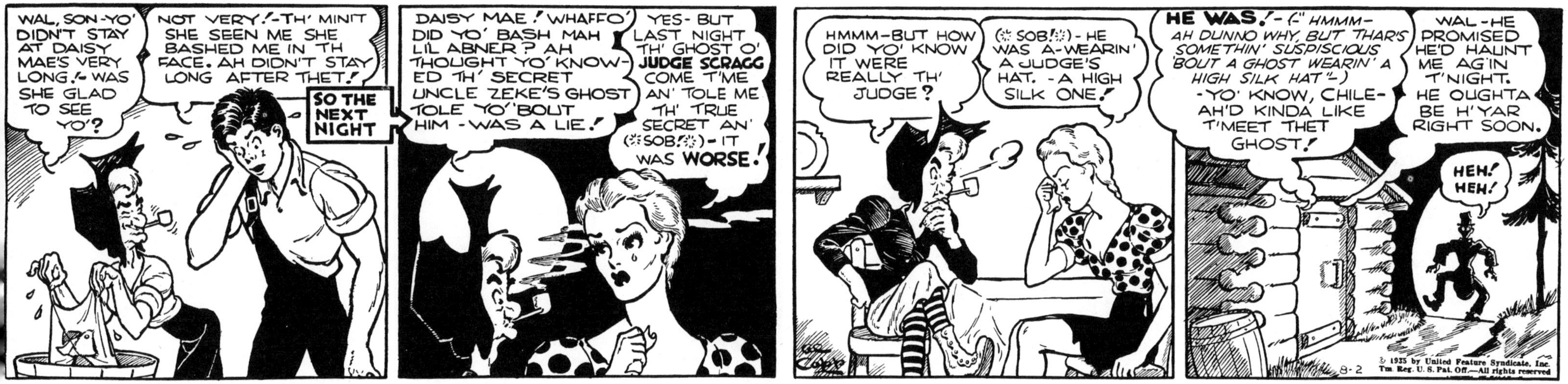

WAL, SON-YO' DIDN'T STAY AT DAISY MAE'S VERY LONG!-WAS SHE GLAD TO SEE YO'?
NOT VERY!-TH' MINIT SHE SEEN ME SHE BASHED ME IN TH FACE. AH DIDN'T STAY LONG AFTER THET!
SO THE NEXT NIGHT
DAISY MAE! WHAFFO' DID YO' BASH MAH LI'L ABNER? AH THOUGHT YO' KNOW-ED TH' SECRET UNCLE ZEKE'S GHOST TOLE YO' BOUT HIM-WAS A LIE!
YES-BUT LAST NIGHT TH' GHOST O' JUDGE SCRAGG COME T'ME AN' TOLE ME TH' TRUE SECRET AN' (SOB!)-IT WAS WORSE!
HMMM-BUT HOW DID YO' KNOW IT WERE REALLY TH' JUDGE?
(SOB!)-HE WAS A-WEARIN' A JUDGE'S HAT. -A HIGH SILK ONE!
HE WAS!-("HMMM-AH DUNNO WHY, BUT THAR'S SOMETHIN' SUSPISCIOUS 'BOUT A GHOST WEARIN' A HIGH SILK HAT"-)
-YO' KNOW, CHILE-AH'D KINDA LIKE T'MEET THET GHOST!
WAL-HE PROMISED HE'D HAUNT ME AG'IN T'NIGHT. HE OUGHTA BE H'YAR RIGHT SOON.
HEH! HEH!
8-2
© 1935 by United Feature Syndicate, Inc. Tm. Reg. U. S. Pat. Off.—All rights reserved

LI'L ABNER Caught In the Act By Al Capp

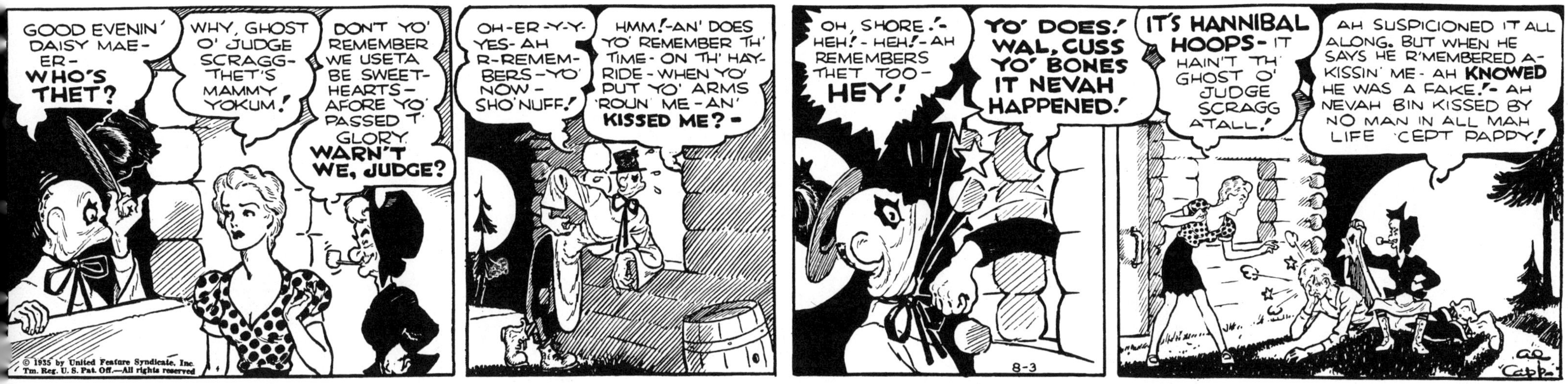

GOOD EVENIN' DAISY MAE-ER-WHO'S THET?
WHY, GHOST O' JUDGE SCRAGG-THET'S MAMMY YOKUM!
DON'T YO' REMEMBER WE USETA BE SWEET-HEARTS-AFORE YO' PASSED T' GLORY. WARN'T WE, JUDGE?
OH-ER-Y-Y-YES-AH R-REMEM-BERS-YO' NOW-SHO'NUFF!
HMM!-AN' DOES YO' REMEMBER TH' TIME-ON TH' HAY-RIDE-WHEN YO' PUT YO' ARMS 'ROUN ME-AN' KISSED ME?-
OH, SHORE!-HEH!-HEH!-AH REMEMBERS THET TOO-HEY!
YO' DOES! WAL, CUSS YO' BONES IT NEVAH HAPPENED!
IT'S HANNIBAL HOOPS-IT HAIN'T TH' GHOST O' JUDGE SCRAGG ATALL!
AH SUSPICIONED IT ALL ALONG. BUT WHEN HE SAYS HE R'MEMBERED A-KISSIN' ME-AH KNOWED HE WAS A FAKE!-AH NEVAH BIN KISSED BY NO MAN IN ALL MAH LIFE 'CEPT PAPPY!
© 1935 by United Feature Syndicate, Inc. Tm. Reg. U. S. Pat. Off.—All rights reserved
8-3

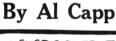

LI'L ABNER Did Yo' Say "Nevah," Boy? **By Al Capp**

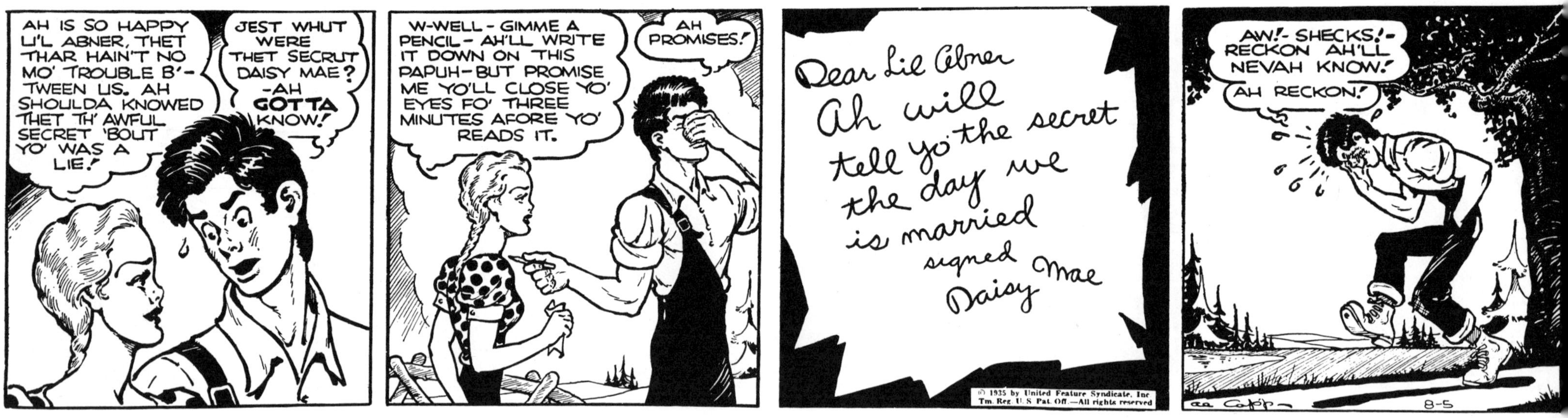

AH IS SO HAPPY LI'L ABNER, THET THAR HAIN'T NO MO' TROUBLE B'-TWEEN US. AH SHOULDA KNOWED THET TH' AWFUL SECRET 'BOUT YO' WAS A LIE!
JEST WHUT WERE THET SECRUT DAISY MAE? -AH GOTTA KNOW!
W-WELL - GIMME A PENCIL - AH'LL WRITE IT DOWN ON THIS PAPUH - BUT PROMISE ME YO'LL CLOSE YO' EYES FO' THREE MINUTES AFORE YO' READS IT.
AH PROMISES!
Dear Lil Abner
Ah will tell yo the secret the day we is married
signed Daisy Mae
© 1935 by United Feature Syndicate, Inc. Tm. Reg. U.S. Pat. Off.—All rights reserved
AW! - SHECKS! - RECKON AH'LL NEVAH KNOW!
AH RECKON!
Al Capp
8-5

LI'L ABNER It's the Gallows! **By Al Capp**

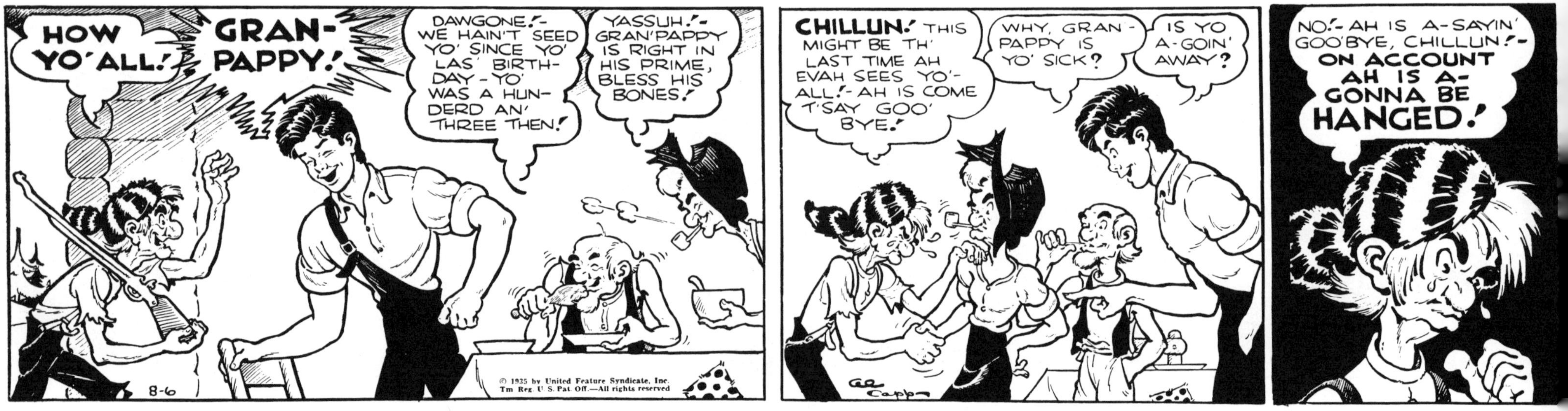

HOW YO' ALL!
GRAN-PAPPY!
DAWGONE! - WE HAIN'T SEED YO' SINCE YO' LAS' BIRTH-DAY - YO' WAS A HUN-DERD AN' THREE THEN!
YASSUH! - GRAN'PAPPY IS RIGHT IN HIS PRIME, BLESS HIS BONES!
8-6
© 1935 by United Feature Syndicate, Inc. Tm. Reg. U.S. Pat. Off.—All rights reserved
CHILLUN! THIS MIGHT BE TH' LAST TIME AH EVAH SEES YO'-ALL! - AH IS COME T'SAY GOO' BYE!
WHY, GRAN-PAPPY IS YO' SICK?
IS YO A-GOIN' AWAY?
Al Capp
NO! - AH IS A-SAYIN' GOO'BYE, CHILLUN! - ON ACCOUNT AH IS A-GONNA BE HANGED!

LI'L ABNER

Gran'pappy's Story—Part One

By Al Capp

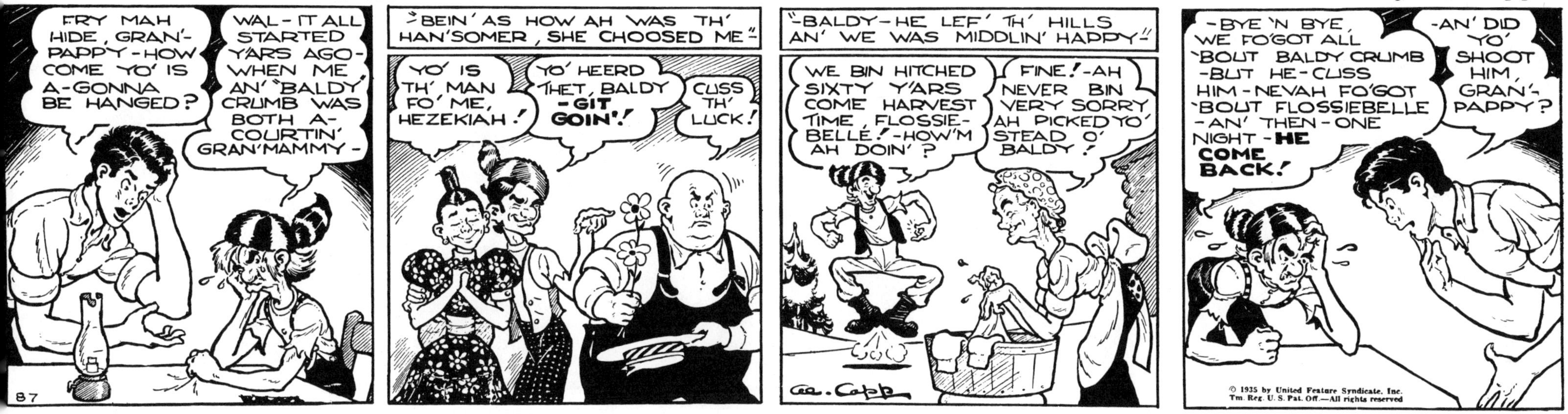
FRY MAH HIDE, GRAN'-PAPPY-HOW COME YO' IS A-GONNA BE HANGED?
WAL-IT ALL STARTED Y'ARS AGO-WHEN ME AN' "BALDY" CRUMB WAS BOTH A-COURTIN' GRAN'MAMMY-
87
"BEIN' AS HOW AH WAS TH' HAN'SOMER, SHE CHOOSED ME"
YO' IS TH' MAN FO' ME, HEZEKIAH!
YO' HEERD THET, BALDY -GIT GOIN'!
CUSS TH' LUCK!
"BALDY-HE LEF' TH' HILLS AN' WE WAS MIDDLIN' HAPPY!"
WE BIN HITCHED SIXTY Y'ARS COME HARVEST TIME, FLOSSIE-BELLE!-HOW'M AH DOIN'?
FINE!-AH NEVER BIN VERY SORRY AH PICKED YO' STEAD O' BALDY!
Al. Capp
-BYE 'N BYE, WE FO'GOT ALL 'BOUT BALDY CRUMB -BUT HE-CUSS HIM-NEVAH FO'GOT 'BOUT FLOSSIEBELLE -AN' THEN-ONE NIGHT-HE COME BACK!
-AN' DID YO' SHOOT HIM, GRAN'-PAPPY?
© 1935 by United Feature Syndicate, Inc. Tm. Reg. U. S. Pat. Off.—All rights reserved

LI'L ABNER

Gran'pappy's Story—Part Two

By Al Capp

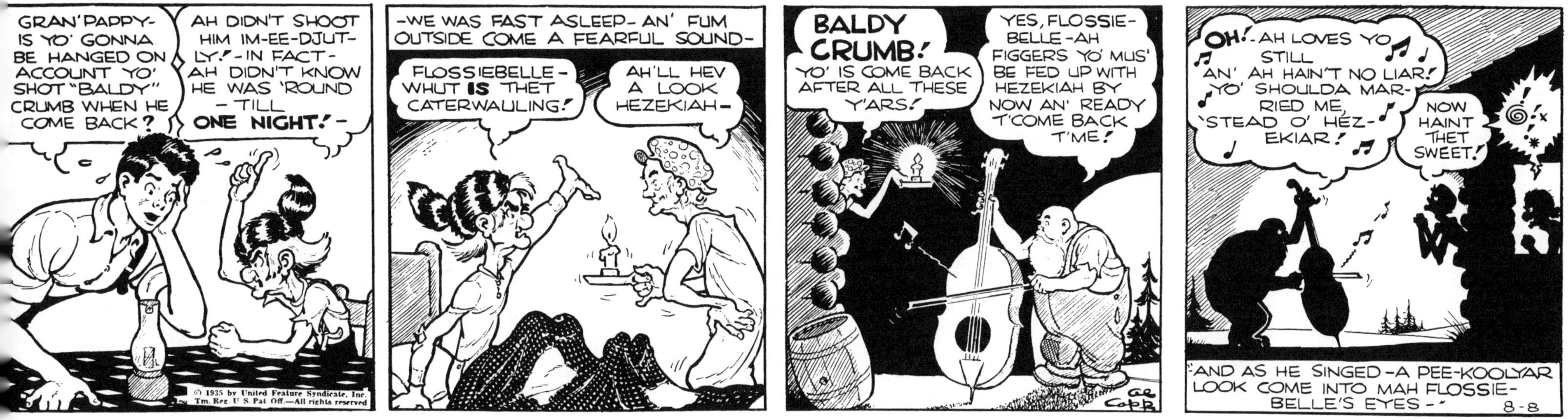
GRAN'PAPPY-IS YO' GONNA BE HANGED ON ACCOUNT YO' SHOT "BALDY" CRUMB WHEN HE COME BACK?
AH DIDN'T SHOOT HIM IM-EE-DJUT-LY!-IN FACT-AH DIDN'T KNOW HE WAS 'ROUND -TILL ONE NIGHT!-
© 1935 by United Feature Syndicate, Inc. Tm. Reg. U. S. Pat. Off.—All rights reserved
-WE WAS FAST ASLEEP-AN' FUM OUTSIDE COME A FEARFUL SOUND-
FLOSSIEBELLE-WHUT IS THET CATERWAULING!
AH'LL HEV A LOOK HEZEKIAH-
BALDY CRUMB! YO' IS COME BACK AFTER ALL THESE Y'ARS!
YES, FLOSSIE-BELLE-AH FIGGERS YO' MUS' BE FED UP WITH HEZEKIAH BY NOW AN' READY T'COME BACK T'ME!
Al Capp
OH!-AH LOVES YO STILL AN' AH HAIN'T NO LIAR! YO' SHOULDA MAR-RIED ME, 'STEAD O' HEZ-EKIAR!
NOW HAINT THET SWEET!
"AND AS HE SINGED-A PEE-KOOLYAR LOOK COME INTO MAH FLOSSIE-BELLE'S EYES-"
8-8

LI'L ABNER Gran'pappy's Story—Part Three By Al Capp

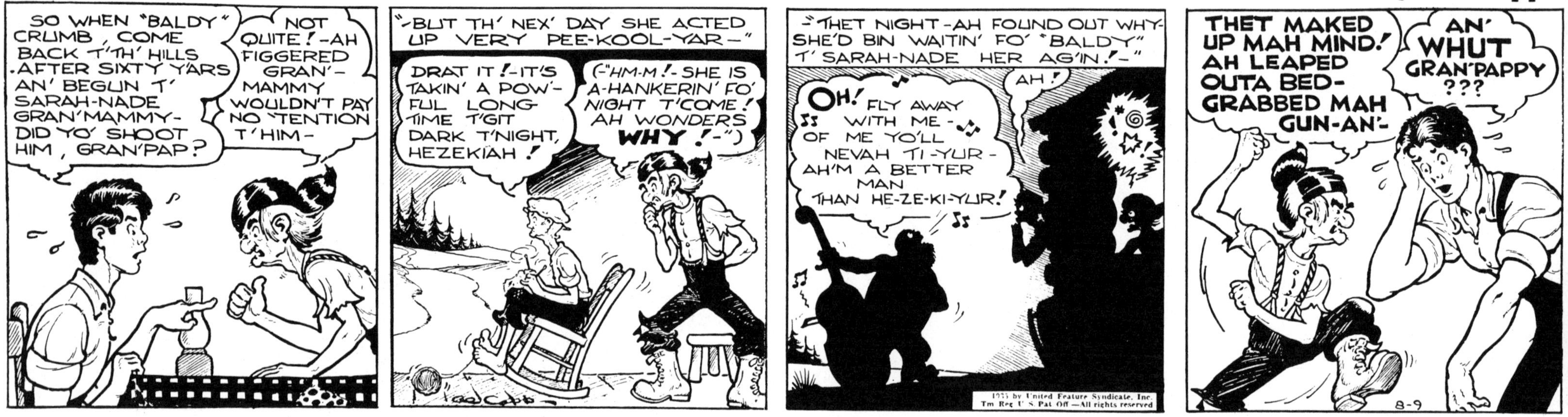

SO WHEN "BALDY" CRUMB, COME BACK T'TH' HILLS AFTER SIXTY YARS AN' BEGUN T' SARAH-NADE GRAN'MAMMY- DID YO' SHOOT HIM, GRAN'PAP?
NOT QUITE!-AH FIGGERED GRAN'-MAMMY WOULDN'T PAY NO 'TENTION T'HIM-
"-BUT TH' NEX' DAY SHE ACTED UP VERY PEE-KOOL-YAR-"
DRAT IT!-IT'S TAKIN' A POW-FUL LONG TIME T'GIT DARK T'NIGHT, HEZEKIAH!
("HM-M!-SHE IS A-HANKERIN' FO' NIGHT T'COME! AH WONDERS WHY!-")
"THET NIGHT-AH FOUND OUT WHY-SHE'D BIN WAITIN' FO' "BALDY" T' SARAH-NADE HER AG'IN!-"
OH! FLY AWAY WITH ME - OF ME YO'LL NEVAH TI-YUR - AH'M A BETTER MAN THAN HE-ZE-KI-YUR!
AH!
1935 by United Feature Syndicate, Inc. Tm Reg U S Pat Off —All rights reserved
THET MAKED UP MAH MIND! AH LEAPED OUTA BED- GRABBED MAH GUN-AN'-
AN' WHUT GRAN'PAPPY ???
8-9

LI'L ABNER Trouble Ahead and Danger Behind By Al Capp

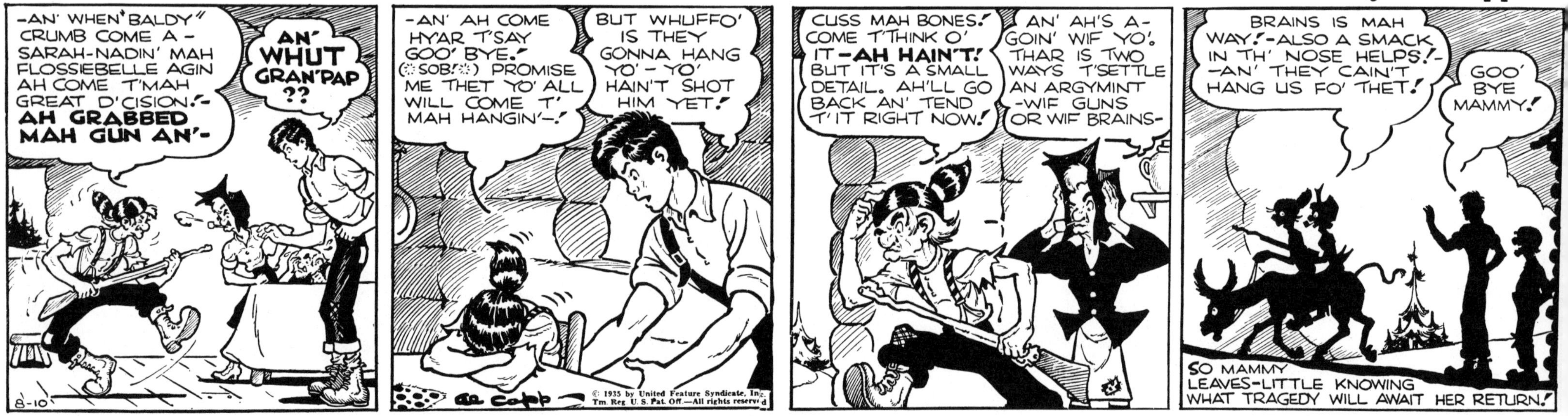

-AN' WHEN "BALDY" CRUMB COME A-SARAH-NADIN' MAH FLOSSIEBELLE AGIN AH COME T'MAH GREAT D'CISION!- AH GRABBED MAH GUN AN'-
AN' WHUT GRAN'PAP ??
8-10
-AN' AH COME HYAR T'SAY GOO' BYE.- (SOB!) PROMISE ME THET YO' ALL WILL COME T' MAH HANGIN'-!
BUT WHUFFO' IS THEY GONNA HANG YO'- YO' HAIN'T SHOT HIM YET!
© 1935 by United Feature Syndicate, Inc. Tm. Reg. U.S. Pat. Off.—All rights reserved
CUSS MAH BONES! COME T'THINK O' IT-AH HAIN'T! BUT IT'S A SMALL DETAIL. AH'LL GO BACK AN' TEND T'IT RIGHT NOW!
AN' AH'S A-GOIN' WIF YO'. THAR IS TWO WAYS T'SETTLE AN ARGYMINT -WIF GUNS OR WIF BRAINS-
BRAINS IS MAH WAY!-ALSO A SMACK IN TH' NOSE HELPS!- -AN' THEY CAIN'T HANG US FO' THET!
GOO' BYE MAMMY!
SO MAMMY LEAVES-LITTLE KNOWING WHAT TRAGEDY WILL AWAIT HER RETURN!

LI'L ABNER A Sign of Trouble **By Al Capp**

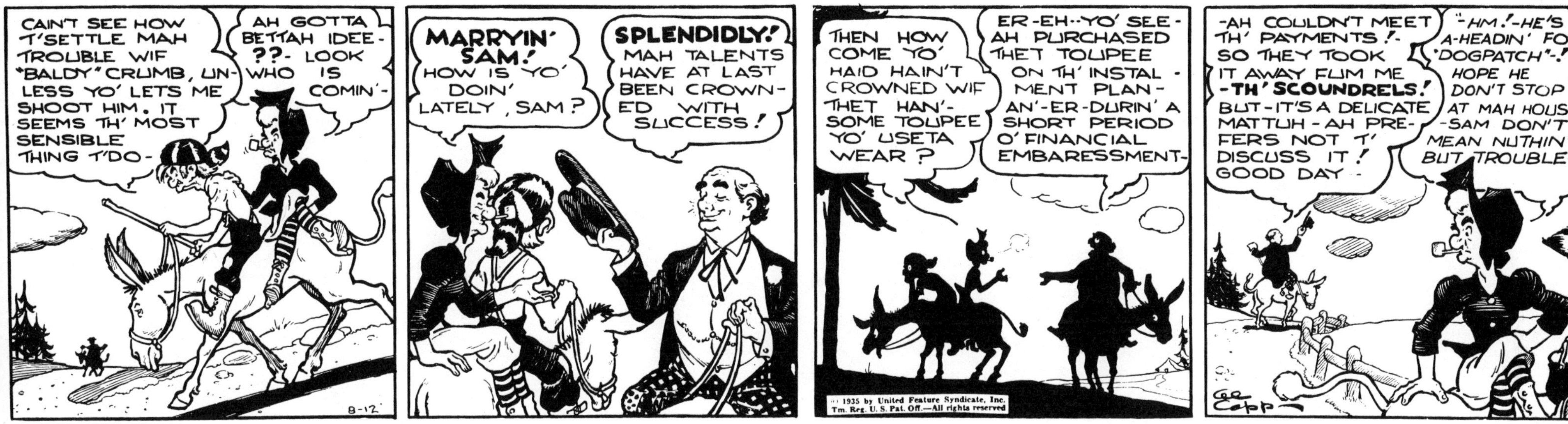
CAIN'T SEE HOW T'SETTLE MAH TROUBLE WIF "BALDY" CRUMB, UNLESS YO' LETS ME SHOOT HIM. IT SEEMS TH' MOST SENSIBLE THING T'DO-
AH GOTTA BETTAH IDEE- ??- LOOK WHO IS COMIN'-
8-12
MARRYIN' SAM! HOW IS YO' DOIN' LATELY, SAM?
SPLENDIDLY! MAH TALENTS HAVE AT LAST BEEN CROWNED WITH SUCCESS!
THEN HOW COME YO' HAID HAIN'T CROWNED WIF THET HANSOME TOUPEE YO' USETA WEAR?
ER-EH--YO' SEE-AH PURCHASED THET TOUPEE ON TH' INSTALMENT PLAN-AN'-ER-DURIN' A SHORT PERIOD O' FINANCIAL EMBARESSMENT-
© 1935 by United Feature Syndicate, Inc. Tm. Reg. U. S. Pat. Off.—All rights reserved
-AH COULDN'T MEET TH' PAYMENTS!- SO THEY TOOK IT AWAY FUM ME -TH' SCOUNDRELS! BUT-IT'S A DELICATE MATTUH-AH PREFERS NOT T' DISCUSS IT! GOOD DAY-
-HM!-HE'S A-HEADIN' FO' "DOGPATCH"-! HOPE HE DON'T STOP AT MAH HOUSE -SAM DON'T MEAN NUTHIN' BUT TROUBLE-!
Al Capp

LI'L ABNER Enter the Serpent **By Al Capp**

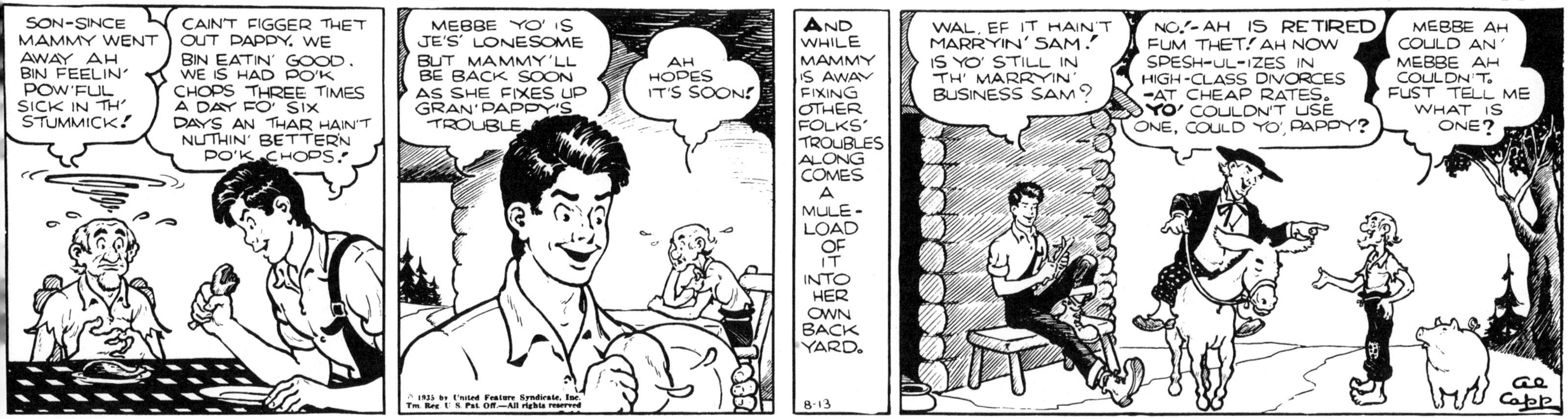
SON-SINCE MAMMY WENT AWAY AH BIN FEELIN' POW'FUL SICK IN TH' STUMMICK!
CAIN'T FIGGER THET OUT PAPPY. WE BIN EATIN' GOOD. WE IS HAD PO'K CHOPS THREE TIMES A DAY FO' SIX DAYS AN THAR HAIN'T NUTHIN' BETTER'N PO'K CHOPS!
MEBBE YO' IS JE'S' LONESOME BUT MAMMY'LL BE BACK SOON AS SHE FIXES UP GRAN'PAPPY'S TROUBLE.
AH HOPES IT'S SOON!
© 1935 by United Feature Syndicate, Inc. Tm. Reg. U. S. Pat. Off.—All rights reserved
AND WHILE MAMMY IS AWAY FIXING OTHER FOLKS' TROUBLES ALONG COMES A MULE-LOAD OF IT INTO HER OWN BACK YARD.
8-13
WAL, EF IT HAIN'T MARRYIN' SAM! IS YO' STILL IN TH' MARRYIN' BUSINESS SAM?
NO!-AH IS RETIRED FUM THET! AH NOW SPESH-UL-IZES IN HIGH-CLASS DIVORCES -AT CHEAP RATES. YO' COULDN'T USE ONE, COULD YO', PAPPY?
MEBBE AH COULD AN' MEBBE AH COULDN'T. FUST TELL ME WHAT IS ONE?
Al Capp

LI'L ABNER

He Nevah Shoulda Mentioned It

By Al Capp

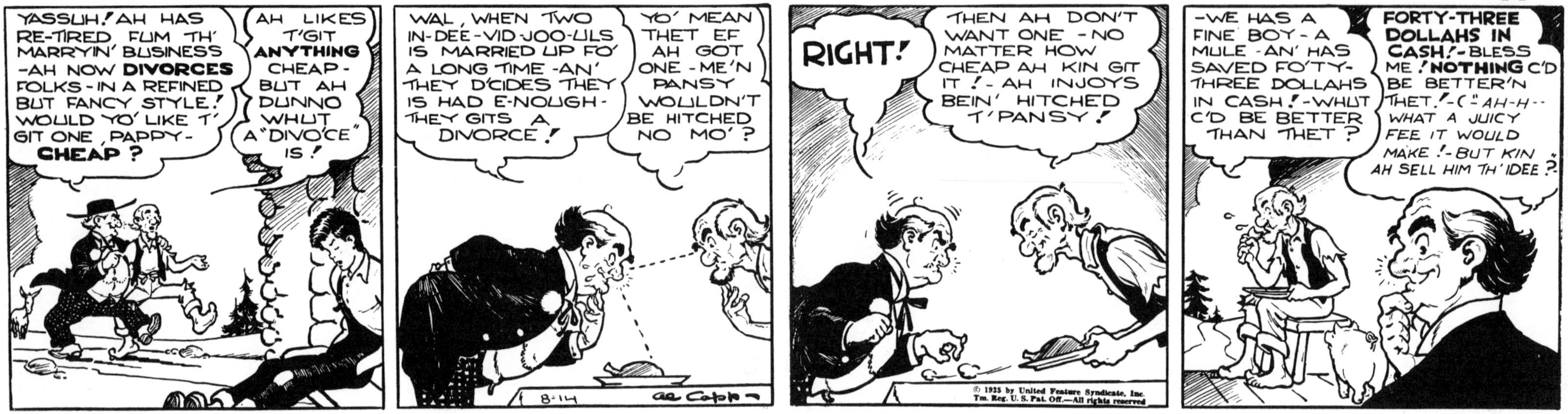

YASSUH! AH HAS RE-TIRED FUM TH' MARRYIN' BUSINESS -AH NOW **DIVORCES** FOLKS - IN A REFINED BUT FANCY STYLE! WOULD YO' LIKE T' GIT ONE, PAPPY- **CHEAP**?
AH LIKES T'GIT **ANYTHING** CHEAP- BUT AH DUNNO WHUT A "DIVO'CE" IS!
WAL, WHEN TWO IN-DEE-VID-JOO-ULS IS MARRIED UP FO' A LONG TIME -AN' THEY D'CIDES THEY IS HAD E-NOUGH- THEY GITS A DIVORCE!
YO' MEAN THET EF AH GOT ONE - ME'N PANSY WOULDN'T BE HITCHED NO MO'?
8-14
Al Capp
RIGHT!
THEN AH DON'T WANT ONE -NO MATTER HOW CHEAP AH KIN GIT IT! - AH INJOYS BEIN' HITCHED T'PANSY!
© 1935 by United Feature Syndicate, Inc. Tm. Reg. U. S. Pat. Off.—All rights reserved
-WE HAS A FINE BOY - A MULE -AN' HAS SAVED FO'TY-THREE DOLLAHS IN CASH! -WHUT C'D BE BETTER THAN THET?
FORTY-THREE DOLLAHS IN CASH! -BLESS ME! **NOTHING** C'D BE BETTER'N THET! -(" AH-H -- WHAT A JUICY FEE IT WOULD MAKE! - BUT KIN AH SELL HIM TH' IDEE?")

LI'L ABNER

Jest Practice Fo' Poppy

By Al Capp

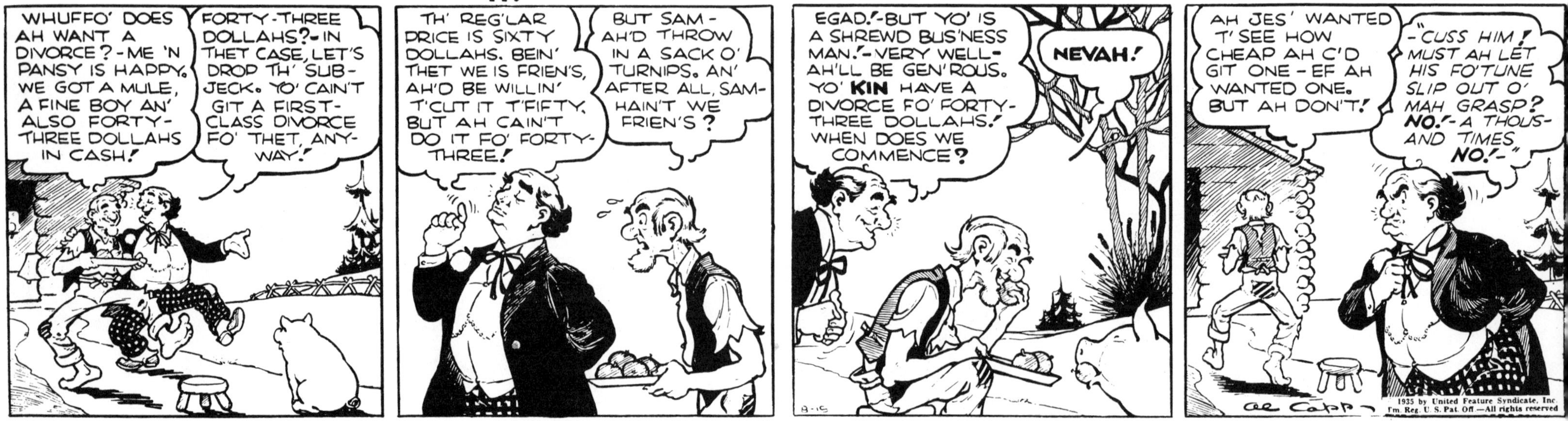

WHUFFO' DOES AH WANT A DIVORCE? - ME 'N PANSY IS HAPPY. WE GOT A MULE, A FINE BOY AN' ALSO FORTY-THREE DOLLAHS IN CASH!
FORTY-THREE DOLLAHS? - IN THET CASE, LET'S DROP TH' SUB-JECK. YO' CAIN'T GIT A FIRST-CLASS DIVORCE FO' THET, ANY-WAY!
TH' REG'LAR PRICE IS SIXTY DOLLAHS. BEIN' THET WE IS FRIEN'S, AH'D BE WILLIN' T'CUT IT T'FIFTY. BUT AH CAIN'T DO IT FO' FORTY-THREE!
BUT SAM - AH'D THROW IN A SACK O' TURNIPS. AN' AFTER ALL, SAM- HAIN'T WE FRIEN'S?
EGAD! - BUT YO' IS A SHREWD BUS'NESS MAN! - VERY WELL - AH'LL BE GEN'ROUS. YO' **KIN** HAVE A DIVORCE FO' FORTY-THREE DOLLAHS! WHEN DOES WE COMMENCE?
NEVAH!
8-15
AH JES' WANTED T'SEE HOW CHEAP AH C'D GIT ONE - EF AH WANTED ONE. BUT AH DON'T!
-"CUSS HIM! MUST AH LET HIS FO'TUNE SLIP OUT O' MAH GRASP? **NO!** - A THOUS-AND TIMES **NO!**-"
Al Capp
1935 by United Feature Syndicate, Inc. Tm. Reg. U. S. Pat. Off.—All rights reserved

LI'L ABNER Drumming Up Business By Al Capp

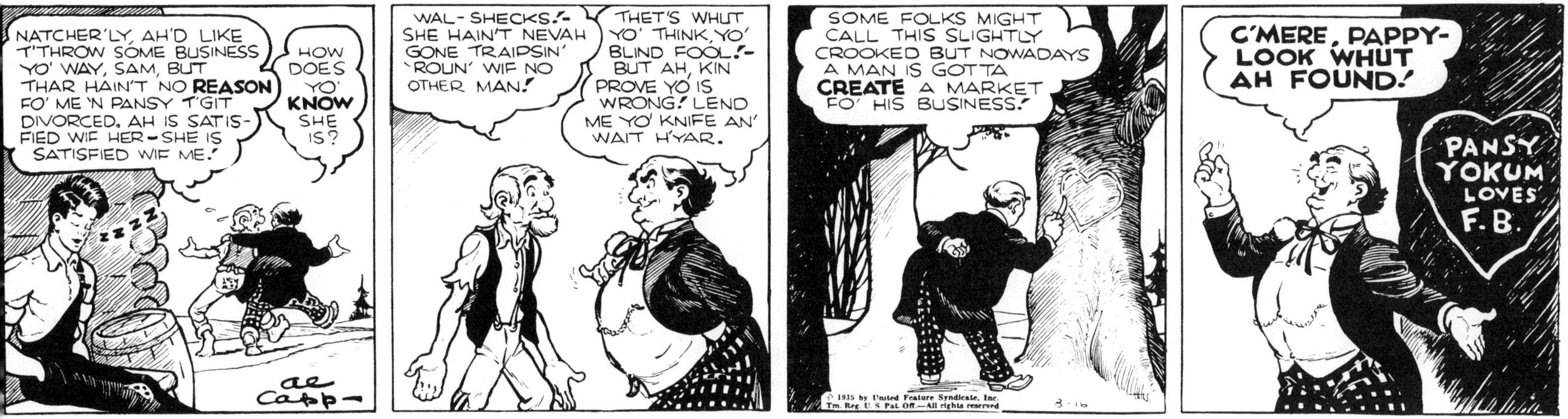

NATCHER'LY, AH'D LIKE T'THROW SOME BUSINESS YO' WAY, SAM, BUT THAR HAIN'T NO **REASON** FO' ME 'N PANSY T'GIT DIVORCED. AH IS SATISFIED WIF HER – SHE IS SATISFIED WIF ME!
HOW DOES YO' **KNOW** SHE IS?
ZZZZ
WAL-SHECKS!– SHE HAIN'T NEVAH GONE TRAIPSIN' 'ROUN' WIF NO OTHER MAN!
THET'S WHUT YO' THINK, YO' BLIND FOOL!– BUT AH, KIN PROVE YO' IS WRONG! LEND ME YO' KNIFE AN' WAIT H'YAR.
SOME FOLKS MIGHT CALL THIS SLIGHTLY CROOKED BUT NOWADAYS A MAN IS GOTTA **CREATE** A MARKET FO' HIS BUSINESS!
© 1935 by United Feature Syndicate, Inc. Tm. Reg. U.S. Pat. Off.—All rights reserved
8-16
C'MERE, PAPPY– LOOK WHUT AH FOUND!
PANSY YOKUM LOVES F.B.

LI'L ABNER The Disturber By Al Capp

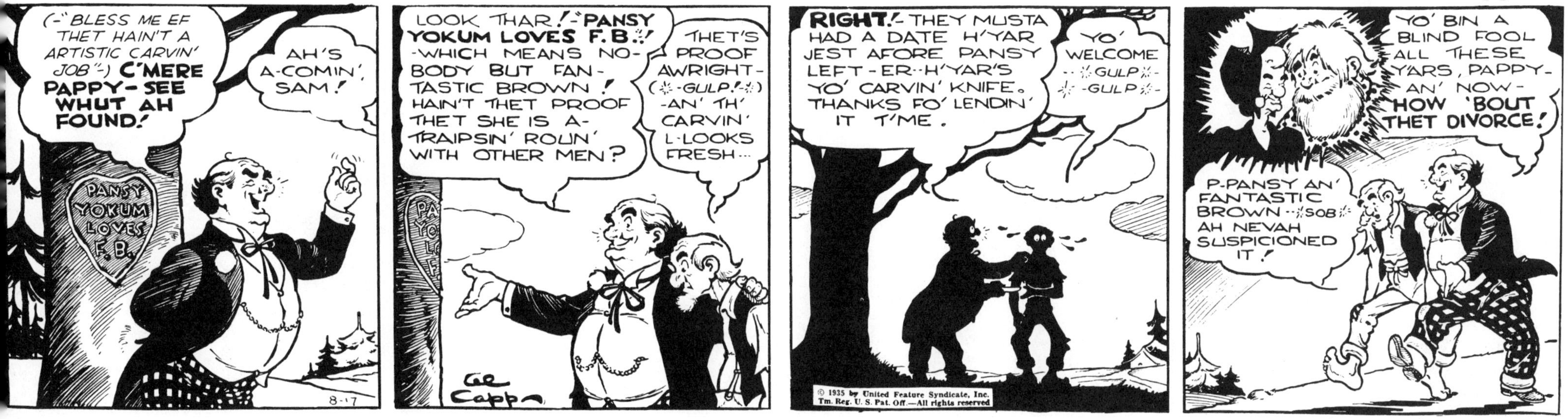

(–"BLESS ME EF THET HAIN'T A ARTISTIC CARVIN' JOB"–) **C'MERE PAPPY– SEE WHUT AH FOUND!**
AH'S A-COMIN', SAM!
PANSY YOKUM LOVES F.B.
8-17
LOOK THAR!–"**PANSY YOKUM LOVES F.B.**"! –WHICH MEANS NOBODY BUT FANTASTIC BROWN! HAIN'T THET PROOF THET SHE IS A-TRAIPSIN' ROUN' WITH OTHER MEN?
THET'S PROOF AWRIGHT– (–GULP!–) –AN' TH' CARVIN' L-LOOKS FRESH...
RIGHT!– THEY MUSTA HAD A DATE H'YAR JEST AFORE PANSY LEFT–ER–H'YAR'S YO' CARVIN' KNIFE. THANKS FO' LENDIN' IT T'ME.
YO' WELCOME – –GULP– –GULP–
© 1935 by United Feature Syndicate, Inc. Tm. Reg. U.S. Pat. Off.—All rights reserved
YO' BIN A BLIND FOOL ALL THESE YARS, PAPPY– AN' NOW– **HOW 'BOUT THET DIVORCE!**
P-PANSY AN' FANTASTIC BROWN – SOB – AH NEVAH SUSPICIONED IT!

LI'L ABNER While Abner Sleeps By Al Capp

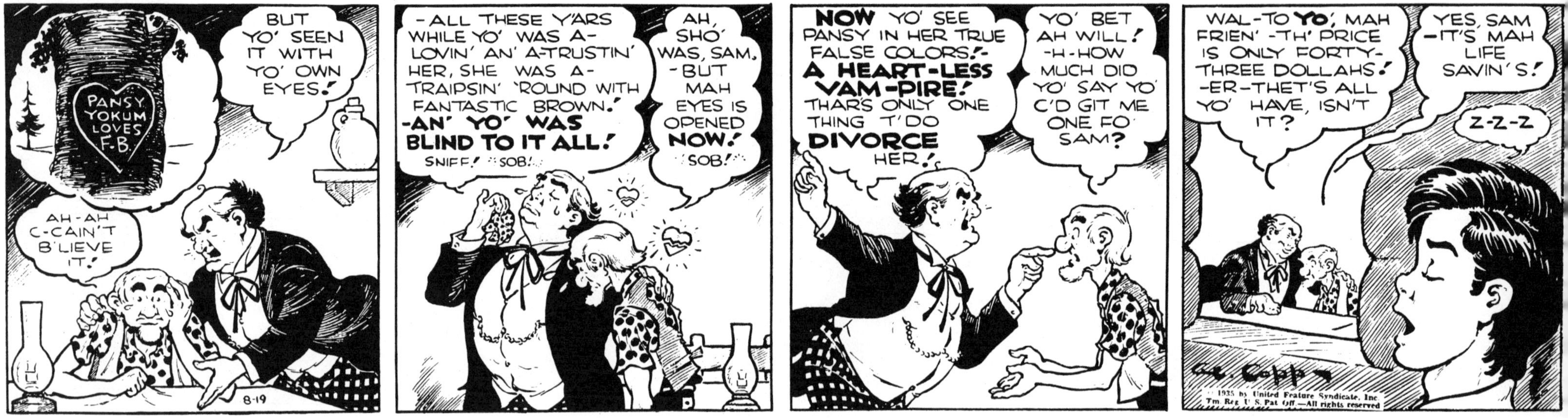
PANSY YOKUM LOVES F.B.
BUT YO' SEEN IT WITH YO' OWN EYES!
AH-AH C-CAIN'T B'LIEVE IT!
8-19
-ALL THESE Y'ARS WHILE YO' WAS A-LOVIN' AN' A-TRUSTIN' HER, SHE WAS A-TRAIPSIN' 'ROUND WITH FANTASTIC BROWN! -AN' YO' WAS BLIND TO IT ALL!
SNIFF! SOB!
AH, SHO' WAS, SAM, -BUT MAH EYES IS OPENED NOW!
SOB!
NOW YO' SEE PANSY IN HER TRUE FALSE COLORS!- A HEART-LESS VAM-PIRE! THAR'S ONLY ONE THING T'DO DIVORCE HER!
YO' BET AH WILL! -H-HOW MUCH DID YO' SAY YO' C'D GIT ME ONE FO' SAM?
WAL-TO YO', MAH FRIEN' -TH' PRICE IS ONLY FORTY-THREE DOLLAHS! -ER-THET'S ALL YO' HAVE, ISN'T IT?
YES, SAM -IT'S MAH LIFE SAVIN'S!
Z-Z-Z
Al Capp
© 1935 by United Feature Syndicate, Inc. Tm Reg. U.S. Pat. Off.—All rights reserved

LI'L ABNER Willing To Compromise By Al Capp

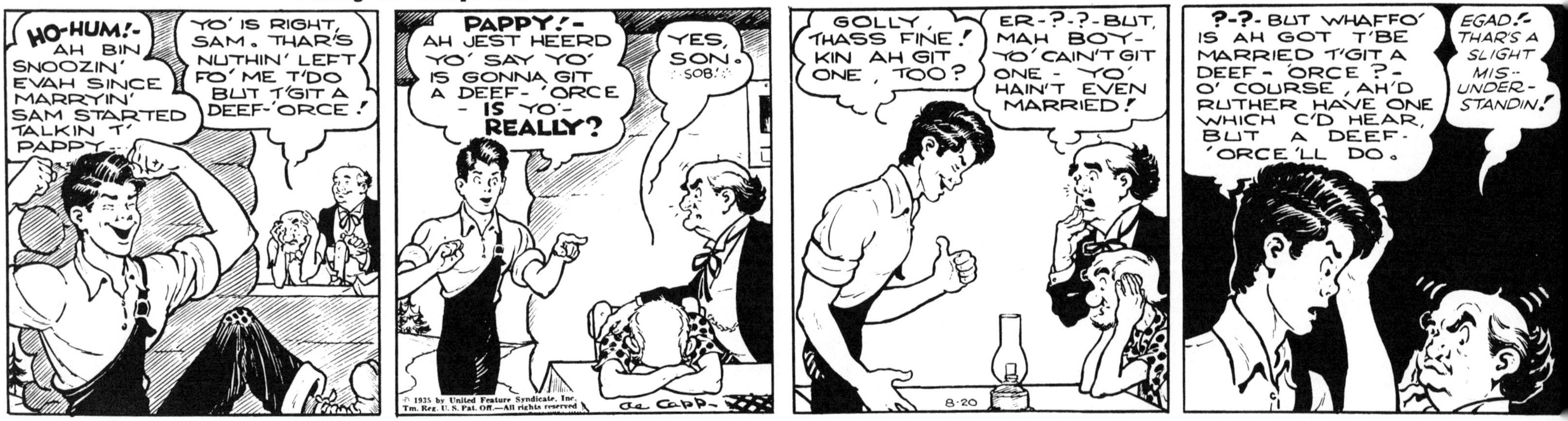
HO-HUM!- AH BIN SNOOZIN' EVAH SINCE MARRYIN' SAM STARTED TALKIN T' PAPPY--
YO' IS RIGHT, SAM. THAR'S NUTHIN' LEFT FO' ME T'DO BUT T'GIT A DEEF-'ORCE!
PAPPY!- AH JEST HEERD YO' SAY YO' IS GONNA GIT A DEEF-'ORCE - IS YO'- REALLY?
YES, SON.
SOB!
© 1935 by United Feature Syndicate, Inc. Tm. Reg. U.S. Pat. Off.—All rights reserved
Al Capp
GOLLY, THASS FINE! KIN AH GIT ONE, TOO?
ER-?-?-BUT, MAH BOY- YO' CAIN'T GIT ONE - YO' HAIN'T EVEN MARRIED!
8-20
?-?- BUT WHAFFO' IS AH GOT T'BE MARRIED T'GIT A DEEF-'ORCE?- O' COURSE, AH'D RUTHER HAVE ONE WHICH C'D HEAR, BUT A DEEF-'ORCE'LL DO.
EGAD!- THAR'S A SLIGHT MIS-UNDER-STANDIN!

LI'L ABNER Hold Yo' Punch! By Al Capp

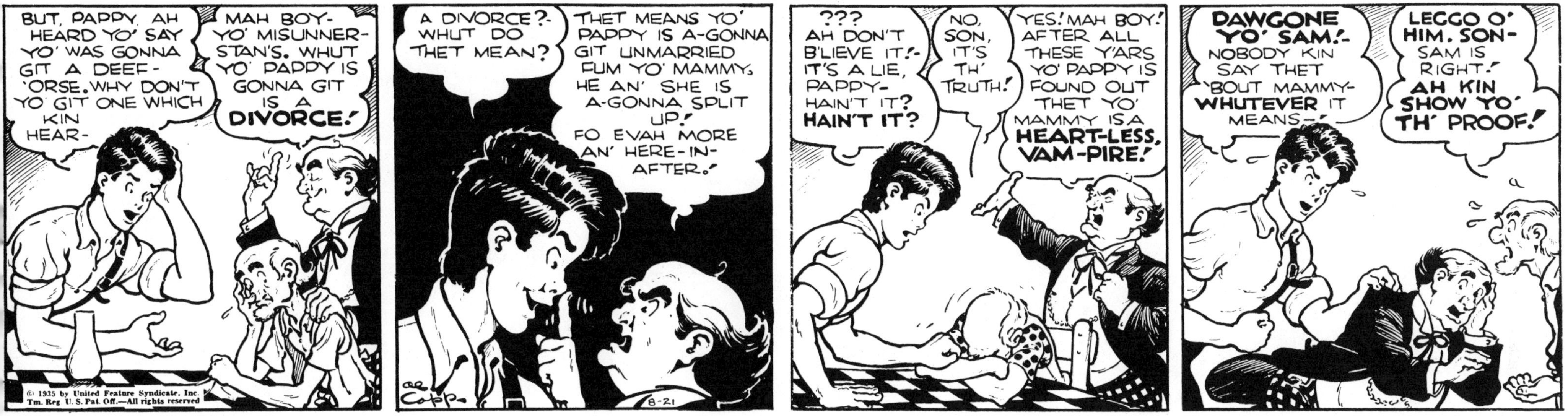

BUT, PAPPY, AH HEARD YO' SAY YO' WAS GONNA GIT A DEEF-'ORSE. WHY DON'T YO' GIT ONE WHICH KIN HEAR-
MAH BOY-YO' MISUNNER-STAN'S. WHUT YO' PAPPY IS GONNA GIT IS A DIVORCE!
© 1935 by United Feature Syndicate, Inc. Tm. Reg. U. S. Pat. Off.—All rights reserved
A DIVORCE?-WHUT DO THET MEAN?
THET MEANS YO' PAPPY IS A-GONNA GIT UNMARRIED FUM YO' MAMMY, HE AN' SHE IS A-GONNA SPLIT UP! FO EVAH MORE AN' HERE-IN-AFTER.!
AL CAPP
8-21
??? AH DON'T B'LIEVE IT!-IT'S A LIE, PAPPY-HAIN'T IT? HAIN'T IT?
NO, SON, IT'S TH' TRUTH!
YES! MAH BOY! AFTER ALL THESE Y'ARS YO' PAPPY IS FOUND OUT THET YO' MAMMY IS A HEART-LESS, VAM-PIRE!
DAWGONE YO' SAM!- NOBODY KIN SAY THET 'BOUT MAMMY-WHUTEVER IT MEANS-!
LEGGO O' HIM, SON-SAM IS RIGHT! AH KIN SHOW YO' TH' PROOF!

LI'L ABNER Technical Error, Sam By Al Capp

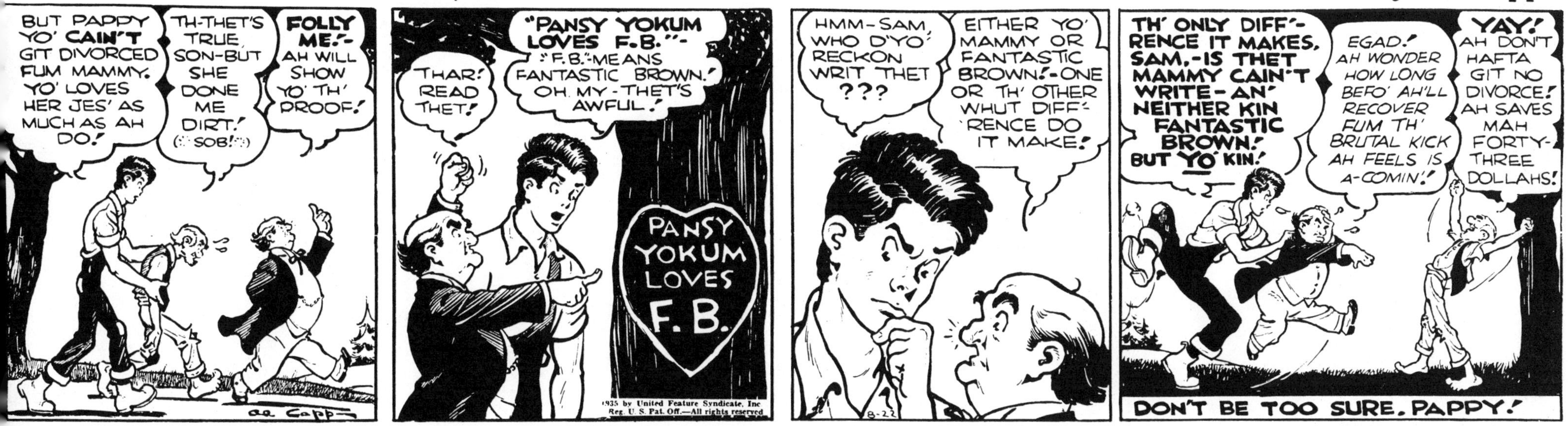

BUT PAPPY YO' CAIN'T GIT DIVORCED FUM MAMMY. YO' LOVES HER JES' AS MUCH AS AH DO!
TH-THET'S TRUE, SON-BUT SHE DONE ME DIRT! (SOB!)
FOLLY ME!- AH WILL SHOW YO' TH' PROOF!
AL CAPP
THAR! READ THET!
"PANSY YOKUM LOVES F.B."-"F.B." MEANS FANTASTIC BROWN! OH, MY-THET'S AWFUL!
PANSY YOKUM LOVES F. B.
1935 by United Feature Syndicate, Inc Reg. U. S. Pat. Off.—All rights reserved
HMM-SAM, WHO D'YO' RECKON WRIT THET ???
EITHER YO' MAMMY OR FANTASTIC BROWN!-ONE OR TH' OTHER WHUT DIFF-'RENCE DO IT MAKE!
8-22
TH' ONLY DIFF-'RENCE IT MAKES, SAM,-IS THET MAMMY CAIN'T WRITE-AN' NEITHER KIN FANTASTIC BROWN! BUT YO' KIN!
EGAD! AH WONDER HOW LONG BEFO' AH'LL RECOVER FUM TH' BRUTAL KICK AH FEELS IS A-COMIN'!
YAY! AH DON'T HAFTA GIT NO DIVORCE! AH SAVES MAH FORTY-THREE DOLLAHS!
DON'T BE TOO SURE, PAPPY!

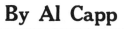

LI'L ABNER The Green Serpent By Al Capp

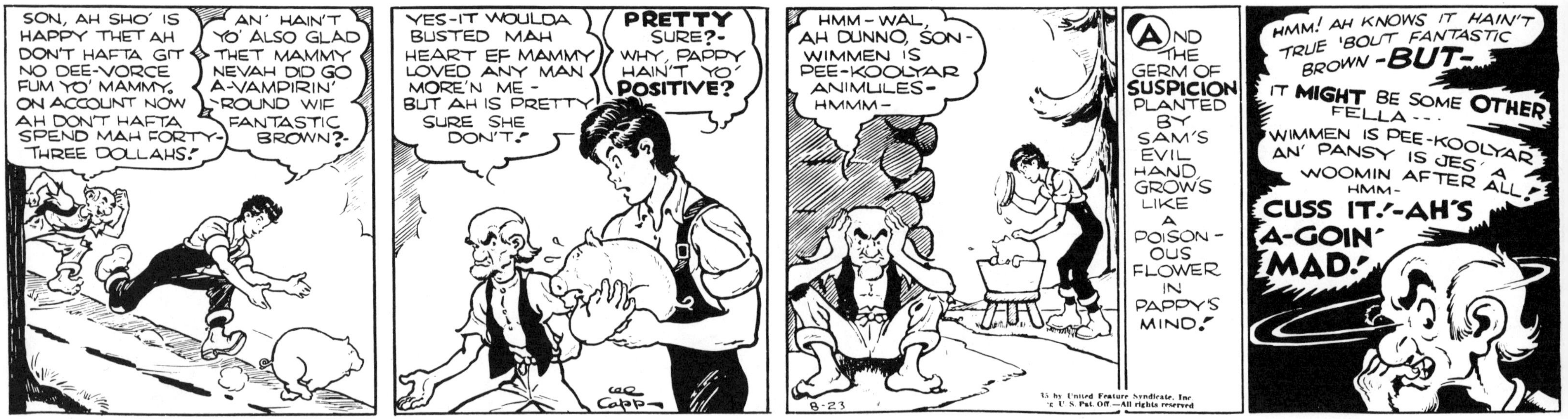

SON, AH SHO' IS HAPPY THET AH DON'T HAFTA GIT NO DEE-VORCE FUM YO' MAMMY. ON ACCOUNT NOW AH DON'T HAFTA SPEND MAH FORTY-THREE DOLLAHS!
AN' HAIN'T YO' ALSO GLAD THET MAMMY NEVAH DID GO A-VAMPIRIN' 'ROUND WIF FANTASTIC BROWN?-
YES-IT WOULDA BUSTED MAH HEART EF MAMMY LOVED ANY MAN MORE'N ME - BUT AH IS PRETTY SURE SHE DON'T!
PRETTY SURE?- WHY, PAPPY HAIN'T YO' POSITIVE?
CAPP
HMM - WAL, AH DUNNO, SON - WIMMEN IS PEE-KOOLYAR ANIMULES - HMMM -
8-23
AND THE GERM OF SUSPICION PLANTED BY SAM'S EVIL HAND, GROWS LIKE A POISON-OUS FLOWER IN PAPPY'S MIND!
HMM! AH KNOWS IT HAIN'T TRUE 'BOUT FANTASTIC BROWN -BUT-
IT MIGHT BE SOME OTHER FELLA - - -
WIMMEN IS PEE-KOOLYAR AN' PANSY IS JES' A WOOMIN AFTER ALL! HMM-
CUSS IT!-AH'S A-GOIN' MAD!

LI'L ABNER Try, Try Again By Al Capp

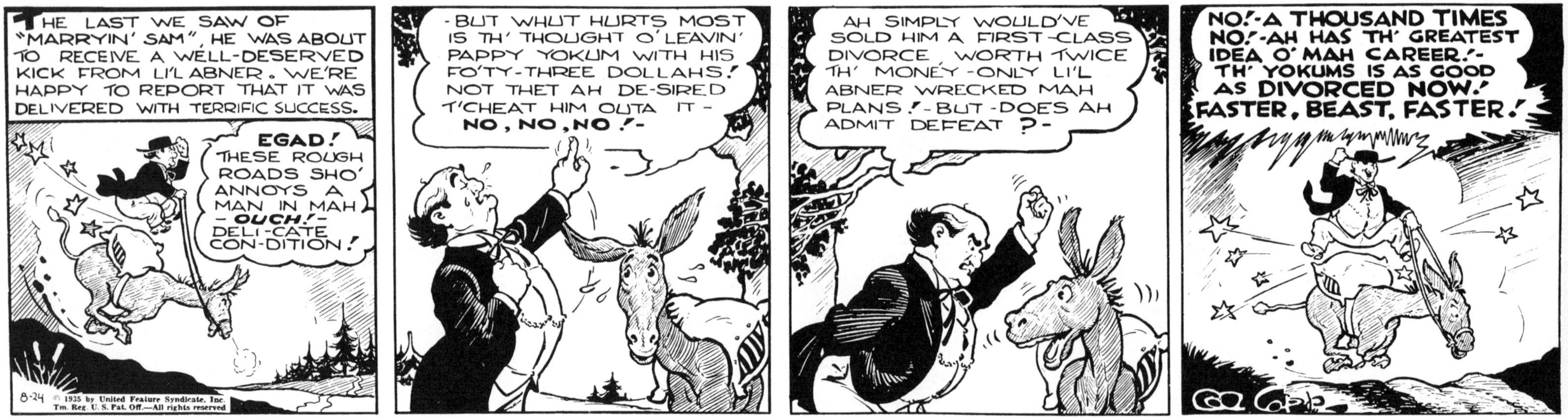

THE LAST WE SAW OF "MARRYIN' SAM", HE WAS ABOUT TO RECEIVE A WELL-DESERVED KICK FROM LI'L ABNER. WE'RE HAPPY TO REPORT THAT IT WAS DELIVERED WITH TERRIFIC SUCCESS.
EGAD! THESE ROUGH ROADS SHO' ANNOYS A MAN IN MAH -OUCH!- DELI-CATE CON-DITION!
8-24
-BUT WHUT HURTS MOST IS TH' THOUGHT O' LEAVIN' PAPPY YOKUM WITH HIS FO'TY-THREE DOLLAHS! NOT THET AH DE-SIRED T'CHEAT HIM OUTA IT - NO, NO, NO!-
AH SIMPLY WOULD'VE SOLD HIM A FIRST-CLASS DIVORCE, WORTH TWICE TH' MONEY -ONLY LI'L ABNER WRECKED MAH PLANS!-BUT-DOES AH ADMIT DEFEAT ?-
NO!-A THOUSAND TIMES NO!-AH HAS TH' GREATEST IDEA O' MAH CAREER!- TH' YOKUMS IS AS GOOD AS DIVORCED NOW! FASTER, BEAST, FASTER!
AL CAPP

LI'L ABNER The Villain Still Pursues By Al Capp

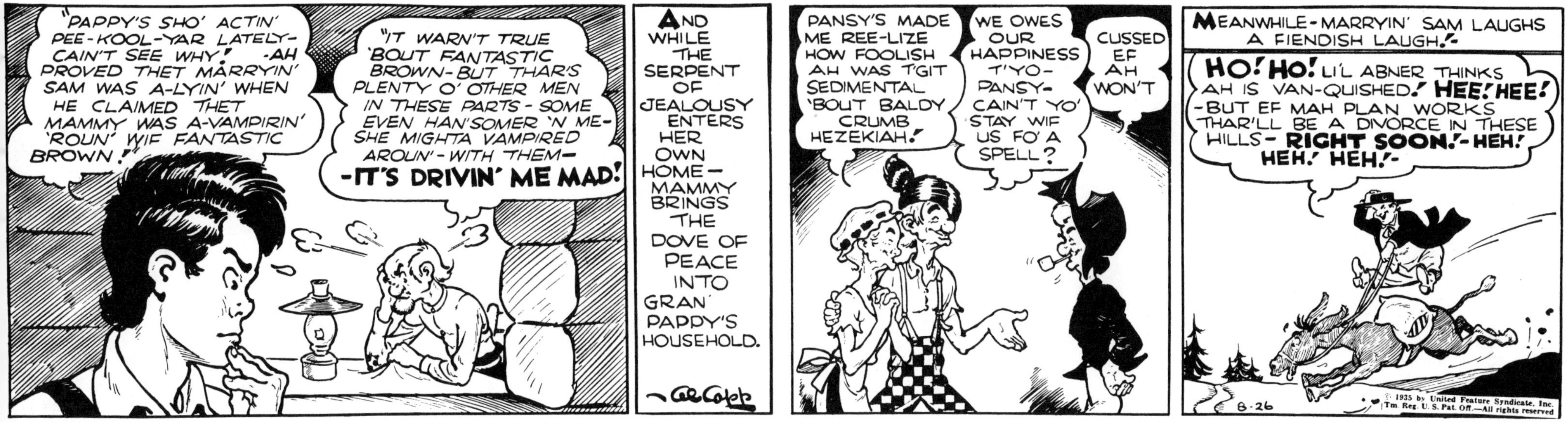

"PAPPY'S SHO' ACTIN' PEE-KOOL-YAR LATELY- CAIN'T SEE WHY! -AH PROVED THET MARRYIN' SAM WAS A-LYIN' WHEN HE CLAIMED THET MAMMY WAS A-VAMPIRIN' 'ROUN' WIF FANTASTIC BROWN!"
"IT WARN'T TRUE 'BOUT FANTASTIC BROWN-BUT THAR'S PLENTY O' OTHER MEN IN THESE PARTS - SOME EVEN HAN'SOMER 'N ME- SHE MIGHTA VAMPIRED AROUN'-WITH THEM-
-IT'S DRIVIN' ME MAD!
AND WHILE THE SERPENT OF JEALOUSY ENTERS HER OWN HOME-MAMMY BRINGS THE DOVE OF PEACE INTO GRAN' PAPPY'S HOUSEHOLD.
AL CAPP
PANSY'S MADE ME REE-LIZE HOW FOOLISH AH WAS T'GIT SEDIMENTAL 'BOUT BALDY CRUMB HEZEKIAH!
WE OWES OUR HAPPINESS T'YO-PANSY- CAIN'T YO' STAY WIF US FO'A SPELL?
CUSSED EF AH WON'T
MEANWHILE-MARRYIN' SAM LAUGHS A FIENDISH LAUGH!-
HO! HO! LI'L ABNER THINKS AH IS VAN-QUISHED! HEE! HEE! -BUT EF MAH PLAN WORKS THAR'LL BE A DIVORCE IN THESE HILLS- RIGHT SOON!-HEH! HEH! HEH!-
8-26
© 1935 by United Feature Syndicate, Inc. Tm Reg. U. S. Pat. Off.—All rights reserved

LI'L ABNER A Broken Blossom By Al Capp

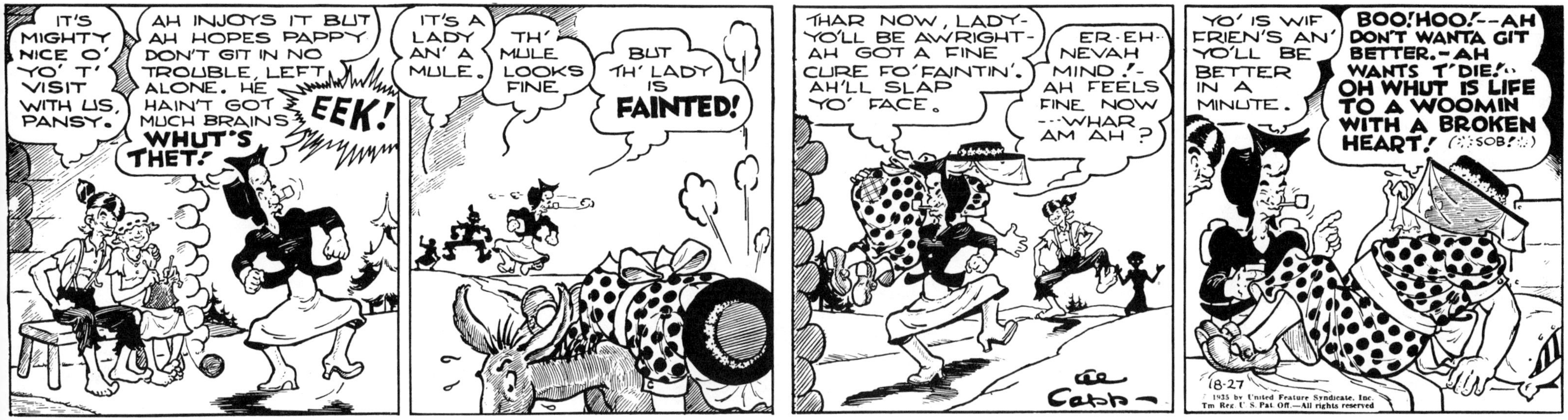

IT'S MIGHTY NICE O' YO' T' VISIT WITH US, PANSY.
AH INJOYS IT BUT AH HOPES PAPPY DON'T GIT IN NO TROUBLE, LEFT ALONE. HE HAIN'T GOT MUCH BRAINS
EEK!
WHUT'S THET!
IT'S A LADY AN' A MULE.
TH' MULE LOOKS FINE
BUT TH' LADY IS FAINTED!
THAR NOW, LADY- YO'LL BE AWRIGHT- AH GOT A FINE CURE FO' FAINTIN'. AH'LL SLAP YO' FACE.
ER-EH- NEVAH MIND!- AH FEELS FINE NOW ---WHAR AM AH?
AL CAPP
YO' IS WIF FRIEN'S AN' YO'LL BE BETTER IN A MINUTE.
BOO! HOO!--AH DON'T WANTA GIT BETTER.-AH WANTS T'DIE!- OH WHUT IS LIFE TO A WOOMIN WITH A BROKEN HEART! (SOB!)
8-27
© 1935 by United Feature Syndicate, Inc. Tm Reg. U. S. Pat. Off.—All rights reserved

LI'L ABNER The Man In the Case By Al Capp

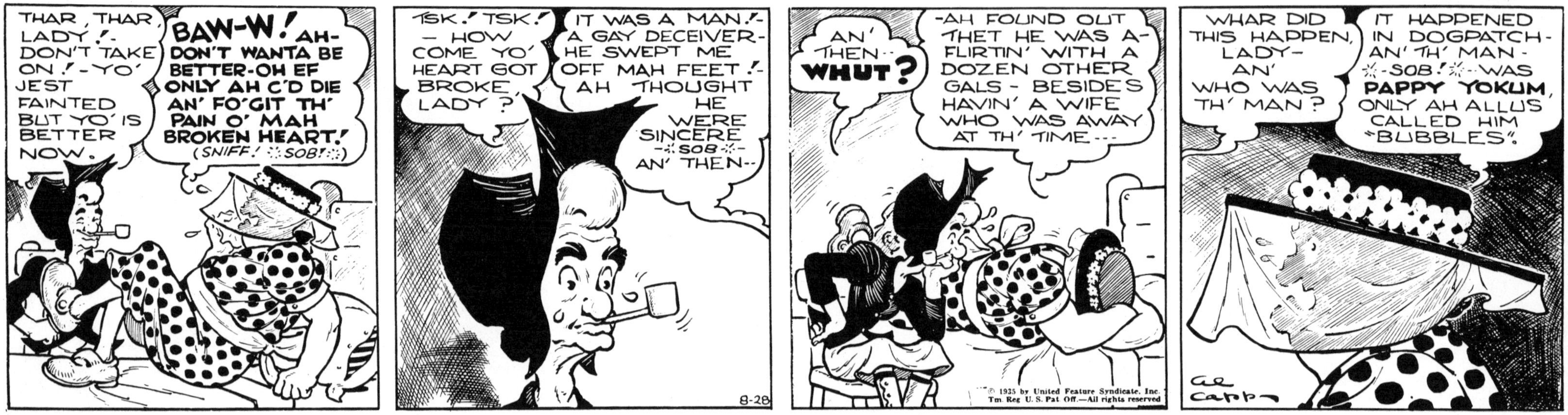

THAR, THAR, LADY!- DON'T TAKE ON!-YO' JEST FAINTED BUT YO'IS BETTER NOW.
BAW-W! AH- DON'T WANTA BE BETTER-OH EF ONLY AH C'D DIE AN' FO'GIT TH' PAIN O' MAH BROKEN HEART! (SNIFF! SOB!)
TSK! TSK! — HOW COME YO' HEART GOT BROKE, LADY?
IT WAS A MAN!- A GAY DECEIVER- HE SWEPT ME OFF MAH FEET!- AH THOUGHT HE WERE SINCERE -SOB- AN' THEN--
8-28
AN' THEN-- WHUT?
-AH FOUND OUT THET HE WAS A-FLIRTIN' WITH A DOZEN OTHER GALS - BESIDES HAVIN' A WIFE WHO WAS AWAY AT TH' TIME---
© 1935 by United Feature Syndicate, Inc. Tm. Reg. U.S. Pat. Off.—All rights reserved
WHAR DID THIS HAPPEN, LADY- AN' WHO WAS TH' MAN?
IT HAPPENED IN DOGPATCH- AN' TH' MAN- -SOB!- WAS PAPPY YOKUM, ONLY AH ALLUS CALLED HIM "BUBBLES".
Al Capp

LI'L ABNER Try, Try Again By Al Capp

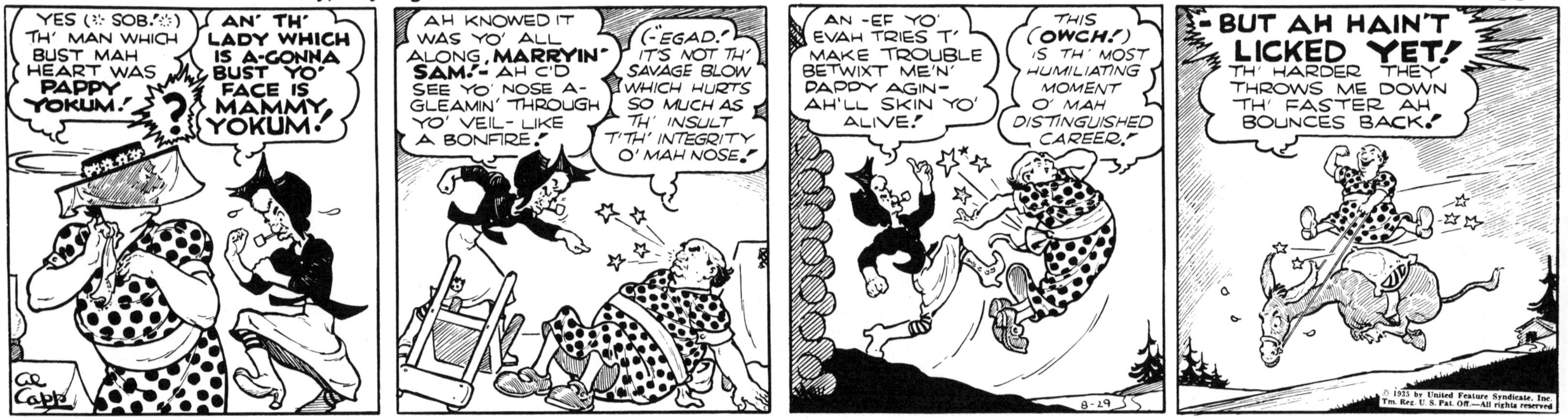

YES (SOB!) TH' MAN WHICH BUST MAH HEART WAS PAPPY YOKUM!
?
AN' TH' LADY WHICH IS A-GONNA BUST YO' FACE IS MAMMY YOKUM!
Al Capp
AH KNOWED IT WAS YO' ALL ALONG, MARRYIN' SAM!- AH C'D SEE YO' NOSE A-GLEAMIN' THROUGH YO' VEIL- LIKE A BONFIRE!
(-EGAD!- IT'S NOT TH' SAVAGE BLOW WHICH HURTS SO MUCH AS TH' INSULT T'TH' INTEGRITY O' MAH NOSE!
AN -EF YO' EVAH TRIES T' MAKE TROUBLE BETWIXT ME'N' PAPPY AGIN- AH'LL SKIN YO' ALIVE!
THIS (OWCH!) IS TH' MOST HUMILIATING MOMENT O' MAH DISTINGUISHED CAREER!
8-29
-BUT AH HAIN'T LICKED YET! TH' HARDER THEY THROWS ME DOWN TH' FASTER AH BOUNCES BACK!
© 1935 by United Feature Syndicate, Inc. Tm. Reg. U.S. Pat. Off.—All rights reserved

LI'L ABNER Comforting Words **By Al Capp**

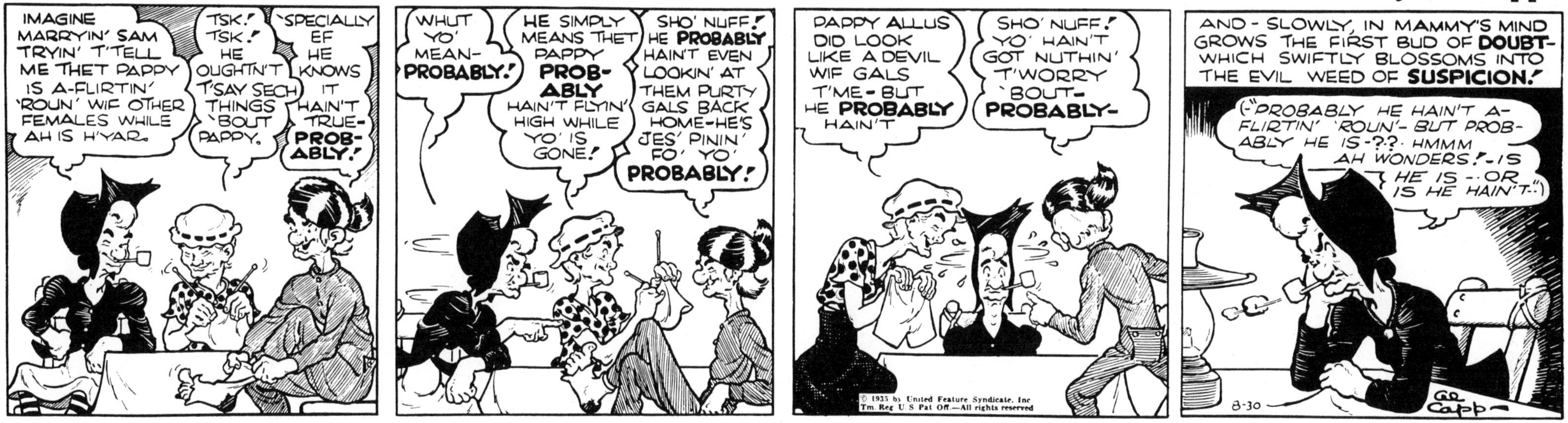
IMAGINE MARRYIN' SAM TRYIN' T'TELL ME THET PAPPY IS A-FLIRTIN' 'ROUN' WIF OTHER FEMALES WHILE AH IS H'YAR.
TSK! TSK! HE OUGHTN'T T'SAY SECH THINGS 'BOUT PAPPY.
'SPECIALLY EF HE KNOWS IT HAIN'T TRUE- PROB-ABLY!
WHUT YO' MEAN- PROBABLY!
HE SIMPLY MEANS THET PAPPY PROB-ABLY HAIN'T FLYIN' HIGH WHILE YO' IS GONE!
SHO' NUFF! HE PROBABLY HAIN'T EVEN LOOKIN' AT THEM PURTY GALS BACK HOME-HE'S JES' PININ' FO' YO' PROBABLY!
PAPPY ALLUS DID LOOK LIKE A DEVIL WIF GALS T'ME-BUT HE PROBABLY HAIN'T
SHO' NUFF! YO' HAIN'T GOT NUTHIN' T'WORRY 'BOUT- PROBABLY-
© 1935 by United Feature Syndicate, Inc. Tm. Reg. U.S. Pat. Off.—All rights reserved
AND-SLOWLY, IN MAMMY'S MIND GROWS THE FIRST BUD OF DOUBT- WHICH SWIFTLY BLOSSOMS INTO THE EVIL WEED OF SUSPICION!
(-"PROBABLY HE HAIN'T A-FLIRTIN' 'ROUN'- BUT PROB-ABLY HE IS-??- HMMM AH WONDERS!-IS HE IS --OR IS HE HAIN'T-")
8-30
Al Capp

LI'L ABNER Looks Good For Sam **By Al Capp**

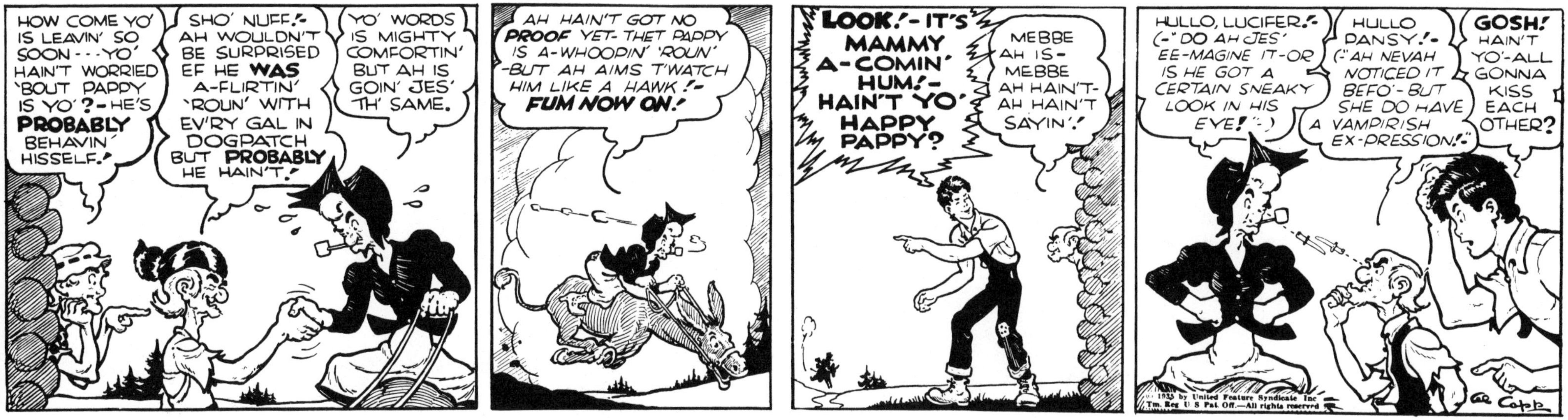
HOW COME YO' IS LEAVIN' SO SOON---YO' HAIN'T WORRIED 'BOUT PAPPY IS YO'?-HE'S PROBABLY BEHAVIN' HISSELF!
SHO' NUFF!- AH WOULDN'T BE SURPRISED EF HE WAS A-FLIRTIN' 'ROUN' WITH EV'RY GAL IN DOGPATCH BUT PROBABLY HE HAIN'T!
YO' WORDS IS MIGHTY COMFORTIN' BUT AH IS GOIN' JES' TH' SAME.
AH HAIN'T GOT NO PROOF YET- THET PAPPY IS A-WHOOPIN' 'ROUN' -BUT AH AIMS T'WATCH HIM LIKE A HAWK!- FUM NOW ON!
LOOK!-IT'S MAMMY A-COMIN' HUM!- HAIN'T YO' HAPPY PAPPY?
MEBBE AH IS- MEBBE AH HAIN'T- AH HAIN'T SAYIN'!
© 1935 by United Feature Syndicate, Inc. Tm. Reg. U.S. Pat. Off.—All rights reserved
HULLO, LUCIFER!- (-"DO AH JES' EE-MAGINE IT-OR IS HE GOT A CERTAIN SNEAKY LOOK IN HIS EYE!"-)
HULLO DANSY!- (-"AH NEVAH NOTICED IT BEFO'-BUT SHE DO HAVE A VAMPIRISH EX-PRESSION!"-)
GOSH! HAIN'T YO'-ALL GONNA KISS EACH OTHER?
Al Capp

LI'L ABNER Sam Speeds 'Em Up By Al Capp

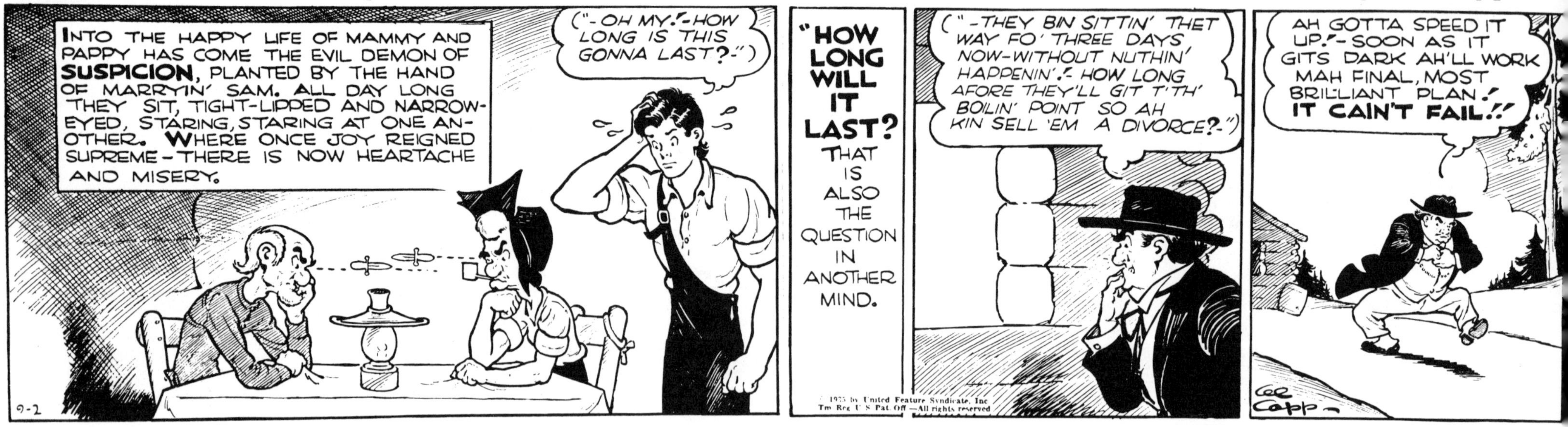
INTO THE HAPPY LIFE OF MAMMY AND PAPPY HAS COME THE EVIL DEMON OF SUSPICION, PLANTED BY THE HAND OF MARRYIN' SAM. ALL DAY LONG THEY SIT, TIGHT-LIPPED AND NARROW-EYED, STARING, STARING AT ONE ANOTHER. WHERE ONCE JOY REIGNED SUPREME – THERE IS NOW HEARTACHE AND MISERY.
("–OH MY!–HOW LONG IS THIS GONNA LAST?–")
9-2
"HOW LONG WILL IT LAST? THAT IS ALSO THE QUESTION IN ANOTHER MIND.
("–THEY BIN SITTIN' THET WAY FO' THREE DAYS NOW–WITHOUT NUTHIN' HAPPENIN'.!–HOW LONG AFORE THEY'LL GIT T'TH' BOILIN' POINT SO AH KIN SELL 'EM A DIVORCE?–")
© 1935 by United Feature Syndicate, Inc. Tm Reg U S Pat. Off —All rights reserved
AH GOTTA SPEED IT UP.!–SOON AS IT GITS DARK AH'LL WORK MAH FINAL, MOST BRILLIANT PLAN.! IT CAIN'T FAIL.!!
Al Capp

LI'L ABNER The Other Woman By Al Capp

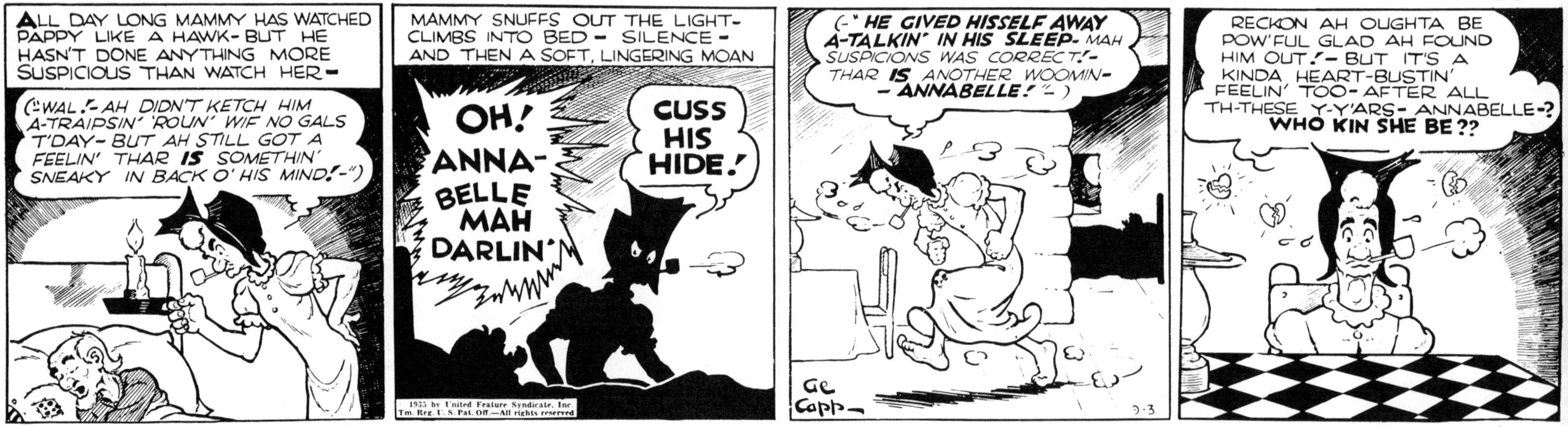
ALL DAY LONG MAMMY HAS WATCHED PAPPY LIKE A HAWK – BUT HE HASN'T DONE ANYTHING MORE SUSPICIOUS THAN WATCH HER –
("–WAL.!–AH DIDN'T KETCH HIM A-TRAIPSIN' 'ROUN' WIF NO GALS T'DAY – BUT AH STILL GOT A FEELIN' THAR IS SOMETHIN' SNEAKY IN BACK O' HIS MIND!–")
MAMMY SNUFFS OUT THE LIGHT – CLIMBS INTO BED – SILENCE – AND THEN A SOFT, LINGERING MOAN
OH! ANNA-BELLE MAH DARLIN'
CUSS HIS HIDE!
© 1935 by United Feature Syndicate, Inc. Tm. Reg. U. S. Pat. Off.—All rights reserved
(–"HE GIVED HISSELF AWAY A-TALKIN' IN HIS SLEEP – MAH SUSPICIONS WAS CORRECT!– THAR IS ANOTHER WOOMIN – ANNABELLE!"–)
Al Capp
9-3
RECKON AH OUGHTA BE POW'FUL GLAD AH FOUND HIM OUT.!– BUT IT'S A KINDA HEART-BUSTIN' FEELIN' TOO – AFTER ALL TH-THESE Y-Y'ARS – ANNABELLE–? WHO KIN SHE BE??

LI'L ABNER Don't Do It, Mammy! By Al Capp

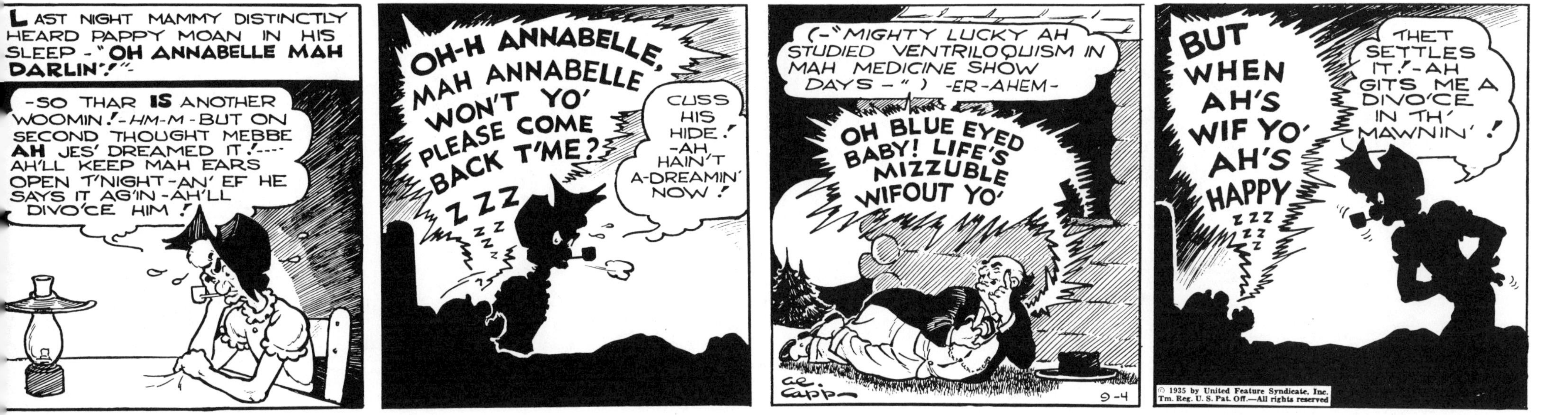

LAST NIGHT MAMMY DISTINCTLY HEARD PAPPY MOAN IN HIS SLEEP -"OH ANNABELLE MAH DARLIN'!"-
-SO THAR IS ANOTHER WOOMIN!-HM-M-BUT ON SECOND THOUGHT MEBBE AH JES' DREAMED IT!---- AH'LL KEEP MAH EARS OPEN T'NIGHT-AN' EF HE SAYS IT AG'IN-AH'LL DIVO'CE HIM!
OH-H ANNABELLE, MAH ANNABELLE WON'T YO' PLEASE COME BACK T'ME?
ZZZ
CUSS HIS HIDE! -AH HAIN'T A-DREAMIN' NOW!
(-"MIGHTY LUCKY AH STUDIED VENTRILOQUISM IN MAH MEDICINE SHOW DAYS-") -ER-AHEM-
OH BLUE EYED BABY! LIFE'S MIZZUBLE WIFOUT YO'
AL CAPP
9-4
BUT WHEN AH'S WIF YO' AH'S HAPPY
ZZZ
THET SETTLES IT!-AH GITS ME A DIVO'CE IN TH' MAWNIN'!
© 1935 by United Feature Syndicate, Inc. Tm. Reg. U. S. Pat. Off.—All rights reserved

LI'L ABNER Fare-Thee-Well Annabelle By Al Capp

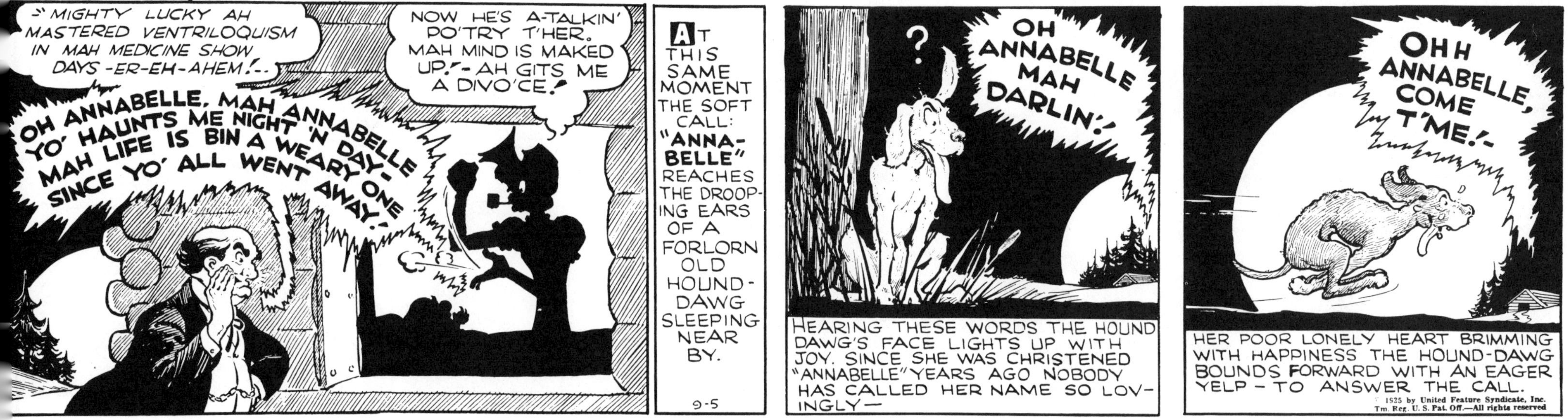

-"MIGHTY LUCKY AH MASTERED VENTRILOQUISM IN MAH MEDICINE SHOW DAYS-ER-EH-AHEM!-
OH ANNABELLE, MAH ANNABELLE YO' HAUNTS ME NIGHT 'N DAY- MAH LIFE IS BIN A WEARY ONE SINCE YO' ALL WENT AWAY!
NOW HE'S A-TALKIN' PO'TRY T'HER. MAH MIND IS MAKED UP!-AH GITS ME A DIVO'CE!
AT THIS SAME MOMENT THE SOFT CALL: "ANNA-BELLE" REACHES THE DROOPING EARS OF A FORLORN OLD HOUND-DAWG SLEEPING NEAR BY.
9-5
?
OH ANNABELLE MAH DARLIN'!
HEARING THESE WORDS THE HOUND DAWG'S FACE LIGHTS UP WITH JOY. SINCE SHE WAS CHRISTENED "ANNABELLE" YEARS AGO NOBODY HAS CALLED HER NAME SO LOVINGLY—
OHH ANNABELLE, COME T'ME!-
HER POOR LONELY HEART BRIMMING WITH HAPPINESS THE HOUND-DAWG BOUNDS FORWARD WITH AN EAGER YELP - TO ANSWER THE CALL.
© 1935 by United Feature Syndicate, Inc. Tm. Reg. U. S. Pat. Off.—All rights reserved

LI'L ABNER A Villain of the Old School By Al Capp

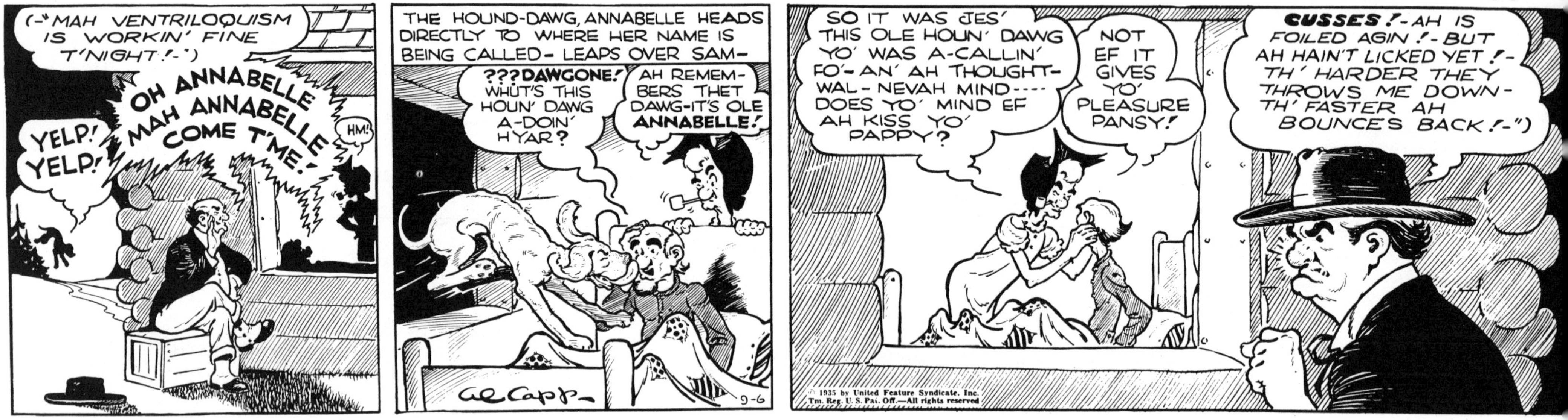
(-"MAH VENTRILOQUISM IS WORKIN' FINE T'NIGHT!-")
YELP! YELP!
OH ANNABELLE MAH ANNABELLE COME T'ME!
HM!
THE HOUND-DAWG, ANNABELLE HEADS DIRECTLY TO WHERE HER NAME IS BEING CALLED- LEAPS OVER SAM-
???DAWGONE! WHUT'S THIS HOUN' DAWG A-DOIN' HYAR?
AH REMEMBERS THET DAWG-IT'S OLE ANNABELLE!
9-6
SO IT WAS JES' THIS OLE HOUN' DAWG YO' WAS A-CALLIN' FO'- AN' AH THOUGHT- WAL- NEVAH MIND---- DOES YO' MIND EF AH KISS YO' PAPPY?
NOT EF IT GIVES YO' PLEASURE PANSY!
© 1935 by United Feature Syndicate, Inc. Tm. Reg. U. S. Pat. Off.—All rights reserved
CUSSES!-AH IS FOILED AGIN!-BUT AH HAIN'T LICKED YET!- TH' HARDER THEY THROWS ME DOWN- TH' FASTER AH BOUNCES BACK!-")

LI'L ABNER The Snake Again By Al Capp

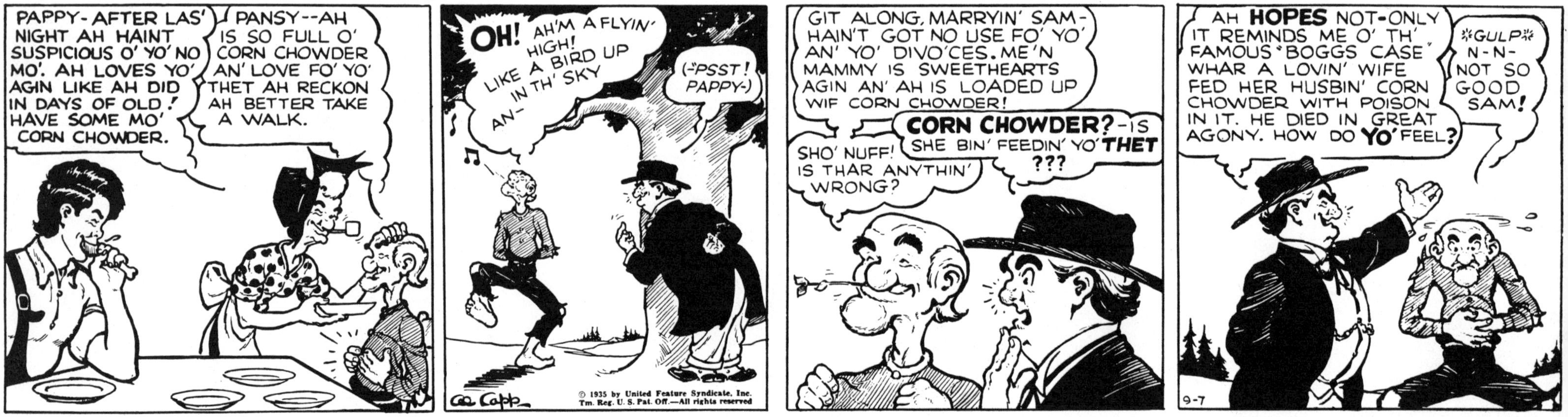
PAPPY- AFTER LAS' NIGHT AH HAINT SUSPICIOUS O' YO' NO MO'. AH LOVES YO' AGIN LIKE AH DID IN DAYS OF OLD! HAVE SOME MO' CORN CHOWDER.
PANSY--AH IS SO FULL O' CORN CHOWDER AN' LOVE FO' YO' THET AH RECKON AH BETTER TAKE A WALK.
OH! AH'M A FLYIN' HIGH! LIKE A BIRD UP IN TH' SKY AN-
(-"PSST! PAPPY-)
© 1935 by United Feature Syndicate, Inc. Tm. Reg. U. S. Pat. Off.—All rights reserved
GIT ALONG, MARRYIN' SAM- HAIN'T GOT NO USE FO' YO' AN' YO' DIVO'CES. ME'N MAMMY IS SWEETHEARTS AGIN AN' AH IS LOADED UP WIF CORN CHOWDER!
CORN CHOWDER?-IS SHE BIN' FEEDIN' YO' THET ???
SHO' NUFF! IS THAR ANYTHIN' WRONG?
AH HOPES NOT-ONLY IT REMINDS ME O' TH' FAMOUS "BOGGS CASE" WHAR A LOVIN' WIFE FED HER HUSBIN' CORN CHOWDER WITH POISON IN IT. HE DIED IN GREAT AGONY. HOW DO YO' FEEL?
GULP N-N-NOT SO GOOD SAM!
9-7

LI'L ABNER A Horrible Example By Al Capp

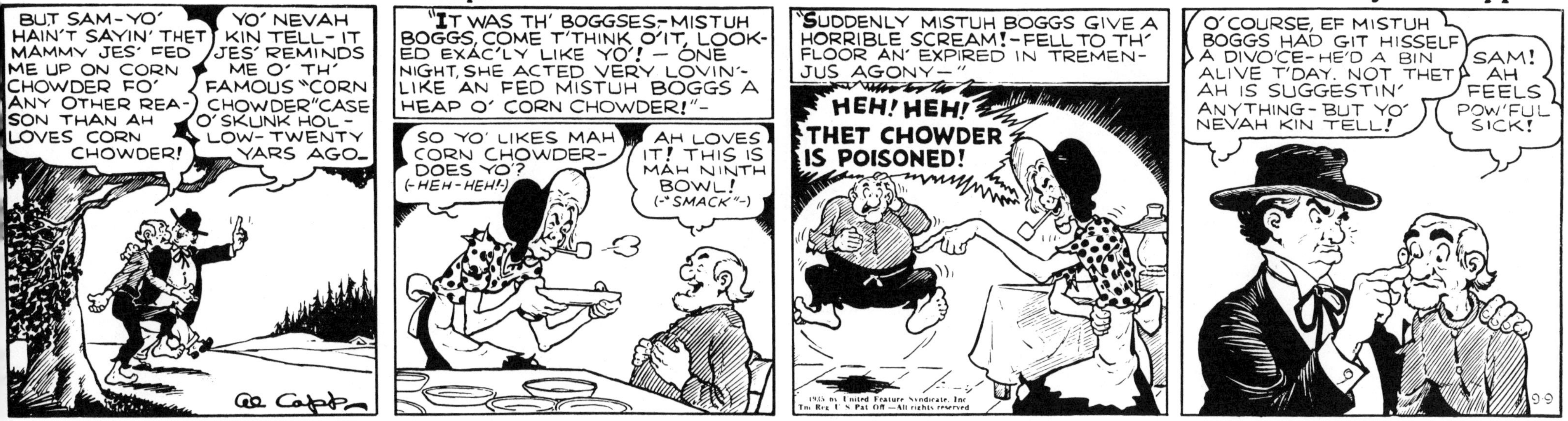

BUT SAM-YO' HAIN'T SAYIN' THET MAMMY JES' FED ME UP ON CORN CHOWDER FO' ANY OTHER REASON THAN AH LOVES CORN CHOWDER!
YO' NEVAH KIN TELL-IT JES' REMINDS ME O' TH' FAMOUS "CORN CHOWDER" CASE O' SKUNK HOLLOW-TWENTY YARS AGO-
Al Capp
"IT WAS TH' BOGGSES-MISTUH BOGGS, COME T'THINK O'IT, LOOKED EXAC'LY LIKE YO'! - ONE NIGHT, SHE ACTED VERY LOVIN'-LIKE AN FED MISTUH BOGGS A HEAP O' CORN CHOWDER!"-
SO YO' LIKES MAH CORN CHOWDER-DOES YO'? (-HEH-HEH!-)
AH LOVES IT! THIS IS MAH NINTH BOWL! (-"SMACK"-)
"SUDDENLY MISTUH BOGGS GIVE A HORRIBLE SCREAM!-FELL TO TH' FLOOR AN' EXPIRED IN TREMENJUS AGONY-"
HEH! HEH! THET CHOWDER IS POISONED!
1935 by United Feature Syndicate, Inc Tm Reg U S Pat Off—All rights reserved
O' COURSE, EF MISTUH BOGGS HAD GIT HISSELF A DIVO'CE-HE'D A BIN ALIVE T'DAY. NOT THET AH IS SUGGESTIN' ANYTHING-BUT YO' NEVAH KIN TELL!
SAM! AH FEELS POW'FUL SICK!
9-9

LI'L ABNER What's In the Chowder? By Al Capp

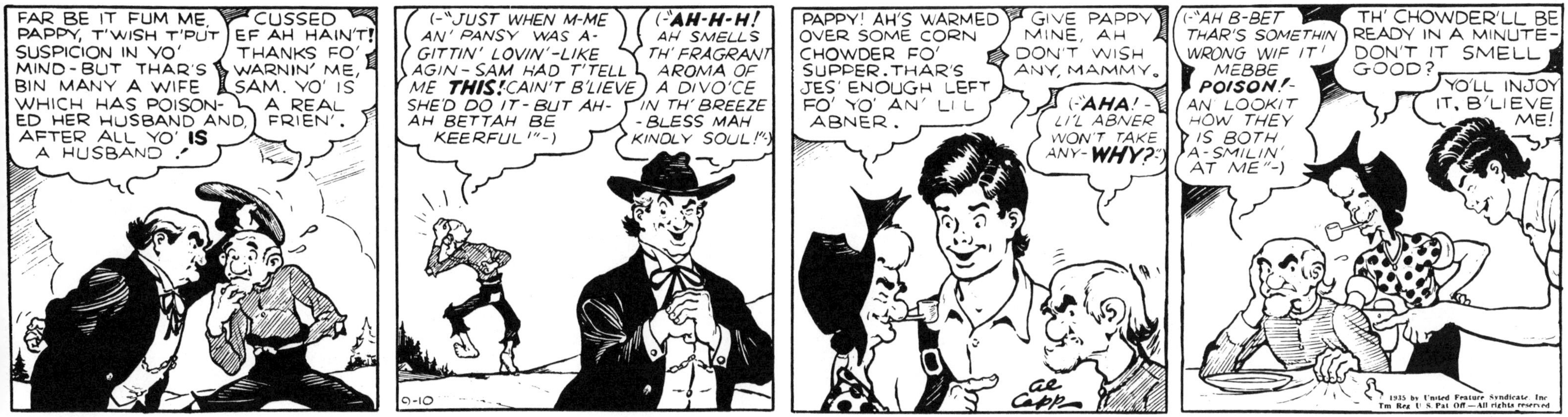

FAR BE IT FUM ME, PAPPY, T'WISH T'PUT SUSPICION IN YO' MIND-BUT THAR'S BIN MANY A WIFE WHICH HAS POISONED HER HUSBAND AND, AFTER ALL YO' IS A HUSBAND!
CUSSED EF AH HAIN'T! THANKS FO' WARNIN' ME, SAM. YO' IS A REAL FRIEN'.
(-"JUST WHEN M-ME AN' PANSY WAS A-GITTIN' LOVIN'-LIKE AGIN-SAM HAD T'TELL ME THIS! CAIN'T B'LIEVE SHE'D DO IT-BUT AH-AH BETTAH BE KEERFUL!"-)
(-"AH-H-H! AH SMELLS TH' FRAGRANT AROMA OF A DIVO'CE IN TH' BREEZE-BLESS MAH KINDLY SOUL!"-)
9-10
PAPPY! AH'S WARMED OVER SOME CORN CHOWDER FO' SUPPER. THAR'S JES' ENOUGH LEFT FO' YO' AN' LI'L ABNER.
GIVE PAPPY MINE, AH DON'T WISH ANY, MAMMY.
(-"AHA!-LI'L ABNER WON'T TAKE ANY-WHY?"-)
Al Capp
(-"AH B-BET THAR'S SOMETHIN WRONG WIF IT! MEBBE POISON!-AN' LOOKIT HOW THEY IS BOTH A-SMILIN' AT ME"-)
TH' CHOWDER'LL BE READY IN A MINUTE-DON'T IT SMELL GOOD?
YO'LL INJOY IT, B'LIEVE ME!
1935 by United Feature Syndicate, Inc Tm Reg U.S. Pat Off—All rights reserved

LI'L ABNER Pappy's Scream Test **By Al Capp**

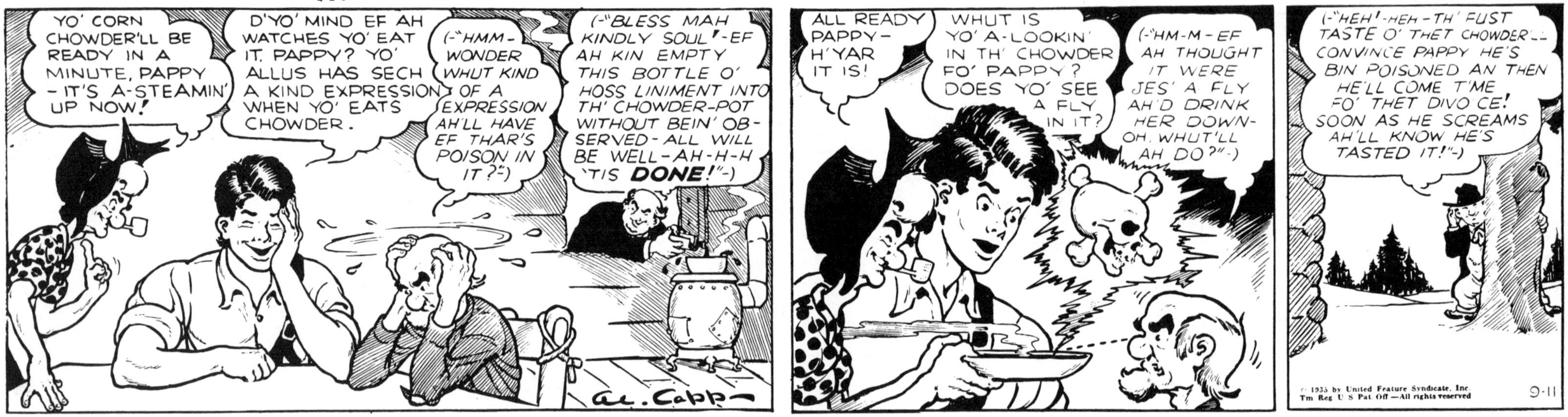

YO' CORN CHOWDER'LL BE READY IN A MINUTE, PAPPY - IT'S A-STEAMIN' UP NOW!
D'YO' MIND EF AH WATCHES YO' EAT IT, PAPPY? YO' ALLUS HAS SECH A KIND EXPRESSION WHEN YO' EATS CHOWDER.
(-"HMM - WONDER WHUT KIND OF A EXPRESSION AH'LL HAVE EF THAR'S POISON IN IT?"-)
(-"BLESS MAH KINDLY SOUL'-EF AH KIN EMPTY THIS BOTTLE O' HOSS LINIMENT INTO TH' CHOWDER-POT WITHOUT BEIN' OB-SERVED - ALL WILL BE WELL-AH-H-H 'TIS DONE!"-)
Al Capp
ALL READY PAPPY - H'YAR IT IS!
WHUT IS YO' A-LOOKIN' IN TH' CHOWDER FO' PAPPY? DOES YO' SEE A FLY IN IT?
(-"HM-M-EF AH THOUGHT IT WERE JES' A FLY AH'D DRINK HER DOWN - OH, WHUT'LL AH DO?"-)
(-"HEH'-HEH-TH' FUST TASTE O' THET CHOWDER-- CONVINCE PAPPY HE'S BIN POISONED AN THEN HE'LL COME T'ME FO' THET DIVO'CE! SOON AS HE SCREAMS AH'LL KNOW HE'S TASTED IT!"-)
© 1935 by United Feature Syndicate, Inc. Tm Reg U S Pat Off —All rights reserved
9-11

LI'L ABNER The Fatal Chowder **By Al Capp**

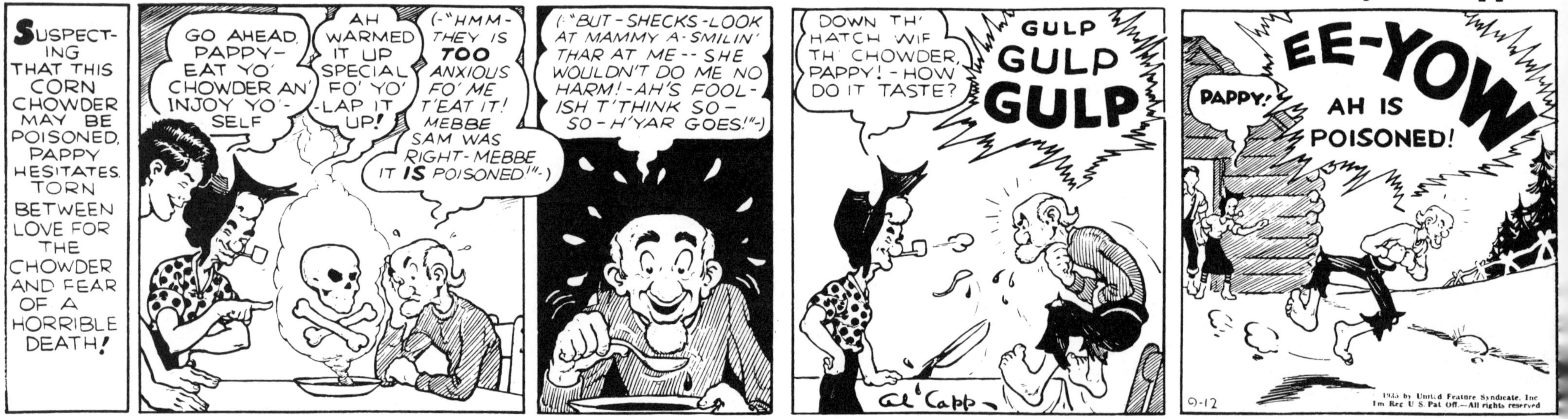

SUSPECTING THAT THIS CORN CHOWDER MAY BE POISONED, PAPPY HESITATES, TORN BETWEEN LOVE FOR THE CHOWDER AND FEAR OF A HORRIBLE DEATH!
GO AHEAD, PAPPY - EAT YO' CHOWDER AN' INJOY YO'-SELF
AH WARMED IT UP SPECIAL FO' YO' - LAP IT UP!
(-"HMM - THEY IS TOO ANXIOUS FO' ME T'EAT IT! MEBBE SAM WAS RIGHT - MEBBE IT IS POISONED!"-)
(-"BUT-SHECKS-LOOK AT MAMMY A-SMILIN' THAR AT ME -- SHE WOULDN'T DO ME NO HARM! - AH'S FOOL-ISH T'THINK SO - SO - H'YAR GOES!"-)
DOWN TH' HATCH WIF TH' CHOWDER, PAPPY! - HOW DO IT TASTE?
GULP
GULP
GULP
Al Capp
PAPPY!
EE-YOW
AH IS POISONED!
9-12
© 1935 by United Feature Syndicate, Inc. Tm Reg U S Pat Off.—All rights reserved

LI'L ABNER A Brainy Decision By Al Capp

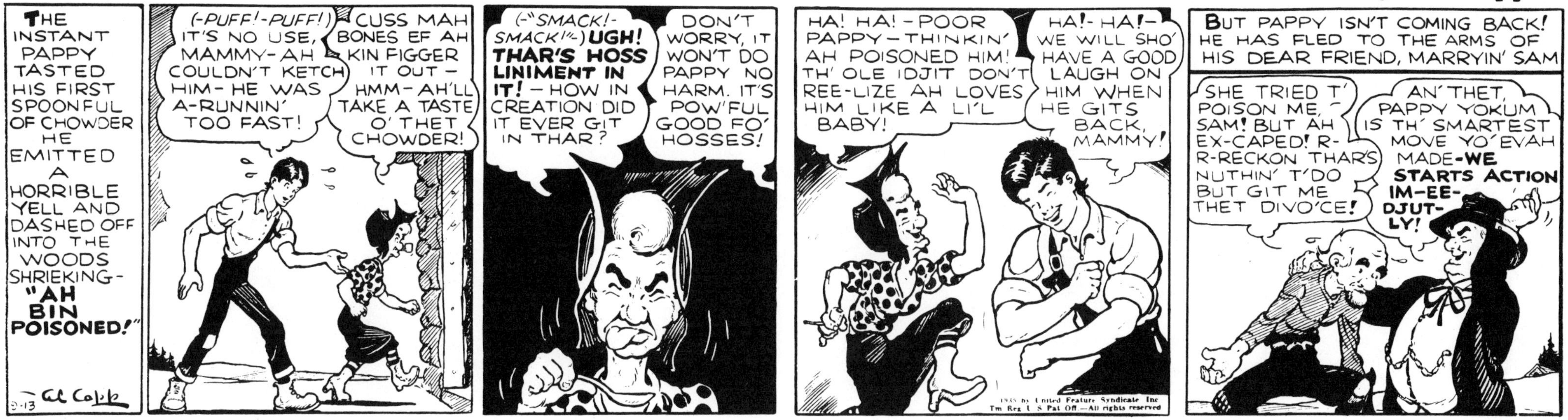
THE INSTANT PAPPY TASTED HIS FIRST SPOONFUL OF CHOWDER HE EMITTED A HORRIBLE YELL AND DASHED OFF INTO THE WOODS SHRIEKING- "AH BIN POISONED!"
9-13
Al Capp
(-PUFF!-PUFF!) IT'S NO USE, MAMMY-AH COULDN'T KETCH HIM- HE WAS A-RUNNIN' TOO FAST!
CUSS MAH BONES EF AH KIN FIGGER IT OUT- HMM-AH'LL TAKE A TASTE O' THET CHOWDER!
(-"SMACK!-SMACK!"-) UGH! THAR'S HOSS LINIMENT IN IT!-HOW IN CREATION DID IT EVER GIT IN THAR?
DON'T WORRY, IT WON'T DO PAPPY NO HARM. IT'S POW'FUL GOOD FO' HOSSES!
HA! HA!-POOR PAPPY-THINKIN' AH POISONED HIM! TH' OLE IDJIT DON'T REE-LIZE AH LOVES HIM LIKE A LI'L BABY!
HA!-HA!-WE WILL SHO' HAVE A GOOD LAUGH ON HIM WHEN HE GITS BACK, MAMMY!
1935 by United Feature Syndicate Inc
Tm Reg U S Pat Off—All rights reserved
BUT PAPPY ISN'T COMING BACK! HE HAS FLED TO THE ARMS OF HIS DEAR FRIEND, MARRYIN' SAM
SHE TRIED T' POISON ME, SAM! BUT AH EX-CAPED! R-R-RECKON THAR'S NUTHIN' T'DO BUT GIT ME THET DIVO'CE!
AN' THET, PAPPY YOKUM IS TH' SMARTEST MOVE YO' EVAH MADE-WE STARTS ACTION IM-EE-DJUT-LY!

LI'L ABNER Anything Can Happen Now By Al Capp

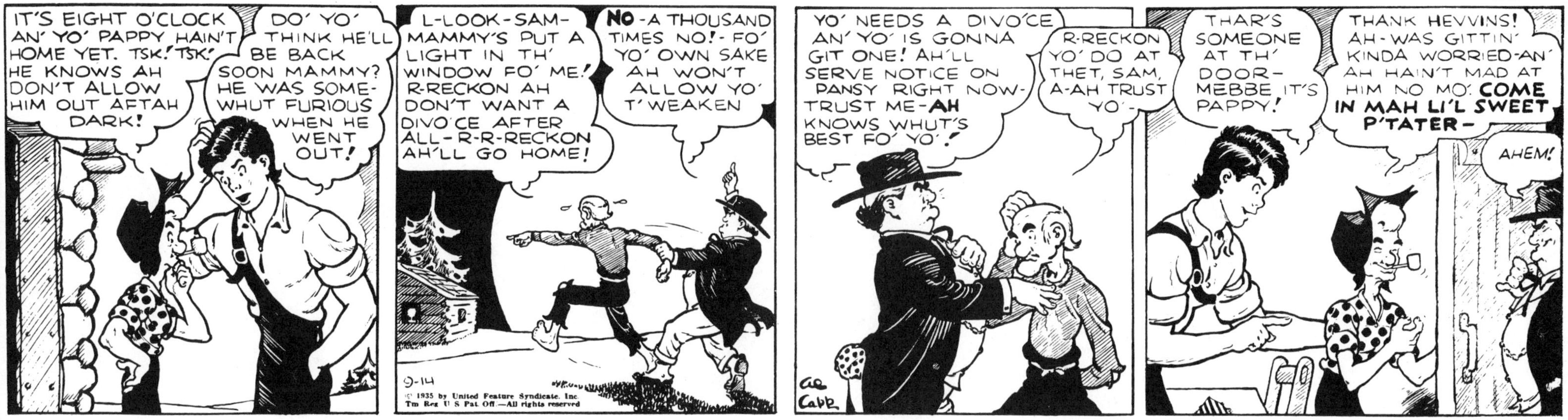
IT'S EIGHT O'CLOCK AN' YO' PAPPY HAIN'T HOME YET. TSK! TSK! HE KNOWS AH DON'T ALLOW HIM OUT AFTAH DARK!
DO' YO' THINK HE'LL BE BACK SOON MAMMY? HE WAS SOME-WHUT FURIOUS WHEN HE WENT OUT!
L-LOOK-SAM-MAMMY'S PUT A LIGHT IN TH' WINDOW FO' ME! R-RECKON AH DON'T WANT A DIVO'CE AFTER ALL-R-R-RECKON AH'LL GO HOME!
NO-A THOUSAND TIMES NO!-FO' YO' OWN SAKE AH WON'T ALLOW YO' T' WEAKEN
9-14
© 1935 by United Feature Syndicate, Inc
Tm Reg U S Pat Off—All rights reserved
YO' NEEDS A DIVO'CE AN' YO' IS GONNA GIT ONE! AH'LL SERVE NOTICE ON PANSY RIGHT NOW-TRUST ME-AH KNOWS WHUT'S BEST FO' YO'!
R-RECKON YO' DO AT THET, SAM, A-AH TRUST YO'-
Al Capp
THAR'S SOMEONE AT TH' DOOR-MEBBE IT'S PAPPY!
THANK HEVVINS! AH-WAS GITTIN' KINDA WORRIED-AN' AH HAIN'T MAD AT HIM NO MO'. COME IN MAH LI'L SWEET P'TATER-
AHEM!

LI'L ABNER Ambassador of Ill Will By Al Capp

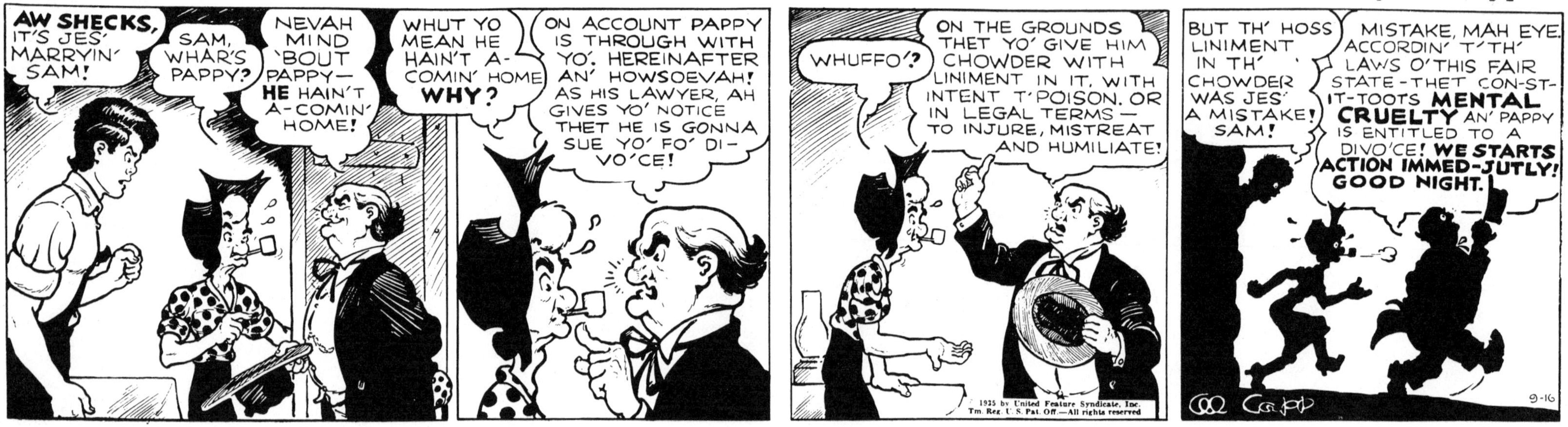
AW SHECKS, IT'S JES' MARRYIN' SAM!
SAM, WHAR'S PAPPY?
NEVAH MIND 'BOUT PAPPY—HE HAIN'T A-COMIN' HOME!
WHUT YO MEAN HE HAIN'T A-COMIN' HOME WHY?
ON ACCOUNT PAPPY IS THROUGH WITH YO'. HEREINAFTER AN' HOWSOEVAH! AS HIS LAWYER, AH GIVES YO' NOTICE THET HE IS GONNA SUE YO' FO' DI-VO'CE!
WHUFFO'?
ON THE GROUNDS THET YO' GIVE HIM CHOWDER WITH LINIMENT IN IT, WITH INTENT T' POISON. OR IN LEGAL TERMS — TO INJURE, MISTREAT AND HUMILIATE!
1935 by United Feature Syndicate, Inc. Tm. Reg. U.S. Pat. Off.—All rights reserved
BUT TH' HOSS LINIMENT IN TH' CHOWDER WAS JES' A MISTAKE! SAM!
MISTAKE, MAH EYE. ACCORDIN' T' TH' LAWS O' THIS FAIR STATE - THET CON-ST-IT-TOOTS MENTAL CRUELTY AN' PAPPY IS ENTITLED TO A DIVO'CE! WE STARTS ACTION IMMED-JUTLY! GOOD NIGHT.
9-16

LI'L ABNER Nobody Loves Pappy By Al Capp

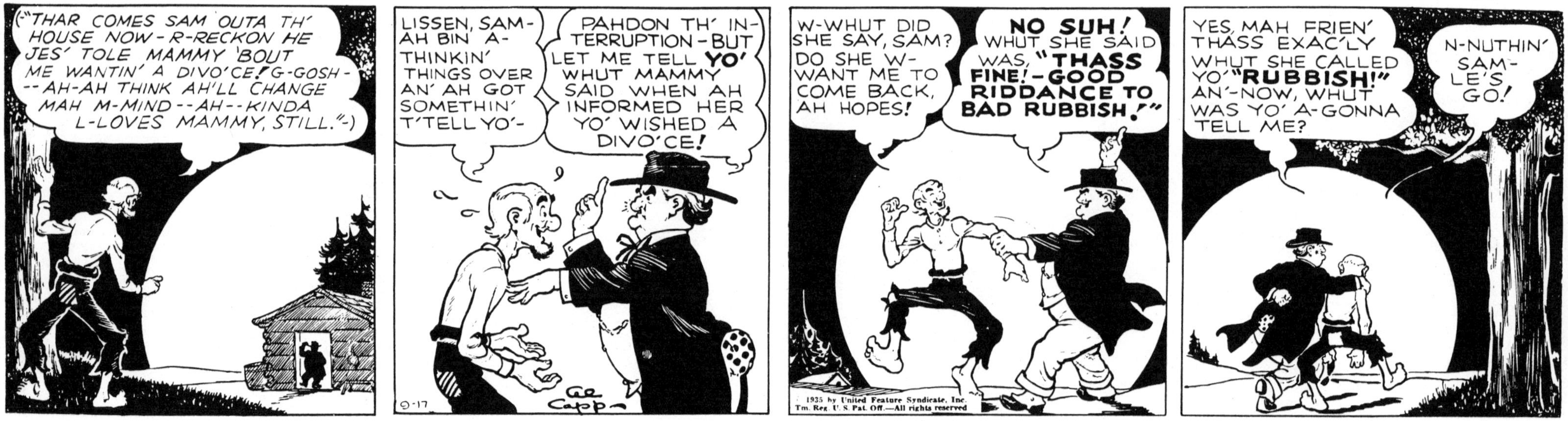
("THAR COMES SAM OUTA TH' HOUSE NOW - R-RECKON HE JES' TOLE MAMMY 'BOUT ME WANTIN' A DIVO'CE! G-GOSH - - AH-AH THINK AH'LL CHANGE MAH M-MIND - - AH - - KINDA L-LOVES MAMMY, STILL." -)
LISSEN, SAM - AH BIN A-THINKIN' THINGS OVER AN' AH GOT SOMETHIN' T' TELL YO' -
PAHDON TH' IN-TERRUPTION - BUT LET ME TELL YO' WHUT MAMMY SAID WHEN AH INFORMED HER YO' WISHED A DIVO'CE!
9-17
W-WHUT DID SHE SAY, SAM? DO SHE W-WANT ME TO COME BACK, AH HOPES!
NO SUH! WHUT SHE SAID WAS, "THASS FINE! - GOOD RIDDANCE TO BAD RUBBISH!"
1935 by United Feature Syndicate, Inc. Tm. Reg. U.S. Pat. Off.—All rights reserved
YES, MAH FRIEN' THASS EXAC'LY WHUT SHE CALLED YO' "RUBBISH!" AN' - NOW, WHUT WAS YO' A-GONNA TELL ME?
N-NUTHIN' SAM - LE'S GO!

LI'L ABNER Pappy Ex-capes By Al Capp

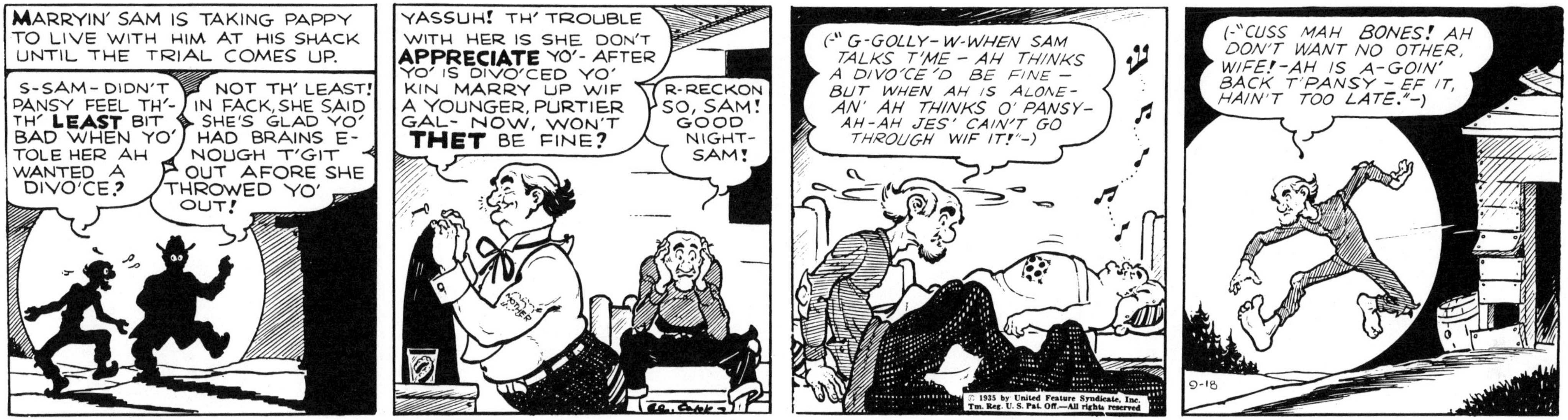
MARRYIN' SAM IS TAKING PAPPY TO LIVE WITH HIM AT HIS SHACK UNTIL THE TRIAL COMES UP.
S-SAM-DIDN'T PANSY FEEL TH'-TH' LEAST BIT BAD WHEN YO' TOLE HER AH WANTED A DIVO'CE?
NOT TH' LEAST! IN FACK, SHE SAID SHE'S GLAD YO' HAD BRAINS E-NOUGH T'GIT OUT AFORE SHE THROWED YO' OUT!
YASSUH! TH' TROUBLE WITH HER IS SHE DON'T APPRECIATE YO'- AFTER YO' IS DIVO'CED YO' KIN MARRY UP WIF A YOUNGER, PURTIER GAL- NOW, WON'T THET BE FINE?
R-RECKON SO, SAM! GOOD NIGHT- SAM!
(-"G-GOLLY-W-WHEN SAM TALKS T'ME - AH THINKS A DIVO'CE'D BE FINE - BUT WHEN AH IS ALONE- AN' AH THINKS O' PANSY- AH-AH JES' CAIN'T GO THROUGH WIF IT!"-)
© 1935 by United Feature Syndicate, Inc. Tm. Reg. U. S. Pat. Off.—All rights reserved
(-"CUSS MAH BONES! AH DON'T WANT NO OTHER, WIFE!-AH IS A-GOIN' BACK T'PANSY - EF IT, HAIN'T TOO LATE."-)
9-18

LI'L ABNER Who's A-knockin' at My Door? By Al Capp

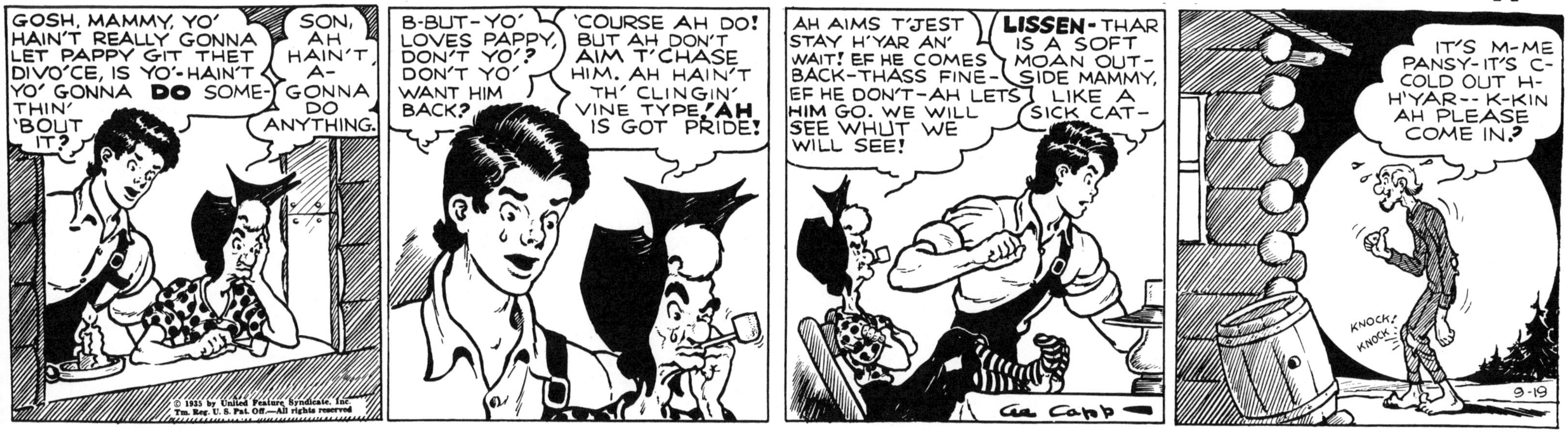
GOSH, MAMMY, YO' HAIN'T REALLY GONNA LET PAPPY GIT THET DIVO'CE, IS YO'-HAIN'T YO' GONNA DO SOME-THIN' 'BOUT IT?
SON, AH HAIN'T, A-GONNA DO ANYTHING.
© 1935 by United Feature Syndicate, Inc. Tm. Reg. U. S. Pat. Off.—All rights reserved
B-BUT-YO' LOVES PAPPY, DON'T YO'? DON'T YO' WANT HIM BACK?
'COURSE AH DO! BUT AH DON'T AIM T'CHASE HIM. AH HAIN'T TH' CLINGIN' VINE TYPE, AH IS GOT PRIDE!
AH AIMS T'JEST STAY H'YAR AN' WAIT! EF HE COMES BACK-THASS FINE-EF HE DON'T-AH LETS HIM GO. WE WILL SEE WHUT WE WILL SEE!
LISSEN-THAR IS A SOFT MOAN OUT-SIDE MAMMY, LIKE A SICK CAT-
IT'S M-ME PANSY-IT'S C-COLD OUT H-H'YAR--K-KIN AH PLEASE COME IN?
KNOCK! KNOCK
9-19

LI'L ABNER Whar Kin Pappy Be? By Al Capp

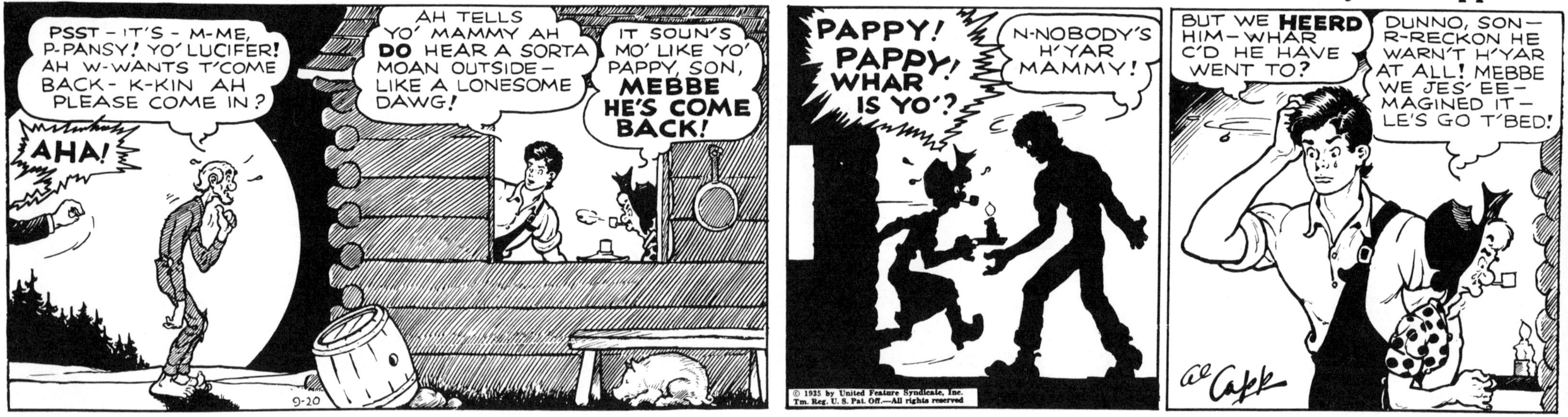

PSST - IT'S - M-ME, P-PANSY! YO' LUCIFER! AH W-WANTS T'COME BACK- K-KIN AH PLEASE COME IN?
AHA!
AH TELLS YO' MAMMY AH DO HEAR A SORTA MOAN OUTSIDE— LIKE A LONESOME DAWG!
IT SOUN'S MO' LIKE YO' PAPPY, SON, MEBBE HE'S COME BACK!
9-20
PAPPY! PAPPY! WHAR IS YO'?
N-NOBODY'S H'YAR MAMMY!
© 1935 by United Feature Syndicate, Inc. Tm. Reg. U. S. Pat. Off.—All rights reserved
BUT WE HEERD HIM—WHAR C'D HE HAVE WENT TO?
DUNNO, SON— R-RECKON HE WARN'T H'YAR AT ALL! MEBBE WE JES' EE-MAGINED IT— LE'S GO T'BED!
Al Capp

LI'L ABNER His Pal to the End By Al Capp

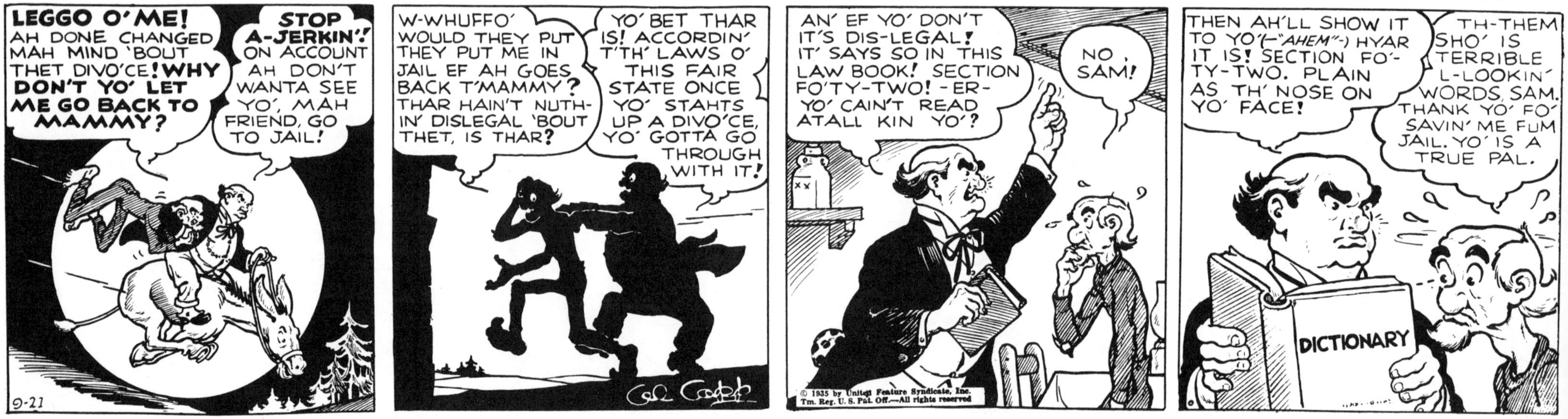

LEGGO O'ME! AH DONE CHANGED MAH MIND 'BOUT THET DIVO'CE! WHY DON'T YO' LET ME GO BACK TO MAMMY?
STOP A-JERKIN'! ON ACCOUNT AH DON'T WANTA SEE YO', MAH FRIEND, GO TO JAIL!
9-21
W-WHUFFO' WOULD THEY PUT THEY PUT ME IN JAIL EF AH GOES BACK T'MAMMY? THAR HAIN'T NUTH-IN' DISLEGAL 'BOUT THET, IS THAR?
YO' BET THAR IS! ACCORDIN' T'TH' LAWS O' THIS FAIR STATE ONCE YO' STAHTS UP A DIVO'CE, YO' GOTTA GO THROUGH WITH IT!
Al Capp
AN' EF YO' DON'T IT'S DIS-LEGAL! IT'S SAYS SO IN THIS LAW BOOK! SECTION FO'TY-TWO! -ER- YO' CAIN'T READ ATALL KIN YO'?
NO, SAM!
© 1935 by United Feature Syndicate, Inc. Tm. Reg. U. S. Pat. Off.—All rights reserved
THEN AH'LL SHOW IT TO YO'(—"AHEM"—) HYAR IT IS! SECTION FO'-TY-TWO. PLAIN AS TH' NOSE ON YO' FACE!
TH-THEM SHO' IS TERRIBLE L-LOOKIN' WORDS, SAM. THANK YO' FO' SAVIN' ME FUM JAIL. YO' IS A TRUE PAL.
DICTIONARY

LI'L ABNER Meet Hairless Joe By Al Capp

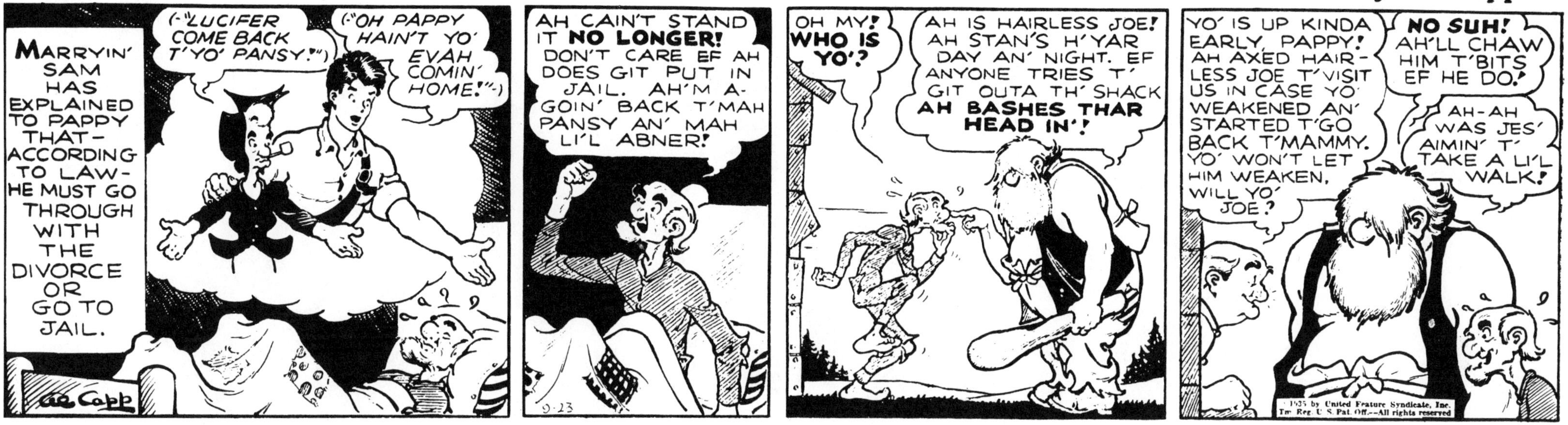

MARRYIN' SAM HAS EXPLAINED TO PAPPY THAT—ACCORDING TO LAW—HE MUST GO THROUGH WITH THE DIVORCE OR GO TO JAIL.
(-"LUCIFER COME BACK T'YO' PANSY!")
(-"OH PAPPY HAIN'T YO' EVAH COMIN' HOME!"-)
AH CAIN'T STAND IT NO LONGER! DON'T CARE EF AH DOES GIT PUT IN JAIL. AH'M A-GOIN' BACK T'MAH PANSY AN' MAH LI'L ABNER!
OH MY! WHO IS YO'?
AH IS HAIRLESS JOE! AH STAN'S H'YAR DAY AN' NIGHT. EF ANYONE TRIES T' GIT OUTA TH' SHACK AH BASHES THAR HEAD IN'!
YO' IS UP KINDA EARLY, PAPPY! AH AXED HAIRLESS JOE T'VISIT US IN CASE YO' WEAKENED AN' STARTED T'GO BACK T'MAMMY. YO' WON'T LET HIM WEAKEN, WILL YO' JOE?
NO SUH! AH'LL CHAW HIM T'BITS EF HE DO!
AH-AH WAS JES' AIMIN' T' TAKE A LI'L WALK!
©1935 by United Feature Syndicate, Inc. Tm Reg. U.S. Pat. Off.—All rights reserved

LI'L ABNER Sam's Ingratitude By Al Capp

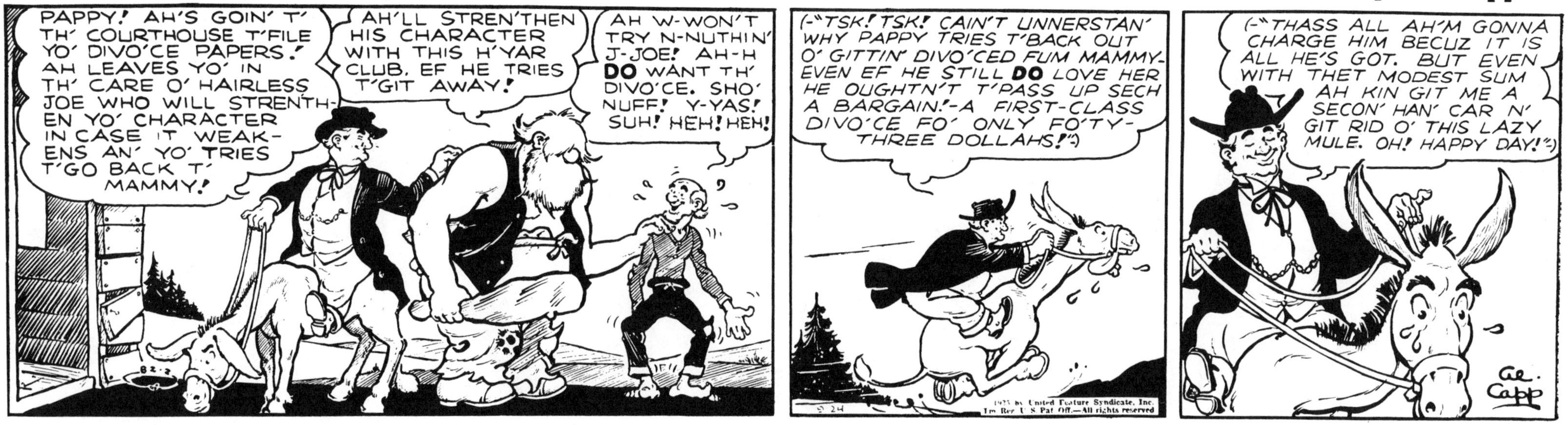

PAPPY! AH'S GOIN' T' TH' COURTHOUSE T'FILE YO' DIVO'CE PAPERS! AH LEAVES YO' IN TH' CARE O' HAIRLESS JOE WHO WILL STRENTHEN YO' CHARACTER IN CASE IT WEAKENS AN' YO' TRIES T'GO BACK T' MAMMY!
AH'LL STREN'THEN HIS CHARACTER WITH THIS H'YAR CLUB, EF HE TRIES T'GIT AWAY!
AH W-WON'T TRY N-NUTHIN' J-JOE! AH-H DO WANT TH' DIVO'CE. SHO' NUFF! Y-YAS! SUH! HEH! HEH!
(-"TSK! TSK! CAIN'T UNNERSTAN' WHY PAPPY TRIES T'BACK OUT O' GITTIN' DIVO'CED FUM MAMMY-EVEN EF HE STILL DO LOVE HER HE OUGHTN'T T'PASS UP SECH A BARGAIN!-A FIRST-CLASS DIVO'CE FO' ONLY FO'TY-THREE DOLLAHS!")
(-"THASS ALL AH'M GONNA CHARGE HIM BECUZ IT IS ALL HE'S GOT. BUT EVEN WITH THET MODEST SUM AH KIN GIT ME A SECON' HAN' CAR N' GIT RID O' THIS LAZY MULE. OH! HAPPY DAY!")
©1935 by United Feature Syndicate, Inc. Tm Reg. U.S. Pat. Off.—All rights reserved

LI'L ABNER — A True-Blue Pal — By Al Capp

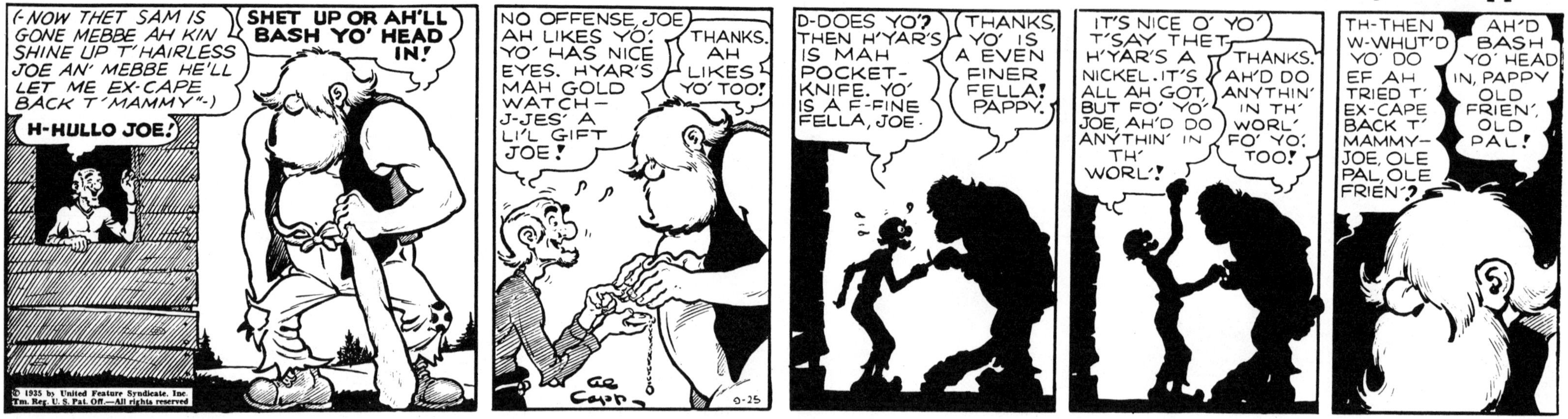

(-NOW THET SAM IS GONE MEBBE AH KIN SHINE UP T'HAIRLESS JOE AN' MEBBE HE'LL LET ME EX-CAPE BACK T'MAMMY"-)
SHET UP OR AH'LL BASH YO' HEAD IN!
H-HULLO JOE!
© 1935 by United Feature Syndicate, Inc. Tm. Reg. U. S. Pat. Off.—All rights reserved
NO OFFENSE, JOE AH LIKES YO'. YO' HAS NICE EYES. HYAR'S MAH GOLD WATCH— J-JES' A LI'L GIFT JOE!
THANKS. AH LIKES YO' TOO!
9-25
D-DOES YO'? THEN H'YAR'S IS MAH POCKET-KNIFE. YO' IS A F-FINE FELLA, JOE.
THANKS, YO' IS A EVEN FINER FELLA! PAPPY.
IT'S NICE O' YO' T'SAY THET. H'YAR'S A NICKEL. IT'S ALL AH GOT, BUT FO' YO' JOE, AH'D DO ANYTHIN' IN TH' WORL'!
THANKS. AH'D DO ANYTHIN' IN TH' WORL' FO' YO', TOO!
TH-THEN W-WHUT'D YO' DO EF AH TRIED T' EX-CAPE BACK T' MAMMY— JOE, OLE PAL, OLE FRIEN'?
AH'D BASH YO' HEAD IN, PAPPY OLD FRIEN', OLD PAL!

LI'L ABNER — Pappy Uses His Brains — By Al Capp

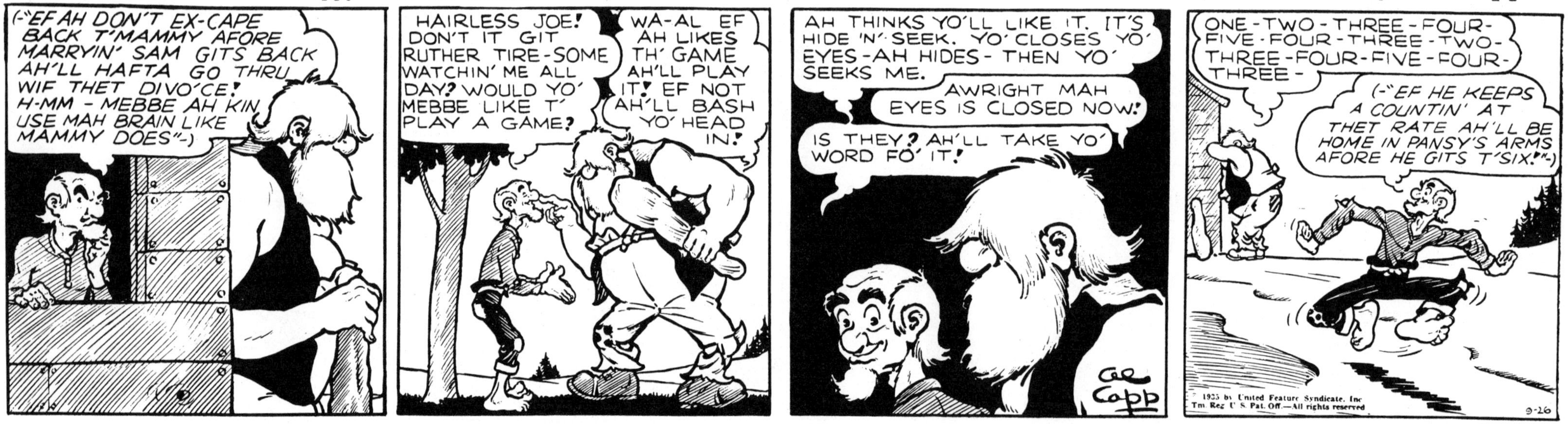

(-"EF AH DON'T EX-CAPE BACK T'MAMMY AFORE MARRYIN' SAM GITS BACK AH'LL HAFTA GO THRU WIF THET DIVO'CE! H-MM - MEBBE AH KIN USE MAH BRAIN LIKE MAMMY DOES"-)
HAIRLESS JOE! DON'T IT GIT RUTHER TIRE-SOME WATCHIN' ME ALL DAY? WOULD YO' MEBBE LIKE T' PLAY A GAME?
WA-AL EF AH LIKES TH' GAME AH'LL PLAY IT! EF NOT AH'LL BASH YO' HEAD IN!
AH THINKS YO'LL LIKE IT. IT'S HIDE 'N' SEEK. YO' CLOSES YO' EYES-AH HIDES- THEN YO' SEEKS ME.
AWRIGHT MAH EYES IS CLOSED NOW!
IS THEY? AH'LL TAKE YO' WORD FO' IT!
ONE-TWO-THREE-FOUR-FIVE-FOUR-THREE-TWO-THREE-FOUR-FIVE-FOUR-THREE-
(-"EF HE KEEPS A COUNTIN' AT THET RATE AH'LL BE HOME IN PANSY'S ARMS AFORE HE GITS T'SIX!"-)
© 1935 by United Feature Syndicate, Inc. Tm. Reg. U. S. Pat. Off.—All rights reserved
9-26

LI'L ABNER An Ambitious Scholar By Al Capp

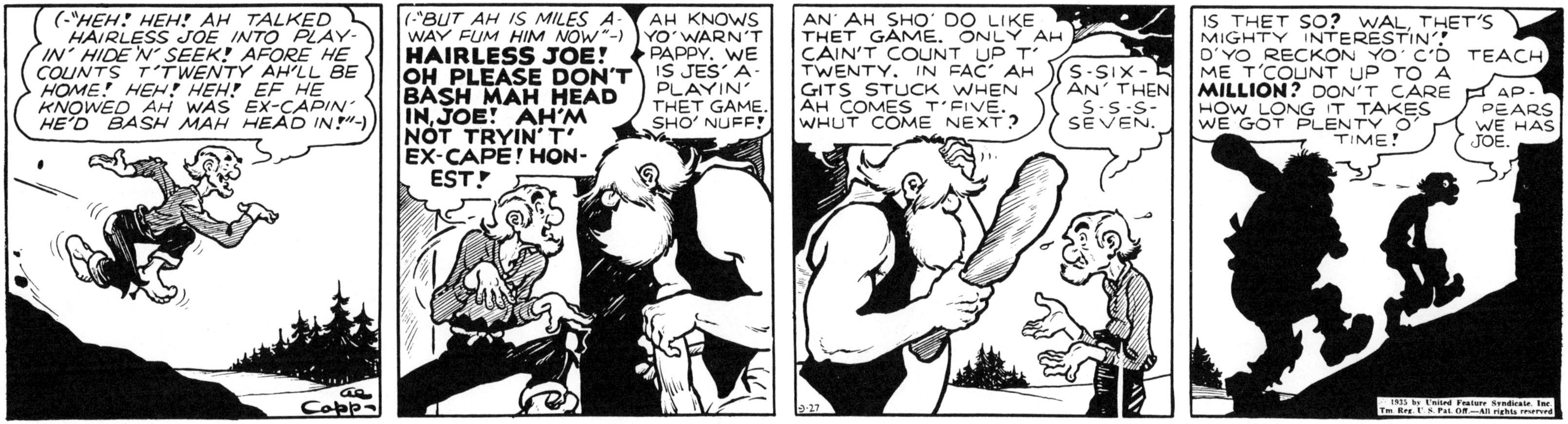

(-"HEH! HEH! AH TALKED HAIRLESS JOE INTO PLAY-IN' HIDE'N' SEEK! AFORE HE COUNTS T'TWENTY AH'LL BE HOME! HEH! HEH! EF HE KNOWED AH WAS EX-CAPIN' HE'D BASH MAH HEAD IN!"-)
Capp
(-"BUT AH IS MILES A-WAY FUM HIM NOW"-) HAIRLESS JOE! OH PLEASE DON'T BASH MAH HEAD IN, JOE! AH'M NOT TRYIN' T' EX-CAPE! HON-EST!
AH KNOWS YO' WARN'T PAPPY. WE IS JES' A-PLAYIN' THET GAME. SHO' NUFF!
AN' AH SHO' DO LIKE THET GAME. ONLY AH CAIN'T COUNT UP T' TWENTY. IN FAC' AH GITS STUCK WHEN AH COMES T'FIVE. WHUT COME NEXT?
S-SIX-AN' THEN S-S-S-SEVEN.
9-27
IS THET SO? WAL, THET'S MIGHTY INTERESTIN'! D'YO RECKON YO' C'D TEACH ME T'COUNT UP TO A MILLION? DON'T CARE HOW LONG IT TAKES WE GOT PLENTY O' TIME!
AP-PEARS WE HAS JOE.
1935 by United Feature Syndicate, Inc. Tm Reg. U.S. Pat. Off.—All rights reserved

LI'L ABNER A Pleasant Fortnight Ahead By Al Capp

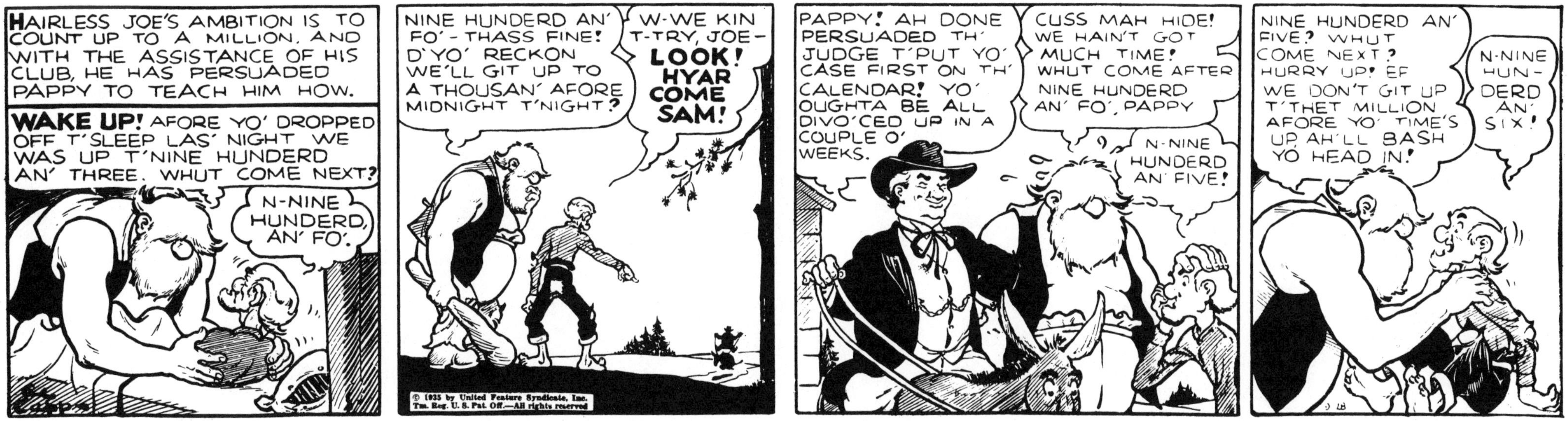

HAIRLESS JOE'S AMBITION IS TO COUNT UP TO A MILLION, AND WITH THE ASSISTANCE OF HIS CLUB, HE HAS PERSUADED PAPPY TO TEACH HIM HOW.
WAKE UP! AFORE YO' DROPPED OFF T'SLEEP LAS' NIGHT WE WAS UP T'NINE HUNDERD AN' THREE. WHUT COME NEXT?
N-NINE HUNDERD, AN' FO'.
Capp
NINE HUNDERD AN' FO' - THASS FINE! D'YO' RECKON WE'LL GIT UP TO A THOUSAN' AFORE MIDNIGHT T'NIGHT?
W-WE KIN T-TRY, JOE-
LOOK! HYAR COME SAM!
© 1935 by United Feature Syndicate, Inc. Tm. Reg. U.S. Pat. Off.—All rights reserved
PAPPY! AH DONE PERSUADED TH' JUDGE T'PUT YO' CASE FIRST ON TH' CALENDAR! YO' OUGHTA BE ALL DIVO'CED UP IN A COUPLE O' WEEKS.
CUSS MAH HIDE! WE HAIN'T GOT MUCH TIME! WHUT COME AFTER NINE HUNDERD AN' FO', PAPPY
N-NINE HUNDERD AN' FIVE!
NINE HUNDERD AN' FIVE? WHUT COME NEXT? HURRY UP! EF WE DON'T GIT UP T'THET MILLION AFORE YO' TIME'S UP, AH'LL BASH YO HEAD IN!
N-NINE HUN-DERD AN' SIX!
9-28

LI'L ABNER — Li'l Abner Makes Up His Mind — By Al Capp

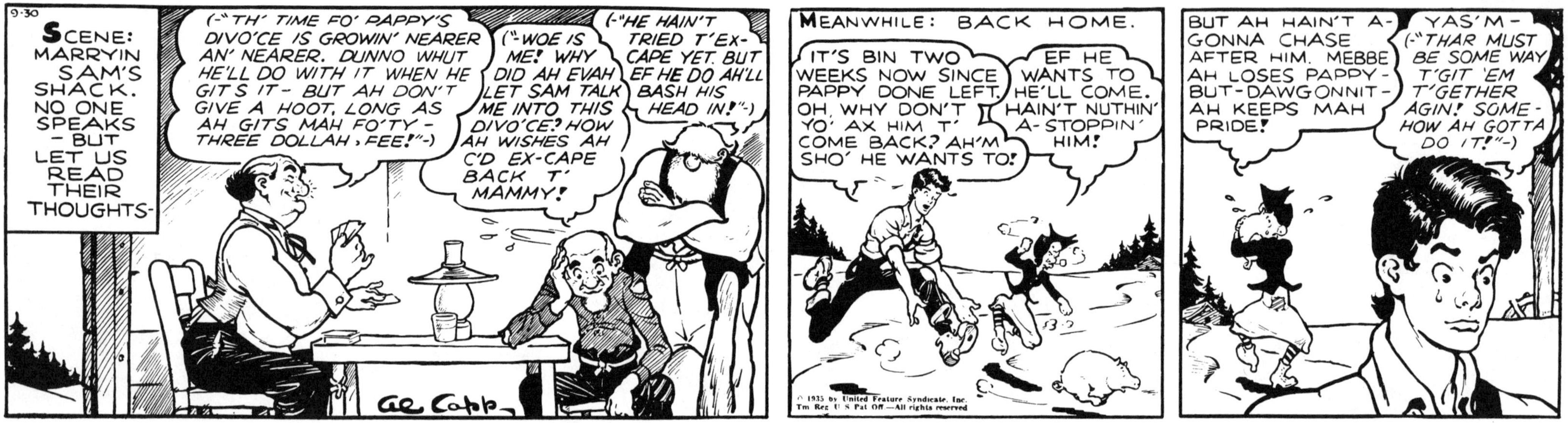
9-30
SCENE: MARRYIN SAM'S SHACK. NO ONE SPEAKS – BUT LET US READ THEIR THOUGHTS–
(-"TH' TIME FO' PAPPY'S DIVO'CE IS GROWIN' NEARER AN' NEARER. DUNNO WHUT HE'LL DO WITH IT WHEN HE GIT'S IT – BUT AH DON'T GIVE A HOOT, LONG AS AH GITS MAH FO'TY-THREE DOLLAH, FEE!"-)
("-WOE IS ME! WHY DID AH EVAH LET SAM TALK ME INTO THIS DIVO'CE? HOW AH WISHES AH C'D EX-CAPE BACK T' MAMMY!
(-"HE HAIN'T TRIED T'EX-CAPE YET. BUT EF HE DO AH'LL BASH HIS HEAD IN!"-)
MEANWHILE: BACK HOME.
IT'S BIN TWO WEEKS NOW SINCE PAPPY DONE LEFT. OH, WHY DON'T YO' AX HIM T' COME BACK? AH'M SHO' HE WANTS TO!
EF HE WANTS TO HE'LL COME. HAIN'T NUTHIN' A-STOPPIN' HIM!
© 1935 by United Feature Syndicate, Inc. Tm Reg U S Pat Off—All rights reserved
BUT AH HAIN'T A-GONNA CHASE AFTER HIM. MEBBE AH LOSES PAPPY – BUT – DAWGONNIT – AH KEEPS MAH PRIDE!
YAS'M – (-"THAR MUST BE SOME WAY T'GIT 'EM T'GETHER AGIN! SOME-HOW AH GOTTA DO IT!"-)

LI'L ABNER — A Stroke of Genius — By Al Capp

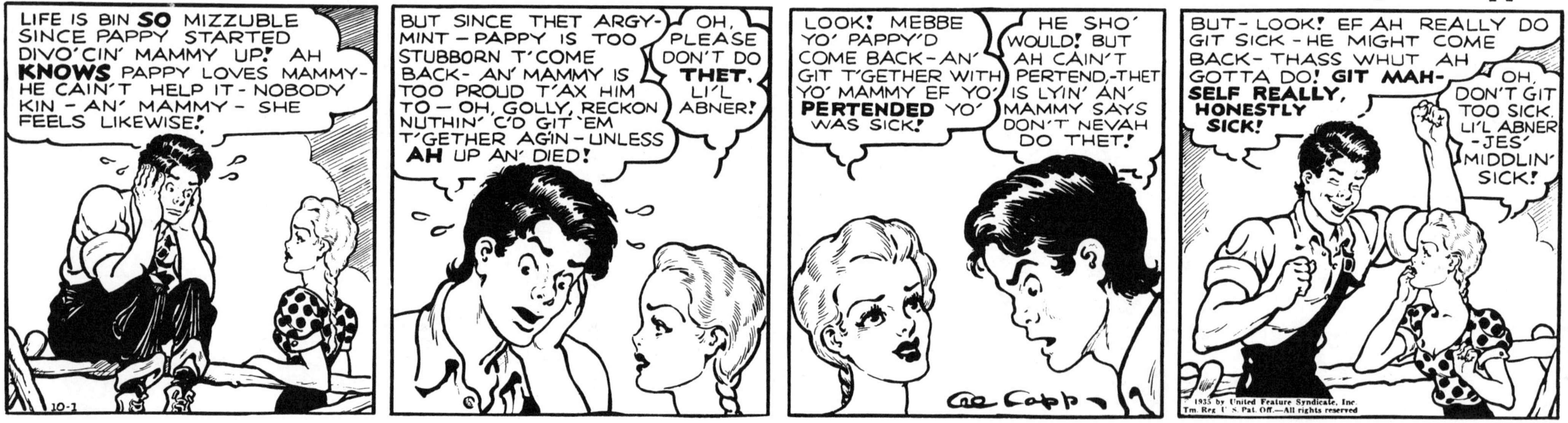
LIFE IS BIN SO MIZZUBLE SINCE PAPPY STARTED DIVO'CIN' MAMMY UP! AH KNOWS PAPPY LOVES MAMMY – HE CAIN'T HELP IT – NOBODY KIN – AN' MAMMY – SHE FEELS LIKEWISE!
10-1
BUT SINCE THET ARGY-MINT – PAPPY IS TOO STUBBORN T'COME BACK – AN' MAMMY IS TOO PROUD T'AX HIM TO – OH, GOLLY, RECKON NUTHIN' C'D GIT 'EM T'GETHER AGIN – UNLESS AH UP AN' DIED!
OH, PLEASE DON'T DO THET, LI'L ABNER!
LOOK! MEBBE YO' PAPPY'D COME BACK – AN' GIT T'GETHER WITH YO' MAMMY EF YO' PERTENDED YO' WAS SICK!
HE SHO' WOULD! BUT AH CAIN'T PERTEND, – THET IS LYIN' AN' MAMMY SAYS DON'T NEVAH DO THET!
BUT – LOOK! EF AH REALLY DO GIT SICK – HE MIGHT COME BACK – THASS WHUT AH GOTTA DO! GIT MAH-SELF REALLY, HONESTLY SICK!
OH, DON'T GIT TOO SICK. LI'L ABNER – JES' MIDDLIN' SICK!
© 1935 by United Feature Syndicate, Inc. Tm. Reg. U. S. Pat. Off.—All rights reserved

LI'L ABNER Noo-mo-nia, Hyar Ah Come ! By Al Capp

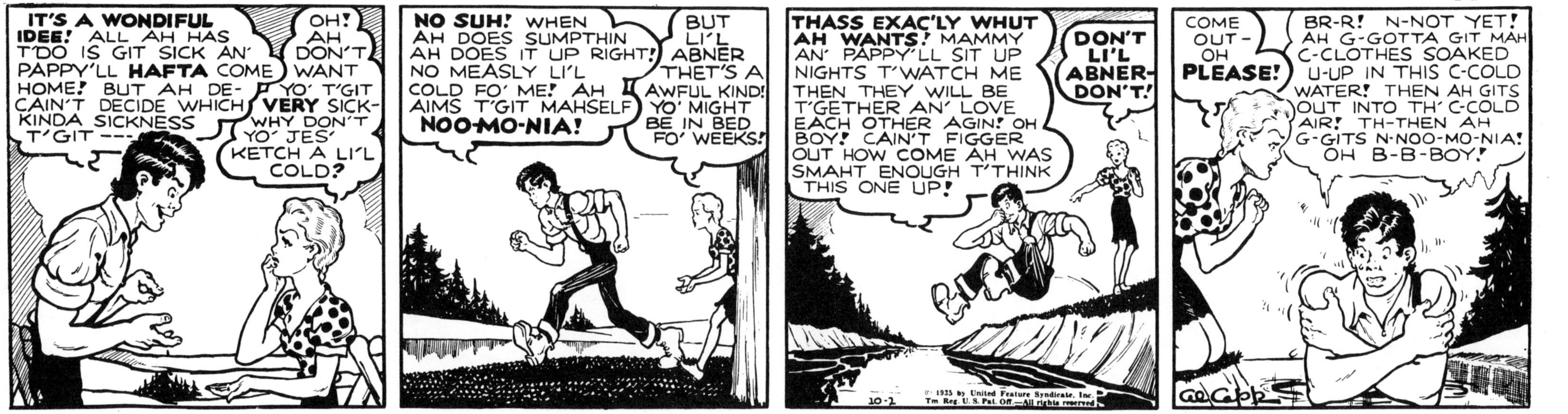
IT'S A WONDIFUL IDEE! ALL AH HAS T'DO IS GIT SICK AN' PAPPY'LL HAFTA COME HOME! BUT AH DE- CAIN'T DECIDE WHICH KINDA SICKNESS T'GIT ---
OH! AH DON'T WANT YO' T'GIT VERY SICK- WHY DON'T YO' JES' KETCH A LI'L COLD?
NO SUH! WHEN AH DOES SUMPTHIN AH DOES IT UP RIGHT! NO MEASLY LI'L COLD FO' ME! AH AIMS T'GIT MAHSELF NOO-MO-NIA!
BUT LI'L ABNER THET'S A AWFUL KIND! YO' MIGHT BE IN BED FO' WEEKS!
THASS EXAC'LY WHUT AH WANTS! MAMMY AN' PAPPY'LL SIT UP NIGHTS T'WATCH ME THEN THEY WILL BE T'GETHER AN' LOVE EACH OTHER AGIN! OH BOY! CAIN'T FIGGER OUT HOW COME AH WAS SMAHT ENOUGH T'THINK THIS ONE UP!
DON'T LI'L ABNER- DON'T!
10-2
(c) 1935 by United Feature Syndicate, Inc. Tm Reg. U. S. Pat. Off.—All rights reserved
COME OUT- OH PLEASE!
BR-R! N-NOT YET! AH G-GOTTA GIT MAH C-CLOTHES SOAKED U-UP IN THIS C-COLD WATER! THEN AH GITS OUT INTO TH' C-COLD AIR! TH-THEN AH G-GITS N-NOO-MO-NIA! OH B-B-BOY!
Al Capp

LI'L ABNER Bigger and Better By Al Capp

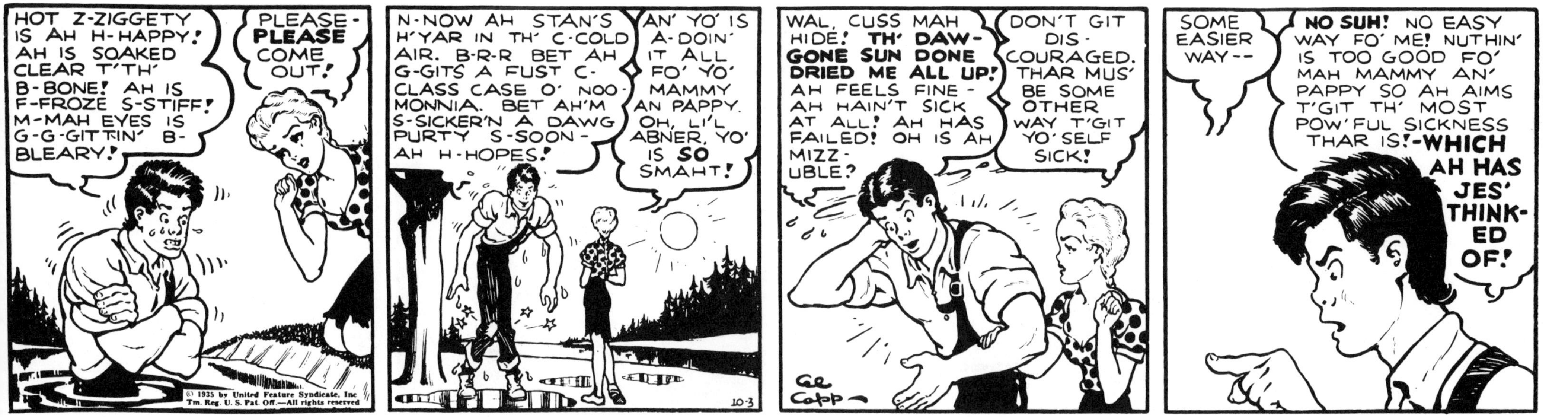
HOT Z-ZIGGETY IS AH H-HAPPY! AH IS SOAKED CLEAR T'TH' B-BONE! AH IS F-FROZE S-STIFF! M-MAH EYES IS G-G-GITTIN' B-BLEARY!
PLEASE- PLEASE COME OUT!
(c) 1935 by United Feature Syndicate, Inc Tm. Reg. U. S. Pat. Off.—All rights reserved
N-NOW AH STAN'S H'YAR IN TH' C-COLD AIR. B-R-R BET AH G-GITS A FUST C-CLASS CASE O' NOO-MONNIA. BET AH'M S-SICKER'N A DAWG PURTY S-SOON- AH H-HOPES!
AN' YO' IS A-DOIN' IT ALL FO' YO' MAMMY AN PAPPY. OH, LI'L ABNER, YO' IS SO SMAHT!
10-3
WAL, CUSS MAH HIDE! TH' DAW-GONE SUN DONE DRIED ME ALL UP! AH FEELS FINE- AH HAIN'T SICK AT ALL! AH HAS FAILED! OH IS AH MIZZ-UBLE?
DON'T GIT DIS-COURAGED. THAR MUS' BE SOME OTHER WAY T'GIT YO'SELF SICK!
Al Capp
SOME EASIER WAY--
NO SUH! NO EASY WAY FO' ME! NUTHIN' IS TOO GOOD FO' MAH MAMMY AN' PAPPY SO AH AIMS T'GIT TH' MOST POW'FUL SICKNESS THAR IS!-WHICH AH HAS JES' THINK-ED OF!

LI'L ABNER All Heart and Brains By Al Capp

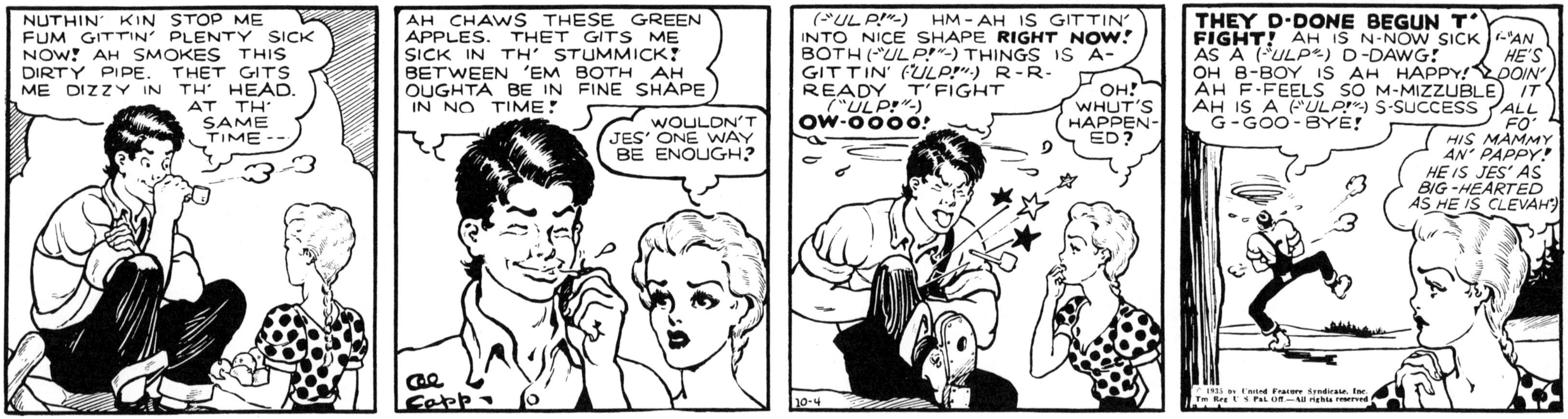

NUTHIN' KIN STOP ME FUM GITTIN' PLENTY SICK NOW! AH SMOKES THIS DIRTY PIPE. THET GITS ME DIZZY IN TH' HEAD. AT TH' SAME TIME--
AH CHAWS THESE GREEN APPLES. THET GITS ME SICK IN TH' STUMMICK! BETWEEN 'EM BOTH AH OUGHTA BE IN FINE SHAPE IN NO TIME!
WOULDN'T JES' ONE WAY BE ENOUGH?
(-"ULP!"-) HM-AH IS GITTIN' INTO NICE SHAPE RIGHT NOW! BOTH (-"ULP!"-) THINGS IS A-GITTIN' (-"ULP!"-) R-R-READY T'FIGHT (-"ULP!"-) OW-OOOO!
OH! WHUT'S HAPPEN-ED?
THEY D-DONE BEGUN T' FIGHT! AH IS N-NOW SICK AS A (-"ULP"-) D-DAWG! OH B-BOY IS AH HAPPY! AH F-FEELS SO M-MIZZUBLE AH IS A (-"ULP!"-) S-SUCCESS G-GOO-BYE!
(-"AN HE'S DOIN' IT ALL FO' HIS MAMMY AN' PAPPY! HE IS JES' AS BIG-HEARTED AS HE IS CLEVAH")
10-4
© 1935 by United Feature Syndicate, Inc. Tm Reg U S Pat Off.—All rights reserved

LI'L ABNER We Shall See What We Shall See! By Al Capp

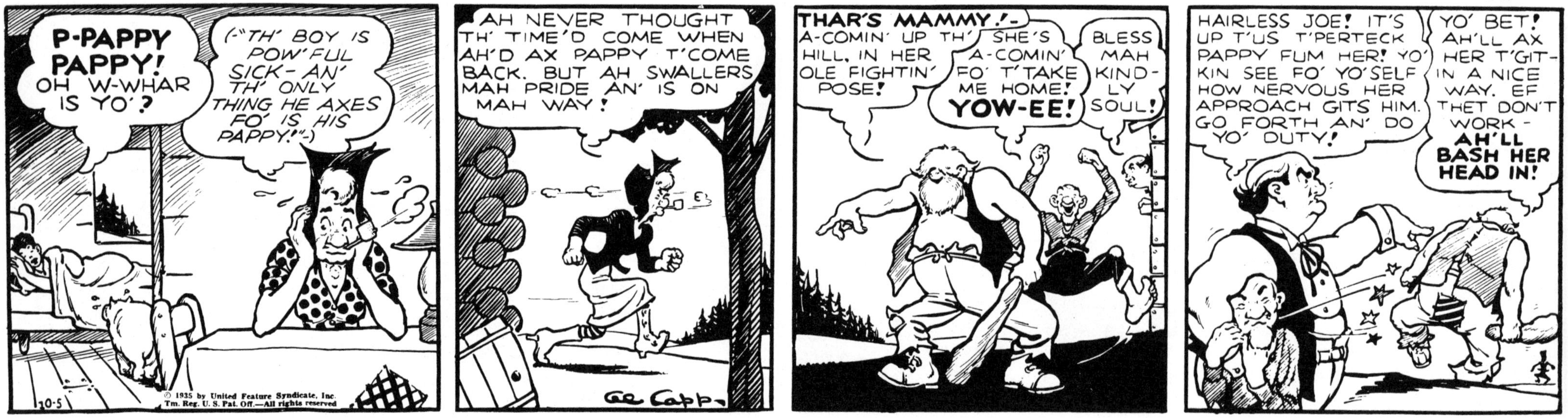

P-PAPPY PAPPY! OH W-WHAR IS YO'?
(-"TH' BOY IS POW'FUL SICK-AN' TH' ONLY THING HE AXES FO' IS HIS PAPPY!"-)
10-5
© 1935 by United Feature Syndicate, Inc. Tm. Reg. U. S. Pat. Off.—All rights reserved
AH NEVER THOUGHT TH' TIME'D COME WHEN AH'D AX PAPPY T'COME BACK. BUT AH SWALLERS MAH PRIDE AN' IS ON MAH WAY!
THAR'S MAMMY!- A-COMIN' UP TH' HILL, IN HER OLE FIGHTIN' POSE!
SHE'S A-COMIN' FO' T'TAKE ME HOME! YOW-EE!
BLESS MAH KINDLY SOUL!
HAIRLESS JOE! IT'S UP T'US T'PERTECK PAPPY FUM HER! YO' KIN SEE FO' YO'SELF HOW NERVOUS HER APPROACH GITS HIM. GO FORTH AN' DO YO' DUTY!
YO' BET! AH'LL AX HER T'GIT IN A NICE WAY. EF THET DON'T WORK - AH'LL BASH HER HEAD IN!

LI'L ABNER A Puffick Combination By Al Capp

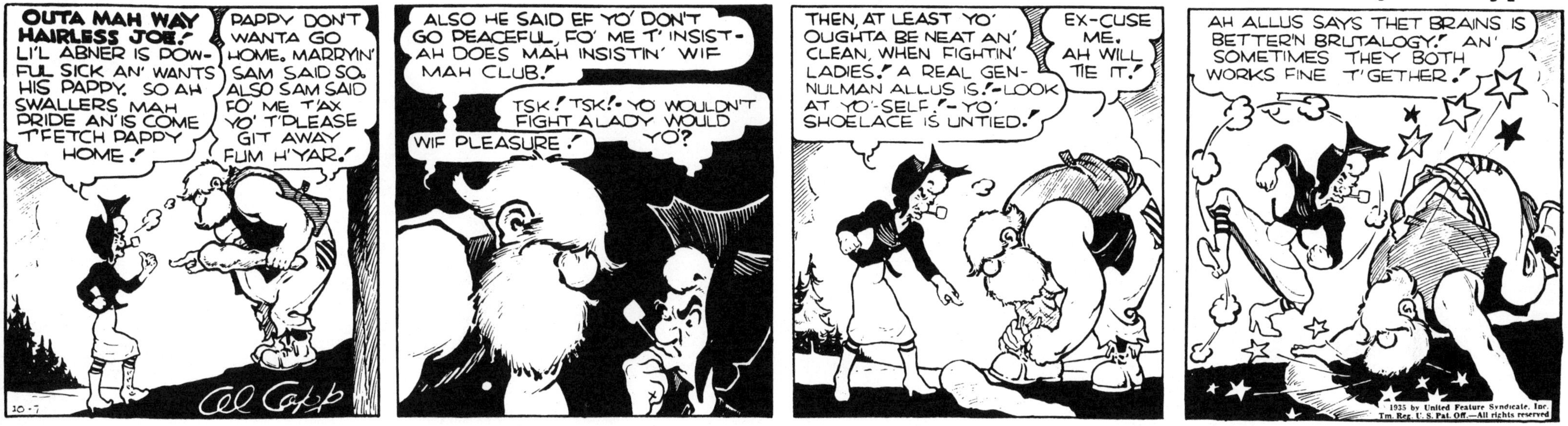
OUTA MAH WAY HAIRLESS JOE! LI'L ABNER IS POWFUL SICK AN' WANTS HIS PAPPY. SO AH SWALLERS MAH PRIDE AN' IS COME T'FETCH PAPPY HOME!
PAPPY DON'T WANTA GO HOME. MARRYIN' SAM SAID SO. ALSO SAM SAID FO' ME T'AX YO' T'PLEASE GIT AWAY FUM H'YAR!
ALSO HE SAID EF YO' DON'T GO PEACEFUL, FO' ME T' INSIST- AH DOES MAH INSISTIN' WIF MAH CLUB!
TSK! TSK!- YO WOULDN'T FIGHT A LADY WOULD YO?
WIF PLEASURE!
THEN, AT LEAST YO' OUGHTA BE NEAT AN' CLEAN, WHEN FIGHTIN' LADIES! A REAL GENNULMAN ALLUS IS!-LOOK AT YO'-SELF!- YO' SHOELACE IS UNTIED!
EX-CUSE ME. AH WILL TIE IT!
AH ALLUS SAYS THET BRAINS IS BETTER'N BRUTALOGY! AN' SOMETIMES THEY BOTH WORKS FINE T'GETHER!
1935 by United Feature Syndicate, Inc. Tm. Reg. U. S. Pat. Off.—All rights reserved

LI'L ABNER Battle of Wits By Al Capp

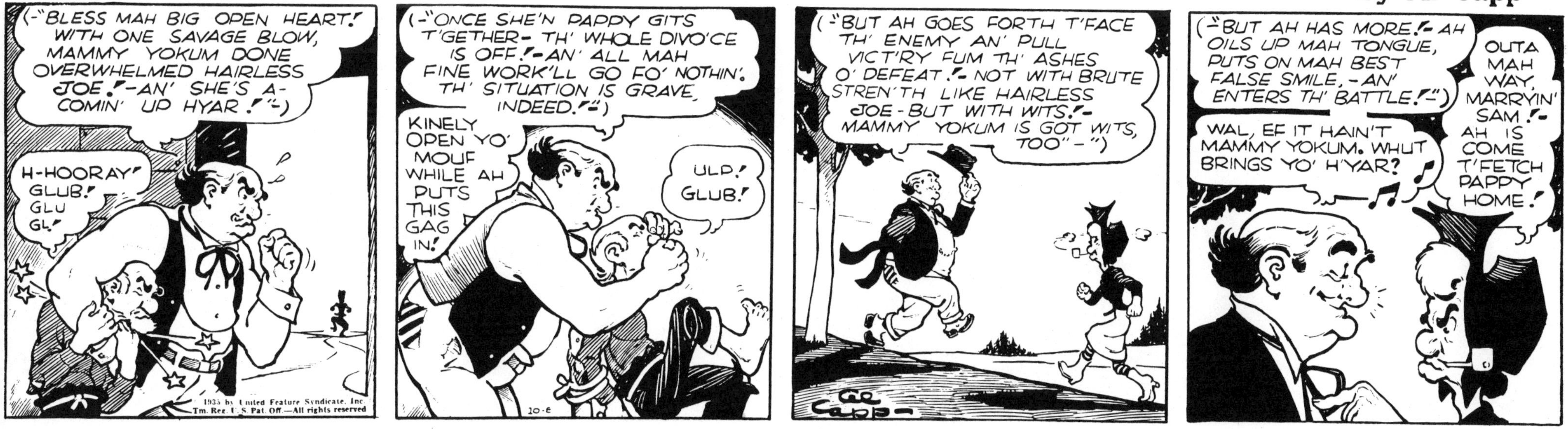
(-"BLESS MAH BIG OPEN HEART! WITH ONE SAVAGE BLOW, MAMMY YOKUM DONE OVERWHELMED HAIRLESS JOE!"-AN' SHE'S A-COMIN' UP HYAR!"-)
H-HOORAY! GLUB! GLU GL!
1935 by United Feature Syndicate, Inc. Tm. Reg. U. S. Pat. Off.—All rights reserved
(-"ONCE SHE'N PAPPY GITS T'GETHER- TH' WHOLE DIVO'CE IS OFF!-AN' ALL MAH FINE WORK'LL GO FO' NOTHIN'. TH' SITUATION IS GRAVE, INDEED!"-)
KINELY OPEN YO' MOUF WHILE AH PUTS THIS GAG IN!
ULP! GLUB!
(-"BUT AH GOES FORTH T'FACE TH' ENEMY AN' PULL VICT'RY FUM TH' ASHES O' DEFEAT!- NOT WITH BRUTE STREN'TH LIKE HAIRLESS JOE-BUT WITH WITS!- MAMMY YOKUM IS GOT WITS, TOO"-")
(-"BUT AH HAS MORE!- AH OILS UP MAH TONGUE, PUTS ON MAH BEST FALSE SMILE,-AN' ENTERS TH' BATTLE!"-)
WAL, EF IT HAIN'T MAMMY YOKUM. WHUT BRINGS YO' H'YAR?
OUTA MAH WAY, MARRYIN' SAM!- AH IS COME T'FETCH PAPPY HOME!

LI'L ABNER The Leopard Changes His Spots! By Al Capp

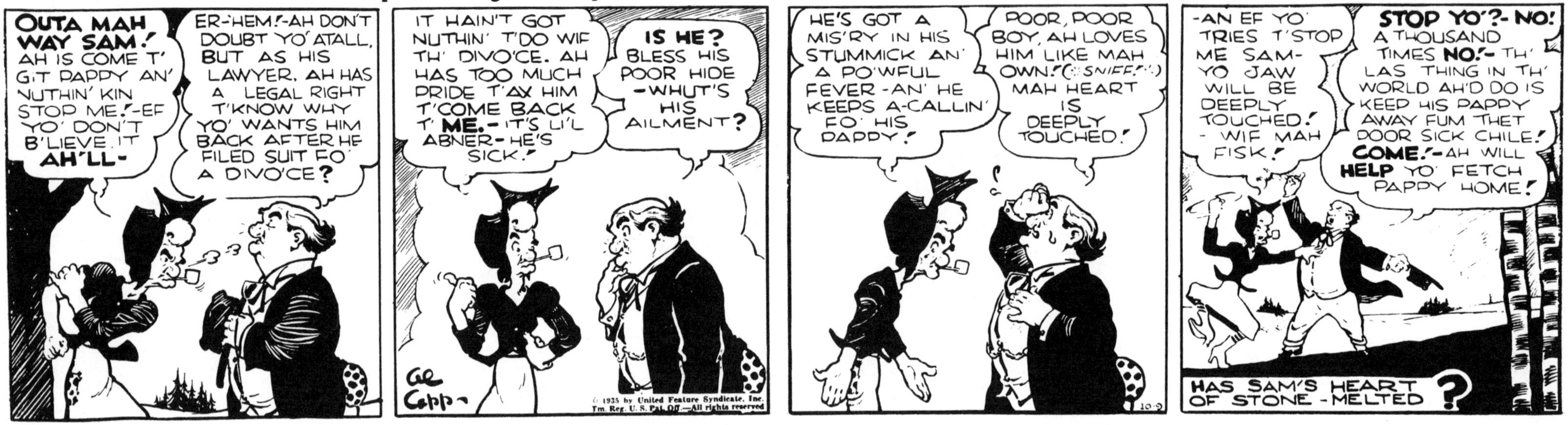

OUTA MAH WAY SAM! AH IS COME T' GIT PAPPY AN' NUTHIN' KIN STOP ME!-EF YO' DON'T B'LIEVE IT AH'LL-
ER-HEM!-AH DON'T DOUBT YO' ATALL, BUT AS HIS LAWYER, AH HAS A LEGAL RIGHT T'KNOW WHY YO' WANTS HIM BACK AFTER HE FILED SUIT FO' A DIVO'CE?
IT HAIN'T GOT NUTHIN' T'DO WIF TH' DIVO'CE. AH HAS TOO MUCH PRIDE T'AX HIM T'COME BACK T' ME.- IT'S LI'L ABNER- HE'S SICK.!
IS HE? BLESS HIS POOR HIDE -WHUT'S HIS AILMENT?
Al Capp
© 1935 by United Feature Syndicate, Inc. Tm. Reg. U. S. Pat. Off.—All rights reserved
HE'S GOT A MIS'RY IN HIS STUMMICK AN' A PO'WFUL FEVER -AN' HE KEEPS A-CALLIN' FO' HIS PAPPY!
POOR, POOR BOY, AH LOVES HIM LIKE MAH OWN!(SNIFF!) MAH HEART IS DEEPLY TOUCHED!
10-9
-AN EF YO' TRIES T'STOP ME SAM- YO JAW WILL BE DEEPLY TOUCHED! - WIF MAH FISK!
STOP YO'?- NO! A THOUSAND TIMES NO!- TH' LAS THING IN TH' WORLD AH'D DO IS KEEP HIS PAPPY AWAY FUM THET POOR SICK CHILE! COME!-AH WILL HELP YO' FETCH PAPPY HOME!
HAS SAM'S HEART OF STONE-MELTED?

LI'L ABNER Mammy Is Through! By Al Capp

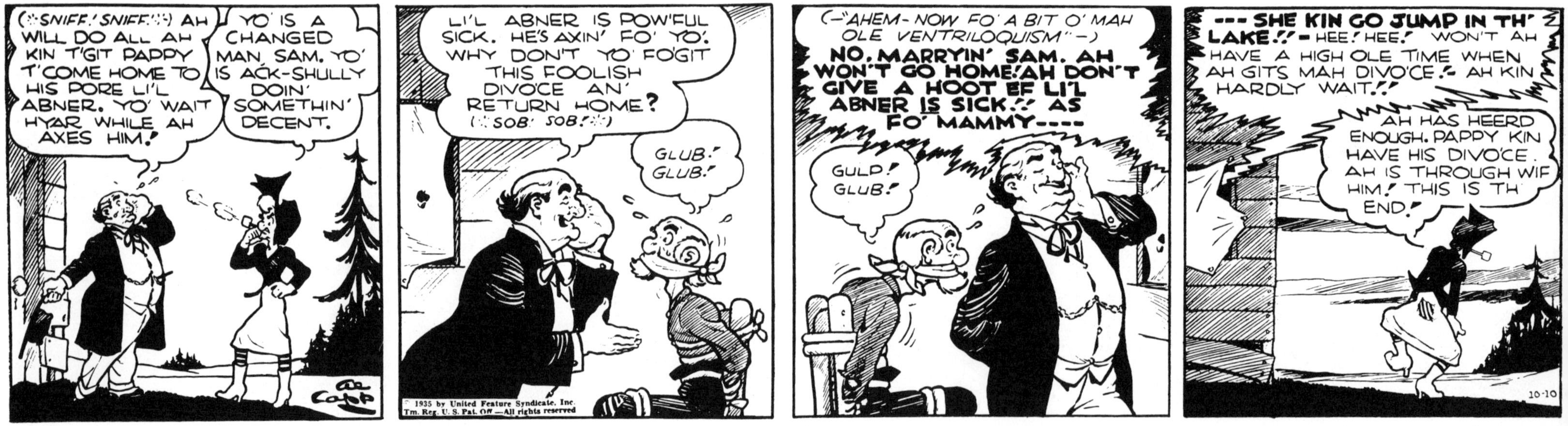

(SNIFF! SNIFF!) AH WILL DO ALL AH KIN T'GIT PAPPY T'COME HOME TO HIS PORE LI'L ABNER. YO' WAIT HYAR WHILE AH AXES HIM!
YO' IS A CHANGED MAN SAM. YO' IS ACK-SHULLY DOIN' SOMETHIN' DECENT.
Al Capp
LI'L ABNER IS POW'FUL SICK. HE'S AXIN' FO' YO'. WHY DON'T YO' FO'GIT THIS FOOLISH DIVO'CE AN' RETURN HOME? (SOB! SOB!)
GLUB! GLUB!
© 1935 by United Feature Syndicate, Inc. Tm. Reg. U. S. Pat. Off.—All rights reserved
(-"AHEM- NOW FO' A BIT O' MAH OLE VENTRILOQUISM"-)
NO, MARRYIN' SAM. AH WON'T GO HOME! AH DON'T GIVE A HOOT EF LI'L ABNER IS SICK!! AS FO' MAMMY----
GULP! GLUB!
--- SHE KIN GO JUMP IN TH' LAKE!! - HEE! HEE! WON'T AH HAVE A HIGH OLE TIME WHEN AH GITS MAH DIVO'CE!- AH KIN HARDLY WAIT!!
AH HAS HEERD ENOUGH. PAPPY KIN HAVE HIS DIVO'CE. AH IS THROUGH WIF HIM! THIS IS TH' END!
10-10

LI'L ABNER Farewell To Pappy By Al Capp

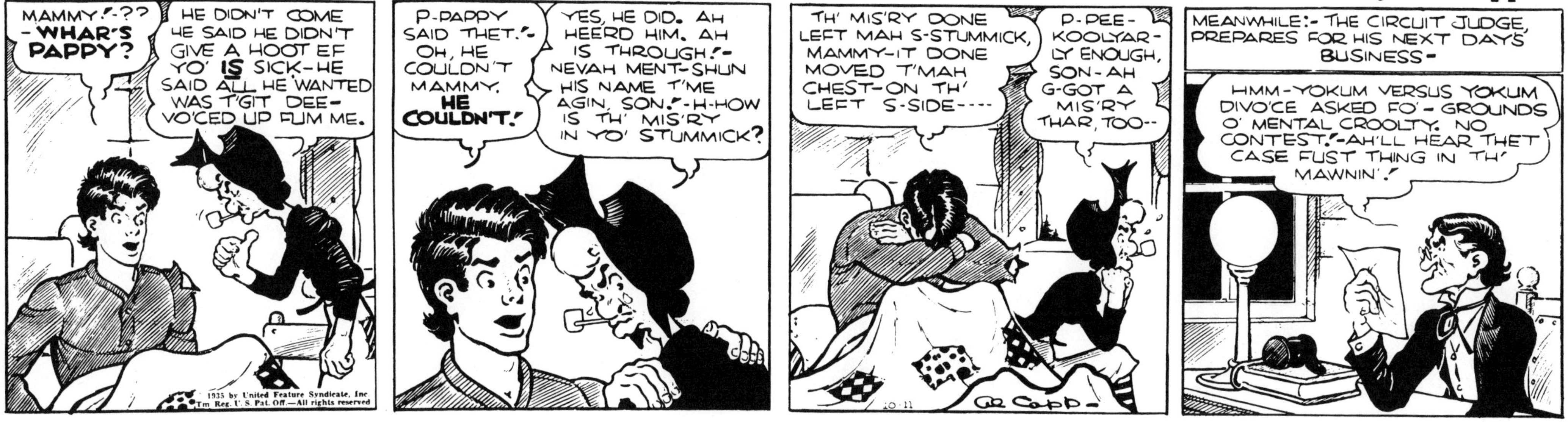

MAMMY!-?? -WHAR'S PAPPY?
HE DIDN'T COME HE SAID HE DIDN'T GIVE A HOOT EF YO' IS SICK-HE SAID ALL HE WANTED WAS T'GIT DEE-VO'CED UP FUM ME.
© 1935 by United Feature Syndicate, Inc Tm. Reg. U.S. Pat. Off.—All rights reserved
P-PAPPY SAID THET!- OH, HE COULDN'T MAMMY. HE COULDN'T!
YES, HE DID. AH HEERD HIM. AH IS THROUGH!- NEVAH MENT-SHUN HIS NAME T'ME AGIN, SON!-H-HOW IS TH' MIS'RY IN YO' STUMMICK?
TH' MIS'RY DONE LEFT MAH S-STUMMICK, MAMMY-IT DONE MOVED T'MAH CHEST-ON TH' LEFT S-SIDE----
P-PEE-KOOLYAR-LY ENOUGH, SON-AH G-GOT A MIS'RY THAR, TOO--
10-11
Al Capp
MEANWHILE:- THE CIRCUIT JUDGE, PREPARES FOR HIS NEXT DAYS BUSINESS-
HMM-YOKUM VERSUS YOKUM DIVO'CE ASKED FO'- GROUNDS O' MENTAL CROOLTY. NO CONTEST!-AH'LL HEAR THET CASE FUST THING IN TH' MAWNIN'!

LI'L ABNER Mammy's Too Proud To Fight By Al Capp

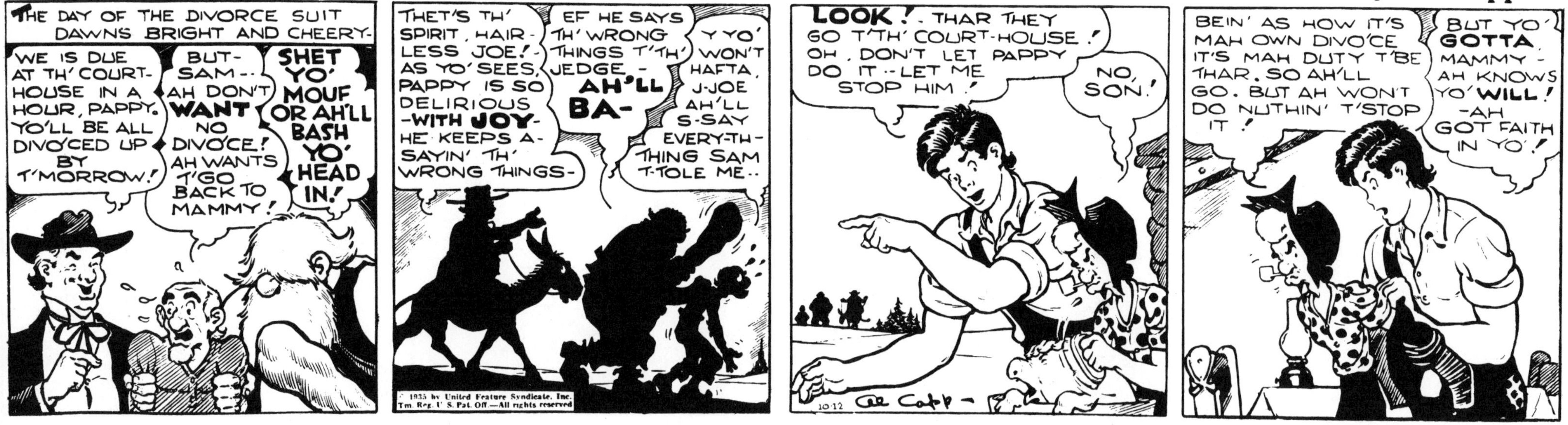

THE DAY OF THE DIVORCE SUIT DAWNS BRIGHT AND CHEERY-
WE IS DUE AT TH' COURT-HOUSE IN A HOUR, PAPPY. YO'LL BE ALL DIVO'CED UP BY T'MORROW!
BUT-SAM--AH DON'T WANT NO DIVO'CE! AH WANTS T'GO BACK TO MAMMY!
SHET YO' MOUF OR AH'LL BASH YO' HEAD IN!
THET'S TH' SPIRIT, HAIR-LESS JOE!- AS YO' SEES, PAPPY IS SO DELIRIOUS -WITH JOY- HE KEEPS A-SAYIN' TH' WRONG THINGS-
EF HE SAYS TH' WRONG THINGS T'TH' JEDGE.- AH'LL BA-
Y-YO' WON'T HAFTA, J-JOE AH'LL S-SAY EVERY-TH-THING SAM T-TOLE ME..
© 1935 by United Feature Syndicate, Inc. Tm. Reg. U.S. Pat. Off.—All rights reserved
LOOK!- THAR THEY GO T'TH' COURT-HOUSE! OH, DON'T LET PAPPY DO IT--LET ME STOP HIM!
NO, SON!
10-12
Al Capp
BEIN' AS HOW IT'S MAH OWN DIVO'CE IT'S MAH DUTY T'BE THAR. SO AH'LL GO. BUT AH WON'T DO NUTHIN' T'STOP IT!
BUT YO' GOTTA, MAMMY- AH KNOWS YO' WILL! -AH GOT FAITH IN YO'!

LI'L ABNER The Law Speaks! By Al Capp

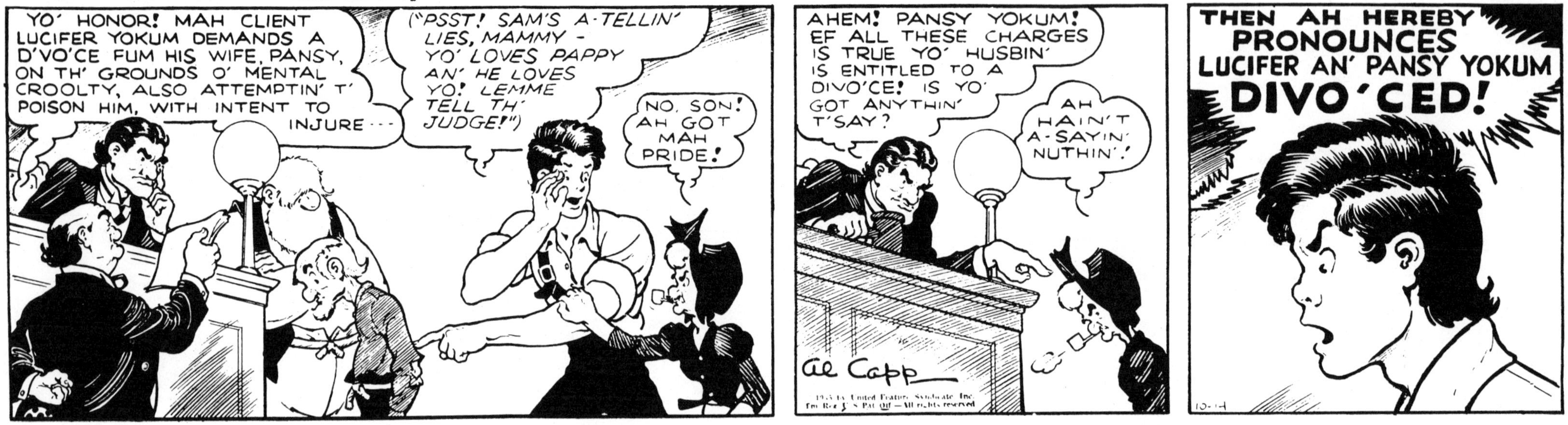

YO' HONOR! MAH CLIENT LUCIFER YOKUM DEMANDS A D'VO'CE FUM HIS WIFE, PANSY, ON TH' GROUNDS O' MENTAL CROOLTY, ALSO ATTEMPTIN' T' POISON HIM, WITH INTENT TO INJURE---
("PSST! SAM'S A-TELLIN' LIES, MAMMY - YO' LOVES PAPPY AN' HE LOVES YO! LEMME TELL TH' JUDGE!")
NO, SON! AH GOT MAH PRIDE!
AHEM! PANSY YOKUM! EF ALL THESE CHARGES IS TRUE YO' HUSBIN' IS ENTITLED TO A DIVO'CE! IS YO' GOT ANYTHIN' T'SAY?
AH HAIN'T A-SAYIN' NUTHIN'!
THEN AH HEREBY PRONOUNCES LUCIFER AN' PANSY YOKUM DIVO'CED!
Al Capp

LI'L ABNER Crime Doesn't Pay! By Al Capp

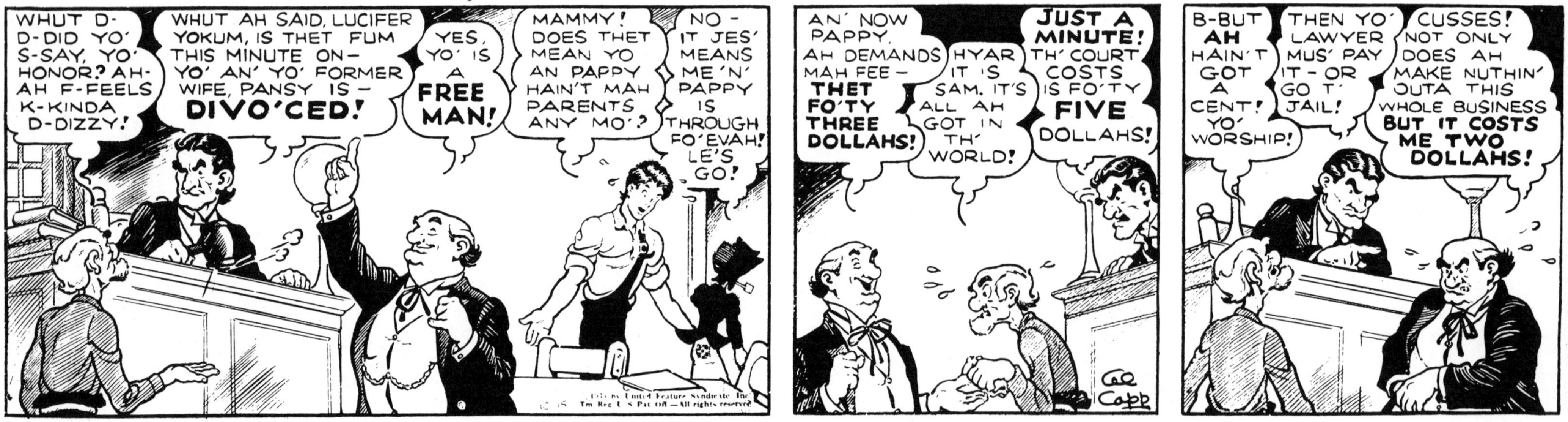

WHUT D-D-DID YO' S-SAY, YO' HONOR? AH-AH F-FEELS K-KINDA D-DIZZY!
WHUT AH SAID, LUCIFER YOKUM, IS THET FUM THIS MINUTE ON— YO' AN' YO' FORMER WIFE, PANSY, IS— DIVO'CED!
YES, YO' IS A FREE MAN!
MAMMY! DOES THET MEAN YO AN PAPPY HAIN'T MAH PARENTS ANY MO'?
NO - IT JES' MEANS ME 'N' PAPPY IS THROUGH FO'EVAH! LE'S GO!
AN' NOW PAPPY, AH DEMANDS MAH FEE— THET FO'TY THREE DOLLAHS!
HYAR IT IS SAM. IT'S ALL AH GOT IN TH' WORLD!
JUST A MINUTE! TH' COURT COSTS IS FO'TY FIVE DOLLAHS!
Al Capp
B-BUT AH HAIN'T GOT A CENT! YO' WORSHIP!
THEN YO' LAWYER MUS' PAY IT - OR GO T' JAIL!
CUSSES! NOT ONLY DOES AH MAKE NUTHIN' OUTA THIS WHOLE BUSINESS BUT IT COSTS ME TWO DOLLAHS!

LI'L ABNER

Whut Kin It Mean?

By Al Capp

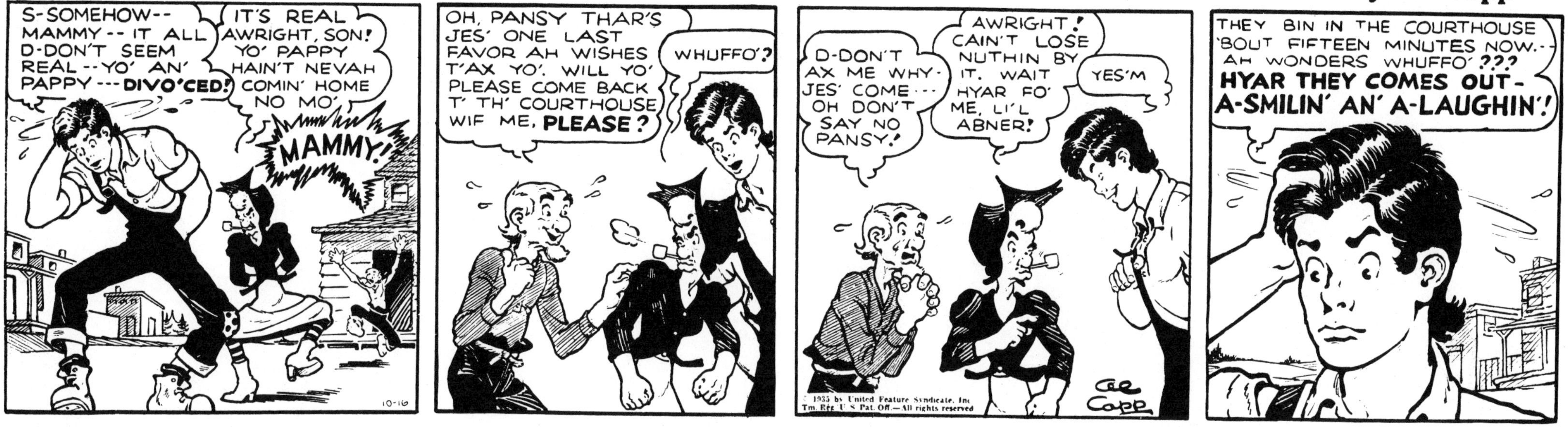

S-SOMEHOW-- MAMMY-- IT ALL D-DON'T SEEM REAL--YO' AN' PAPPY---DIVO'CED!
IT'S REAL AWRIGHT, SON! YO' PAPPY HAIN'T NEVAH COMIN' HOME NO MO'
MAMMY!
10-16
OH, PANSY THAR'S JES' ONE LAST FAVOR AH WISHES T'AX YO'. WILL YO' PLEASE COME BACK T' TH' COURTHOUSE WIF ME, PLEASE?
WHUFFO'?
D-DON'T AX ME WHY- JES' COME--- OH DON'T SAY NO PANSY!
AWRIGHT! CAIN'T LOSE NUTHIN BY IT. WAIT HYAR FO' ME, LI'L ABNER!
YES'M
© 1935 by United Feature Syndicate, Inc. Tm. Reg. U.S. Pat. Off.—All rights reserved
Al Capp
THEY BIN IN THE COURTHOUSE 'BOUT FIFTEEN MINUTES NOW.-- AH WONDERS WHUFFO'??? HYAR THEY COMES OUT- A-SMILIN' AN' A-LAUGHIN'!

LI'L ABNER

All's Swell That Ends Well

By Al Capp

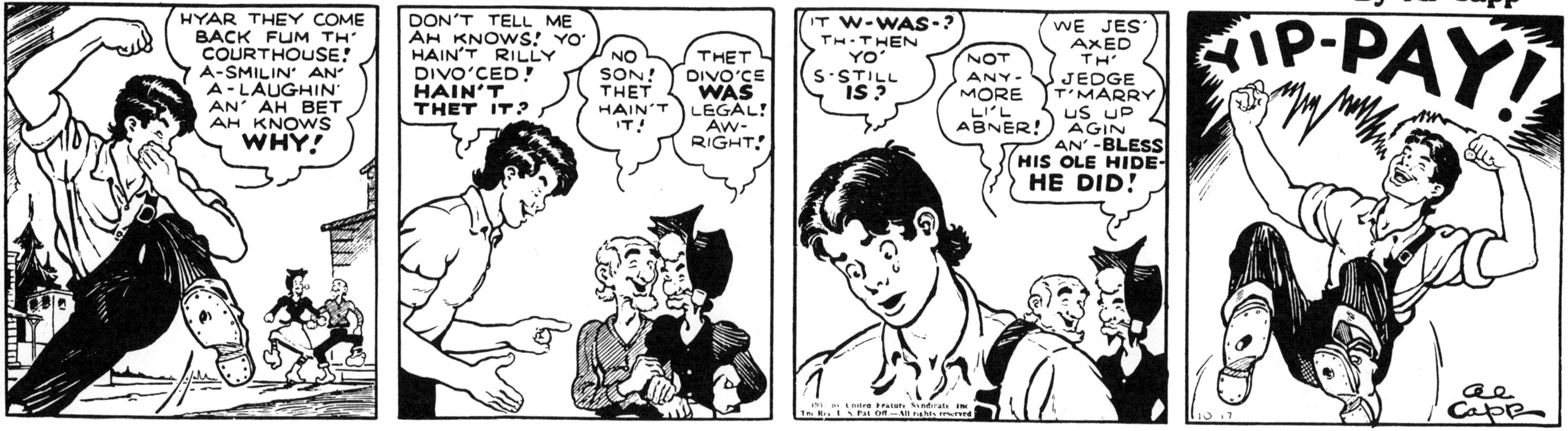

HYAR THEY COME BACK FUM TH' COURTHOUSE! A-SMILIN' AN' A-LAUGHIN' AN' AH BET AH KNOWS WHY!
DON'T TELL ME AH KNOWS! YO' HAIN'T RILLY DIVO'CED! HAIN'T THET IT?
NO SON! THET HAIN'T IT!
THET DIVO'CE WAS LEGAL! AW-RIGHT!
IT W-WAS-? TH-THEN YO' S-STILL IS?
NOT ANY-MORE LI'L ABNER!
WE JES' AXED TH' JEDGE T'MARRY US UP AGIN AN'-BLESS HIS OLE HIDE-HE DID!
United Feature Syndicate, Inc. Tm. Reg. U.S. Pat. Off.—All rights reserved
YIP-PAY!
10-17
Al Capp

LI'L ABNER Granny's Prophecy By Al Capp

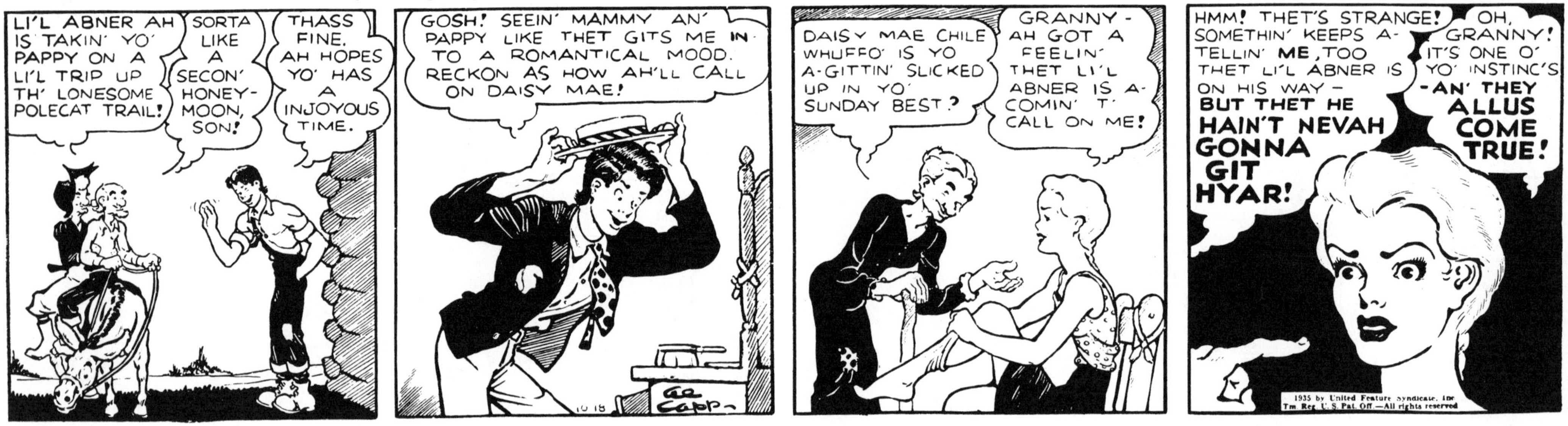
LI'L ABNER AH IS TAKIN' YO' PAPPY ON A LI'L TRIP UP TH' LONESOME POLECAT TRAIL!
SORTA LIKE A SECON' HONEY-MOON, SON!
THASS FINE. AH HOPES YO' HAS A INJOYOUS TIME.
GOSH! SEEIN' MAMMY AN' PAPPY LIKE THET GITS ME IN-TO A ROMANTICAL MOOD. RECKON AS HOW AH'LL CALL ON DAISY MAE!
10 18
Al Capp
DAISY MAE CHILE WHUFFO' IS YO A-GITTIN' SLICKED UP IN YO' SUNDAY BEST?
GRANNY - AH GOT A FEELIN' THET LI'L ABNER IS A-COMIN' T' CALL ON ME!
HMM! THET'S STRANGE! SOMETHIN' KEEPS A-TELLIN' ME, TOO THET LI'L ABNER IS ON HIS WAY - BUT THET HE HAIN'T NEVAH GONNA GIT HYAR!
OH, GRANNY! IT'S ONE O' YO' INSTINC'S - AN' THEY ALLUS COME TRUE!
1935 by United Feature Syndicate, Inc. Tm Reg. U.S. Pat. Off.—All rights reserved

LI'L ABNER A Lady Drops In By Al Capp

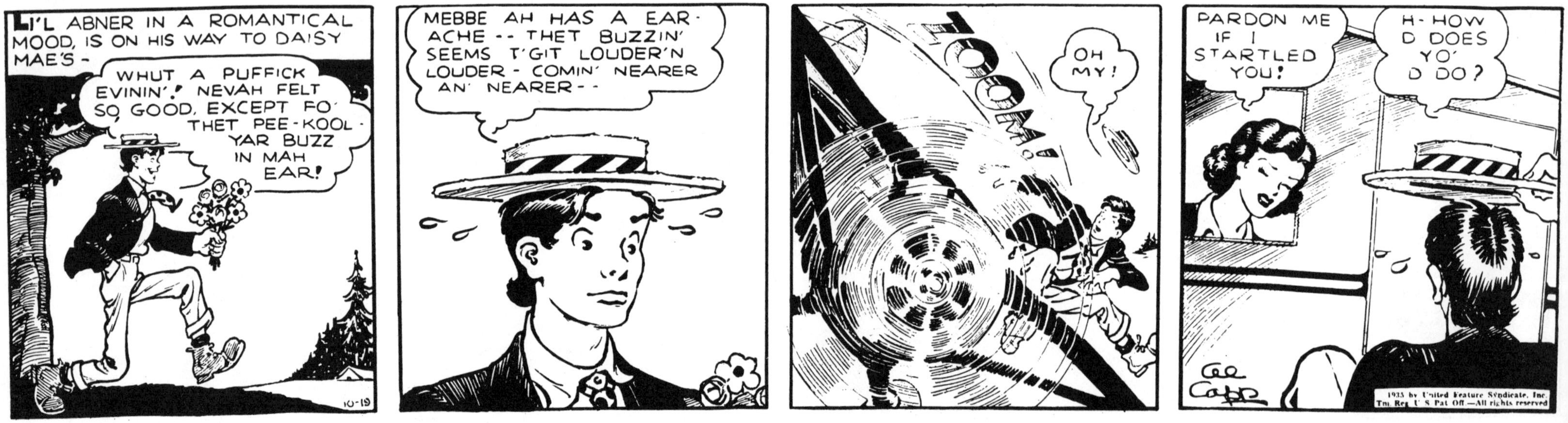
LI'L ABNER IN A ROMANTICAL MOOD, IS ON HIS WAY TO DAISY MAE'S -
WHUT A PUFFICK EVININ'! NEVAH FELT SO GOOD, EXCEPT FO' THET PEE-KOOL-YAR BUZZ IN MAH EAR!
10-19
MEBBE AH HAS A EAR-ACHE -- THET BUZZIN' SEEMS T'GIT LOUDER'N LOUDER - COMIN' NEARER AN' NEARER --
ZOOM!
OH MY!
PARDON ME IF I STARTLED YOU!
H-HOW D DOES YO' D DO?
Al Capp
1935 by United Feature Syndicate, Inc. Tm. Reg. U.S. Pat. Off.—All rights reserved

LI'L ABNER

So Near, Yet So Far

By Al Capp

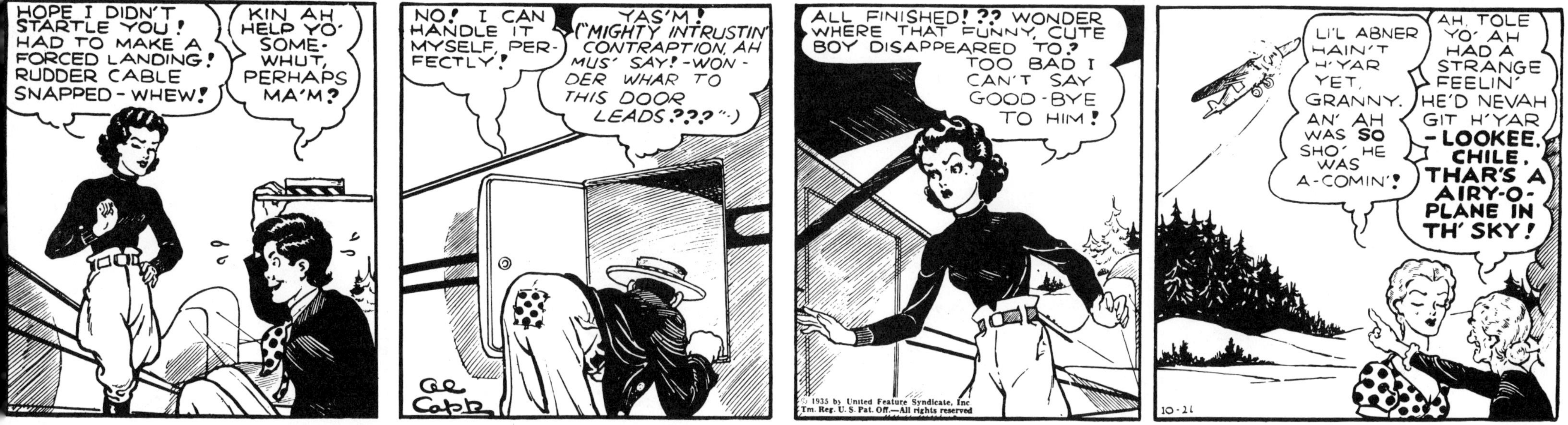
HOPE I DIDN'T STARTLE YOU! HAD TO MAKE A FORCED LANDING! RUDDER CABLE SNAPPED - WHEW!
KIN AH HELP YO' SOME-WHUT, PERHAPS MA'M?
NO! I CAN HANDLE IT MYSELF, PER-FECTLY!
YAS'M! ("MIGHTY INTRUSTIN' CONTRAPTION, AH MUS' SAY! - WON-DER WHAR TO THIS DOOR LEADS???")
AL CAPP
ALL FINISHED! ?? WONDER WHERE THAT FUNNY, CUTE BOY DISAPPEARED TO? TOO BAD I CAN'T SAY GOOD-BYE TO HIM!
© 1935 by United Feature Syndicate, Inc Tm. Reg. U. S. Pat. Off.—All rights reserved
LI'L ABNER HAIN'T H'YAR YET, GRANNY. AN' AH WAS SO SHO' HE WAS A-COMIN'!
AH TOLE YO' AH HAD A STRANGE FEELIN' HE'D NEVAH GIT H'YAR - LOOKEE, CHILE, THAR'S A AIRY-O-PLANE IN TH' SKY!
10-21

LI'L ABNER

Happy Landings

By Al Capp

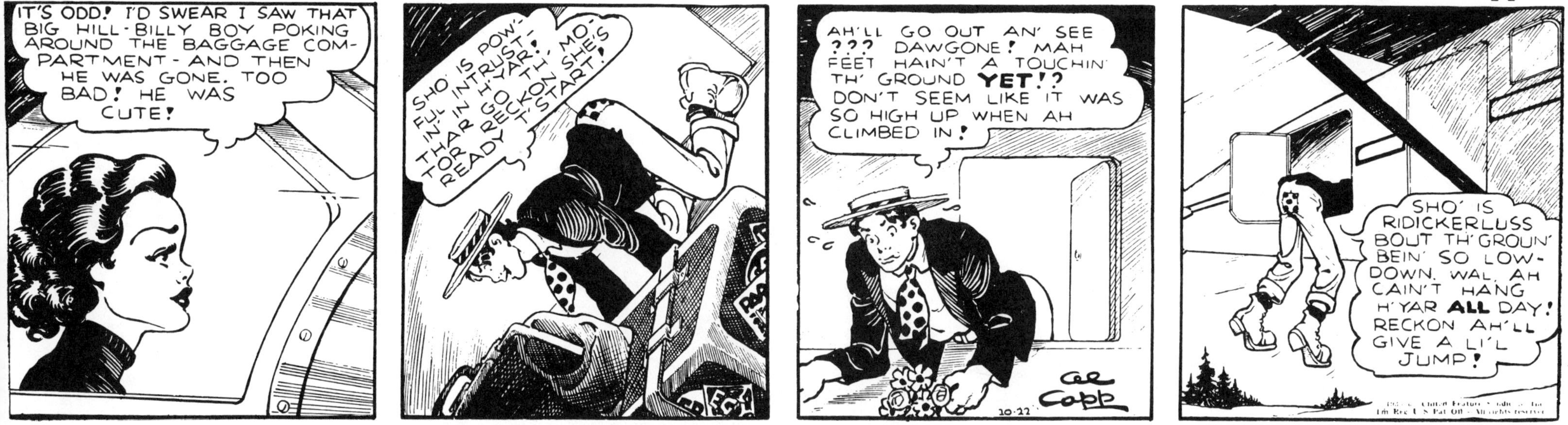
IT'S ODD! I'D SWEAR I SAW THAT BIG HILL-BILLY BOY POKING AROUND THE BAGGAGE COM-PARTMENT - AND THEN HE WAS GONE. TOO BAD! HE WAS CUTE!
SHO' IS POW-FUL INTRUST-IN' IN H'YAR! THAR GO TH' MO-TOR. RECKON SHE'S READY T'START!
AH'LL GO OUT AN' SEE ??? DAWGONE! MAH FEET HAIN'T A TOUCHIN' TH' GROUND YET!? DON'T SEEM LIKE IT WAS SO HIGH UP WHEN AH CLIMBED IN!
AL CAPP
10-22
SHO' IS RIDICKERLUSS BOUT TH' GROUN' BEIN' SO LOW-DOWN. WAL, AH CAIN'T HANG H'YAR ALL DAY! RECKON AH'LL GIVE A LI'L JUMP!

LI'L ABNER It's A Tough Life ! By Al Capp

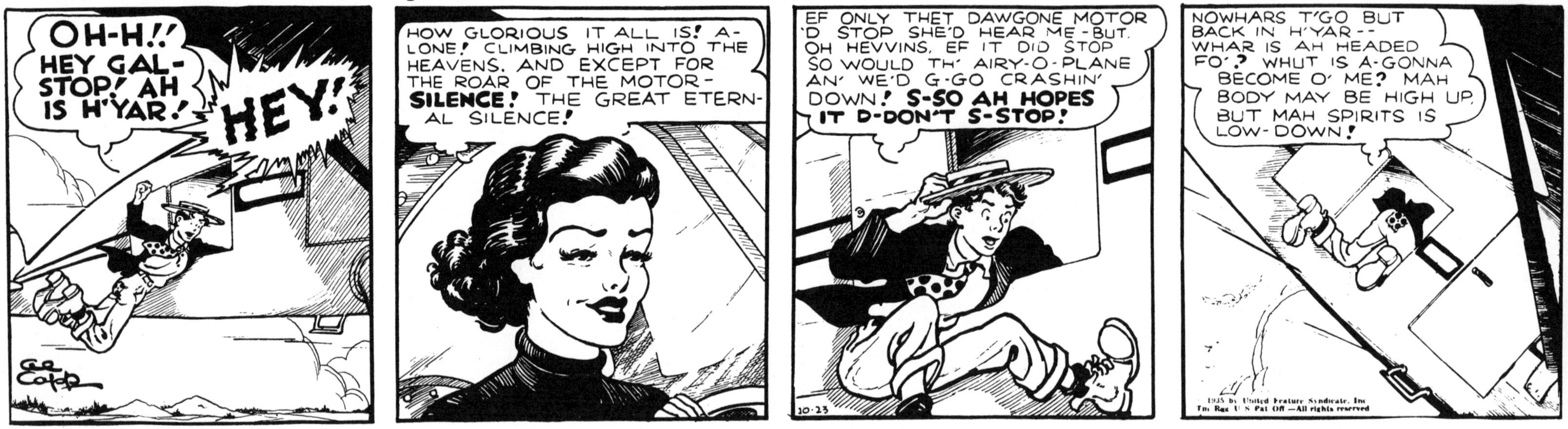
OH-H!! HEY GAL-STOP! AH IS H'YAR!
HEY!
HOW GLORIOUS IT ALL IS! A-LONE! CLIMBING HIGH INTO THE HEAVENS. AND EXCEPT FOR THE ROAR OF THE MOTOR-SILENCE! THE GREAT ETERNAL SILENCE!
EF ONLY THET DAWGONE MOTOR 'D STOP SHE'D HEAR ME-BUT. OH HEVVINS, EF IT DID STOP SO WOULD TH' AIRY-O-PLANE AN' WE'D G-GO CRASHIN' DOWN! S-SO AH HOPES IT D-DON'T S-STOP!
10-23
NOWHARS T'GO BUT BACK IN H'YAR-- WHAR IS AH HEADED FO'? WHUT IS A-GONNA BECOME O' ME? MAH BODY MAY BE HIGH UP, BUT MAH SPIRITS IS LOW-DOWN!
© 1935 by United Feature Syndicate, Inc
Tm Reg U S Pat Off —All rights reserved

LI'L ABNER A Ghost With A Straw Hat By Al Capp

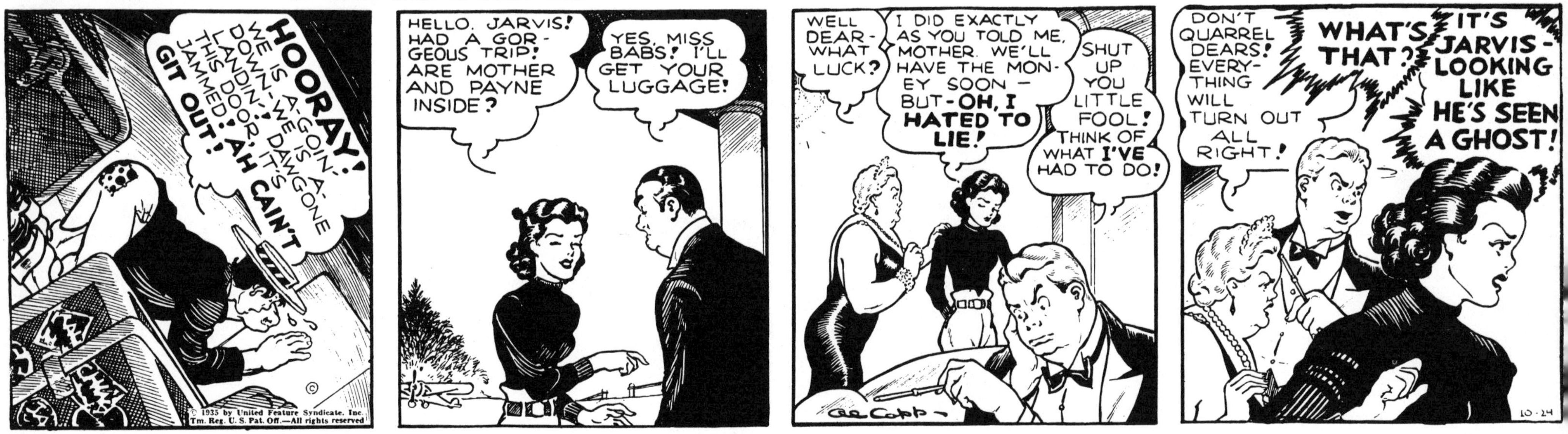
HOORAY! WE IS A-GOIN' DOWN-WE IS A-LANDIN'! DAWGONE THIS DOOR, IT'S JAMMED! AH CAIN'T GIT OUT!
© 1935 by United Feature Syndicate, Inc.
Tm. Reg. U.S. Pat. Off.—All rights reserved
HELLO, JARVIS! HAD A GORGEOUS TRIP! ARE MOTHER AND PAYNE INSIDE?
YES, MISS BABS! I'LL GET YOUR LUGGAGE!
WELL DEAR-WHAT LUCK?
I DID EXACTLY AS YOU TOLD ME, MOTHER. WE'LL HAVE THE MONEY SOON - BUT-OH, I HATED TO LIE!
SHUT UP YOU LITTLE FOOL! THINK OF WHAT I'VE HAD TO DO!
DON'T QUARREL DEARS! EVERYTHING WILL TURN OUT ALL RIGHT!
WHAT'S THAT?
IT'S JARVIS-LOOKING LIKE HE'S SEEN A GHOST!
10-24

LI'L ABNER Unwelcome Stranger By Al Capp

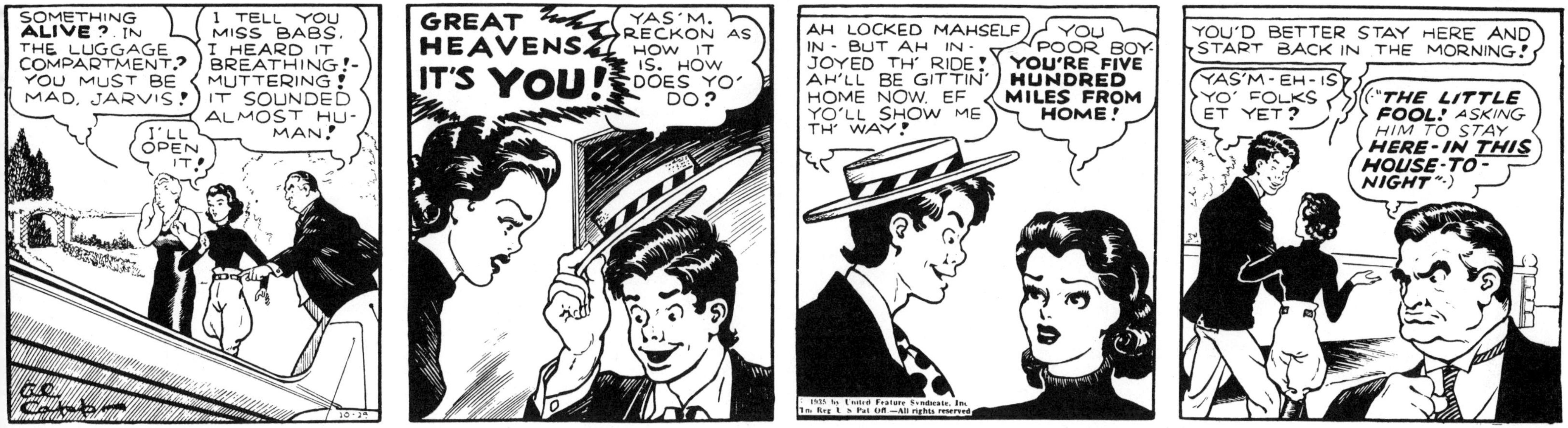
SOMETHING ALIVE? IN THE LUGGAGE COMPARTMENT? YOU MUST BE MAD, JARVIS!
I TELL YOU MISS BABS. I HEARD IT BREATHING!- MUTTERING! IT SOUNDED ALMOST HU-MAN!
I'LL OPEN IT!
10-24
GREAT HEAVENS IT'S YOU!
YAS'M. RECKON AS HOW IT IS. HOW DOES YO' DO?
AH LOCKED MAHSELF IN - BUT AH IN-JOYED TH' RIDE! AH'LL BE GITTIN' HOME NOW. EF YO'LL SHOW ME TH' WAY!
YOU POOR BOY- YOU'RE FIVE HUNDRED MILES FROM HOME!
© 1935 by United Feature Syndicate, Inc. Tm Reg U S Pat Off—All rights reserved
YOU'D BETTER STAY HERE AND START BACK IN THE MORNING!
YAS'M - EH - IS YO' FOLKS ET YET?
("THE LITTLE FOOL! ASKING HIM TO STAY HERE - IN THIS HOUSE - TO-NIGHT"-)

LI'L ABNER Orders From A Servant! By Al Capp

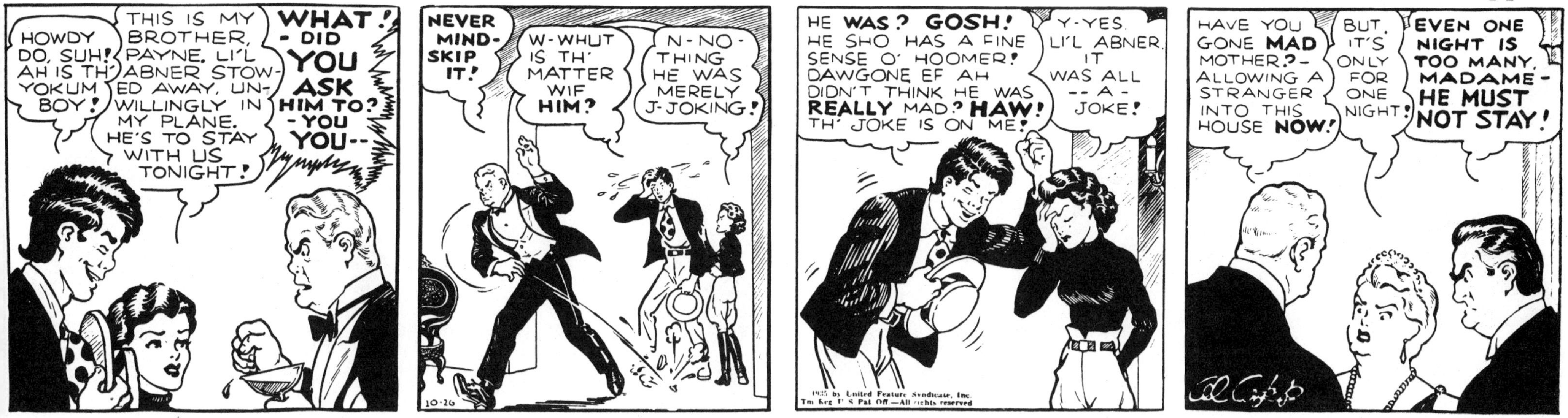
HOWDY DO, SUH! AH IS TH' YOKUM BOY!
THIS IS MY BROTHER, PAYNE. LI'L ABNER STOW-ED AWAY, UN-WILLINGLY IN MY PLANE. HE'S TO STAY WITH US TONIGHT!
WHAT! - DID YOU ASK HIM TO? - YOU YOU--
NEVER MIND-SKIP IT!
W-WHUT IS TH' MATTER WIF HIM?
N-NO-THING HE WAS MERELY J-JOKING!
10-26
HE WAS? GOSH! HE SHO HAS A FINE SENSE O' HOOMER! DAWGONE EF AH DIDN'T THINK HE WAS REALLY MAD? HAW! TH' JOKE IS ON ME!
Y-YES. LI'L ABNER. IT WAS ALL -- A - JOKE!
© 1935 by United Feature Syndicate, Inc. Tm Reg U S Pat Off—All rights reserved
HAVE YOU GONE MAD MOTHER?- ALLOWING A STRANGER INTO THIS HOUSE NOW!
BUT, IT'S ONLY FOR ONE NIGHT!
EVEN ONE NIGHT IS TOO MANY, MADAME - HE MUST NOT STAY!

LI'L ABNER Please Stay—But Not Long By Al Capp

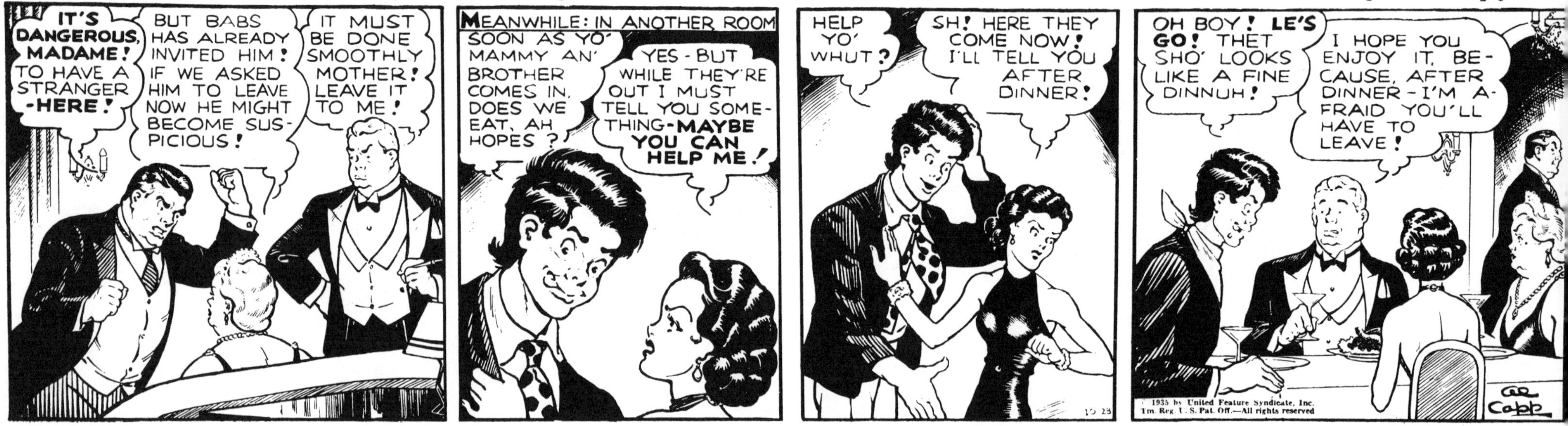

IT'S DANGEROUS, MADAME! TO HAVE A STRANGER -HERE!
BUT BABS HAS ALREADY INVITED HIM! IF WE ASKED HIM TO LEAVE NOW HE MIGHT BECOME SUSPICIOUS!
IT MUST BE DONE SMOOTHLY MOTHER! LEAVE IT TO ME!
MEANWHILE: IN ANOTHER ROOM
SOON AS YO' MAMMY AN' BROTHER COMES IN, DOES WE EAT, AH HOPES?
YES - BUT WHILE THEY'RE OUT I MUST TELL YOU SOMETHING-MAYBE YOU CAN HELP ME!
HELP YO' WHUT?
SH! HERE THEY COME NOW! I'LL TELL YOU AFTER DINNER!
OH BOY! LE'S GO! THET SHO' LOOKS LIKE A FINE DINNUH!
I HOPE YOU ENJOY IT, BECAUSE, AFTER DINNER - I'M AFRAID YOU'LL HAVE TO LEAVE!
© 1935 by United Feature Syndicate, Inc. Tm Reg. U.S. Pat. Off.—All rights reserved

LI'L ABNER Abner Ketches On By Al Capp

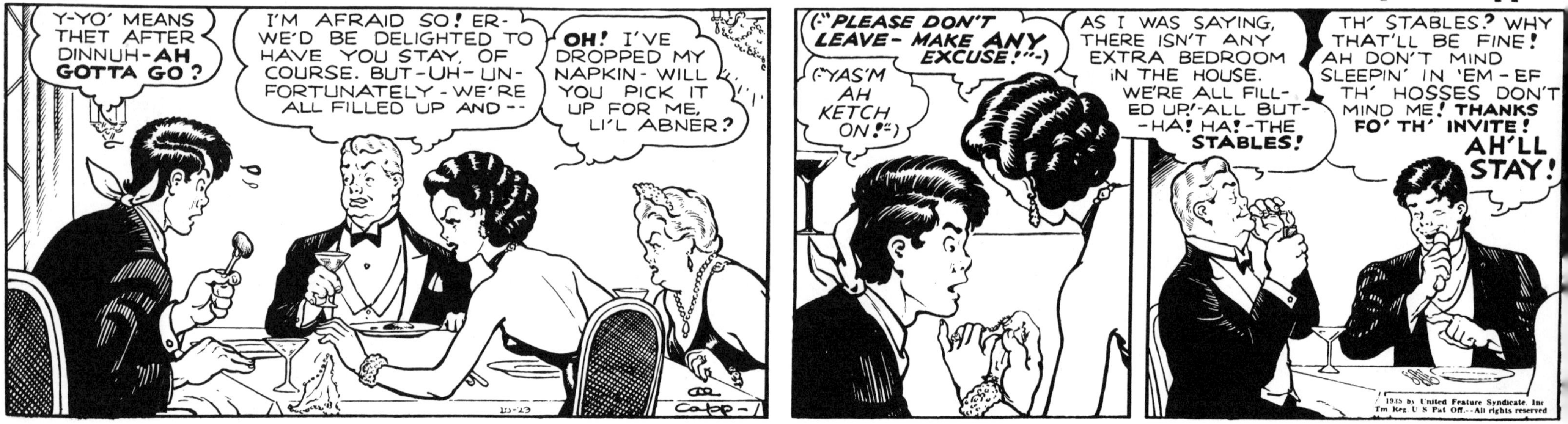

Y-YO' MEANS THET AFTER DINNUH-AH GOTTA GO?
I'M AFRAID SO! ER- WE'D BE DELIGHTED TO HAVE YOU STAY, OF COURSE. BUT-UH-UNFORTUNATELY - WE'RE ALL FILLED UP AND--
OH! I'VE DROPPED MY NAPKIN- WILL YOU PICK IT UP FOR ME, LI'L ABNER?
("PLEASE DON'T LEAVE- MAKE ANY EXCUSE!"-)
("YAS'M AH KETCH ON!"-)
AS I WAS SAYING, THERE ISN'T ANY EXTRA BEDROOM IN THE HOUSE. WE'RE ALL FILLED UP!-ALL BUT- -HA! HA!-THE STABLES!
TH' STABLES? WHY THAT'LL BE FINE! AH DON'T MIND SLEEPIN' IN 'EM - EF TH' HOSSES DON'T MIND ME! THANKS FO' TH' INVITE! AH'LL STAY!
© 1935 by United Feature Syndicate, Inc. Tm Reg. U.S. Pat. Off.--All rights reserved

LI'L ABNER It's a Matter of Opinion, Fella By Al Capp

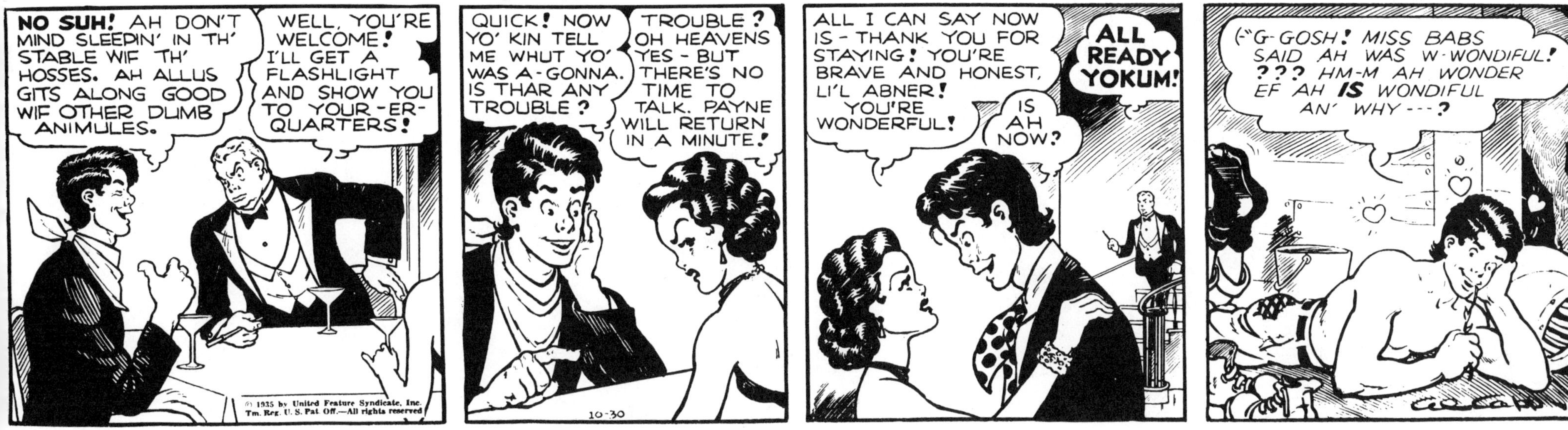

NO SUH! AH DON'T MIND SLEEPIN' IN TH' STABLE WIF TH' HOSSES. AH ALLUS GITS ALONG GOOD WIF OTHER DUMB ANIMULES.
WELL, YOU'RE WELCOME! I'LL GET A FLASHLIGHT AND SHOW YOU TO YOUR-ER-QUARTERS!
© 1935 by United Feature Syndicate, Inc. Tm. Reg. U. S. Pat. Off.—All rights reserved
QUICK! NOW YO' KIN TELL ME WHUT YO' WAS A-GONNA. IS THAR ANY TROUBLE?
TROUBLE? OH HEAVENS YES - BUT THERE'S NO TIME TO TALK. PAYNE WILL RETURN IN A MINUTE!
10-30
ALL I CAN SAY NOW IS - THANK YOU FOR STAYING! YOU'RE BRAVE AND HONEST, LI'L ABNER! YOU'RE WONDERFUL!
IS AH NOW?
ALL READY YOKUM!
"G-GOSH! MISS BABS SAID AH WAS W-WONDIFUL! ??? HM-M AH WONDER EF AH IS WONDIFUL AN' WHY---?

LI'L ABNER It Were No Ghost By Al Capp

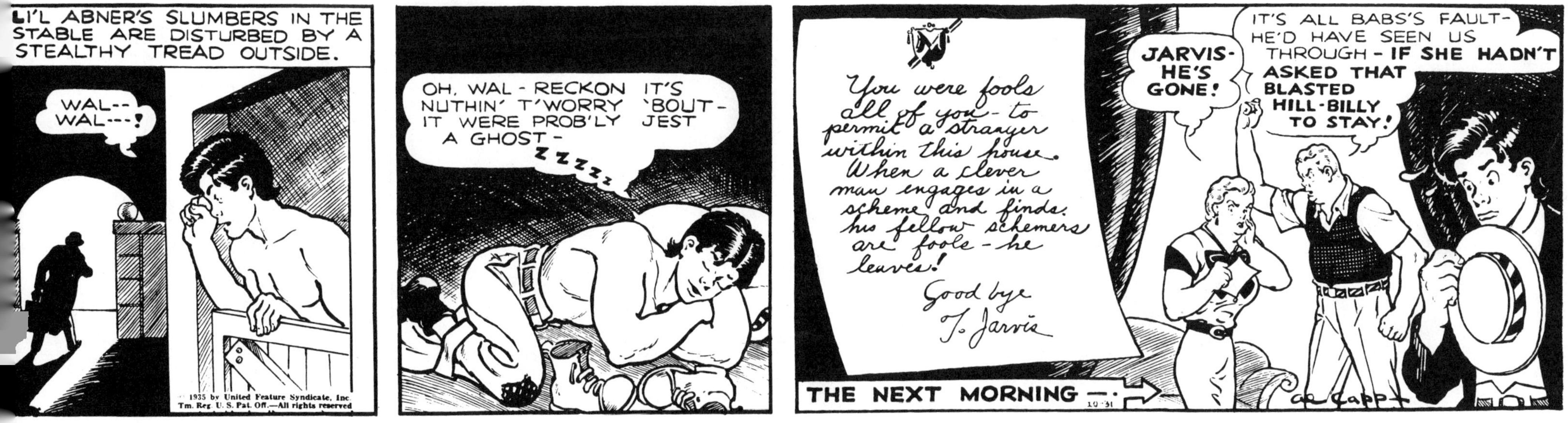

LI'L ABNER'S SLUMBERS IN THE STABLE ARE DISTURBED BY A STEALTHY TREAD OUTSIDE.
WAL-- WAL---!
© 1935 by United Feature Syndicate, Inc. Tm. Reg. U. S. Pat. Off.—All rights reserved
OH, WAL - RECKON IT'S NUTHIN' T'WORRY 'BOUT - IT WERE PROB'LY JEST A GHOST -
ZZZZZ
You were fools all of you - to permit a stranger within this house. When a clever man engages in a scheme and finds his fellow schemers are fools - he leaves!
Good bye T. Jarvis
JARVIS - HE'S GONE!
IT'S ALL BABS'S FAULT - HE'D HAVE SEEN US THROUGH - IF SHE HADN'T ASKED THAT BLASTED HILL-BILLY TO STAY!
THE NEXT MORNING —
10-31

LI'L ABNER Babs Puts One Over By Al Capp

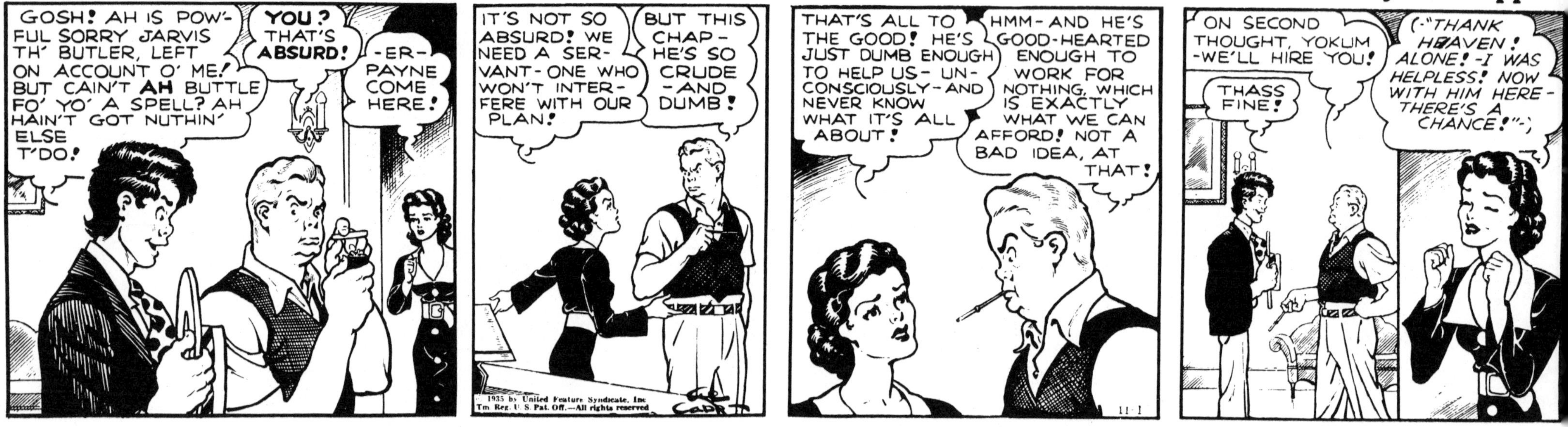
GOSH! AH IS POW-FUL SORRY JARVIS TH' BUTLER, LEFT ON ACCOUNT O' ME! BUT CAIN'T AH BUTTLE FO' YO' A SPELL? AH HAIN'T GOT NUTHIN' ELSE T'DO!
YOU? THAT'S ABSURD!
-ER-PAYNE COME HERE!
IT'S NOT SO ABSURD! WE NEED A SER-VANT-ONE WHO WON'T INTER-FERE WITH OUR PLAN!
BUT THIS CHAP-HE'S SO CRUDE-AND DUMB!
© 1935 by United Feature Syndicate, Inc. Tm. Reg. U.S. Pat. Off.—All rights reserved
THAT'S ALL TO THE GOOD! HE'S JUST DUMB ENOUGH TO HELP US-UN-CONSCIOUSLY-AND NEVER KNOW WHAT IT'S ALL ABOUT!
HMM-AND HE'S GOOD-HEARTED ENOUGH TO WORK FOR NOTHING, WHICH IS EXACTLY WHAT WE CAN AFFORD! NOT A BAD IDEA, AT THAT!
11-1
ON SECOND THOUGHT, YOKUM-WE'LL HIRE YOU!
THASS FINE!
(-"THANK HEAVEN! ALONE!-I WAS HELPLESS! NOW WITH HIM HERE-THERE'S A CHANCE!"-)

LI'L ABNER Big Brother By Al Capp

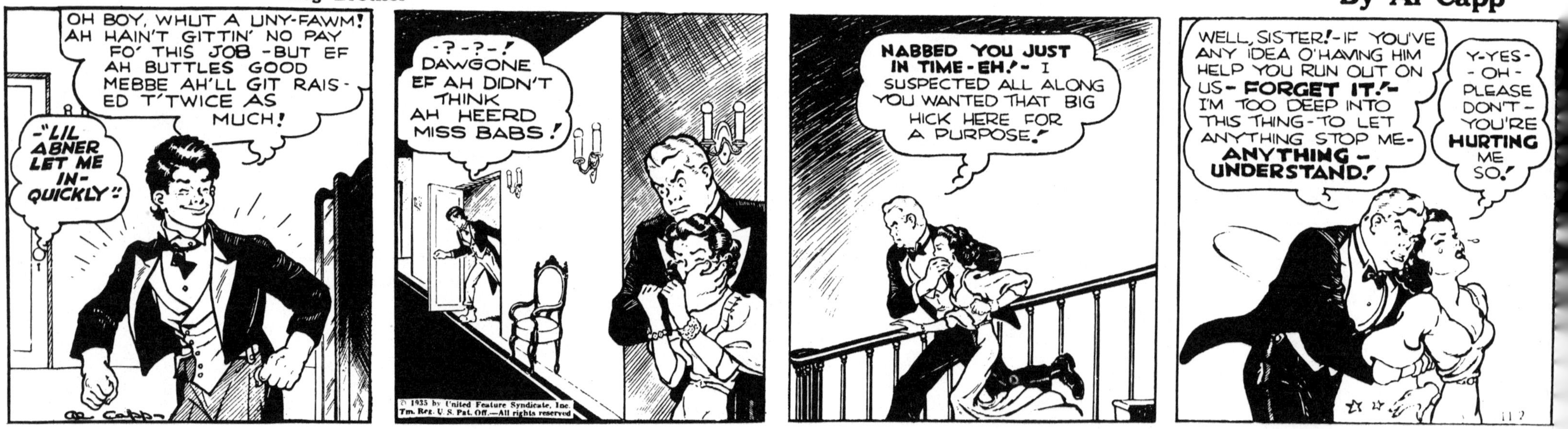
OH BOY, WHUT A UNY-FAWM! AH HAIN'T GITTIN' NO PAY FO' THIS JOB-BUT EF AH BUTTLES GOOD MEBBE AH'LL GIT RAIS-ED T'TWICE AS MUCH!
-"LIL ABNER LET ME IN-QUICKLY"-
-?-?-! DAWGONE EF AH DIDN'T THINK AH HEERD MISS BABS!
© 1935 by United Feature Syndicate, Inc. Tm. Reg. U.S. Pat. Off.—All rights reserved
NABBED YOU JUST IN TIME-EH!- I SUSPECTED ALL ALONG YOU WANTED THAT BIG HICK HERE FOR A PURPOSE!
WELL, SISTER!-IF YOU'VE ANY IDEA O'HAVING HIM HELP YOU RUN OUT ON US-FORGET IT!-I'M TOO DEEP INTO THIS THING-TO LET ANYTHING STOP ME-ANYTHING-UNDERSTAND!
Y-YES-OH-PLEASE DON'T-YOU'RE HURTING ME SO!
11-2

LI'L ABNER — A Gal On His Mind — By Al Capp

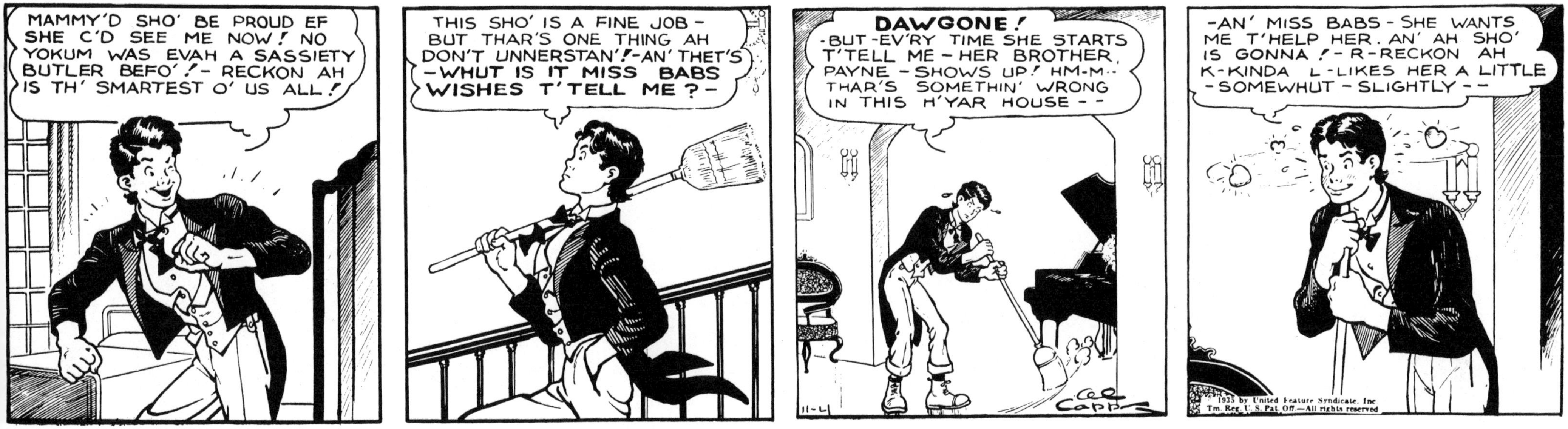

MAMMY'D SHO' BE PROUD EF SHE C'D SEE ME NOW! NO YOKUM WAS EVAH A SASSIETY BUTLER BEFO'! - RECKON AH IS TH' SMARTEST O' US ALL!
THIS SHO' IS A FINE JOB - BUT THAR'S ONE THING AH DON'T UNNERSTAN'! - AN' THET'S - WHUT IS IT MISS BABS WISHES T'TELL ME? -
DAWGONE! - BUT - EV'RY TIME SHE STARTS T'TELL ME - HER BROTHER, PAYNE - SHOWS UP! HM-M - THAR'S SOMETHIN' WRONG IN THIS H'YAR HOUSE - -
11-4
AL CAPP
- AN' MISS BABS - SHE WANTS ME T'HELP HER. AN' AH SHO' IS GONNA! - R-RECKON AH K-KINDA L-LIKES HER A LITTLE - SOMEWHUT - SLIGHTLY - -
© 1935 by United Feature Syndicate, Inc
Tm. Reg. U.S. Pat. Off.—All rights reserved

LI'L ABNER — The Very Best People — By Al Capp

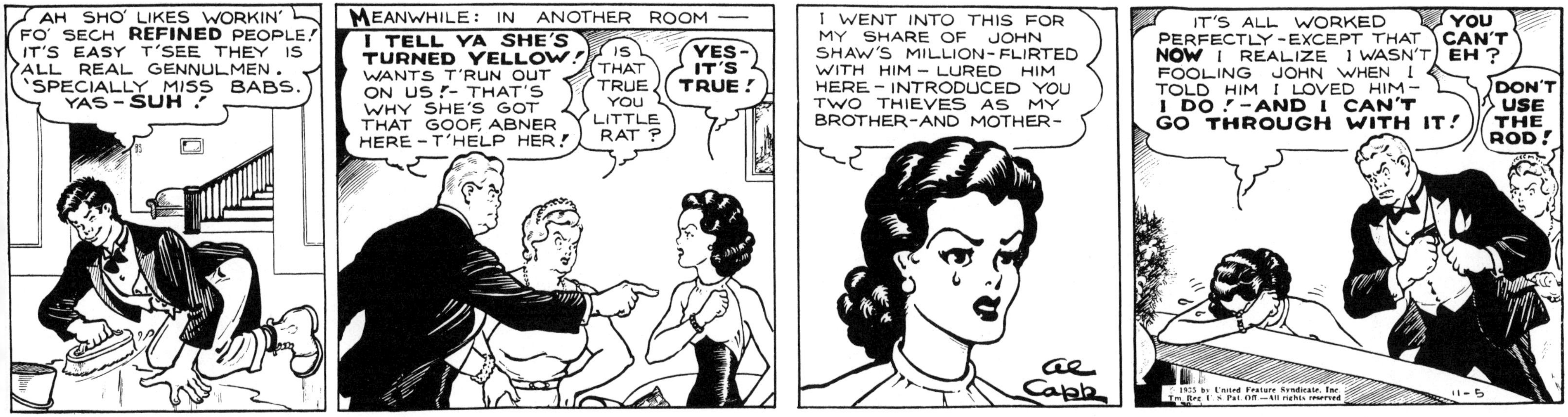

AH SHO' LIKES WORKIN' FO' SECH REFINED PEOPLE! IT'S EASY T'SEE THEY IS ALL REAL GENNULMEN. 'SPECIALLY MISS BABS. YAS - SUH!
MEANWHILE: IN ANOTHER ROOM —
I TELL YA SHE'S TURNED YELLOW! WANTS T'RUN OUT ON US! - THAT'S WHY SHE'S GOT THAT GOOF, ABNER HERE - T'HELP HER!
IS THAT TRUE YOU LITTLE RAT?
YES - IT'S TRUE!
I WENT INTO THIS FOR MY SHARE OF JOHN SHAW'S MILLION - FLIRTED WITH HIM - LURED HIM HERE - INTRODUCED YOU TWO THIEVES AS MY BROTHER - AND MOTHER -
AL CAPP
IT'S ALL WORKED PERFECTLY - EXCEPT THAT NOW I REALIZE I WASN'T FOOLING JOHN WHEN I TOLD HIM I LOVED HIM - I DO! - AND I CAN'T GO THROUGH WITH IT!
YOU CAN'T EH?
DON'T USE THE ROD!
© 1935 by United Feature Syndicate, Inc
Tm. Reg. U.S. Pat. Off.—All rights reserved
11-5

LI'L ABNER

Red-Hot Culture

By Al Capp

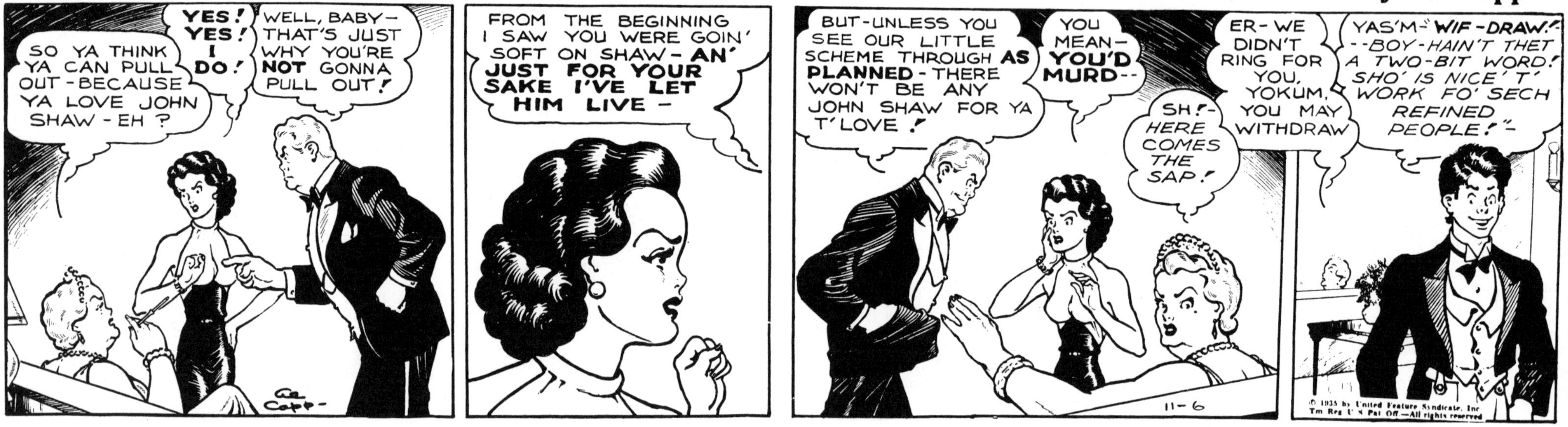

SO YA THINK YA CAN PULL OUT - BECAUSE YA LOVE JOHN SHAW - EH ?
YES! YES! I DO!
WELL, BABY - THAT'S JUST WHY YOU'RE NOT GONNA PULL OUT!
Al Capp
FROM THE BEGINNING I SAW YOU WERE GOIN' SOFT ON SHAW - AN' JUST FOR YOUR SAKE I'VE LET HIM LIVE -
BUT - UNLESS YOU SEE OUR LITTLE SCHEME THROUGH AS PLANNED - THERE WON'T BE ANY JOHN SHAW FOR YA T'LOVE!
YOU MEAN - YOU'D MURD- -
SH! - HERE COMES THE SAP!
11-6
ER - WE DIDN'T RING FOR YOU, YOKUM, YOU MAY WITHDRAW
YAS'M - WIF-DRAW! - - BOY - HAIN'T THET A TWO-BIT WORD! SHO' IS NICE 'T' WORK FO' SECH REFINED PEOPLE! -
© 1935 by United Feature Syndicate, Inc. Tm Reg U S Pat Off — All rights reserved

LI'L ABNER

Bring In the Sap

By Al Capp

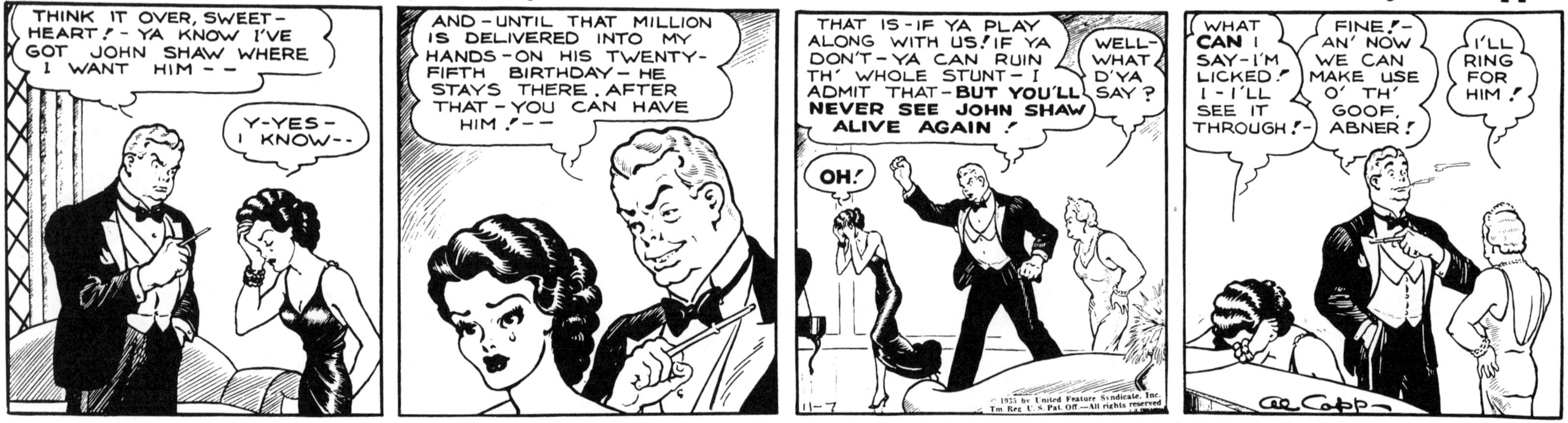

THINK IT OVER, SWEET-HEART! - YA KNOW I'VE GOT JOHN SHAW WHERE I WANT HIM - -
Y-YES - I KNOW - -
AND - UNTIL THAT MILLION IS DELIVERED INTO MY HANDS - ON HIS TWENTY-FIFTH BIRTHDAY - HE STAYS THERE. AFTER THAT - YOU CAN HAVE HIM! - -
THAT IS - IF YA PLAY ALONG WITH US! IF YA DON'T - YA CAN RUIN TH' WHOLE STUNT - I ADMIT THAT - BUT YOU'LL NEVER SEE JOHN SHAW ALIVE AGAIN!
WELL - WHAT D'YA SAY?
OH!
11-7
© 1935 by United Feature Syndicate, Inc. Tm Reg U.S. Pat. Off. — All rights reserved
WHAT CAN I SAY - I'M LICKED! I - I'LL SEE IT THROUGH! -
FINE! - AN' NOW WE CAN MAKE USE O' TH' GOOF, ABNER!
I'LL RING FOR HIM!
Al Capp

LI'L ABNER Into the Web By Al Capp

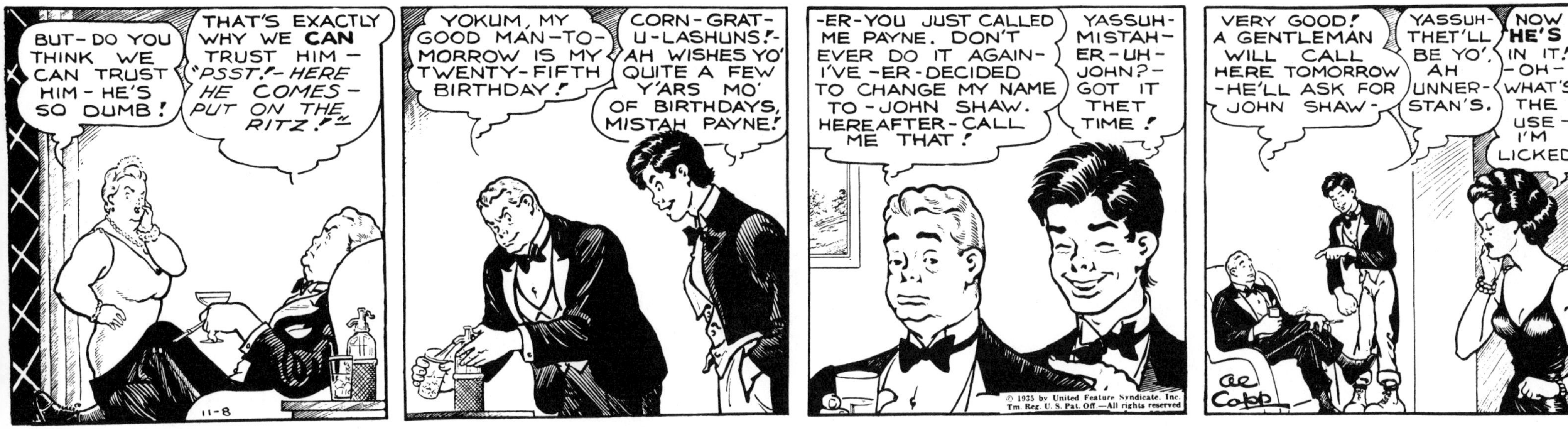
BUT-DO YOU THINK WE CAN TRUST HIM-HE'S SO DUMB!
THAT'S EXACTLY WHY WE **CAN** TRUST HIM-"PSST!-HERE HE COMES-PUT ON THE RITZ!"-
11-8
YOKUM, MY GOOD MAN-TO-MORROW IS MY TWENTY-FIFTH BIRTHDAY!
CORN-GRAT-U-LASHUNS!-AH WISHES YO' QUITE A FEW Y'ARS MO' OF BIRTHDAYS, MISTAH PAYNE!
-ER-YOU JUST CALLED ME PAYNE. DON'T EVER DO IT AGAIN-I'VE-ER-DECIDED TO CHANGE MY NAME TO-JOHN SHAW. HEREAFTER-CALL ME THAT!
YASSUH-MISTAH-ER-UH-JOHN?-GOT IT THET TIME!
© 1935 by United Feature Syndicate, Inc. Tm. Reg. U. S. Pat. Off.—All rights reserved
VERY GOOD! A GENTLEMAN WILL CALL HERE TOMORROW-HE'LL ASK FOR JOHN SHAW-
YASSUH-THET'LL BE YO', AH UNNER-STAN'S.
NOW **HE'S** IN IT!-OH-WHAT'S THE USE-I'M LICKED!

LI'L ABNER Danger Ahead By Al Capp

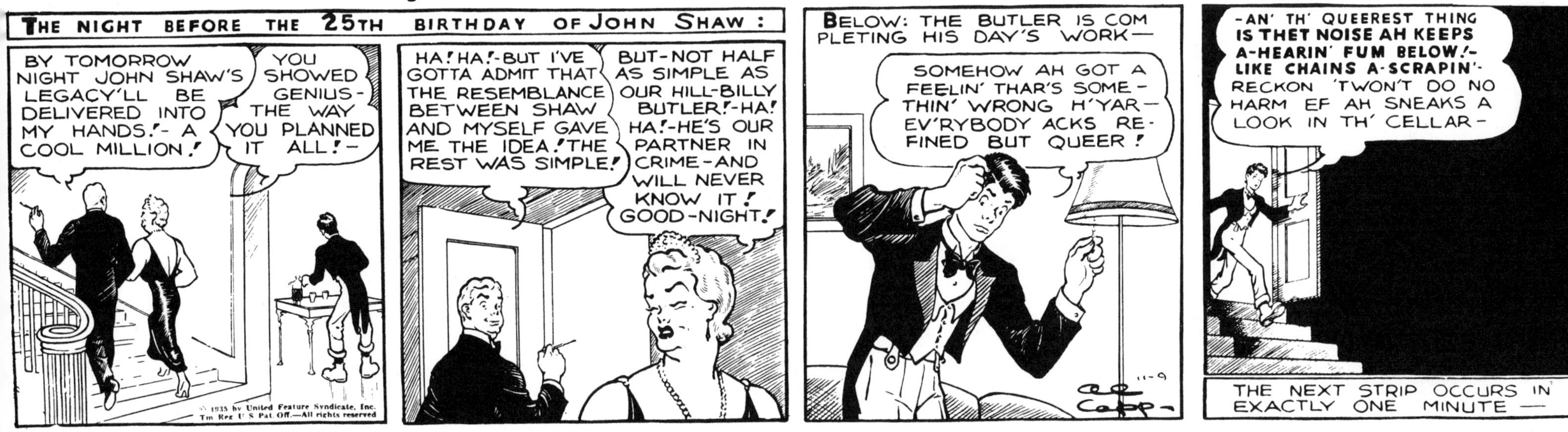
THE NIGHT BEFORE THE 25TH BIRTHDAY OF JOHN SHAW:
BY TOMORROW NIGHT JOHN SHAW'S LEGACY'LL BE DELIVERED INTO MY HANDS!-A COOL MILLION!
YOU SHOWED GENIUS-THE WAY YOU PLANNED IT ALL!-
© 1935 by United Feature Syndicate, Inc. Tm. Reg. U. S. Pat. Off.—All rights reserved
HA! HA!-BUT I'VE GOTTA ADMIT THAT THE RESEMBLANCE BETWEEN SHAW AND MYSELF GAVE ME THE IDEA! THE REST WAS SIMPLE!
BUT-NOT HALF AS SIMPLE AS OUR HILL-BILLY BUTLER!-HA! HA!-HE'S OUR PARTNER IN CRIME-AND WILL NEVER KNOW IT! GOOD-NIGHT!
BELOW: THE BUTLER IS COMPLETING HIS DAY'S WORK—
SOMEHOW AH GOT A FEELIN' THAR'S SOME-THIN' WRONG H'YAR-EV'RYBODY ACKS RE-FINED BUT QUEER!
11-9
-AN' TH' QUEEREST THING **IS THET NOISE AH KEEPS A-HEARIN' FUM BELOW!-LIKE CHAINS A-SCRAPIN'**-RECKON 'TWON'T DO NO HARM EF AH SNEAKS A LOOK IN TH' CELLAR-
THE NEXT STRIP OCCURS IN EXACTLY ONE MINUTE —

LI'L ABNER No Dumb Animule By Al Capp

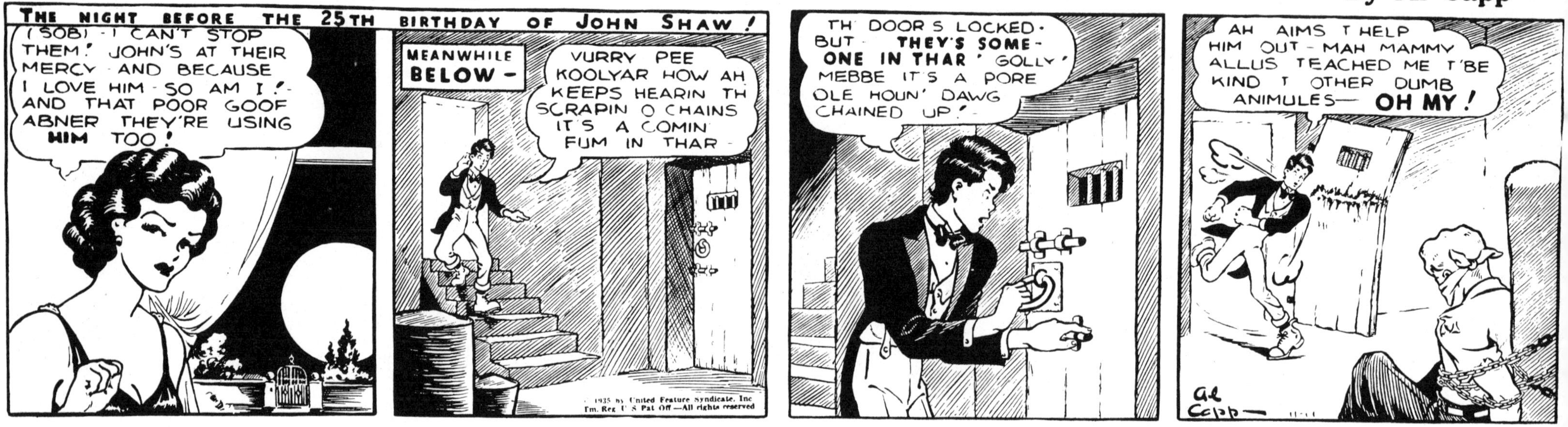
THE NIGHT BEFORE THE 25TH BIRTHDAY OF JOHN SHAW!
(SOB) - I CAN'T STOP THEM! JOHN'S AT THEIR MERCY - AND BECAUSE I LOVE HIM - SO AM I! - AND THAT POOR GOOF ABNER THEY'RE USING HIM TOO!
MEANWHILE BELOW -
VURRY PEE KOOLYAR HOW AH KEEPS HEARIN TH SCRAPIN O CHAINS IT'S A COMIN FUM IN THAR -
© 1935 by United Feature Syndicate, Inc
Tm. Reg. U S Pat Off —All rights reserved
TH DOOR'S LOCKED - BUT - THEY'S SOME-ONE IN THAR' GOLLY! MEBBE IT'S A PORE OLE HOUN' DAWG CHAINED UP! -
AH AIMS T HELP HIM OUT - MAH MAMMY ALLUS TEACHED ME T'BE KIND T OTHER DUMB ANIMULES— OH MY!
Al Capp

LI'L ABNER Abner Don't Get It By Al Capp

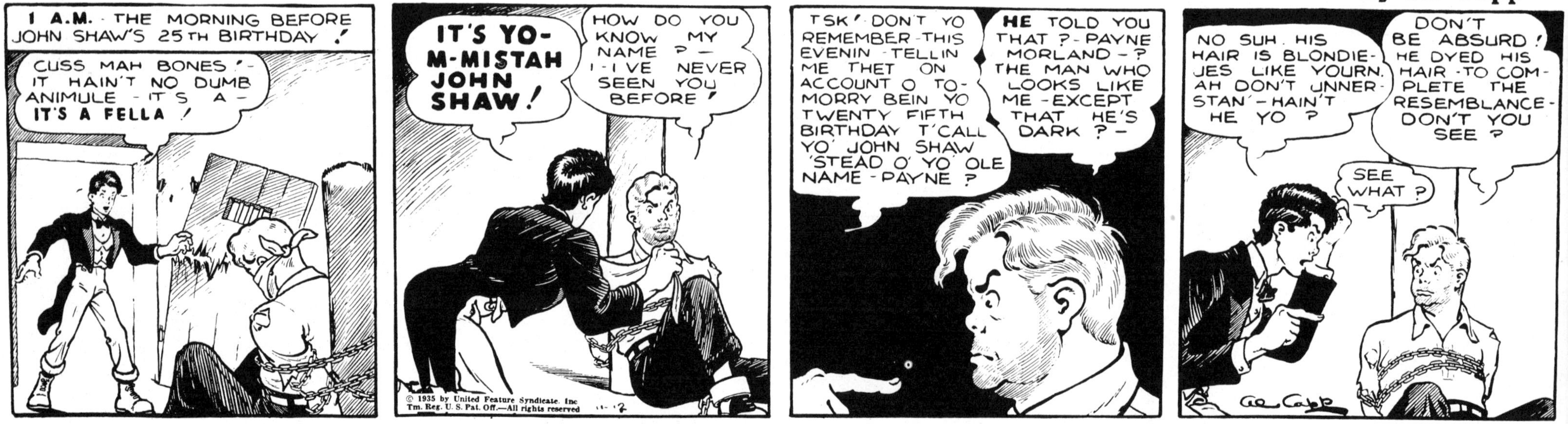
1 A.M. - THE MORNING BEFORE JOHN SHAW'S 25TH BIRTHDAY!
CUSS MAH BONES! - IT HAIN'T NO DUMB ANIMULE - IT'S A - IT'S A FELLA!
IT'S YO-M-MISTAH JOHN SHAW!
HOW DO YOU KNOW MY NAME? - I - I'VE NEVER SEEN YOU BEFORE!
© 1935 by United Feature Syndicate, Inc
Tm. Reg. U. S. Pat. Off.—All rights reserved
TSK! DON'T YO REMEMBER - THIS EVENIN - TELLIN ME THET ON ACCOUNT O TO-MORRY BEIN YO TWENTY FIFTH BIRTHDAY T'CALL YO' JOHN SHAW 'STEAD O' YO' OLE NAME - PAYNE?
HE TOLD YOU THAT? - PAYNE MORLAND -? THE MAN WHO LOOKS LIKE ME - EXCEPT THAT HE'S DARK? -
NO SUH. HIS HAIR IS BLONDIE-JES LIKE YOURN. AH DON'T UNNER-STAN' - HAIN'T HE YO?
DON'T BE ABSURD! HE DYED HIS HAIR - TO COM-PLETE THE RESEMBLANCE - DON'T YOU SEE?
SEE WHAT?
Al Capp

LI'L ABNER The Mystery Revealed By Al Capp

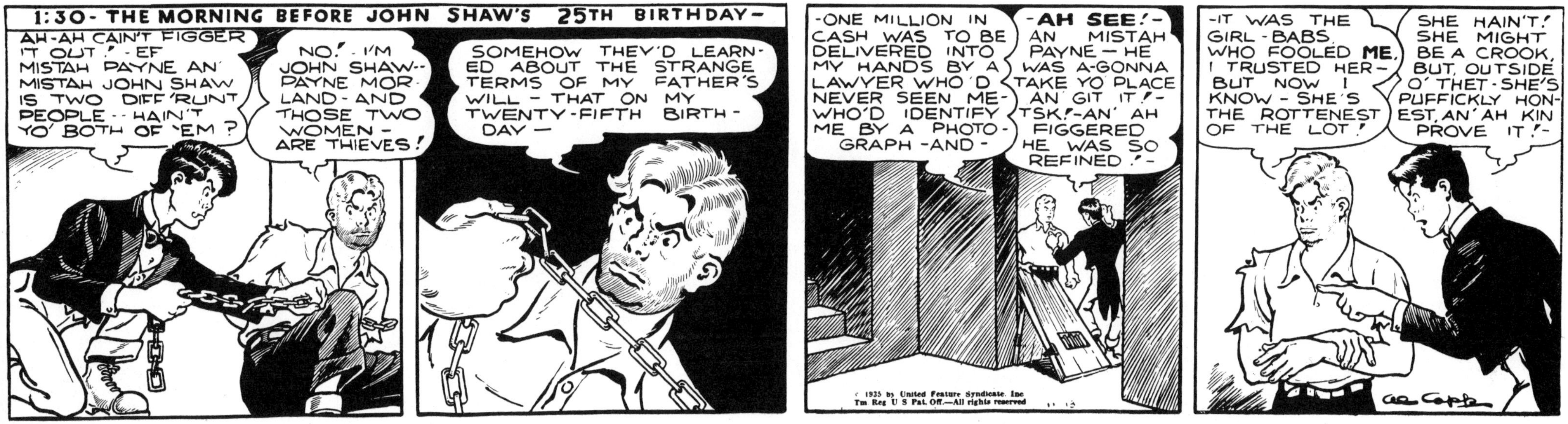

1:30 - THE MORNING BEFORE JOHN SHAW'S 25TH BIRTHDAY -
AH-AH CAIN'T FIGGER IT OUT! - EF MISTAH PAYNE AN' MISTAH JOHN SHAW IS TWO DIFF'RUNT PEOPLE - - HAIN'T YO' BOTH OF 'EM ?
NO! - I'M JOHN SHAW - - PAYNE MORLAND - AND THOSE TWO WOMEN - ARE THIEVES!
SOMEHOW THEY'D LEARNED ABOUT THE STRANGE TERMS OF MY FATHER'S WILL - THAT ON MY TWENTY-FIFTH BIRTHDAY -
-ONE MILLION IN CASH WAS TO BE DELIVERED INTO MY HANDS BY A LAWYER WHO'D NEVER SEEN ME - WHO'D IDENTIFY ME BY A PHOTOGRAPH - AND -
-AH SEE! - AN MISTAH PAYNE - HE WAS A-GONNA TAKE YO' PLACE AN' GIT IT! - TSK! - AN' AH FIGGERED HE WAS SO REFINED! -
-IT WAS THE GIRL - BABS WHO FOOLED ME. I TRUSTED HER - BUT NOW I KNOW - SHE'S THE ROTTENEST OF THE LOT!
SHE HAIN'T! SHE MIGHT BE A CROOK, BUT, OUTSIDE O' THET - SHE'S PUFFICKLY HONEST, AN' AH KIN PROVE IT! -
© 1935 by United Feature Syndicate, Inc
Tm Reg U S Pat. Off.—All rights reserved

LI'L ABNER Sleeves That Pass In the Night By Al Capp

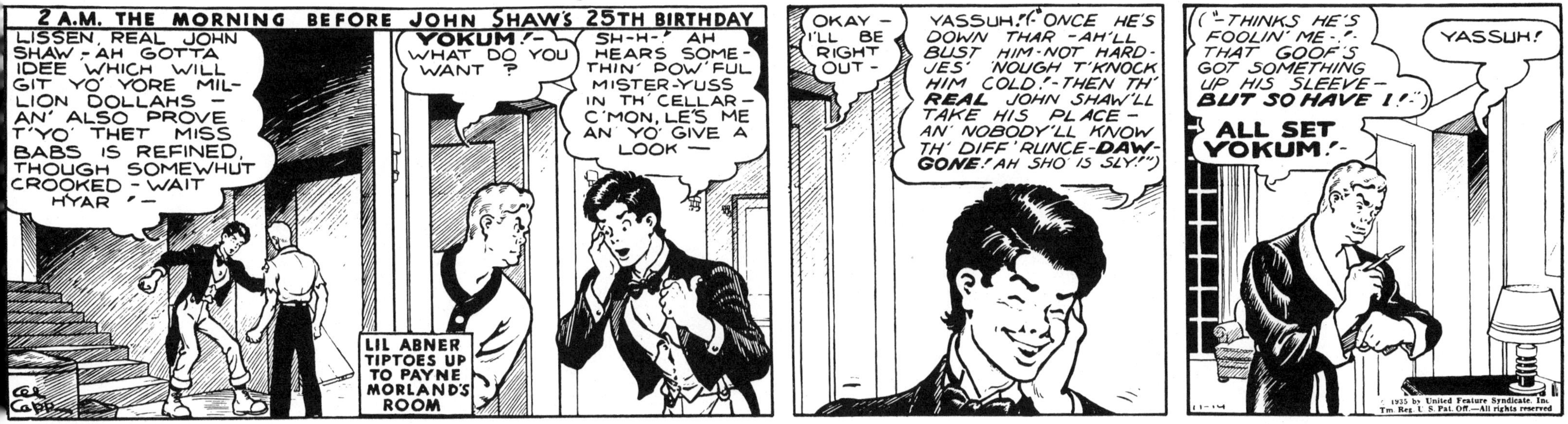

2 A.M. THE MORNING BEFORE JOHN SHAW'S 25TH BIRTHDAY
LISSEN, REAL JOHN SHAW - AH GOTTA IDEE WHICH WILL GIT YO' YORE MILLION DOLLAHS - AN' ALSO PROVE T'YO' THET MISS BABS IS REFINED, THOUGH SOMEWHUT CROOKED - WAIT HYAR ' -
YOKUM! - WHAT DO YOU WANT ?
SH-H-! AH HEARS SOMETHIN' POW'FUL MISTER-YUSS IN TH' CELLAR - C'MON, LE'S ME AN' YO' GIVE A LOOK -
LIL ABNER TIPTOES UP TO PAYNE MORLAND'S ROOM
OKAY - I'LL BE RIGHT OUT -
YASSUH! ("ONCE HE'S DOWN THAR - AH'LL BUST HIM - NOT HARD - JES' 'NOUGH T'KNOCK HIM COLD! - THEN TH' REAL JOHN SHAW'LL TAKE HIS PLACE - AN' NOBODY'LL KNOW TH' DIFF'RUNCE - DAWGONE! AH SHO' IS SLY!")
("- THINKS HE'S FOOLIN' ME -! - THAT GOOF'S GOT SOMETHING UP HIS SLEEVE - BUT SO HAVE I! -")
YASSUH!
ALL SET YOKUM! -
© 1935 by United Feature Syndicate, Inc
Tm Reg U S Pat. Off.—All rights reserved

LI'L ABNER Reverse Surprise By Al Capp

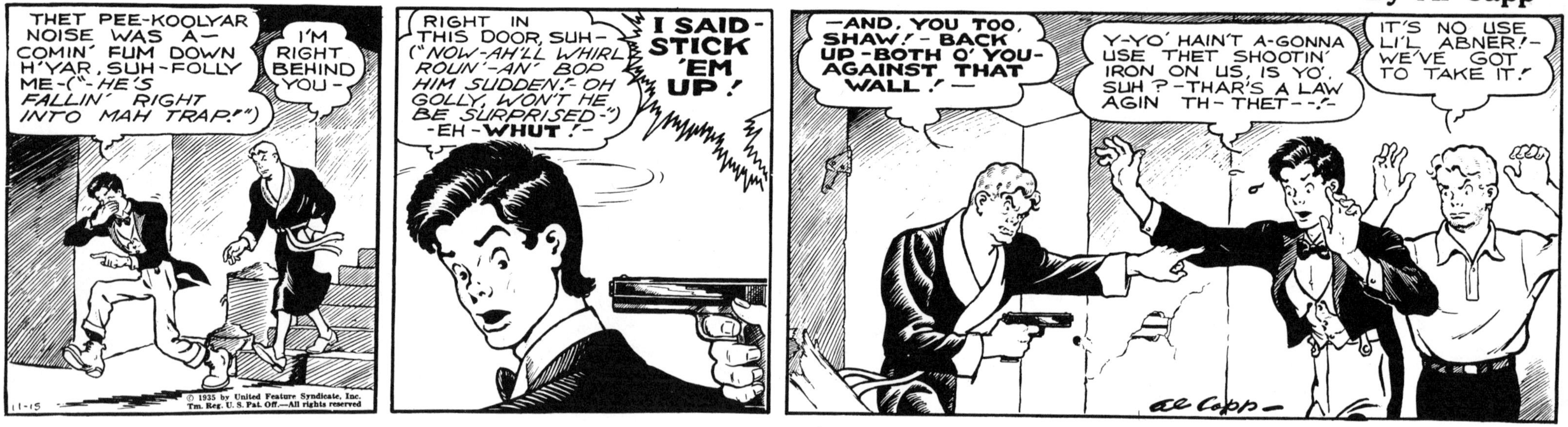
THET PEE-KOOLYAR NOISE WAS A-COMIN' FUM DOWN H'YAR, SUH-FOLLY ME-("-HE'S FALLIN' RIGHT INTO MAH TRAP!")
I'M RIGHT BEHIND YOU-
11-15
© 1935 by United Feature Syndicate, Inc. Tm. Reg. U. S. Pat. Off.—All rights reserved
RIGHT IN THIS DOOR, SUH-("NOW-AH'LL WHIRL ROUN'-AN' BOP HIM SUDDEN!-OH GOLLY, WON'T HE BE SURPRISED-") -EH-WHUT!-
I SAID-STICK 'EM UP!
-AND, YOU TOO, SHAW!-BACK UP-BOTH O' YOU-AGAINST THAT WALL!-
Y-YO' HAIN'T A-GONNA USE THET SHOOTIN' IRON ON US, IS YO', SUH?-THAR'S A LAW AGIN TH-THET--!-
IT'S NO USE LI'L ABNER!-WE'VE GOT TO TAKE IT!
Al Capp

LI'L ABNER Direct Hit By Al Capp

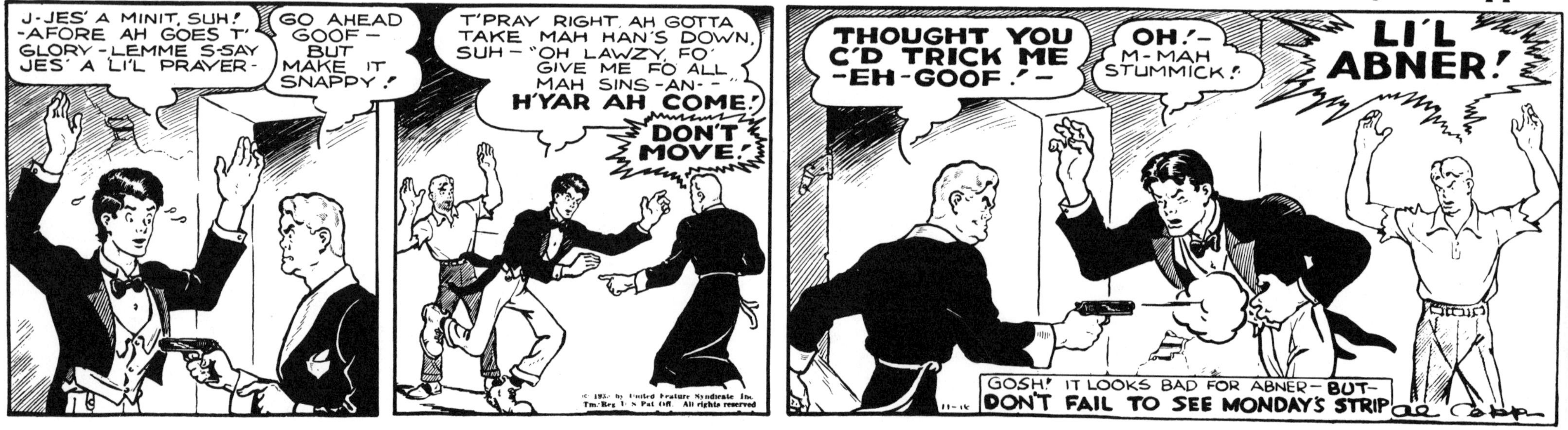
J-JES' A MINIT, SUH!-AFORE AH GOES T' GLORY-LEMME S-SAY JES' A LI'L PRAYER-
GO AHEAD GOOF-BUT MAKE IT SNAPPY!
T'PRAY RIGHT, AH GOTTA TAKE MAH HAN'S DOWN, SUH-"OH LAWZY, FO' GIVE ME FO ALL MAH SINS-AN--" H'YAR AH COME!
DON'T MOVE!
© 1935 by United Feature Syndicate Inc. Tm. Reg. U. S. Pat. Off. All rights reserved
THOUGHT YOU C'D TRICK ME -EH-GOOF!-
OH!-M-MAH STUMMICK!
LI'L ABNER!
GOSH! IT LOOKS BAD FOR ABNER-BUT-DON'T FAIL TO SEE MONDAY'S STRIP
Al Capp

LI'L ABNER Valuable To His Mammy By Al Capp

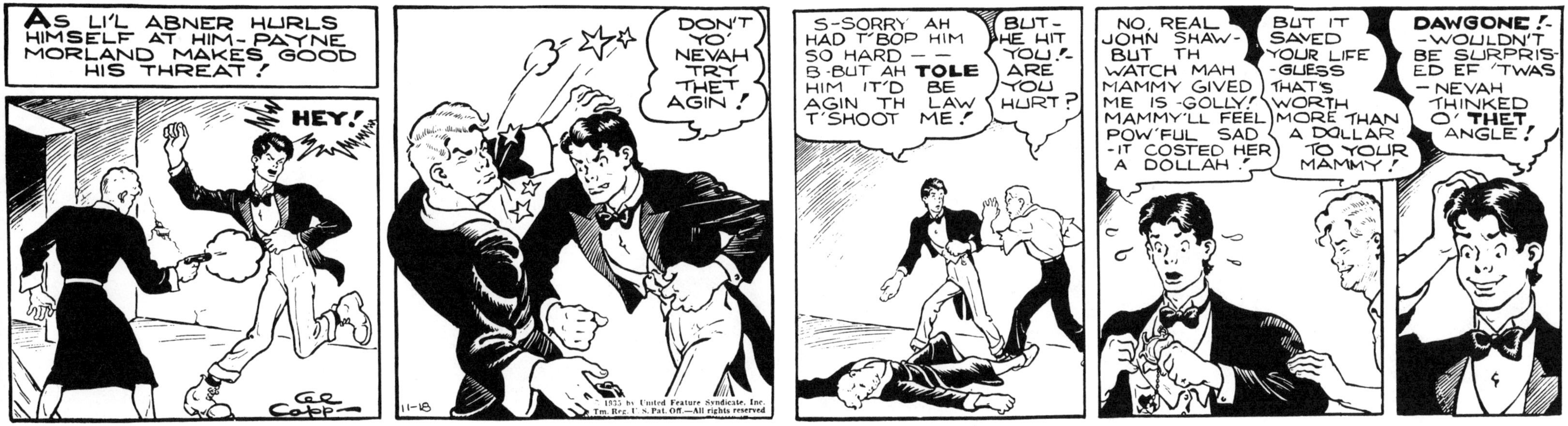

AS LI'L ABNER HURLS HIMSELF AT HIM - PAYNE MORLAND MAKES GOOD HIS THREAT!
HEY!
DON'T YO' NEVAH TRY THET AGIN!
11-18
© 1935 by United Feature Syndicate, Inc. Tm. Reg. U.S. Pat. Off.—All rights reserved
S-SORRY AH HAD T'BOP HIM SO HARD — — B-BUT AH TOLE HIM IT'D BE AGIN TH LAW T'SHOOT ME!
BUT - HE HIT YOU! - ARE YOU HURT?
NO, REAL JOHN SHAW - BUT TH WATCH MAH MAMMY GIVED ME IS - GOLLY! MAMMY'LL FEEL POW'FUL SAD - IT COSTED HER A DOLLAH!
BUT IT SAVED YOUR LIFE - GUESS THAT'S WORTH MORE THAN A DOLLAR TO YOUR MAMMY!
DAWGONE! - - WOULDN'T BE SURPRISED EF 'TWAS - NEVAH THINKED O' THET ANGLE!

LI'L ABNER Two Minds With But A Single Thought By Al Capp

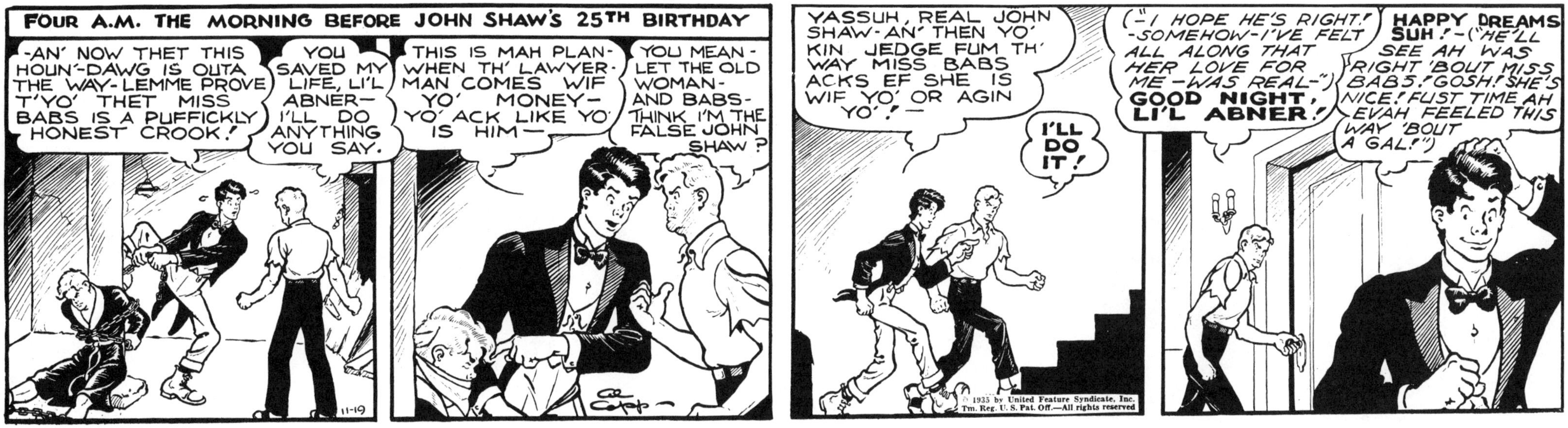

FOUR A.M. THE MORNING BEFORE JOHN SHAW'S 25TH BIRTHDAY
-AN' NOW THET THIS HOUN'-DAWG IS OUTA THE WAY - LEMME PROVE T'YO' THET MISS BABS IS A PUFFICKLY HONEST CROOK!
YOU SAVED MY LIFE, LI'L ABNER — I'LL DO ANYTHING YOU SAY.
11-19
THIS IS MAH PLAN - WHEN TH' LAWYER-MAN COMES WIF YO' MONEY - YO' ACK LIKE YO' IS HIM —
YOU MEAN - LET THE OLD WOMAN - AND BABS - THINK I'M THE FALSE JOHN SHAW?
YASSUH, REAL JOHN SHAW - AN' THEN YO' KIN JEDGE FUM TH' WAY MISS BABS ACKS EF SHE IS WIF YO' OR AGIN YO'! —
I'LL DO IT!
© 1935 by United Feature Syndicate, Inc. Tm. Reg. U.S. Pat. Off.—All rights reserved
("- I HOPE HE'S RIGHT! - SOMEHOW - I'VE FELT ALL ALONG THAT HER LOVE FOR ME - WAS REAL -") GOOD NIGHT, LI'L ABNER!
HAPPY DREAMS SUH! - ("HE'LL SEE AH WAS RIGHT 'BOUT MISS BABS! GOSH! SHE'S NICE! FUST TIME AH EVAH FEELED THIS WAY 'BOUT A GAL!")

LI'L ABNER The Showdown By Al Capp

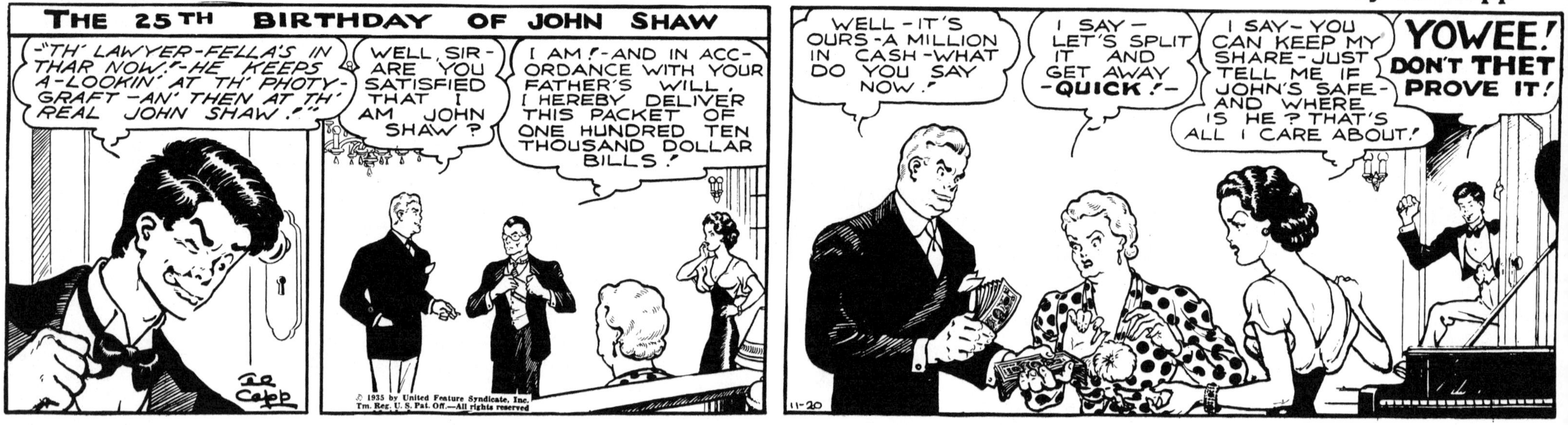
THE 25TH BIRTHDAY OF JOHN SHAW
-"TH' LAWYER-FELLA'S IN THAR NOW!-HE KEEPS A-LOOKIN' AT TH' PHOTY-GRAFT-AN' THEN AT TH' REAL JOHN SHAW!"
WELL, SIR-ARE YOU SATISFIED THAT I AM JOHN SHAW?
I AM!-AND IN ACCORDANCE WITH YOUR FATHER'S WILL, I HEREBY DELIVER THIS PACKET OF ONE HUNDRED TEN THOUSAND DOLLAR BILLS!
© 1935 by United Feature Syndicate, Inc. Tm. Reg. U. S. Pat. Off.—All rights reserved
WELL-IT'S OURS-A MILLION IN CASH-WHAT DO YOU SAY NOW!
I SAY-LET'S SPLIT IT AND GET AWAY -QUICK!-
I SAY-YOU CAN KEEP MY SHARE-JUST TELL ME IF JOHN'S SAFE-AND WHERE IS HE? THAT'S ALL I CARE ABOUT!
YOWEE! DON'T THET PROVE IT!
11-20

LI'L ABNER Three, Li'l Abner—Is A Crowd! By Al Capp

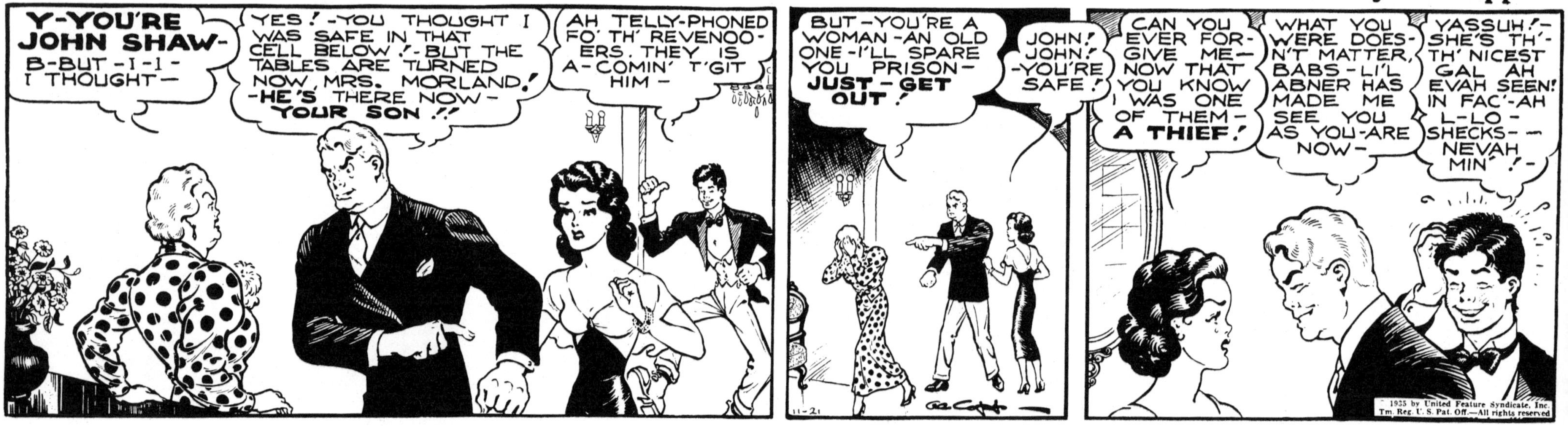
Y-YOU'RE JOHN SHAW-B-BUT-I-I-I THOUGHT-
YES!-YOU THOUGHT I WAS SAFE IN THAT CELL BELOW!-BUT THE TABLES ARE TURNED NOW, MRS. MORLAND!-HE'S THERE NOW-YOUR SON!!
AH TELLY-PHONED FO' TH' REVENOOERS. THEY IS A-COMIN' T'GIT HIM-
BUT-YOU'RE A WOMAN-AN OLD ONE-I'LL SPARE YOU PRISON-JUST-GET OUT!
JOHN! JOHN! -YOU'RE SAFE!
11-21
CAN YOU EVER FORGIVE ME-NOW THAT YOU KNOW I WAS ONE OF THEM-A THIEF!
WHAT YOU WERE DOESN'T MATTER, BABS-LI'L ABNER HAS MADE ME SEE YOU AS YOU-ARE NOW-
YASSUH!-SHE'S TH'-TH' NICEST GAL AH EVAH SEEN! IN FAC'-AH L-LO-SHECKS--NEVAH MIN'!-
1935 by United Feature Syndicate, Inc. Tm. Reg. U. S. Pat. Off.—All rights reserved

LI'L ABNER C-c-con-g-gratulations ! **By Al Capp**

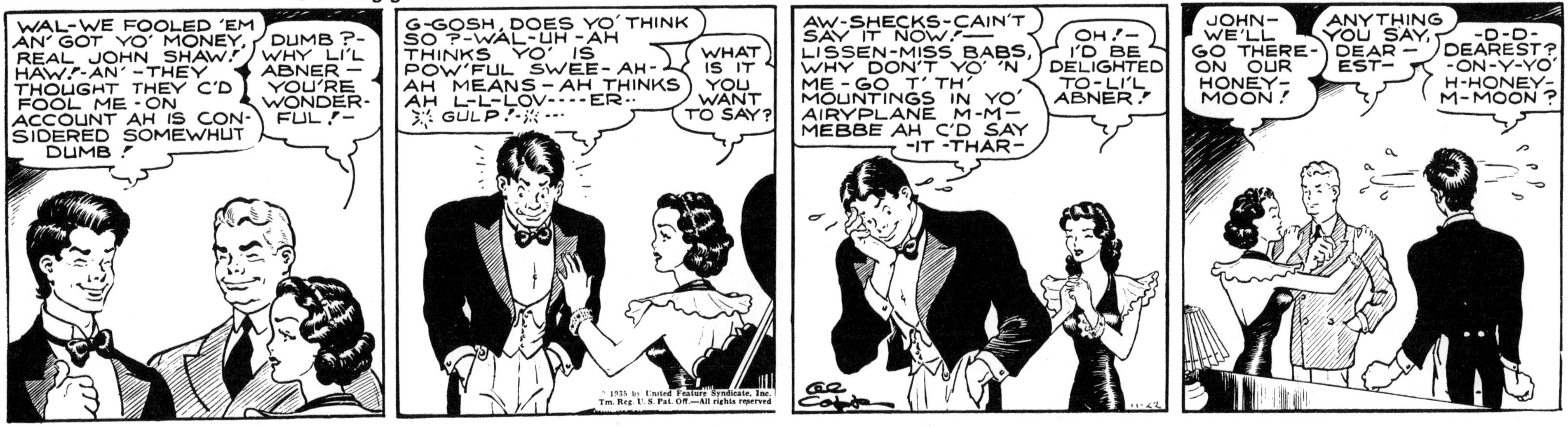

WAL-WE FOOLED 'EM AN' GOT YO' MONEY, REAL JOHN SHAW! HAW!-AN'-THEY THOUGHT THEY C'D FOOL ME-ON ACCOUNT AH IS CONSIDERED SOMEWHUT DUMB!
DUMB?-WHY LI'L ABNER-YOU'RE WONDERFUL!-
G-GOSH, DOES YO' THINK SO?-WAL-UH-AH THINKS YO' IS POW'FUL SWEE-AH-AH MEANS-AH THINKS AH L-L-LOV----ER.. GULP!- ---
WHAT IS IT YOU WANT TO SAY?
© 1935 by United Feature Syndicate, Inc. Tm. Reg. U. S. Pat. Off.—All rights reserved
AW-SHECKS-CAIN'T SAY IT NOW!— LISSEN-MISS BABS, WHY DON'T YO' 'N ME-GO T' TH' MOUNTINGS IN YO' AIRYPLANE M-M-MEBBE AH C'D SAY -IT-THAR-
OH!-I'D BE DELIGHTED TO-LI'L ABNER!
JOHN-WE'LL GO THERE-ON OUR HONEYMOON!
ANYTHING YOU SAY, DEAR-EST-
-D-D-DEAREST?-ON-Y-YO' H-HONEY-M-MOON?

LI'L ABNER Where Yo' Be Goin', Boy ? **By Al Capp**

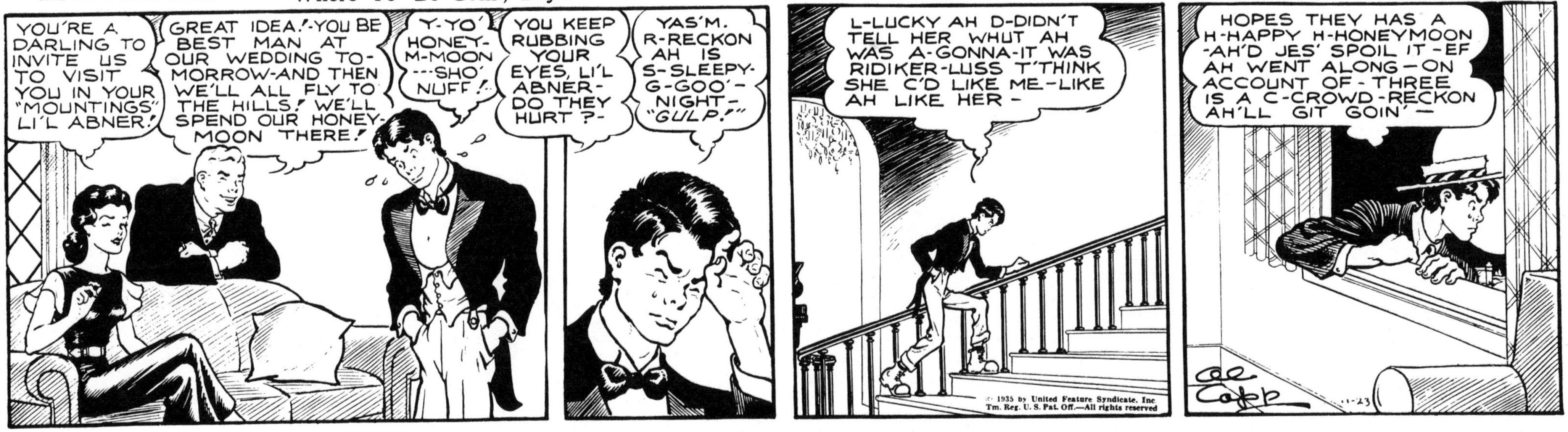

YOU'RE A DARLING TO INVITE US TO VISIT YOU IN YOUR "MOUNTINGS" LI'L ABNER!
GREAT IDEA!-YOU BE BEST MAN AT OUR WEDDING TOMORROW-AND THEN WE'LL ALL FLY TO THE HILLS! WE'LL SPEND OUR HONEYMOON THERE!
Y-YO' HONEY-M-MOON ---SHO' NUFF!
YOU KEEP RUBBING YOUR EYES, LI'L ABNER-DO THEY HURT?-
YAS'M. R-RECKON AH IS S-SLEEPY-G-GOO'-NIGHT-"GULP!"
L-LUCKY AH D-DIDN'T TELL HER WHUT AH WAS A-GONNA-IT WAS RIDIKER-LUSS T'THINK SHE C'D LIKE ME-LIKE AH LIKE HER-
© 1935 by United Feature Syndicate, Inc Tm. Reg. U. S. Pat. Off.—All rights reserved
HOPES THEY HAS A H-HAPPY H-HONEYMOON -AH'D JES' SPOIL IT-EF AH WENT ALONG-ON ACCOUNT OF-THREE IS A C-CROWD-RECKON AH'LL GIT GOIN'—

LI'L ABNER Company For the Gorilla By Al Capp

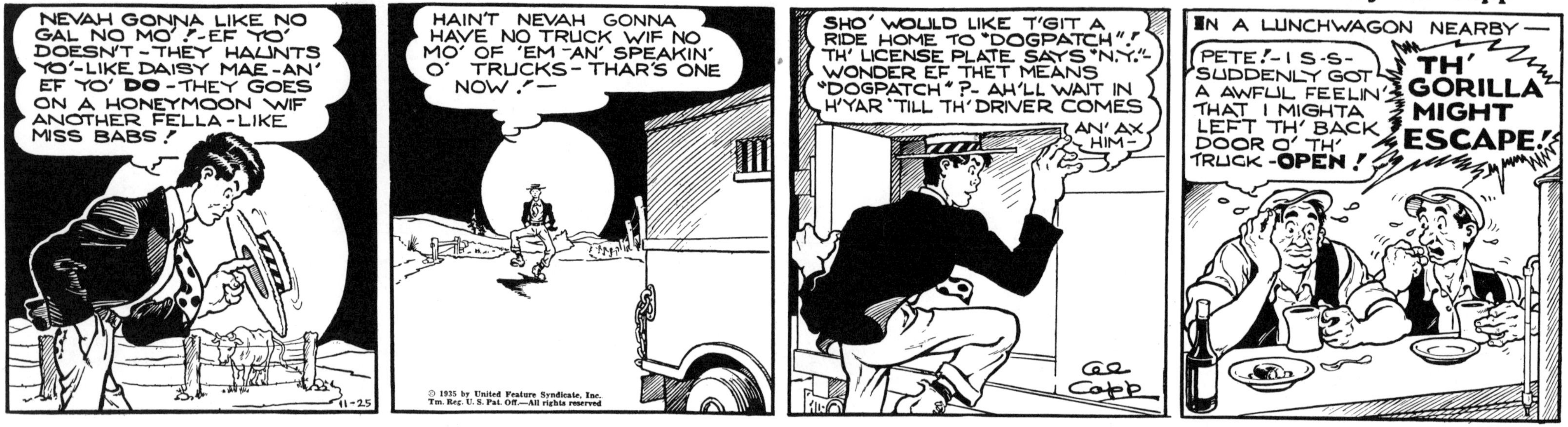

NEVAH GONNA LIKE NO GAL NO MO'!-EF YO' DOESN'T-THEY HAUNTS YO'-LIKE DAISY MAE-AN' EF YO' **DO**-THEY GOES ON A HONEYMOON WIF ANOTHER FELLA-LIKE MISS BABS!
11-25
HAIN'T NEVAH GONNA HAVE NO TRUCK WIF NO MO' OF 'EM-AN' SPEAKIN' O' TRUCKS-THAR'S ONE NOW!-
© 1935 by United Feature Syndicate, Inc. Tm. Reg. U. S. Pat. Off.—All rights reserved
SHO' WOULD LIKE T'GIT A RIDE HOME TO "DOGPATCH"! TH' LICENSE PLATE SAYS "N.Y."-WONDER EF THET MEANS "DOGPATCH"?- AH'LL WAIT IN H'YAR 'TILL TH' DRIVER COMES AN' AX HIM-
Al Capp
IN A LUNCHWAGON NEARBY—
PETE!-I S-S-SUDDENLY GOT A AWFUL FEELIN' THAT I MIGHTA LEFT TH' BACK DOOR O' TH' TRUCK-**OPEN**!
TH' GORILLA MIGHT ESCAPE!

LI'L ABNER The Call of the Wild By Al Capp

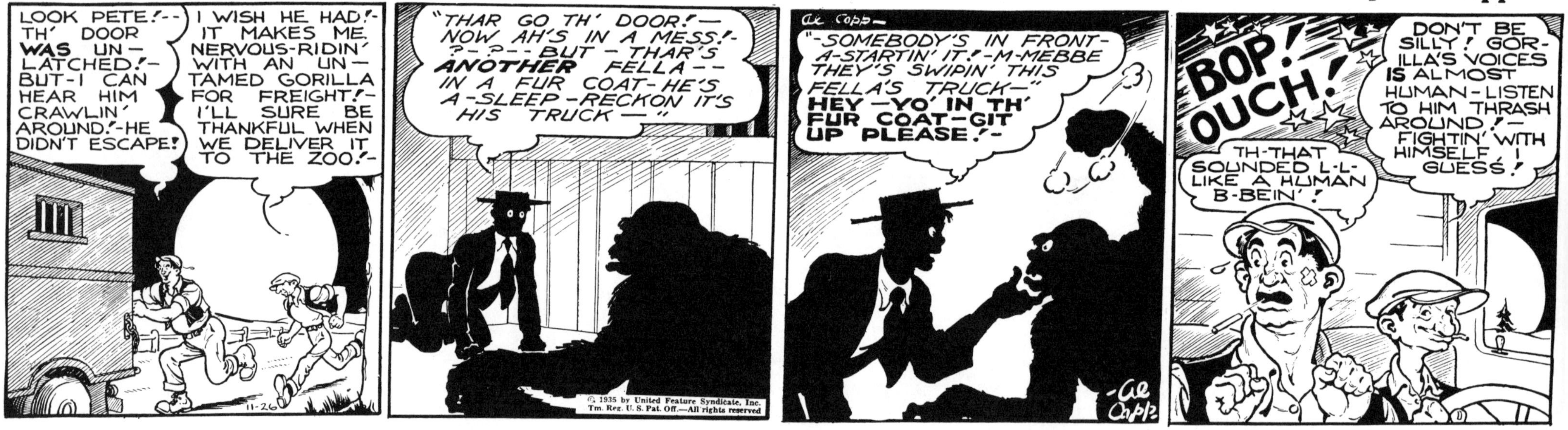

LOOK PETE!--TH' DOOR **WAS** UN-LATCHED!-BUT-I CAN HEAR HIM CRAWLIN' AROUND!-HE DIDN'T ESCAPE!
I WISH HE HAD!-IT MAKES ME NERVOUS-RIDIN' WITH AN UN-TAMED GORILLA FOR FREIGHT!-I'LL SURE BE THANKFUL WHEN WE DELIVER IT TO THE ZOO!-
11-26
"THAR GO TH' DOOR!-NOW AH'S IN A MESS!-?-?--BUT-THAR'S **ANOTHER** FELLA--IN A FUR COAT-HE'S A-SLEEP-RECKON IT'S HIS TRUCK--"
© 1935 by United Feature Syndicate, Inc. Tm. Reg. U. S. Pat. Off.—All rights reserved
Al Capp
"-SOMEBODY'S IN FRONT-A-STARTIN' IT!-M-MEBBE THEY'S SWIPIN' THIS FELLA'S TRUCK-"
HEY-YO' IN TH' FUR COAT-GIT UP PLEASE!-
Al Capp
BOP! OUCH!
TH-THAT SOUNDED L-L-LIKE A HUMAN B-BEIN'!
DON'T BE SILLY! GOR-ILLA'S VOICES **IS** ALMOST HUMAN-LISTEN TO HIM THRASH AROUND!-FIGHTIN' WITH HIMSELF, I GUESS!

LI'L ABNER Is Abner Havin' Fun, Too? By Al Capp

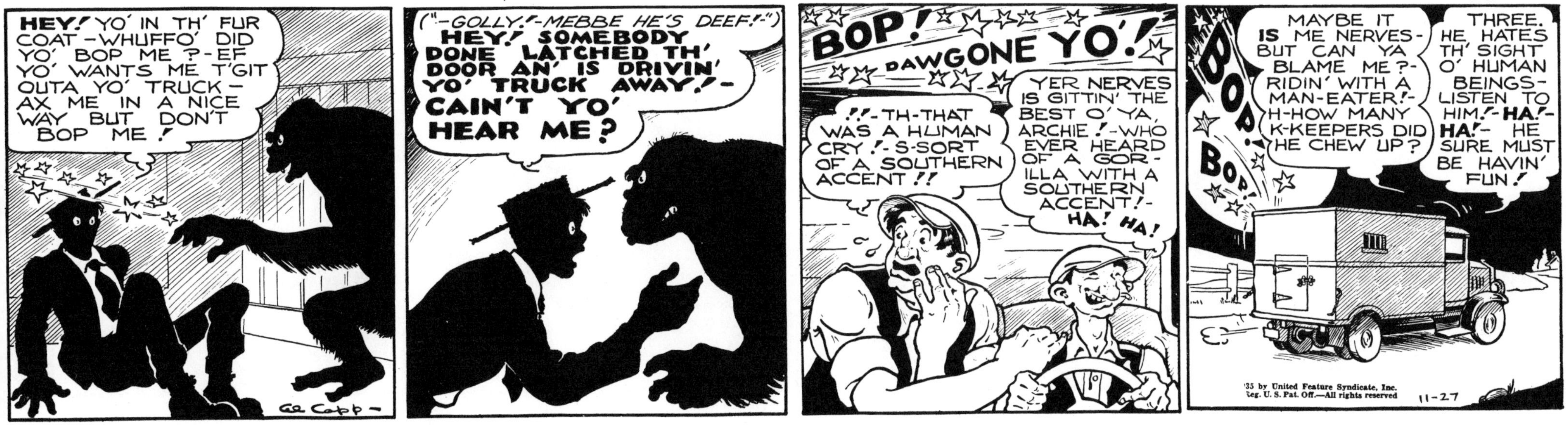

HEY! YO' IN TH' FUR COAT - WHUFFO' DID YO' BOP ME? - EF YO' WANTS ME T'GIT OUTA YO' TRUCK - AX ME IN A NICE WAY BUT DON'T BOP ME!
Al Capp
("-GOLLY!-MEBBE HE'S DEEF!-")
HEY! SOMEBODY DONE LATCHED TH' DOOR AN' IS DRIVIN' YO' TRUCK AWAY! - CAIN'T YO' HEAR ME?
BOP! DAWGONE YO'!
!!-TH-THAT WAS A HUMAN CRY!-S-SORT OF A SOUTHERN ACCENT!!
YER NERVES IS GITTIN' THE BEST O' YA, ARCHIE!-WHO EVER HEARD OF A GORILLA WITH A SOUTHERN ACCENT!- HA! HA!
BOP! BOP!
MAYBE IT IS ME NERVES- BUT CAN YA BLAME ME?- RIDIN' WITH A MAN-EATER!- H-HOW MANY K-KEEPERS DID HE CHEW UP?
THREE. HE HATES TH' SIGHT O' HUMAN BEINGS- LISTEN TO HIM!-HA!-HA!- HE SURE MUST BE HAVIN' FUN!
'35 by United Feature Syndicate, Inc. Reg. U. S. Pat. Off.—All rights reserved
11-27

LI'L ABNER Now—Anything Might Happen! By Al Capp

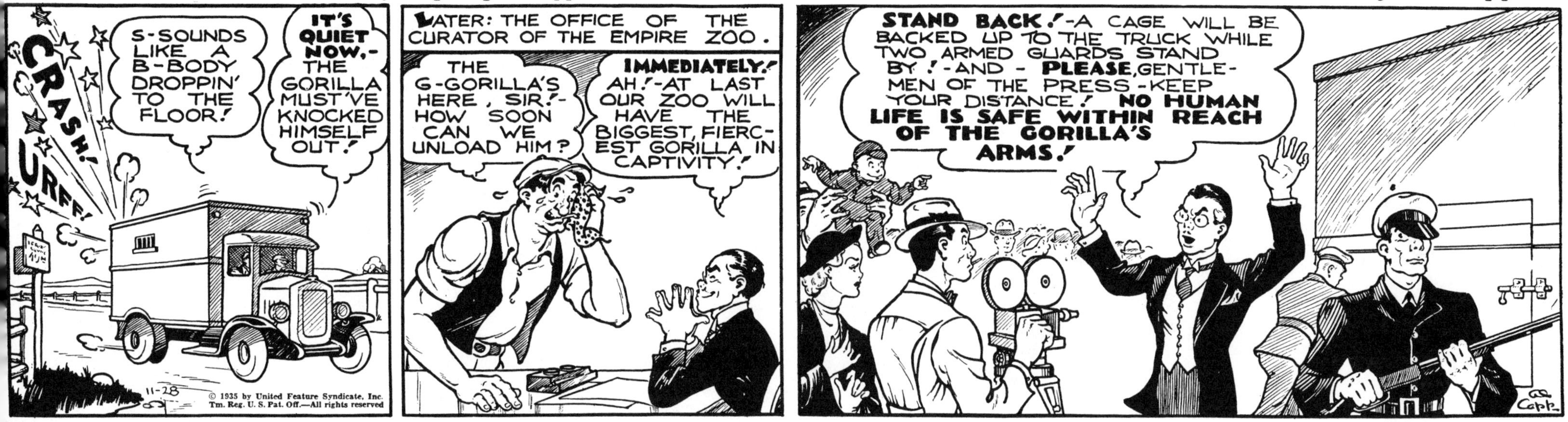

CRASH! URFF!
S-SOUNDS LIKE A B-BODY DROPPIN' TO THE FLOOR!
IT'S QUIET NOW,- THE GORILLA MUST'VE KNOCKED HIMSELF OUT!
11-28
© 1935 by United Feature Syndicate, Inc. Tm. Reg. U. S. Pat. Off.—All rights reserved
LATER: THE OFFICE OF THE CURATOR OF THE EMPIRE ZOO.
THE G-GORILLA'S HERE, SIR!- HOW SOON CAN WE UNLOAD HIM?
IMMEDIATELY! AH!-AT LAST OUR ZOO WILL HAVE THE BIGGEST, FIERCEST GORILLA IN CAPTIVITY!
STAND BACK!-A CAGE WILL BE BACKED UP TO THE TRUCK WHILE TWO ARMED GUARDS STAND BY!-AND- PLEASE, GENTLEMEN OF THE PRESS-KEEP YOUR DISTANCE! NO HUMAN LIFE IS SAFE WITHIN REACH OF THE GORILLA'S ARMS!
Al Capp

LI'L ABNER He Hain't Seen No Gorilla By Al Capp

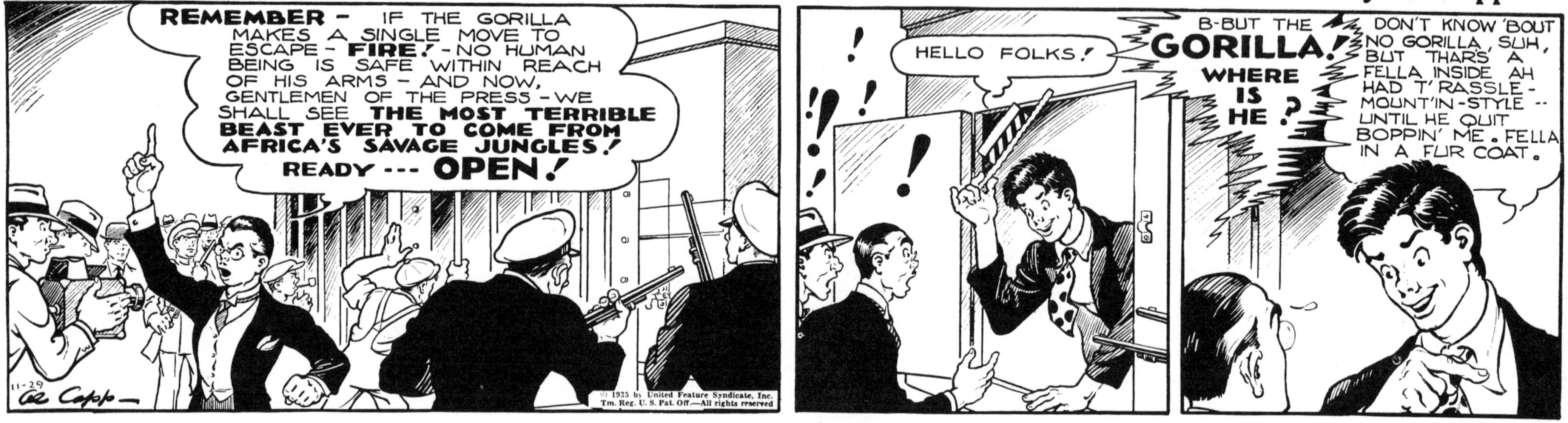
REMEMBER - IF THE GORILLA MAKES A SINGLE MOVE TO ESCAPE - FIRE! - NO HUMAN BEING IS SAFE WITHIN REACH OF HIS ARMS - AND NOW, GENTLEMEN OF THE PRESS - WE SHALL SEE THE MOST TERRIBLE BEAST EVER TO COME FROM AFRICA'S SAVAGE JUNGLES! READY --- OPEN!
HELLO FOLKS!
B-BUT THE GORILLA! WHERE IS HE ?
DON'T KNOW 'BOUT NO GORILLA, SUH, BUT THAR'S A FELLA INSIDE AH HAD T' RASSLE - MOUNT'IN-STYLE -- UNTIL HE QUIT BOPPIN' ME. FELLA IN A FUR COAT.
© 1935 by United Feature Syndicate, Inc. Tm. Reg. U. S. Pat. Off.—All rights reserved

LI'L ABNER But—Can They ? By Al Capp

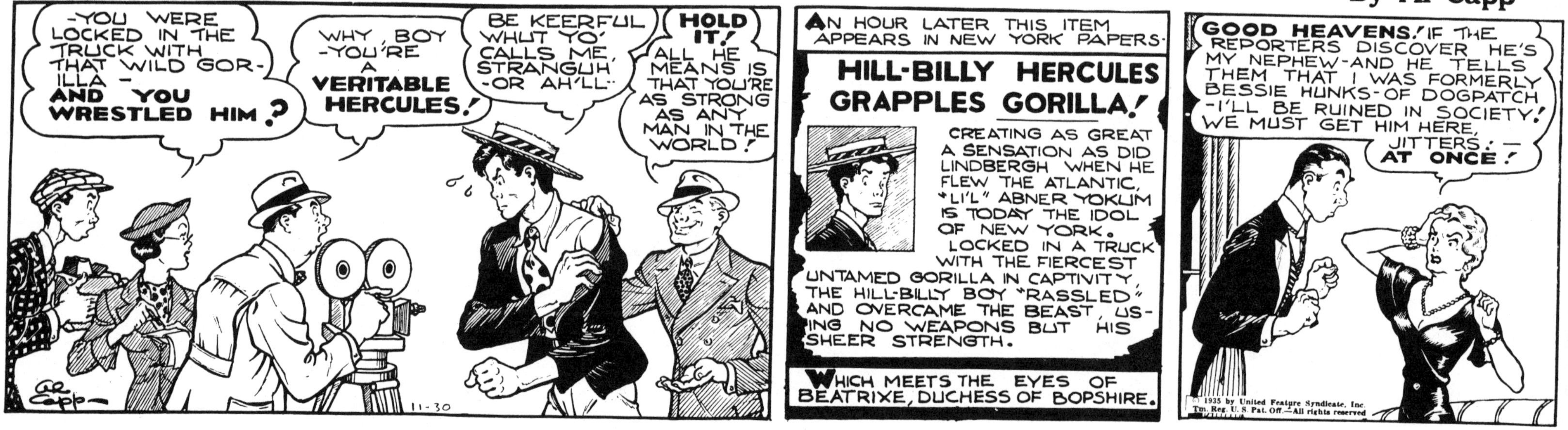
-YOU WERE LOCKED IN THE TRUCK WITH THAT WILD GORILLA - AND YOU WRESTLED HIM ?
WHY, BOY -YOU'RE A VERITABLE HERCULES!
BE KEERFUL WHUT YO' CALLS ME, STRANGUH -OR AH'LL-
HOLD IT! ALL HE MEANS IS THAT YOU'RE AS STRONG AS ANY MAN IN THE WORLD!
AN HOUR LATER THIS ITEM APPEARS IN NEW YORK PAPERS-
HILL-BILLY HERCULES GRAPPLES GORILLA!
CREATING AS GREAT A SENSATION AS DID LINDBERGH WHEN HE FLEW THE ATLANTIC, "LI'L" ABNER YOKUM IS TODAY THE IDOL OF NEW YORK. LOCKED IN A TRUCK WITH THE FIERCEST UNTAMED GORILLA IN CAPTIVITY, THE HILL-BILLY BOY "RASSLED" AND OVERCAME THE BEAST, USING NO WEAPONS BUT HIS SHEER STRENGTH.
WHICH MEETS THE EYES OF BEATRIXE, DUCHESS OF BOPSHIRE.
GOOD HEAVENS! IF THE REPORTERS DISCOVER HE'S MY NEPHEW-AND HE TELLS THEM THAT I WAS FORMERLY BESSIE HUNKS-OF DOGPATCH -I'LL BE RUINED IN SOCIETY! WE MUST GET HIM HERE, JITTERS. - AT ONCE!
© 1935 by United Feature Syndicate, Inc. Tm. Reg. U. S. Pat. Off.—All rights reserved

LI'L ABNER The Pride of His People By Al Capp

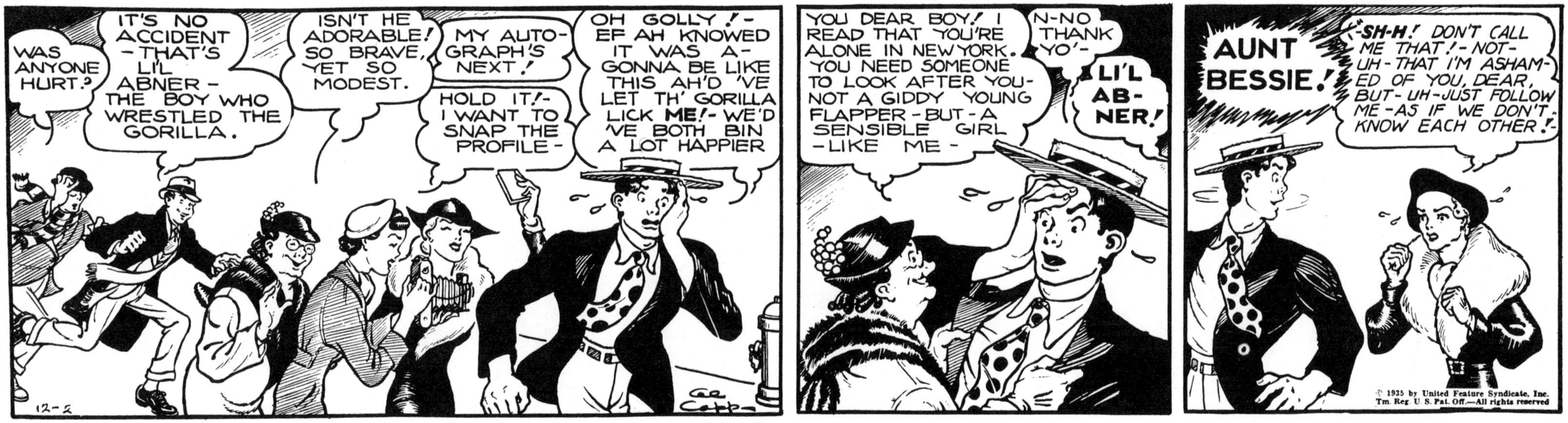
WAS ANYONE HURT?
IT'S NO ACCIDENT - THAT'S LI'L ABNER - THE BOY WHO WRESTLED THE GORILLA.
ISN'T HE ADORABLE! SO BRAVE, YET SO MODEST.
MY AUTO-GRAPH'S NEXT!
HOLD IT!- I WANT TO SNAP THE PROFILE -
OH GOLLY!- EF AH KNOWED IT WAS A-GONNA BE LIKE THIS AH'D 'VE LET TH' GORILLA LICK ME!- WE'D 'VE BOTH BIN A LOT HAPPIER
YOU DEAR BOY! I READ THAT YOU'RE ALONE IN NEW YORK. YOU NEED SOMEONE TO LOOK AFTER YOU-NOT A GIDDY YOUNG FLAPPER - BUT - A SENSIBLE GIRL - LIKE ME -
N-NO THANK YO'-
LI'L AB-NER!
AUNT BESSIE!
SH-H! DON'T CALL ME THAT!- NOT- UH - THAT I'M ASHAMED OF YOU, DEAR, BUT - UH - JUST FOLLOW ME - AS IF WE DON'T KNOW EACH OTHER!-
© 1935 by United Feature Syndicate, Inc. Tm. Reg. U. S. Pat. Off.—All rights reserved

LI'L ABNER Like A Lamb To the Slaughter By Al Capp

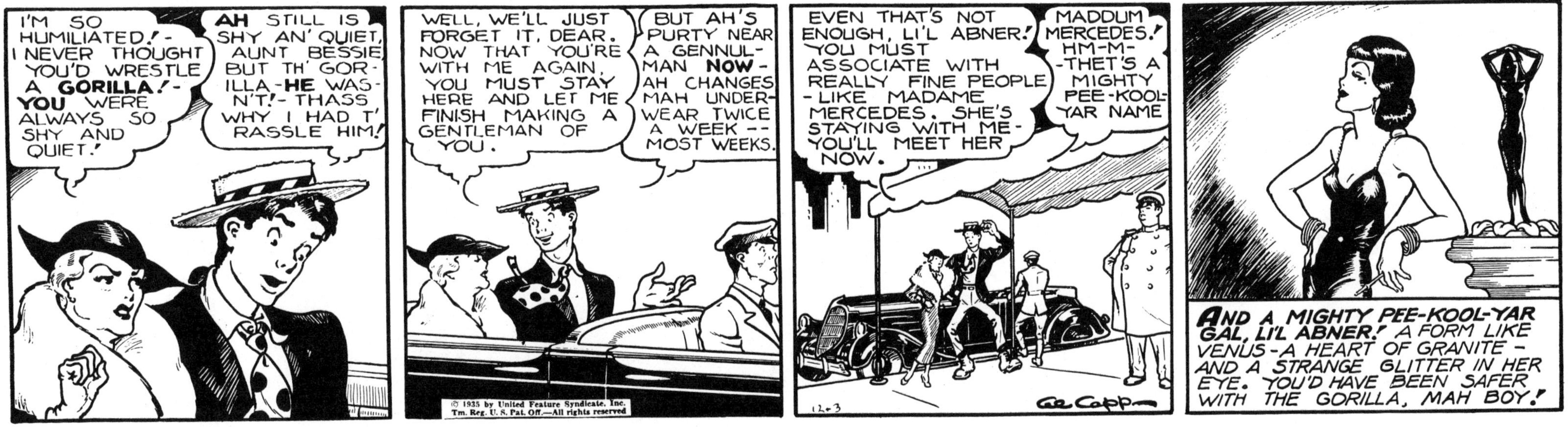
I'M SO HUMILIATED!- I NEVER THOUGHT YOU'D WRESTLE A GORILLA!- YOU WERE ALWAYS SO SHY AND QUIET!
AH STILL IS SHY AN' QUIET, AUNT BESSIE BUT TH' GORILLA - HE WASN'T!- THASS WHY I HAD T' RASSLE HIM!
WELL, WE'LL JUST FORGET IT, DEAR. NOW THAT YOU'RE WITH ME AGAIN, YOU MUST STAY HERE AND LET ME FINISH MAKING A GENTLEMAN OF YOU.
BUT AH'S PURTY NEAR A GENNULMAN NOW - AH CHANGES MAH UNDERWEAR TWICE A WEEK -- MOST WEEKS.
© 1935 by United Feature Syndicate, Inc. Tm. Reg. U. S. Pat. Off.—All rights reserved
EVEN THAT'S NOT ENOUGH, LI'L ABNER! YOU MUST ASSOCIATE WITH REALLY FINE PEOPLE - LIKE MADAME MERCEDES. SHE'S STAYING WITH ME - YOU'LL MEET HER NOW.
MADDUM MERCEDES! HM-M- THET'S A MIGHTY PEE-KOOL-YAR NAME
AND A MIGHTY PEE-KOOL-YAR GAL, LI'L ABNER! A FORM LIKE VENUS - A HEART OF GRANITE - AND A STRANGE GLITTER IN HER EYE. YOU'D HAVE BEEN SAFER WITH THE GORILLA, MAH BOY!

LI'L ABNER Dangerous Curves Ahead **By Al Capp**

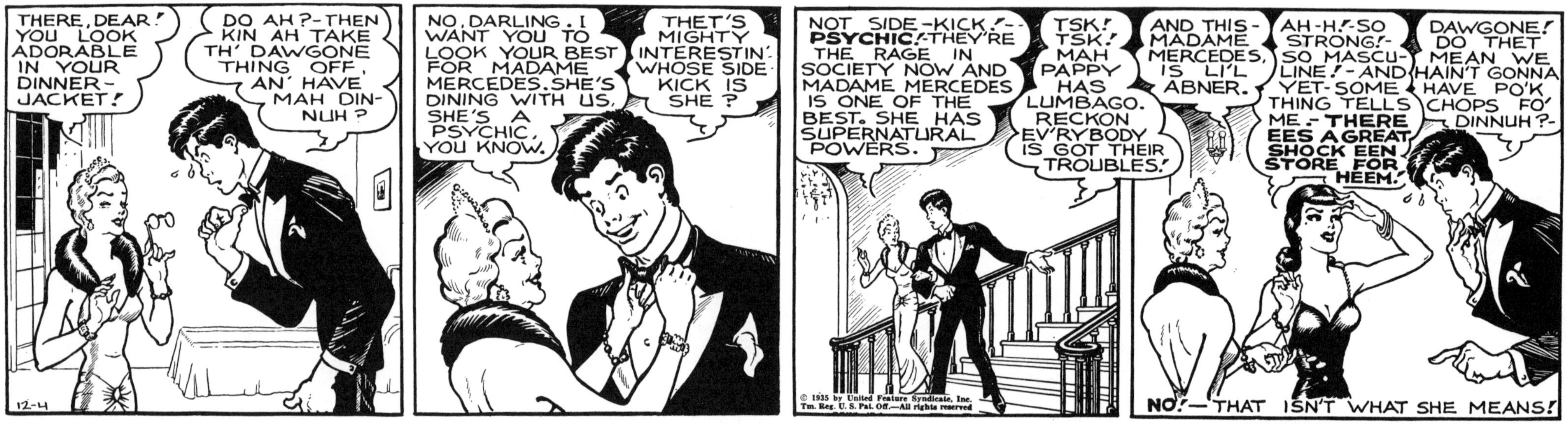
THERE, DEAR! YOU LOOK ADORABLE IN YOUR DINNER-JACKET!
DO AH?-THEN KIN AH TAKE TH' DAWGONE THING OFF, AN' HAVE MAH DIN-NUH?
12-4
NO, DARLING. I WANT YOU TO LOOK YOUR BEST FOR MADAME MERCEDES. SHE'S DINING WITH US. SHE'S A PSYCHIC, YOU KNOW.
THET'S MIGHTY INTERESTIN'. WHOSE SIDE KICK IS SHE?
NOT SIDE-KICK!-- **PSYCHIC!**-THEY'RE THE RAGE IN SOCIETY NOW AND MADAME MERCEDES IS ONE OF THE BEST. SHE HAS SUPERNATURAL POWERS.
TSK! TSK! MAH PAPPY HAS LUMBAGO. RECKON EV'RYBODY IS GOT THEIR TROUBLES!
© 1935 by United Feature Syndicate, Inc. Tm. Reg. U. S. Pat. Off.—All rights reserved
AND THIS - MADAME MERCEDES, IS LI'L ABNER.
AH-H!-SO STRONG!-SO MASCULINE!-AND YET-SOMETHING TELLS ME.-**THERE EES A GREAT SHOCK EEN STORE FOR HEEM!**
DAWGONE! DO THET MEAN WE HAIN'T GONNA HAVE PO'K CHOPS FO' DINNUH?-
NO!—THAT ISN'T WHAT SHE MEANS!

LI'L ABNER A Great Entertainer **By Al Capp**

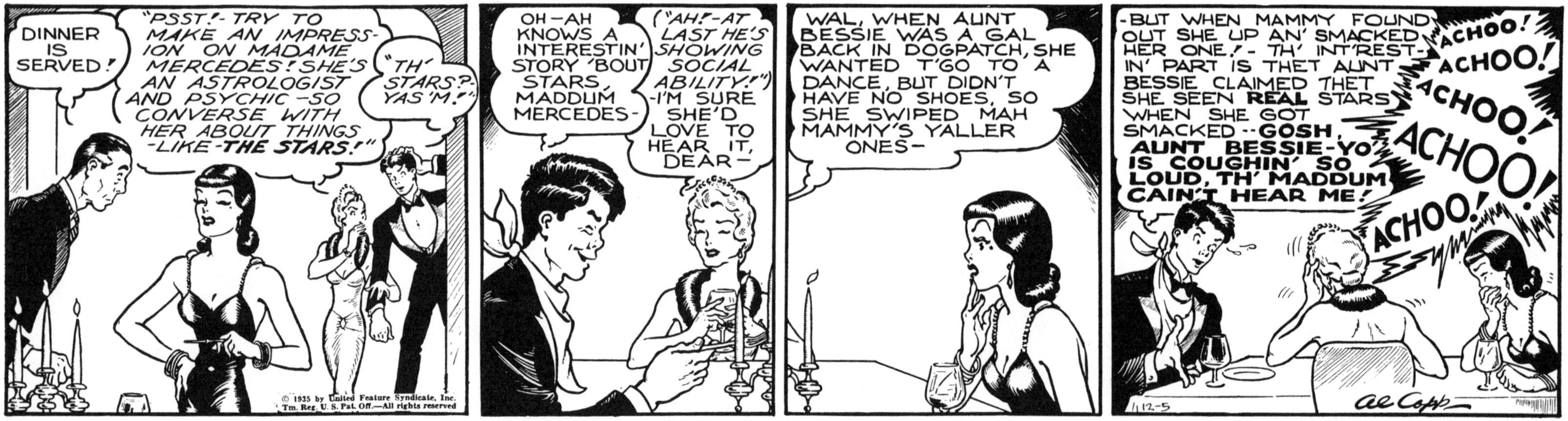
DINNER IS SERVED!
*"PSST!-TRY TO MAKE AN IMPRESSION ON MADAME MERCEDES! SHE'S AN ASTROLOGIST AND PSYCHIC-SO CONVERSE WITH HER ABOUT THINGS -LIKE-**THE STARS!**"*
"TH' STARS?-YAS'M!"
© 1935 by United Feature Syndicate, Inc. Tm. Reg. U. S. Pat. Off.—All rights reserved
OH-AH KNOWS A INTERESTIN' STORY 'BOUT STARS, MADDUM MERCEDES-
("AH!-AT LAST HE'S SHOWING SOCIAL ABILITY!")-I'M SURE SHE'D LOVE TO HEAR IT, DEAR-
WAL, WHEN AUNT BESSIE WAS A GAL BACK IN DOGPATCH, SHE WANTED T'GO TO A DANCE, BUT DIDN'T HAVE NO SHOES, SO SHE SWIPED MAH MAMMY'S YALLER ONES-
-BUT WHEN MAMMY FOUND OUT SHE UP AN' SMACKED HER ONE!-TH' INT'REST-IN' PART IS THET AUNT BESSIE CLAIMED THET SHE SEEN **REAL** STARS WHEN SHE GOT SMACKED--**GOSH, AUNT BESSIE-YO' IS COUGHIN' SO LOUD, TH' MADDUM CAIN'T HEAR ME!**
ACHOO! ACHOO! ACHOO! ACHOO! ACHOO!
12-5
Al Capp

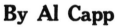

LI'L ABNER His Unlucky Star By Al Capp

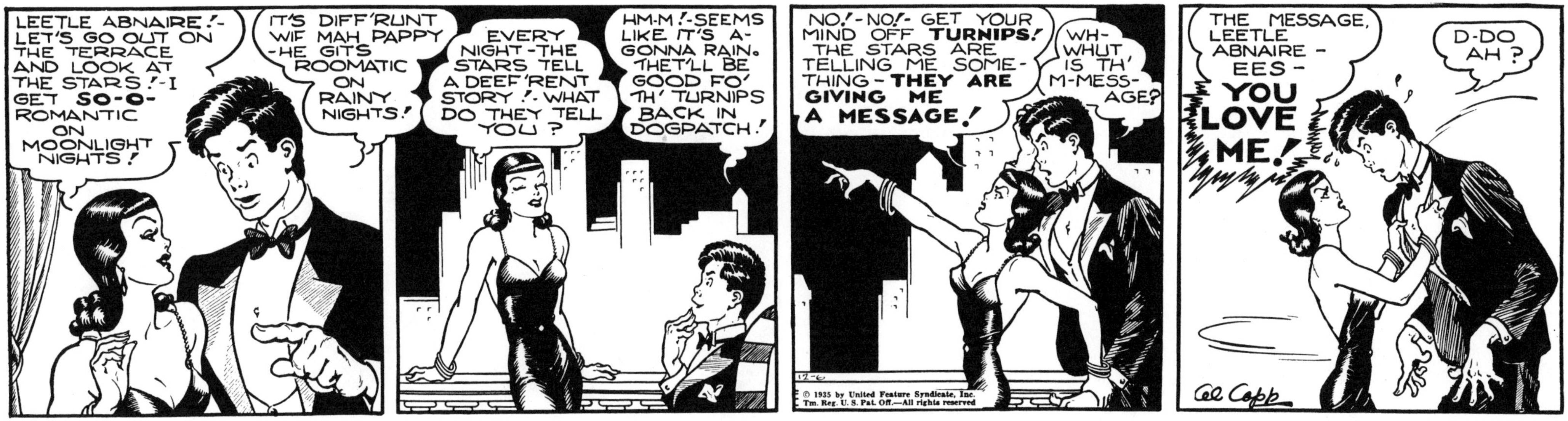

LEETLE ABNAIRE!- LET'S GO OUT ON THE TERRACE AND LOOK AT THE STARS!- I GET **SO-O-** ROMANTIC ON MOONLIGHT NIGHTS!
IT'S DIFF'RUNT WIF MAH PAPPY -HE GITS ROOMATIC ON RAINY NIGHTS!
EVERY NIGHT-THE STARS TELL A DEEF'RENT STORY!- WHAT DO THEY TELL YOU?
HM-M!-SEEMS LIKE IT'S A-GONNA RAIN. THET'LL BE GOOD FO' TH' TURNIPS BACK IN DOGPATCH!
NO!-NO!- GET YOUR MIND OFF **TURNIPS!** THE STARS ARE TELLING ME SOME-THING- **THEY ARE GIVING ME A MESSAGE!**
WH- WHUT IS TH' M-MESS-AGE?
THE MESSAGE, LEETLE ABNAIRE - EES -
YOU LOVE ME!
D-DO AH?
© 1935 by United Feature Syndicate, Inc. Tm. Reg. U. S. Pat. Off.—All rights reserved
Al Capp

LI'L ABNER A Credit To His People By Al Capp

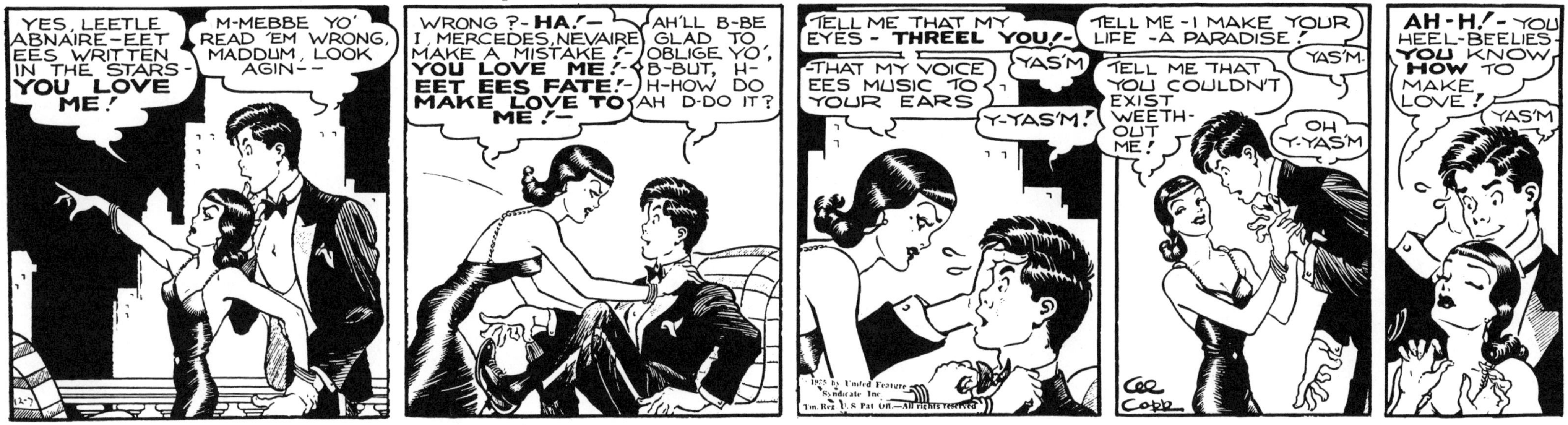

YES, LEETLE ABNAIRE-EET EES WRITTEN IN THE STARS- **YOU LOVE ME!**
M-MEBBE YO' READ 'EM WRONG, MADDUM. LOOK AGIN--
WRONG?- **HA!**— I, MERCEDES, NEVAIRE MAKE A MISTAKE!- **YOU LOVE ME!- EET EES FATE!- MAKE LOVE TO ME!**—
AH'LL B-BE GLAD TO OBLIGE YO', B-BUT, H-H-HOW DO AH D-DO IT?
TELL ME THAT MY EYES - **THREEL YOU!**-
YAS'M
-THAT MY VOICE EES MUSIC TO YOUR EARS
Y-YAS'M!
TELL ME -I MAKE YOUR LIFE -A PARADISE!
YAS'M-
TELL ME THAT YOU COULDN'T EXIST WEETH-OUT ME!
OH Y-YAS'M
AH-H!- YOU HEEL-BEELIES- **YOU** KNOW **HOW** TO MAKE LOVE!
YAS'M
Al Capp

LI'L ABNER Fancy Meeting Youse Here! By Al Capp

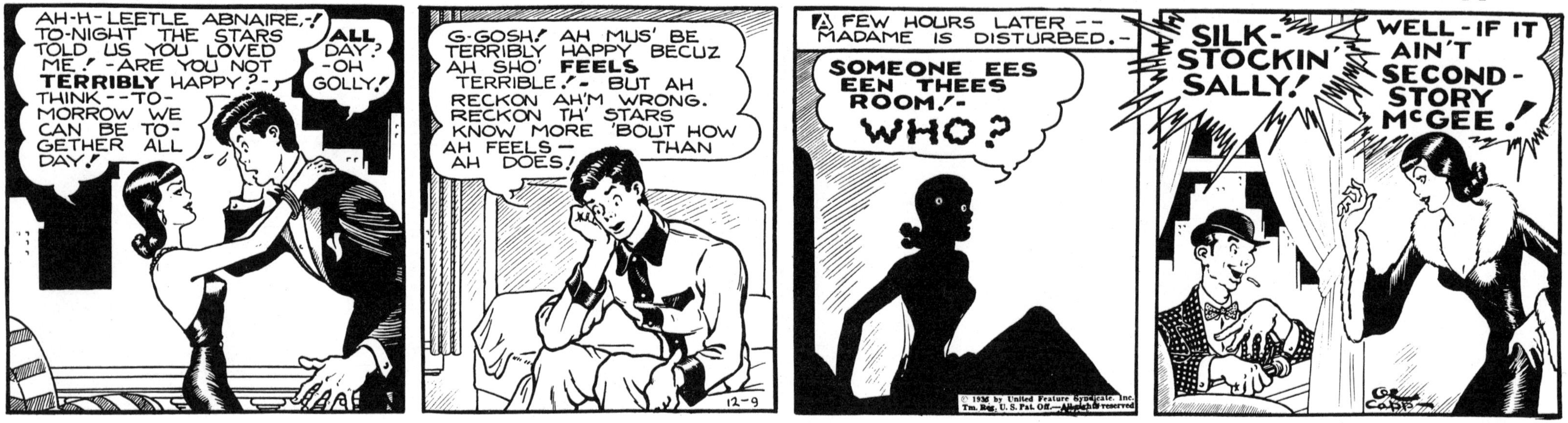
AH-H- LEETLE ABNAIRE,-! TO-NIGHT THE STARS TOLD US YOU LOVED ME.! -ARE YOU NOT TERRIBLY HAPPY?- THINK--TO-MORROW WE CAN BE TO-GETHER ALL DAY!
ALL DAY? -OH GOLLY!
G-GOSH! AH MUS' BE TERRIBLY HAPPY BECUZ AH SHO' FEELS TERRIBLE.!- BUT AH RECKON AH'M WRONG. RECKON TH' STARS KNOW MORE 'BOUT HOW AH FEELS— THAN AH DOES!
12-9
A FEW HOURS LATER -- MADAME IS DISTURBED.-
SOMEONE EES EEN THEES ROOM!- WHO?
© 1936 by United Feature Syndicate, Inc. Tm. Reg. U. S. Pat. Off.—All rights reserved
SILK-STOCKIN' SALLY!
WELL-IF IT AIN'T SECOND-STORY McGEE!
Al Capp

LI'L ABNER Dishonorable Intentions By Al Capp

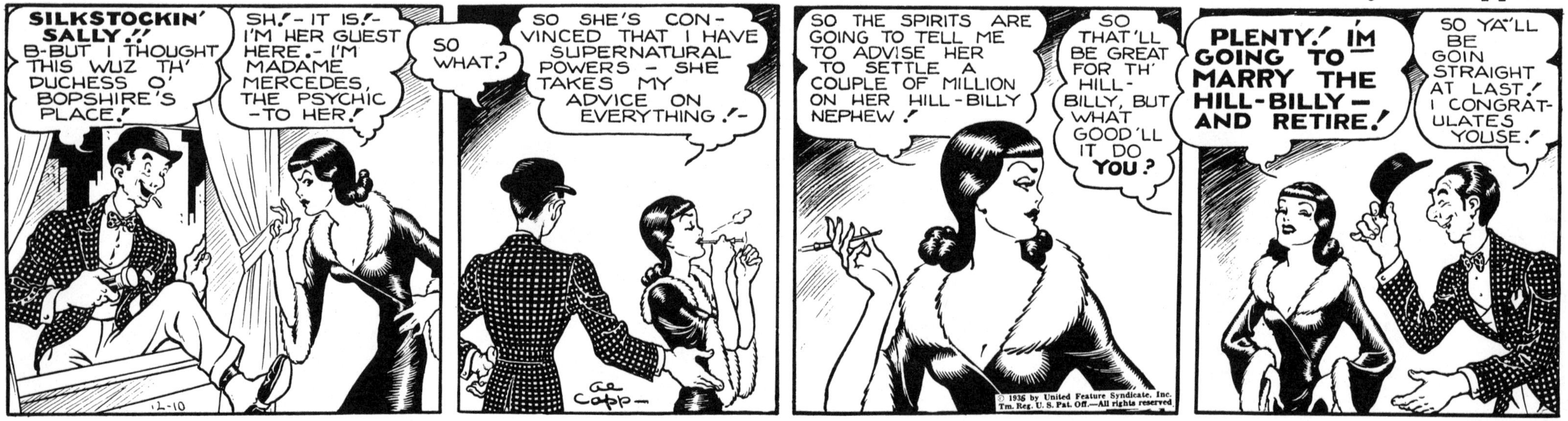
SILKSTOCKIN' SALLY.!! B-BUT I THOUGHT THIS WUZ TH' DUCHESS O' BOPSHIRE'S PLACE!
SH!- IT IS!- I'M HER GUEST HERE.- I'M MADAME MERCEDES, THE PSYCHIC -TO HER!
12-10
SO WHAT?
SO SHE'S CON-VINCED THAT I HAVE SUPERNATURAL POWERS - SHE TAKES MY ADVICE ON EVERYTHING.!-
Al Capp
SO THE SPIRITS ARE GOING TO TELL ME TO ADVISE HER TO SETTLE A COUPLE OF MILLION ON HER HILL-BILLY NEPHEW!
SO THAT'LL BE GREAT FOR TH' HILL-BILLY, BUT WHAT GOOD'LL IT DO YOU?
© 1936 by United Feature Syndicate, Inc. Tm. Reg. U. S. Pat. Off.—All rights reserved
PLENTY! I'M GOING TO MARRY THE HILL-BILLY — AND RETIRE!
SO YA'LL BE GOIN STRAIGHT AT LAST! I CONGRAT-ULATES YOUSE!

LI'L ABNER Reverse Proposal By Al Capp

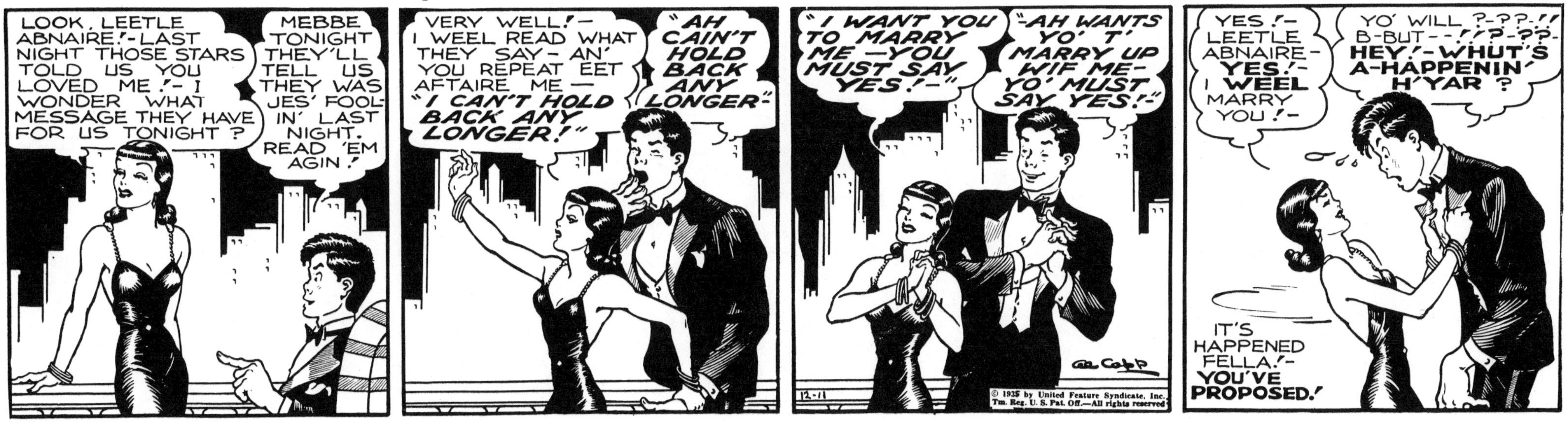

LOOK, LEETLE ABNAIRE!–LAST NIGHT THOSE STARS TOLD US YOU LOVED ME!–I WONDER WHAT MESSAGE THEY HAVE FOR US TONIGHT?
MEBBE TONIGHT THEY'LL TELL US THEY WAS JES' FOOL-IN' LAST NIGHT. READ 'EM AGIN!
VERY WELL!–I WEEL READ WHAT THEY SAY–AN' YOU REPEAT EET AFTAIRE ME–"I CAN'T HOLD BACK ANY LONGER!"
"AH CAIN'T HOLD BACK ANY LONGER"–
"I WANT YOU TO MARRY ME–YOU MUST SAY YES!–"
"–AH WANTS YO' T' MARRY UP WIF ME–YO' MUST SAY YES!–"
AL CAPP
12-11
© 1935 by United Feature Syndicate, Inc. Tm. Reg. U. S. Pat. Off.—All rights reserved
YES!–LEETLE ABNAIRE–YES!–I WEEL MARRY YOU!–
YO' WILL ?-??-!! B-BUT--!!?-??-HEY!–WHUT'S A-HAPPENIN' H'YAR?
IT'S HAPPENED FELLA!–YOU'VE PROPOSED!

LI'L ABNER Nothing To Worry About Now By Al Capp

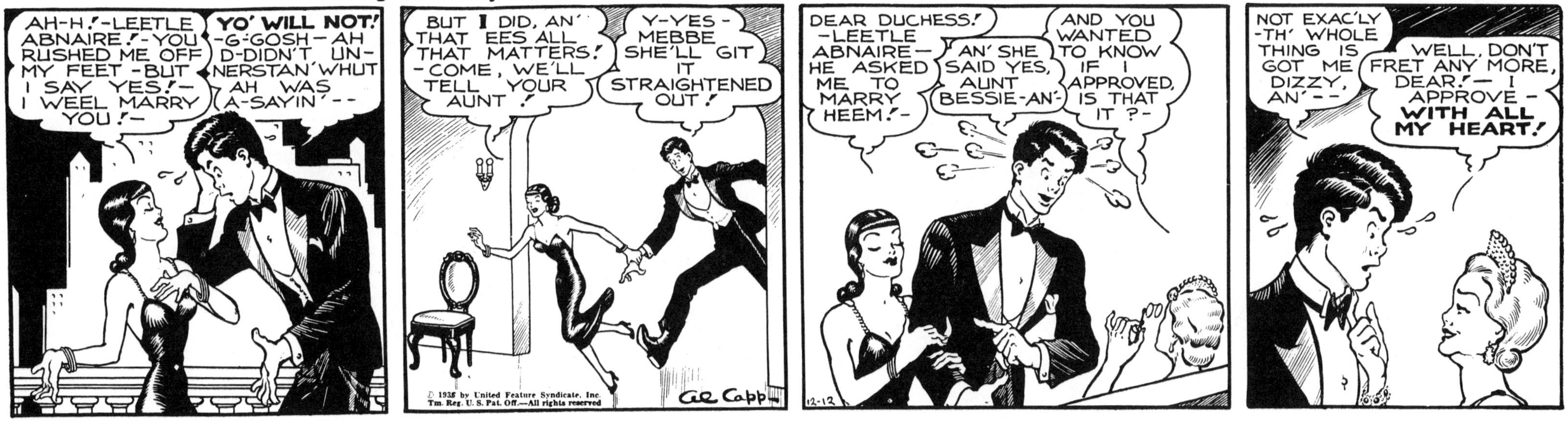

AH-H!–LEETLE ABNAIRE!–YOU RUSHED ME OFF MY FEET–BUT I SAY YES!–I WEEL MARRY YOU!–
YO' WILL NOT!–G-GOSH–AH D-DIDN'T UN-NERSTAN' WHUT AH WAS A-SAYIN'--
BUT I DID, AN' THAT EES ALL THAT MATTERS!–COME, WE'LL TELL YOUR AUNT!
Y-YES–MEBBE SHE'LL GIT IT STRAIGHTENED OUT!
© 1935 by United Feature Syndicate, Inc. Tm. Reg. U. S. Pat. Off.—All rights reserved
AL CAPP
DEAR DUCHESS!–LEETLE ABNAIRE–HE ASKED ME TO MARRY HEEM!–
AN' SHE SAID YES, AUNT BESSIE–AN'–
AND YOU WANTED TO KNOW IF I APPROVED, IS THAT IT?–
12-12
NOT EXAC'LY–TH' WHOLE THING IS GOT ME DIZZY, AN'--
WELL, DON'T FRET ANY MORE, DEAR!–I APPROVE–WITH ALL MY HEART!

LI'L ABNER Don't Mind Me **By Al Capp**

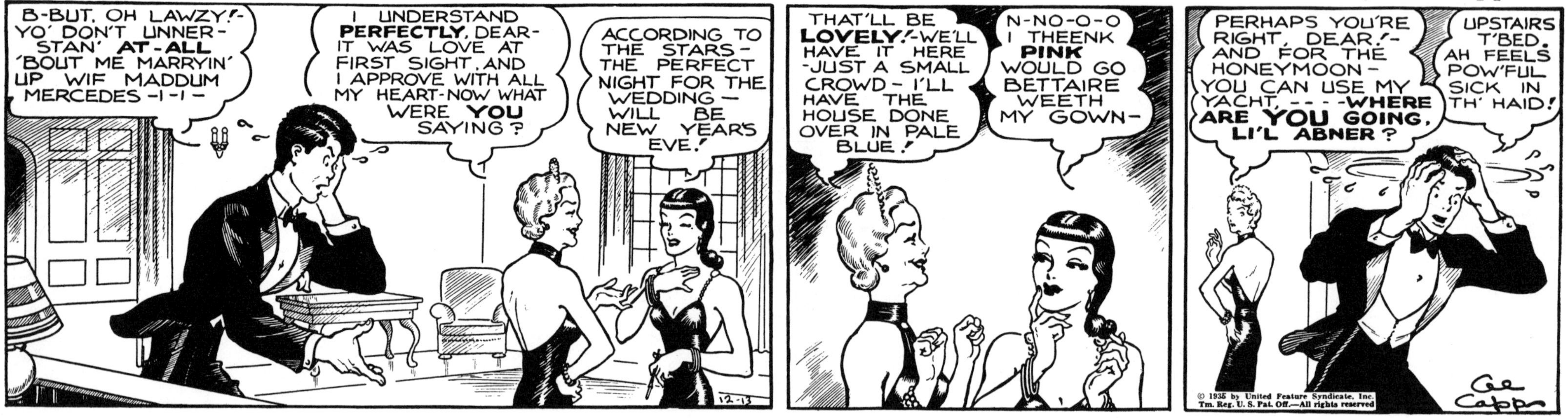

B-BUT, OH LAWZY!- YO' DON'T UNNER-STAN' AT-ALL 'BOUT ME MARRYIN' UP WIF MADDUM MERCEDES -I-I-
I UNDERSTAND PERFECTLY, DEAR- IT WAS LOVE AT FIRST SIGHT, AND I APPROVE WITH ALL MY HEART-NOW WHAT WERE YOU SAYING?
ACCORDING TO THE STARS - THE PERFECT NIGHT FOR THE WEDDING - WILL BE NEW YEAR'S EVE!
12-13
THAT'LL BE LOVELY!-WE'LL HAVE IT HERE -JUST A SMALL CROWD - I'LL HAVE THE HOUSE DONE OVER IN PALE BLUE!
N-NO-O-O I THEENK PINK WOULD GO BETTAIRE WEETH MY GOWN-
PERHAPS YOU'RE RIGHT, DEAR!- AND FOR THE HONEYMOON - YOU CAN USE MY YACHT, - - - -WHERE ARE YOU GOING, LI'L ABNER?
UPSTAIRS T'BED. AH FEELS POW'FUL SICK IN TH' HAID!
© 1935 by United Feature Syndicate, Inc. Tm. Reg. U. S. Pat. Off.—All rights reserved
Al Capp

LI'L ABNER A Mizzuble Sitchee-ay-shun **By Al Capp**

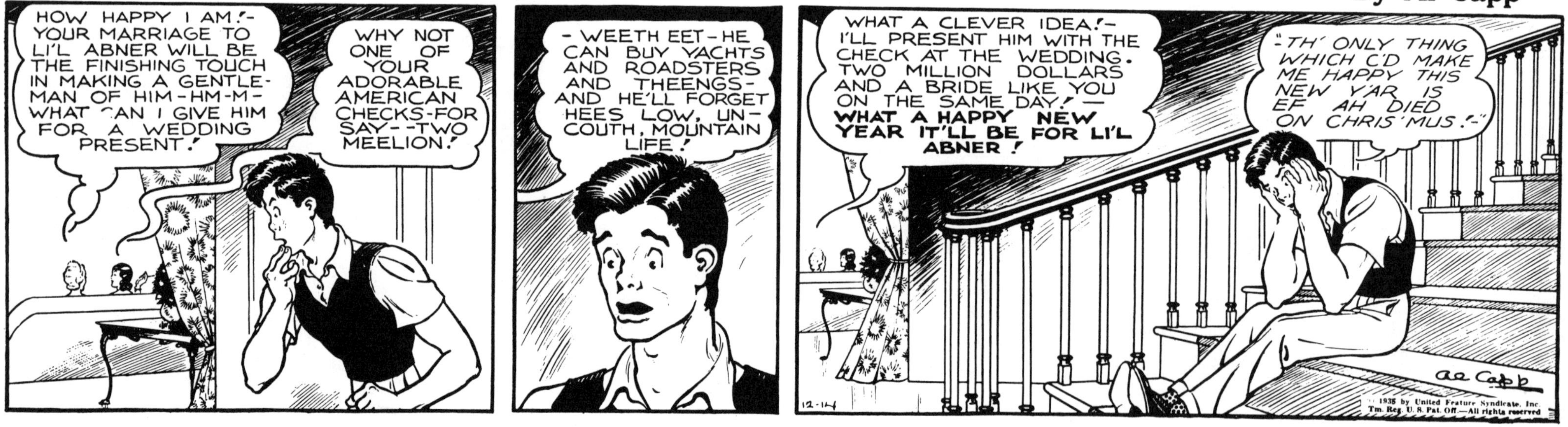

HOW HAPPY I AM!- YOUR MARRIAGE TO LI'L ABNER WILL BE THE FINISHING TOUCH IN MAKING A GENTLE-MAN OF HIM-HM-M-WHAT CAN I GIVE HIM FOR A WEDDING PRESENT!
WHY NOT ONE OF YOUR ADORABLE AMERICAN CHECKS-FOR SAY--TWO MEELION!
- WEETH EET-HE CAN BUY YACHTS AND ROADSTERS AND THEENGS- AND HE'LL FORGET HEES LOW, UN-COUTH, MOUNTAIN LIFE!
WHAT A CLEVER IDEA!- I'LL PRESENT HIM WITH THE CHECK AT THE WEDDING. TWO MILLION DOLLARS AND A BRIDE LIKE YOU ON THE SAME DAY!- WHAT A HAPPY NEW YEAR IT'LL BE FOR LI'L ABNER!
-TH' ONLY THING WHICH C'D MAKE ME HAPPY THIS NEW Y'AR IS EF AH DIED ON CHRIS'MUS!-
12-14
Al Capp
© 1935 by United Feature Syndicate, Inc. Tm. Reg. U. S. Pat. Off.—All rights reserved

LI'L ABNER A Sincere Invitation By Al Capp

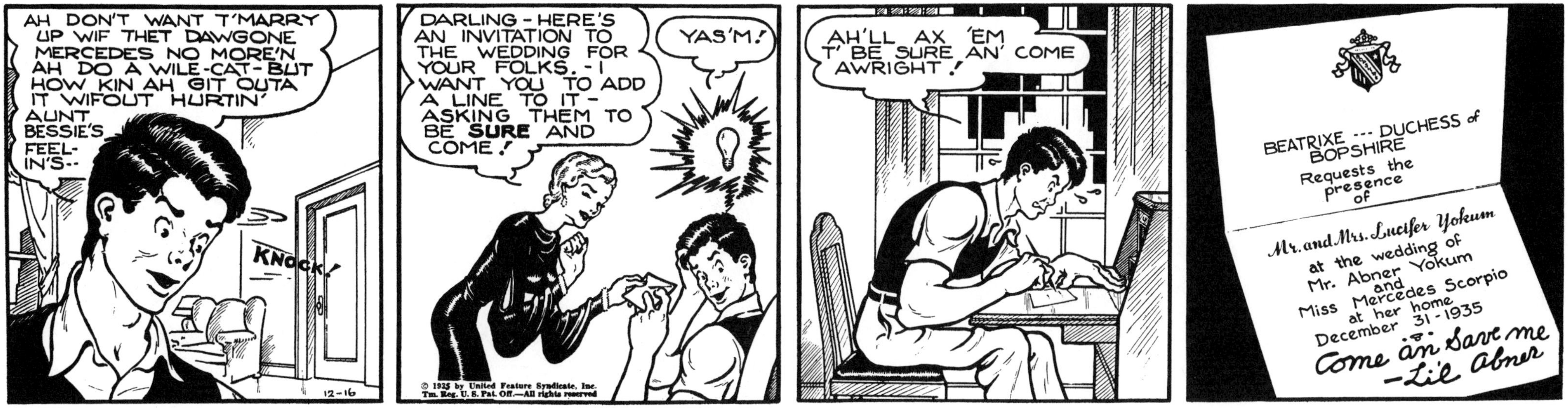
AH DON'T WANT T'MARRY UP WIF THET DAWGONE MERCEDES NO MORE'N AH DO A WILE-CAT-BUT HOW KIN AH GIT OUTA IT WIFOUT HURTIN' AUNT BESSIE'S FEEL-IN'S--
KNOCK!
12-16
DARLING-HERE'S AN INVITATION TO THE WEDDING FOR YOUR FOLKS.-I WANT YOU TO ADD A LINE TO IT-ASKING THEM TO BE **SURE** AND COME!
YAS'M!
© 1935 by United Feature Syndicate, Inc. Tm. Reg. U. S. Pat. Off.—All rights reserved
AH'LL AX 'EM T' BE SURE AN' COME AWRIGHT!
BEATRIXE --- DUCHESS of BOPSHIRE
Requests the presence of
Mr. and Mrs. Lucifer Yokum
at the wedding of Mr. Abner Yokum and Miss Mercedes Scorpio at her home December 31-1935
Come an Save me
-Li'l Abner

LI'L ABNER No Loss By Al Capp

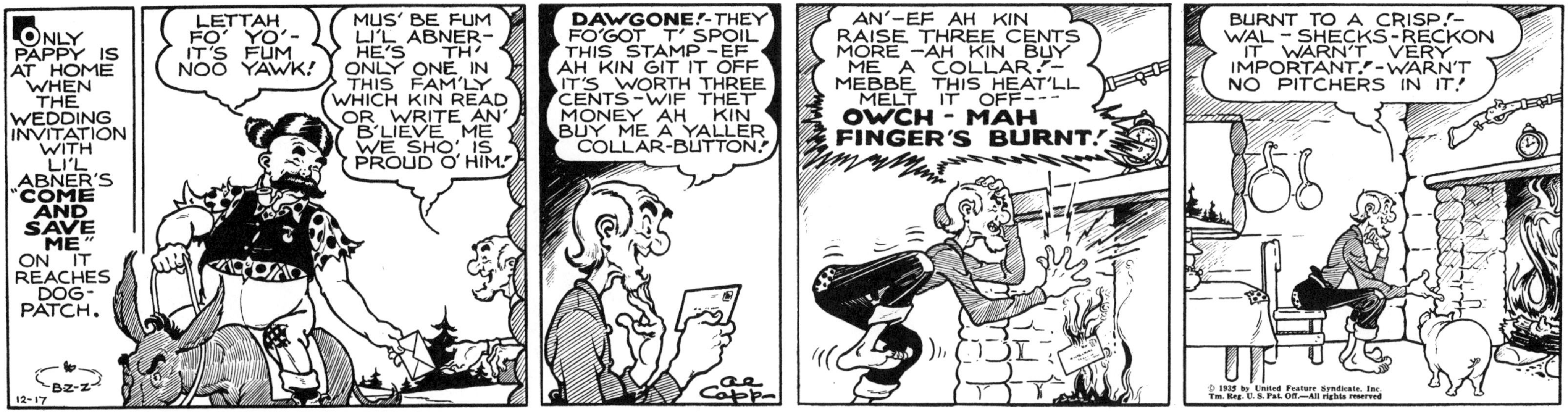
ONLY PAPPY IS AT HOME WHEN THE WEDDING INVITATION WITH LI'L ABNER'S "**COME AND SAVE ME**" ON IT REACHES DOG-PATCH.
LETTAH FO' YO'-IT'S FUM NOO YAWK!
MUS' BE FUM LI'L ABNER-HE'S TH' ONLY ONE IN THIS FAM'LY WHICH KIN READ OR WRITE AN' B'LIEVE ME WE SHO' IS PROUD O' HIM!
B-Z-Z
12-17
DAWGONE!-THEY FO'GOT T' SPOIL THIS STAMP-EF AH KIN GIT IT OFF IT'S WORTH THREE CENTS-WIF THET MONEY AH KIN BUY ME A YALLER COLLAR-BUTTON!
Al Capp
AN'-EF AH KIN RAISE THREE CENTS MORE-AH KIN BUY ME A COLLAR!-MEBBE THIS HEAT'LL MELT IT OFF---
OWCH-MAH FINGER'S BURNT!
BURNT TO A CRISP!-WAL-SHECKS-RECKON IT WARN'T VERY IMPORTANT!-WARN'T NO PITCHERS IN IT!
© 1935 by United Feature Syndicate, Inc. Tm. Reg. U. S. Pat. Off.—All rights reserved

LI'L ABNER A Mere Detail By Al Capp

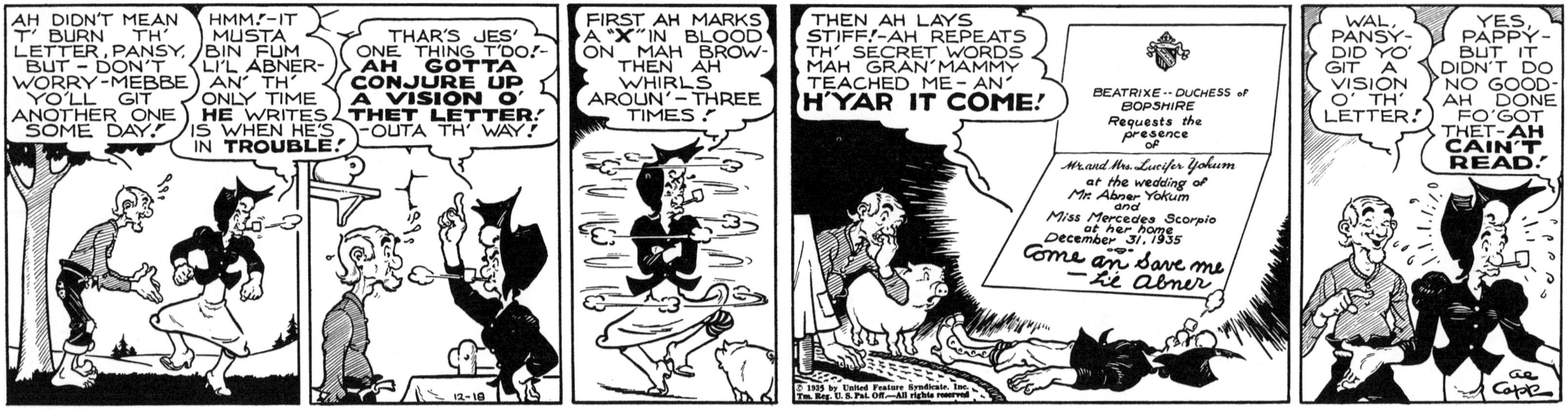

AH DIDN'T MEAN T' BURN TH' LETTER, PANSY, BUT - DON'T WORRY - MEBBE YO'LL GIT ANOTHER ONE SOME DAY!
HMM!-IT MUSTA BIN FUM LI'L ABNER- AN' TH' ONLY TIME HE WRITES IS WHEN HE'S IN TROUBLE!
THAR'S JES' ONE THING T'DO!- AH GOTTA CONJURE UP A VISION O' THET LETTER! -OUTA TH' WAY!
12-18
FIRST AH MARKS A "X" IN BLOOD ON MAH BROW- THEN AH WHIRLS AROUN' - THREE TIMES!
THEN AH LAYS STIFF!-AH REPEATS TH' SECRET WORDS MAH GRAN'MAMMY TEACHED ME - AN' H'YAR IT COME!
BEATRIXE -- DUCHESS of BOPSHIRE Requests the presence of
Mr. and Mrs. Lucifer Yokum at the wedding of Mr. Abner Yokum and Miss Mercedes Scorpio at her home December 31, 1935
Come an' Save me — Li'l Abner
© 1935 by United Feature Syndicate, Inc. Tm. Reg. U. S. Pat. Off.—All rights reserved
WAL, PANSY- DID YO' GIT A VISION O' TH' LETTER!
YES, PAPPY- BUT IT DIDN'T DO NO GOOD- AH DONE FO'GOT THET- AH CAIN'T READ!

LI'L ABNER A Woman of Her Word By Al Capp

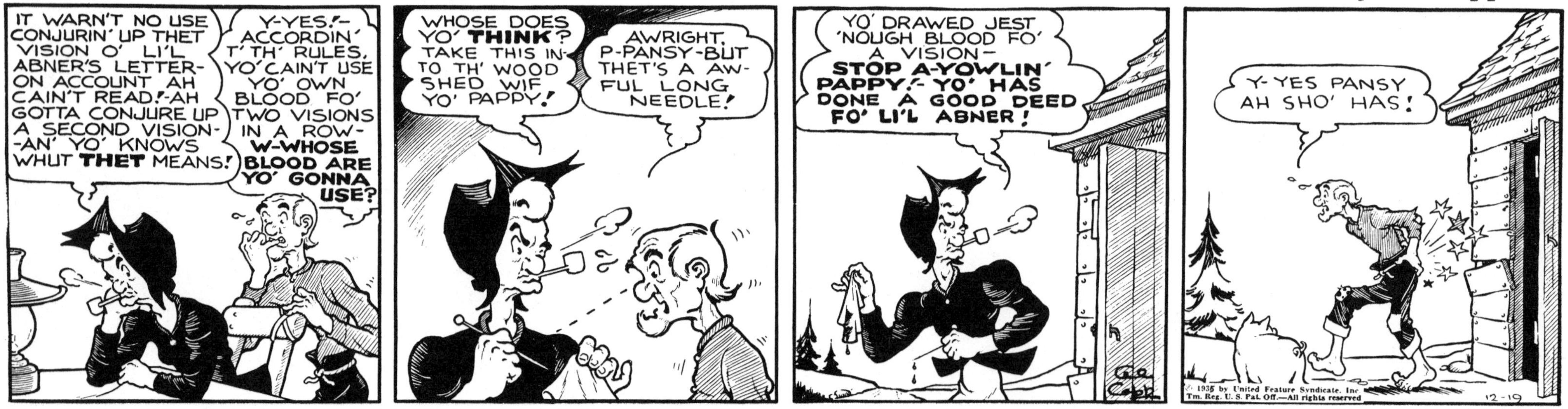

IT WARN'T NO USE CONJURIN' UP THET VISION O' LI'L ABNER'S LETTER- ON ACCOUNT AH CAIN'T READ!-AH GOTTA CONJURE UP A SECOND VISION- -AN' YO' KNOWS WHUT THET MEANS!
Y-YES!- ACCORDIN' T' TH' RULES, YO' CAIN'T USE YO' OWN BLOOD FO' TWO VISIONS IN A ROW- W-WHOSE BLOOD ARE YO' GONNA USE?
WHOSE DOES YO' THINK? TAKE THIS IN- TO TH' WOOD SHED WIF YO' PAPPY!
AWRIGHT, P-PANSY-BUT THET'S A AW- FUL LONG NEEDLE!
YO' DRAWED JEST 'NOUGH BLOOD FO' A VISION- STOP A-YOWLIN' PAPPY!- YO' HAS DONE A GOOD DEED FO' LI'L ABNER!
Y-YES PANSY AH SHO' HAS!
© 1935 by United Feature Syndicate, Inc Tm. Reg. U. S. Pat. Off.—All rights reserved
12-19

LI'L ABNER Narrow Escape By Al Capp

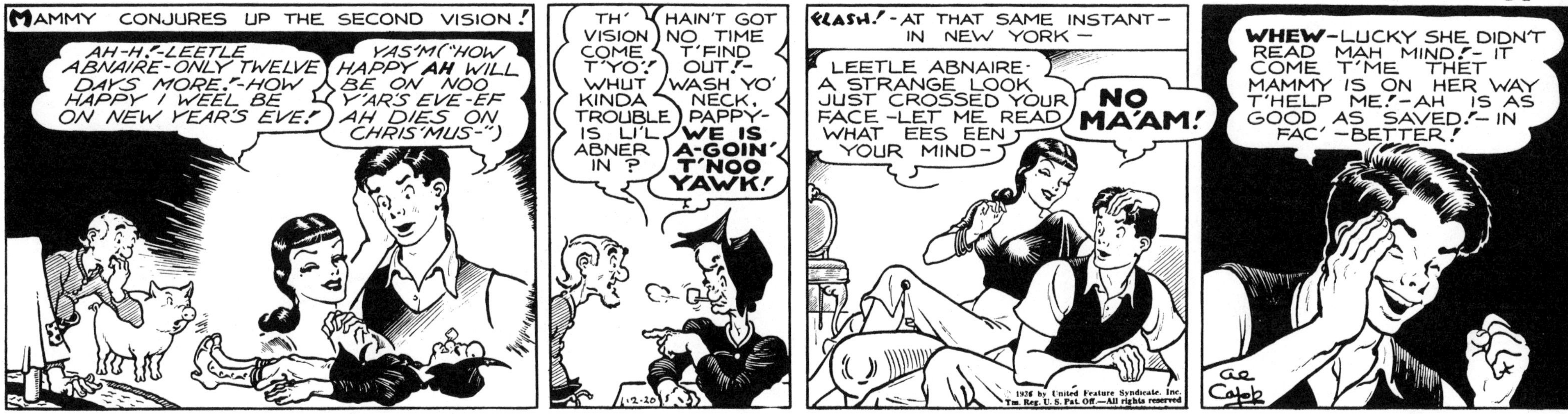
MAMMY CONJURES UP THE SECOND VISION!
AH-H!-LEETLE ABNAIRE-ONLY TWELVE DAYS MORE!-HOW HAPPY I WEEL BE ON NEW YEAR'S EVE!
YAS'M("HOW HAPPY AH WILL BE ON NOO Y'AR'S EVE-EF AH DIES ON CHRIS'MUS-")
TH' VISION COME T'YO'! WHUT KINDA TROUBLE IS LI'L ABNER IN?
HAIN'T GOT NO TIME T'FIND OUT!-WASH YO' NECK, PAPPY-WE IS A-GOIN' T'NOO YAWK!
FLASH!-AT THAT SAME INSTANT-IN NEW YORK-
LEETLE ABNAIRE-A STRANGE LOOK JUST CROSSED YOUR FACE-LET ME READ WHAT EES EEN YOUR MIND-
NO MA'AM!
WHEW-LUCKY SHE DIDN'T READ MAH MIND!-IT COME T'ME THET MAMMY IS ON HER WAY T'HELP ME!-AH IS AS GOOD AS SAVED!-IN FAC'-BETTER!

LI'L ABNER Nothing of Value By Al Capp

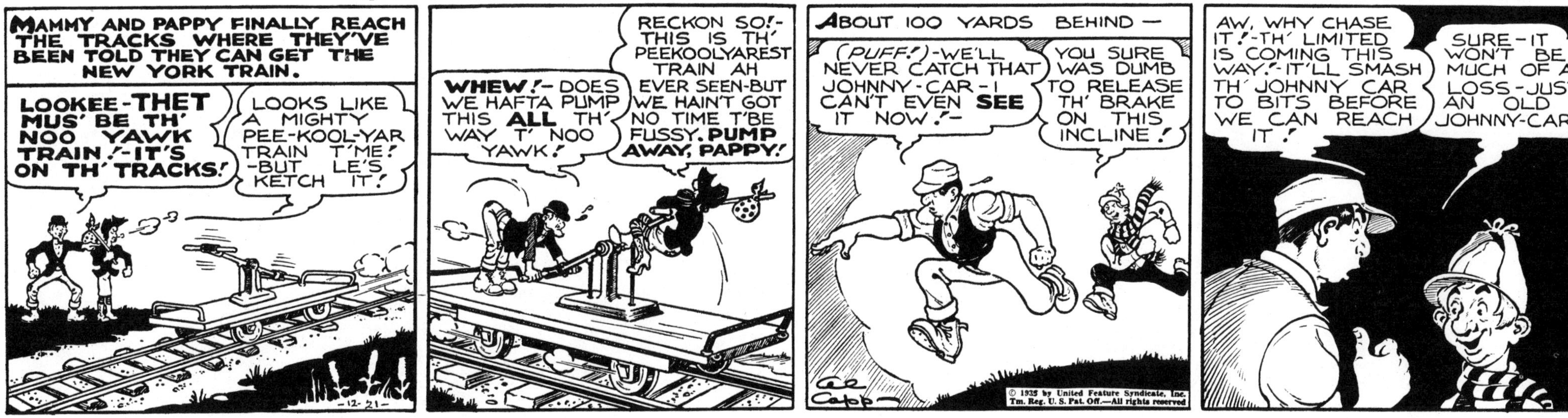
MAMMY AND PAPPY FINALLY REACH THE TRACKS WHERE THEY'VE BEEN TOLD THEY CAN GET THE NEW YORK TRAIN.
LOOKEE-THET MUS' BE TH' NOO YAWK TRAIN!-IT'S ON TH' TRACKS!
LOOKS LIKE A MIGHTY PEE-KOOL-YAR TRAIN T'ME!-BUT LE'S KETCH IT!
WHEW!-DOES WE HAFTA PUMP THIS ALL TH' WAY T' NOO YAWK?
RECKON SO!-THIS IS TH' PEEKOOLYAREST TRAIN AH EVER SEEN-BUT WE HAIN'T GOT NO TIME T'BE FUSSY. PUMP AWAY, PAPPY!
ABOUT 100 YARDS BEHIND-
(PUFF!)-WE'LL NEVER CATCH THAT JOHNNY-CAR-I CAN'T EVEN SEE IT NOW!-
YOU SURE WAS DUMB TO RELEASE TH' BRAKE ON THIS INCLINE!
AW, WHY CHASE IT?-TH' LIMITED IS COMING THIS WAY!-IT'LL SMASH TH' JOHNNY CAR TO BITS BEFORE WE CAN REACH IT!
SURE-IT WON'T BE MUCH OF A LOSS-JUST AN OLD JOHNNY-CAR!

LI'L ABNER There'll Be Two New Hill-Billies In Heaven By Al Capp

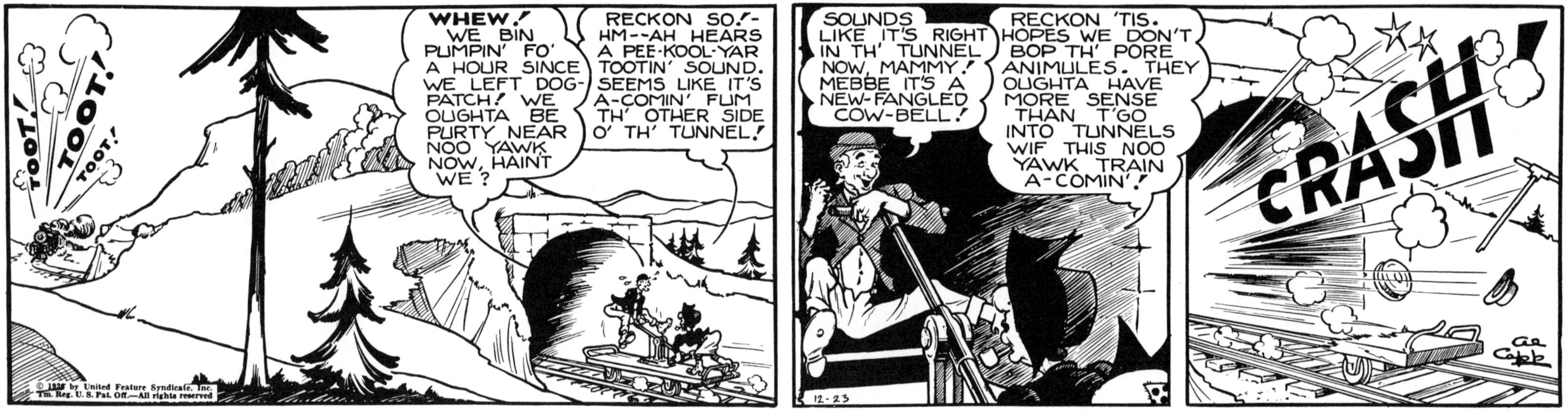

TOOT! TOOT! TOOT!
WHEW! WE BIN PUMPIN' FO' A HOUR SINCE WE LEFT DOG-PATCH! WE OUGHTA BE PURTY NEAR NOO YAWK NOW, HAINT WE?
RECKON SO!-HM--AH HEARS A PEE-KOOL-YAR TOOTIN' SOUND. SEEMS LIKE IT'S A-COMIN' FUM TH' OTHER SIDE O' TH' TUNNEL!
© 1935 by United Feature Syndicate, Inc. Tm. Reg. U. S. Pat. Off.—All rights reserved
SOUNDS LIKE IT'S RIGHT IN TH' TUNNEL NOW, MAMMY! MEBBE IT'S A NEW-FANGLED COW-BELL!
RECKON 'TIS. HOPES WE DON'T BOP TH' PORE ANIMULES. THEY OUGHTA HAVE MORE SENSE THAN T'GO INTO TUNNELS WIF THIS NOO YAWK TRAIN A-COMIN'!
12-23
CRASH!
Al Capp

LI'L ABNER A Close Shave! By Al Capp

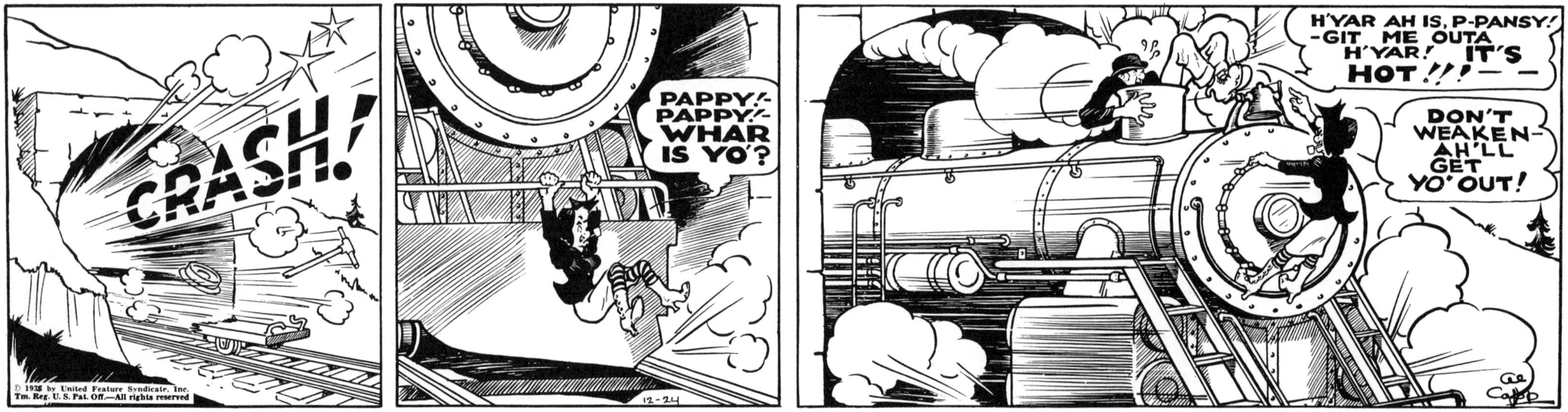

CRASH!
© 1935 by United Feature Syndicate, Inc. Tm. Reg. U. S. Pat. Off.—All rights reserved
PAPPY!- PAPPY!- WHAR IS YO'?
12-24
H'YAR AH IS, P-PANSY! -GIT ME OUTA H'YAR! IT'S HOT!!!——
DON'T WEAKEN- AH'LL GET YO' OUT!
Al Capp

LI'L ABNER

Huge-Hearted Hannibal

By Al Capp

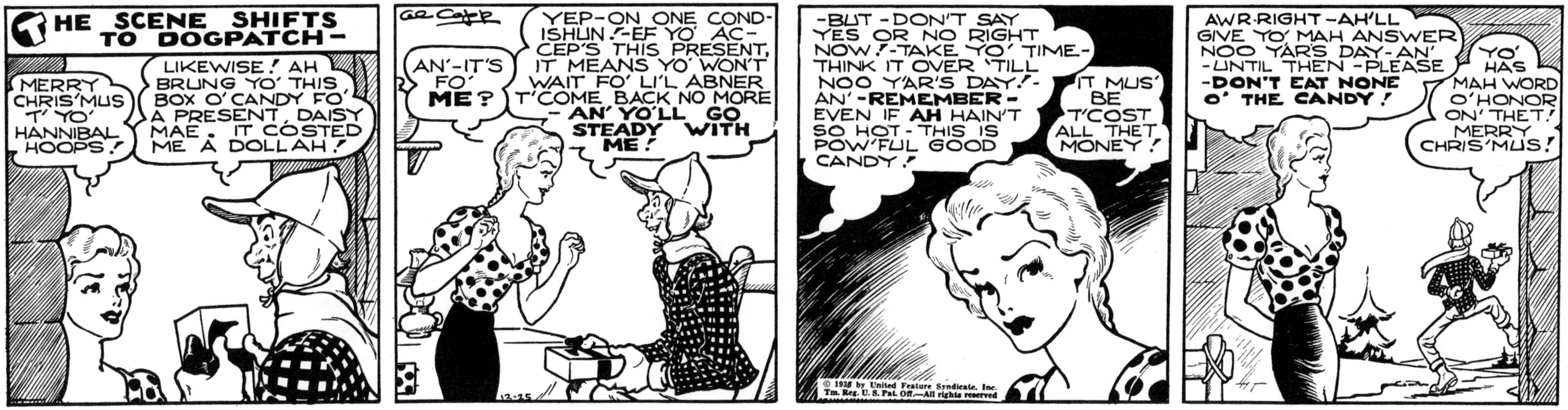
THE SCENE SHIFTS TO DOGPATCH—
MERRY CHRIS'MUS T' YO' HANNIBAL HOOPS!
LIKEWISE! AH BRUNG YO' THIS BOX O' CANDY FO' A PRESENT, DAISY MAE. IT COSTED ME A DOLLAH!
AN'-IT'S FO' ME?
YEP-ON ONE CONDISHUN!-EF YO' ACCEP'S THIS PRESENT, IT MEANS YO' WON'T WAIT FO' LI'L ABNER T'COME BACK NO MORE — AN' YO'LL GO STEADY WITH ME!
12-25
-BUT -DON'T SAY YES OR NO RIGHT NOW!-TAKE YO' TIME-THINK IT OVER 'TILL NOO YAR'S DAY!- AN' -REMEMBER- EVEN IF AH HAIN'T SO HOT- THIS IS POW'FUL GOOD CANDY!
IT MUS' BE T'COST ALL THET MONEY!
© 1936 by United Feature Syndicate, Inc. Tm. Reg. U. S. Pat. Off.—All rights reserved
AWR-RIGHT-AH'LL GIVE YO' MAH ANSWER NOO YAR'S DAY-AN' -UNTIL THEN -PLEASE -DON'T EAT NONE O' THE CANDY!
YO' HAS MAH WORD O'HONOR ON' THET! MERRY CHRIS'MUS!

LI'L ABNER

A Friend In Need

By Al Capp

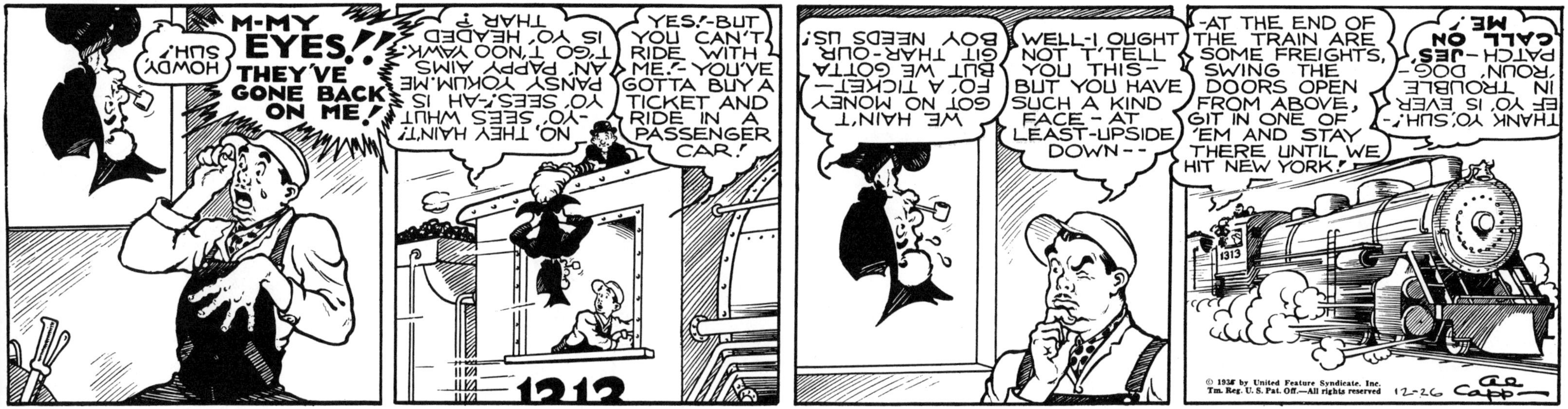
HOWDY, SUH!
M-MY EYES!! THEY'VE GONE BACK ON ME!
NO, THEY HAIN'T! -YO' SEES WHUT YO' SEES!-AH IS PANSY YOKUM. ME AN' PAPPY AIMS T'GO T' NOO YAWK. IS YO' HEADED THAR?
YES!-BUT YOU CAN'T RIDE WITH ME!-YOU'VE GOTTA BUY A TICKET AND RIDE IN A PASSENGER CAR!
1313
WE HAIN'T GOT NO MONEY FO' A TICKET— BUT WE GOTTA GIT THAR-OUR BOY NEEDS US!
WELL-I OUGHT NOT T' TELL YOU THIS- BUT YOU HAVE SUCH A KIND FACE- AT LEAST-UPSIDE DOWN--
-AT THE END OF THE TRAIN ARE SOME FREIGHTS, SWING THE DOORS OPEN FROM ABOVE, GIT IN ONE OF 'EM AND STAY THERE UNTIL WE HIT NEW YORK!
THANK YO', SUH!- EF YO' IS EVER IN TROUBLE 'ROUN' DOG-PATCH-JES' CALL ON ME!
1313
© 1936 by United Feature Syndicate, Inc. Tm. Reg. U. S. Pat. Off.—All rights reserved
12-26

LI'L ABNER A Mysterious Disappearance By Al Capp

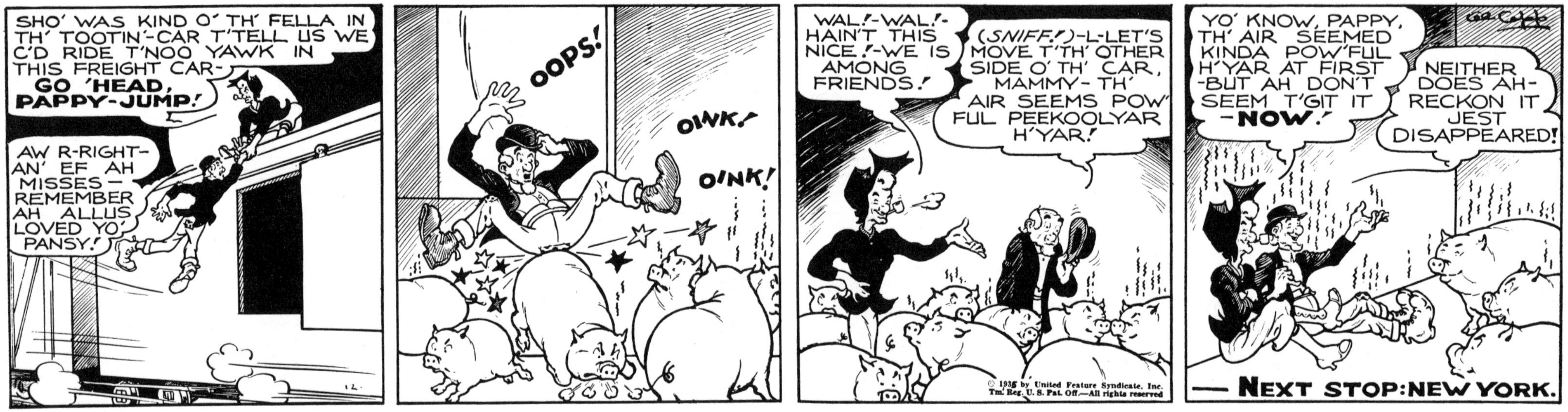

SHO' WAS KIND O' TH' FELLA IN TH' TOOTIN'-CAR T'TELL US WE C'D RIDE T'NOO YAWK IN THIS FREIGHT CAR- GO 'HEAD, PAPPY-JUMP!
AW R-RIGHT- AN' EF AH MISSES- REMEMBER AH ALLUS LOVED YO' PANSY!
OOPS!
OINK!
OINK!
WAL!-WAL!- HAIN'T THIS NICE!-WE IS AMONG FRIENDS!
(SNIFF!)-L-LET'S MOVE T'TH' OTHER SIDE O' TH' CAR, MAMMY- TH' AIR SEEMS POW'FUL PEEKOOLYAR H'YAR!
YO' KNOW, PAPPY, TH' AIR SEEMED KINDA POW'FUL H'YAR AT FIRST -BUT AH DON'T SEEM T'GIT IT -NOW!
NEITHER DOES AH- RECKON IT JEST DISAPPEARED!
— NEXT STOP: NEW YORK.
© 1938 by United Feature Syndicate, Inc. Tm. Reg. U. S. Pat. Off.—All rights reserved

LI'L ABNER His Expression Is Bound To Be Good By Al Capp

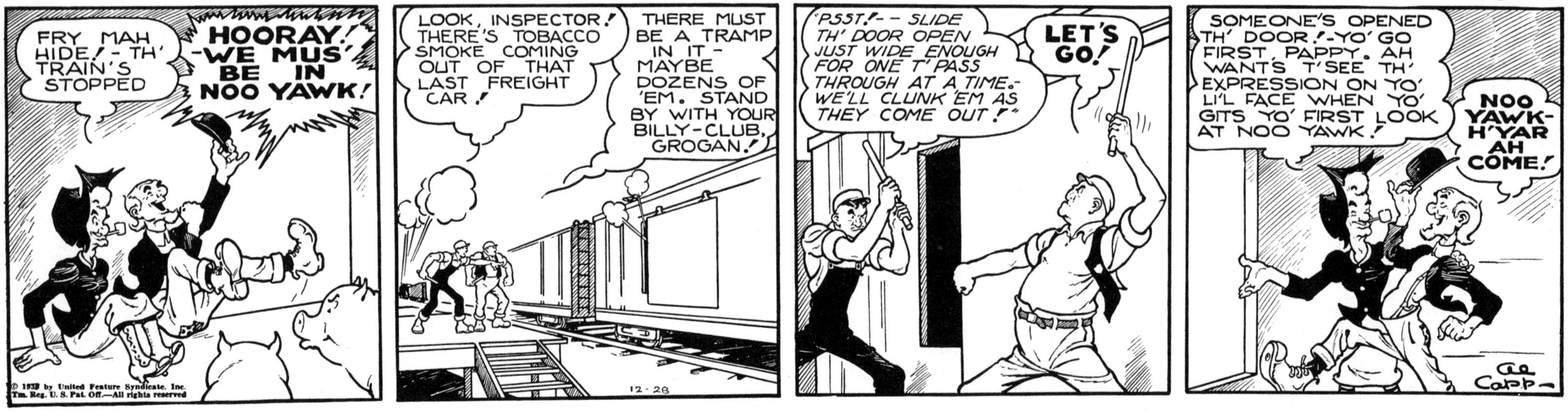

FRY MAH HIDE!-TH' TRAIN'S STOPPED
HOORAY!-WE MUS' BE IN NOO YAWK!
LOOK, INSPECTOR! THERE'S TOBACCO SMOKE COMING OUT OF THAT LAST FREIGHT CAR!
THERE MUST BE A TRAMP IN IT - MAYBE DOZENS OF 'EM. STAND BY WITH YOUR BILLY-CLUB, GROGAN!
"PSST!-- SLIDE TH' DOOR OPEN JUST WIDE ENOUGH FOR ONE T' PASS THROUGH AT A TIME.- WE'LL CLUNK 'EM AS THEY COME OUT!"
LET'S GO!
SOMEONE'S OPENED TH' DOOR!-YO' GO FIRST, PAPPY. AH WANTS T'SEE TH' EXPRESSION ON YO' LI'L FACE WHEN YO' GITS YO' FIRST LOOK AT NOO YAWK!
NOO YAWK- H'YAR AH COME!
© 1938 by United Feature Syndicate, Inc. Tm. Reg. U. S. Pat. Off.—All rights reserved

LI'L ABNER Welcome To the Big City By Al Capp

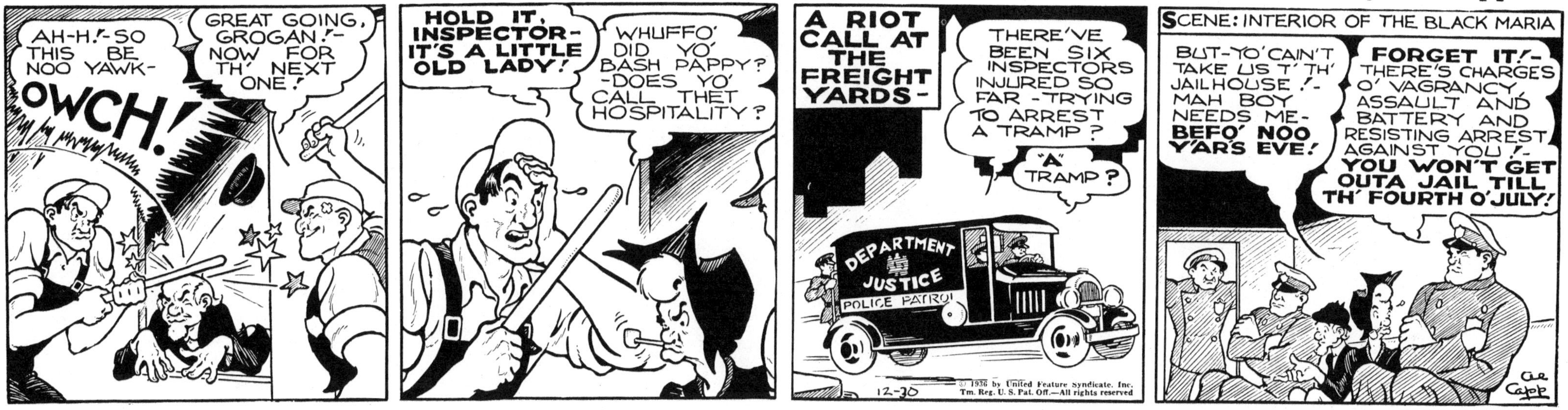

AH-H!-SO THIS BE NOO YAWK-
OWCH!
GREAT GOING, GROGAN!-NOW FOR TH' NEXT ONE!
HOLD IT, INSPECTOR-IT'S A LITTLE OLD LADY!
WHUFFO' DID YO' BASH PAPPY? -DOES YO' CALL THET HOSPITALITY?
A RIOT CALL AT THE FREIGHT YARDS-
THERE'VE BEEN SIX INSPECTORS INJURED SO FAR -TRYING TO ARREST A TRAMP?
"A" TRAMP?
DEPARTMENT JUSTICE
POLICE PATROL
12-30
© 1936 by United Feature Syndicate, Inc. Tm. Reg. U. S. Pat. Off.—All rights reserved
SCENE: INTERIOR OF THE BLACK MARIA
BUT-YO' CAIN'T TAKE US T' TH' JAILHOUSE!-MAH BOY NEEDS ME-BEFO' NOO Y'AR'S EVE!
FORGET IT!-THERE'S CHARGES O' VAGRANCY, ASSAULT AND BATTERY AND RESISTING ARREST AGAINST YOU!-YOU WON'T GET OUTA JAIL TILL TH' FOURTH O'JULY!

LI'L ABNER The Getaway By Al Capp

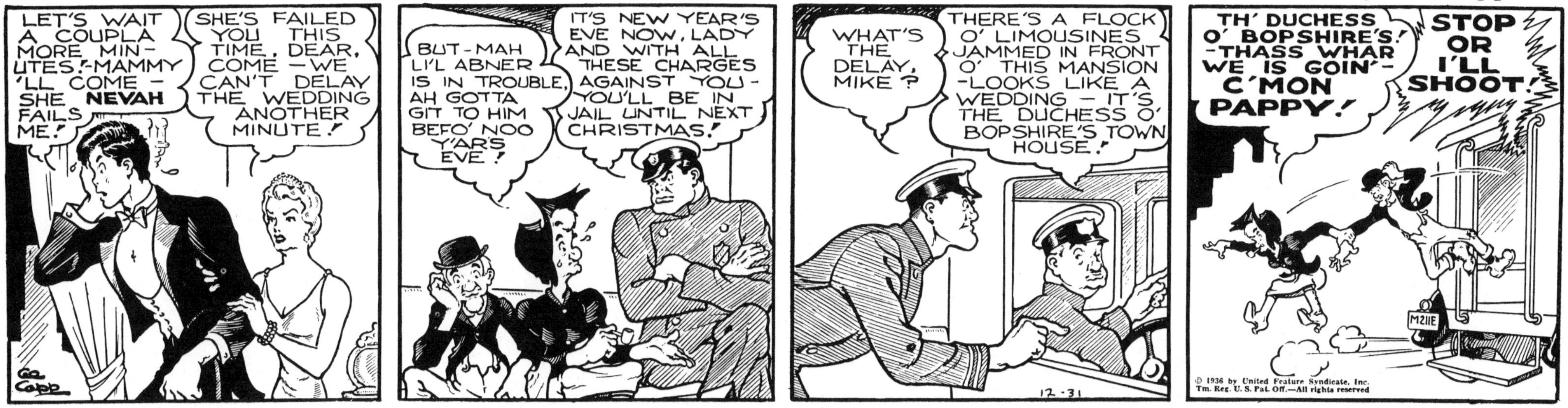

LET'S WAIT A COUPLA MORE MIN-UTES!-MAMMY 'LL COME-SHE NEVAH FAILS ME!
SHE'S FAILED YOU THIS TIME, DEAR, COME-WE CAN'T DELAY THE WEDDING ANOTHER MINUTE!
BUT-MAH LI'L ABNER IS IN TROUBLE, AH GOTTA GIT TO HIM BEFO' NOO Y'AR'S EVE!
IT'S NEW YEAR'S EVE NOW, LADY AND WITH ALL THESE CHARGES AGAINST YOU-YOU'LL BE IN JAIL UNTIL NEXT CHRISTMAS!
WHAT'S THE DELAY, MIKE?
THERE'S A FLOCK O' LIMOUSINES JAMMED IN FRONT O' THIS MANSION -LOOKS LIKE A WEDDING - IT'S THE DUCHESS O' BOPSHIRE'S TOWN HOUSE!
12-31
TH' DUCHESS O' BOPSHIRE'S!-THASS WHAR WE IS GOIN'-C'MON PAPPY!
STOP OR I'LL SHOOT!
M211E
© 1936 by United Feature Syndicate, Inc. Tm. Reg. U. S. Pat. Off.—All rights reserved

LI'L ABNER The Seasons Greetings ! **By Al Capp**

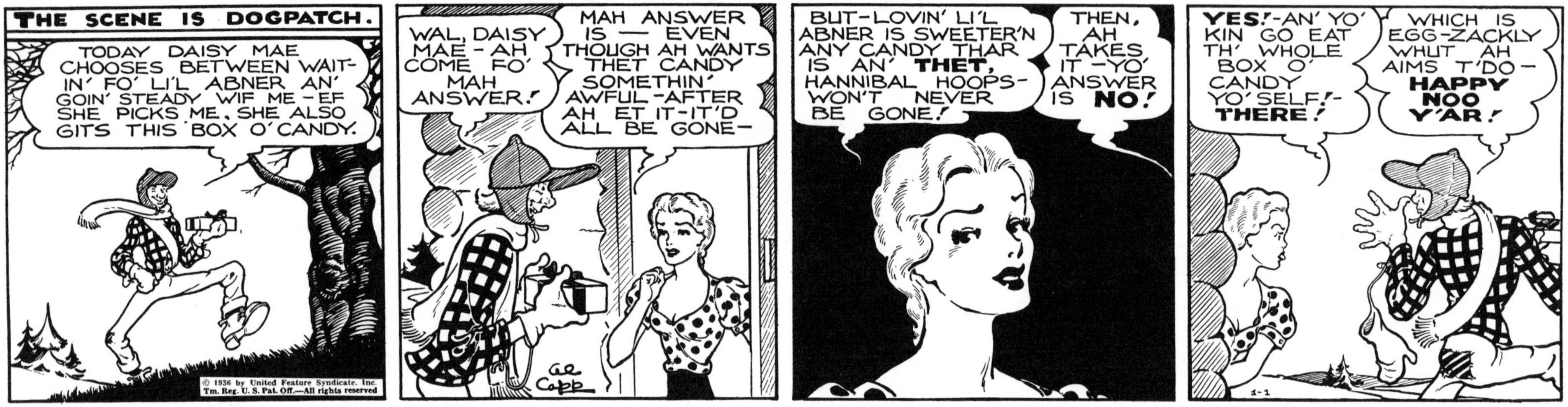
THE SCENE IS DOGPATCH.
TODAY DAISY MAE CHOOSES BETWEEN WAITIN' FO' LI'L ABNER AN' GOIN' STEADY WIF ME - EF SHE PICKS ME, SHE ALSO GITS THIS BOX O' CANDY.
© 1936 by United Feature Syndicate, Inc. Tm. Reg. U. S. Pat. Off.—All rights reserved
WAL, DAISY MAE - AH COME FO' MAH ANSWER!
MAH ANSWER IS — EVEN THOUGH AH WANTS THET CANDY SOMETHIN' AWFUL - AFTER AH ET IT - IT'D ALL BE GONE -
Al Capp
BUT - LOVIN' LI'L ABNER IS SWEETER'N ANY CANDY THAR IS AN' THET, HANNIBAL HOOPS - WON'T NEVER BE GONE!
THEN, AH TAKES IT - YO' ANSWER IS NO!
YES! - AN' YO' KIN GO EAT TH' WHOLE BOX O' CANDY YO'SELF! - THERE!
WHICH IS EGG-ZACKLY WHUT AH AIMS T'DO - HAPPY NOO Y'AR!
1-1

LI'L ABNER The Important Thing **By Al Capp**

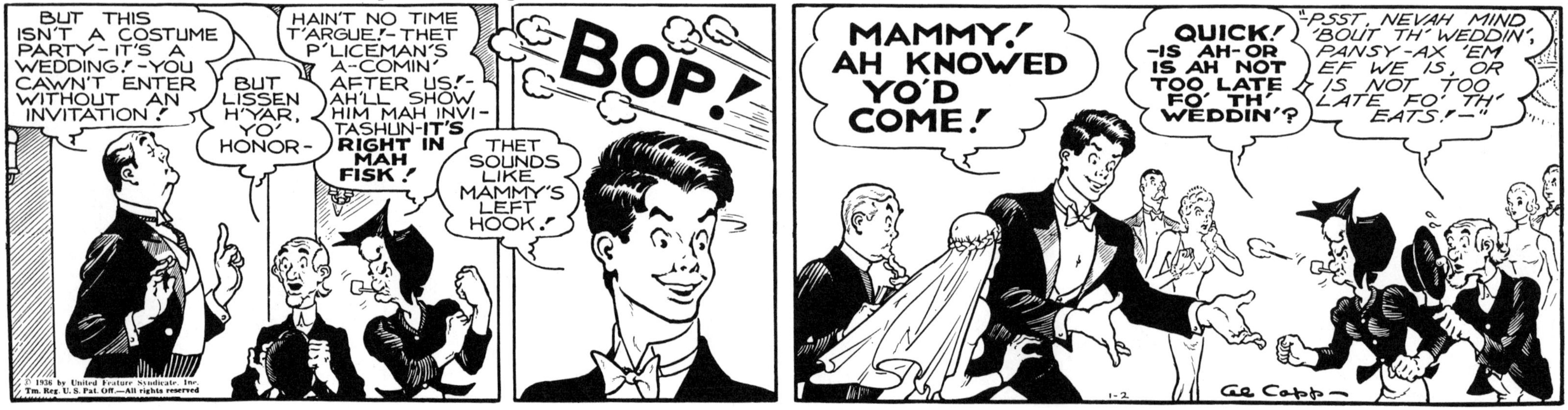
BUT THIS ISN'T A COSTUME PARTY - IT'S A WEDDING! - YOU CAWN'T ENTER WITHOUT AN INVITATION!
BUT LISSEN H'YAR, YO' HONOR -
HAIN'T NO TIME T'ARGUE! - THET P'LICEMAN'S A-COMIN' AFTER US! - AH'LL SHOW HIM MAH INVITASHUN - IT'S RIGHT IN MAH FISK!
© 1936 by United Feature Syndicate, Inc. Tm. Reg. U. S. Pat. Off.—All rights reserved
THET SOUNDS LIKE MAMMY'S LEFT HOOK!
BOP!
MAMMY! AH KNOWED YO'D COME!
QUICK! - IS AH - OR IS AH NOT TOO LATE FO' TH' WEDDIN'?
"PSST, NEVAH MIND 'BOUT TH' WEDDIN', PANSY - AX 'EM EF WE IS, OR IS NOT TOO LATE FO' TH' EATS! -"
1-2
Al Capp -

LI'L ABNER Doomed ! By Al Capp

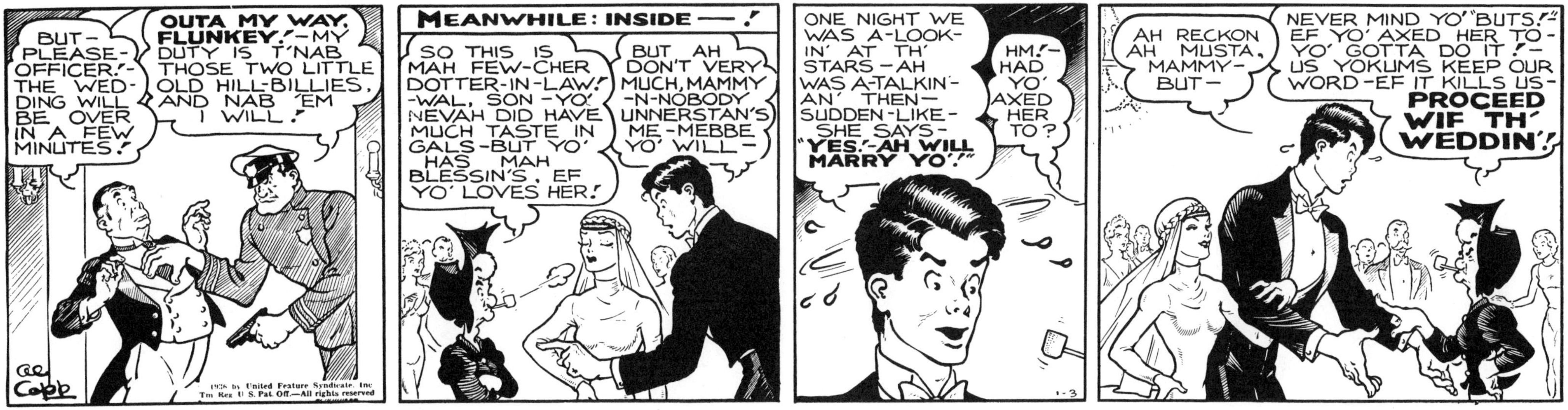

BUT— PLEASE— OFFICER!— THE WEDDING WILL BE OVER IN A FEW MINUTES!
OUTA MY WAY, FLUNKEY!—MY DUTY IS T'NAB THOSE TWO LITTLE OLD HILL-BILLIES, AND NAB 'EM I WILL!
Al Capp
1936 by United Feature Syndicate, Inc Tm Reg U S. Pat. Off.—All rights reserved
MEANWHILE: INSIDE —!
SO THIS IS MAH FEW-CHER DOTTER-IN-LAW!—WAL, SON—YO' NEVAH DID HAVE MUCH TASTE IN GALS—BUT YO' HAS MAH BLESSIN'S, EF YO' LOVES HER!
BUT AH DON'T VERY MUCH, MAMMY—N-NOBODY UNNERSTAN'S ME—MEBBE YO' WILL—
ONE NIGHT WE WAS A-LOOKIN' AT TH' STARS—AH WAS A-TALKIN'—AN' THEN—SUDDEN-LIKE—SHE SAYS—"YES!—AH WILL MARRY YO'!"
HM!—HAD YO' AXED HER TO?
1-3
AH RECKON AH MUSTA, MAMMY—BUT—
NEVER MIND YO' "BUTS!"—EF YO' AXED HER TO—YO' GOTTA DO IT!—US YOKUMS KEEP OUR WORD—EF IT KILLS US—PROCEED WIF TH' WEDDIN'!

LI'L ABNER Giving the Bride Away By Al Capp

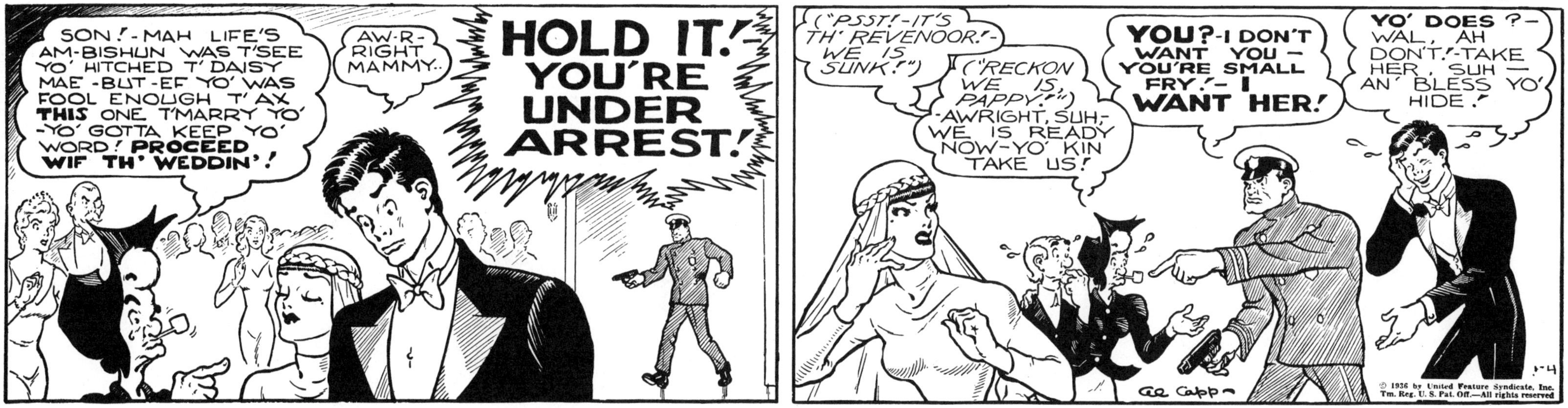

SON!—MAH LIFE'S AM-BISHUN WAS T'SEE YO' HITCHED T' DAISY MAE—BUT—EF YO' WAS FOOL ENOUGH T' AX THIS ONE T'MARRY YO'—YO' GOTTA KEEP YO' WORD! PROCEED WIF TH' WEDDIN'!
AW-R-RIGHT MAMMY..
HOLD IT!—YOU'RE UNDER ARREST!
("PSST!—IT'S TH' REVENOOR!—WE IS SUNK!")
("RECKON WE IS, PAPPY!")—AWRIGHT, SUH,—WE IS READY NOW—YO' KIN TAKE US!
YOU?—I DON'T WANT YOU—YOU'RE SMALL FRY!—I WANT HER!
YO' DOES?—WAL, AH DON'T!—TAKE HER, SUH—AN' BLESS YO' HIDE!
Al Capp
1-4
© 1936 by United Feature Syndicate, Inc. Tm. Reg. U. S. Pat. Off.—All rights reserved

LI'L ABNER

Abner Thinks They're Fine

By Al Capp

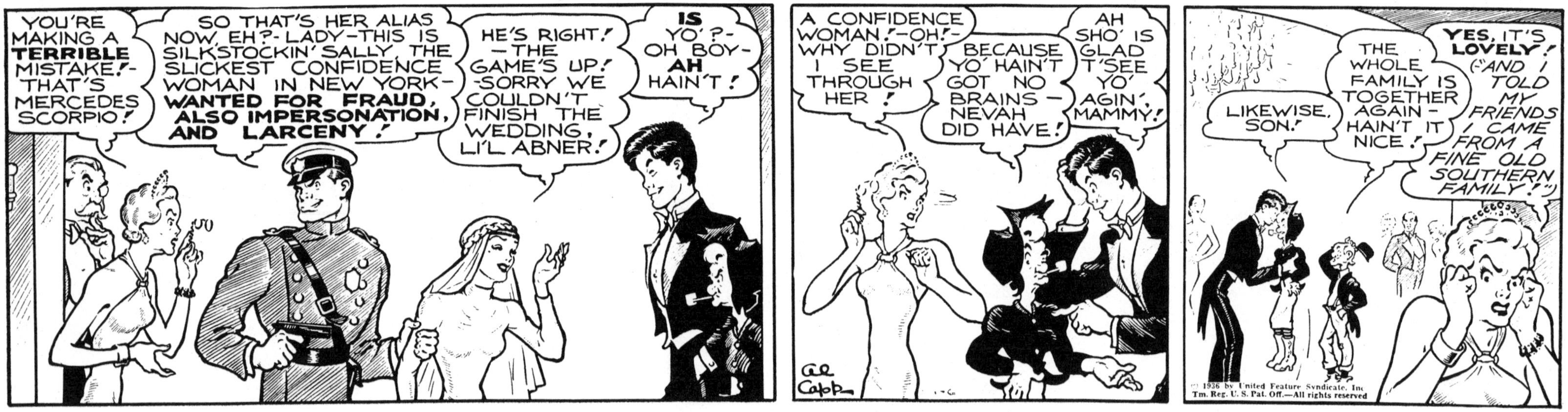

YOU'RE MAKING A **TERRIBLE** MISTAKE!-THAT'S MERCEDES SCORPIO!
SO THAT'S HER ALIAS NOW, EH?-LADY-THIS IS SILKSTOCKIN' SALLY, THE SLICKEST CONFIDENCE WOMAN IN NEW YORK-**WANTED FOR FRAUD, ALSO IMPERSONATION, AND LARCENY!**
HE'S RIGHT!-THE GAME'S UP!-SORRY WE COULDN'T FINISH THE WEDDING, LI'L ABNER!
IS YO'?-OH BOY-**AH** HAIN'T!
A CONFIDENCE WOMAN!-OH!-WHY DIDN'T I SEE THROUGH HER!
BECAUSE YO' HAIN'T GOT NO BRAINS-NEVAH DID HAVE!
AH SHO' IS GLAD T'SEE YO' AGIN', MAMMY!
LIKEWISE, SON!
THE WHOLE FAMILY IS TOGETHER AGAIN-HAIN'T IT NICE!
YES, IT'S LOVELY! *("AND I TOLD MY FRIENDS I CAME FROM A FINE OLD SOUTHERN FAMILY!")*
© 1936 by United Feature Syndicate, Inc
Tm. Reg. U. S. Pat. Off.—All rights reserved

LI'L ABNER

Don't Go, Pappy!

By Al Capp

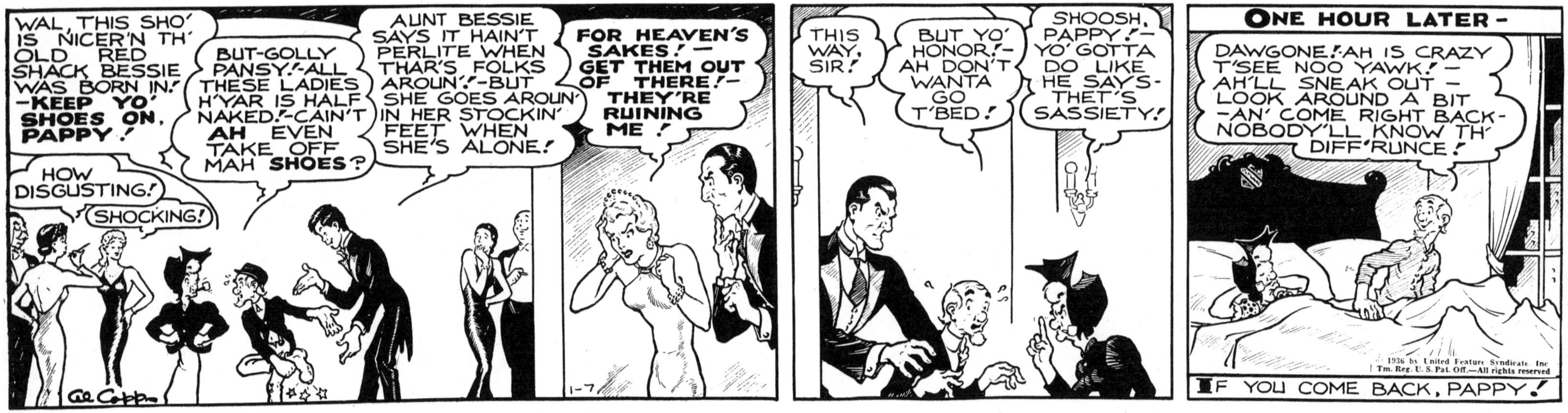

WAL, THIS SHO' IS NICER'N TH' OLD RED SHACK BESSIE WAS BORN IN!-**KEEP YO' SHOES ON, PAPPY!**
BUT-GOLLY PANSY!-ALL THESE LADIES H'YAR IS HALF NAKED!-CAIN'T **AH** EVEN TAKE OFF MAH **SHOES**?
AUNT BESSIE SAYS IT HAIN'T PERLITE WHEN THAR'S FOLKS AROUN'!-BUT SHE GOES AROUN' IN HER STOCKIN' FEET WHEN SHE'S ALONE!
HOW DISGUSTING!
SHOCKING!
FOR HEAVEN'S SAKES!-GET THEM OUT OF THERE!-THEY'RE RUINING ME!
THIS WAY, SIR!
BUT YO' HONOR!-AH DON'T WANTA GO T'BED!
SHOOSH, PAPPY!-YO' GOTTA DO LIKE HE SAYS-THET'S SASSIETY!
ONE HOUR LATER-
DAWGONE!-AH IS CRAZY T'SEE NOO YAWK!-AH'LL SNEAK OUT-LOOK AROUND A BIT-AN' COME RIGHT BACK-NOBODY'LL KNOW TH' DIFF'RUNCE!
© 1936 by United Feature Syndicate, Inc
Tm. Reg. U. S. Pat. Off.—All rights reserved
IF YOU COME BACK, PAPPY!